HIDDEN PARADIGMS

Comparing Epic Themes, Characters, and Plot Structures

A South Indian Folk Legend Viewed through Many Lenses

Understanding an epic story's key belief patterns can reveal community-level values, the nature of familial bonds, and how divine and human concerns jockey for power and influence. These foundational motifs remain understudied as they relate to South Asian folk legends, but are nonetheless crucial in shaping the values exemplified by such stories' central heroes and heroines.

In *Hidden Paradigms*, anthropologist Brenda E.F. Beck describes *The Legend of Ponnivala*, an oral epic from rural South India. Recorded in 1965, this story was sung to a group of village enthusiasts by a respected pair of local bards. This grand legend took more than thirty-eight hours to complete over eighteen nights. Bringing this unique example of Tamil culture to the attention of an international audience, Beck compares this virtually unknown South Indian epic to five other culturally significant works – the Ojibwa Nanabush cycle, the Mahabharata, an Icelandic Saga, the Bible, and the Epic of Gilgamesh – establishing this foundational Tamil story as one that engages with the same universal human struggles and themes present throughout the world. Copiously illustrated, *Hidden Paradigms* provides a fresh example of the power of comparative thinking, offering a humanistic complement to scientific reasoning.

BRENDA E.F. BECK is an adjunct professor in the Department of Anthropology at the University of Toronto Scarborough.

BRENDA E.F. BECK

Hidden Paradigms

Comparing Epic Themes, Characters, and Plot Structures

A South Indian Folk Legend Viewed through Many Lenses

UNIVERSITY OF TORONTO PRESS
Toronto Buffalo London

© University of Toronto Press 2023
Toronto Buffalo London
utorontopress.com

ISBN 978-1-4875-2933-8 (cloth)   ISBN 978-1-4875-2936-9 (EPUB)
ISBN 978-1-4875-2934-5 (paper)   ISBN 978-1-4875-2935-2 (PDF)

Library and Archives Canada Cataloguing in Publication

Title: Hidden paradigms : comparing epic themes, characters, and plot structures /
  Brenda E.F. Beck.
Names: Beck, Brenda E.F., author.
Description: Includes bibliographical references and index.
Identifiers: Canadiana (print) 20220426759 | Canadiana (ebook) 20220426767 |
  ISBN 9781487529338 (cloth) | ISBN 9781487529345 (paper) |
  ISBN 9781487529369 (EPUB) | ISBN 9781487529352 (PDF)
Subjects: LCSH: Epic literature – Themes, motives. | LCSH: Epic literature – History
  and criticism. | LCSH: Legends – Themes, motives. | LCSH: Aṉṉaṉmār Cuvāmi katai.
Classification: LCC PN56.E65 B43 2023 | DDC 809/.9337–dc23

Every effort has been made to contact copyright holders; in the event of an error or
omission, please notify the publisher.

We wish to acknowledge the land on which the University of Toronto Press operates. This
land is the traditional territory of the Wendat, the Anishnaabeg, the Haudenosaunee, the
Métis, and the Mississaugas of the Credit First Nation.

University of Toronto Press acknowledges the financial support of the Government of
Canada, the Canada Council for the Arts, and the Ontario Arts Council, an agency of
the Government of Ontario, for its publishing activities.

Contents

Introduction 3

Part One: Multiple Epics Compared

1 Summarizing an Epic Legend: The Legend of Ponnivala Nadu 11
2 Character and Plot Structures: The Mahabharata 39
3 Human Life as a Balancing Act: The Epic of Gilgamesh 109
4 Seven Great Phases of History: The Bible's Old and New Testament Stories 137
5 Landscapes and Identity Formation: The Vatnsdaela Saga 168
6 Human versus Extra-Human Powers: The Nanabush Story Cycle 224

Part Two: Hidden Paradigms

7 Splitting, Replicating, and Twinning of Gods and Animals 245
8 The Story Told by the Stars: Babylonian Star-Lore and the Hindu Nakshatras 277
9 The Shining Lotus Plant: A Visual Approach to Finding Hidden Paradigms 309
10 The Monsoon Rains: Filling a Lotus Pond and Nourishing a Golden River 357
Conclusion 405

Appendix: Names of the Central Ponnivala Nadu Story Characters 409

Notes 411

Annotated Bibliography of Primary Epic Story Sources, by Chapter 435

General Bibliography 443

Image Credits 449

Index 453

HIDDEN PARADIGMS

Introduction

Some have claimed that you can find an entire world inside a single acorn or by examining one grain of sand. In the long journey that led me to write this book I have experienced something similar. One single epic, a story I discovered accidentally early in 1965, has become the central focus of this entire volume. Readers might well wonder what could have triggered my fascination with this particular tale. It began just as I settled into a village of Tamil speakers, deep in the interior of South India, to begin two years of PhD field research. I had taken an audio tape recorder with me although I had never intended to study folk epics. Nonetheless, accidental discoveries often drive innovative research. Soon a mysterious Tamil legend simply revealed itself, right before my eyes.[1] One night under a full moon, a singing bard accompanied by his assistant drummer sat in the middle of a large open space in the centre of the village where I had just rented a small house. Those two men were telling a story and a considerable crowd of admiring fans had gathered around to listen. I had not yet found any other good use for my tape recorder and there was little else to occupy my mind each evening. Furthermore, because my tiny home was lit only with a couple of oil lamps, reading a book after dark was not easy. And so, I thought, why not record these two men's singing and storytelling? I asked their permission after showing them how my tape recorder, packaged in a not-so-little box, could capture the sound both of their voices and of the drum beats they were using. The two men were fascinated and quickly agreed to my proposal. They asked me what story I wanted to hear. I had no idea, of course, and so I turned to the audience. The curious listeners who had formed a wide circle around the two singers unanimously asked for the Annanmar Kathai, the Tamil name for the epic story I later came to call, in English, the Land of the Golden River, or the Legend of Ponnivala Nadu.[2]

I had assumed that this would be a one-hour tale, but I quickly learned that that first night was just an opening instalment. To my surprise, the Annanmar story morphed into a thirty-eight-hour performance and completing it required a full eighteen nights of singing! The two bards continued to unfold their long tale night after night and every evening I set up my tape recorder faithfully, ready to document each ensuing segment. Fortunately, I had brought enough tape with me to cover this project, though there was little left when it was all over. And I got lucky in another way as well. An angel appeared on what, I think, was the third night. He called himself a "line man" and he proceeded to offer me an illegal connection to the major electrical line that he knew how to access at the side of a nearby road. The government had not yet approved the electrification of the village where I was staying, but it had promised that one day this would happen. That angelic lineman produced a long wire, and from that he constructed a jerry-rigged connection between my little tape recorder and that huge overhead line. He never asked for a single rupee in compensation. It was his gift! This offer of help turned out to be a life saver as it allowed me to complete all eighteen nights of recording without having to source hundreds of batteries to keep my hungry machine running. On the nineteenth night, when the story was complete, local story fans conducted a ritual puja. They wanted to honour my recording machine and all the tapes I had used. I stacked those tapes beside the machine and many ritual oblations were conducted. Then, I began to wonder: What do I do now?

I knew I had something important on those recorded tapes, but I had had no training in this kind of research. I was a social anthropologist, not a literary scholar or a folk music collector. Furthermore, there was no way I could continue to use that secretive and highly illegal connection to a main electrical line without incurring government rage and, besides, I did not want to "scrub" these now valuable tapes by trying to listen to the story over and over for its every detail. Moreover, at that time I still had only a very thin knowledge of the Tamil language and had understood only a little when the bard and his companion had actually been singing. So, I chose the obvious path. I asked my research assistant (who spoke only Tamil) to sit down with me and explain the story patiently, step by step, scene by scene. I took copious notes as he retold it using simple Tamil sentences I could understand. Soon, I had acquired an elementary grasp of the entire tale. But that was just the beginning. At that point I never imagined that I would continue working on this story for the next fifty-four years. That is my count of the time I have spent thinking about this wonderful legend, as of the day I write these words.

Somehow this Annanmar story slowly crept into my heart and made its home there. I now reference it, mentally, at every turn in my own life. Indeed, it plays out as a backdrop to almost everything I actively do or even just experience happening around me. Perhaps I always needed a keystone legend to serve as an anchor for my own life. Certainly, this epic has played that role for me over the years. My identification with it has only grown as I have aged. Perhaps this is because, even though I was raised a nominal Christian, I was never really taught the corpus of Old and New Testament stories in a memorable way. How a story is told is so very important. The teller needs to capture the listener's imagination. Those Christian tales never stuck with me. They never managed to weave a cohesive pictorial tapestry in my imagination, in a way that would create an integrated worldview, a set of meanings that I could carry around in life and use for guidance. The Ponnivala Nadu legend, by contrast, has long since taken over that role in my head and has gradually become a fundamental reference point for much of my day-to-day thinking.

In the chapters that follow I try to share with my readers some of the many ways I have explored this epic story, finding many new meanings and fresh insights year after year. In sum, this folk legend serves, at least for me, as a kind of cornucopia. An equivalent image, familiar to the residents of the village area where I lived, would be the Pongal pot. That is the name given to a ritual container of fresh milk which is boiled using a hot flame until it overflows. When the milk nearly explodes, bubbling over in abundance, it is understood to signify the hope for everlasting richness and joy. The Pongal pot represents a state of well being that people wish would fill their lives more generally. The Annanmar story has played a role in my life that is something like an overflowing Pongal pot. It has afforded me a vast intellectual journey through both space and time and has also been the source of much inspiration. In the following pages I explain the many different questions I have asked of this legend over time and some of the answers I have found. It is time to share the wide variety of ideas that have spilled forth from this tale resulting from my constant engagement with it.

My hope is that my own discoveries can help guide others who also wish to explore the power of epics and of epic storytelling. I also hope that the various personal findings, brought to light while seeking to understand this one legend in depth, will help stimulate others to make experimental and fresh types of story comparisons for themselves. If we seek to understand human differences in terms of the variety of thought-frames people use, then the comparative study of epics becomes a worthwhile way to explore cultural differences more broadly. As suggested earlier by the grain of sand, what looks to be just one small ant-sized doorway into the soil can sometimes turn out to be a tunnel that leads to a gold mine hidden below. One simply needs to find good questions to ask, queries likely to lead to an ever-deeper exploration of a story's inner passageways. Diving into a tunnel and following its path can also lead to the mapping of overall patterns, and of course, to eventually describing an entire anthill's architecture. Myriad separate pathways are bound to eventually meet, perhaps abruptly, at some unexpected crossing point. There will be fresh signage located there, markers that point to those ants' community hall. Once in that special space, if lucky, we may discover a surprising stash of buried treasure, a bundle of ideas and unique symbols they have compiled over many eons and are now willing to share, as long as we agree to honour and respect their unique value.

The following chapters detail several different approaches to the study of epics all of which can be used to think comparatively about the contributions made by grand legends told by remarkable poets from different lands. The ideas addressed have been organized under two broad headings, as laid out in the table of contents. Chapters 1 to 6 compare this book's core tale with several other much better-known heroic legends collected elsewhere around the world, pointing out similarities and contrasts. Chapters 7 through 10 unpack a variety of significant paradigms found hidden inside the main tale featured throughout this study. Together these two halves are designed to explore both what makes the Land of the Golden River a unique epic and what, at the same time, makes it an attempt to confront universal themes such as heroism, family survival, and life beyond death. In its second half *Hidden Paradigms* explores four topics: twinship, the stars, the lotus symbol, and the monsoon rains. Each of these subjects evokes cultural specifics as well as universal themes. Both levels of understanding operate at one and the same time, providing a bundle of interwoven perspectives that can be best understood if carefully untangled.

When we examine post hunter-gatherer legends, and legend cycles, a key theme repeatedly emerges: what did mankind give up when people decided to abandon a previous, relatively mobile, community-focused lifestyle? What problems resulted from the decision to shift to a denser, tied-to-one-place plan for living? That choice carried with it a clear downside, the need to work within (and under) many more layers of human hierarchy. And all that new social complexity also entailed a new kind of economy, one dependent on larger scale food production. Ploughing, seeding, and weeding, and all back-breaking types of work became necessary and routine. Such changes also meant that the hunter-gatherer lifestyle associated with more natural landscapes became secondary to deliberate, well-organized modes of food production that transformed the natural terrain and also created the need for a more centralized social system. Furthermore, there was always the looming issue of climate change. Large swaths of ploughed fields now left the soil vulnerable to the harsh drying effects of wind and sunlight. Those laboriously tilled fields, as they grew larger and covered more acreage, also came to require labour intensive irrigation systems, just to keep the earth moist. These new economic patterns also entailed new transportation needs. Now animal-drawn carts were required, just to transport the foods harvested from well-tilled fields to distant consumer locations. No wonder fresh stories, focused on wars, kings, and local heroes, were needed to explain all this and to suggest ways of coping with the enormous amount of upheaval such changes brought in their wake. What happened when wild and unmanaged forests were transformed into vast stretches of ploughed fields?

How have humans artfully bent and strategically transformed core non-human animal and plant energies in order to better harness them to serve to human needs?" Ethically, what have humans had to sacrifice to achieve this new end? Each epic story examined in the following pages will, when looked at deeply, be found to address a different dimension of this same basic human history, each offering its own unique view of this larger evolutionary challenge.

The first epic to be compared with the Legend of Ponnivala Nadu is the Mahabharata, a culturally fundamental story that has come down to us from ancient India. Here the overlap between the two is primarily based on family and kinship norms, and with that, on the similarities between the personalities of several of the Mahabharata's key characters and the protagonists who dominate the three generations of family in the Ponnivala Nadu or *Land of the Golden River* story. The second comparison contrasts the Ponnivala legend with the Story of Gilgamesh. This latter tale lacks the all important focus on family structure and descent line themes that are central to the Mahabharata, and instead describes the importance of a walled city-state, an entity that is likened to a ruler's personal cattle pen. The need for timber for building temples and other cultural monuments, along with the slave labour needed to accomplish those phenomenal tasks, is also made explicit. The third comparison looks at the biblical tale of mankind's repeated efforts to improve the human condition overall. The many historic struggles, related by both the Old and New Testament texts, are focused on the complex nature of the moral issues that loom large over human behaviour. Those same texts also depict the social pain entire ethnic communities experienced when specific groups rose up to either confront or flee from one another.

The fourth epic to be examined is from Iceland, the Vatnsdaela Saga, a story of pioneering in a pristine wilderness where the influence of non-human powers is intensely felt. Here ideas of magic and the fearsome nature of the non-human environment are explored, along with concepts such as a heroes' raw ability to dominate or to show resilience in the face of repeated adversity. Finally, the fifth epic considered in this book is a North American Native cycle of stories that describe the exploits of the Ojibwa culture hero Nanabush. This last choice is an outlier in some respects as it reflects the perspective of First Peoples prior to their encounter with colonialists whose key focus was on cutting trees and then ploughing local lands. But even this hunting-gathering perspective is caught up in trying to answer the broadest question of all: What, in the end, makes us human beings special? All the stories to be discussed ahead, furthermore, struggle to understand the occasional unavoidable "intrusion of chaos" that all human social systems confront when change is forced on them. It is hoped that reading these chapters, each different in what it uncovers, will reveal a few new insights. It is also hoped that the multiple approaches presented will inspire fresh questions, perhaps ones that others will also wish to vigorously pursue in the future.

PART ONE

Multiple Epics Compared

1 Summarizing an Epic Legend: The Legend of Ponnivala Nadu

It is never easy to summarize a long, long story. One has to choose a perspective or interpretive angle. Then one must decide which incidents and which scenes are most climatic and most memorable. And finally, one must retell the tale in a way that makes it unforgettable. Can the audience recall who the key characters were, recall what they experienced, and finally, answer simple questions about how the story concluded? Here then is a summary of the Legend of Ponnivala Nadu, the focal story that this book is built around.

Superficially, the Legend of Ponnivala Nadu is about a line of male heroes and their willingness to stand up to their local rivals. In large part, their challengers are lineal male cousins, men who are jealous because they claim that the original responsibility for farming the territory of Ponnivala Nadu, allocated to nine brothers, had been unjustly split up between them. That initial division favoured just one man, the eldest son, grandfather to the twin heroes Ponnar and Shankar in the third generation. But there are also struggles that pit this heroic family against local, indigenous artisans and against hunters who live in a nearby hilly and well-forested tract. Other parts of the story show the twins being unjustly insulted by a powerful neighbouring king. But underneath all these tensions lies a deeper theme. The males in this story are deeply dependent on women: for their insights, for their resilience in times of hardship and, of course, for their unique ability to birth family successors. This last trait links those women to a wider set of beliefs about the nature of divine power and the organization of the cosmos at large. After years of study, I am now convinced that a largely hidden female energy drives the Legend of Ponnivala Nadu forward at many of its most critical moments.

Aside from the above core themes, it is also important to mention a set of questions that have proven to be particularly useful, especially when comparing a variety of important and famous epic stories with the unique and rich content of The Legend of Ponnivala Nadu. The questions, categorized under seven key concepts and used repeatedly in the study ahead, are as follows:

1 **Roots**: What spiritual or cosmic origin story do the key characters recognize as uniquely their own?
2 **Reclamation**: What have these characters lost that they are now trying to understand and reclaim?
3 **Resistance**: What core challenges confront those characters and threaten to prevent them reaching their goals?
4 **Resilience**: In what ways do a story's main characters demonstrate their focus and their fortitude?
5 **Relationships**: What intricate mesh of relationships are the above characters embedded in? Which human bonds link them together and why?
6 **Reflection**: What mirrors operate in the story? What do we see doubled, stretched, or skewed? Do these imperfect reflections present windows that help one uncover a story's deepest themes?
7 **Revelation**: When we do identify one or more core concepts threaded through a story, what do these themes mean? What are they trying to tell us about the nature of human life and death on earth today?

In the following pages, each of the above concepts will be discussed in relation to the Legend of Ponnivala Nadu story. To facilitate this, seven panels of a display designed to present the entire sweep of this epic will be used for reference. Each of these pieces presents at least one example of the concept under discussion, while also summarizing one distinctive part of the larger Ponnivala Nadu story. Each concept has been presented using a unique collage of story illustrations; all are images previously used in varied lecture and presentation settings (see figure 1.1). Viewers young and old have responded well to being asked to focus their attention on this display. These visuals help newcomers to the epic develop an interest in learning more about its content. Each of these seven panels will be discussed, in turn.[1]

Panel One: Roots

The story begins with the goddess Parvati, seen in the tree leaves at the top of the first panel (figure 1.3). She is busy creating nine brothers who are given the status of clan ancestors (lower circle). Their descendants will become a group of agnatic cousins. Significantly, these men are set down in a deep forest, on the steps of an old temple. Ganesh (called by the Tamil name Vinayakar in this story) is Parvati's eldest son. He is the god associated with "new beginnings." But more important, Parvati sends these men down to earth, far away from her own domain high above. Lightning and thunder are involved, signifying the cosmic power associated with this first creative act. Here we see her floating in the upper branches of a large banyan tree. That tree, a cosmic pillar of sorts, appears in all seven panels and connects them together. Its aerial roots link heaven and earth. New roots sprout frequently, and they always grow downwards hoping to touch the ground, while this tree's branches, of course, stretch upwards.[2]

The Legend of Ponnivala Nadu   13

a

b

Figure 1.1. Author's presentation at a school in the Toronto area.

14   Multiple Epics Compared

THE LEGEND OF PONNIVALA
An Ancient folk epic sung in the Kongu region of Tamilnadu, India

Displayed in columns on searate banners:
SEVEN KEY THEMES IN THIS STORY

○ Initial Event   ○ Subsequent example

ROOTS   RECLAMATION   RESISTANCE   RESILIENCY   RELATIONSHIPS   REFLECTION   REVELATION

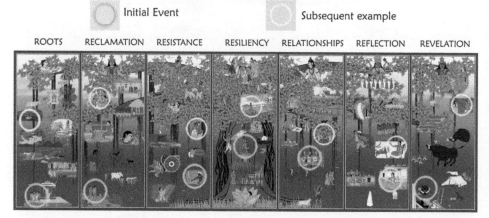

Figure 1.2. Handout the author has used when speaking in both school and university contexts.

Somewhat later, wives are also generated by the same goddess and they all are sent to earth too, one to marry each of the original nine men. But then an unfortunate event occurs, a kind of "original sin." Seven poor hungry cows die by trying to leap over an iron fence covered with spikes. This was a barrier built around the eldest brother's first sugarcane field, something he was very proud of. But he was a little too proud and thus he had ordered the fence built without much forethought. The cows were hungry and tried to jump the fence but were impaled on it and died. The spirits of those poor cows then complain to Parvati's husband, Lord Shiva, who resides high above. Shiva decides to curse that clan ancestor (the eldest brother) and his descendants to childlessness for seven generations. (This act against generation one in effect ensures that any descendants will be sired, in part, by the gods. Thus all the heroes in this story, including those in the third generation, are semi-divine.) Later Shiva's heart softens a bit, and he decides to create a son for this man. Shiva hides the infant under a pile of rocks in his back field (upper circle) where the small baby is nursed by drinking the milk of a kind cow who has been left to graze nearby. Later the baby, who is in good health and appears to be a normal, if inexplicably orphaned, child, is found there by the eldest of those original nine brothers. The child is adopted by that brother (as per Shiva's intention) and grows up to be the key male hero of the Ponnivala Nadu

The Legend of Ponnivala Nadu 15

Figure 1.3. Panel 1: Roots.

story's second generation of heroes. Notably therefore, he, like his father, was created by the gods above and then sent down to earth to serve their grander purpose. Soon after a woman is produced in the clouds for him to wed (see panel 4, figure 1.6) and then also sent directly to earth by Shiva and Parvati.

Shiva and Parvati's love play, high in the skies, was involved in creating this wife-to-be for the hero of the second generation. During their interaction some "love liquid" fell to earth and landed on a lotus flower where it transformed quickly into a beautiful baby girl. As we will see later, the third generation of males in this story is also "created" in heaven, but in a slightly different way. This time Lord Shiva immaculately places a set of male twins in the womb of the lotus-born heroine, Tamarai. But she first had to sit on a high pillar praying to Shiva, begging him for children for a full twenty-one years (see panel 4). A sister for those twins is Shiva's final gift of life. He also places her, in pre-birth embryo form, in Tamarai's womb. Lying beside her brothers-to-be, this little girl shares their womb space and becomes the triplet in this third-generation cluster of key characters. The heroine Tamarai then descends to earth and roughly nine months later all three of her children are born together on the same day. The memorable point here is that all three generations of key characters in this story are sky created, but their destiny is to become earth-dwelling humans. Thus, by implication, the roots of human existence as described by this story lie in the sky. But these are not brand-new lives. Rather, the gods have taken the spirit essence of lives that have lived on earth before and recycled them. At least in the third generation, the triplets born to Tamarai contain the essence of previous heroic beings who have walked this earth before or at least have previously lived as spirits in the sky. That is what is meant in this story by "Roots," namely a description of where the human lives described in this legend ultimately came from. The banyan tree's roots are a traditional Indian way of visualizing and expressing this core idea. Furthermore, where these beings were born is also part of this Roots concept. In the second and third generations of this epic tale, the heroes were physically "born" in the land of Ponnivala itself. And the role of a key goddess, the great Parvati, the wife of Lord Shiva, plays a notable role in all of that creation activity. She is the original source of the heroes' human family in this epic account. She is the creatrix behind it all!

Panel Two: Reclamation

This next segment of the story focuses on finding identity through locating a place and a set of values that a family can claim as their own. In this story there are several themes of this kind that require mention: a) Kunnutaiya, the son of the first ancestor, Kolatta, was born (under a pile of rocks) on the heroes' family lands, b) After a period in exile early on, Kunnutaiya, now married to Tamarai, the little girl who was born in a lotus flower, returns with her to reclaim Kolatta's fields, the locale where he had been born. The couple enjoy their first fine view of this area from the top of a rock promontory (lower circle), c) They have become a farming family, dedicated to ploughing and planting crops that will make the land prosper, d) Tamarai finds jewels inside the sheaths of the couple's first maize crop, e) This key female is generous and kind to beggars. She defines the family's goodness by showing empathy for those who are in need and come to her door for help, and f) This young family gradually begins to command wealth and respect. They do well, despite resistance from Kunnutaiya's lineal cousins, and eventually they manage to build a fine home. This process of respect building culminates in a scene where the

Figure 1.4. Panel 2: Reclamation.

neighbouring Chola monarch offers the local hero Kunnutaiya a small crown. Hence this second-generation male now attains the status of a minor king. He is pronounced a Chola ally, as he was willing to pledge loyalty to that prestigious overlord (upper circle). The heroine Tamarai is central to this reclamation process as well. She was the one to find the jewels in their maize crop while her husband noticed nothing unusual about the plants there. She is then the one to ask that a palace be built. She is also the one on whom the family's prosperity will ultimately rest. But Tamarai is haunted by a curse that makes her unable to become pregnant. That fate must be understood to be a measure of counter justice, Shiva's punishment for the loss of seven cows' lives early in the story. Their deaths were not Tamarai's fault, but she has been chosen to suffer for another's mistake. And the punishment is not just confined to her for as mentioned earlier, that curse of barrenness is due to last for seven generations. Later (panel 4) this same heroine will be tested seven times, losing her life during each trial but being quickly revived by Vishnu afterwards. Finally, Tamarai is rewarded for her devotion and her patience and is invited to meet Lord Shiva in person. She will visit him while he sits in his cloud-covered mountain abode, known as Kailasa. The main theme that runs throughout this panel is the heroine's dedication to family. Her overall concern for their welfare lies at the very heart of this kingdom's prosperity. When the king's family flourishes, the entire area will prosper as well. She, and the goddess who backs her, are the central forces behind the hero's reclamation efforts and they are, together, responsible for the high status her husband eventually wins as the first king of Ponnivala Nadu.

Panel Three: Resistance

The heroic family in the Ponnivala Nadu story meet plenty of resistance. Local artisans try to block their takeover of local lands. But the heroes ignore the local residents' claim to having been there first. The newcomers assert their skills as ploughmen and promise agricultural abundance. Meanwhile, the family perseveres, even though the heroes' agnatic cousins resist their farming efforts. Their strength and devotion to the local goddess Cellatta count for a lot. Both Kunnutaiya and his wife Tamarai place their heads under the wheels of a great temple cart to demonstrate their faith in the goddess above, the deity who is riding on it (lower circle). Their faith is an expression of their devotion to her and to their resistance to their adversaries who hope they will be crushed. Despite the jealousies that swirl around this family, they are devout and hence the local goddess always protects them. Miraculously, her heavy cart takes flight at the last minute, saving this couple from sure death. Instead, their enemies die as the huge temple cart flies about like a whirlwind and strikes them. Furthermore (in the next generation), the tribal hunters who live in a nearby area, try to kidnap a maid who works for this family when they mistake her for the family's only daughter, a young princess named Tangal (the triplet mentioned earlier) who is living in the family palace. Happily, that maid is rescued by the family's principal assistant (Shambuga) before any serious harm can be done to her (upper circle). Thus, we see that the goddess herself, her female human "daughter," and her "granddaughter" all have key roles to play in assuring this family's survival. Multiple threats develop: the cousins, the artisans, and the aboriginals all hope to prevent the heroes' successful establishment in the Ponnivala Nadu area. But underneath, the earthly women in this story are also very important. In each generation, women provide a hidden source of resistance. Somehow, they are able to manoeuvre

The Legend of Ponnivala Nadu 19

Figure 1.5. Panel 3: Resistance.

around all the male-on-male jealousies that surround them. The women are this story's mediators par excellence.

Panel Four: Resilience

This panel is key to understanding the role of female power in the Ponnivala Nadu epic. As already mentioned above, Tamarai, the baby found lying on the lotus flower (and whose name translates as lotus) becomes the wife of the second-generation hero. Due to her barrenness, she undertakes a long pilgrimage to find Lord Shiva and ask for his help. That pilgrimage involves climbing a high pillar and praying to Lord Shiva for twenty-one years (lower circle). She is hoping he

20 Multiple Epics Compared

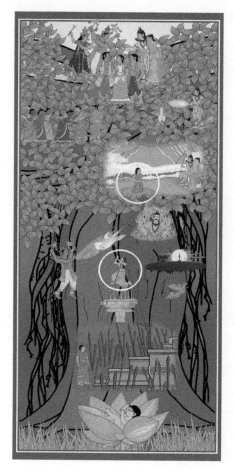

Figure 1.6. Panel 4: Resilience.

will give her a child. Lord Vishnu, Shiva's brother-in-law and a powerful god in his own right, tries to help her, using a fiery torch to burn him as he sits in deep meditation in the forest. But Shiva responds with his own fire. His rage results in Tamarai being burnt, chopped up, and desiccated seven times (his way of testing her dedication and steadfastness). But Tamarai survives all seven assaults with the help of Lord Vishnu, who cools her and moistens her surviving bones each time with precious Ganges water. This allows Tamarai to come back to life and then begin praying once more atop her high pillar. Finally, after these seven trials, Shiva has a change of heart and allows Tamarai to enter his council chambers to make her formal request. There Tamarai asks for three children (upper circle). Lord Shiva consents and then miraculously places the embryos of two sons and one daughter in Tamarai's womb. Lord Shiva also gives Tamarai a pot of sacred Ganges water that she will carry back down to earth with her. There she gives that water, drop by drop, to other women in her area who also hope for pregnancy. With this, we see certain themes begin to repeat themselves. Once again, life is generated in the heavens and travels down to earth by various means. Even many secondary women are granted happiness by means of the water that Tamarai brings down from heaven in the magical pot Shiva gave her.

One further theme requires discussion here. Think of what a lotus plant is and how it grows. Initially, a rhizome sits in the mud at the bottom of a pond or lake. Its first shoots start to grow laterally, but soon a central stem will grow upward. When it finds the surface of the water and the sun touches it, it will grow a flower that floats and basks in light shining down from above. What a beautiful metaphor for woman this is: each female is a stem that struggles upward, reaching for sunlight. When it eventually achieves enough height, a flower sitting on that stem will burst forth, just as Tamarai blossomed as she sat on her penance pillar. Her twenty-one years of meditation there present us with a vivid image of resiliency and determination. Her dedication serves both as a devotional and liberating symbol of human willpower. Tamarai is the heroic mother figure in this epic story. It is no accident then that she has been named after a lotus blossom. Her character is the central example of resilience seen in this Ponnivala Nadu story.

Panel Five: Relationships

Next in this panel sequence is the story of the birth and adolescent adventures of the twin grandsons, the true heroes of this epic story. Just minutes after birth they are seized and carried to a dark and secret cave beneath the temple of the local goddess Cellatta. There she arranges to have the boys fed on tigers' milk. She also gives them lessons in the martial arts. Later the two are returned to their human "parents" where they learn horseback riding and swordsmanship on the family farm. Then, at age sixteen, both boys are put through a set of wedding rituals by their mother, and two cousin-sisters are pronounced to be their wives (lower circle). But their simultaneous marriages are never consummated and instead these two women remain chaste hostages in a separate palace where they spend the rest of their lives spinning. That image, though cruel, symbolizes the importance of women in generating protection via the threads they produce. Their metaphorical spider webs are implicitly understood to both guard (as webs that trap evil influences) and magically empower their virgin husbands. Furthermore, the two wives' lifelong chastity also generates a fierce energy that will supernaturally transfer added force to their husbands' swords, important tools they will then use in battle.

Despite what has been said above, male-to-male relationships also play a central role in this story. The father-son bond is one such theme. We see this in panel 5, at the bottom right, where these two young heroes ride on their father's right and left shoulders respectively (see figure 1.7). This image nicely expresses that core

22 Multiple Epics Compared

Figure 1.7. Panel 5: Relationships.

relationship. The brother-to-brother connection is another important theme in the Ponnivala Nadu story. It is no accident that these two adolescent boys, now just sixteen, are twins. One sibling is mild tempered, thoughtful, and patient. The other one is aggressive, impulsive, and easily angered (see him killing the Chola king, near the top, left side of this panel). Also depicted in this illustration is one of these two heroes' multiple war expeditions (upper circle). That image nicely expresses the broader view of brotherhood presented by this epic story: one brother serves as the dominant actor, while the other provides a counter point to his aggressive style by being pliant and restrained. The two boys inherit their father's kingdom together and thus the question is how will they agree to share their power? Neither personality type is likely to find success in isolation but, instead, a mix or a balance of traits is needed. In the all-important third generation of this epic account there is no single ruler. Instead, the brothers govern the lands of Ponnivala Nadu together. The elder twin does much of the day-to-day management of the kingdom. He is liked and he is kind. But the younger twin occupies the lead position in any violent engagement, and he is always seen out front as they ride together into a fight (upper circle). To be even more metaphorical, the elder brother's goodness draws rain from the skies (see chapter 10) while the younger one draws blood from battle fields on earth. The complementarity these brothers display in their relationship with one another, furthermore, echoes an ancient Indo-European theme that regularly featured not one but rather a pair of complementary rulers or, mythologically speaking, a pair of counterbalanced semi-gods.

Dicing is another theme mentioned repeatedly in the Ponnivala story. But here the game is often played by a threesome (seen in the centre between the two heroes as they study their game board). It is as if the heroes and the gods are contesting their powers and trying to divine who will win, or at least be able to direct the larger game of life itself. This game of dice shifts in character as the story progresses. Vishnu initially tries to help these two heroes on many occasions, but he gradually pulls away as they near the end of their lives, at age sixteen. This was Lord Shiva's public ruling as he placed these two boys in their mother's womb as embryos. Towards the end of this epic account Vishnu "jumps ship," so to speak, and decides to support the two brothers' adversaries, the forest hunters, instead. This god already knows what these twin heroes' common fate will be and that it will happen soon. Furthermore, the relationship between Vishnu and Shiva, brothers-in-law in this story, is another theme that highlights this story's focus on a need for balance. The great goddess herself stands between these two as the sister of one of them and the wife of the other. She both mediates and conspires, taking pains to help both her brother and her husband in alternation. Again, if one looks behind the surface of the events described, it is often a woman whose influence determines the outcome of the day. Parvati, thus, plays a role at a cosmic level similar to the one the heroine Tamarai performs on earth. Both are caught between a brother (or brothers) and a close male comrade (or husband), making women in this story key to understanding the hidden role of the goddess at large. Tamarai must be seen to play a critical role if one wants to truly appreciate the human relationships underlying this story's important kinship bonds.

Panel Six: Reflection

The name of the most important woman seen in panel 6 (lower circle) is Tangal, which simply means "younger sister" (see figure 1.8). She is the triplet born alongside her two brothers in panel 5. Of all the women in this epic legend, Tangal is the most important female protagonist. But who is she? The answer is Tangal is an earthly form of one of the Pleiades sisters, a set of near-identical women associated with the constellation of the same name. This is a star cluster important to many cultures around the world. In South India these seven females are most often portrayed as a line-up of young girls (top centre). Above them is an image of Durga, a principal Hindu goddess and also a form of Parvati. We will discuss the significance of these seven women at some length in chapters 7 and 8. However, here it is important to note that Tangal, the youngest of the seven sisters, is the specific female spirit Lord Shiva decided to place in Tamarai's womb. Tangal thus descends to earth inside Tamarai and is then born as her daughter. While Tangal's two brothers rush about on earth, ride horses, fight with swords, and play gambling games (panel 5), Tangal mostly sits in a swing that hangs in the palace courtyard. Her cradle (a style of bed her brothers never sleep in) hangs mysteriously from above (bottom centre). Tangal's feet, even as she grows into a teenage girl, rarely touch the ground. She is a creature of dreams, of fantasies, and of the sky. Importantly, she can see the sky from the very place where her swing is located (an open courtyard). Her will and her manipulation of events have a clear impact on her brothers, particularly in ways they may not always notice. Tangal gradually grows dissatisfied with her brothers: a) for the lack of attention they give her, b) for their refusal to bring her sisters-in-law into the palace to assuage her loneliness (they are housed separately and she never sees them), c) for her brothers' mistake in not asking for her blessing before placing their swords in their scabbards, d) because they decide to go to war against her wishes, e) because they lack of interest in seeing her married, and f) because they ignore her favourite little pet, a female dog named Ponnacci.

Furthermore, the theme of reflection becomes important and more apparent as one examines this panel. Note that there is a second female (upper circle) just above the first (lower circle). She is Viratangal (the fierce or brave Tangal), a clear (almost) mirror-image of the first heroine, but with a different personality. And this second woman is located in a quite different environment. She is a forest girl, daughter of the tribal chief. Viratangal is surrounded by wild animals, especially tigers, cobras, and a huge wild boar. She also interacts with a flock of wild parrots that have descended from the gates of heaven to live in her family's great forest banyan tree. Tangal, in contrast to this natural lifestyle, lives beside fine ploughed fields that her brothers' farm workers till and cultivate for her and her brothers' economic benefit. This reflection shows the similarity, but also the difference, that exist between a forest female and a farm girl who is also a princess. These two images are meant to contrast wild and tame, or forest versus ploughed fields. The context of the tale is now seen to have expanded from the simple opposition of twin brothers, one mild and one violent, to one of two different lifestyles, brought together inside a larger story frame.

Tamil poems that describe these young women (the Kannimar or sisters of the Pleiades) also support the idea that each sister has two sides to her personality. This folk poetry makes it clear that they have all come from far away, from the heavens where the stars are like fish in a great sea. They must cross a vast watery expanse each time they decide to descend to earth. Once having descended, the mission of these girls is to protect and support. One might compare their role to what a loyal police force is supposed to do for a local king. Furthermore, these seven girls work

Figure 1.8. Panel 6: Reflection.

for a senior woman, just as daughters may try to help their mother. This is exactly how these seven are seen in temple shrines, usually seated next to a larger icon of a well-known goddess like Durga, Kali, or Saraswati. More evidence to this effect will be presented in chapter 7. Here let it simply be said that the Kannimar provide an important underbelly for the entire Ponnivala Nadu story. The young Tangal is an unmarried virgin girl, one of the group of seven, and it is her job to monitor and (try) to direct her brothers' impetuous behaviour. Near the end of the story Tangal, the farm princess, crosses over into the forest after her two brothers die. At this point Tangal takes on some of the bravery and wildness of her counterpart Viratangal. seeming to almost merge with her. As the story concludes, the forest

26   Multiple Epics Compared

is essentially declared by Vishnu to be durable and everlasting. Tangal and Viratangal's subtle interaction is central to that broader theme. At the end of the story the power, magic and fertility of the forest is given recognition and its cosmic role acknowledged. Tangal (symbolic of the farmland) and Viratangal (symbolic of the forest) reflect each other, but they can also be understood to merge, towards the end, into a combined, semi-divine, pre-puberty female essence.

Panel Seven: Revelation

Panel 7 provides the final key to understanding this epic story (see figure 1.9). In this last collage we find that two important concluding events are depicted nearly side-by-side. A great wild boar is beheaded, and the heroic twins take their own lives. Both are powerful, sacrificial events. We also learn more about Tangal and her inner powers as one of the seven "sisters" belonging to the Pleiades star cluster. As Tangal sleeps (bottom left) she has a horrific dream. A huge forest-dwelling boar (the male pet of her rival, Viratangal) has cursed her own twin brothers and threatened to pierce each of them with one of his sharp white tusks (lower circle). Soon Tangal's little female pet dog steps in. That tiny dog sends Tangal's twin brothers a curse in the shape of a dream-ghost (seen just above the white tent). This curse serves as a kind of alter ego for Tangal herself. It forces these two men to abandon their hunt for that marauding boar due to high fevers and dizziness. After a time, the little dog steps in and bites the boar's testicles, severely weakening him. Meanwhile, the twin brothers recover from their illness and can now accomplish the final kill using the family's great boar spear. It is clear the sister and her tiny female dog are actually responsible for this demon's demise, but the scene is engineered so that Tangal's two brothers can take the credit for this grand achievement. However, the tables soon turn again. Very soon, Lord Vishnu drags away the severed head of that monster boar (right side, just below the centre). That head, the epic implies, will soon be offered to the goddess of the forest, a woman who represents a mix of Kali, Bhudevi, and Kottravai (all three of whom are important in the larger corpus of South Indian mythology). This blended form of several goddesses, in turn, uses this head as a seed to help restart a fresh yuga, and jump start the next grand era in cosmic time. That restart is much needed. Just before the goddess receives the offering of a powerful head-cum-seed, a huge fight breaks out between Viratangal's one hundred brothers and Tangal's only two siblings, the heroic farmer-twins. But Vishnu steps in and makes this illusory, a kind of mental vision that harms no one. As a result, the hunters and their forest are not destroyed. They will live on, unlike the heroes' own family, who like the great boar will now pass from the earth without leaving any kinsmen as successors. There will soon be a reset for all who live in the Land of the Golden River: a new, fresh era and a new beginning for all, now lies on the horizon.

The heroic twins survive what Vishnu led them to believe was a terrible fight, but soon afterwards (following a special signal from this god) they decide to take their

The Legend of Ponnivala Nadu 27

Figure 1.9. Panel 7: Revelation.

own lives while still in the forest. This makes their deaths parallel to that of the boar. Both are forest sacrifices. Each hero falls forward deliberately on his own sword and dies on the spot (upper circle). This offering of their personal lives echoes what the wild boar had earlier threatened in Tangal's dream. Both of Tangal's siblings die on the points of tusklike spears. Tangal, the sister of the heroes, soon learns of their deaths in another dream. With great sadness and anger, she conducts their funeral rites. Then she sets off into the deep forest, alone, to find her brothers' bodies. Once there she meets a sun maiden who has been praying on top of a pillar for many months. This woman descends from her perch when she sees Tangal and offers her help. The sun maiden first tells Tangal to go and fetch seven tiered pots. When Tangal returns with these seven requested vessels (upper circle) the sun maiden magically fills them with life-giving substances. These seven gifts represent an array of life-giving foods, mainly liquids, that she has obtained from the sky via her prayers. Tangal takes her filled pots and flies away, using her new friend's loyal goose as her vehicle. During that flight Tangal metaphorically passes to the land of the dead. There she soon finds the spot where her brothers' corpses lie. Now she uses her seven magical substances to resurrect the two men. These heroic warriors spring back to life, but only briefly. Their resurrection lasts long enough, however, for the three siblings to talk to one another for a short time. In their brief conversation the two men tell their sister why they have decided to take their own lives. After that they slump back to the ground.

The Ponnivala story's key revelation, as we have just seen, is that the two heroines Shiva earlier sent to earth, the mother Tamarai and her daughter Tangal, collaborate with the gods in a well-intentioned attempt to achieve a more just society. The story makes clear that death is a necessity to allow for an untarnished and largely unstructured cosmic renewal process that will take place soon. As we have seen, when men fail to follow the rules and become excessively violent or verbally aggressive, women emerge as community gatekeepers and trusted guardians. Sometimes a total renewal is necessary because the earth has, over time, undergone so much decay. But that renewal first requires deconstruction, an event that allows the earth to be cleansed and the seeds of regrowth to gather new energy. The great goddess will always utilize the blood spilled by previous heroes to allow all humans to grow up tall once more. First, she will first plant a seed here on earth, in this case the head of a wild boar, and then she will nourish it with the blood of heroic warriors.[3] The goddess is able to use such gifts, here expressed as a tangible presentation of the two heroes' own life energies, to start the cyclical processes of life over once again. In that process of renewal both the farm imagery of planting seeds and the forest imagery of wildness-through-sacrifice are involved. Both are important to cosmic continuity, as are the stars above. In sum, a divine sense of cosmic purpose is displayed throughout this story. The energy inherent in the sky and in the blessings received through rain flows to earth via steadfast devotees like the sun maiden who knows how to source sacred liquids that serve to re-energize life on earth. More about how all this comes together will be discussed in the final three chapters.

Additional Basic Themes Imbedded in The Ponnivala Nadu Story

There are three further themes that have been found to be quite useful when discussing this story, especially when thinking of using this epic in a classroom context and particularly when studying it with Canadian students.

Multiple Generations of Immigrants

The story is about three generations in one family. The first generation is made up of pioneers, men who enter a remote region as ploughmen backed by a powerful

South Indian Chola king. They confront many challenges as new settlers. They are opposed by the people who live in the area already, people who feel that the newcomers pose a threat to their own local economy and livelihoods. They do not like the fact that these immigrants are cutting down trees and taking over control of the land. The original residents, furthermore, eventually lose status. They are now forced to participate in a new agricultural economy where they are treated as lowly "workers." In this transformation they lose their sense of independence and of personal pride. They no longer control territory, nor can they continue to set what they believe to be a fair price on their knowledge and their artistic skills. This is the old and familiar story of colonial conquest, well known not only to Canadians but around the world.

The second generation differs from the first as now the new settlers are born locally on the land in question. In this generation the newcomers thrive. Furthermore, they manage to build on their parents' hard work. At this point the early immigrant-pioneers' gains are consolidated. The revered independent farming family model gains respect and, likewise, the Ponnivala family begins to prosper. Its members grow wealthy; the heroes build a fine palace and now they can afford to hire others rather than doing the work of ploughing by themselves. The family also gains recognition from the Chola king, the same monarch who initially backed the family's initial migration into the area. The family is given respectful gifts by that king and also a small, symbolic crown. This gives the family a new status. They are now minor kings.

In the third generation, things change again. Now the young twin grandsons take control. These men have been well schooled (for their time) and they grow up with a knowledge of the martial arts, of horseback riding, and more. These young heroes no longer want to be farmers, but they do want to defend their family and its prestigious position. In sum, they want to become heroic warriors. They also know that family life may inhibit the independence they dream of and so, although they marry, they chose to remain celibate and never start families of their own. They are modern men who want to strike out and achieve something new. They do not want to be labelled immigrants but rather they want to embody pride, physical strength, and independence.

This depiction of three generations in the lives of an immigrant family compares nicely with what many recent North American immigrants, especially those from Asia, often experience. This pattern of progression provides a good topic of discussion with students, both recent immigrants as well as those from other backgrounds.

First Peoples versus Colonizers

A second, somewhat related perspective on the Ponnivala Nadu story especially appeals to students in Canada. That is to view this story as one about the experience of a family of immigrants who enter a remote area backed by a distant king.

These newcomers believe they have a manifest destiny as farmers. They believe it is their responsibility to advance into what is to them a remote and unfamiliar land, colonize it, and then initiate a new plough-based economy there. This is the story of French and British colonizers in North America, and it resembles the history of Australia, parts of Africa, and many other locales as well. Furthermore, the Legend of Ponnivala Nadu is told from the colonizers' perspective, just as is most history around the world. The typical story is one where a group of hard-working immigrants, mainly farmers, are depicted as brave and strong, while any original peoples inhabiting the area they have entered are barely mentioned or worse, are negatively portrayed and their interests ignored. Those indigenous locals simply fail to resist encroachment and eventually become subordinated to the newcomers' modern farming skills and related technical knowledge.

The end of the Ponnivala Nadu story, however, provides a different perspective on this common legend. If one looks deeply into the ending of the Golden River legend, one could argue that it is really the immigrants who loose. The twin heroes and all their relatives disappear and everyone and everything else around them fades away. Here we see Vishnu ensuring that the forest hunters and their way of life continues. They are the one group who are destined to always be there, if only in the background. In the final battle Vishnu sends in substitute, imagined fighters for the twin heroes to kill off while the real native hunters remain untouched and hidden amongst the trees. Was it the immigrants' mistake to move in and marginalize those whose lifestyles (that of the artisans and the hunters) were both different and more ancient than their own? Was a sustainable lifestyle and a sense of well-being (somewhat naively imagined, perhaps) enjoyed by this planet's early inhabitants? This second perspective can be extracted from the background references in this story and used for a lively classroom discussion. This idea may appeal to teachers who want to show students that what happened in North America was not an isolated case. Poor treatment has been meted out to indigenous First Peoples everywhere. This could be a meaningful way to include an in-depth review of the Legend of Ponnivala in a year-long study theme defined under a broader theme such as social justice. Observant students, once alerted to the idea, will be able to find many issues relating to social justice deeply embedded in this rich and interesting epic legend.

Other possible approaches an astute teacher or student can use when discussing the Legend of Ponnivala Nadu include treating it as: a) a story about kings that asks what makes for a good leader; b) a story about human fate that asks who actually controls key decisions in one's life; c) a story that explores the relationship between a possible divine realm and an opposing human realm more generally; and/or d) a story about good and evil that explores the impact of this dichotomy on family life across the generations. In sum, there is much to discover in this magnificent folk epic. Everyone can identify a preferred and personalized topic of their own to pursue. The possibilities are (nearly) endless.[4]

Other Authors' Paradigms

The perceptive reader will want to revisit the seven themes identified earlier. They will be reused and referenced repeatedly in the chapters ahead: *Roots, Reclamation, Resistance, Resilience, Relationships, Reflection,* and *Revelation*. Personal experience suggests that these seven concepts can help a researcher identify a story's multiple dimensions of meaning, and also assist in locating where in a story various deeper understandings may be hidden. Usually, these seven concepts function more like threads than lumps. They aid in discovery when one follows trails of tiny breadcrumbs across many scenes. The relevant details needed to formulate ideas that relate to these seven themes are rarely found clustered together in one big lump. At the same time, it is important to understand that these concepts do not, by themselves, constitute a predictive theory nor they constitute, in themselves, a *hidden paradigm*. These seven suggestions are tools of enquiry that help one to formulate research questions and enhance a reader's sensitivity to detail. The focus of this book is to locate those larger meanings in an attempt to grow one's understanding of one particular cultural locale and this one, much-honoured, heritage story. But building a deeper and larger understanding of one example always requires contrast and comparison. For this reason, this book lays many other stories out as samples for parallel study. The challenge is to use comparison wisely, so that it does not just uncover story differences but truly prompts one to look for similarities as well. The seven dimensions listed above will all be examined repeatedly in the chapters that follow in part 1 of this book.

We must now also consider what these seven thematic questions are not. If one or more of themes outlined above are not present in a given story's case, it does not mean that question is not useful. Rather it means one should ask WHY that topic or theme is not addressed. Why it was avoided or left out can be interesting in itself. A paradigm is a different matter. If a paradigm predicts something, then that something should be present. One should be able to point to the evidence that the theme identified has indeed been built into that story. Otherwise, the paradigm does not work for that case. Much like a hypothesis in the hard sciences, if the idea does not work it should then either be adjusted or, perhaps, abandoned entirely. Part 2 of this book deals specifically with four key paradigm concepts: 1) twin characters whose actions embody contrastive value sets but who also need each other, 2) a wild boar that is two-faced. He is both fertilizing and destructive almost at the same instant in time, 3) a lotus-like tree that reaches up in order to separate sea from sky but also connects those two realms, and 4) the earth itself, which needs the sun's light and heat, but also requires the dark clouds that result in rain and flooding. These four concepts each come with opposing poles that oscillate back and forth in power, each duo helping to maintain life on earth for all.[5]

These four paradigms lend emotive feeling and personal meaning to the Legend of Ponnivala Nadu. All four are rich with complexity and all involve a tension

32 Multiple Epics Compared

between opposites. We must also ask, however, how the seven terms used throughout this book relate to other studies of epic structure, especially ones that claim to have discovered a paradigm-like key to understanding epic-length stories in general. Joseph Campbell is one such author. In his famous work *The Hero with a Thousand Faces,* Campbell presents a grand scheme, a kind of meta paradigm, that he argues suitably describes the core stages of any heroic journey, worldwide. Do his conclusions apply to the Legend of Ponnivala, a story he had never heard of? How does his approach apply to the ideas used in this book? In our view, Campbell's grand argument describes the adventures, yearnings, and eventual fate of the Ponnivala epic heroes reasonably well. The problem is first, that his approach does not yield many insights, and second, that the conclusions reached from applying his grand chart to the Ponnivala Nadu example are quite bland. All that can be said is that there is some fit. Here is the matchup that I was able to find:

Sequential Stages: The Hero's Quest - as per Campbell	Sequential Stages: The Lives of the Ponnivala Nadu Heroes
The hero sets out on a journey to acquire some object or attain some sort of divine wisdom.	Kolatta, the clan ancestor, sets out to find a new home after a bad drought makes life in a primeval, heavily forested area untenable. This theme matches with **Roots** and **Reclamation** (where life began and how a group's story and identity can be retained after migration).
The hero undergoes great trials and tribulations during the course of his quest.	Kolata and his descendants (his son and two grandsons) end up in a region named Ponnivala Nadu, but their right to stay there are contested by: a) First, its pre-existing residents (craftsmen) b) Second, related kinsmen (who rival them for land control) c) Third, a group of neighbouring forest hunters (Vettuvas) **Resistance** (struggles to establish family rights)
The hero undergoes a spiritual (and sometimes literal) death and rebirth, and then transforms to become an entirely new being.	Vishnu reveals to the heroes (the two grandsons of Kolatta) that they forgot to include the family's loyal pet, Ponnacci, when setting off to hunt down a black boar named Komban. In the end they realize their mistake with help from Vishnu, humble themselves, call Ponnacci to their forest hunting camp and apologize to her. She then succeeds in bringing about the death of that boar-demon. **Relationships** (respect owed to family members, even pets). Death and rebirth occur later in this chart, under the "revelation" theme below.

(Continued)

Sequential Stages: The Hero's Quest - as per Campbell	Sequential Stages: The Lives of the Ponnivala Nadu Heroes
The hero gains new powers, and with those powers, achieves his goal.	Ponnacci helps conquer the great wild boar. The grandsons use a huge, magical boar spear for the kill. Other revelations follow. Vishnu finally sends the two brothers a signal (a flowered arrow) indicating that their lives are nearing their final moments and that it is time now to gift their spirits to the gods. **Resilience** (the spirits of these brave heroes will live on in Kailasa, their version of heaven)
The hero returns home to share this heavenly reward with his people.	Both grandsons commit suicide (responding to Vishnu's flowered-arrow command) but both are then later brought back to life by their sister Tangal. She asks them to return to the family palace, but the younger brother (who takes the lead) refuses permanent revival. He clarifies that they must both die without returning home. They realize it is now time to pass the torch on to others through engineering their own deaths. **Revelation** (why death is inevitable – the purpose it serves)
All mankind is redeemed	The heroes' deaths allow the goddess to start a new yuga, in turn allowing the survivors to flourish. **Reflection** (the new era will duplicate but also somewhat modify the previous one)

Campbell, however, is not the only scholar to propose a "grand scheme" or pattern that can be applied across many cultures and areas of the world. A second proposal of this kind has been generated by Michael Witzel, Wales Professor of Sanskrit at Harvard. He has focused on mythological tales in general, rather than on heroes from a culture's story traditions per se. But these two concepts, one of myths held dear and one of heroes glorified by a legend, are interrelated. Furthermore, Witzel's 2012 work *The Origins of the World's Mythologies* presents, roughly speaking, a modern revision of Sir James Frazer's much older but very extensive 1890 publication, *The Golden Bough*. Witzel and Frazer both focus on the worldwide corpus of myths. And their conclusions are rather similar: For both the goal was to find a single overarching pattern that would, more-or-less accurately, encompass a huge number of specific examples. Frazer attempted to develop a world-wide frame for all myths that address how human life arose and how man's place on earth relates to the stars and the planets. He also discussed the role of plants, of the sun and moon, of animals and more in these grand myths. Witzel's

34   Multiple Epics Compared

conclusions differ somewhat from Frazer's in that he outlines two separate patterns; one he calls the Laurasian architype and the other the Gondwana alternative. And there is another distinguished author, Bruce Lincoln, who has published a similar schematic analysis entitled *Myth, Cosmos and Society* in 1986.[6] Although Witzel and Lincoln reached somewhat different conclusions, when looked at from a certain level their works are rather similar. Both Lincoln and Witzel rely heavily on Indo-European source materials and, not surprisingly, the grand patterns they identify can be seen to be culturally related in a general way. They diverge because Lincoln stresses the link between mythology and social structure, a connection Witzel largely ignores. Both authors ideas, however, more-or-less fit the structure of the Ponnivala legend. The Ponnivala Nadu account can be called a heroic legend that has been decorated with several mythical overtones. It is not based on a single, integrated myth, nor does it present a scrambled corpus of many myths. The truth lies somewhere in between these two possibilities. Furthermore, when trying to uncover a specific story's mythical backdrop and bring that to the fore, Frazer, Lincoln, and Witzel can all be seen to share a certain core approach. Here is a very brief outline of an effort made by the author of the present work, at a three-way comparison:

Frazer, *The Golden Bough*: the king was the incarnation of a god who died and then was revived, https://en.wikipedia.org/wiki/Solar_deity, a solar deity who underwent a mystic marriage to a goddess of the Earth (**X1**). He died at the harvest (**X2**) and was reincarnated in the spring (**X3**). Frazer claims that this legend of rebirth is central to almost all the world's mythologies[7] Places where Frazer's conclusions match Witzel's and Lincoln's have been marked with an X.

Lincoln, *Myth, Cosmos and Society*: the overarching info-European myth structure describes a creation, the human hero and his family appear, the earth and sky are separated, a divine figure is dismembered in a sacrificial setting, the resulting pieces are considered to embody or symbolize three separate social tiers (priests / kings, warriors, and commoners), then there is a flood, the killing of a demon, and lastly, a grand renewal.

Witzel, *Origins of the World's Mythologies*: mythic time recounts the fortunes of generations of deities across four or five ages plus human beings' own creation and fall. All culminates in the end of that universe and, occasionally, there is hope for a new world expressed.

Table 1.1 surveys, in an abbreviated chart form, these various predictive theories that attempt to generalize about human mytho-heroic stories, nearly worldwide. Both authors are somewhat successful in representing the Ponnivala Nadu epic, an example that was not studied by either one. However, I do not find their results very informative. Their generalizations are so broad and so vaguely constructed that

Table 1.1. Application of Witzel's and Lincoln's analysis to the Ponnivala Nadu story

Witzel's outline of a universal mythic story (the Laurasian version only)[a] [Lincoln's scheme is referenced in Italics][b]	Matching mythical themes embedded in the Ponnivala story (showing how the seven key questions used in this book line up – very roughly – with Witzel & Lincoln's thinking.
1. Creation from nothing or from chaos 1. *A creation story is provided*	The (mother) goddess Parvati creates (from nothing) nine men and then nine women destined to be their wives. The name of the lead male is Kolatta. **Roots** (how the family line came to be)
2. Father heaven/Mother earth created and separated	The great god and goddess take the form of two antelopes and make love in the sky. Semen from this love-play drops to earth and engenders a woman named Tamarai who rises from a lotus flower as a babe. Thus a daughter of the sky drops to earth as a tiny baby. She is adopted by Kolatta's wife's brother and will later be the mother of the next generation when she marries Kunnutaiya (see below). **Reclamation** (mother's origin reasserts the family's divine connections)
3. Father heaven engenders several generations 3. *At the human level a family and a hero emerge*	Shiva (the father god) further creates a male child and hides it under a pile of rocks. He is named Kunnutaya and he is adopted by the childless Kolatta and his wife. Kunnutaiya is cruelly beaten after his parents die, but eventually weds his (marriageable) cross-cousin Tamarai anyway. Their family forms a bridge that links the first and third generations (**X1**). **Relationships** (marriage and future heirs become the key to family succession)
4. Heaven pushed up – sun released 4. *There is a macrocosmic description that depicts order at a cosmic level (linking heaven and earth)*	Tamarai climbs a tall pillar reaching high into the sky and performs penance there for twenty-one years. The sun beats down upon her as she sits there, motionless. **Resistance** (this woman cannot be deterred)
5. Current gods defeat/kill predecessors 5. *An important figure with divine qualities is sacrificed / dismembered and these pieces then used to describe key categories of that society's social organization*	Shiva, angered, has his assistants kill Tamarai seven times as she prays on that pillar. The last of these deaths is accomplished by beheading her. But each time Vishnu revives Tamarai by having her bathe in Ganges water.c **Resilience** (this woman even survives beheading)

(Continued)

Witzel's outline of a universal mythic story (the Laurasian version only)[a] [Lincoln's scheme is referenced in Italics][b]	Matching mythical themes embedded in the Ponnivala story (showing how the seven key questions used in this book line up – very roughly – with Witzel & Lincoln's thinking.
8. A hero (or god) shows hubris and is punished by a flood 2. *There is a huge destructive flood event*	The heroes' family are farmers and show hubris by disrespecting the trees and animals of the forest, as well as the hunters who dwell there. They cut down many trees and their ploughs cut channels across the sacred earth. The forest boar Komban, in anger, then breaks open their irrigation dam, creating a huge flood. **More Resistance** (forest beings resist the encroachment of a plough-based culture)
9. A trickster deity (or deities) manages to introduce culture to mankind. As a result, a more "civilized" lifestyle takes hold across the land.	Vishnu announces to the twin grandsons that they will not succeed in their hunt for the demon Komban because they have shown disrespect towards their loyal family pet, a small female dog. Once they renounce their hubris and honour her, the little dog joins them in the challenge they are engaged in, a hunt for the demonic wild boar. The dog's assistance is vital to an eventual kill and the meat used as a sacrificial offering. The little dog is the trickster. (This piece of the story reflects both Frazer's and Lincoln's emphasis on there being a sacrificial offering, featuring the death of a powerful figure whose butchered remains must be offered up to the gods. Somewhat later both heroes also offer up their own lives, which can be understood to be another type of sacrifice, this time a cultured and human-focused one. The twin heroes' bodies are not dismembered (**X2**). **Relationships** and **Reflection** (the family bonds that exist in heaven and on earth closely resemble one another, but with some differences)
6. A dragon is killed and a sacred drink appears *(For Lincoln, this stage links to his #5 above)*	The two heroic grandsons have killed the wild forest boar Komban. Later a sun maiden climbs her sun pillar and brings down sacred, magical, life-giving liquid(s) that are later used by the heroes' sister to help resurrect and revive them. **Revelation** (live-producing liquids originate above and flow downwards. These liquids have life-giving properties)

(*Continued*)

Witzel's outline of a universal mythic story (the Laurasian version only)[a] [Lincoln's scheme is referenced in Italics][b]	Matching mythical themes embedded in the Ponnivala story (showing how the seven key questions used in this book line up – very roughly – with Witzel & Lincoln's thinking.
7. Humans become descendants of a sun god	The liquids, obtained earlier from the sun maiden, are carried to the heroes' place of death by their sister Tangal using seven pristine pots. The two heroes' lives return when she sprinkles these liquids on their prone bodies. **(X3) Revelation** (life-giving drops can restart life in what appears to be a dead body)
10. A final destruction of the world brings about a new heaven and earth. 6. *A grand renewal is achieved*	The heroes realize they cannot take back their lives. Instead, they willingly return to death after a brief resurrection, and leave the land of Ponnivala Nadu to the rest of humanity still living there. **Reflection** (the new era will reflect the old one but will hopefully be plentiful, very green and peaceful.

[a] Adopted from Table 5.3 as per Witzel, p. 323. Note that the sequence of numbers indicates Witzel's ordering while the order displayed on the right side of the chart is roughly the order of events in the Ponnivala Nadu story.

[b] Broadly interpreted and liberally condensed from Lincoln 1986, pp. 1–40 and pp. 119–40.

[c] There is no relation between Tamarai's sacrifice and social organization in the Kongu area. The later sacrifice of the wild boar Komban (segment nine in the chart) does bear some vague relationship with the famous purusa story (RgVeda 10.90.12) where a great giant in the sky is divided to create the so-called varna hierarchy (Brahmins, Kshatriyas, Vaishyas, and Shudras). In the present story Komban's meat is similarly divided, but this time into seven portions that depict the heroes' immediate family and community relationships but not a rigid social hierarchy. The portions, named in the present text, go to: 1) Ponnar, 2) Shankar, 3) Tangal, 4) Vishnu, 5) all the households located in Ponnivala Nadu taken together, 6) Ponnacci, the loyal family she-dog, and 7) Shambuga, the heroes' loyal minister and assistant who is a Dalit by caste. Here we see a strong concept of sibling loyalty expressed, along with a sense of belonging granted by that family to all those who serve them loyally, including the helper god Vishnu! That family is at the centre of the world here, not the wider society.

a great deal of variety can be covered by any one of them. A very rough correlation of the seven terms used in this study with these men's conclusions is possible, but only when the concepts being surveyed are treated very loosely indeed. Though they have some merit, these grandiose maps are not very helpful if one is trying to develop a feeling for the richness of an individual epic. But what about a related and somewhat complementary approach, the search for *specific cultural paradigms* that underlie a particular epic story? This latter type of investigation will more likely uncover some brightly coloured patterns of meaning and of structural patterning. The unique patterns, specific to a particular people and locale, are extremely interesting and valuable. Unwrapping the variety of such hidden paradigms buried inside one particular folk epic is the distinctive task assigned to part 2 of this book.

What more can we gain from the comparative exploration of epic stories? The ensuing chapters attempt to answer this question thoroughly. But, in short, there are four benefits: First, comparison generates new insights, not the least of which are the new understandings that are bound to emerge regarding the primary story itself. While working on this volume, I was repeatedly surprised to discover that there were still further depths of meaning to discover within the Legend of Ponnivala Nadu. This search proved very productive, precisely because thinking comparatively has helped me to uncover new gems, repeatedly, over many years. Second, the cross-cultural examination of any corpus of story similarities and differences supports the development of a better and richer understanding of epic tales in other cultures as well. Third, comparisons assist us in making discoveries about our shared human roots. We all need guideposts that can assist us in building good human interactions and better social outcomes. Finding and applying flexible frame concepts can help people better negotiate the diverse set of social networks modern life presents. These outcomes can also help us better interface with whole communities. Fourth, such comparisons help us to grasp how the story specifics of context, time, and place can have an impact on any individual's imaginative inner landscape.

Major cultural narratives are never black and white, and they do not have simplistic moral outcomes. Instead, epics are more like philosophical debates where the illustrations used stem from a string of adventures experienced sequentially by a well-defined character. Taken as a whole, epic stories wrestle with key moral dilemmas and invite competing interpretations. Good epic stories are Socratic structures that reward both questioning thoughts and vigorous debate. They are meant to tease and puzzle at first, and then to reveal deeper meanings to those thoughtful enough to search for them. An epic story must be played before the mind's eye numerous times before it gradually begins to lead one towards its buried treasure. The full appreciation of a truly epic story takes years, but persistence reveals many important but often concealed added layers, its hidden paradigms. In the next chapter we will see, in the case of the Mahabharata, how the Ponnivala Nadu story has borrowed and woven into its own fabric some of the Mahabharata's own exemplary themes.

2 Character and Plot Structures: The Mahabharata

(A Major Heritage Story Known throughout South and Southeast Asia)[1]

A National versus a Regional Martial Epic

One might ask why we should compare a major, exceptionally large, ancient heritage epic like the Mahabharata with a virtually unknown local folk legend composed in a remote region of Tamil Nadu centuries later. The cultural weight and universal recognition of the Mahabharata seem to make the Ponnivala Nadu story unworthy even of mention in parallel with such a famous ancestral model. The bonds that tie these two epic stories together, however, are multiple and fascinating. We can learn a lot about cultural creativity, local identity, and the interaction of stories and story tellers across regions by comparing these two, seemingly disparate, legends. The Mahabharata is a highly prestigious story that has influenced nearly all dimensions of South Asian culture for several millennia. This great epic ancestor references numerous ancient textual sources[2] and long predates the Ponnivala legend both in terms of its origin date and in terms of the lifestyle described. When we look at the more recent regional legend, however, we can readily see the background influence of that hugely important early story tradition. The opening songs of the Legend of Ponnivala Nadu reference the Mahabharata at the very start, citing this forerunner in the invocation itself. Clearly the local region's poet-singers wish to honour this larger tradition and link their own story to it. This opening homage creates an aura of ancient divine wisdom and conjures it up as a worthy backdrop for any current storytelling event. Furthermore, the similarities noted in the following pages are clearly unidirectional. The Mahabharata influenced the Legend of Ponnivala Nadu, but the former story, of course, knew nothing about the latter, a local epic that only came together as a unified and culturally distinctive story many centuries later.

Although the Ponnivala Nadu story starts out by referencing the Mahabharata, that does not mean that it has absorbed that story wholesale. Instead, there is a likely counter dynamic at play. Local poets, and their audiences, wanted to understand their unique identity and glorify their own distinct and local identity. The following pages will argue that the bards of the Kongu area built, in large part, on what they believed to be their own region's unique heroes and, in addition, on a significant local corpus of historical memories. They have then stretched these around the edges, much as one might stretch a skin or a cloth while attaching it to a fixed larger frame. A local poet's purpose in doing this is to enhance their own immediate audience's understanding of history, but also to give his local area added prestige by linking it to an all-encompassing super legend. The story of Ponnivala Nadu, Land of the Golden River, both is and is not a retelling of the great Mahabharata. And to make the matter more complex, there are multiple ways in which the Ponnivala story can be read as a rebellious tale that inverts and even jokes about this great pan-national epic. The Ponnivala legend has its own perspective: it affirms the primacy of agrarian life and of the Kongu area's fine cattle. Furthermore, it projects a picture of this distinctive area as being independent and unique. By attending to a range of colourful details found within this folk story, we can learn much about how a localized tradition has found creative ways both to mimic and to distort, even invert, the core themes the Mahabharata presents. The exercise in story comparison that follows, will attempt to demonstrate precisely how the Ponnivala Nadu legend celebrates its own special constellation of images and actions. It will also show how these several important dimensions of the local story play out in their own unique space.

Alf Hiltebeitel has written at length about the importance of the Mahabharata as a frame story that appears to inspire and inform much of the content of India's more localized oral, martial epics. He focuses on regional legends whose origins seem to lie in India's medieval period (twelfth to sixteenth century), a timeframe that fits well with the Ponnivala Nadu story's own likely period of formation. Much of what Hiltebeitel has to say is accurate and thought provoking,[3] but he does tend to see these story relationships from a Sanskrit scholar's perspective. While I am not schooled in Sanskrit or in India's classical literature, I am deeply familiar with the local Ponnivala Nadu account. From my perspective, the similarities between these two epic legends stems from a whole host of largely decorative add-ons. The Mahabharata references serve as jewelry, glittering bits that have been attached in order to beautify this local epic account without influencing its core themes or basic action trajectory to any great degree. Their function is largely to enhance the power and awe of the Ponnivala story, which likely started life as a straightforward folktale about two heroic brothers. To enhance their stature, it would appear, the poets eventually gave these two heroes parents and grandparents. Those added generations were shaped to echo the family history of the five famous Pandava brothers of Mahabharata fame. In essence, it is likely that this folk epic was built backwards, starting with the adventures of two heroes and then, later, adding information to satisfy local listeners' curiosity to learn more about these characters' family background.

Significantly, the women described by the Ponnivala story remain largely unique and are much more independent of possible Mahabharata counterparts than are the lives of the story's central male figures. For example, both the Mahabharata and the regional epic describe a core antagonism between lineal male cousins. But this is such a common social issue for men born into a landowning community that this specific correspondence between the two epics is hardly surprising. Problems caused by male cousins or half-brothers arise in both stories but are not unique to those two accounts; cousin-to-cousin rivalry is a core theme described in many, many Indian stories. It is also fair to say that women "suffer" in most Indian stories. But the nature of female suffering in the Mahabharata and in the Ponnivala Nadu epic is quite different. We will return to this topic in later paragraphs. Hiltebeitel's take on the relationship between the Mahabharata and the Ponnivala story differs from mine as he is convinced of the Mahabharata's primacy and its extensive influence over this local tale. In contrast, I believe the Ponnivala story is a largely independent legend, one that draws not only on this famous forerunner, but also on several additional myths and stories that are important to India's larger cultural heritage. This disagreement is only a matter of degree, however, and not one of stark contrast.

Hiltebeitel's key ideas are found throughout his book, *Rethinking India's Oral and Classical Epics*,[4] and the main points are summarized below:

1 Regional epics are re-emplotments that only tell fragments of the frame (Mahabharata) story.
2 These oral legends translate the Mahabharata frame story and re-present its classical themes using regional and vernacular terminology and imagery. This frame undergoes "reality testing" at the local level by the embedding of localized castes, sectarian rivalries, kinship patterns, family dramas, plus cross-cousin and mother-son relationships where there were none originally.
3 The localized epics disjoin classical epics and turn them inside out. Central characters from the Mahabharata become reincarnated in these local stories but now the "newer stories" turn the old frame around. Old grudges are revived and now winners are seen to lose and losers are seen to win.
4 These oral epics "innovate from the darker areas" that the Sanskrit epics leave open. In particular, Hiltebeitel is referring here to a Draupadi cult that is found in the Gingee area of Taminadu. There Draupadi re-emerges as an angry, vengeful, and dangerous character. Hiltebeitel also speaks of a sort of "sub-text" that wells up in local epics that relates to the "Liebestod mythology" of Kālī. This is the story of the goddess in her form as Durga, and the buffalo demon that she is attracted to but later kills.

All of Hiltebeitel's summary statements ring true to some extent when we examine the Ponnivala legend, and he makes some good points. However, various matters of "degree" and "theme" beg discussion. Scattered illustrations of all the points Hiltebeitel has made can be found in the Ponnivala story, but those bits and pieces by no means overwhelm or dominate this local story. Rather, the influence of the Mahabharata on this particular local legend is relatively light, subtle, and intermittent. And as a "trajectory," Hiltebeitel sees the Mahabharata's bigger epic frame as essentially "mothering" this and other "infant" stories that were developed later. He sees them as residing within the Mahabharata's large, encompassing, womb-like cultural envelope. But to suggest another dynamic, I will contrast this view with the idea that local hero stories grow bigger and display more and more embroidery across their surfaces, over time. According to the latter view, the larger and older story serves more like a status marker or ancient family name, than like a close, warm, and nurturing mother. My choice of a male image, suggesting that the Mahabharata serves as a venerable clan ancestor rather than as a loving, indulgent mother, is appropriate. The images the Ponnivala epic borrows from this great epic story are largely male, both in name and in tone. They function something like a fine gold necklace that a king might wear, here appropriated by a regional royal. That monarch will be proud of his locally woven lower cloth, tied on firmly using his own area's distinctive wrapping style. But he will be happy to wear an expensive royal necklace on his chest as a sign of his dignity, wealth, and high status within his own regional community.

Local bards, casting about for new ways to elaborate on a core story (ornament it, to use a musical term) readily borrow and play with other singers' story materials. Each draws on a broad cultural corpus of shared imagery that a local audience will already be familiar with. Such embellishments help to stretch out a region-based tale and make it more memorable. Employing a "reincarnation" concept that is already very familiar to Hindu listeners, for example, can provide a teller with many ready-made images and resonating details. But creative local bards will even go further. They know how to warp or twist known themes, even invert them, when that strategy seems advantageous. As Claude Levi-Strauss has suggested many times in his writings, inversions of various broad cultural motifs and images are a convenient way of defining a distinctive locale, lending it a memorable identity. References that a creative teller decides to import from other stories can also deepen a listener's potential understanding of both tales, making them both more interesting. The mechanism is similar to the one this book also employs: comparisons cause one to think more deeply and to ask new questions. Overall, freshly embedded foreign-story reference points provide echoes of other times and places, giving a listener more to remember and review during moments of personal reflection.

Ponnivala Nadu bards are not bound by a fixed text, nor by versification, nor even by a detailed and rigorous sequence of events. Unlike the singers of classically "fixed" tales like the Mahabharata, they are free to "borrow" pieces from others and then to use those interesting "bits" as they wish. The villagers of the Kongu

Nadu area, for example, give great prominence to the goddesses of Hinduism and, especially to forms of Kāli. It is only natural, therefore, that references to her provide a popular means of story expansion. So too do the many heroes and heroines of other Tamil legends. Of course, all local story characters also exhibit social traits that are partially "pre-structured" by popular stereotypes, personality styles, and local rivalries. Here are some examples of "borrowing" from other great South and Southeast Asian epic known in this area.

References to the Ramayana

A hunchbacked midwife: The Ponnivala king named Kunnutaiya suffers from the taunts of some mean lineage rivals. When those distant cousins notice that his queen is pregnant, they devise a plan to kill what could be Kunnutaiya's firstborn son. If the child is male, that new family member would stand to inherit the kingdom upon his father's death. The cousin's plot involves a devious hunchbacked midwife whose behaviour obviously echoes that of the servant Mantara in the Ramayana. In that well-known story Mantara is not a midwife who plots to kill any newborn sons of the king, but this servant does try to poison the mind of Kaikeyi (third wife of King Dasharatha) in order to make her feel hatred towards the story's main hero, Ram. The larger dilemma facing these two families is similar: which family line will inherit the rights to local land and thus the throne? Ram is the son of King Dasharatha's first wife, Kausilya. If Ram were to die or abdicate then Bharata, son of Kaikeyi, Dasharatha's third wife, might have a chance to rule. Similarly, in the local epic, if Kunnutaiya' wife never bears a son, then one of the sons born to a male cousin might win the chance to rule Ponnivala Nadu. The hunched back midwife in this local epic was bribed by the king's male cousins to participate in a plot to kill any newborn males that Ponnivala's reigning queen might birth. An attempt by this midwife to execute that plan fails, just as Mantara's plot to install Bharata on the throne also failed. The details of the two plots are very different but the basic purpose of these two women's plans and the hunchback theme are similar.

The "Monkey God" Hanuman: Hanuman, Ram's major assistant and helper, resembles Shambuga, the first minister of the Ponnivala Nadu heroes. Both Hanuman and Shambuga are loyal and both are good fighters. Furthermore, both are very large and each sometimes acts like a buffoon. More important, perhaps, both are of "low" status and both carry with them various hints of their forest-linked ancestry. Hanuman is a monkey, Shambuga is an untouchable (a Paraiyar or Dalit by caste). Each commands a large group of fighters and serves the reigning king as a kind of army general. The low formal ranking these characters share does not seem to be accidental. Neither does the extreme respect both assistants enjoy for their loyal service and special magical abilities. Nonetheless, the similarities between these two are very abstract, while in terms of story details the two characters are clearly very different.

Brothers: Rama and Laksmana are the key pair of brothers in the Ramayana. Rama is the senior and more prominent character. Although Rama is a Kshatriya by caste, he seems to cross over into the Brahmin category in many respects. He is both a wise king and a prominent warrior and as such he blends these two varna categories through his behaviour, if not strictly in terms of his birth. His younger brother Laksmana serves as Rama's aid and assistant and is the subordinate figure. In the local epic Shankar is the younger twin, yet his wishes and assertive personality almost always triumph. The Ponnivala story's inversion of elder and junior siblings' roles may draw inspiration from the politics of the locally dominant farming community in the Kongu region. The members of the Kongu Vellalar caste in Ponnivala Nadu are sometimes called younger brothers by their powerful Vellalar caste associates living beyond this region's borders. Those higher status and more Brahminical Vellalar associates reside in the rich delta areas lying to the South and East of the Kongu area. Their soil and water resources are generally superior to what exists locally. However, the Kongu Vellalars of Ponnivala Nadu take great pride in their ploughing ability and fearsome fighting skills and do not accept the idea that they are lower status younger brothers. Thus in the Ponnivala Nadu story, local residents give the younger brother great power. Ponnar, the elder brother in the local legend, is somewhat like a Brahmin, while his younger brother resembles a fearsome, rather stereotypical Kshatriya warrior. Ponnar is the elder but has a mild and unassertive personality. His strengths are that he is wise and rather Brahmin-like. Songs about the twin brothers are often in the singular and seem to point to Ponnar as the ruler. Shankar is featured in songs about battles and where a confrontation with enemies is described. Laksmana, the younger brother of Rama, is more Brahman-like in that great epic. When Shankar is compared with Rama, therefore, we can see clear differences. Personality traits that are combined in Rama, are separated and used to characterize the opposed and contrasted twins of the Ponnivala Nadu story. The local story thus lies closer to the original concept of a varna hierarchy where the Brahmin would be considered the elder sibling and the Kshatriya, though stronger and more violent, would be understood to act as his junior partner.[5]

A woman who requests the capture of a beautiful animal (and later regrets it): In the Ramayana, Sita sees a beautiful deer while in the forest with her husband Rama. She asks him to catch it so the deer can become her pet. Rama then tries to catch the lovely animal, but to do so he leaves his wife alone and vulnerable to attack by the agents of a demon king. The story unfolds from this point with drastic consequences for Sita. Similarly, in the Ponnivala Nadu story, the twin heroes' sister Tangal dreams of a beautiful pair of parrots she wishes could keep her company. She asks her brothers to go and catch two of these colorful birds. The brothers' resulting quest leads them into a forest controlled by enemy hunters, and although they do manage to trap one female parrot (Rama never catches that deer), the hunters of the forest become angry. The great conflict the two Ponnivala brothers are later drawn into unfolds from this simple parrot hunt and ends up defining the climax of the larger story. The Ramayana incident involving the deer does somewhat parallel the Ponnivala parrot episode, however, because it too leads to war. Sita (who is certainly as beautiful as a parrot) is captured by demonic forces when she is left alone in the forest, and that abduction starts the war that defines that classic South Asian epic as well.

The Cilappatikaram Story

The Ponnivala epic clearly contains overtones of other famous local legends as well, most specifically echoing the story of Kannagi in the Cilappatikaram. There the heroine takes a fireball drawn from her own breast and burns the great king responsible for unjustly killing her husband. In the Ponnivala account the heroine Tangal was chosen by Lord Shiva to be the youngest of the seven sisters of the Pleiades precisely because she had "fire in her breast." And Tangal does not use her fire that differently from the way Kannagi does. Distraught, she burns down her own family palace after her brothers' deaths. She also burns down the palace of her sisters-in-law. At the end of this epic legend Tangal is then lifted to heaven in a golden chariot. Kannagi is said to have risen to heaven at the end of her life in a similar chariot. The list of echoes and borrowings ends here, but they are enough to suggest that the local poets who composed the Ponnivala Nadu story were very knowledgeable about their culture's broader corpus, and they were not shy about linking their own account to this wider and very rich story frame

Creative Story Engineering

Innovative local bards are simultaneously poets and entrepreneurs. But they do not just seek out parallels. They also look for opportunities to differentiate their own local stories from other better-known tales they have been exposed to. It is perfectly reasonable that they would want to make their own story special. And the local singers, who are professional story tellers, work hard at this. Indeed, when this version of the Ponnivala Nadu epic was tape recorded, it was generally considered to be the most popular story circulating in the area. The bards might sing other stories, but the Ponnivala Nadu tale was the one everyone wanted to hear again and again. It was a matter of pride, as well as a matter of local heritage. Of course, we can never know for sure how historically accurate this epic legend is, but interviews done with local bards who sing the Ponnivala Nadu story today are revealing. These bards believe that they are telling a true story that amounts to a true history of the Kongu area. When these singers discuss their own skills and repertoire, they begin by describing their teachers and their personal intellectual lineages. They will name known local gurus of song and story, men that they began to study with as young children, often from the age of about ten. These bards recount how they travelled with and learned from those teachers, practising daily by taking on bit roles or singing a few of the story's most important songs. The bards will also sometimes explain that their own families were innovators, that their fathers or uncles had added small scenes to their own evolving version of the story that a neighbouring school of singers never referenced. Furthermore, these living singers are quite candid about their need to engage the audiences they performed for. They need audience donations to be plentiful, so that they can make a good living. These singers also add small rituals that they ask their audiences to perform at the end of a night of storytelling, like lighting a lamp. What the audience wants, in other words, influences what the bards choose to do to enhance audience interest and participation. They are eager to tell stories, but of course, must generate interest in order to make a living by practicing their trade.

The Mahabharata

It is now time to turn our attention to the Mahabharata itself. This story has provided significant inspiration for bards singing the Legend of Ponnivala Nadu especially when they try to engage their audiences by adding fresh story details. As discussed previously, one method of elaboration was likely generated by questions asked by audience participants themselves. As people became familiar with the life story of the Ponnivala twins, they began to want to know more about the two heroes' ancestry. One of the easiest and most effective routes for this kind of plot development would have been for a bard to suggest that these local heroes were reincarnations of other legendary protagonists who were already locally known and had preceded the twin brothers in older legends. In this case, selecting two of the Pandava brothers for a reincarnation story would have been an obvious choice. A large number of possible Ponnivala and Mahabharata add-ons will be discussed in depth, below.

KEY CHARACTER RELATIONSHIPS IN THE MAHABHARATA AND IN THE LEGEND OF PONNIVALA NADU: SEVEN THEMES EXPLORED

Theme 1: Roots

A root has a mission – to grow towards a nutrient source and establish a corridor for the transfer of benefits from that background source to the centre of a growing plant. Roots also offer stability. In epic terms a root can be an origin myth or any other kind of story about beginnings or perhaps about the core geographic locale the story identifies with.

The Ponnivala Nadu epic is first and foremost about farmers. Initially, as the story begins, the goddess Parvati creates nine farming brothers and gives them a

Figure 2.1. The twins as they prepare to kill the Chola monarch.

plough, telling them to use it to convert the landscape that surrounds them from stands of trees to tillable fields. In the second generation the son of the eldest brother becomes a proud and successful overlord. In the third generation, twin grandsons choose to become warriors, though they are still farmers by heritage. Their new focus becomes defending their inherited landholdings against multiple challengers. Perhaps even more important, these third-generation twins rebel against their overlord, a neighbouring Chola monarch, and eventually kill him (figure 2.1). This provides independence for the small kingdom and removes an overlord who had been pompous, mean, and overbearing when dealing with these two teenage kings. This outcome serves to bolster the self-image of local residents who want to believe that their region is truly the equal of any other area nearby. In truth, the Kongu area has no extended historical record of having been ruled by any famous line of kings, homegrown or otherwise. Instead, in the past, a variety of powerful dynasties (mainly Chola, Chera, and Pandya kings) fought among themselves for control of this distinctive region. Kongu was a key geographic prize, not good for much agriculture, but host to valuable raw resources and also to a number of important trade routes that crossed the area. Indigenous artisans also made trade goods, especially out of metal, wood, and precious stones, that were considered valuable. As a result, the area changed hands often. Traditionally, Kongu was a marginal and quite dry place, despite its lovely river. And its people, frequently described in early Tamil literature, were considered to be fiercely independent. For comparison, the Mahabharata also describes the Pandava heroes' region as one that residents were proud of, but that epic's Kurukshetra does not compare easily with the Kongu area. Any correspondence between the two stories in this regard would have to reference a very general concept of home locale, basically a homeland theme that is common to almost all epic tales.

48   Multiple Epics Compared

Figure 2.2. The local goddess Cellatta.

Goddesses: The story of Ponnivala Nadu gives much more centrality to the goddesses of the heroes' area than does the Mahabharata. Parvati, Lord Shiva's wife who resides with him in Kailasa, explicitly tells the original nine farmers she has created that they are to worship their local goddess daily. And that lovely divinity, named Cellatta, is significant through most of the story (figure 2.2). Cellatta is involved in all the family's life cycle ceremonies and festivals. Towards the end of the epic, however, a fiercer form of Cellatta, named Kali, steps in. Black Kali is associated with the well-forested mountainous areas. She is the goddess the heroes' rivals, the forest-dwelling Vettuvas, turn to. Temples dedicated to her surround the heroes' lands on at least two sides. There is no similar emphasis on the power of local goddesses in the Mahabharata, either to ones that belong to their homeland, or to ones worshipped by their enemies.

Human Heroines: There is a strong implication that the key women in the Ponnivala story are themselves goddesses, but ones who have taken human form. Both the mother of the twin heroes, and their sister have the power to call fire to their aid when they are angry. In the Mahabharata Arjuna is known for his burning of a forest. But in the Ponnivala case it is only women who use hot flames to burn people or things. There is no burning of a forest, or of plants of any kind. Furthermore, only Tamarai has the strength to walk all the way to Shiva's council chambers high in the Himalayas (a strength her husband does not share). Only she has the spiritual patience to meditate for twenty-one years and to endure seven deaths inflicted on her by Shiva himself. Furthermore, Tamarai eventually does succeed in her heroic effort to obtain the gift of three children from this god. Similarly, Tamarai's daughter Tangal can see into the future while her brothers cannot. She is the dreamy sibling (figure 2.3). Only she can call upon the gods to bring forth a punishing rain. Only she can fly across the land on a great golden bird and locate the spot where her two siblings died, a place that lies hidden deep within a

The Mahabharata   49

Figure 2.3. Tangal as she foresees the future in a dream.

great forest. Only she has the power to revive her brothers (just briefly) in order to talk to them. Female animals in the Ponnivala Nadu story also have special powers. In sum, several types of actions that are associated with male characters in the Mahabharata are instead allocated to females in this Ponnivala Nadu epic.

Lord Vishnu: Krishna, an avatar of Lord Vishnu, is very important in the Mahabharata. He comes to visit the Pandava heroes frequently and is essentially a human figure. In the Ponnivala story, by contrast, Vishnu is less human and behaves more like a separate and superior divine figure. Vishnu does appear before Tamarai when she asks him for help, but he also takes on many other disguises, some human and some not (such as a fly on the wall). Vishnu is a key actor in the final battle fought by the heroes of both epics. Strikingly, however, Vishnu switches sides late in the Ponnivala epic account and instead fights alongside the heroes' enemies. Until this point, Vishnu always visits earth with a mission to help the heroes. But there is the difference. In the Ponnivala story Vishnu makes short visits, unlike in the Mahabharata where Krishna manifests himself as a fully human character who is constantly near at hand. In the Ponnivala Nadu legend, when Vishnu does show himself visibly to any member of the ruling family, it is usually (but not always) while using his recognizably divine form (as seen in figure 2.4 where he is pictured travelling down from the sky on his favourite vehicle, an eagle-like bird). And even then, Vishnu's visits often last for just a few minutes. Each of these special moments of divine-human contact, furthermore, is treated as a favour granted to one of the story's two key heroines, something he only rarely offers human male equivalents. For all the above reasons, the role Vishnu plays in the classical and in the folk epic are very different.

Lord Shiva: Shiva is important in both epic stories as well, but again he behaves in very different ways in these two accounts. In the Mahabharata Shiva is the key god that the Pandavas worship. The heroes' family enjoys festivals dedicated to

50 Multiple Epics Compared

Figure 2.4. Lord Vishnu as he flies to earth.

this god and his presence in shrines on earth is a matter for celebration. In the Ponnivala Nadu legend, by contrast, Shiva is important only as a distant, rather frightening, and authoritative figure. Here Lord Shiva makes almost all the life and death decisions that affect the story's key characters, but he does so from his sky-high, snowy Himalayan abode. He sits there, in his lofty council chambers, receiving guests and listening to the demands of penitents. If he is not there, then Shiva is in the forest meditating and does not want to be disturbed. Penitents who try to gain his attention use the heat generated by their own yogic concentration to try to burn him. When things get too hot Shiva generally responds with anger. But those who persist long enough eventually do win his attention and he finally does agree to help them. Frequently Lord Vishnu, who is always referred to as Shiva's brother-in-law, plays the key role of go-between. Vishnu will plead the cause of someone suffering on earth (usually a story heroine) and only then will Shiva do something, using the excuse that he feels obliged to help his brother-in-law. The goddess Parvati, Shiva's wife and Vishnu's sister, is also (occasionally) seen acting in the role of principal human-divine mediator.

Vishnu tries to convince Lord Shiva to grant the heroine, Tamarai, three children. But the later drives a hard bargain by demanding that Lord Vishnu hand over his conch and powder box. Shiva takes these magical tools and holds them in hock throughout the years that the Ponnivala twin heroes and their sister Tangal are all active down on earth. Only when Vishnu returns the spirits of the two key male heroes to Shiva at their deaths, does Shiva give him back these sacred items (figure 2.5). They are the collateral that Shiva takes to assure that he retains ultimate control over the twins while they walk the earth below. And he also does not want his brother-in-law Vishnu to become too powerful or proud. After all, Vishnu is the only god who will interact regularly with all the story's heroic human characters. Shiva is worried, it seems, that this alliance and closeness to

Figure 2.5. Shiva (arms on right) giving back a powder box and conch shell to Vishnu.

humankind could get out of hand, causing Vishnu to think a little too much of his own power to control events. None of these interesting dynamics, all key to understanding how these two great gods interact in the Ponnivala epic, are present in the Mahabharata.

Dicing: One of the most interesting things Vishnu does in the Ponnivala Nadu story, something else that has no parallel in the Mahabharata, is to play dice with the heroes in their palace gaming room (figure 2.6). During Vishnu's visits to that room, he places restraints on the more violent twin (Shankar) to keep him from becoming disruptive. We are never told exactly why Vishnu plays dice, but we do learn that he enjoys this pastime, just as the twin heroes do. Nine distinct references are given to different dice games played at various points in the story. Vishnu is present for the first four and for the sixth, but absent for the fifth, seventh, eighth, and ninth gaming sessions. Also, after every one of those nine dice games the heroes (or just one hero in two cases) get called away because of an emergency of some sort. That emergency always has negative consequences. Nothing is explicitly said about this predictable sequence of the two men engaging in dicing, followed immediately by a serious and unforeseen problem. However, it seems likely that their gambling pastime does somehow bring about the serious consequences which inevitably follow. It is likely that Vishnu's role is to try to keep those dice games under control. He tries to constrain Shankar's anger, a mood shift that inevitably surfaces during these games. In the first few instances of Lord Vishnu's participation in these games of dice he succeeds in maintaining control. But as the story events move forward, Vishnu either becomes less interested in constraint, more careless, or perhaps just more resigned to letting things unfold. Of course, Vishnu already realizes that all will fall apart in the end. To sum up, these dice games seem to function as a clever way of gradually moving the fateful outcome of the heroes' time on earth towards its inevitable end.

Figure 2.6. Lord Vishnu plays dice with the two Ponnivala Nadu heroes.

Dicing is equally central to the Mahabharata story. But the several gaming scenarios described there are very different. In the Mahabharata, the heroes play against their adversaries, who place competing bets on the outcome. Readers familiar with that story will know about the terrible consequences of losing a dice game in that account. As well, in the Mahabharata story the gods are not present during the core contest, making their appearance only to protect Draupadi after the game has been lost. No god ever plays dice with the heroes directly. And the Pandavas never play among themselves in private, either. Finally, there are only two or three dice games in this great story, rather than nine as in the Ponnivala Nadu case. The two epics share an emphasis on this theme, therefore, but their separate ways of using the dice game to advance the overall story are quite different.

Deaths of the main heroes: In the Ponnivala Nadu story the key characters all die natural deaths, that is, until the third and final generation. At this point the twin heroes fight what appears to be a great battle with their hunter enemies. But during that confrontation Lord Vishnu shows himself briefly to Ponnar and Shankar and reveals that he has been busy conjuring a scene before their eyes and creating the perception that enemies are attacking. The attackers are in fact emerging, one by one, from his own right palm. There are also other indications that Vishnu has made an about face and is about to bring this story, and the lives of these twin heroes, to an abrupt end. First, Vishnu absents himself from the last few dice games the heroes play (see above). Second, he takes the form of a washerman and, after speaking briefly with the heroes, drags away the head of the great black boar (King Komban) that they have just killed. Shankar, the younger brother, quickly recognizes this loss of the boar's head is a sign that they are about to lose their own lives too. Then, without the heroes' knowledge, Vishnu appears in front of those hunter-enemies, at their home temple, a forest shrine dedicated

Figure 2.7. Vishnu shooting the flowered arrow that removes the younger twin's chest thread.

to Kāli, and offers to lead their fight against these two brothers. It is just after this, as mentioned above, that Vishnu shows the heroes (as a private revelation) how he, himself, has created the hundreds of enemy warriors now advancing towards them. Vishnu then asks the two men to fight just a little longer, seemingly in order to preserve their desire for dignity and self-respect as heroic warriors. The brothers soon decide that they have had enough of that fighting and assume (incorrectly, we can conclude) that every single enemy fighter is now dead. The twin heroes then leave that gory scene where blood is everywhere and go to bathe in a nearby river.

But then, in a big surprise, the very next scene depicts Lord Vishnu sitting on a branch overhanging the river where they are bathing. From there he shoots a flowered arrow at Shankar (figure 2.7). This arrow removes just one (ritual) thread from Shankar's bare chest. He notices this change, of course, and quickly recognizes this as a sign from god that his and his brother's lives must now be ended. The two men climb back onto firm ground and confirm to each other the meaning of what has just happened. Then both brothers (the younger one first) fall forward on their own sword tips, instantly taking their own lives. Their devoted first minister, Shambuga, finds their prone bodies there moments later. He rapidly fashions a pointed branch taken from a nearby Vanni tree and with that he takes his own life too, falling forward on its equally sharp and spear-like tip. Later, when the two heroes are brought back to life by their sister, they quickly tell her that they cannot remain on earth any longer. It is better for them to give up their own lives, they state, than go back to a kingdom full of widows[6] and to a place where there are no proud, fighting men left.

The Mahabharata story has a very different ending. In that epic the Pandavas continue to rule Hastinapur for thirty-six years and their lineage continues even

Figure 2.8. The vision of hell that Tamarai sees with the help of Lord Vishnu.

beyond that point. In the Ponnivala Nadu account, by contrast, no prominent men survive the great war, and just a few male servants are left to tend the family palace. Now both the lineage and the clan that the twin heroes were born into cease to exist. Hence, the endings given these two stories do not align well at all. In the Mahabharata, furthermore, there are no suicides. Unlike the Ponnivala twins, Yudhisthira dies of depression. Interestingly, of the five brothers, he alone has the spiritual power to reach heaven before abandoning his physical body. There is, one might argue, possibly a faint parallel to be found in that all four of Yudhisthira's younger brothers (including Bhima and Arjuna) gradually will their own deaths through their powers of ascetic renunciation. But they all die slowly and non-violently, providing a rather tepid match, at best, to the twin Ponnivala heroes' dramatic and near-instantaneous gift of their lives to the gods and to their stated wish for a future renewal.

There is one interesting parallel to be discovered between Yudhisthira, the eldest Pandava brother, and the folk epic's queen-mother Tamarai. As Yudhisthira climbs up the Himalayas towards the gates of Shiva's high abode he looks down and sees people suffering in the gloom of hell below him. As Tamarai climbs a set of steps towards that same set of gates, with Lord Vishnu at her side, she too looks down (ignoring Vishnu's warnings) and sees a vision of hell. Following this transgression, Vishnu walks her through a "hell cave," a place where she sees up close the same human suffering as Yudhisthira did (figure 2.8). This experience of hell is Vishnu's punishment, it seems, because Tamarai disobeyed this god's strict warning not to look around. This is a tiny plot detail that the Ponnivala bards may have possibly lifted from the Mahabharata story, albeit implanted in quite a different spot and linked to a female character.

Marriages and romance: The marriages described in these two epic accounts are very different as well. The five Pandava brothers marry one wife, due to a kind of verbal accident. The decision is initially made at a swayamvara archery contest that Arjuna (brother number three) wins. But looking a little further into the larger story there are other marriages that are also of interest. Arjuna actually marries many women (some sources say as many as forty-two). His father, Pandu, had two official wives, and his grandfather Vichitravirya also had two. And there are side stories where key women such as Arjuna's own mother and grandmother also become pregnant by other men and/or by various gods. In the Ponnivala story no hero has more than one wife and the twins, though technically they do marry, never so much as touch their wives with their little fingers. This, in contrast to the Mahabharata account, is a very, very chaste epic that is careful to describe only a very mild degree of sexual attraction, and that only once and in the context of the heroes' father, a short romantic interlude that does not even occur once in their own generation!

The theme of becoming pregnant via a god is important in both the Mahabharata and the Ponnivala account. It must be said, however, that this kind of story is common in Indian mythology more generally. Indeed, how else can one easily explain the magical or divine characteristics a hero embodies? But when it comes to earthly marriages, the contrast between these two epic accounts is stark. In the Ponnivala Nadu legend there are no multiple marriages of any kind where human males are concerned. There are also no marriage contests set up that allow a male hero to win his bride by exhibiting his superior fighting skills. Only three weddings are described in this entire story. In the first the clan grandfather is married by the simple act of putting a garland around his chosen partner's neck, a minimalistic ritual that takes just seconds. The other two weddings, however, conform to local wedding standards, at least to some degree. Nonetheless, each of these is also odd in significant ways. Kunnutaiya, the twin heroes' father, had to wander about as a child orphan and did not know his own true ancestry. Eventually Vishnu helps him out and identifies the woman, Tamarai, that he is destined to marry. Vishnu tells him that she is his own mother's brother's daughter, the girl who, according to South Indian tradition, is a man's the ideal marital partner. Kunnutaiya likes this girl but is afraid to ask for her hand. Vishnu intervenes and shores up Kunnutaiya's courage. Eventually the marriage takes place, but it is conducted in secret, in a forest, by Vishnu himself, because Tamarai's brothers are firmly opposed to this union. They think that Kunnutaiya is an orphan with no family wealth and therefore they do not agree that he is a proper marital match for their young sister. The wedding proceeds with Vishnu's help, but there are no wedding guests and the ceremony performed is greatly abbreviated. As the couple leave, lines are drawn in the dirt and the many wedding gifts presented purposely insult the newly wedded pair. They are ordered to never to return to the bride's village. When Tamarai does try, years later, to go back to her natal home, anger and violence erupt in an effort to prevent her from re-entering. The bitter relationship between these two in-law families, therefore, never really turns positive. However, Tamarai does enforce a kind of compromise at the end of that aborted visit. She forces her brothers to kneel before her and apologize for their transgression.

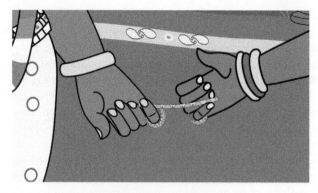

Figure 2.9. The finger extensions the heroes use so as not to have to touch their brides as they walk around the wedding fire.

In the case of the twin heroes' own marriages, the ritual proceedings unfold oddly once again. These men's mother, Tamarai, has long since secured two potential daughters-in-law for her sons to marry. The local rules are then followed, as custom dictates. But because of Tamarai's outlaw position, she must go to great lengths to make the wedding arrangements work. Tamarai had long ago turned her two daughters-in-law-to-be into stone statues, keeping them chaste while they await their marriage. Just moments before the wedding, Tamarai returns those two sisters to their original flesh and blood form, albeit once more with a little added help from Lord Vishnu. But this happy turn of events does not last long. The wedding is very peculiar. It takes place in the same kind of no man's land as did their mother's wedding. However, this time Lord Vishnu does not preside, and he does not even try to bless the twins and their new wives. Nonetheless, this caring god does supply the basic wedding paraphernalia needed for the big event. Though his lesser role this time is not explained, one can guess that it is likely due to a strange vow the twins have taken. They have told their mother that they will never touch their brides. And indeed, they have special finger extensions made so that they do not even need to join hands as they walk around the sacred wedding fire (figure 2.9). Furthermore, no sooner are the two girls married than their bridegrooms order the first minister of Ponnivala to lock them away in a specially built palace. There they are destined to do nothing except spin thread for the rest of their lives. They never once exit their jail-like home and their husbands never visit them. By these various devices the brothers manage to remain 100 per cent chaste throughout their entire lives, enhancing (we may assume) their warrior-like virility. But the flip side of all this, which of course upsets the boys' parents, is that there can be no family heirs since their two wives have been permanently locked away.

In sum, the marriage arrangements described by both the Mahabharata and the Ponnivala Nadu story can certainly be called unusual. Nonetheless, that is about all the two stories share regarding this central theme. In the case of the Mahabharata there is an excess of wives and of love alliances. At the same time at least one key woman has more than one husband. In the case of the Ponnivala Nadu story there is an excess of chastity and of sexual restraint. Indeed, there are no romantic passages or love scenes at all, except for a few mythical images of love making depicted between Shiva and his wife Parvati. The closest this story comes to romance is in a scene where Kunnutaiya (as a household servant) pushes the swing of a lovely young maid in the garden of her palace, the girl that he will eventually marry. Any personal feelings evoked by this are fully left to the imagination of the story's listeners.

It is interesting to note, however, that there are a few (if infrequent) overtones of romance in several Ponnivala epic scenes where Vishnu interacts with Tamarai. In these instances, the god does such things as tease her or visit her while she is alone in her palace. He also offers to carry her over the Himalayas on her way to the gates of Shiva's council chambers. Significantly, perhaps, that last scene occurs shortly after Vishnu himself has turned Tamarai's official husband into a stone and left him by the wayside. Ostensibly, earlier events that occur during their journey, like a scorpion bite, have exhausted him. Perhaps Vishnu does harbour some romantic feelings when it comes to Tamarai, but that is as far as it ever goes. Nowhere is the possible affection he feels for her made explicit, unlike the popular scenes of "lila" or love play that Krishna enjoys with his many gopis. Those scenes are widely popular in Vaisnava mythology but are not referenced here. When we consider questions about **Roots**, therefore, we can find very little in common between these two stories except that the same divine characters and a slightly similar geographical motherland appear in both accounts.

Theme 2: Reclamation

Reclamation involves the retrieval of something of value, repossessing something left aside earlier, perhaps even something non-physical like a former state of well-being or of self-respect.

Reclaiming family rights to local lands and local leadership: This is a core area of overlap between the Mahabharata and the Ponnivala Nadu stories. The Mahabharata is about the Pandava's right to rule Hastinapura. In this case the line of rule starts by following a direct male descent regime for three generations. But after those rights descend onto the shoulders of Vichitravirya that descent pattern is interrupted, because Vyasa (his half brother), not Vichitravirya himself, sires Pandu. Shortly after his marriage, Vichitravirya died of consumption and left no sons. As a result the sage Vyasa was asked to biologically father a son with Vichitravirya's surviving wives. One wife gave birth to Dhritarashtra, who was blind from birth. Then in the same way, Ambalika, the other wife, gave birth to Pandu. He was anaemic and very pale as a child and later also suffered from a curse that meant he could not bear children. Vichitravirya's half-brother Bhishma could have inherited the descent line, but that plan was aborted when he became a self-declared ascetic and announced that he would never sire children. Nonetheless, Bhishma obligingly raised his brother's children, Dhritarashtra and Pandu, despite that neither one was a blood-line Kuru. This meant the throne was up for grabs. Dhritarashtra was the eldest, but because he was born blind no one believed he could fulfil this important leadership role. How could a blind man rule a vast kingdom? Thus, Pandu was chosen to be heir to the throne, and he was eventually crowned king. Happily, he became a good and just ruler who held this position for a long period of time. He was a good king who managed to expand his empire through war, helping it prosper, despite his paleness. His reputation rested heavily on the fact that he was a skilled archer and a fighter.

Kunnutaiya, the king of Ponnivala Nadu and father of the twin Ponnivala Nadu heroes was also a successful ruler. He was not pale or anaemic like Pandu but the two exhibit other similarities. Kunnutaiya, like Pandu, was a good and gentle king who gradually built up Ponnivala's prosperity, enhancing his family's status in the area. Kunnutaiya was not physically anaemic, but he was gentle and kind to a fault. More importantly, his roots lay in farming. He was not a warrior. He had been orphaned as a child and therefore had had to accept all manner of odd jobs. He had absolutely no training in how to fight. The story does not even once describe him as having engaged in physical combat. In essence, the Ponnivala legend is about a farming (Vellalar) community and is focused on its claim to the lands the family's ancestors had tilled. Kunnutaiya never lifted a sword or a bow during his entire life. But he did hold the plough as a young man. As he grew older and became a powerful landowner, however, story references to his doing any ploughing work cease. Workers now do this for him. Finally, in middle age, Kunnutaiya is crowned a small king by the neighbouring Chola ruler. Furthermore, Kunnutaiya becomes a ruler where no such leader had existed before. This meant that he did not have to face any biological succession issues except the jealousy of his lineal cousins, in order to become a small king.

Furthermore, Kunnutaiya, even at the height of his power, was little more than a sub-king. He had to answer to the great Chola monarch nearby, the man to whom he owed his crown. Nonetheless, Kunnutaiya's two sons had an (unspoken) desire to be recognized as Kshatriyas, that is, they wished to claim to be descendants of a family with warrior status. Notably, all descendants of farmers were technically classified as Shudras according to the Brahminical law books of the time. This meant that they were believed to be less worthy than "twice-born" people, referring to those who were assigned to the three varna categories that ranked higher up on the social ladder than they did as Shudras. But that implicit Shudra status was not satisfactory for the twin heroes of Ponnivala. These two men, the sons of Kunnutaiya, wanted to be true kings. It seems they knew that to achieve that status they had to be Kshatriyas, a community of would-be warriors who

Figure 2.10. The two brothers conduct a ritual to prepare their sacred threads.

others acknowledged as having a higher varna status. By donning protective chest threads as they left for a (hunting) war against a great black boar, Kunnutaiya's two sons find a clever way to make their own claim to being twice-born (figure 2.10). This is an important detail. These two Ponnivala heroes are not just declaring that they have inherited their father's status as landowning men of substance. They are also attempting to raise their own public status in a substantial and significant way. The wearing of a thread hung from the shoulder over the chest was a symbol of twice-born status. This highly symbolic pre-war gesture the two heroes make goes to the heart of their identity claims. But there is a subtle difference. Twice-born chest threads normally hang from the left shoulder and then cross over the chest to touch the right side of that male's waistline. The twin brothers in the Ponnivala story, by contrast, hang their threads directly down from the neck like a long necklace. It is a subtle but important difference, because in doing this these twins find a way to assert their warrior status without wearing this thread exactly like real Kshatriya men did (figure 2.11).

This is a significant issue in this local epic because the larger story makes an implicit claim on behalf of all of Kongu's local agricultural landowners suggesting that they are really Kshatriyas. The way these men wear their protective thread accomplished this without issuing a direct challenge to others. The two wealthy farmer-brothers just want to be respected as mighty rulers. Although this attempt to parallel the status of Pandu's sons in the Mahabharata is not stated openly, one can certainly argue that these twin brothers wanted to be like them. Indeed, their God-given birth connection to Bhima and Arjuna states as much. The Pandava brothers were respected warriors, men with a fighting ancestry comparable with the (presumed) ancestors of the great Chola king nearby. The twin heroes' own Kshatriya claim is never put into words, however, it is clearly symbolized by their putting on chest threads for the first time. It is interesting that the artist chose to

Figure 2.11. The two brothers put newly made protective threads on their chests.

depict the two as wearing these threads in the form of a necklace, not as slung over one shoulder. He knew that this difference, though subtle, was important. Not adopting the local Brahmin tradition of wearing this thread in the conventional way clearly suggests that some ambiguity about the heroes' real Kshatriya status underlies the larger epic story. By contrast, there is no ambiguity whatsoever in the Pandava's case. Those Pandava heroes were genuine Kshatriyas.

The male blood line: Pandu dies because he crossed the line, a line laid down when he was cursed. That curse laid out that he must never pursue a woman (even a wife) with sexual intent. When he did so, he died. Kunnutaiya's death is different. It just happens naturally when old age sets in. Furthermore, Kunnutaiya himself never suffers directly from a curse, though significantly, his descent line is threated by one: no women in his family will bear children for seven generations due to a curse Shiva laid on his father Kolatta. The matter is more subtle than it might seem at first blush, however. What that curse amounted to was that there would be no descendants sired by the males in Kolatta's family. The work around (unspoken) was that each new generation would instead either be gifted to the family directly by a god (Kunnutaiya's story) or be sired by a god and borne by the family's wives (the story of Tamarai's triplets). This situation has a direct parallel in the Mahabharata. Pandu, the Pandava's human father, could not sire children. Similarly, the mother of the twin Ponnivala heroes, Tamarai, could not conceive children. Technically speaking, a female in this folk epic is thus given a handicap equivalent to that which was allocated earlier to a male character in the Mahabharata. Both find the same work around, which is that their children are born on earth but before that are quietly sired by a god.

Kunnutaiya's status as an orphan also bears some slight resemblance to the Mahabharata's famous orphan, Karna. Karna was born out of wedlock to Pandu's wife Kunti before her marriage to Pandu. He was sired by the sun god himself. Kunti

The Mahabharata   61

Figure 2.12. The babe Kunnutaiya, hidden under rocks by Lord Shiva, being fed by a compassionate cow.

later deliberately abandoned this first child, a boy, placing him in a basket that she let float down a nearby river. Karna was found and raised by foster parents and later became one of the Pandava brothers' key adversaries in the great epic war that followed. Kunnutaiya, by contrast, has no biological mother. He was found under a rock pile after having been created whole by Shiva and then left in this unusual spot (figure 2.12). Kunnutaiya is orphaned, similar to Karna, but not until age five when his parents die. His mother never deliberately abandoned him, as Pandu's wife had done when she cast away her illegitimate child prior to her marriage to Pandu. Furthermore, Kunnutaiya becomes a loving parent and father who is very loyal to the family line. He is never a Ponnivala family adversary like Karna turned out to be for the Pandavas.

It is important as well, of course, that in both stories the initial involvement of the gods in siring a set of heroic brothers later evolves into a succession entanglement. In the Pandava case one could argue that this problem actually starts a war, while in the Ponnivala case it creates a bitter feud between two sets of cousins that, while not exactly a war, does involve mean tricks and a lot of violence. By featuring this theme, both stories implicitly point to a larger cultural ambiguity: When a direct male heir is lacking, who deserves precedence in matters of succession? Is a blood relative in the male line (namely a king's brother or brother's son) the rightful heir? Or, on the other hand, should a magically (or divinely) sired boy, one who was then lovingly raised as if he were the king's own biological son, be eligible? In other words, is adoption (via any of a variety of means) a legitimate route to becoming the heir of a ruling sovereign? Both stories essentially side with the adoption argument. Nonetheless, an adopted son may have to struggle for recognition, including fighting for his right to ascend the throne. Both stories also implicitly assert that the loving upbringing of a young boy born to the queen

62   Multiple Epics Compared

and accepted by the ruler's family should have a legitimate claim to be the king's successor. This liberal perspective points to an underlying value code: socialization counts for a lot. It also points to a way to legitimize adoption by claiming that the child has a god as a father instead of a human one. This underlying perspective is embedded in both stories and constitutes a cultural theme that remains relevant to succession issues in India (and elsewhere) to this day, although in some cases now the rights of female heirs may also be at issue.

Growing jealousy: In the case of Ponnivala Nadu the eldest in the ancestral brotherhood of nine men, Kolatta, had jealous siblings. From the start they felt slighted and believed that the land Kolatta was given should have been more fairly divided among all nine brothers. Furthermore, at Kolatta's death, because this eldest male had no biological children, his rivals asserted that his lands should become theirs, rather than the adopted Kunnutaiya's when he comes of age. They then pass those feelings on to their sons, Kunnutaiya's lineal cousins. Precisely because Kolatta died when Kunnutaiya was still young, an opportunity opens for these uncles and cousins to try to move in and grab his land rights. These jealous men beat the orphaned boy, exploit him, and demand that he work for them in order to earn his keep. Furthermore, they tear down Kunnutaiya's father's fine family home, plough the remains under, and plant castor oil seeds as a way of insulting his memory. This marks the start of a life-long enmity between Kunnutaiya and his cousins and is the reason why these cousins play many mean tricks on Kunnutaiya later. At the tender age of about six, Kunnutaiya ran away from his uncles' and cousins' torture and lived in exile, supporting himself by doing many odd jobs. Finally, Kunnutaiya married. He then returned with his new bride to reclaim his father's family fine fields. It was a struggle, but Kunnutaiya eventually succeeded in recouping his family's old rights. Over time Kunnutaiya also grew stronger and wealthier. Eventually he became a just and respected local ruler. He resembles Pandu in that life path. However, Kunnutaiya is always, at his core, an agricultural estate manager not a warrior like Pandu.

In the Mahabharata case Pandu's half-brother Dhritarashtra (sired by the same Vyasa but with Vichitravirya's first wife) became the father of a hundred sons known as the Kauravas. Dhritarashtra stood in line to inherit the Hastinapura throne. This would have meant that the Kaurava brothers would follow him in time and inherit the leadership of that kingdom. But because Dhritarashtra was born blind and could not use fighting weapons properly, his half-brother Pandu was suggested as the better choice when it came time to nominating an heir. Dhritarashtra, though bitter at the result, willingly conceded the crown to Pandu. But his one hundred Kaurava sons held a big grudge and bitterly resented any claim to the throne made by Pandu's sons, the Pandavas. The great Mahabharata war had its roots in this contest of claims centred around having the right to rule between these two male lines, two groups who were lineal cousins. Although there is also rivalry between the twin Ponnivala heroes and their lineal cousins, this structural,

Figure 2.13. Kunnutaiya's old home destroyed with the remains ploughed under before the planting of castor oil plants.

descent-generated opposition between two male groups is not nearly as central as it is in the Mahabharata story. The two sets of male cousins in Ponnivala Nadu never fight a war. Instead, the enduring opposition in this account is between farmers, represented by the twin heroes, and a group of tribal hunters who live nearby. This rivalry results in a confrontation that is ultimately responsible for the end of the Ponnivala family line. Hence the two epics differ at their core about the fundamental issue at stake: a kinship and succession problem in the first case versus a conflict arising from a gradual economic transition already under way. In Ponnivala Nadu, the struggle arises due to the looming threat to a hunter-gatherer and artisan-based economy from a spreading plough-farming existence that had already occurred in a neighbouring downstream area ruled by a line of Chola kings.

Reproductive Help Gifted by the Gods

The two boys born to Tamarai are spirited away at birth due to the threat of infanticide at the hands of their jealous uncles and cousins. For safety's sake her twin sons are secretly raised underground, for the first five years, by the local goddess. No one except the gods knows of their existence. Meanwhile the same cousins notice that there is only one baby girl (the boys' sister) being raised in the family palace. Those jealous kinsmen seize the opportunity and viciously intimidate the only family members they know of, namely Kunnutaiya, his wife and their baby daughter (figure 2.14). They then send all three into exile in the forest where they are forced to live in a humble hut kindly lent to them by the hunters there. The goddess finds that couple's hideout, however, and she brings the twin boys to them when they are five years old. At that pivotal point, the little family suddenly

Figure 2.14. Kunnutaiya's clansmen enter his home and demand to see him while threatening his wife, Tamarai.

grows from three members to five. Now the family has two sons and so making a claim to their old family lands and their old palace locale now becomes justified. The initial (but distant) parallel with the Mahabharata story is this: the Ponnivala goddess Cellatta hides the two young boys who could claim the Ponnivala crown, while Kunti abandons Karna by letting him float down river in a basket. Although he was adopted, his arrival in Kuru territory as an orphan concealed his true parentage and cancelled any claim he might have later tried to make to the Hastinapura throne as Kunti's first-born son. In both cases the birth stories of these potential male successors are hidden from public view. Remember that Gandhi once called all orphans (and Dalits) "children of god." This was not a random comment. The link between orphans, wanderers, ascetics, outcasts, and gods is a core cultural theme that is certainly present in both these epic accounts, as is the idea of suffering a forest exile.

There is one more point to make. What about women, the wives, and the sisters of these sons who are the family's heroes? Although nowhere in either story do females inherit the throne directly, women are significant king makers in both tales. In each of these epics women connive to advance the rights of their own sons, despite opposition from half-brothers or cousins. It is almost a truism to say that women sometimes rule through their sons or brothers and assert significant power in that indirect way. But in this matter too, we find that the Mahabharata and the Ponnivala Nadu stories diverge significantly. The wives and sisters portrayed in the Ponnivala Nadu story have greater power and more significant roles vis-a-vis their husbands and brothers than their equivalents do in the Mahabharata. Also, those same sisters and wives do not have to connive, like the women in the Mahabharata do. Instead, the Ponnivala heroine Tangal uses her supernatural abilities to transfer magical power to her twin brothers' swords (figure 2.15). The way this female

Figure 2.15. Tangal says a blessing over her brothers' swords as she hands their weapons to them.

character interacts with the twin kings of Ponnivala is therefore significantly different from the roles of female characters in the Mahabharata.

Nonetheless and despite all the contrasts between the two stories related above, the **Reclamation** of land and rights that relate to territorial control, in the face of fierce opposition from agnatic cousins, is a major feature of both stories.

Theme 3: Resistance

Resistance involves conflict, a struggle, or some other expression of opposition to violent or aggressive action, or to the clear threat of such, from a specific individual or from an adversarial group.

Forms of Female Resistance

Draupadi versus Tamarai: Draupadi was born of fire, Tamarai was born from a lotus flower and, thus, both these key heroines have a kind of magico-natural parentage. One is the wife of the five Pandava heroes, the other is the wife of King Kunnutaiya and mother of heroic twins. Furthermore, both women are strong, and both face many hardships, including life in exile. As such, both are paragons of resistance. But the resemblance falls off from there. Tamarai is never sexually humiliated though she is bullied by her husband's cousins in one instance (see figure 2.14). Draupadi is gravely humiliated at least three times. First, this famous Pandava wife is disrobed by her husband's cousins following a dicing match that her eldest husband loses. After this Draupadi and her five husbands are sent into exile. In the first year of this further humiliation, they chose to stay in the neighbouring Matsya Kingdom. There Draupadi is ordered by Kichaka to fetch wine

Figure 2.16. Tangal calling more crows to come to feed on cooked rice. This is one of several prescribed funeral rites performed for her deceased brothers

from his house, despite her protests. On the way, Kichaka accosts her and tries to molest her. Draupadi escapes and runs into the court of Virata. But now Kichaka is angry and he kicks her in front of all the courtiers and in full view of her eldest husband, Yudhishthira. In a third incident, while Draupadi is living in the forest with her five husbands, they leave her to go on a hunt. While they are gone, she is abducted by Jayadratha. Even though Draupadi is saved by her own husbands before being raped by this intruder, the intended insult to her and her family is clear. Tamarai never experiences any of these horrible things, though she is beaten for unjust reasons at several points by her brothers' palace guard, and once by her own husband. She is also slapped and has her hair pulled during an intimidation scene in which her husband's cousins taunt her prior to sending her and her husband into exile. Several other famous scenes that reflect Draupadi's intense sense of humiliation such as her washing her hair in her brother-in-law Dushana's blood as an act of revenge, or her wearing a disguise while in the court of King Virāta, find no parallel in the Ponnivala Nadu story.

Draupadi and Tangal: There is also little to suggest very much resemblance between Draupadi and Tangal. Draupadi is a wife with five husbands and the mother of five sons. Tangal is a young virgin who ascends to Shiva's abode high above at the very end of the story after her brothers die. At that point all three are still just sixteen. Thus, in contrast to Draupadi, Tangal remains a virgin to the bitter end. Also, unlike Draupadi, Tangal is a constant dreamer, a young girl who can see ahead into the future. Using this skill, she aids her brothers in several significant ways. But Tangal's most memorable role is as the sole remaining member of her family after her two brothers' deaths. At that point she takes on the duties and the role of a male, first performing a funeral-related ceremony for her male siblings (figure 2.16) and then wandering alone in the forest in a quest to find

Figure 2.17 Mayavar shows Shankar how he has been busy creating a horde of enemy attackers from his own right palm.

their bodies. When she does finally locate their corpses Tangal manages to revive her twin brothers with various magical liquids and foods. She is a brave woman and at least the equal of her mother in her ability to resist adversity. None of the women in the Mahabharata story bear any significant resemblance to Tangal.

Forms of Male Resistance

Krishna and Arjuna versus Shankar and Vishnu (here called Mayavar): In the Bhavagad Gita segment of the Mahabharata, Krishna addresses Arjuna's reluctance to enter the great battle. In the lengthy conversation that follows Krishna counsels Arjuna not to be a coward but instead to shake off any weakness he feels in his heart and go fight. Krishna tells him clearly that this is his duty, his dharma as a Kshatriya. Arjuna is eventually persuaded and does as Krishna requests. Krishna also briefly displays his wonderous inner form in front of Arjuna's mind-eye using a special magical vision he suddenly creates, called a Visvarupa. Via that holistic vision of the godhead at large, Arjuna sees something overwhelming, a vast patterning of cosmic energies. There is a somewhat similar scene in the Legend of Ponnivala Nadu where Mayavar (a Krishna-like form of Lord Vishnu) presents the younger of the twin brothers, Shankar, with a memorable vision. At the relevant moment Shankar sees a mob of tribal fighters rushing towards him (figure 2.17).

This scene is the Ponnivala Nadu epic's answer to the Mahabharata's famous conversation in the Bhagavad Gita between Krishna and Arjuna. And it is clearly meant to parallel the famous Visvarupa vision provided to Arjuna by Lord Krishna during their conversation about war. But there are important differences. In the Ponnivala case Mayavar does not paint the full picture of cosmic energy that Krishna's scene displays. Instead, Mayavar decides to provide Shankar with a more

Figure 2.18. Vishnu throws Shankar backwards with a gentle shove.

focused revelation, a more specific and substantially narrowed presentation that is easier for him to digest. Essentially, this god's message to Shankar is different. Although no words are provided at this point, Mayavar this time is likely trying to say: "There will always be wars and challengers to any kingdom and to a king's rule. I, myself, am responsible for managing an endless cycle of human struggles in which you must play your part." Shankar's first reaction to this revelation is to try to attack the image of Mayavar that he sees standing directly before him. But first, before doing that, Shankar complains to his brother Ponnar about their dire situation: "This is all his, all Mayavar's doing" he says. Shankar actually raises his sword to threaten the great god, seeming to challenge him to a duel. But Mayavar coolly then pushes Shankar backwards with just one arm (figure 2.18). Shankar, shamed, quickly loses his balance, and falls to the ground.

Next Mayavar speaks to Shankar as he looks down at him. Gazing straight at the younger twin he issues the following order: "You must not do anything to me. These are the only fighters you will see. No more will come. Just strike and kill this one group of warriors that you see now and throw them to the ground." Then Mayavar disappears and the two brothers engage in their last, fierce fight. It is not an equal battle. The two heroes have swords while the tribal fighters, though skilled, carry only sticks. When all these (illusory) challengers have been killed the two Ponnivala leaders quickly leave the scene, wanting to wash the blood off their swords. We can now see a clear difference in how the themes of the Bhagavad Gita are presented. In this folk epic there is no long discourse on the nature of fate or any commentary at all about the deep meaning of dharma. These concepts, all of which are presented in the Bhagavad Gita in abstract and philosophical terms, are here offered in just two of three highly visual vignettes. These are scenes that local listeners can easily grasp and are later able to call to mind and think about. Hence, we can say that the Bhagavad Gita's core ideas are clearly present in the Ponnivala epic, but that the means by which this core message is delivered is unique and fresh. The two heroes resist Mayavar's message at first, but then realize (just as Arjuna did) that they have no choice. They must proceed and so they face their human challengers and engage in a struggle that is meant to symbolize life itself. Lord Vishnu is testing them, setting out for them their last and final challenge. The two heroes must live up to what they face with honour and with self-confidence. After all, these men are the kings of Ponnivala Nadu, and they must behave as such.

Kunnutaiya as a young boy: As a young boy the orphan Kunnutaiya is severely mistreated by many people. Some of his attackers are his own cousins or his cousins' wives. Kunnutaiya also must face the dangers of sleeping in strange cattle sheds, running alone through dark forests, and struggling to find food. Pandu, it seems, had a less challenging childhood, but there is still some overlap. Apparently, Pandu's mother neglected him as a young boy and regularly left him alone in the family's very large palace. Now the contrast is simple and direct. The Ponnivala Nadu legend places great emphasis on how frequently and how well the young Kunnutaiya rises to the challenges he faces. He is a surprisingly strong and wise young boy. The fact that he is orphaned at age five and has to struggle helps prepare him for his later role. This is one reason that he becomes an empathetic and kind king. There is no obvious parallel for this kind of youthful resistance in the face of adversity in the Mahabharata's account of Pandu (or any other key male hero) during their childhood.

Kunnutaiya as an emerging adult leader: Kunnutaiya, as he ages, loses some of his resistant spirit. As an adult, he is always portrayed as a mild-tempered leader, and later when he becomes a king, he is kind, generous, tolerant, and honest, almost to a fault. Kunnutaiya is also respectful of his overlord, the Chola king. He visits him repeatedly, honours him, and takes him small gifts. Kunnutaiya accepts the political hierarchy of his time and does not try to challenge it. Furthermore, when he does face repeated confrontation by his jealous cousins, Kunnutaiya does little to fight back. He never expresses any thoughts of revenge or even of doubt (figure 2.19). Instead, it is Kunnutaiya's wife, Tamarai, who guides and counsels him to be cautious. She frequently advises him to question what his adversaries tell him. She suspects treachery where he perceives nothing but good will. Later, walking out in front as they begin their joint pilgrimage to the Himalayas, she takes the lead. Kunnutaiya is a pliable and agreeable leader who others try to take advantage of. He is, indeed, somewhat like Pandu in that they both exhibit a generous amount of sympathy and tolerance towards others.

The two sons of Kunnutaiya and their Chola overlord: The Chola king provides a significant example of a non-family member who pressures the Ponnivala twin heroes and who they try to resist. This confrontation starts when the neighbouring Chola monarch reminds them that they have not paid any tribute since their father's death. Shankar refuses outright to take him the required gifts because he does not want to bow before this overlord. That would have meant,

70   Multiple Epics Compared

Figure 2.19. Kunnutaiya goes to fetch planting seeds from the rival cousins, despite his wife having cautioned him that they are untrustworthy.

symbolically, that he was the inferior leader and a subordinate of that king. But his elder brother has a softer temperament and is more compliant, taking the required tribute to the Chola king instead. Ponnar, however, ends up in the Chola's private jail as a result of this compliance. Jailing Ponnar, story listeners soon learn, was that Chola ruler's ploy, his chess move. He wanted to force Shankar, the younger twin, to come to his palace in person. He believed that if he put Ponnar in jail, that his brother would soon appear and try to rescue him. Shankar does eventually show up, but he still finds a way to avoid submission. After several further attempts by the Chola king to humiliate and trick these two heroes, they finally turn on him. Both Ponnivala brothers enter his palace with swords drawn and Shankar then stabs the mean monarch, causing him to die (see figure 2.1).

The vicious aggression against their overlord that the twin brothers demonstrate has a purpose. With the Chola's death, the land of Ponnivala Nadu gained independence. The king's demise thus marks a significant turning point in the broader story. With his death the self-confidence of the twin heroes grows by leaps and bounds. But there is a downside to their new independence as well. The twin heroes soon discover that there are other enemies, once held at bay by that overlord, that now wish to openly challenge these two Ponnivala leaders. The first enemy to step forward is a local artisan. He is not a new adversary, but rather a man whose larger community had tried to kill the heroes' parents long ago. These artisans, who are among Ponnivala Nadu's important earlier residents, have never forgotten how they were pushed aside by these two heroes' ancestors, a bunch of homeless immigrant farmers who had arrived suddenly and wanted to take over their lands. And then, just a little bit later, Ponnivala Nadu's neighbouring indigenous hunting population, a group known as Vettuvas, also tries to unseat the heroes. They are angry about how the descendants of those newly arrived farmers had cut down their trees, and then ploughed and planted crops, thus ruining large tracts of their ancestral hunting grounds.

In sum, the Chola king's death morphs into an unexpected disaster for the twin heroes. Without this monarch's overarching reach as a powerful figurehead, the local social order quickly descends into chaos. Once again, then, we find out how different the Ponnivala Nadu story really is from the Mahabharata, though a few faint parallels can be discerned. The Pandavas were, in their own time, also threatened by a variety of non-relatives. They too faced threats from other groups who lived in the vicinity, particularly their own neighbouring tribal groups, people the Mahabharata generally depicts as uncivilized barbarians. However, those indigenous groups are not key Pandava adversaries and no major struggle with them is described. Furthermore, the artisans described by the Mahabharata do not resent the Pandava's presence, while the craftsmen of Ponnivala definitely resent their new farmer neighbours who work to humiliate them and to display their own superior political and economic power. In sum, the theme of **Resistance** in the two stories covers a certain number of reasonably parallel events and actions, but at the same time, a variety of significant differences are readily evident.

Theme 4: Resilience

The term resilience is applied, in this study, to a protagonist that exhibits clear personal goals, and who demonstrates spirit and determination in the face of a powerful opposing force or other significant challenge. In this story a unique female protagonist provides an example of one way in which resilience is expressed through the profound courage and deeply held convictions that this woman demonstrates in the face of her infertility problem.

Draupadi and Tamarai: Draupadi is the joint wife of all five Pandava brothers in the Mahabharata. Because she must try to please all five men, she suffers a lot. She also must undergo exile with her many husbands and endure multiple insults at the hands of their common enemy, the Kauravas. One can certainly argue that Draupadi resembles Tamarai, the mother of the twin heroes of Ponnivala Nadu, in her suffering. But the agony Draupadi and Tamarai undergo result from very different underlying circumstances. The main difference between the two women stems from Tamarai's curse of barrenness. Throughout Tamarai's twenty-one years of penance, she demonstrates a remarkable resilience. Eventually, she manages to overcome her barren fate. Furthermore, unlike Draupadi, Tamarai finds a way to share this good fortune, the boon of pregnancy she received from Lord Shiva. When that great god immaculately impregnated her, he granted her the three children but also gave her a pot of magical water to carry back to earth. She was told to share drops of that precious liquid with every woman in the kingdom of Ponnivala wanting to bear a child. There is no parallel scene in the Mahabharata. Draupadi never shares any sort of gift with all the females of Hastinapura.

However, lets carry this discussion a little further. Having children was never a big issue for Draupadi and not much is said about this matter in the Mahabharata. In fact, she ends up bearing five sons, one sired by each of the Pandava brothers. Some versions of the Mahabharata even say that she also bore one daughter. All of Draupadi's sons are later killed by Ashwatthama during a single terrible night, the night just preceding the last day of the great war. The deaths are unjust; her sons were killed while they were asleep. Now contrast this with Tamarai's experiences. She suffered from barrenness for many years. And when Shiva finally gave her an immaculate impregnation, she bore just two sons along with a daughter. Both sons survive Ponnivala Nadu's several battle scenes. These two heroes, in contrast to Draupadi's sons, suffer a fate that is nearly the opposite of theirs. The two folk heroes deliberately take their own lives. Theirs is a willing sacrifice. They jointly offer themselves to a great goddess just after the worst battle of their lives reaches an end and they both survive. In addition, Tamarai acts alone in many situations, unsupervised by her husband or by her palace guards. In many instances only the odd servant is by her side. By contrast, the Pandavas are (almost) always guarding Draupadi very carefully. In all these respects Tamarai can easily be shown to be very different from her Mahabharata counterpart, and overall, there is very little in the two stories' contrasting details to suggest any strong parallels.

In one larger and some minor ways, however, Tamarai and Draupadi are similar. They both experience multiple years of life in exile. Furthermore, Draupadi suffers many (sexual) insults at the hands of her husband's rivals, the Kauravas. Tamarai does suffer an assault that resembles Draupadi's, in one instance, but only to a minor extent. Like Draupadi, at one point she is attacked by her husband's cousins (figure 2.20). But these aggressive cousins never try to pull off her sari and no sexual innuendoes underlie their threats. Tamarai also endures a very different set of insults, the provocations and mean behaviours of her own brothers. Tamarai is first ridiculed and outcast by her two siblings because of her unorthodox marriage. Then, much later, when she tries to return to her original home for a visit, she is attacked by a palace guard. Upon her arrival a functionary beats her, but he is merely executing her two brothers' joint command to not allow her re-entry into the house. This happens because these brothers believe she going to bring them bad luck due to her barrenness. Furthermore, and again unlike Draupadi, there is absolutely no implication in the Ponnivala epic that Tamarai could possibly be abducted by a family adversary to serve as a sexual partner or slave. Rather, Tamarai is simply the twin heroes' ultra-pure, never-once-sullied, mother. However, her daughter Tangal's situation is a little bit different, as will be seen below.

Draupadi and Tangal: In the next generation, the Ponnivala Nadu story features Tangal, the younger sister of Ponnar and Shankar. The Pandava brothers do not have a sister at all, let alone one to whom Tangal might, in theory, be compared. However, there is some small degree of overlap between Draupadi and Tangal. It is almost as if Draupadi's positive traits have been split between the two

The Mahabharata   73

Figure 2.20 Tamarai is insulted by her husband's cousins.

key Ponnivala women, mother Tamarai and daughter Tangal. For example, there is a well-known Sanskrit stanza that speaks of the virtues of a set of five kanyas or virgins. Their names are Ahalya, Draupadi, Kunti, Tara, and Mandodari. Tangal is an explicit reincarnation of the youngest of seven virgins (called the Kannimar), a very popular set of folk deities in the Kongu Nadu area. Those seven are a cluster of "celestial virgins" in Tamil folk tradition that can be linked to the constellation Pleiades (see chapters 7 and 8 for more details). These seven young women hover around Lord Shiva's council chambers (sometimes they are also said to hang about near Indra's palace) in local Tamil mythology. None of those seven women (the Kritikka) have an explicit presence in the Mahabharata story, but the five kanyas of the Sanskrit tradition are present. Perhaps they reference the same broader concept of multiple virgins. If so, Draupadi could then be called an earthly form of one of those five women, giving her a mythological link that resembles the one Tangal has to the Kritikka. One literary version of the Ponnivala Nadu story, furthermore, does suggest that Tangal reincarnates Draupadi.[7] However, why this is so remains unexplained, as these two women are basically very different. Perhaps this literary reference is just one more way in which a variety of prestigious associations have been welded onto the Ponnivala story's local frame in order to raise its general status and enhance its wished-for respectability.

Like Draupadi, Tangal, undergoes exile. But Tangal is just a baby when this happens and she is accompanied by her parents. She was never old enough to realize that there was any hardship involved in living in a forest. Later in life, furthermore, Tangal does not suffer any real insults, unlike the famous disrobing of Draupadi. However, one sign of possible neglect is that her two brothers never assign guards to protect her when they leave on any of their military exploits. Draupadi, by contrast, is guarded when the Pandavas are not around. The implication is that Tangal would be able to take care of herself should she ever be threatened.

Figure 2.21. Tangal laments over her brothers' dead bodies.

Her brothers believe in her visionary powers and also in her goddess-like resilience. Furthermore, the Ponnivala twins never discuss arranging a marriage for their sister. This is despite undergoing a double-wedding ceremony of their own, something that their mother insisted on. Tangal remains unmarried to the bitter end of the Ponnivala story. Not even one potential suitor is ever mentioned. Draupadi, by contrast, experiences an elaborate wedding ceremony and had many eager suiters vying to wed her.

One faint additional parallel between Draupadi and Tangal can be found in the fact that Tangal engages in an extensive, poetic lament when she finally locates her dead brothers (figure 2.21). This is the moment when she finds her brothers' bodies lying prone and covered with blood, because they decided to fall on their own swords. Draupadi recites a similar lament over the corpses of her own dead sons and dead brothers as they lie at the scene of their deaths. But there are two key contrasts. For one, the Ponnivala Nadu brothers have killed themselves willingly while all the sons Draupadi laments have been killed by the family's adversaries. And another contrast between these two scenes is that Tangal is able to bring her dead brothers back to life, if only briefly, using magical verses and a golden wand that she has obtained from Lord Shiva. Draupadi has no similar power to rejuvenate the dead. This is relevant because the annual ceremonies at many local shrines dedicated to the Ponnivala Nadu brothers today revolve around a re-enactment of that stunning episode where a reincarnation occurs. Tangal's revival of her two brothers highlights the same basic theme: life-renewal. Recall that Tamarai was born of Shiva and Parvati's love play, after Shiva's semen fell on a lotus leaf and quickly transformed into a lovely baby girl. That lotus-leaf-baby theme and its association with the love play of the gods is a common motif in Hindu mythology more generally. It relates, somewhat distantly, to the idea of a cosmic Shiva and Parvati periodically renewing life on earth by letting some of Shiva's semen fall, now and then, into receptive vessels located on earth. Draupadi, by contrast, is born of fire and she emerges from a cluster of hot flames as an adult, not as a tiny infant. This latter set of images is not a common mythological theme. In sum, it is hard to see many strong parallels when comparing either Tangal or her mother Tamarai with the Mahabharata heroine Draupadi. That famous ancestral epic woman is distinct from both key women featured in the Ponnivala epic when we consider their differing personalities and also their very different life experiences.

Draupadi, Tangal, and Dogs: The Pandavas had an agreement that only one brother would enter Draupadi's chamber at a time. Whenever any one of her five husbands was in her chamber, they were to leave their shoes outside the door. There was a strict penalty for a violation of this rule; the offender would have to leave immediately on a solitary, year-long exile. One day when Yudhishthira was in Draupadi's chamber, a dog stole his shoes which he had dutifully placed outside. Arjuna, unaware of that theft, entered the chamber and saw his elder brother making love to Draupadi. Draupadi, furious with the dog that had stolen Yudhishthira's shoes, then cursed all dogs to copulate in public without shame. At one key place in the Ponnivala Nadu story there is also an important story about a dog. This time it describes a tiny palace bitch that is Tangal's chief pet. Note that she is female and that her name translates roughly as "little piece of gold." Ponnacci was a fierce and resilient little animal. Despite her extremely small size, this tiny dog knew that she had hunting skills. But when Tangal's two brothers left to start their chase of Komban, the great wild boar, they did not take Ponnacci with them. Nonetheless, all of the male dogs in Ponnivala's many villages were invited to join that hunt. Ponnacci was angry about this insult. Now, instead of the pet being cursed in the way that Draupadi cursed her dog, the direction the anger flows is reversed and Ponnacci curses Tangal's brothers for their thoughtless mistake. That curse then causes both brothers to suffer a severe illness while they are away on their hunt. The two brothers soon lie side by side in their camp tent, barely able to move. Before the effect of this terrible curse can be halted, the brothers must humble themselves before her and beg Ponnacci to come help them with their great boar quest.

Maybe the Pandava's bedroom incident and Ponnacci's anger are unrelated. But the powerful anger of a righteous female clearly permeates both scenes. When Ponnacci is finally invited to join the heroes in their boar chase she becomes a major contributor. Ponnacci, rather than any of the male dogs who have been accompanying the two brothers from the start, is the one member of the hunting party able to successfully challenge Komban's bullying ways. She is just a tiny little thing crouched on a rock that finds herself looking upward at that boar's huge and frightening body (figure 2.22). It is at this point that Ponnacci exhibits great resilience and courage. Komban speaks first. He says, in a threatening voice: "I could crush you with just one foot." But the little dog does not let him do that. In the Mahabharata, the Pandava's guard dog (who appears to be male) is treated

76 Multiple Epics Compared

Figure 2.22. Komban threatens tiny Ponnacci (seen inside the circle).

as lowly and shameless, while in the Ponnivala Nadu story a much smaller female dog is glorified. Furthermore, Ponnacci is ugly because she was born without ears. Related or not, the Ponnivala Nadu dog story celebrates the victory of a small, ugly female over a great big male bully. Especially suggestive is the fact that Ponnacci wins the day by biting Komban's testicles. If nothing else, this scene presents a clear case of a male/female status reversal, something not present in the Mahabharata. In the Ponnivala Nadu story the female gender trumps the male, tiny trumps the huge, and ugly wins over a much bigger and possibly more handsome bully. Furthermore, Ponnacci uses her magical teeth to combat that huge wild enemy, perhaps a hidden reference to the powerful bow and arrow that Arjuna once used, in a famous Mahabharata scene, to shoot at the huge boar that was charging him.[8] Even at that, Lord Shiva wins this mock contest with Arjuna. Ponnacci also wins her contest in a possible Ponnivala-Mahabharata parallel. Could Ponnacci be understood to be the goddess Parvati in disguise, in other words Shiva's other half? After all, Parvati wins several contests against her husband Shiva in the wider Indian mythological corpus. This pattern repeats itself in many other ways. Indeed, in the Ponnivala Nadu story, the human and animal females appear to blend. The story's male characters, on the other hand, are more differentiated, less resilient, and are certainly never compared with biting dogs.

Arjuna and Tamarai: There is one striking example of resilience that involves a male Pandava, Arjuna. In the folk account the obvious parallel is a female: the heroes' mother, Tamarai. How is that possible? This gender crossover is very interesting. Tamarai spends the first part of her twenty-one-year penance walking towards the Himalayas with her husband Kunnutaiya. They experience various hardships along the way and are helped numerous times by Vishnu. But the going gets harder and harder. Tamarai eventually begins to carry Kunnutaiya on her back, a sure sign of her extraordinary resilience. She starts climbing the Himalayan

Figure 2.23. Tamarai's weakened husband is turned to stone.

foothills with him on her back. But then the couple reach a gate beyond which there are steps leading upwards into the clouds. Tamarai can carry Kunnutaiya no farther but he is too weak to climb those stairs and must stop. Vishnu very gently converts him to stone and has him wait in this frozen state for Tamarai to return (figure 2.23). Then Vishnu leads Tamarai onward alone, climbing that long flight of steps with her. But at one point the two reach a kind of plateau intended for ascetics who are meditating and who are deep in prayer. There Vishnu shows Tamarai the place where Arjuna once performed his famous penance, the very special location where he begged Shiva for his great Pasupata weapon. Arjuna wanted that weapon because he believed it would help him and his brothers achieve victory in the great war that would soon follow.

Vishnu tells Tamarai that this was the very spot where Arjuna had once stood in prayer and meditation. The helpful god then tells Tamarai to put on the saffron robes of an ascetic. After that Tamarai climbs to the top of the very same pillar Arjuna once used. She will now sit there patiently, in prayer, for twenty-one years. Significantly, there are sharp needles at the summit of that pillar. As part of a carving seen in a famous temple located in Perur (near Coimbatore City), Arjuna is depicted standing (placing his big toe on) just such a needle. That carving provides one more hint of a possible Arjuna–Tamarai analogy being suggested here. Furthermore, Arjuna asks Shiva for a great weapon of war. Tamarai, by contrast, asks for two sons and a daughter. What is the similarity in these requests? Perhaps those two sons will be able to serve Tamarai's personal interests in a similar way to Arjuna's Pasupata weapon? Sons could help Tamarai win back her beloved Ponnivala Nadu kingdom from its enemies and could also protect it from harm for decades to come.

It is not such a stretch, then, to suggest that Tamarai be understood as a female Arjuna. Her **Resilience** is just as strong as his was. She is also equally patient and persistent, perhaps even more so than he was. The task of winning the Pasupata, however, took Arjuna just days, while Tamarai had to persist with her prayers for twenty-one years. If there is a parallel between the two stories, it is one containing several inversions and important differences, each contrasting this local story with the Mahabharata original in interesting ways.

Theme 5: Relationships

In the present context, the term relationship is used to describe a significant social bond of kinship, or else a political bond of some sort. In a story, scenes depicting relationships often involve the personality traits of the character portrayed. This same theme may also reflect multiple loyalties, commitments, and responsibilities that identify a particular character.

Understanding the relationship between two protagonists is central to any Mahabharata versus Ponnivala Nadu comparison. We will find more overlap in this segment of our study than can be identified under any other theme featured in this chapter. The overlap is especially striking when it comes to male characters. These multiple similarities will be considered below. Each will be discussed as it can be understood to exist within a wider generational structure fundamental to both stories. First, intergenerational relationships will be discussed, then relationships defined by marriage, then political relationships such as king versus subject, and finally sibling relationships as they sort into subcategories according to a variety of gender and twinning themes.

Parents versus Children

We have already seen, above, that in the second generation the Chola king gives some very wise and helpful advice to Kunnutaiya about how to be a good (minor) king. This happens just after that Chola has honoured the Ponnivala Nadu leader (second generation) with a small crown. The Chola's overall attitude towards Kunnutaiya at this point is supportive and kind. He behaves somewhat like Kunnutaiya's surrogate father. The parents of this hero, Kolatta and Ariyanacci, also hold that same attitude towards Kunnutaiya, expressing loving support of their (adopted) son. Of course, this support only lasts up to their deaths and, unfortunately, Kunnutaiya is just five years old when he is orphaned. The same parental attitudes are reflected in the next generation as well. When Kunnutaiya and Tamarai marry and Tamarai bears a set of triplets, this parental pair become loving and supportive parents of all three of their children.[9] Their affection is spread among their daughter and two sons equally, but only after the two sons join the family at age five. Before that all their parental love is focused on their sole daughter, Tangal. No descriptions of abusive or highly authoritarian attitudes can be attributed to either adult. The only examples of these possible parental

Figure 2.24. As Kunnutaiya and Tamarai prepare to die, they deliver their parting instructions to their two sons.

attitudes appear when Kunnutaiya is taken in by his cousins' various families. There, as an outsider, Kunnutaiya is repeatedly mistreated. But those incidents are only tangential to this enquiry.

Much later, Kunnutaiya and his wife Tamarai provide instructions to their two sixteen-year-old sons. The scene is somewhat parallel to the one where the Chola king offers advice to Kunnutaiya in the previous generation, after his parents have died. This formal advice is presented at the exact point when these two parents realize that their own deaths are near. Now the couple call their sons into their private chamber. Kunnutaiya begins his address to the two teenagers as follows:[10]

> Dear Lords! The end of our time is drawing near. We must leave for the gods' council chambers. Before that we want to tell you a few important things that will help you going forward. Never do anything to harm the king of Chola Nadu. He was the one who helped establish your grandfather Kolatta in this area, He also helped establish the clansmen and gave them lands that neighbour ours. He had the boundaries measured and marked. Therefore, do nothing to harm that Chola monarch. Furthermore, no matter how much harm our clansmen once did to us, they must account for those actions themselves. Don't you do anything to them. Also, always be sure to perform three pujas for our goddess Cellatta each day. The lands of Ponnivala Nadu all belong to her. And lastly, always be patient of heart, no matter what mistakes your relatives might make. Never extract compensatory justice.

Tamarai, the twins' mother, then continues with some further advice regarding the boys' sister: "You both must look after Tangal. Whatever she might say, be patient of heart and do whatever she asks immediately. Do not get angry with her. She will see your future in her dreams and know what will happen to you. She was born with that special power. You are to be both mother and father to her after our deaths. And furthermore, when you find a good match for her, you are to finalize and carry out her marriage."

The two boys agree to follow this parental advice in every respect. They speak respectfully in front of their father and mother. But as soon as the two elders die, their advice is not only ignored, it is directly contradicted. Furthermore, these twins now develop a rebellious attitude toward their parents very quickly. These boys are only sixteen, but they are now, suddenly, the twin rulers of the lands of Ponnivala Nadu. In contrast to their parents' style of gentle rule, these two soon begin to bully and beat their clansmen, even though these clansmen are their own cousins. They also attack the clansmen's sons even as they sit inside their own village school, a scene that is somewhat reminiscent of the several terrorist school attacks described in the news and carried out across North America in recent years. The clansmen and their families, all suffer deep despair because of these attacks. They are also forced into exile following the two brothers' vicious beating of those clansmen's children. Nonetheless, Ponnivala's twin heroes feel justified in having carried out these aggressive acts. They see those attacks as justified revenge, in their own generation, for mean tricks their clansmen's elders once played on their own parents, Kunnutaiya and Tamarai, long ago.

Soon after that first violent school assault, the twin heroes become involved in an even worse act of violence. This time they kill the neighbouring Chola king, a ruler they feel has been arrogant and untruthful. This current Chola ruler has tried to trick them and humble them even though his predecessor (presumably his father) was generous and kind towards these boys' parents and even their grandparents. The ruling Chola at the time had helped them out in several ways. Furthermore, the twins do not remember the instruction their father gave them earlier; that they were to worship the family goddess three times each day. And finally, the two brothers almost completely ignore their sister Tangal. They leave her alone in the palace with just a few servants whenever they depart on one of their many warrior-style adventures. On multiple occasions they refuse to listen to their sister's visionary advice and they never search for a husband that might suit their chaste sister and solve her problem of constant loneliness. Notable too is that in the set of instructions the parents give these two heroes, there is no mention of playing dice. Perhaps this is because it was a pastime they never engaged in. But now the two brothers' dice games are repeatedly described (figure 2.25).

In all the above-listed ways, these two grandsons of Kolatta function as polar opposites to their parents. They now deliberately contradict almost every norm those two seniors had so clearly endorsed. This behavioural shift makes the death of the second generation a significant turning point in the larger story. Everything begins to spiral downhill from that point. Although dicing is a key vice in the Mahabharata as well, the other things mentioned do not find clear parallels in the former account. Such a blatant case of parental rebellion is not seen in the

Figure 2.25. The two heroes, ready for risk taking, begin a game of dice.

Mahabharata story. This unique story feature provides one further example of an important way in which the two tales diverge. Indeed, the Pandava brothers bend over backwards to carry out a central (but seemingly accidental) instruction from their mother: that they are all to marry the same woman even though it was very awkward to execute that order in many situations. More importantly, perhaps, we should perhaps argue that the Ponnivala Nadu story was never intended to model itself after the Mahabharata in these (and many other) particular ways.

Wife versus Husband

First Generation: There are three marriages described in the Ponnivala Nadu story, one in each of the three generations the story describes. The marriage between Kolatta and Ariyanacci in the first generation is unremarkable and peaceful. Ariyanacci, not her husband, for example, is the first to propose that they go and visit the nearby Chola king and seek his help due to a severe local drought when there is a serious lack of food. Kolatta agrees. Later, it is Kolatta who takes the initiative. When the couple visit the Chola king, Kolatta asks him to agree to a work contract. As soon as the king agrees Kolatta asks for a work contract for his wife as well. The Chola king, however, agrees to pay only half of what Kolatta will be paid when it comes to her services. Nonetheless, Ariyanacci agrees to the plan. She also collaborates with her husband in many other ways. Together they lovingly raise their adopted son Kunnutaiya, the baby they find in a back field. These two protagonists also die at the same time (something Lord Yeman engineers) and then they climb a ladder to heaven together.

One key incident that does need mention, however, is the moment when Kolatta orders a spiked fence built to protect his first fine sugarcane crop. Twelve cows leave the Chola's country when a famine breaks out and seven of those poor hungry females find that luscious and ripe sugarcane field. Alas, those seven cows all die trying to jump over the mean barrier Kolatta had built. Soon afterwards, the angry Shiva pronounces a curse: Ariyanacci is to become a barren wife. Here we see that a curse, intended to interrupt Kolatta's descent line, primarily causes suffering for his wife. Ariyanacci takes that infertility seriously. She understands it to be signal that she has personally committed some unknown sin. Meanwhile Kolatta is more resigned and philosophical about this family problem. Ariyanacci, however, feels it is her personal responsibility, not his, to bear children who can carry on the family line. Kolatta is willing to accept an adopted child, but she is distraught about not being able to perform this key service for her family herself. This sad situation does not make the marriage go sour, but it does illustrate how women tend to suffer for faults and mistakes that can clearly be traced back to their husband's actions and not their own. There is a parallel here with Draupadi's situation in the Mahabharata, but only concerning the broad theme of female suffering in general. Draupadi suffers ignominy, sexual embarrassment, and a long exile due to the poor judgement of her most senior husband, Yudhisthira. It is he who gambles her away in a seemingly innocent game of dice. Draupadi's marriage (to five brothers) survives that dice game but Draupadi herself suffers a lot in the wake of her husband's rash actions. Ariyanacci and Tamarai, similarly, suffer greatly due to Kolatta's ill-considered decision to fence his fine sugarcane field with the sharp spikes that end up killing seven cows.

Second generation: In the second generation the marriage between Kunnutaiya and Tamarai is described in much more depth but the overarching themes addressed remain similar. Here Tamarai is a very strong and determined heroine and her rather meek husband tends to live in her shadow. Tamarai warns her husband multiple times about the mean tricks his cousins are likely to play on him. Furthermore, she can see jewels in a field of maize where her husband sees nothing. Tamarai is also more generous with the family's wealth, giving scoops of jewels away to a long line of beggars while Kunnutaiya urges restraint and gets angry. She is the manager of the family's wealth at several later points and she brings out jewels to pay labourers when needed. She is also the more sensitive one when it comes to family status issues. Tamarai wants a palace built, while Kunnutaiya merely complies with her wishes. But the real core of Tamarai's heroism is her twenty-one-year quest to win a gift of pregnancy from Lord Shiva. She is barren at this point, due to Shiva's cruel curse, just as her husband's mother suffered barrenness earlier in the story. That same fate has now fallen on her, because she is the wife of Kolatta's son. Just like Ariyanacci, Tamarai is mortally embarrassed by her apparent infertility, and she suffers a lot of teasing from other local women for this reason. Worst of all, her husband argues with her when she finally suggests to him that she would like to visit her sisters-in-law and at least enjoy playing with their children. Kunnutaiya does not approve. Tamarai goes anyway but returns badly bruised from the beating she receives at the hands of her two brothers. At

The Mahabharata 83

Figure 2.26. Kunnutaiya orders Tamarai to leave the palace.

this point Kunnutaiya is so angry he throws Tamarai out of their palace (figure 2.26). Lord Vishnu later finds a way to help soften Kunnutaiya's anger and coax him back to join his wife again, but this serious marital argument causes Tamarai to attempt suicide. Vishnu helps the couple patch over this fight after rescuing Tamarai from a jump she threatens to make from a high pillar. Later, during the early part of Tamarai's twenty-one-year pilgrimage, she even offers to carry her weak and failing husband on her back. In sum, the Ponnivala story makes it very clear that Tamarai is the stronger, more focused, and more determined partner in this marriage. But she also suffers more hardship and more self-doubt than her husband, similar to the difficulties her mother-in-law and predecessor Ariyanacci faced. If any parallel is to be drawn between this set of women, and those in the Mahabharata it would, once more, be with Draupadi. Overall, however, the similarities to be found between these several females and that ancient heroine are quite thin.

Third Generation: In the third generation there are virtually no parallels to be drawn between the females of the Ponnivala Nadu story and the Mahabharata. The two brothers (Kolatta's grandsons) do marry in the end, but that is a mere formality. Their brides are locked in a separate set of living quarters right after the nuptial rituals conclude. There they are forced to spin and spin some more. They do nothing else. When their two husbands die, their sister Tangal goes to their separate home to inform them of this tragic event. But the two wives refuse to attend their husbands' funeral saying they have had no life at all as married women. Tangal then burns down these two wives' living quarters in retaliation for this refusal, using a magical ball of fire and both wives die in this tragic blaze. Tangal then performs the needed funeral rituals, ceremonies that would normally be conducted by a man (figure 2.27). This is one of several indications of her radical gender transformation at this point. Furthermore, the heroes' two wives

Figure 2.27. Tangal empties the pot containing bones of her two sisters-in-law into the river as a part of the standard funeral rites.

can be compared to suttees, except that here they are unwilling victims of their fiery, joint death. Perhaps we can take this as a folk commentary on the practice of suttee more generally (a ritualistic Indian female widow's suicide act, normally accomplished by walking deliberately into a large, hot fire). Suttee is more of a North Indian tradition than a Tamil one. Several queens commit suttee in the Mahabharata.[11] Pandu's second wife, Madri, immolated herself after the death of her husband. The five wives of Krishna in Hastinapur did the same after news of his death. However, these stories are not well known and thus any parallel with the Ponnivala story feels somewhat forced. The broader similarity here concerns family honour. The heroes' sister does not want to leave behind any vulnerable women who might be subject to defilement or other kinds of mistreatment, now that both of their husbands are dead. Tangal kills them to ensure the good name of the family for posterity. In addition, she is angry that these two sisters-in-law do not express the normally expected sorrow over her dear brothers' deaths, two men that she had dearly loved.

How the key characters are born in each generation: As Ponnivala Nadu's local community advanced both socially and economically, we see that the rules applied to marital matches grow more and more restrictive. The initial nine men and women partner off without any consideration of rank or kin relatedness. The ancestral couple that represents the first generation, furthermore, is made up of fully formed human adults who marry in a pure, beautiful, and natural environment (a forest). Parvati created just nine men, followed by nine women. All are adults and none were born on earth. They were just placed there by her good graces. These humans pair off with no prescriptions or guidelines mentioned. And they marry in the simplest possible way, by just mutually garlanding each other with wreaths of flowers. Parvati, furthermore, gives them just one key instruction

Figure 2.28. Tamarai, as a baby, is found by a stranger, at the edge of a lotus pond.

and it has nothing to do with sexual desire or its restraint. She merely asks them to go and use the plough she has given them to start their farming enterprise. But the larger frame is important here. Parvati tells the nine men to transform the landscape seen around them into ploughed fields. They are to convert the natural world into a tamed one (that is, make a forest into farmed fields, or irkai into cer‑ kai, to use the Tamil words for this). Parvati does not describe her intent exactly, but it does seem that she is basically asking these nine men to "civilize the area" thus making it into a plentiful food basket that can support much human life.

In the second generation as well, none of the key antagonists are born in the acknowledged human way, from a woman's womb on earth. Both Kunnutaiya and Tamarai are created by the gods but then are set down on the earth as newly born infants. These tiny babies are simply found by their adoptive parents. Neither baby has any family ties at that point and each is found in a location that lies beyond the boundaries of a human settlement. The male hero, Kunnutaiya, is found under a pile of rocks (a very male setting, metaphorically speaking) and the female Tamarai (who will later become his wife) appears in a lotus flower that is growing in a lovely pond (a very female setting) (figure 2.28). Both are discovered by members of a human family living not far away, but these tiny children do not appear on protected village land. A group of males find Kunnutaiya while a lone female finds Tamarai. In the first scenario a landowner (Kolatta) happens to be checking on his cows and goats that are grazing in a distant back pasture, while the woman who finds the tiny girl Tamarai has been praying for a child while sitting cross-legged and alone by an isolated pond. Where that pool of water was located is never specified, but it clearly lay well beyond the boundaries of the praying woman's own home village. Both places, therefore, can be described as borderline wilderness areas; both are conveniently situated part way between a genuine forest and the civility of a clustered human settlement. These

Figure 2.29. Tamarai and Kunnutaiya, married deep in the forest by Lord Vishnu himself.

two important second-generation infants are then brought into the village environment and raised there by members of two separate, powerful landowning families. Both their homes symbolize the epitome of fine, civilized life, as it was known at the time. In sum, the hero and heroine of the second generation have a mix of natural and cultural birth traits and therefore constitute a bridge between these two respective norms.

Significantly, the boy in this second Ponnivala generation is later orphaned at the tender age of five. After this he must survive on his own. Fortunately, Kunnutaiya eventually finds work as a shepherd for a large landowner, where he also does many odd jobs. In fact, unbeknownst to Kunnutaiya, he has begun working for the family of that lotus-born girl, and his two bosses are her two elder brothers! As both these protagonists grow into young adults, Tamarai and Kunnutaiya fall in love. We must note, however, that they never spend any intimate time together. The storyteller is very careful to keep the women in each story generation very pure. Tamarai and Kunnutaiya each dream about the other, but they never, ever, physically touch before they are married. Eventually the two do tie the knot, but with substantial resistance being expressed by the girl's two elder brothers. This is because, though appreciated as a good worker, Kunnutaiya is considered to have once been a waif of unknown origin. On her side, furthermore, her elder brothers represent a wealthy landed family, and their daughter could easily be called a local princess. In the end, Lord Vishnu outlines a respectable lineage for the hero to claim. Kunnutaiya tries to explain his respectable ancestry to the girl's brothers. However, they are not convinced and continue to resist the idea of her marriage to Kunnutaiya.

Vishnu eventually conducts their marriage, nonetheless, but the ritual happens at a forest shrine that lies nowhere near the bride's village (figure 2.29). No relatives on either side agree to attend. Only a few tribal girls, out gathering wood, watch the limited proceedings. The circumstances of this second-generation marriage suggest, then, that the rules of marriage, in this second generation, are now more restrictive and more sensitive to matters of social prestige than they were previously. Both politics and economics have become a part of decision process where marriage is concerned. But in the end, Kunnutaiya and Tamarai's wedding ignores or breaks the standard that requires a matched economic and social status between the bride and the groom. Despite the groom being of lower status than his bride, however, the two do manage to marry, albeit with a little help from Lord Vishnu. But the brides' brothers impose penalties. The girl is told never to return to her natal home. She is cast out by her kinsmen precisely because of their strong objections to the groom's inferior status. Furthermore, Tamarai is given several very insulting wedding gifts (a sick, old cow, a blind goat, and more).

In the third generation the key protagonists' birth and marriage arrangements are different again. This time there are two grandsons and one granddaughter to consider. All three are born from the same mother's womb, though Vishnu provides a magical caesarean to assist with those boys' arrival. Furthermore, the two males arrive clothed and holding miniature weapons. But the girl's birth is fully natural. She is born naked, as any other child would be, directly exiting her mother's cervix in the normal way. More important still, the two infant boys are immediately threatened by jealous cousins and must be hidden. Their sister, on the other hand, is safe from any succession threats. Now the developing social mores present in the surrounding society encroach on the wedding event still further. The boys are considered to be in line to inherit land and power, while the girl is not.

When these same boys reach a marriageable age, there are other interesting contrasts with what their parents experienced in their time. The main difference is that they are now compelled by their mother to marry two precise girls, their mother's brothers' daughters. They are the ones considered to be exactly the correct, socially approved marriage partners from both a kinship perspective and an economic one. When their mother insists, therefore, her two boys reluctantly agree to please her. But there is a catch. The two sons say that they will only consent to perform a few limited wedding rituals. There has been no courtship and in fact they have never even met their brides-to-be. In the third generation, therefore, the local kinship rules are fully obeyed, and everything is kept pure and chaste. But then something odd happens. The two boys refuse to touch those girls during the prescribed wedding rituals, even with their little fingers. All the required nuptial procedures are conducted without the two heroes ever physically having contact with their brides. After that, the two female cousins are immediately taken to a separate building and locked inside. They never speak to or even see their husbands again, let alone have a chance to be with them in a situation where they could possibly conceive and produce a subsequent generation. How will the family line carry on?

Tangal, furthermore, is never married at all. Thus, in the third generation, no one produces any offspring and there is no chance at all for social continuity and palace succession. And the family's lands and fine palace are destroyed when the two virgin heroes die. There is no ending of this sort in the Mahabharata. The themes discussed above belong entirely to the Ponnivala Nadu story.

Rulers versus Subjects

The Mahabharata heroes' sociological father, Pandu, resembles the Ponnivala heroes' father Kunnutaiya in several important ways. Both are honourable men, and both are by and large considered to be kind and just rulers. To that extent the first kings of these two epic accounts resemble one another. It is not so easy however, to generalize about their sons. In both stories this junior generation becomes engaged in war and conflict. Furthermore, the male sibling set born to each king is highly differentiated internally. Pandu's and Kunnutaiya's sons each display a range of distinct personalities but their leadership styles are more difficult to characterize. One thing that does compare well is that in both there is a senior brother (Yudhisthira in one case and Ponnar in the other) for whom reason, empathy, and restraint take priority. In both stories, too, it is the younger sibling who is extremely strong, violent, and vengeful (Bhima in the Mahabharata and Shankar in the Ponnivala Nadu account). Conflict arises between those contrasting leadership styles in both epics. To that extent a rather loose degree of similarity or overlap can be seen.

Death of the ruling king: It must be noted that the Ponnivala folk epic has a populist feel and that it expresses the perspective of a regional underdog in its attitude vis-a-vis a wider world. Indeed, this becomes more and more the case as the story progresses. Not long after the twin heroes lose their parents, they manage to murder their overlord, the Chola king. This act of terror would have horrified their elders. And significantly, the Chola's palace is destroyed in the process (figure 2.30). Because many of the heroes' lineal cousins had taken shelter there (after the twins sent them into a forced exile earlier) a whole generation of rival kinsmen was instantly wiped out when the monarch was killed. Hence, the threat posed by the heroes' cousins now evaporates. These rivals are never heard from again. Furthermore, as expected, Shankar and his sidekick Shambuga are front and centre in the scene where the Chola's palace is demolished. Ponnar, the elder and more passive brother, on the other hand, is a mere bystander during this violent event.

The death of the Chola king moves the Ponnivala story to new ground. The tribal Vettuva community living on the edges of Ponnivala Nadu quickly take the place of the heroes now absent cousins. And these hunters are angry. In fact, their antagonism is initiated by the heroes themselves because they now begin to steal from their forest-dwelling neighbours. First the twins' assistant Shambuga

Figure 2.30. The destruction of the Chola palace.

runs off with a valuable stash of iron belonging to this indigenous community – a pile of sturdy iron rods that they had stored near their forest temple. This is their principal shrine, a place dedicated to the goddess who was supposed to guard that very treasure. Implicitly, Kali is offended by this theft and that is likely one reason she later becomes a key facilitator when it comes to the twin heroes' deaths. Next these two men use that stolen iron to make a large hunting net that will soon capture a beautiful female parrot that the Vettuvas believe belongs to them. The farmers must invade the hunters' forest in order to get that bird because it lives in a very beautiful, special, and highly symbolic banyan tree located in the Vettuva forest (figure 2.31). The female parrot's family life is violently interrupted by her abduction and her male partner is left alone to mourn her absence. Implicitly, indeed metaphorically, the rules that uphold orderly family life are being broken in this scene. This signals the beginning of a chaotic downward spiral for all involved.

Because the Chola king has just very recently been killed, his power to control this forest tract and its valuable wildlife is no longer relevant. The heroes had never before invaded this wild area, precisely because this king had exercised oversight there and asserted his own exclusive right, as the only outsider allowed to hunt in this pristine territory. Likely this Vettuva forest had been his own exclusive hunting ground. It may have also been where his elephants and horses grazed and were well cared for by the same indigenous Vettuva community. But now that the Chola king was no more, the two brothers could do what they liked. They could now willfully enter that previously forbidden area and behaved as thieves. The tribal residents, insulted and exasperated by this unruly behaviour, now begin to fight back. The local artisans living in the Ponnivala Nadu area, the same group that had suffered insults from members of two earlier generations in the heroes' family, now join forces with the wronged Vettuva hunters. The resulting confrontation grows quickly and lasts until a war between these opposing groups,

Figure 2.31. The farmers' first forest hunting expedition.

overseen by Vishnu, finally brings the story to a close. In sum, the core themes that are woven through this local epic undergo a shift in the third generation. The challenges to the heroes' family first posed by their lineal cousins now morph into challenges posed by two other significant groups that populate the wider area: a group of indigenous hunters and a group of artisans. That transformation takes the story to a new level, making it still more unlike the Mahabharata. Furthermore, those same changes also help relate this old, medieval tale to various more modern colonial-expansion themes, issues that are still relevant around the world. What is most significant is that while Kunnutaiya had accepted and honoured the Chola king, his sons rebelled and broke the social norms of the day by refusing to pay respect to that monarch and eventually going so far as to murder him.

Marriage Rules: Given the local rules of marriage, in Kongu Nadu, a land where one does not marry a man from one's own lineage, the presence of a separate male line whose clan contains marriable sisters, is always assumed. This is because everyone knows by well-established tradition, that the men of one male descent line should give their sisters to the men of a second, separate male line (one whose men belong to a different descent group). It is also normal for separate clans to have different territorial affiliations. The nine men of the Ponnivala Nadu area were placed on earth by Parvati in an area called Vellivala Nadu. In the first generation she provided the women she wanted them to marry. But in the second generation the story calls the area where marriable women live Valavandi Nadu. Although both Kunnutaiya and Tamarai were orphans, one found under a pile of rocks and the other inside a lotus flower, Lord Vishnu declared that they were marriageable cross cousins whose fathers belonged to different clans. Specifically, Vishnu told Kunnutaiya that Tamarai was the daughter of one of his own mother's brothers. Vishnu then likewise assures Tamarai's elder brothers that their sister can rightly marry Kunnutaiya as he was related to their father's sister's side of the family.

Whether or not Vishnu fabricated this relationship, his offer of a snippet of family genealogy serves to socially legitimize the couple's marriage. But that was only part of the challenge. There was also the issue of wealth and social status. Traditionally, for a marriage relationship to be considered correct, wealth and status differences should be minimal. In fact, cross-cousin marriage was a primary way (not usually verbalized) of controlling and minimizing differences in material well-being that were not likely to be large between closely related families. Vishnu knew this very well and, in a way, he was challenging Tamarai's brothers to do the right and moral thing. Although this logic may seem foreign to a non-Tamil, the underlying rational is clear.

A wedding ritual that expresses the brother-sister bond: The importance of the brother-sister bond is symbolized directly in a local Kongu wedding ritual. During any marriage ceremony conducted by families who take pride in their Kongu identity today, there should first be a preliminary ritual celebrating the bond the groom has with his sister.[12] That ritual is referenced in the description of the twins' wedding. To symbolize the bond between the two of them, Tangal and her elder twin brother Ponnar are visually connected using the ritual wedding sari that the bride herself will later wear. Only after this ceremony is concluded, is the sari given to the bride for her to wear at the wedding. In this ritual the sister, Tangal, also carries a coconut that is used to symbolize her own potential son (figure 2.32). This ritual represents the promise and the hope that her brother will someday produce a daughter who will then be in position to rightfully marry her future son.[13] This tie between brother and sister is so strong that the promise of a future marriage in the next generation is acted out symbolically before the wedding of the couple in question is allowed to proceed. That sibling ceremony is called the innai cir (uniting ritual) in the local dialect spoken in the Kongu area. There is nothing like this described in the Mahabharata story.

We will now examine the several important brother-sister relationships that play out in the Ponnivala epic itself. First, we must look at Tamarai, the twin heroes' mother. Her brothers refused to condone her marriage, but Vishnu does approve and indeed advocates for it. Then he makes sure that it happens. This marriage goes ahead despite all her elder brothers' objections. We have just seen how Vishnu gave Kunnutaiya a special insight into his own family history, allowing him to claim a pre-existing right to marry Tamarai, despite her brothers' protests. The advice that the god gives him was culturally correct and reflects exactly what the innai cir wedding ritual that bonds a brother and sister is intended for. It is meant to pass a very specific right to the children of the next generation such that they (and their parents) will be able to claim that right in the future. This little ceremony is intended to override any economic inequalities or objections that might later develop. This very specific family right is not just formally recognized but is tested later in the story when Tamarai tries to return to her natal home (as discussed previously).

Figure 2.32. The binding ceremony that takes place between a brother his sister before his own wedding can proceed.

When Tamarai does decide that she wants to visit her brothers they break the common rule described above, at least in its general form. They do not welcome their sister but, instead, have her severely beaten by a palace guard. This angers Tamarai and she prays to Lord Shiva for help. Shiva answers to her pleas by sending her a magic wand. Tamarai uses that wand to curse her brothers' children, causing them all to die at once. The brothers soon notice their expired children and are extremely distraught. In time, however, Tamarai manages to extract a humble apology from them for their unethical behaviour towards her and then magically brings her nieces and nephews back to life using the same golden wand. This series of magical events provides a vivid example of the power of a woman when she is driven by righteous anger. A sister is allowed to discipline her own brothers and enforce her traditional kinship rights this way. But there is more. We now learn why Tamarai was so determined to visit her brothers' family. Her true purpose was to take control of two of their daughters, her nieces, and to separate them from the other children in the family. She soon turns the two girls into stone at a nearby shrine and they will only be brought back to life many years hence, when Tamarai's own twin sons (Ponnar and Shankar) have been born, grow up, and are ready for marriage. This exceedingly strong brother-sister bond is deeply embedded in local tradition, a well-known cultural practice in this area that stands squarely behind her claim over those two nubile nieces. They are the rightful marriage partners for her own sons, even though those two sons have not yet been born to her. When it comes to a brother-sister connection, then, this story demonstrates how its importance was strong enough to allow it to override a father's or brother's personal power to control the destiny of his own daughters. This custom has been highlighted here because there is no mention of brother-sister bonds or anything similar to this in the Mahabharata story. There we find that the kin-based rights which descend in the male line are all-powerful, while men's sisters are hardly mentioned at all.

The Mahabharata 93

Figure 2.33. The two heroes' brides are quickly locked in a separate small palace by an assistant.

Marriages that do not produce children: After Ponnivala Nadu's third generation is born and these twin boy heroes mature, the epic then goes on to describe their joint wedding ceremony, where they marry the two girls who had been preserved as stone statues and later revived for this very purpose.[14] The ritual expressing the tie between the heroes' sister Tangal and her brothers (the innai cir) is now explicitly and duly carried out. But, true to the two heroes' characters, the grooms are now the ones to rebel. Shankar, of course, takes the lead as he is the more assertive brother. These two siblings do not want to marry and do so only to conform to expectations. A king should have a wife, that is, a kingdom needs a queen. Thus, they agree to undergo the formalities of the nuptial rites needed but refuse to touch even their brides' little fingers during their joint ceremony. Immediately after those rituals are completed, as already seen, these two women are locked up and their grooms never ever visit them, not even on their wedding night (figure 2.33). As a result, the two brides, after learning of the deaths of their husbands, refuse to conduct any of the normal funeral ceremonies for their husbands.

These women, too, are rebelling against the norms of the day. Of course, we can understand their anger at having been treated in such an inhumane way. But some women would crumble under this kind of social pressure from a sister-in-law who is insisting that they honour their dead husbands no matter how they were treated by them. These two unique brides do not give in. The fact that they are later burnt alive in their locked palace residence is also important. These two poor ladies are made to suffer, through no fault of their own, but because of their husbands' sister's concern to uphold her brothers' honour. Because these two wives refuse to follow protocol, the two brides end up suffering even further when they are burnt and become suttees while trapped in their home. In sum, this incident in the story reinforces the idea that certain key rights and duties irrevocably bond brothers and sisters together. Those rights can override much

Figure 2.34. Cellatta, Vishnu's sister (a form of Parvati), asks her brother to intervene by providing a ball of fire that Tangal will use to burn her sister-in-laws' palace to the ground.

else, including the right of a wife to rebel against inhumane treatment received from her husband,

One of the central principles of the Ponnivala Nadu world, as we have just seen, is that brother-sister bonds are all-powerful. However, another example occurs much earlier in the story, when Cellatta begs her brother Vishnu to help her out. She complains to him that no one has worshipped at her temple for years and that it is in serious disrepair. She wants her brother to find the young orphaned Kunnutaiya and bring that boy back to Ponnivala Nadu to work the lands his father once tilled. Cellatta remembers this boy's good heart and knows that he would take good care of the fields there, and of her temple, if he were to return. She is very unhappy with the fact that his disrespectful cousins have ignored her. Vishnu is sympathetic to his sister's major problem and agrees to help her (figure 2.34).

Cellatta is a form of Parvati that resides on earth. Her focus is the welfare of the crops, plus the need to support the health and prosperity of the local community that cultivates all that bounty. The brother-sister bond that governs much that happens in the gods' domain is similar, but there we see a significant twist. Parvati is the Kailasa-dwelling counterpart of Cellatta, and Vishnu is, of course, brother to both. But now it is Vishnu who solicits his sister's help from time to time, rather than she requesting his. Nonetheless, the loyalty expected between a brother and sister does not change. When Vishnu asks his sister (now Parvati) for help, she predictably agrees to come to his aid. But her help is more indirect. Vishnu usually wants something from his brother-in-law Shiva, but he finds him a hard god to approach and therefore he frequently uses his sister as the go-between, asking Parvati to get Shiva's consent for his request (figure 2.35).

The Mahabharata does include one small story that perhaps bears on this brother-sister issue. It is a minor moment in the larger story there but is significant

Figure 2.35. Parvati interrupts Shiva's forest meditation to ask him to assist Tamarai, the woman her brother Vishnu had taken responsibility for earlier.

in that this case revolves around an indigenous tribal woman, a Rakasha named Hidamba. She belongs to a hunting group despised by the Pandava heroes. Hidamba is stereotyped as an evil character because she is willing to betray her own brother in order to advance her personal and selfish passion for the Pandava hero Bhima. Hidamba is in love with him. The not-so-hidden meaning here is that only an evil woman, and an indigenous woman at that, will betray her own brother, something a self-respecting Pandava hero would never do.[15] Furthermore, Hidamba's betrayal involves her illicit love interest in an inappropriate male partner.

In the Ponnivala epic we find a related example that also features forest hunters' bond with their sister Viratangal. But in the case of this folk epic that brother-sister bond is described in positive terms. Princess Viratangal, a Vettuva by caste, has hundreds of brothers willing to stand beside her. She is their leader; they are her backers and protectors. When the twin heroes steal Vettuva iron and then a beautiful female Vettuva parrot, this forest princess is overcome with anger. In response to these insults, Viratangal calls all her brothers together in front of their common goddess, Kāli. There, in a memorable scene, she asks those numerous male siblings to fight back against these insults. They then carry out her command and set off on a war mission. These hunters' positive support for their angry sister is, in fact, the start of the final confrontation depicted in this epic, a fight that occurs very near the end of this account.

In contrast to Viratangal's brothers' straightforward loyalty, Tangal has a more complex relationship with her own male siblings. For example, near the end of this epic legend, just when the heroic twins are about to commit a double suicide, Ponnar turns to his twin and says: "What shall we do about Tangal?" Shankar answers, "She is like a goddess. She will be able to take care of herself." Tangal does, indeed have goddess-like traits. But Shankar's response does not express the caring attitude he should display towards his sister at this pivotal point, the moment when he is about to depart this earth via suicide. In fact, Shankar has never expressed much concern for Tangal's welfare at any point in this long story. Instead, he has always focused primarily on his own goals as a warrior: on the conquest of challengers and on the vanquishing of family enemies. However, Viratangal (also unlike Hidamba) enjoys an entirely positive relationship with her multiple forest-dwelling brothers. Thus this folk epic does not directly, or indirectly, denigrate these hill-dwelling hunting people. Although there is one instance when Tamarai and Kunnutaiya refuse to eat the foods the Vettuva king offers them, and several other points where the two farmer-kings steal valuable items from this group, the Ponnivala family clearly share a degree of respect this set of rivals. Indeed, their forest brothers embody their own share of magical power. Viratangal knows how to speak to animals and she is kind to them. And the Vettuva's pristine forest domain, too, appears to contain regenerative, life-giving power. That power is something that Vishnu himself believes must be preserved.

Brother versus Brother

First generation: In the Ponnivala Nadu story there are no real brothers in the first generation. Nine men are created at the same time and are called brothers, but they never interact in any significant way. All we learn is that the land the Chola king assigned them is split unequally, such that the eldest brother (and story hero) gets the best, most fertile area. This causes problems in the second generation but nothing much happens for a while. The only key time the nine brothers are seen together in generation one is when they meet in the Chola's guest reception room. The eldest brother, Kolatta, arrives at the Chola palace first, weeks before his siblings follow him there. When the other eight do arrive, the king welcomes them by saying they must be good workers, because their elder brother has performed well. He bases this comment on his appreciation of Kolatta's fine labour, which he has already seen, and so the other eight are hired on that good faith. This tells us that the reputation of one brother was, in this case, assumed to represent the positive qualities of an entire sibling group.

Second generation: In the second generation Kunnutaiya is Kolatta's only son. He has no brothers at all. The only thing that needs to be mentioned here is that the sons of his uncles, the eight brothers of Kolatta, quickly become jealous of their eldest uncle and his adopted son, Kunnutaiya. These male cousin rivals believe that the fine lands that once belonged to their uncle should now pass to them, the biological sons of that man's brothers. According to them, Kunnutaiya is nothing more than a mysteriously born interloper, an orphan found in a back field. This lack of a biological connection is the reasoning these cousins use to launch significant attacks on Kunnutaiya in hopes of laying claim to his father's riches. When Kunnutaiya becomes an orphan again, this time by virtue of

Figure 2.36. The hero Shankar threatens a group of young schoolboys in his cousin's village.

his adoptive parents' deaths, those same cousins destroy his family's small palace. Kunnutaiya is just five or six at the time. This problem with his cousins' jealousy continues for years. But the details that describe this extended period of confrontation are very different from the cousin-to-cousin enmity described in the Mahabharata. Said another way, the concept of two sets of cousins arguing over inheritance rights is present in both epic legends, but the way this confrontation gets fleshed out is very different. Those differences are best seen in the story of the next and final generation.

Third generation: When Kunnutaiya's twin sons are born and the third generation of heroes step onto the stage, the Ponnivala Nadu story begins to diverge from the Mahabharata even more dramatically.[16] Unlike their gentle father Kunnutaiya, Ponnar and Shankar decide on a path of aggressive revenge against their cousin rivals. Their first act, which occurs very soon after their parents' die, is to launch an attack on a schoolhouse where their cousin's young sons are studying (figure 2.36). Shankar and his low caste sidekick Shambuga violently beat those innocent children and soon afterwards the twins intimidate these pupils' parents too. As a next step, the inhabitants of this entire village community, one full of cousin-brother families, is sent into exile. It is Shankar who is the instigator and the leader in this. His elder brother Ponnar hangs back and resists starting a fight. But when Ponnar confronts Shankar, the latter gets angry (figure 2.37). Ponnar then quickly backs down in the face of Shankar's threats and falls in line. This is nothing special. Throughout this epic story, Ponnar behaves as a largely passive second sibling.

The symbolism of twins: Two things are especially important about brother-to-brother relations in the third generation of the Ponnivala story. First, these two brothers are twins by birth and their relationship provides an important commentary on kingship-writ-large. From childhood itself the two brothers consistently

Figure 2.37. Shankar demands his way in speaking with his elder twin.

represent polar opposites in terms of leadership strategies and leadership styles. The elder brother, Ponnar, always advocates compassion, forgiveness, empathy and compromise. He wants to look ahead rather than to right the wrongs of the past. But his junior twin (born just minutes later, but always referred to as younger) wants to right the wrongs of the past. Shankar also contrasts with Ponnar in that he believes in using physical prowess to enforce his understandings about who and what is right. Shankar continually thinks about the events of the past, hoping to punish those he feels have done his family wrong. He also believes that leadership requires the domination of others. According to this worldview, "might makes right." It is important to see that the whole Ponnivala Nadu story builds around this fundamental contrast between Ponnar and Shankar. Which path is morally superior? Which path gets the job done and makes the world a better place? The Ponnivala Nadu epic story does not answer this important question, but it does make one think deeply about the many dimensions that must be considered in finding an answer. A similar tension is embedded in the Pandava brothers' story as well. Yudhisthira is the calm one. He is the thinker and the most gentle and passive among the five Pandava siblings. But that larger issue is not nearly as central to the actions and outcomes of the Mahabharata as it is to outcomes in the folk epic. In the Ponnivala Nadu story this brother-to-brother **Relationship** is constantly referenced and it serves as one of its defining motifs.

Theme 6: Reflection

Reflections are seen in mirrors. A mirror is thought to record a scene accurately, but it can also bend the truth. For starters, a mirror reverses left and right in the eyes of the person looking into it. Lighting makes a big difference too, and if the surface is bumpy or curved, a mirror can also distort the image it reflects in other

Figure 2.38. Tamarai's immaculate conception.

ways. Mirrors are metaphors for situations where a parallel character, initially similar, then becomes altered, inverted, or distorted in some way.

Arjuna becomes Ponnar and Bhima becomes Shankar: Ponnar and Shankar are the male heroes of the Ponnivala Nadu story. They are two brothers that represent explicit reincarnations of the Mahabharata's two most popular male heroes, Arjuna and Bhima. This is made very clear when Lord Shiva himself places the spirits of these two famous Pandavas in the womb of the heroine, making her their new mother-to-be. The immaculate conception of this mother-of-heroes happens as she kneels before that great god in his Himalayan council chambers (figure 2.38). We already know that she wants to be a fertile queen, one who will give birth to men who can eventually succeed her husband and sustain the line of family rule in Ponnivala.

However, we also know that birth order is very significant in Tamil culture and in the Tamil language as well. So why is Bhima, the elder brother in the *Mahabharata*, now made the younger twin in this Ponnivala account? This obvious inversion in the birth order of these two Mahabharata characters cannot be considered accidental. If the bard had wanted to keep the traditional order he could just as well have made Shankar exit his mother's womb first, keeping the strong parallel with Bhima intact. Otherwise, the bard could have described Shiva as choosing the spirit of Yudhisthira, the oldest Pandava of all, and made him the subject of reincarnation as Ponnar. And indeed, in another version of the Ponnivala Nadu story, one that fancies itself to be more literary, Ponnar is indeed described as a reincarnation of Yudhisthira, not a double for Arjuna. It is very interesting to note, therefore, that the more colloquial version studied here is also the more radical in terms of who becomes whom via Shiva's reincarnation work. Another contrast can be seen in the fact that the five Pandavas grow up in Dwarka under Krishna's personal care. The twin heroes of the Ponnivala Nadu story have a different childhood. Their first five years are spent under the care a very different divine figure, Cellatta. She is not a well-known divine figure, and she is female. This epic's reuse of two Mahabharata characters is radical in the sense that both the gender and the fame of the heroes' caretaker goddess in their early years has been altered to better reflect local tastes and value structures.

The choice of Cellatta instead of Krishna for the caretaker role is easy to understand, of course. It echoes the local population's feelings towards their own temple and divine females when it comes to mothering a hero, in contrast to the more distant and grand gods of the standard Hindu pantheon. But why not Yudhisthira instead of Arjuna as the ancestral spirit-source for the elder twin? That choice likely reflects an underlying distaste for Yudhisthira's Brahmin-like character. Kongu Nadu is a region where the non-priestly values of physical strength and support for the violent domination of rivals are highly valued. Ponnar is a key hero and the eldest twin. The character of Arjuna better reflects this area's local image of how a distinguished hero should behave. And choosing him also gives the bard a chance to have fun with a not-so-subtle inversion. In this story, Arjuna's spiritual descendent, Ponnar, is given the senior role, even though Arjuna is the younger Mahabharata brother. Likewise, the people of the Kongu region, called younger brothers in the wider context, are given a chance, via this inversion, to strut and essentially say that "our brave heroes mirror the great Arjuna and Bhima, and to our way of thinking, we belong at the top of the social hierarchy."

Asvathama becomes Shambuga: Shambuga, the young Ponnivala heroes' key assistant and first minister, is a Dalit (Paraiyar) by caste. Basically Shambuga, as a Ponnivala story character, presents a mirror image of the Mahabharata's Asvathama. And this association is officially cemented by the fact that the story's lead bard states that Asvathama's spirit was selected by Shiva when he in the process of creating Shambuga. In the Mahabharata Asvathama is a Brahmin, but his behaviour pulls him downward, religiously speaking. Asvathama, although technically a Brahmin by birth, is treated like a Kshatriya by the Pandava brothers because he grows up to be such a skilled fighter. This behaviour, taken by itself, does not really change Asvathama's assigned social category, however, late in the story ethical considerations get added to the forces pulling his social status downward. Asvathama turns against the Pandavas and tries to murder all five brothers in their sleep. This significantly inverts the common understanding of what a Brahmin is and how he is expected to behave, not only in the world of the Mahabharata but elsewhere as well. Shambuga's life story describes an opposite progression, as if Asvathama, in his Ponnivala reflection, is being viewed upside down. Shambuga was born an outcast but slowly rises in status as the Ponnivala Nadu story progresses. In contrast to Asvathama's treachery towards the Pandavas, Shambuga is very loyal to the twin heroes. In return he wins greater and greater respect from them and is eventually treated as though he were Ponnivala's first minister. In sum, how Asvathama and Shambuga arrive at their ultimate status in these two stories is very different.

This interesting contrast ties in nicely with the broader ethos of local Ponnivala Nadu culture. In the Kongu area of Tamil Nadu Brahmins were (and still are) relatively insignificant players. They enjoy formal respect but are neither wealthy nor politically powerful. However, the Paraiyar caste was traditionally very important, and their presence was required at most ritual events, including many where the Brahmins were not invited at all. Paraiyar men were also key agricultural workers. Local landowners depended on them. Furthermore, there were specific and very personal ties that bonded many specific Paraiyar families to their landed overlords. Those ties usually ran through several generations, as they also do in the Ponnivala story. Shambuga's father served Kunnutaiya, and thus Shambuga inherited that position and served his two sons, Ponnar and Shankar. The Paraiyars of the Kongu area have a reputation of being especially strong and resilient people, unlike the local Brahmin priests who are commonly stereotyped as slight in stature, reserved, and not physically very strong.

But there is one other significant aspect to Shambuga's story of loyalty that is worthy of mention. He is so dedicated to the twin heroes that he even chooses to follow them in death, taking his own life just minutes later than they take theirs and using a similar technique: not having his own sword, he falls forward on the sharpened spear-like branch of a Vanni tree (figure 2.39). But Shambuga also exhibits a fateful weakness. He is too self-confident at a very critical moment, and as a result his desire to be helpful worked to his detriment. He offered to seek out and fight the great boar Komban on his own but then lost all the local village men who followed as his fighters when that fearful wild boar killed all but Shambuga in a forest cul-de-sac. Shambuga failed miserably in this mission to kill Komban precisely because he did not have the two heroes by his side to act as the expedition's real leaders.

Instead of killing the great boar, Shambuga ultimately loses all of Ponnivala's support fighters to that forest beast. His failure, furthermore, has a sociological underpinning. Shambuga lacked any experience in leading others. Yes, this man was the meanest, biggest, and most powerful fighter around, but Shankar had always given him orders. Shambuga's task had been to execute his masters' wishes not to lead others himself. However, one can also argue that this unfortunate turn of events, a moment when all Ponnivala's fine village labourers were lost on one day, was part of a larger divine strategy. Perhaps Vishnu had planned for this to happen. The goddess Kali was the one who initially agreed to let the little dog Ponnacci curse and seriously sicken the two Ponnivala leaders. Ponnacci had gone to Cellatta's temple where Kali had stepped in as Cellatta's sister divinity and given the little dog her permission. Furthermore, Vishnu had earlier promised Shiva that he would return the lives of the two Ponnivala heroes to his Kailasa-based council chambers the moment that they died. This had to happen before the end of their sixteenth year and that time was drawing near. The twin heroes thus, at best, had only months left to live. Komban's[17] and then the heroes' own deaths are

102   Multiple Epics Compared

Figure 2.39. Shambuga praying to the two heroes before taking his own life by falling on a sharpened branch of a Vanni tree.

outcomes that Vishnu himself clearly engineers very soon after that forest massacre occurs. Thus Shambuga, who resembles the Mahabharata character Asvathama in some ways, provides a rather poor mirror image of him when we view his role from the perspective of the larger progression of these central folk epic events.

The Ramayana character named "Shambuga": There is one more side to this story of Shambuga that makes better sense if we consider mirror images as representing the principal idea behind Shambuga's character. In the famous Ramayana story, there is a character who is actually named Shambuga.[18] This man is a rebel and a challenger. He belonged to the lowest of the four varna categories: he was a Shudra, just one rung higher in status than Shambuga, who is a Dalit. But the Ramayana Shambuga decides to perform penance (tapas) in hopes of becoming a Brahmin. In the end, though, Shambuga lost his head because the hero of the Ramayana, Rama, punished him severely for his excessive pride and egotism in attempting rise so high above his real birth status. There is a subtle reflection here of the Shambuga's own behaviour. He, too, was proud and self-confident (figure 2.40), sometimes to a fault. And, just as the Ramayana Shambuga failed to succeed with his penance, so Ponnivala's Shambuga unwittingly fails in his leadership of that large group of farm labourers he recruited to help in the great boar hunt. Instead, they were sacrificed and turned into mincemeat by that angry boar Komban. The only survivor of that massacre was Shambuga, and he was then obliged to return to the heroes' hunting tent alone and deliver the bad news to his two sick masters. When Shankar heard that all his brave fighters had been killed by that wild boar, his principal adversary, he was very, very angry. Indeed, Shankar saw even more meaning in this disaster. He then turns to Shambuga and says: "I warned you, but you took all our men and led them into danger anyway. We can no longer go home to Ponnivala with our heads held high. Instead, we will have

Figure 2.40. Shambuga (right) wrapping on his turban as he proudly prepares to serve his master Shankar.

to kill ourselves. We cannot honourably face all those village wives who have been widowed by this disaster. In response to this disaster we will soon have to commit suicide ourselves, right here, in this forest." Although the death of the two heroes by suicide does not take place right away, this fate hangs over them from that moment forward. To sum up, Shambuga embodies not one but several somewhat distorted **reflections** of other well-known South Asian story heroes inside his own singular character.

Komban, the great boar as the god Ganesh: This third case of Mahabharata mirroring in the legend of Ponnivala Nadu is far less serious and can be taken to be more like a playful joke. But this does not make it any less interesting. In one small scene the great boar Komban decides to send a message to the heroic twin kings and challenge them to war. To do this he first intimidates their gardener, bullies him, and makes this poor man roll in the mud. Then, the boar asks that gardener to turn around so that his bare back faces towards him. Next Komban uses his huge white tusk to scrape his simple words in the dried mud on the man's back, just like a stylus was used in earlier times to write on palmyra-palm leaves. Because everyone knows that the great god Ganesh (Lord Shiva's first-born son) wrote down the story of the Mahabharata using one of his tusks (as he worked as a scribe for the poet Vyasa), this rather silly scene appears to make a fool of that boisterous boar. Komban, here, looks like he is trying to be as grand as the very popular and rotund god Ganesh (figure 2.41). Audiences loves this sub-story and people often request its retelling. It is just a small vignette, but it does show once more how a local epic can play with known elements found in a much older story and link the new story to them in unexpected ways. Though playful, this joke also asserts local identity. It seems to say: "We have a grand boar who believes he is as learned and literary as the great god Ganesh. We may be farmers from a remote

104 Multiple Epics Compared

Figure 2.41a and b. Komban writing on the gardener's back.

area, but our history involves a forest challenger even bigger (and fatter) that the Lord of Beginnings himself."

There is also a brief reference by Komban to himself (an animal who can both speak like a human, as well as write) where he comments that the heroes have sent multiple messengers to locate him, just as the Pandava enemy Duryodhana (in the Mahabharata) sent out multiple scouts hoping to find the exiled Pandava heroes' whereabouts.[19] With these words Komban compares himself to a Pandava hero. This makes it even clearer that the bard is joking while he presents a scene intended to mirror a pre-established and well-accepted substory from the Mahabharata. Komban is bragging. He fancies himself to be as fine as that heroic set of Pandava brothers, great warriors who were spied upon by the famous enemy leader Duryodhana. These links, intended to be comical, speak once more to the pride of people living in the Ponnivala Nadu area who feel some empathy both for Ganesh and for Komban. That identification is also a **reflection** of their own pride in local cultural traditions and shows how undervalued by others they feel their own local culture is.

Theme 7: Revelation

A revelation can come gradually as an unfolding understanding, or suddenly, as a shock that may or may not be pleasant. Revelations are frame concepts intended to touch on one's understanding of the nature of life itself. Such insights may reveal a belief in a much larger cosmic pattern, but oftentimes they can describe down-to-earth human truths as well.

Revelations are ultimate epic story truths, grand patterns that the listener is intended to absorb and think through. Here we search for parallels and for contrasts that paint big pictures, primary concepts that it may be possible to extract from both stories being studied here. In other words, we will now try to discover one or two key messages each of these epics presents. In searching for revelations, we will discover that the last section of the Ponnivala Nadu legend differs greatly from the end scenes of the Mahabharata. In the Ponnivala Nadu story, as soon as the Chola king has been killed the heroes begin to steal from their forest-dwelling neighbours. At the outset, their first minister, Shambuga, runs off with a large cache of iron rods he finds near their neighbours' clan temple. The farmer-heroes then hire artisans to hammer those rods into fine wires from which they plan to make a net for trapping birds. Using their new hunting tool, the heroes then manage to trap and cage a unique, female parrot, again with assistance from Shambuga. Shambuga has a good knowledge of the forest environment. The parrot they want lives in a fine banyan tree that grows near the local hunters' palace. This bird is a symbol. It is a creature of exceptional beauty, born in heaven, and one which descended to earth from paradise. This same parrot, furthermore, had a loving mate. Alas, its idyllic marriage is broken when the twin heroes intrude and steal it. This leaves that parrot's male mate, alone and sad. In distress, he hurriedly flies through the forest searching for the hunters' princess, Viratangal. Of course, when she and her brothers hear of this travesty, the theft of their beautiful female parrot, they want revenge.

Not long afterwards, a huge wild boar named Komban, Viratangal's personal pet, descends from that mountainous forest area onto the plains below. And as boars will do, he then spends hours uprooting the heroes' finest fields. This is his way of expressing anger and his act of revenge. And Komban does not just destroy all those fine, planted fields. He also breaks through the heroes' irrigation dam, behind which a significant amount of water has been stored. That water then floods all the nearby the crops, making a grand watery mess of everything. After finishing this work, Komban declares war in a message scratched in the mud caked on a gardener's back (described above). That message challenges the heroes to come and find him in his forest den. The twin Ponnivala Nadu heroes then take up Komban's challenge and enter the forest with a large group of supportive village men, including all their dogs. But the huge boar kills all those dogs as they try to chase him into his lair.

Then Komban leaves his cave to play tricks on all the inexperienced village fighters who have pursued him but do not know the secrets of the forest. Komban chases this large hunting party and traps all its men in a secret cul-de-sac. There Komban kills those poor, loyal workers who had simply been trying to help and support their masters, the twin heroes of Ponnivala. The sad mess that results from this leaves only Ponnar, his brother Shankar, and their assistant Shambuga alive. But a few days later the two heroes do manage to get revenge. Komban is finally killed with a great spear that Shankar throws at him from atop a small cliff, as he passes by below (figure 2.42). Komban had already been weakened by a poison bite to his testicles which their sister Tangal's little she-dog had just delivered, but the two brothers are not aware that they have received this special assistance with the kill. After his death, the great boar's body is cut into pieces and made into a sacrifice that is offered to multiple forest spirits.

Figure 2.42. Komban, killed by the heroes' great boar-hunting spear.

But now there is a new twist. Komban's head cannot be split into pieces for that set of forest offerings, and so it is simply set to one side. This provides an opening for Lord Vishnu who now appears in the disguise of a washerman. Vishnu drags the boar's left-over head away, casually telling the twin heroes that this prize is intended for his wife who is suffering from pregnancy cravings. Logic suggests that Vishnu' was referring here to his second spouse, Bhudevi, the famous Hindu goddess of the earth. Following this, the two heroes fight off an anticipated band of forest hunters who are angry at the loss of their beloved boar, and seemingly, the heroes defeat those attackers. Then, soon after that, the two heroes take their own lives in a double, sacrificial suicide. This results in there being not even one survivor who can continue the farmer-heroes' family line. Nonetheless, that sacrifice of heroic lives, sad as it is, also brings renewal. The epic ends with a lovely song of regeneration. Now fresh shoots of grass and green bamboo shoots are seen rising anew from the cleansed earth. A new yuga cycle is set to begin.

To Sum Up

The Ponnivala twins are very concerned about their public reputation. They are proud warriors by choice. They do not want to face any sad, mourning widows back in the villages of Ponnivala Nadu, women whose husbands have just recently died in that misguided forest hunt that Shambuga led. The twin heroes of Ponnivala prefer to die right there, in the forest, as brave and courageous fighters who will be remembered forever. They do not want others to think of them as failed rulers who lost their kingdom through their mistakes, especially as this was the same kingdom their ancestors had worked hard to build. Soon after their deaths, the heroes' surviving sister Tangal has a simple shrine built in their honour. It is now a very important place of pilgrimage for story devotees. Those who visit this temple believe in the two brothers' heroism and recognize that their deaths were part of a much-needed renewal process. The twin brothers had given up their lives so that their spirits could rise to Kailasa but, also, they had killed a great boar, a supernatural force whose body could then become the seed that would help the goddess renew and reboot life in the cosmos at large.

The above ending to the Ponnivala story provides a distinct contrast with the ending of the Mahabharata. There the heroes win their war against their cousins and re-establish their kingdom. They and others survive the war, and this allows the Pandava brothers and their descendants to carry on the family line. Furthermore, Lord Krishna, who is Vishnu incarnate as a human being who walked the earth, died from an arrow that hit him in the only spot where he was vulnerable, the sole of his left foot. Nothing like that happens to Vishnu in the Ponnivala story. The ending described for the Pandavas heroes is also quite different. They rule only briefly. Then they leave their lands, planning to renounce their lives and in hopes of this they begin to walk towards heaven. One by one various members of this family group die during this pilgrimage. The ending is somewhat convoluted and difficult to summarize, complicated by issues about who goes to heaven and to which heaven they go (there are several). Some visit hell first, and the story describes who they meet there. These details need not concern us here. Instead, a variety of abstract issues surrounding dharma and compassion for one's enemies is what needs discussion in a conclusion to the Mahabharata-Ponnivala Nadu comparison attempted here. As Devdutt Pattanaik has written, "The (Mahabharata) epic ends not with the victory of the Pandavas over the Kauravas but with Yudhisthira's triumph over himself."[20] Pattanaik is referring to the idea that at least the eldest brother, Yudhisthira, is at last able to conquer his own ego. Even though the two Ponnivala heroes, who commit suicide, have similarly abandoned their own pride and individuality and although they do gift their lives to a goddess, they remain committed to heroism until the bitter end. They want to avoid embarrassment or any taint of disrespect. Instead, they hope to be remembered as having contributed to the much larger and more memorable process of cosmic renewal. In spirit, and in emotional texture, then, the final acts by the heroes of these contrasted stories leave one with two different sets of feelings. In sum, one can reasonably argue that the Pandavas opt for Brahmin-like values as they walk towards their deaths while the Ponnivala heroes identify with the Kshatriya-like set of morals that feature bravery and a fierce, self-confident brand of heroism as they fall on their own swords.

To venture a broad generalization now, the **revelations** woven into the Legend of Ponnivala Nadu identify multiple themes that underly a basic farm-based lifestyle. Although the heroes in the third generation of the Ponnivala story rise above a strict focus on agriculture to become warriors, they still feel the need to honour and protect their peasant roots. Furthermore, these heroes never question one core assumption: that it is ultimately the good character of the ruler in a specific area like theirs, that underlies its prosperity, abundance, and general well-being. The Ponnivala Nadu epic paints a clear picture of a South Indian medieval social landscape roughly divided into three categories: farmers, artisans, and hunters. Multiple relationships within the heroes' own family are also detailed: these are made up of three generations of family members who are fathers, mothers, brothers, sisters, wives, husbands, sons and daughters. Clansmen and in-laws also constitute important categories. Beyond that, a complex geography is outlined, including a detailed description of the path that leads directly to the gates of Lord Shiva's celestial abode. Underneath all, however, a medieval, plough-based agricultural economy remains this story's primary anchor. That economic base is contrasted with the deep and dangerous forest, a mysterious, energized, and liminal space that lies beyond the boundaries of a village's ploughed ground. The forest space serves to counterbalance a tilled, planted, and thus a tamed land. The cooler, darker landscape that lies beyond those fields is timeless but also much less travelled, wilder, and much more dangerous.

The Mahabharata, by contrast, depicts a society full of forests, but one that has scattered kingdoms situated around the forest's edges. That story tells us little about the central importance of an agrarian lifestyle and much more about warring family clans. Furthermore, that epic ends by pointing to abstract, somewhat individualized truths relating to life in the hereafter. The rituals described are Brahmanical, linked to ancient texts and focused on fire rituals and wild, roaming horses. The kings of that story focus on the wars that incessantly threaten to break out between rival kingdoms. Meanwhile the forests described are less wild, less foreboding, and more inhabitable. The rituals described in the Ponnivala epic, provide an interesting contrast too. They put much less emphasis on fire, and instead emphasize the importance of the yearly planting of crops. Many Ponnivala Nadu metaphors compare humans with cows and bulls that live in a farmer's cattle pen. Temples are far more important in this latter story as well, as are visits to worship the gods that dwell within them. Hence these two epics are very different in terms of their core visions of social life. The next chapter will consider another great epic, the story of Gilgamesh. There, we will discover a greater degree of economic and political overlap with the Ponnivala account, but less similarity when it comes to kinship, particularly since Gilgamesh offers us almost no information regarding basic human family bonds.

3 Human Life as a Balancing Act: The Epic of Gilgamesh

(Oldest Epic in the World Whose Written Words Have Survived)

The Epic of Gilgamesh was set down in written form earlier than any other epic in the world. The first Gilgamesh texts date from roughly 1600 BCE, whereas the oral poems underlying these surviving tablets are known to have been in existence well before that, say by roughly the start of the third millennium BCE.[1] We will explore the ideas this epic builds on using the same seven broad themes used to examine the Mahabharata, and that are then also applied to other epics to be studied in ensuring chapters, namely: Roots, Reclamation, Resistance, Resilience, Relationships, Reflection, and Revelation. This approach will hopefully help the reader match the following analysis with observations on other stories to be discussed in this book.

Background

A core theme common to both the Ponnivala Nadu epic and the Epic of Gilgamesh is the effort both make to depict the background social principles governing life in that setting. Unlike the Mahabharata, the story of Gilgamesh comes from an era and a locale that had undergone a recent and rapid economic transition. Those changes had revolutionized the nature of local life. Not long before King Gilgamesh ruled, the natural world in this region had been filled with forests and swampy wetlands populated by small clusters of hunter-gathers and mobile pastoralists. These human groups had learned to coexist with other non-human forms of life that lived in their midst. They knew how to adjust to the regular pattern of seasonal changes that largely determined the behaviour of the animals and plants around them. They knew that they could not fully master and control their environment, and that its resources had to be shared among all the creatures that swam, crept, walked, or flew across the land. But suddenly the world had been dramatically transformed. It had become a very different place. Most people now found themselves working as labourers in a social environment governed by a distant and powerful ruler who behaved like a god and expected to be treated that way. A few people enjoyed high status, but most were living in poverty. There were multitudes of peasant laborers. Some local residents had even sunk into abject slavery. Previously people had tended small hand-planted field plots filled with grains or tubers that were harvested and mostly consumed by the same people who had gown and cared for them. There were also small, settled clusters of artisans linked by trade routes that merchants vied for and controlled. Those artisans made tools, weapons, and body ornaments, in a word, anything locals needed for their fields or their animals that they could not make for themselves. Those artisans were paid in kind with various edible foods and animals either kept in local pens or gathered from the lands nearby. But now the landscape was no longer dominated by small kin-related clusters of humans, proud and largely egalitarian people who moved here and there with the seasons. Instead, many locals had moved into villages and towns. Families were no longer mobile. Their lives had changed. The urban dwellers suffered from overcrowding and the majority were governed by powerful overlords, men who enjoyed new categories of privileges that were hierarchically ranked. Those privileges served to demonstrate a person's importance, or more often, his or her lack thereof.

The majority of the Mesopotamian population saw these changes as a sign of advancement. They thought of themselves as living in a civilized society ruled by fine kings and rich merchants.[2] However, the goals of most urban residents had also changed. Instead of a person's individual skills in hunting or in a given craft being greatly admired, the most respected and powerful people were not makers of goods or producers of food. Instead, they were organizers who worked through and for others who were still further removed from daily life. Kings did very little administrative work. Instead, they advanced their personal and family interests through appointing effective ministers and managers who did that work for them. Those men were go-betweens whose job was to extract products and labour on behalf of the king who had appointed them. The accumulation of money and other material goods now become much more important. Furthermore, many new rungs had been added to the ladder that had to be climbed in search of social success. These changes troubled thoughtful people, and their concerns are reflected, I will argue, in the Epic of Gilgamesh. Similar issues are also present in the Ponnivala Nadu story. This makes a comparison of these two epic accounts relatively straightforward.

Theme One: Roots

In both Ponnivala Nadu and in Ancient Sumeria, there was a strong nostalgia for the old way of life. One very old image of status, the shepherd and his flock, had by this time taken on new meaning. Now a king was described as the most skilful and respected shepherd of all, a man who managed a very large cattle pen. That pen, however, was now metaphorical. Poets described it as the walled urban settlement of the area's biggest city. And inside that enclosure were the humans who could offer a king all the fine services a prestigious a ruler could want. Speaking poetically, these helpers were his family bulls, cows, sheep, and goats. In the Gilgamesh case, the city of Uruk was exactly this: the king's great cattle pen. Instead of a simple fence, Uruk was contained inside a great wall. In the Ponnivala story the peasant society described had also become nucleated. Ponnivala Nadu was a very small kingdom with no grand cities. But its rulers built themselves a fine family palace and that ruling family grew to control the surrounding outlying villages. Those settlements were small and populated by ploughmen, field labourers, and a few craftsmen like potters, stone masons, and wood cutters. In that local South Indian universe, just as in the Mesopotamian world of Gilgamesh, the size of one's cattle herd functioned as a significant status marker. The term for herd ownership, furthermore, also functioned as a metaphor for a king's control of his resident laborers. Thus, when we examine the epic of Gilgamesh, we will find many more social similarities with the Ponnivala epic, this book's core story, than we were able to locate when discussing Ponnivala's similarities to the *Mahabharata*.

For example, the clan grandfather of the twin Ponnivala heroes (Kolatta), enjoyed great respect because he owned twelve handsome black cows. Later, when Kolatta's son Kunnutaiya was orphaned at age six, he found employment managing the cattle and sheep that belonged to two wealthy farm-owning brothers. Kunnutaiya's respect grew by leaps and bounds when these men discovered how skilled he was in managing their cattle pen. Their animals were prospering under Kunnutaiya's care and the cattle's well-being was thought to reflect the fine inner character of their shepherd. The two brothers who hired Kunnutaiya considered him to be blessed by the gods because he was a skilled cattle manager. His inner goodness was somehow transferred to those cows, making them grow fat, contented, and full of milk. The great Chola king, whose kingdom lay nearby, had a fine herd of cows too and they were considered to be a reflection of his fine character, using a similar reasoning. In sum, cattle were equally important to life in Ponnivala Nadu and to life in the Gilgamesh era in Mesopotamia. A shepherd's skills were linked through metaphor and song to multiple poetic images that extolled the merits and inner spiritual goodness of their owners and managers.

The importance given to the health and beauty of cattle was naturally linked to the importance of the animal's role in daily life: local farmers needed strong oxen to drag their ploughs, draw their water, help with threshing, and pull their all-important farm carts that were loaded with produce. Oxen also had a significant role as the draught animal of choice when one needed to haul trade goods to faraway places. The routes that criss-crossed Ponnivala Nadu were important ancient pathways that were popular with ox cart owners. Many carts had master drivers who were respected and often wealthy, travelling merchants.

The cattle pen theme is still expressed in rituals practised to this day in the barnyards of local Kongu Nadu farmers. In Uruk, Sumeria's central city between 4000 and 2390 BCE, the bull and the cow were also key religious symbols.[3] They play an important role in the Epic of Gilgamesh, but even stronger evidence is provided by the many carved images that celebrate these animals in the royal artwork of that time. The decorations found on the fine stone walls of Uruk can also be seen on the seals exchanged by businessmen and used to preserve records of their important commercial transactions. Even the metaphors used by poets in these two cultural regions seem similar: fine women were likened to fine cows, while fine warriors were likened to bulls, both in medieval South India and in ancient Sumeria.

The family ancestry of the heroes and heroines that populate both epics is also similar. Gilgamesh and the Ponnivala brothers resemble one another as, in both cases, the heroes depicted are half-divine, half-human figures. The Ponnivala twins were sired by Lord Shiva (a god who is strongly associated with his bull vehicle Nandi) while their father, Kunnutaiya was also created by Shiva and nursed by a magical cow. In the Sumerian case, the hero Gilgamesh was born to the goddess Ninsun, whose best-known epithet was "Wild Cow." This gave him a divine sky-dwelling mother who was also the fine cow who had nursed him. In both cases, as well, the story heroes end up being battle-hardened warriors and successful local kings. This leads us to also compare their respective deaths. Both epics ask: should the story's semi-divine heroes have to die at all, and if so, where did they go upon their demise? These two epic stories agree in their answers: a hero's death is necessary, even though he may well have a divine ancestry. In both epics the story heroes become minor gods and are honoured after their deaths. During the Early Dynastic period in Sumer, Gilgamesh was worshipped as a god. The Ponnivala heroes are also worshipped to this day in many temples across the area where their story is told. All these parallels will grow more specific and more interesting as we begin to look at these similarities in more depth.

Another important resemblance can be seen in the two kings' respective male sidekicks: Enkidu in the Gilgamesh case, and Shambuga in the Ponnivala story. Enkidu was a wild man, a character without human parents. He was born in a forest, among the animals there, thanks to the blessings of a goddess. Initially Enkidu lived in an all-but-naked fashion in a mountainous area. In the descriptions provided, Enkidu was supernaturally strong. He also had an uncanny knowledge of the dark, uncharted, wooded tracks that surrounded the city of Uruk. In time, however, Enkidu was deliberately tamed by a prostitute and brought to the great city of Uruk by her. There Enkidu becomes a loyal partner-helper who works alongside Gilgamesh, that city's great king. The two men form a strong and respectful bond, even though it is always clear that Gilgamesh wields the upper hand, as he is the king. Gilgamesh is the one who manages the city's polity and oversees all political matters. He also enjoys first rights in various cultural and ceremonial celebrations.

Ponnivala's Shambuga has similar characteristics. Although he was not born in a forest as a wild man in the version of the story referenced here, another account does suggest that this might be where Shambuga originated as well. All story versions agree, furthermore, that Shambuga's family came from a very lowly background. Everything about him suggests that he was a kind of a wild man, someone who moved at the boundaries of Ponnivala Nadu's civilized arena.[4] Shambuga is able to run as fast as a horse and lives in the horse stable located near the heroes' palace. He drinks prodigiously, and on occasion can be as fearsome as a tiger. Furthermore, Shambuga serves as a skilled guide for the Ponnivala heroes during their several trips into unknown wooded areas. Shambuga's father had previously worked as an assistant to the heroes' family serving the Ponnivala twins' father Kunnutaiya for years before his son's birth. Shambuga inherits that position and serves the twin heroes in a similar fashion, from a very young age. The story also makes it clear that Shambuga maintains his loyalty to Ponnivala's lead family from his early days as a child, right through to the moment of his death. And, despite his technically low status, he is treated very well by those two masters. A bond exists between all three men that is quite remarkable. However, there is one point, late in the story, where Shambuga does abuse his masters' trust. This is when he is asked to lead a group of local village fighters in a significant forest hunt, the aim of which is to kill the great wild boar named Raja Komban. Instead of succeeding in killing that boar, all the fighters Shambuga led to the boar's hideout end up being killed by that fierce beast. Shambuga is the only survivor, aside from the boar, of that great confrontation. This outcome was humiliating for him, but perhaps occurred because Shambuga felt that he had a secret affinity or friendship with that boar? Perhaps he didn't really want to kill him? We will never know the answer, but what is clear is that he was the Ponnivala heroes' key assistant and that he was a man who was part wild, or in other words part forest, at his core.

Shambuga and Enkidu, therefore, are strikingly similar. They are both wild men who change into a non-threatening, civilized human in order to serve as a king's tamed ally. Both men offer the king their physical strength and, by implication, the male sexual energy that would have governed a life in the wild but that is now well-controlled. In each case, therefore, the wild is made to partner with the tame. This could be considered a strategy used by a king to enhance his own power. Both assistants could have helped their king extend his influence over a neighbouring wild area that he could not conquer or control alone. In sum, both Enkidu and Shambuga lend their ruler their personal wild powers without appearing to threaten or dominate their more civilized master. Historically speaking, this kind of relationship likely developed many times. A king, motivated by an ambition to expand his terrain, would reach out to a leader living on the periphery of his kingdom and woo him into forming an alliance. This would allow a monarch to absorb some of the energy of that wild area nearby and bring it into his realm via a partnership that was basically hierarchical and well-suited to his own interests.

The deaths of Enkidu and of Shambuga also bear some similarity. Enkidu died due to a curse from a wild boar named Humbaba. That forest beast was angry because Enkidu, his old friend, had left for the city and then had returned to the forest to betray him. Gilgamesh became grief stricken when Enkidu died and later died himself due to his sorrow over that loss. In Shambuga's case the Ponnivala heroes were the ones to die first and Shambuga was the one who felt a terrible grief. But in this case he followed his masters into death very quickly, immediately fashioning a pointed stick set at an angle guaranteed to deeply penetrate his own chest as he dove forward on it (see figure 2.39).[5] In both stories, then, the alliance that a king (or kings) worked to build between themselves and a more natural or wild human became so strong that this relationship continued beyond their separate deaths.

Theme Two: Reclamation

A second important similarity between the Gilgamesh and Ponnivala stories arises directly from the near-parallel situations in which the heroes of each account meet with death. In both legends a huge forest animal, a supernatural beast that has not been tamed, is killed by the story's king (or twin kings) and their wild ally, acting together. In each case the great battle, with that beast, furthermore, ends with a large knife or spear. Komban, a wild boar, is very big. He is also black in colour, has a loud voice, and has a fearful set of tusks. Komban is associated with darkness and his role is to protect a primeval forest that the king was never supposed to enter in the first place. He acts as the proud protector of that wild domain and knows how to intimidate an intruder with his loud bellows. In addition, Komban has acute hearing and an exceptional sense of smell. Indeed, he is a big bully who has vowed to bring death to any challenger. In the Gilgamesh case Humbaba also seems to be a boar with large tusks. In his case, furthermore, the forest he rules is full of cedar trees, a species that creates an exceptionally dark area under its wide-spreading canopy. In sum, the key similarities between these two wild boars and the parallel threats that the two demon-like figures pose is quite clear.

And there is also a similarity in these two epic-sized wild beasts' ability to curse others. Komban's mother laid a curse on the kingdom's twin kings, Ponnar and Shankar, even before her son was born. Humbaba laid his curse on the king's assistant, Enkidu. However, the reason Enkidu was targeted was to ensure that the true king, Gilgamesh, would suffer great grief when his ally died, a sorrow so great that it would cause Gilgamesh himself to die. Such is the revenge both wild boars, each king of his own forest domain, extracted in exchange for their own demise. There is likely a central symbolic message here that goes beyond just the simple idea that if the king on one side must die, then the one on the other side of the conflict must die as well. It also suggests that when the wild energy of nature is stifled, then the leader and the occupants of the civilized space nearby will suffer greatly as a result. In other words, mankind needs the forests and the many animals who live there. Furthermore, betrayal is a key element in both outcomes. Each of these two fearsome wild beasts dies with the help of an intermediary who is, himself, semi-wild. That person knows the forest well but then becomes a traitor from the perspective of the hunted beast. The traitor left his home, the place where he really belonged, and switched his loyalty to align himself with a plow-dependent kingdom that had little regard for forests. And finally, in both cases, it is the hero himself (Shankar in the Ponnivala case) who wields the spear that finally kills that grand beast. The hero himself is made responsible for delivering that fateful blow, one that changes the surrounding economy and it associated social values, forever.

We can now argue that there is an even broader frame of reference operating in both these stories. Human culture necessitates human death, while nature (raw, pristine life without rules) is in some sense everlasting, if not disturbed. When rules are broken, and the forest gets invaded, even great men who lead the civilized world are destined to suffer death because of this disruption of natural cycles. This cosmic message is not much different from the one conveyed by the biblical Garden of Eden story, as well as by Christ's own ultimate crucifixion as its' grand hero (see chapter 4). The idea of death as a necessary consequence of civilized life, that is, life outside the garden of Eden, constitutes a deep paradigm that operates in the background of many Indo-European legends. Whether a woman is the one responsible for this fall, however, is more debatable. Eve bears the blame for mankind's original sin in the biblical account. Perhaps the prostitute that tempts Enkidu out of his pristine forest plays a similar role in the Gilgamesh story?

If there is any possibility of a Ponnivala parallel to this idea of female fault however, it is well hidden. However, possibly the central woman in the Ponnivala Nadu story, the twins' sister Tangal, has a similar role, if we look deeply enough into this story's details. Tangal is certainly not a prostitute, nor is she one to disobey a god's command. On the contrary, Tangal is an extremely chaste woman. She also has a tame and gentle appearance, most of the time. At the end of the story, after her brothers' deaths, however, we see something different. Now, she burns her two sisters-in-law alive, sets fire to her own palace, and more. These hidden traits had begun to surface much earlier, however, and they do have an impact on her siblings' decisions.

Tangal's first real step in manipulating her brothers' fate occurs as a result of a dream she has about parrots. As a result of that dream she asks her brothers to capture a parrot from the forest in order to save her from loneliness. That demand requires her brothers to violate nature's autonomy, enter a forest where they have never been, and rob that pristine area of a lovely female bird. Metaphorically she is asking her brothers to capture a rival female and subjugate it by putting it in a cage. Even she wonders if this request is really justified, and she later tries to change her mind. But by then her two brothers have already taken all the preliminary steps needed to execute a hunt and they realize that they cannot now reverse course without embarrassment. So, they proceed. As a result, these two men do end up kidnapping a female parrot, breaking apart a beautiful and natural relationship with a mate that would have lasted for life. Tangal's seemingly innocent request, therefore, leads to the destruction of a romantic bond. When the male parrot complains to his forest-dwelling mistress, the hunter-princess, she quickly orders an all-out war be fought by her loyal Vettuva brothers against the farmers. That war ultimately leads to a fateful boar hunt where Komban's great curse is seen by Tangal in the form of a dream (see figure 2.1). In the dream she is made to realize that the breaking of the free and romantic bond between wild natural creatures and the destruction of forest harmony will ultimately lead to the Ponnivala twin heroes' own deaths.

Komban, the wild boar discussed above is backed by and allied with this same forest princess whose name is Viratangal. She is Tangal's wild double. Tangal, furthermore, is linked by her birth story to the Krittika or Pleiades star cluster. In local astrological terms these seven stars are called the seven virgin goddesses or seven Kannimar. Those young women are fierce fighters who are also said to live deep inside a forest.[6] And Komban has a star on his tongue, suggesting his own link to a great boar constellation in the sky.[7] He also has a tulasi plant tucked into his navel[8] and a ring of flowers on his tail, marking him as a potential sacrifice. In the parallel case of Gilgamesh, Humbaba is backed by seven auras who can take human form and are ready to fight for him in battles. It seems that the stars are aligned with Humbaba too. That cluster of stars is the well-known Pleiades constellation. Could these seven bright points of light in the sky be the unspoken arbitrators of a central nature versus culture contest that colours both these epic accounts? Has this constellation been stationed in the sky with a unique mission, that of protecting wild spaces and processes, especially perhaps protecting new human embryos just in the process of forming? We return to this topic and will cite additional evidence for its importance in chapter 8.

Returning to the reclamation theme, it is also important to point out that both Humbaba and Komban are closely allied with a key divinity. In Humbaba's case this is Utu the Sun god who raised him lovingly.[9] For Komban it is the goddess Kali who gave the blessing that caused him to be born. In both tales this beast had tusks and was considered king of the forest. In the Ponnivala Nadu story we know for certain that the monster was a wild boar. In the case of Humbaba this seems like a reasonable guess, although images of this protagonist often depict him as having a humanlike face where no tusks can be seen. Similarly, in both stores the head of both Komban and Humbaba is given great significance. In Humbaba's story, his tusks are treated as booty and they are carried back to the city of Uruk after he is killed.[10] In the Ponnivala Nadu parallel, Komban's complete head is offered to the goddess, here likely Vishnu's second wife Bhudevi, while his tusks are still attached. Humbaba's head is offered to Enlil, the god of the forest. Reading further into the story, at least in the South Indian case, this important sacrificial offering has a double meaning. It is the conquest of a monster but also a sacrifice that will allow life renewal, especially agricultural renewal.

Bhudevi is the earth goddess and the head of the sacrificial beast she receives appears to be treated like a powerful seed that will soon be planted. Indeed, in South Indian rituals for the famous and very ancient village goddess Mariyamman, a symbolic black buffalo or goat is beheaded for just this purpose. Its visceral pounding into a hole in the ground visually symbolizes the intent to renew the life energy lost through this sacrifice in the coming year, by treating it like a fresh seed.[11] It also seems to open the way for the ruling heroes who perform the sacrifice to rise into the heavens at their deaths. Gilgamesh, like Ponnar and Shankar, was deified after his demise. What is especially interesting is that after Gilgamesh kills Humbaba he cuts down a forest of grand cedar trees and from the best of those he has a fine door made that is destined to become a grand gateway leading to Enlil's sanctuary in Nippur.[12] Enkidu declares that this new doorway will make the people rejoice. In chapter 10 we will see that passing through a grand gateway to enter a temple is compared with passing into a divine space situated in the sky. Thus it seems that Humbaba's death is what will now grant worshippers a new and specially blessed access to Enlil's temple. In Komban's case the gift of his head to the great goddess Bhudevi paves the way for an entire kingdom's renewal and rebirth. These two ideas are suggestively similar. Temple gateways in Indian architecture have always been a central design feature that receives extensive design attention.

Further, the goddess in her role as a queen and divine creatrix accepts the wild beast's head as a sacrificial offering made specifically to her. This is *her* moment of **reclamation**, the point at which she takes back control of the lives that cycle all around her. If we can presume to read her mind, this is the goddess's response to an oversexed and threatening wild male who has been trying to sow seed on his own. But now his head is taken from him and will subsequently serve her and become a seed she plants. That seed becomes like her embryo, her child, with the earth now serving as her womb. It is important that in the Ponnivala Nadu case the severing of that head is understood to be an act that will engender and invigorate the sprouting of a new agricultural season. It will begin a new year in the relentless cycle of life that surrounds the goddess and steadily moves forward.[13] The core idea is that when first severed, the head can be powerful and dangerous. But if it is properly handled in a ritualized way, that power can be converted to a good end. The theme of a great life-seed that gets replanted will be discussed further in chapter 9.

Later, in the Gilgamesh story, when a second animal is sacrificed, a similar symbolism seems intended. The second animal is the Bull of Heaven and its heart, rather than the head as in the case of Humbaba killed earlier is the focus of attention. This bull's heart is offered to the goddess Ishtar, along with a piece of its own leg. Furthermore, this bull may have once been the goddess' lover, but now he is presented to Ishtar in a very humble and dismembered form. That bull had been tamed by death and its head and one haunch were then set before Ishtar's image in the city's main shrine. A similar ritual is preserved in some South Indian villages today, where animals are sacrificed, and a piece of the victim's foreleg then placed in its mouth just as its head is laid before the shrine of the great creatrix, Mariyamman. In my fieldwork this goddess is the local divinity who manages the agricultural cycle for the village lands nearby. Mariyamman, the equivalent of Cellatta in the epic story, is a form of the great goddess Parvati, wife of Lord Shiva.

Parvati does the initial work of creation in the Ponnivala Nadu story, setting nine clan brothers down in a forest on earth. Next she commands them all to plough that land and to bring forth beautiful harvests. Parvati knew that this would require cutting the trees where they stood. A serious drought ensues, and although the story does not say so directly, it is quite likely the tree cutting and the drought that followed had some connection. The situation is somewhat similar in the Gilgamesh account. The father of the gods, Anu, sends down a Bull of Heaven. It was a symbol that personified seven years of drought, and the bull's presence was Anu's punishment of Gilgamesh for killing Humbaba and cutting down of the sacred cedar trees in his forest. Similarly, Kolatta migrates due to a terrible drought, which, we might speculate, was also a punishment for forest mismanagement. Kolatta only later reaches Ponnivala Nadu and begins to plough the land around him. Nonetheless, a related underlying theme seems to be at work. Both epics express the same basic idea: man is destined to tame the wild forest and its threats and to convert and transform that raw energy for human benefit. Kolatta is the first to do this in the Ponnivala story and that makes him the first plough-farmer to rule this tale's lovely riverine locale. Gilgamesh, in parallel, has a very valuable cedar forest cut down and the great trunks of those trees transported to the gates of Uruk, his grand city, on rafts. Gilgamesh is the more powerful and prominent king, but the location of both kingdoms near a primal forest that is exploited and violated plays a central role in both accounts. Here the shared idea is that reclamation was no longer possible. The damage had been done; the trees were gone. Human death and the suffering of those two kings was the inevitable result, in each case.

Theme Three: Resistance

When it comes to matters of resistance, the overlap between these two stories can best be observed by studying the personalities of its main heroes. In the Gilgamesh story the king is tyrannical. He is described from very early on in the tale as: "Surpassing all other kings, heroic in stature, a brave scion of Uruk and a wild bull on the rampage."[14] Gilgamesh endlessly harried the young men in his domain and his tyranny grew harsher by the day. He was large in stature and strong. He feared no one. He ordered great ramparts be built around his city that were made of fine, fired brick and he had a grand temple built to honour the goddess Ishtar. Significantly, her temple was constructed inside the city's boundary wall, the metaphoric cattle pen where Gilgamesh ruled. Enkidu was initially untamed, a forest bull that was later civilized when taken from his homeland and enticed by a prostitute to serve the Uruk king. When Enkidu came to the city, Gilgamesh soon challenged him to a fight. The two were well matched. Enkidu was Gilgamesh's physical equal. After a time, however, Enkidu accepted the king's supremacy, while at the same time Gilgamesh, the great king, showed this wild man an exceptional degree of respect. Each recognized the other's prowess. They became friends.

But Gilgamesh was still restless. He wanted more fame and glory. And so, he proposed to Enkidu that they go together to the cedar forest to slay the great demon Humbaba who lurked there. With considerable effort, and led by Enkidu, the two entered the forest. There, with the help of the latter, who knew the habits of beasts in the wild, the two managed to defeat that monster. But with Humbaba killed, the good luck of Gilgamesh and his partner turned. That huge wild creature cursed those two men before falling to earth and dying. That spell would eventually bring death to both men, but to Enkidu first. However, another event followed before that could happen. The Bull of Heaven was now brought to earth by the goddess Ishtar herself. She was upset that Gilgamesh, the great king now made even more famous by his killing of Humbaba, had rebuffed her amorous approaches. To symbolize his rejection of the goddess, Gilgamesh decided he would kill the wild bull she had brought with her. The king then speared the Bull of Heaven, killing it, which only added to the goddess's anger. Trying to appease her, Gilgamesh and Enkidu gave her that dead bull's fine heart and a part of its hind quarters, laying those gifts at the door of her temple shrine. But their gesture of respect had an unintended consequence. With this move they did not realize that they were also magically handing over the power to control future events to Ishtar, a power that had previously resided with the great Bull of Heaven himself. From that point forward, Gilgamesh's fate turns downward. The goddess is now determined to demonstrate that she has a wider vision and wider powers than he does. She is determined not to let a mere king, even the great Gilgamesh, override her ultimate primacy. Ishtar has to make sure that she, not he, held the right to manage all life recycling and renewal work and that Gilgamesh's death will symbolize his submission to her.

The parallel with the Ponnivala Nadu story here is quite clear. Of the twin kings ruling Ponnivala, the one born second (Shankar) was the more powerful, ambitious, and boastful. Shankar was a rebel who had disobeyed his parents' wishes and attacked his rivals viciously and unfairly. In particular, he was the twin who had initiated an attack on a schoolhouse full of innocent children. He had also attacked and killed a nearby Chola monarch who he believed had insulted him. Shankar strongly resembles Gilgamesh in these ways. Later, Shankar and his timid elder brother (Ponnar) together enter a neighbouring forest area belonging to local hunters. There the two brothers kill tigers and cobras, and other animals, who (like Humbaba) were put there precisely to protect that forest area from harm. Even worse, their assistant Shambuga stole the Vettuva hunters' important stash of iron rods. Now the three acting together, steal a beautiful female parrot. But Shankar is the leader in that kidnapping attack. Later he is the one to wield the fateful spear that kills the wild boar Komban himself. Some will argue that Shankar is not a very likeable hero as he is the lead brother when it comes to any violent acts. Much like Gilgamesh, however, it is precisely his outlandish bravado and aggressive bullying that give him prominence.[15]

In the Ponnivala Nadu story too, the killing of a monster is what really acts as that story's fulcrum. King Komban (Humbaba's double) is responsible for this change in story direction. Komban's mother cursed Ponnivala's twin brothers, saying that each was destined to die on one of her own son's very white tusks. Although this wild boar eventually dies first (just as Humbaba dies before either Enkidu or Gilgamesh) those curses live on in both accounts. However, some further discussion is needed. In the Gilgamesh story there are two killings, the forest beast Humbaba is brought down by a knife to his throat. Then, somewhat later, the Bull of Heaven is killed with a spear aimed at the back of his neck. In the first case it is not clear where the body of Humbaba went, but we do know that his tusks were valued by the heroes and taken as booty. More important, that monster's death gives Gilgamesh and Enkidu access to the trees of the cedar forest Humbaba had once protected. The two heroes lose no time in starting to fell those trees and that very useful, high-quality wood was then quickly taken back to Uruk. It was there that the second slaughter, that of the Bull of Heaven, occurred.

By contrast, in the Ponnivala story, just one animal is killed, the huge forest boar Komban. In effect the two animals slaughtered in the Gilgamesh case, when considered together, roughly equate to the one killing described by the Ponnivala story where Komban is both speared and just a bit later, beheaded. Furthermore, in the Gilgamesh legend, Gilgamesh and Enkidu start felling trees almost immediately. But in the Ponnivala Nadu case the heroes' resulting assault on the forest is more subtle, because the felling of forested areas near the heroes' home has long since commenced. It had begun right alongside the introduction of plough farming in the area two generations previously. Therefore, in the Ponnivala case, tree felling is an assumed ongoing background fact, not something overtly described right at the point in the story when Komban is killed. Instead, Komban is taking revenge for a process that had started to threaten his forest homeland in the time of the twin's grandfather.

Significantly, in Komban's lifetime, the two Ponnivala Nadu heroes invade the primeval forest near them for a second time. On that second occasion they do not harm the trees. Instead they steal the local hunters' valued cache of iron rods, and just a little later, after killing numerous tigers and cobras who were told by Viratangal to guard her pristine domain, they kidnap and cage a lovely wild parrot. It is important to read these acts symbolically as an intensification of the previous travesty. Now the heroes are attacking animals and birds, not just trees. Furthermore, in the Ponnivala story Komban's body is treated in a way opposite to the body of Humbaba. While Humbaba's head was used to make a sacred offering to Ishtar, Komban's head was cut off and then ignored. Only his body was sliced up and offered to the local forest spirits. The true parallel with the Gilgamesh epic, however, does not take long to emerge. Lord Vishnu himself intervenes and his actions make clear that the heroes did not do what they should have done right after killing that hugely symbolic boar. In the Ponnivala Nadu the story the gift of Komban's head to a goddess happens only when Vishnu interferes and even then he only vaguely describes his real intention.

We cannot be completely sure who the intended goddess was who Vishnu promptly offered Komban's head to. Very likely, however, it was Bhudevi, the divine goddess who represents the earth itself and who is commonly known as Vishnu's second wife. In both legends, a sacrificial part related to the head of the boar is used to placate a powerful goddess, even though in the second case that offering was not planned or carried out by the two heroes themselves.[16] Most interesting of all, however, is that Shankar quickly concludes upon seeing the head dragged away that he and his brother have made a grave mistake. He realizes, within minutes, that losing control of Komban's head means that he and his brother Ponnar will very soon have to relinquish their own heads in a parallel sacrificial set of deaths. They, too, will soon become corpses laid out and offered to the gods above. In both stories we can conclude that the same thing happens, though in somewhat different ways: 1) as an offering of one wild male animal's tusks and the heart of second (Gilgamesh); or 2) an offering of just one, wild male head that includes an impressive set of tusks (Ponnivala Nadu). Both instances of killing these beasts, each of which embodied the forest itself and whose great mission in life was to protect it, leads to the death of the heroes who were responsible and to the death of a tamed (turncoat) forest ally, as well.

These differences in how the beast's bodies and heads are treated in the two stories are relatively minor. Basically, the killings are similar in their symbolic intent. We see this in that the Bull's death is mourned by the goddess Ishtar because he was her pet. She was also a want-to-be lover of Gilgamesh himself. Similarly, the wild boar's death in the Tamil legend is mourned by a lovely (likely semi-divine) woman named Viratangal. Komban is definitely her special pet and although not overtly her lover, there may be overtones of that hidden under the story's surface. The female deity in each of these stories, furthermore, finds a way to take revenge for the killing of a huge male beast that she adored. In the Ponnivala case Viratangal, lady of the forest, orders hundreds of her hunter-brothers to go to the edge of the woods and attack the twin heroes directly. In the case of the goddess of Uruk, the female revenge plan is more subtle: Enkidu starts to suffer from bad dreams. But lying at the heart of both stories is a larger semi-hidden paradigm: both sets of male human heroes pose a cosmic threat to the ongoing life of the forest nearby. Civilization has advanced. In both cases towns and villages control the farming spaces around those human settlements as well as determine the nature of the crops they depend on.[17]

Of added significance in the Ponnivala Nadu legend is the fact that Lord Vishnu, brother-in-law of the great Lord Shiva, decides to switch his allegiance and act against the heroes very soon after the great boar's death. Previously their greatest backer, Vishnu now steals the boar's head from them and then he leads a fierce group of angry hunters who wish to attack them. His real intent becomes clear quite quickly. Just after the heroes begin to wash their swords following what they believe has been a great and heroic struggle against the forest dwellers, Vishnu shoots an arrow at Shankar. This happens while the hero is standing in the water of a small nearby river, symbolically both taking his last bath before death and referencing his crossing of a river when ready to die. Vishnu uses the symbols of Kama (the Indian version of Cupid) in this scene. His tools are a bow made of sugarcane and an arrow fashioned from flowers. That arrow carries away Shankar's chest thread, and with it, his magical protection. Shankar noticed this loss immediately, and he is quick to understand this god's larger message. Shankar now turns to his brother, who stands close by, and explains that the arrow that was sent towards his chest thread/heart came from Lord Vishnu himself.

Now, suddenly, Shankar realizes that it is time to submit his own life to the gods. When Shankar falls on his sword he dies instantly. His elder twin and loyal assistant follow suit. It does remain a bit unclear who the Ponnivala Nadu twins offer their lives to. Perhaps it is Shiva, as they will soon ascend to his council chambers for their afterlife? Perhaps it is Vishnu, the god who sent the flowered arrow? Or it could be the goddess Bhudevi or Kali, or even their own sister, Tangal, who they reminded each other is herself a goddess just minutes before they die. A good resolution to this dilemma, I think, is to say it is all these and that their real intent is to offer up their lives for recycling to the cosmos at large.

Finally, it is important to understand that the Ponnivala Nadu story does not end at this point. After the heroes' deaths the two brothers' virginal, unmarried sister finds their bodies lying deep within the forest. She now uses magical verses and other special substances to resurrect them and allow some time for a last conversation. When she then talks to her revived brothers, they both (and, in particular, Shankar) explain to her that they cannot live any longer. Others in Ponnivala Nadu, they declare, must now take their place. After this conversation, the two men again fall to the ground. Lord Vishnu, who is waiting nearby, then carries off their spirit lives in a small gold box and delivers that to Lord Shiva, who is standing watch in his council chambers high above. Meanwhile, the heroes' two physical bodies are carried in procession down out of the mountains to a convenient spot where their sister then builds a temple in their memory. That temple is the place of an important local festival to this day.

The parallel of these heroes' deaths with that of Gilgamesh story may not be obvious at first, but it seems likely that there is a significant similarity here as well. It is unconventional to claim that Gilgamesh committed suicide before taking off on a kind of dreamy, shadow-life journey seeking to learn the secret he believes will allow him to live forever. But there is a line in the translation consulted here that says "[That night he] lay down, then woke from a dream. In the presence of the moon he grew glad of life, he took up his axe in his hand, [and] he drew forth [the dirk from] his belt. Like an arrow among them he fell, he smote the [lions, he] killed them and scattered them."[18] It is only after this that Gilgamesh's wandering begins. That wandering resembles an extended dream or perhaps a resurrection moment, as happens to the Ponnivala Nadu twins.

Following this supernatural adventure period, however, both Gilgamesh, and the Ponnivala heroes finally come to realize that death is a must. Their **resistance** wans at this point and they accept their fate. In each case they also learn that there will be some kind of renewal after they depart for the divine world. In both cases, too, a mother goddess is implicated in birthing the new lives that will follow.[19] Gilgamesh is recognized as a divine being very soon after he dies. In the Ponnivala Nadu story, the heroes rise to the sky to become a pair of folk gods who dwell in Kailasa, resting near to Lord Shiva himself. Gilgamesh, by contrast, enters the underworld. There he becomes a minor deity, overseeing the lives of others who have also died and descended into the depths. Thought of in this way, the endings of these two epics are not really that different, notwithstanding the minor proviso that the first epic describes the heroes' ascent into the sky while in the other, the hero undergoes a descent and becomes part of the world below.

Theme Four: Resilience

In comparing Ponnivala and Gilgamesh, it seems evident that the themes of **resistance** and **resilience** can largely be grouped together. The key male heroes in both the Ponnivala Nadu and Gilgamesh stories combine social and mental strength with personal physical resilience in battle. The core issue, in both stories, is the need to prevent a takeover of the heroes' respective kingdoms by outsiders. The heroes, especially Gilgamesh and Shankar, are proud, strong, and admired for their ability to impress others. They also dare to challenge fate. In the Ponnivala Nadu case the main hero in this quest is the younger twin Shankar and not the elder Ponnar. Ponnar is calmer, softer, and more concerned about his duty towards others. Therefore Ponnar is different. He is honoured by the Ponnivala story in a different way. He is the one mentioned in praise songs that talk about the beauty of the land and its prosperity. His younger brother, Shankar, is the one highlighted in action sequences that involve battles and bravery.

The women in both stories show their share of resistance and resilience. Gilgamesh's sister is the goddess Innana. Similarly, the Ponnivala twins' sister is Tangal, who is also one of the seven Pleiades goddesses. Both sisters appear to be goddesses who have come to earth for a limited time. And in both epics, the sisters display two sides: warm and gentle on the one hand, but on the other, fierce and demanding when needed. This makes them resilient. They are able to adapt to any given situation by showing the side that is appropriate to the moment. The women of both stories are also very patient, unlike their male counterparts. They wait and watch. They are not impetuous, at least not until they get angry. But there is one difference. Sexually, the women of the Gilgamesh story are active agents. One example is the prostitute that entices Enkidu to leave his forest ways for the glitter and excitement of urban life. But the personality of Innana is by far the more important one to reference here. She tries to seduce Gilgamesh, though without success. She becomes angry when she fails and so she finds other ways to badger and (ultimately) control him.

The two best examples of female behaviour in the Ponnivala Nadu story are the actions attributed to Tamarai and Tangal. Tamarai, mother of the heroes, is exceptional. It is as if she were the goddess Parvati (perhaps in her version as Sati) hiding in human disguise. Tamarai's exceptional patience and resilience shine during her twenty-one years of penance, during which time she sits on a high pillar and begs Lord Shiva for a child (much like Sati prays to become the wife of Shiva, against her father's wishes). Meanwhile, Shiva is very mean to Tamarai, ignoring her completely, except for a few moments now and then when he asks his assistants to torture her. Each time poor Tamarai is injured so badly that Vishnu must come to her aid and rescue her dried up and de-fleshed bones. In each of these instances, Vishnu ends up reviving her by soaking those dried remains in a nearby river. It is only after Shiva's wife, Parvati, begs Shiva to soften his heart that he finally relents. After that he invites Tamarai to enter his heavenly council chambers, a place where many of his ministers also sit. There, in front of all, Shiva immaculately impregnates Tamarai, placing two male and one female spirit-fetuses in her womb using a beam of light (as one local artist has imagined this moment). This is his gift to her: a set of triplets-to-be.

But before Tamari's much-wished-for impregnation could happen, she first had to leave her husband and spend twenty-one years alone, begging him for help. After receiving those three fetuses from him, however, her mood lifts. She returns to earth where she bears and then raises those three children lovingly, behaving as a model mother. In sum, Tamarai embodies resilience par excellence. However, it is also important to point to her occasional anger. When Tamarai's two elder brothers refuse to allow her to enter the home where she was born and raised, she is furious. Tamarai burns the palace guard who is preventing her entry and she also ritually freezes her many nieces and nephews who are innocently playing inside, making them all appear as if dead. Later she revives them, but only after her two male siblings make a formal apology to her for their unbrotherly behaviour. Both men dramatically drop to their knees and beg her forgiveness while the goddess of her local community watches carefully.

When Tamarai's three children are finally born in her own palace, however, she finds herself faced with many further trials. We will focus here on her daughter,

Tangal, who is called the "little sister." Tangal is raised more or less alone in her family home, because her two brothers are always out and about pursuing their youthful adventures. They ride around the family lands on horseback and meanwhile Tangal simply sits on her palace swing. She is very different from her two brothers. She is a dreamer who spends her days waiting for visions and then uses these to foretell the fate of her two siblings. She frequently warns them to temper their aggressive habits and describes to them the dangers she believes lie in wait. She is patient, they are not. Furthermore, they listen to her less and less as time passes. After these three siblings lose their parents to old age, things only become worse. Eventually Tangal, via a dream, discovers that Komban is threatening to kill her two brothers with his tusks. She warns them but they ignore her. She is also very lonely. Her brothers do not tend to her safety, nor do they recognize her need for company. Shankar thinks only about the glory that he hopes his personal exploits will bring him. Eventually Tangal gives up and her brothers leave on the hunt she has warned them against. She knows that it is a dangerous expedition but, nonetheless, she does not bless their swords before the they depart. She knows that her two brothers will never return and her lack of a blessing at this key moment clearly has something to do with its sad outcome.

After Ponnar and Shankar's deaths Tangal's personality changes. Now she quickly transforms into an angry and very determined woman. She is so upset that she immediately burns down her own family palace as well as the smaller and simpler abode that her two sisters-in-law are kept inside. There are other instances of Tangal's anger as well. Eventually, she wanders through the deep forest alone, exhibiting an unheard degree of resilience for a young, nubile woman. When she eventually does find her brothers bodies, Tangal uses her magical powers to resurrect them. But as a result she learns the sad truth: they have willed their own deaths and she has no choice but to continue on earth without them. Despite this disappointment, Tangal decides to build her two siblings a shrine and to conduct the first worship rituals ever in their honour. After completing that task, Lord Shiva sends down his personal chariot and raises her to the heavens in his own lovely golden vehicle. Thus, unlike her two brothers, Tangal never experiences death. Generalizing, we can say that the heroic men of both epic stories focus on **resistance** to domination while the women exhibit extraordinary **resilience** in pursuit of their core commitment to life's renewal.

Theme Five: Relationships

A comparative exploration of family relationships depicted in the Gilgamesh and Ponnivala stories also yields interesting results. This volume is called *Hidden Paradigms* and now that theme will be further explored. The three powerful examples that follow will help underline the appropriateness of this book's main title. First, consider the three-generation timeframe that underlies both the Uruk story and the Ponnivala Nadu account. Enmerkar is the founder of the city of Uruk. He easily blends in with his predecessor Meski'ang-gasher, founder of the larger dynasty. Together those two men, both founders, represent the first generation of humans in that story. The second generation is represented by the outstanding figure of Lugalbanda, the son of Enmerkar who also becomes an eminent and respected ruler. And for a third generation we have Gilgamesh, builder of the great Uruk city wall. All three of these men descend from the same source, the sun god Utu. This broad picture matches very nicely with the genealogy of the Ponnivala heroes. There Kolatta, the dynasty founder serves as the heroes' clan ancestor, alongside his eight younger brothers. Kolatta, furthermore, is the first pioneer farmer to migrate to Ponnivala Nadu and settle there. His son, Kunnutaiya, becomes the eminent, just, and kind ruler of generation two. And finally two grandsons, Ponnar and Shankar, follow in this line and become leaders in generation three. Both Gilgamesh, Uruk's third generation ruler, and the Ponnivala heroes, have reputations as powerful warriors. Both also work to preserve their region's proud heritage. This way of looking at the two stories suggests a strong parallel in the underlying paradigm used: both are epic tales in which the central heroes inherit their status via a distinguished descent line. The main heroes stand at the end of this line, as the rightful rulers and protectors of the family's third generation. They represent that family's good name and substantial material assets.

The second paradigm that emerges from this comparison relates to the strong brother-sister bond that pervades both stories. We have already demonstrated, in chapter 2, that a fundamental brother-sister connection lies at the heart of the Ponnivala Nadu legend. The same appears to be true of the Gilgamesh story, though this concept is more visible in the ancillary tales and myths and tales that circulate around this foundational epic. The brother-sister relationship is a more difficult concept to describe because it can involve overtones of brother-sister incest and in depicting that cross-gender sibling bond the line between brother-sister, brother-wife, and brother-mistress easily becomes blurred. The whole matter is perhaps more easily discussed at the mythological level than at the human one.

If we first consider the Ponnivala Nadu story, *all* references to sexual attraction between human characters in that epic are suppressed to the point of invisibility. Here the three siblings, two brothers and a sister, all remain strict virgins to the very end. There are not even hints of flirtation. In this super chaste universe, romantic feelings are not even seen in dreams. Furthermore, although the heroes do marry, as previously discussed, they go to great lengths never to touch their wives. There is not even any touching of fingers during their wedding rituals and soon afterwards both women are locked inside a lonely home built especially for them, where they spend the rest of their lives in total isolation. When these poor wives finally hear of their husbands' deaths, they cry out, complaining that they have never known even a single day of wedded pleasure. Feelings of sexual desire in this epic, then, are always turned inward. Once directed toward herself, that sexual power is then used by Tangal to enhance her brothers' virility. The Ponnivala twin heroes clearly benefit from both their sister's and their wives' absolute sexual purity. Their own sexual purity also contributes to their magical power.

Despite the absence of amorous references in the Ponnivala text, however, there are reasons to give the sister-brother bond a unique importance. In the region the story comes from, a Kongu man must, before his marriage, first undergo a ritual that literally ties him to his sister using the wedding sari (later given to the bride). That sari gets stretched between the brother and his sister first, as described in the previous chapter (see figure 2.32).[20] Furthermore, all brothers are responsible for their sisters' sons and must give them repeated ritual gifts. In the Ponnivala Nadu epic, the mother of the heroes takes for granted that her brothers will welcome her back into their home at any time, no matter what the circumstances. This is particularly true should she happen to be suffering for whatever reason. When Tamarai is distraught over being childless and goes to visit her two brothers, she is shocked and horrified that they refuse to let her in. They even order their palace guard to beat her. As discussed earlier, in a bitter act of revenge, Tamarai magically kills all her brothers' children and revives them only when she has been shown formal the respect she deserves.

A similar tension exists in the next generation, between the heroine Tangal and her two brothers. After the simultaneous deaths of their parents, the three children continue to live together in the old family home. Tangal is considered to have a unique power to bless her brothers' swords, and her observance of this tradition was understood to give her brothers' fine weapons added magical power. Her blessings were thought to utilize and redirect her own sexual energy, converting it into a fighting force for these brothers' use. But there is no reciprocity. That is the unexpected part of the story. Instead of caring for her welfare the two brothers largely ignore her and, despite her parents' dying request to arrange their sister's wedding, the two brothers never find a bridegroom for her. Yet, after her two siblings die, Tangal wanders through the forest for days until she finds their bodies. There, on the spot, she returns them, briefly, to life. Again, she uses her own innate, life-giving, essentially female power to do this. To sum up, Tangal's bond with her two brothers, if not overtly sexual, does have sexual undertones that are of great importance. The brothers need her power and presumably do not want to find her a husband because after that, Tangal's magic would instead be expected to flow to her new husband.

Moving to the level of the gods in the Ponnivala Nadu story, we can now see the dynamics of the brother-sister bond even more clearly. Now the story is about Lord Shiva, his wife Parvati, and Parvati's brother Vishnu. Vishnu repeatedly approaches his brother-in-law and begs that he pay attention to the childless Tamarai. It must be remembered that Tamarai is, in essence, a form of the goddess Parvati, Vishnu's real sister. Parvati's spirit essence descended to earth and took on an added form: that of the (apparently) human wife Tamarai. But then, due to her childlessness, Tamarai and her husband Kunnutaiya make a heroic pilgrimage to Shiva's chambers in Kailasa to ask for help. Tamarai remains strong throughout that pilgrimage, but her husband weakens quickly. Vishnu finally must step in and put him to sleep by turning him to stone. This happens just at the foot of a long staircase leading into the clouds. Tamarai, now alone, must climb these steps if she is to reach her goal: Shiva's council chambers.

As Tamarai starts to ascend the staircase leading to Kailasa, step by step, Lord Vishnu quickly appears at her side to help her out. He does many things both to tease and to taunt her along the way, but it is a loving type of teasing. He also reassures her repeatedly and uses tactics much like a shrewd lover might employ while trying to seduce a forbidden girl. Remember, Vishnu is essentially (perhaps metaphorically) Tamarai's own brother, because she is likely a form of Parvati, Vishnu's sister. Eventually Tamarai reaches a pillar close to Kailasa and she sits on that, meditating there for many years. When Shiva finally invites her into his council chambers, his heart softens, and he then agrees to immaculately grant this prayerful woman triplets. Note that Shiva is behaving like Tamarai's husband, and this is fully appropriate because he the husband of Parvati, who is her double. But Tamarai is also his own daughter because when he and Parvati played together some years earlier, a drop of semen fell to earth and quickly grew into baby Tamarai lying in the petals of a lotus flower. Thus, in a sense, Shiva is impregnating his own daughter by placing those three embryos in her. Such is the nature of myth, but myth is often used to express human feelings and human dreams. Shiva then assigns Vishnu the job of looking after Tamarai's three children after their births (acting, in essence, as their mother's brother). This too is appropriate given that the mother's brother bears a special responsibility towards his sister's children. True to this logic, Vishnu comes to the aid of the triplets time and again during all sixteen years that they spend on earth.

Shiva, however, cunningly sets up a contract with Vishnu before letting Tamarai begin her journey back to earth. He tells Vishnu that he must hand over his precious conch shell for safe storage. The conch, of course, is one of Vishnu's most powerful tools. Shiva promises to give it back, but only after Vishnu has returned the lives of the two sons born to Tamarai, to him, at their deaths. This is expressive of their (mostly friendly) brother-in-law rivalry. Shiva explicitly states that he does not want Vishnu to have too much power in his new role as the uncle of those three children. No wonder. We have just seen, above, how he later starts behaving, in some subtle ways, like a secret lover of Tamarai, their mother.[21] Furthermore, when Tamarai prays to Vishnu complaining of her barrenness, Vishnu (almost) always arranges to appear before her at moments when she is alone. This, too, suggests a not-so-subtle competition between Shiva and Vishnu for Parvati's affection. As a wife in one case and sister in the other, Parvati is the woman who stands between these two great gods. And as the daughter of Shiva, Tamarai is also caught in this web. Now we can understand why Tangal, Shiva's granddaughter one might argue, is also called Parvati by her brothers late in the story. The whole family is caught up in this complex web of kinship that makes all three women versions of one another. They are all embodiments of one central divine feminine force that keeps reincarnating and re-representing itself in various ways throughout the Ponnivala Nadu story.

It is also important to know that Kongu Nadu is a predominantly "Saivite" or Shiva-worshipping region of South India. This means that it is an area where Shiva is presumed, by most, to be the supreme god. Vishnu is seen as more of co-god who works as Shiva's ally. This rivalry reaches deep into Hindu mythology more generally, and it begs the question: Who is the greater and the more powerful: the husband or the brother of a beautiful woman? Shiva and Vishnu display a stereotypical joking relationship for precisely this reason. This same joking relationship between brothers-in-law is reported by anthropologists to exist in many, many cultures around the world.

Nonetheless, whatever sexual undertones between brother-sister exist in the Ponnivala story, they are well hidden from view. For this reason looking at this theme through the comparative lens of the Gilgamesh epic can be very helpful. There Utu is the sun god and his twin sister Innana is the most powerful goddess of the time. Utu presents a strong echo of Lord Shiva in several ways. Shiva is strongly associated with the bull that he rides, while Utu is sometimes addressed by the epithet "wild bull." Furthermore, Utu is known to have been married to Ninsun, whose common name was Lady Wild Cow. With that name she is, of course, an appropriate match for the great Utu, a son of An and progenitor par excellence. An was also famous for his role as the keeper of the great Bull of Heaven. Indeed, an association of the king, ruler, or hero of Babylon with a great sky bull runs through the entire history of the Uruk family line.

As Utu is the sun god, then logically he has a personality that makes him a traveller. This is appropriate because the sun travels across the sky by day and was (at the time) believed to cross back under the earth each night. As well, therefore, Utu had two personalities, one bright and one dark. He was both straightforward and secretive. This makes sense because half the time he was hidden by darkness. Perhaps that hiding suggests that Utu may also have had a few illicit or uncultured behavioural traits, just as Lord Shiva is known for. For example, Shiva is a mendicant famous for his wandering. And he certainly has a dark side as he haunts graveyards. His body is dark blue, and he often covers it with ash. Furthermore, Shiva dances on the graves of the dead late at night. He is a rule breaker that poets often refer to as a shameless, naked man. Shiva is also bi-sexual when seen in his famous Ardhanarishvara form. In that body Shiva is female on his left side and male on his right, clearly demonstrating his nature as a deeply bi-valent character.

Now consider Innana, Utu's sister. Dumuzi is Innana's lover and some-time husband. He is also, by this reasoning, Utu's brother-in-law, which makes him, at times, Utu's competitor. It is important to note that entire line of kings mentioned earlier (Enmerkar, Lugalbanda, and Gilgamesh) all become identified with

Dumuzi in various stories. Each in turn has a romantic attraction of some kind to Innana. Like Parvati, the goddess Innana stands between her twin brother Utu (whose other name is Shamash) and her lover, a king. She has to mediate the ongoing contest for power that plays out between her brother Utu (the sun) and her own lovers, all of whom are kings. All the great rulers of Uruk are drawn to Innana, just as Vishnu is drawn to Tamarai (a form of Parvati). But that attraction is never allowed to reach its culmination in stories generated by either tradition. Innana's lovers (Dumuzi and his stand-ins) are all fearful of the consequences of approaching her. To embrace Innana would be to court the wrath of Utu, the potential brother-in-law. Furthermore, Innana herself has a conflict. She sees the three Uruk kings through two lenses, for one as her lovers, but for another, also as descendants of her brother Utu, making all of them both brothers and nephews, from her perspective. Gilgamesh, the king, is similarly fearful of Innana's advances, perhaps sensing a potential for incest. He rejects her love-signals and instead he connives to kill the Bull of Heaven, Innana's pet. But Innana has other plans. She brings that bull down from the skies on a lead rope, in hopes of forcing Gilgamesh into submission at the sight of her powerful and dangerous pet.

Woods has written a very interesting article about this conscious and extensive blurring of the lines between brother, sister, and brother-in-law in Babylonian tradition,[22] and also discusses various related examples of incestuous overtones in Uruk mythology. He writes, for example, that Innana was a sister-lover of the king of Uruk.[23] Elsewhere he finds instances of Innana's brother being compared with the king of heaven and a form of the Sun. In the Ponnivala story, Parvati's role is equally complex. Her brother Vishnu appears to be attracted not to Parvati herself, but to her daughter Tamarai who is Ponnivala's queen. As stated earlier, Tamarai is the mother of Tangal, a lovely young woman who is simultaneously a daughter of Lord Shiva, the king of heaven. All this may seem complex, as myths often are, but the main point is that a clear tension exists in this story between Vishnu and Shiva, relating to a rivalry over the women who belong to their joint family cluster. Similarly, in the Gilgamesh case, Dumuzi claims to be Utu's equal, while from Utu's perspective, of course, he alone is the supreme being.[24] The hidden paradigm that covers both these cases is the ambivalent brother-sister bond that makes the sexual attraction towards a forbidden female who relations with would obviously be incestuous a salacious overtone.

The possibility of confusing a husband with a brother always lurks in the background where the divine Hindu triad is described, at least in the Kongu area. Maybe this answers the question of why Shiva feels the need to take Vishnu's conch away from him and hold it in hock until he physically brings these two heroic spirits back to his council chambers after their sixteen years of life on earth have finished. In another Shiva-Utu parallel, Woods writes that Utu provides Gilgamesh and Enkidu with seven warriors who lead them both through the mountain passes, making their long journey possible.[25] In the Ponnivala Nadu story Shiva places one of the seven Pleiades sisters (one of the seven Kannimar) in Tamarai's womb. This youngest Pleiades sister, born as Tangal, shows herself to be a very fierce and self-confident woman near the end of the story. Setting aside the male/female ambiguity here, there is a larger parallel to be observed here between Gilgamesh getting seven warriors from Utu, and Shiva giving the Ponnivala Nadu twins one of the seven Pleiades sisters as their private guide in life. All these parallels have to do with key social **relationships**.

Theme Six: Reflection

There is one more important aspect of the Bull of Heaven story not touched on above. The great progenitor-god An is clearly associated with the Bull of Heaven in Sumerian tradition (he represents the Taurus constellation). But Utu made the mistake of lending his partner-bull to his sister Innana when she begged her father for it. As we have seen, Innana wanted to use that bull to challenge and intimidate Gilgamesh, the handsome hero on earth who had been ignoring her seductive messages. Innana got her father An's agreement for this plan to borrow the bull. She then led the great bull to earth by a rope threaded through his nose. Surely that served as a sign that she was now its master, and that she had somehow managed to tame him. But Innana then unleashed that bull either inside or very near the city of Uruk, where it caused havoc. With his wild partner Enkidu at his side, however, Gilgamesh eventually found the bull's weak spot and killed it. Gilgamesh managed to thrust a knife blade between the horns of that bull and thence through the centre of its skull. Perhaps his success in killing it had something to do with the fact that Innana had previously reduced its wild ferocity by using her nose rope? In any event, that ended Innana's plan to kill Gilgamesh while using her bull-pet as bait. Instead, she was left to mourn the death of her pet. Her sorrow began when she saw the bull's heart, which Gilgamesh had torn from its chest and laid in front of Utu the all-powerful sun god himself.

What has all this got to do with reflection? In the Gilgamesh story, there appears to be a deliberate juxtapositioning of the Bull of Heaven with the other huge and powerful animal that Gilgamesh successfully killed, the great tusked Humbaba. Humbaba, king of the dark forest, was likely an animal meant to provide a strong reflection of the famous and wild star-bull of the night sky, Taurus. Each was a king in his own domain. The great bull and the great boar in this story are not opposed. They also never fight or even meet. Instead, they are different-yet-similar wild beings. Each is a kind of reflection of the other. Together they were meant to suggest some kind of balance. These two animals constitute the only two great animal conquests of Gilgamesh's career. Now consider their differences. Humbaba was killed first, deep in the forest. He was struck in the neck. The Bull of Heaven was killed later, in or near the city of Uruk, the place he was taken to in order to cause chaos. He was struck in the head, but not before he managed to dry up the woods, the reed beds, and the many marshes surrounding Uruk due to his great thirst, according to the surviving text. And because of his prodigious drinking, it is said that the river that flowed near Uruk was lowered by seven full cubits.

In these images, we perhaps see a recorded memory of the severe effects of a great local drought. This is something that can happen when a forest is cut down and ceases to attract rain clouds. That same Bull of Heaven, it is said, also opened up a huge pit when he snorted and that pit then swallowed one hundred Uruk men. However, in contrast to Humbaba, this powerful bull was not assigned to protect forests and the wild animals associated with them. This bull was not the opposite of Humbaba, but nonetheless, his strategy and his goals were quite different. His task was not to protect nature but rather to destroy what men of civilization had built their agricultural kingdom upon. His mission was one of retribution. Perhaps he was upset at being tamed and asked to become a pet and, more metaphorically, a draught animal? Perhaps we could go so far as to suggest there was wide discomfort with the unpleasant fact that Uruk had been castrating bulls in order to make them into docile workers? The angry bull figure that so troubled Uruk can be understood to reflect a response sent from the heavens high above earth to punish human hubris down below. It seems that the Bull of Heaven came to earth with a message: humans are too proud and too disrespectful of nature. Pride has its limits. All men must die, gods need not. Killing the Bull of Heaven was an act against nature that went against what people believed the gods had willed and signalled through their construction of the star-signs that moved and could be observed, quite predictably, high above.[26] We will return to this topic in chapter 8.

Humbaba was different from the great bull. He did not attack Uruk. He was not the aggressor. Instead, he dwelt quietly in his own realm, but nonetheless he was willfully hunted down by an Uruk king. Furthermore, soon after the bull's death Enkidu also died. Seeing this, Gilgamesh experienced great anguish. He suffered greatly from Humbaba's curse. He then set off on a very lonely and unsuccessful journey, hoping to find the secret to immortality. However, to flush out the parallel between the two stories and to understand their respective and dramatic animal sacrifices, one more thing must be mentioned. Although Komban was technically killed by Shankar's boar-spear, Komban had been severely weakened in advance by a tiny female dog named Ponnacci (described in more depth previously). What is significant here is that she attacked Komban's testicles, biting them with her sharp, poisoned teeth. Poor Komban could barely walk after that assault, let alone run. This made him easy prey for the hero Shankar's final spear throw. There is likely a message hidden in this sub-story as well. Komban was a symbol of male testosterone and male aggression writ large. Ponnacci took this power from him, taming him using a castration technique she alone was able to apply (with her teeth). Her bite on his testicles is always a favourite with epic singers' local audiences. They laugh at her clever answers when he tries to bully her with his huge size and dark colour, and they celebrate her vicious bite.

Like the Bull of Heaven, Ponnacci's story appears to touch on some deep paradigms. Becoming civilized is something like being castrated. One loses the benefits and the freedom of wildness and unconstrained sexual pleasure for the sake of a stable food supply and a safe city life. More abstractly, perhaps humans also lost the secret key to immortality that the forest held when they decided to leave it and begin a life of virtual slavery to the plough and all the hard work that new lifestyle demanded. Men hailing from civilized agricultural centres are bound to die, just as the plants in the fields of farmers die each year. The wild animals of the forest, however, are rarely seen to die of old age. They just disappear, perhaps like a boar, a clever beast that simply hides in a cave that takes him underground for the winter. Animals naturally appear again in the spring while dead humans do not. Is this underlying message of mortality a kind of theme or paradigm that underlies both these epics? Yes, I would argue that the problem of human death is there, kept somewhat under wraps, but what is more important in these two stories is their consideration of humankind's move to a civilized, plough-based economy, a shift that required changing to a peasant, clustered-dwelling lifestyle. This theme provides a backdrop, or perhaps more aptly, a link to an important underlying paradigm that spans and informs both stories. If the tilled fields and the forest exist in a hoped-for state of balance, the divinities that populate the heavens and the heroes that roam the earth can then **reflect** each other in significant ways.

Theme Seven: Revelation

In discussing the final theme of this chapter, the focus of discussion now shifts to the topic of twins and twinning. It appears that the heroes of the Ponnivala story are twins for good reason. And one can also include their sister, their triplet in this kin-cluster. However, the relationship between the two brothers Ponnar and Shankar is what must be discussed next. Ponnar is kind and unaggressive. He listens to his parents' words. He is uncomfortable using a sword. He is praised in songs that describe the area's agricultural prosperity. He rules the region as a good and well-respected king. He closely resembles his father Kunnutaiya in having those key personality traits. Hindus might say that he is the "Brahmin" in the family. By contrast, his brother, called younger because he was born a few minutes later, is quite different. Shankar has a violent temper and is impatient. He bullies his elder brother and always takes the lead when a dangerous expedition is underway. Shankar is quick to draw his sword and quick to challenge enemies. He is the one to kill the Chola king while his brother simply stands to one side (see figure 2.1). The few times that these two brothers discuss their sister, furthermore, they largely voice worry about her being alone in their palace. Ponnar is the one to express a special concern for her welfare when she seems endangered, not Shankar. Interestingly, at one-point Shankar responds by saying essentially: "Don't worry. She is a goddess. She can take care of herself." He knows the value of her blessings and that they energize his sword. Why worry about her? Ponnar is less interested in his sword. He expresses empathy for his sister and knows he bears a responsibility to care for her. Shankar is less worried about others and more focused on making sure that his family continues to wield its considerable local power.

What is the meaning, then, of this heroic twin-ship? The answer would seem fairly simple. This pairing of brothers provides a commentary on the nature of kingship itself. The story asks, implicitly: Overall, what makes for a successful leader and ruler? The twins split into two a single bundle of qualities that all contribute to a ruler's success. How should these traits be balanced? Woods put it very well when he wrote that "the whole is greater than its parts" and that the union of complementary opposites can be used as a means of depicting a transcendent concept.[27] This concept, of course, is not new, especially when it comes to a king's role as a leader. It constitutes yet one more hidden paradigm that underpins both the Gilgamesh and the Ponnivala Nadu stories.

There are two other major examples of this twinning concept displayed by the Ponnivala epic that must also be mentioned. For one, Tangal serves as a responsible and magical sister for her two brothers and, for another, Tangal functions as a balance mechanism or opposing weight in relation to her forest equal, Viratangal. In the first instance we have a woman who tries to reign in and constrain a very active set of brothers, story heroes who are physically energetic. They are always going here and there pursuing exciting adventures. When young, they are busy learning the martial arts and practicing bareback horsemanship. When they are a little older and their parents die, the two men start to play dice. Since dicing is considered to be a dangerous pursuit that brings trouble, they are not demonstrating the qualities favoured in good kings when they do this. In fact, after every game they play, something fearful and dangerous happens. By contrast, their sister Tangal never engages in a dice game, ever.

Spatially, too, there is a significant contrast displayed between the two brothers and their sister. The brothers physically travel across the lands of Ponnivala Nadu in all directions, but they never even dream about other possible kinds of travel. They never go underground except as children when the goddess takes them into her cave to raise them, nor do they ever fly. Their sister is different. She sits day after day in her palace swing. Her feet are generally off the ground. She sways gently back and forth and dreams constantly. It is as if she is suspended by invisible ropes dangling from the sky. Furthermore, Tangal descended to earth after an earlier life where she is said to have lived in the clouds near Lord Shiva's Himalayan council chambers. There she was one the seven virgin sisters of the Pleiades. Tangal never goes underground physically, though her mother does walk through a long and dark tunnel (said to be an image of hell) at one point. However, Tangal does talk with the king of the cobras, the ultimate creature thought to rule underground. Later she flies on a golden goose, crossing a boundary that separates life from death. And later still Lord Shiva lifts her back up to his high abode, hidden in the clouds, using a flying, gold-coloured chariot. Thus, again, the whole is more than its parts. Seen together this set of triplets combine male and female gender traits that, though different, balance each other's excesses. When united, these differences strengthen the Ponnivala Nadu family as a whole.

To pursue this topic a bit further, it is worth noting that Ponnivala's twin boys have reality-tested, down-to-earth skills, while their sister is full of dreamy insights but little action. Her mental flights and constant oscillation fit well with the fact that she is the only one to undergo mind travel to distant realms. Tangal's mother, Tamarai, shares some of these skills, though to a lesser degree. Leaving her husband on earth Tamarai manages to reach Lord Shiva's snowy abode high atop Mount Kailasa by calling on her supernatural powers of meditation and prayer. As discussed previously, once there she sat on a very high pillar that seemed to almost touch the sky, staying for a full twenty-one years. That was her way of moving vertically as opposed to horizontally. Both mother and daughter thus exemplify an ability to cross boundaries. Furthermore, they both use rain and fire in constructive and destructive ways to achieve their ends. These themes play a role in how these heroines complement their male counterparts. Taken together, the three siblings, Tangal, Ponnar, and Shankar, are much more than the sum of the three constituent sibling parts that make up this triad.

Lastly, there is the interesting unspoken but obvious twinning of Tangal, the little sister who is princess of Ponnivala Nadu, with Viratangal, the fierce little sister who is a woman of the same age but who is even more beautiful and who lives in a dark forest. Viratangal does not sit on a swing. Instead, she spends her time with her pet, a huge wild boar. Together they frequently visit the Kali temple that has been built near her place in the forest. Although Viratangal does not fight, when she gets angry she does incite her brothers to start a war, telling them to challenge those who have wronged her and her forest brothers. Viratangal also knows how to speak to animals. She has conversations with birds and commands lions and cobras, asking them to protect her beloved mountainous domain. Unlike the more civilized Tangal, Viratangal has no genealogy, no ancestors, and no birth story. She, her brothers, and her father just "are." She does not live in a Nadu (a formal and well-bounded territory), but in the mountains among the trees and the wildlife there. Tangal worships the calm and well-mannered Cellatta, mother-goddess of the village settlement where she lives. Viratangal worships Kali, a fierce goddess whose shrine lies deep, deep within the trees. Furthermore, Viratangal and her brothers were wronged by the farming rulers of Ponnivala Nadu who cut down their trees, stole iron from them, and then captured and caged their beloved forest-dwelling parrot. But Viratangal does not sit still and just accept all this. She tries to right those wrongs directly by inciting her brothers to action. When we contrast Tangal with Viratangal we see that this field-forest opposition constitutes a basic theme that underlies both stories. Comparing these two settings and similar protagonists helps lift both stories to a higher plane, one where the great sweep of history starts to come into view.

This field-forest contrast, or civilized life versus life in the wild, is equally important in the Gilgamesh epic. We have already described the obvious opposition this second story depicts between the Bull of Heaven and the wild beast Humbaba. It bears some similarity to the relation of Tangal to her fierce forest counterpart Viratangal. But that duality is even better expressed through the story of Enkidu. He is the wild man who was won over from the forest and brought to the city of Uruk by a prostitute. That is surely not an accident. The fact that his transformation is accomplished with the help of a scheming prostitute speaks to the idea that there is less duplicity operating in the wild. Enkidu was betrayed, in essence, by having his sexual appetite teased. His desire for fancy human foods and nice clothes only enhanced the attraction that civilized life held out to him. Once tempted, Enkidu turns about face and employs his new self to return to the forest to deceive Humbaba, the beast who had once trusted him implicitly and innocently. Enkidu gave away the location where Humbaba could be found, telling Gilgamesh all he knew. In this epic tale the wild is portrayed as simple, direct, honest, and unselfish. Civilization, by contrast, is plagued by the opposite qualities. It has become stained by human schemes of self-aggrandizement, self-indulgence, and duplicity.

It is important to note that the Gilgamesh story does not reject the merits of the forest and its wild inhabitants. Indeed, it is quite the opposite. The wild is valued. Humanity's move away from the forest can now be placed in its larger context. The forest and its purity of form provide civilization with needed balance and perspective. The forest provides a counter rhythm that allows us so called more evolved humans to reconsider the merits of mankind's village and town-based values. It is the same with the Ponnivala Nadu story. There too, the pairing of these two archetypes, field and forest, places emphasis once more on the broader theme that underlies both epic accounts: the need to combine opposites in order to strengthen a larger cosmic whole. These two stories, one Sumerian and one medieval South Indian, share this basic perspective. They agree, in large part, about the core trajectory of human history. These same two legends also agree that the forest must continue to exist if mankind itself is to survive. That is the core **revelation** that both these story texts share.

The next chapter carries this idea further by examining what can arguably be called the underlying message of the Bible. There human sins and crass egoism are seen carried to their limit, to the utmost dissatisfaction of the great father god who is constantly watching humans from the sky. And there, the underlying paradigm structuring human behaviour is seen to be morality, defined as obedience to god's greater purpose. His overpowering determination is to make sure the norms of human culture conform to his own social guidelines. The forest is also valued in the Bible as a place of refuge, but its most important purpose there was seen to be as a valuable source of timber for building temples, walls, and individual homes, all human-focused, highly civilized ends.[28]

4 Seven Great Phases of History: The Bible's Old and New Testament Stories

(A Key Text with Middle East Origins, Now Known around the World)

Some readers will certainly argue that the Bible is not really an epic story. One objection might be that there is no central cast of players, while others will contend that it covers too many generations or is about too many different places to be a unified epic story. Of course, the opposite assertion is also reasonable: that this vast assemblage of short stories is all about one thing, the Christian deity's grand plan. What that plan is has been defined somewhat differently by various interpreters. However, the central theme the Bible embodies has been more-or-less consistently outlined by scholars since at least the time of St Augustine, who lived roughly sixteen centuries ago.[1] Augustine's argument, simply put, is that the Old and New Testaments, combined, present the story of God's* multiple efforts to teach and ultimately reward human beings for leading moral, loving, caring lives. God wanted his people, the humans he had created, to be good, to be honest, to be upright and to behave as fine, shining citizens who would reflect his own inner essence. Furthermore, the number seven has always been a sacred and special number in Middle and Near-Eastern thought, and so it is not surprising that this "Story of Salvation," as many call it, speaks of six different eras that have unfolded to date, as well as of a seventh one yet to come. In each of those distinct eras, God created one or more special leaders and then proceeded to test them.[2]

The sixth stage, out of the seven eras the Bible describes, was the era in which Christ lived. According to most theologians, we are still living in that sixth time period. The seventh stage, usually called the Second Coming, has yet to occur. God's prophecy, according to this way of reading the biblical story, is that he will soon

---

* Since the Christian deity referred to in the Bible is called "God" and has no other specific proper noun names, the term "God" will be capitalized when referring to that deity to accommodate a Western spelling convention. It must not be interpreted as diminishing the respect rightfully accorded any other god or goddess mentioned in this book.

create a new heaven and new earth. At that moment he will sponsor a grand event that will include a Judgement Day. This will then open phase seven, the final chapter in the human story.[3] Throughout these seven stages of history, the Christian concept of the great being known as God is always given the central role. His offer of salvation, many theologians say, has been presented multiple times but his people remain obstinate, quarrelsome, greedy, and distracted by self-interest. There are other approaches to understanding the great sweep of history the Bible describes, and several have come into prominence recently. However, for the sake of this study, and for a comparison of this broad biblical story with that told in the Ponnivala Nadu legend, we will focus solely on this one, especially well-known, approach to what the Bible is said to be telling its readers. That approach argues that the Old and New Testaments, taken together, tell a unified and intentional story of human history. It also notes and celebrates the constant presence, throughout its long text, of a righteous, demanding, God-the-Father figure. This omnipotent, larger-than-life male presence is thought to hover in upper world but be largely invisible. Furthermore, he is always depicted as a senior male figure who is all-powerful.

Frei and Fahs have both outlined Augustine's seven great ages of time as follows:

1 **God created the world** but then, soon afterwards, mankind's first sin occurred when Eve (and then Adam) disobeyed his first command (**Roots**).
2 **Noah built an ark** that saved God's chosen people from a great flood but then he had to punish those whom the ark saved, due to their subsequent quarreling and debauchery (attempted **Reclamation** of a previous golden era).
3 **Abraham led the chosen people into the land of Canaan**, but then God had to punish them again for their subsequent immorality, stemming from their inability to resist temptation (lack of **Resistance**).
4 **Moses helped the chosen people escape into the desert** after a long period of slavery in Egypt. But they began to worship false idols and so God had to punish them once more (helping to build up their **Resilience**).
5 **Joshua emerged as a new leader who engineered the take-over of Jerusalem**. David followed by establishing a new kingdom in the land of Canaan. But following these events the chosen people again committed many sins, both by engaging in war and by colluding with foreigners. This brought forth God's wrath once more (and so he placed a new emphasis on **Relationships**).
6 **God now sent a saviour named Christ**, in the form of his own divine son. God now made himself human and hoped that Christ would atone for those many sins committed by his own example. Many challenging years on earth culminated in his painful death, but Christ's life did demonstrate the need to submit to his father's will. At last God was pleased with the result. The Christian church was established (as a **Reflection** of his goodness).
7 **God will soon announce a Day of Judgment timed to coincide with his Second Coming**. God will return, rule for a thousand years and grant his

people great rewards that will last forever, at least, that is, as long as they continue to obey his word and henceforth lead moral lives (his key **Revelation**).

The seven categories or themes suggested as a useful tool for comparative analysis at the start of this book, match reasonably well with these seven eras or defined stages of the Christian story.[4] A loose correspondence will be good enough to make that case. What is more surprising is to discover a significant overlap between the Ponnivala legend and the Biblical story writ large. This South Indian folk epic focuses more on moral dilemmas and less on God's wrath and punishment than the Bible does, but the kinds of moral issues raised and the progressive unfolding of the many struggles the heroes undergo is broadly similar. This is especially so when one considers the life of Christ, the key character of the New Testament, and the lives of the twin heroes Ponnar and Shankar in the Ponnivala story. That overlap is particularly visible when comparing the mode of death of the divine Ponnivala twins with the crucifixion of Jesus in the New Testament. Furthermore, the similarity is not trivial if we ask how both legends operate in a modern-day context. The key figures in both accounts are worshipped, in each case, by a large community of contemporary followers. In both cases, these storied heroes' own life-messages serve as a significant guide to their devotees' current thinking, In the following pages these similarities will be discussed, in more depth.

Theme One: Roots – Beginnings and the "Original" Sin

A Pristine Place of Origin

The two stories we are about to compare both speak of a beautiful location that starts the human experience off in a pleasing, dreamy way. The Ponnivala legend speaks of a lush, green, virginal forest (figure 4.1) while the Bible describes a Garden of Eden. The goddess Parvati (in the Hindu tale) specifically creates a primal ancestor (Kolatta) and places him in this lovely forest, along with eight younger brothers. The Bible story, similarly, describes how a male god created Adam, the first man, and placed him in a beautiful garden. Furthermore, in the Ponnivala legend, just a little bit later, the same goddess creates nine females for these many brothers to marry. That nuptial ritual is simple, using just a small gift exchange. Each of the nine men just places a flower garland on the female of his choice (figure 4.2). Somehow this works. There is no fighting or jealousy described as to who will get which partner. The nine just naturally select the mate the goddess has assigned them. The resulting unions are affirmed in a gentle and loving way. There is no expense, no decorations are needed, no music is played, and no special clothing is referenced. Each couple simply exchanges flower garlands.

The biblical story does not provide any information about how the first couple's wedding was celebrated. Adam and Eve just exist as a couple, right from the

Figure 4.1. The idyllic forest garden where the goddess Parvati places the first nine (ancestral) men of Ponnivala.

Figure 4.2. The first man, Kolatta, garlands his wife-to-be.

start. Also notable is the fact that Adam and Eve are said to be totally naked at the start (unlike the nine first couples described in the Ponnivala Nadu story). Another difference is that in the biblical case God creates Eve from one of Adam's ribs. This appears to mark her as a somewhat subordinate figure vis-a-vis her husband. In the Ponnivala case, each of the nine wives has their own separate creation moment. Nonetheless, the big picture is remarkably similar. Eve and the nine Ponnivala women, are similar in that all were created as an afterthought. They are ancillary figures. while their husbands are central to the big human-creation event that starts things off. However, a few other details are also significant. In the biblical case the first female (Eve) is fashioned from "just one small part" of her husband Adam, that is from one of his many ribs. Her creator, furthermore, is a very authoritarian male god, not a gentle, kind female like the Parvati, the goddess who undertakes all the needed creation work in the Ponnivala case. Nonetheless, these initial gender differences between the two stories gradually dissipate, while the similarities to be found across the two accounts continue to build.

The first thing the goddess Parvati tells the nine men she created is that they are to focus their efforts on converting the lovely forest that surrounds them into a bountiful and productive food source. They are to do this using the plough that she gives them at the start, on day one, and it is intended to launch their very first farming efforts. That constitutes these brothers' first tool and is a gift from the goddess herself. In the case of the Old Testament, the Christian God orders Adam and Eve to go forth and fill the earth with descendants. On the surface this is a different project, one focused on reproducing the human species rather than one concerned with food production. Nonetheless at a higher, albeit metaphorical level, ploughing and sexual intercourse form a familiar pair of images. That association is a familiar one that is used elsewhere, by both cultural traditions.[5]

Now comes the matter of disobedience and the harsh curse that will follow mankind's first misstep. The biblical account is well-known. God leaves the idyllic couple alone in their lovely garden with one commandment: they are never to pick fruit from a certain forbidden tree. But a scheming serpent, an underground creature (that has phallic overtones, of course) wishes to counter God's supreme authority. He soon climbs the forbidden tree and tempts Eve to taste its fruit (figure 4.3). After some hesitation, she agrees to pick a single, succulent low-hanging one, while Adam looks on. The couple then proceed to taste their forbidden harvest. But God has also been watching carefully. This was his great test, and he is greatly angered by the couple's wilful disobedience. God then decides to punish them telling Adam and Eve that they must now leave the garden of Eden and struggle to make their way outside this sheltered place. No longer can they live in innocence, without clothes, without hard labour, and without death. Instead, Adam and Eve are now cursed to enter the not-so-comfortable wider world lying beyond that beautiful garden.

In sum, during the initial age in this biblical story, the first couple learn four things: 1) God's anger is waiting and will be felt whenever a human disobeys his word; 2) All humans, henceforth, will be created via sexual union, but this raw act of intercourse will also be a source of embarrassment. Unclothed, natural bodies will incite desire and hence cause shame. Thus, going forward, at least some minimal form of clothing will be required; 3) Women must accept that their lot will be worse than that of men. In particular, they alone will suffer the physical pain of childbearing; and 4) As a result of all the above, there is now to be a separation between human life and life in a pure or natural state. People will no longer exist in a beautiful garden where no pain or hard labour is required. Thus, the nature/culture distinction now begins. And the extra difficult fate that every female carries with her can (implicitly) be explained because Eve, not Adam, was the one to pick

Figure 4.3. Eve picks a forbidden fruit in the Garden of Eden.

that first forbidden fruit. She transgressed and broke God's will first. Somehow, too, the serpent comes to represent the reason why Eve decided to break God's commandment. Because the serpent symbolizes raw, sexual desire (or so it would seem), lust and fornication now become the hallmarks of moral transgression and women (especially the sight of them while naked) will henceforth be understood as the root cause underlying much of mankind's sinful behaviour.

In the Ponnivala Nadu story, by contrast, the reason why the nine initial human families find that they must leave their original, very beautiful, forest seems different. Yet in both stories these first humans actually face a similar situation. These nine Ponnivala men, along with their wives, must likewise abandon the place where the goddess decided to set them down. And the reason for leaving such a beautiful locale is described quite similarly in these two epic stories: something shocking happened. In the Ponnivala case, Parvati's initial creation work was followed, after only a year or two, by a severe drought. Thus, the two stories agree that something went terribly wrong in paradise, but what went wrong is different. In the South Indian case the problem that arose does not appear to have been the nine families' fault. They did not transgress a moral rule. Nature itself seems to have come up with this glitch. There was not enough food to eat, and despite having tried their best, all nine brothers and their wives had to leave their idyllic forest setting because of a severe dry spell. That is the superficial conclusion.

But underneath the simple idea that a terrible drought could just happen unpredictably in paradise, there is likely a hidden truth. We know that the nine families had been told to use the plough they were given to produce fine crops. Although technically the goddess does not tell them to cut down trees, that preliminary act is obviously required if one is going to begin ploughing in a forest. Knowledgeable readers may speculate, therefore, that the initial felling of a primal forest, done in order to make way for fields, might have something to do with the drought that quickly beset those poor nine families.[6] This possible link is not mentioned by

Figure 4.4. The hero and his new wife leave their original home to search for work due to a severe drought.

the story tellers, but we do know that farmers are the most frequent sponsors of local performances They are the ones to pay the singers liberally. Maybe this is the reason that there is no hint given that cutting trees in order to plough could have caused the disaster. Local farmers would likely be uncomfortable with the implication that their lifestyle could relate to the severe local dry spells they periodically suffer but nowadays cannot escape.

Nonetheless, the Ponnivala Nadu story does make clear that a severe drought did indeed cause those first nine families to abandon their beautiful, well-forested homeland. The most senior brother, Kolatta, and his wife Ariyanacci, left first (figure 4.4). They are the ones to explore the options and send news back to the younger brothers who stayed behind, waiting for direction from their eldest sibling. This first couple now travel on foot in search of a better life. They soon locate a fine king who is ruling nearby, and he takes the couple in as agricultural workers. Specifically, Kolatta and Ariyanacci are hired to help with the ploughing and planting of his vast expanse of ploughed fields. This king belonged to a famous Chola line of South Indian rulers (which king is not made clear). Kolatta and his wife became labourers and must work under his authority. Kolatta's wife accompanies him to the fields daily and works just as hard as he does. However, she is paid much less than he is, a differential that is taken for granted by the couple and they do not complain. Thus the Ponnivala story clearly establishes a conventional gender-based labour hierarchy at this point, one that values a man's labour more than it does a woman's. This new situation continues and becomes integrated into the broader story. Now the political and economic hierarchy seen to operate in a world ruled by kings is on display. Ploughmen and their wives are located on its bottom rung. When the other eight men and their wives follow this first couple, they meet the same fate and must accept the same new social structure, one in which political and gender differences are now highly visible.

144   Multiple Epics Compared

Figure 4.5. Seven cows die on the spiked fence the first man, Kolatta, had ordered built.

Finding a Homeland

Following the first couple's loss of their idyllic first habitat in the South Indian story, a second migration is described. This happens when the Chola king selects Kolatta as a favourite among his workers and asks him to go forth as a pioneer to help to open up and settle a new territory that lies upstream of his palace. That new place had already been given the name Ponnivala Nadu, meaning (roughly) "the land where the golden river flows." The river referred to is the famous Kaveri, one of the most important rivers in Tamil Nadu. A rough comparison is appropriate here with the central place of the Jordan river in the Bible. Furthermore, Palestine and Jerusalem represented a homeland for the Jews of that time in the same way that Ponnivala Nadu is the homeland for Kolatta and his family. As a result of their pioneering settlement work, Kolatta and his descendants remain in Ponnivala Nadu from then on. They become emotionally attached to this new place, despite the extended periods of exile they later have to endure. The bards telling this story repeatedly sing beautiful songs describing the heroes' positive feelings towards this new land.

After Kolatta settled in, however, he soon began to struggle once again. At first, he was a humble pioneer who worked to build himself a simple home. Beside that new dwelling he constructed a small temple. Then he planted his first crop of sugarcane. But just before the first harvest was ready, on one terrible morning, Kolatta found that his fine field had been trampled during the night (figure 4.5). Many sugarcane stalks had been chewed off or stepped on and crushed. He did not know what kind of animal was responsible for all this destruction. In anger and without any further research, Kolatta called in a group of artisans and asked them to construct a protective iron fence around his precious sugarcane field.

To be sure that the new fence would protect his crop from any further intrusions, Kolatta asked that the new barrier be topped with sharp metal spearpoints. That fence was quickly built. But the very same night the culprits came back. Unbeknownst to Kolatta, many hungry cows had been set loose by their master, the Chola king. These were honoured (sacred) cows that were due protection from anyone who encountered them. They were refugees because the Chola king's own lands were now afflicted by a severe drought! Those poor cows, desperate for food, were determined to find a place to graze. They were very hungry. Seven of those cows encountered Kolatta's mean, spiked fence, and as fate would have it, every one of them died trying to leap over those vicious, sharp points. Their souls then cried out and ascended to heaven. There the cows pleaded with Lord Shiva, complaining about this injustice and asking for compensation. That great male god then cursed Kolatta. Hence, the biblical account and the Ponnivala legend meet here once again. In both stories the anger of a great male god has been triggered by the selfish behaviour of someone who disobeyed a rule. In this case the rule was to not kill cows, something known to all South Indians as a basic moral principle.

The Original Sin

Killing cows, thought of as angelic souls in much of India, is a great sin for Hindus. Lord Shiva was very angry at Kolatta for the death of seven cows who tried to jump his spiked fence, both for his greed in refusing to share that sweet sugarcane in the first place and because he had not done enough advance research to discover who had been trying to eat it. After all, Kolatta could have figured out what creatures had been in his sugarcane field the previous night. It was his failure that he did not make further inquiries before hastily ordering the construction of that cruel fence. So, Shiva now gave Kolatta an ultimatum. It was a severe punishment. He announced that there were to be no children born in Kolatta's family line for seven generations. One might reasonably ask how his family line could continue to exist if this rule was enforced. The answer is that there was the possibility of finding certain workarounds. There could be a magical birth instead, for one. Several such tricks are introduced into the Ponnivala story at a later point, all framed as gestures of divine grace. But the original curse was devastating, nonetheless. And that curse would particularly affect the women who married into Kolatta's family. It was those women who would be held responsible for the family's lack of children. Their sins, if there were any at all, are never described in this story, but these females bear the brunt of god's retribution anyway. The curse of barrenness that descended on the heroes' family stemmed from Kolatta's misstep. It was a man who had misjudged the situation and ordered a deadly fence built to begin with. But it is his wife who then suffers most for this error. This is little different from the biblical story about God's curse of Adam and Eve, where once again, a woman bears the brunt of a great god's anger. In fact, the result of Eve's misstep was that all the world's women would have to suffer the pain of every childbirth henceforth.

To sum up, both the Bible and the Ponnivala legend describe a natural beginning where the first human couple is placed in a dreamland of beauty and abundance. There they would be free from hunger and no wider social order is described where they would have to serve as field labours and obey the whims of some distant ruler. Both stories suggest that at first there was no social hierarchy. All were equal, at least all males were. Moving from that natural state at the beginning of time to a social state where rules and responsibilities were prevalent is treated by both stories as an abrupt change that brings on suffering, especially on the part of women. Each story, furthermore, carries with it an acknowledgment of the importance of this transition. Civilized community life constituted a new social order, a new milieu that necessarily entailed restraints on instinctual human desires for fine food, sexual pleasure, wealth, and yes, power over others. These truisms underlie both story traditions. They provide one with fresh insight into the **roots** of human communal norms: we are all destined to lead social lives that involve others, including unseen beings or powers whose presence is felt by most, but whose extra-terrestrial demands may remain obscure and not be fully understood.

Theme Two: Reclamation – Descendants of the First Ancestor Achieve a New Status

There Is One Chosen Survivor, after a Major Disaster

In the biblical story, there was much hatred and distrust across the land of Yeravan, the place where Noah lived. This enmity seemed to grow stronger with each generation. So, God chose just one family, Noah's, and asked him to build an ark. There was to be just one sexually active couple to represent each type of living being allowed on board. Each such pair was told to bring along only the essentials that they would need to start life again (figure 4.6). All the other living beings on earth were destined to die in the great flood that was about to overtake everything.

In Ponnivala, Kunnutaiya was a child of Lord Shiva's own creation. So, in a sense, he too was chosen by a god, just like Noah was. Shiva had hidden Kunnutaiya as a baby under some rocks in a back field where Ponnivala's original clan ancestor, Kolatta, would be sure to find him (figure 4.7). Earlier Shiva had cursed Kolatta to have no natural offspring. So, this was the god's workaround. He would create a special child and make sure Kolatta would find and adopt him as his own. Kunnutaiya, as the baby was named, would become the single heir to the fine lands ruled by his father. However, as luck would have it, at the age of six his father and mother suddenly died. Kunnutaiya's cousins promised the Chola king that they would look

The Bible's Old and New Testament Stories 147

Figure 4.6. The long line of animal pairs waiting to board Noah's ark.

Figure 4.7. A magical baby hidden under rocks in Kolatta's back field by Lord Shiva.

after the little orphaned boy. But their real intention was to exploit Kunnutaiya and make him into a servant, and thus he was treated very badly. His several paternal uncles feared that he might one day assume the role of ruler of the fine fertile valley lands the Chola king had originally given his father to plough. Kunnutaiya's uncles plotted several times about how to reverse this, each time devising a new way to avoid the expected succession that they all dreaded. Executing their initial plan, they proceeded to tear down Kunnutaiya's boyhood home. Those mean uncles even ploughed the land where that family home had once stood and then planted castor oil seeds there, just for good measure.[7] It was as if to say, good riddance. Kunnutaiya himself, furthermore, experienced many harsh beatings at the hands of these same men (figure 4.8). Eventually he was forced to run away and wander as a waif.

In both stories we see that a major problem arose that would threaten the descendants of the first couple. With the help of a god, however, at least one male

Figure 4.8. Kunnutaiya, soon an orphan, was beaten by his uncles and treated like a slave.

in each family line finds a way to survive. Noah and three of his sons surmount and conquer the great flood by using a specially built boat. But later the first-born of Noah's sons (Ham) turned to drink along with his father and thus they both became degenerate, immoral men. Fortunately, Noah's other two sons, Shem and Japheth were better. Eventually their descendants wandered eastward, deciding it would be wise to travel far away and search for a better life. They were hoping to replace the very primitive existence their family had first endured after that great flood. In time, after much wandering, Shem and Japheth came upon a fertile plain and decided to settle down as farmers there. They worked together, prospered and felt fortunate. As a result, those two descendants of Noah developed a plan to build a tower. It was a tower of thanks and they hoped it would reach the heavens. But, alas as time passed, these men, and their many relatives, all became proud and ambitious. As a result, they ceased to get along. This displeased God and he decided to make the various competing groups that had formed speak different languages. This interrupted communication and interfered with their big building project. Confusion (babel) was the result and therefore that great tower was never finished. Then, from this group, God is said to have chosen just one man, Abraham, a good and devout shepherd who remembered to worship God each day, to lead his people forward. God instructed Abraham to take his flocks towards the land of Canaan. But despite God's choice of such a good man, Abraham's twelve sons could not live in peace either. Once in the land of Canaan, Joseph, a son of Jacob and Rachel, lived alongside one full brother, ten half-brothers and at least one half-sister. Many of those half-brothers disliked Joseph and hoped for his ruin. Eventually they sold Joseph to a gang that took him to Egypt and there he became a slave (figure 4.9).

In the Ponnivala Nadu case, Kunnutaiya wandered about as an orphan for a long time. Finally, he located a sympathetic rural family headed by two wealthy brothers.

The Bible's Old and New Testament Stories   149

Figure 4.9. Joseph is sold and taken to Egypt to become a slave.

They invited this young boy to become their fulltime farm hand. Kunnutaiya was happy to accept, and the two men treated him well. He gathered and chopped wood for their maids' kitchen fire, milked the cows and more. But after a time Kunnutaiya fell in love with his masters' younger sister. He wanted to marry this lovely girl. After much hesitation, he asked her two brothers for her hand. But Kunnutaiya's masters were horrified and beat him badly for this overreach. They felt he had become too proud and that he harboured ambition far beyond what was suitable, given his lowly station in life. With Lord Vishnu's help, however, the loving couple managed a wedding ceremony anyway. But the bride's family quickly ostracized the bride for marrying someone so lowly. They told the young couple that they must never again set foot in her natal village, let alone step inside her previous home.

Thus, a serious bitterness grew between these two related families. Kunnutaiya was exiled from the farm where he had been working and was forced to take his new wife and search for his father's original lands. Kunnutaiya eventually finds the right spot, but his old palace home there lay in ruins. Furthermore, the family temple had been left uncared for. But the honest couple worked hard, reclaimed some of the fields that were rightfully theirs, cleaned the local temple and committed to the daily worship of the local goddess inside. Kunnutaiya started to grow crops and his old family lands gradually began to prosper again. He was always mindful, however, of the power of the nearby Chola king. He knew it was important to acknowledge the help this monarch had once offered his father. So Kunnutaiya regularly took the king tribute. The monarch was pleased and considered Kunnutaiya to be a promising ally. Because this king's generous support, Kunnutaiya's reputation gradually grew. He also matured and eventually he became become an outstanding leader, a good, kind, and gentle ruler. In time the Chola king formally recognized this and presented Kunnutaiya with a small crown (figure 4.10). He also honoured Kunnutaiya with a new title: King of Ponnivala Nadu.

150   Multiple Epics Compared

Figure 4.10. Kunnutaiya becomes a respected leader after being given a crown by the Chola king.

Figure 4.11. Joseph being honoured by the Egyptian pharaoh.

In a similar scenario, Joseph did well in Egypt. For some reason the pharaoh there was very impressed and eventually promoted him to a trusted position. At that point he was given a new name: Israel (Genesis 32:28). In time Joseph became the second most powerful man in Egypt (figure 4.11). His position and power there caused many other Israelites to leave Canaan and settle in Egypt, hoping his good luck would spread to them. The relationship grew into one of loyalty and trust, not dissimilar to the relationship Kunnutaiya managed to build with the Chola ruler in his time.

In sum, in both the biblical and the Ponnivala Nadu cases, we can see that a male descendant of the first couple finally **reclaims** his family's earlier level of status and respect. In each story, furthermore, we see a shepherd-son of the original ancestor lives through hardship and then gradually transforms into a respected leader. In time, both men receive authentication from a powerful king. Both legends, therefore, describe the second stage of their larger tale as one where pride was re-established and the good reputation of their family line was guaranteed. These were recognized families whose legitimacy rested on the shoulders of a key earlier ancestor, Kolatta in one case and Noah in the other.

Theme Three: Resistance – There Are Renewed Difficulties

Disaster Strikes Again

The Pharaoh and his lands in Egypt were doing well, but the many relatives of Joseph who were still living in the neighbouring area called Canaan underwent a great famine. Hearing of Joseph's successful rise to power in Egypt, many of his relatives decided to move there as well. They were hoping to find work, of course, and thereby survive the local disaster that was afflicting Canaan. This strategy worked for a while and the new immigrants did find relative peace as Jews in Egypt, at least so long as Jacob and Joseph were alive. But after their deaths a new Pharaoh came to power and his respect for the workers from Canaan waned. The new Pharaoh forced this large group of immigrants to become his slaves. Their painful existence lasted for several generations. In fact, the descendants of Jacob lived in Egypt for more than 450 years and they gradually came to identify themselves as a separate nation: the nation of Israel. But at the same time the Egyptians began to see them as a threat and gradually began to tighten their control. Eventually, in an attempt to reduce their numbers, the Egyptian pharaoh issued an order that new-born Israelite babies be drowned, regularly, in the River Nile. God visited famines and plagues upon those cruel Egyptians, but this did not stop their terrible deeds.

According to the biblical story, Moses (backed by God) now began to perform various miracles. This further frightened the Pharaoh. Eventually the ruler agreed to let those Hebrews go free, hoping to rid his kingdom of their upstart local leader, Moses. Understanding that this situation was very serious Moses succeeded in leading his people out of Egypt, even though it took much preliminary effort on his part to prepare for this exodus. He had been so angered by seeing the unfair treatment of his people all around him that in a fit of aggression, he reacted by killing an Egyptian guard. Of course, this irritated the Pharaoh even more. Moses was forced to flee the Pharoah's new threats by going to the land of Midian. One day, during that exile, when Moses was alone in the desert, he heard the voice of God speaking to him through a magical bush. The bush expressed itself by throwing flames into the air without, itself, getting burnt up. Moses understood this as God's direct order to him to lead his people out of Egyptian slavery and into a new land. Returning to Egypt, Moses now demanded that the Pharaoh grant freedom to his people. Trying to bring the Pharoah to loosen his grip, God then unleashed

Figure 4.12. Local women gossip about Tamarai and reject her. Head lowered, she is followed by her maid.

nine different plagues on Egypt. But the Pharaoh continued to refuse to let the Israelites leave. The biblical list of scourges that beset Egypt at this time are, in turn: toxic red water, frogs, biting insects, wild animals, livestock diseases, boils, fiery hail, locusts, and overall darkness.

The multiple disasters that threatened the Pharaoh can be interpreted as similar, in a general way, to the curse of barrenness Lord Shiva laid on Ponnivala after seven cows had met their deaths on Kolatta's spiked fence. The curse on Kolatta's family was destined to last for seven generations. It is no wonder, then, that when the curse reached his son Kunnutaiya, his wife Tamarai suffered terribly. She yearned for a child and was never entirely sure why she had been made to suffer so much. She could not think of what she had done wrong, especially anything so serious that it merited this terrible fate. And it was not just she who was barren. No births were occurring anywhere across the land, not even in the nests and the cattle pens of the many fine animals who lived in Ponnivala Nadu as well. Tamarai tried many different strategies to find a cure for her difficulty, but no matter where she turned the people of Ponnivala rejected her. They feared that interacting with someone so inauspicious would bring their own families bad luck (figure 4.12). Tamarai was teased and even beaten for her sterile condition. Even her husband, rejected her. Finally, poor queen Tamarai decided to commit suicide. Fortunately, Lord Vishnu appeared at just the right moment and rescued her by dissuading her from committing such act. He did this by turning her mind around, asking her to focus on preparing a list of good deeds she could do for others. As a result, Tamarai ordered new wells dug, shelters built, and asked that many public rituals be performed. She also held feasts for the poor (figure 4.13). But nothing relieved her plight of barrenness nor helped anyone else in the land of Ponnivala Nadu conceive. The people living there continued to suffer. And not a single animal

Figure 4.13. Tamarai providing a feast for the poor in the courtyard of her palace.

managed to give birth either. The prosperity of the Ponnivala kingdom declined rapidly. People's hopes faded. They began to think that there would never be a birth in the palace, and that their kingdom was doomed to fail. None of Tamarai's efforts had yielded results.

In both stories, as we can see, the local people tried to endure the terrible hardships they were experiencing. Somehow, they persevered. Moses and Kunnutaiya were both leaders in their respective communities. But neither one experienced any personal joy. The best that could be done was to **resist** the terrible fate that seemed to confront them and all the people around them as well. They worried about the sad state of affairs they faced, oppression by a pharaoh in one case and barrenness across the land in the other. Each tested out a variety of survival strategies, both for themselves and for their kingdom's suffering people. But god's anger and the resulting misfortunes they were each undergoing, seemed unrelenting.

Theme Four: Resilience – The New Difficulties Are Surmounted

Finally, a Determined New Leader Arises and Accepts a Gift from God for His People

After nine plagues, the God of the Israelites made a final effort. He now unleashed a tenth scourge – the plague of the firstborn. The sons of the Israelites believed that they could save themselves and their families, however, if they quickly marked their door posts with the blood of a sacrificed lamb. This mark was to be made by killing and eating a lamb that very night, along with bitter herbs and unleavened bread, a rite that is now remembered by the Jewish festival of Passover. This sacrifice worked and the Jewish families were saved from disaster by God's grace. But with the threat of firstborn sons dying still hanging over the entire land, Moses again demanded that the Pharaoh let the Israelites leave. That cruel ruler, badly frightened at last,

154   Multiple Epics Compared

Figure 4.14. Moses leads his people out of Egypt and into the desert.

finally allowed Moses to gather the Jews together and lead them out of Egypt. God helped by parting the waters of the Red Sea to let them pass. But the Pharaoh soon changed his mind and sent his army after those fleeing refugees. Fortunately, God had a surprise for the mean warriors who were trying to follow and recapture those who had just left. He allowed the freed slaves to walk across a divinely emptied sea channel. However, as soon as they safely reached the other side, that deep channel's water quickly returned in the form of large waves. Those waves destroyed all six hundred of the Pharaoh's chariots that were in hot pursuit and just then crossing the miraculously emptied riverbed. In sum, Moses, a great grandson of Jacob, successfully led his suffering people out of Egypt and across the Red Sea at great risk to his own life. He took the Jews into the desert of the Sinai Peninsula, a place where they would then wander for forty years (figure 4.14)

Similarly, Tamarai and Kunnutaiya decided to leave their fine Ponnivala Nadu palace and begin a pilgrimage into the high Himalayas, in hopes of seeking help from Shiva for their plight. Although the people and the animals of Ponnivala Nadu did not follow them in bodily form, as the Jews followed Moses, many Ponnivala residents did make requests of their queen, hoping for help with their own plight of barrenness. Tamarai carried all those personal requests with her faithfully, and she did not forget to present their cases to the great god when the critical moment finally arrived. At the start of their long pilgrimage, Tamarai and Kunnutaiya walked together. But when Kunnutaiya was bitten by a scorpion, he became tired and was in pain. As the poison spread, he found he could not go any further (figure 4.15). So, Lord Vishnu turned him into a stone at the foot of a long staircase leading into the sky towards Shiva's Himalayan council chambers. Tamarai would now have to continue alone, while Kunnutaiya remained there for twenty-one years awaiting her return.

In the biblical parallel, the time the suffering travelers spent wandering in the desert was forty years. However, in both stories, there was a resilient leader,

The Bible's Old and New Testament Stories   155

Figure 4.15. During the pilgrimage Tamarai tries to help her exhausted husband, but finally has to leave him behind.

someone who sought to re-establish prosperity for the entire community and free all from despair. In one story that leader is Moses, a male Jew, and in the other it is Tamarai, a female Hindu queen. Both were **resilient**. Both crossed bravely into an unknown, liminal, and semi-magical space. One led a multitude of followers, the other represented an entire kingdom but traveled into that unknown space (almost) alone.

Theme Five: Relationships – New Bonds Are Built within God's Favoured Family

After crossing the Red Sea and travelling about in the desert for nearly three months, the Israelites camped at the foot of Mount Sinai. From there Moses set out to climb up that mountain on his own. On the way God appeared to him and proposed a covenant. He declared that the Israelites were his chosen people but that in appreciation of this special status that they must agree to always listen to him and obey his laws. God then showed Moses the two stone tablets that his ten commandments were carved on (figure 4.16). That set of edicts outlined the basic principles that were to govern all Israelite lives henceforth. God told Moses that if his people obeyed the commandments and worshipped him only, then in return he would help them and lead them to the promised land. That covenant was considered by his people to be God's great gift to mankind.

In Ponnivala Nadu the basic story is similar. Tamarai spent twenty-one years in prayer on a high pillar, trying hard to get Shiva's attention (figure 4.17). At first the great god responded with angry and violent rebuffs. Finally, exasperated, Vishnu threw some fiery flames at Shiva and this great god became frightened by that burning heat. That fire caused Shiva to finally respond, inviting Tamarai for an audience inside his Himalayan council chambers. Shiva sat there,

156   Multiple Epics Compared

Figure 4.16. Moses presents the ten commandments to his people.

Figure 4.17. Tamarai during her twenty-one years of penance on a high pillar.

amongst his many councillors, and listened to her. He asked Tamarai what she wanted, and she replied by begging him for two sons plus one daughter. Tamarai also asked for fertility for all the others in her kingdom who were hoping for progeny. Quickly resolving these several issues, the great god chose three spirit souls, each of which he immaculately placed In Tamarai's womb. Then he gave the queen a magical water pot as well. The heroine carried that sacred vessel back to her palace in Ponnivala and distributed drops of Shiva's fertility-granting liquid to all the people and animals in her kingdom who wanted children. As a result of her magical liquid gifts, Tamarai symbolically became a mother to all the living beings in her kingdom. At the same time, while still in his council chambers, Shiva made a pact with Vishnu, his brother-in-law. He assigned Vishnu the job of being Tamarai's helper. He was to step in from time to time to assist the queen's family with their problems. From then on Vishnu would be responsible

Figure 4.18. Tamarai gives a drop of precious liquid to every female in her kingdom who is hoping for a pregnancy.

for providing special counsel both to Tamarai and her children-to-be, for the rest of their earthbound lives.

In sum, the story of how a bond developed between a visionary leader and the people of a chosen land functions as a focal theme in both stories. And in each epic legend, the people resident in the kingdom concerned do agree to trust their visionary director. That leader, in turn, appeals to an almighty god for help, climbing to the summit of a high and very remote place to do so. And soon after that, an important conversation with that great being occurs. In both cases that male god also responds with a gift. Yahweh, god of the Israelites, gives his chosen people the ten commandments and, in return, expects the entire community to obey his will. If they follow his words carefully, then he will allow them entry into the promised land. That was the land the Jews had long dreamt of, a concept that referred both to a specific Jewish heritage territory and also to each community member's potential spiritual afterlife. Similarly, in the Ponnivala legend, Lord Shiva gifts fertility to the people through their representative envoy, Tamarai (figure 4.18). This gift of progeny was limited to the people who lived in a special geographic area: the kingdom of Ponnivala Nadu. But Shiva also offered the promise of perpetual regeneration to his especially chosen earth-bound devotees. That would occur when the three souls placed in the queen's womb were returned to him at the end of their allocated sixteen years on earth. The two heroic sons would then become small divinities, residing close to Shiva himself, high in the Himalayas. Their special responsibility would remain the land of Ponnivala Nadu, and they would become divine entities to whom devotees could pray, stating their own wishes for eternal life as they did so.[8] Ultimately, then, both stories build on the special **relationship** a chosen people believe they have with a great god, a relationship that unfolds through a long sequence of key events in each epic legend.

This hoped-for bond underscores a fundamental belief that the listeners hold: that a special relationship exists between god and his chosen human descent line, a line that is localized in a specific territory and that belongs to a particular social group of loosely related people.

Theme Six: Reflection – God Sends Several More Leaders, the Last Being a Saviour That Is a Reflection of Himself

According to the Bible, God next raised up another brave leader named Joshua. He gave Joshua magical powers that first allowed him to divide the waters of the Jordan River so that the people could cross easily. Second, he could cause the walls of Jericho to fall at the sound of his trumpet's signal. These blessings allowed Joshua's people to burn Jericho and destroy its wicked inhabitants. Indeed, in time, a large section of Canaan was conquered by the Israelites and then a strong line of kings took hold (Saul, David, and then Solomon). But there were also many Hebrew leaders who did not heed god's warnings. God now sent a whole chain of prophets: Elijah, Elisha, Amos, Isaiah, Jeremiah, and others, one following another. But the people would not heed their warnings and so God repeatedly punished them with pestilences and famines. He even allowed other nations to invade the land of the Jews. King after king continued to do what was evil in the sight of the lord, causing God's people to sin. Over three and a half centuries the Jewish nation, now divided into two parts, grew weaker. It was rare that a good king ruled. Thousands of people were killed and many others were led to Babylon where they would have to endure slavery. The history of the Hebrew people became a never-ending story of battles and conquests. The people of God had once more become a people of sorrows.

In a parallel set of episodes, Ponnivala Nadu's two new overlords, twin sons, take the helm at age sixteen. They become the joint rulers of Ponnivala when their aged parents die rather suddenly. Just as in the Israelites case, Lord Vishnu now steps in and gives these leaders magical powers. In particular, he makes sure that a supernatural energy resides inside their fine swords (figure 4.19). The twins enjoyed prestige and power as a result. They also managed a wide swath of productive croplands. But like the leaders of Israel, those two brothers did not use their powers very wisely. Tamarai and Kunnutaiya had told their twin sons the following: 1) Never do harm to the Chola king. He is the one who brought us to this place and helped us to settle here; 2) No matter how much harm your clansmen have done to us, do not do anything to harm them; 3) Be sure to worship our family goddess every day, three times. The land here belongs to her; 4) Be good rulers and whoever makes a mistake, be patient of heart and do not demand compensatory justice; 5) Look after your sister and do whatever she asks immediately without getting angry. She has the power to see your future in her dreams; and 6) Arrange her marriage when you find the right match.

The Bible's Old and New Testament Stories   159

Figure 4.19. The twin rulers enjoyed using the finest of swords and two magical horses as well.

Figure 4.20. The heroes' assistant, Shambuga, terrorizes the school children by entering their classroom through the roof, while the twin brothers guard its normal entrances.

But alas, the two young rulers soon disobey their parents' commands. Instead, they pompously rode into one of their cousin's villages and attacked the children there while those poor kids stood helplessly at their school benches (figure 4.20). Soon that whole village, full of the heroes' own clansmen, was routed and all those suffering families were sent into exile as refugees. Divisions started to emerge between those twin kings as well. The elder always preferred to follow his dying parents' good words while the younger son wanted to fight and seek revenge for the wrongs of history. It was always the younger one whose wishes won the day. Because the twin heroes did not faithfully follow the instructions their parents had issued, matters in the kingdom of Ponnivala Nadu, just like in the land of Canaan, began to deteriorate once again.

Now the Hero Makes a Personal Sacrifice for His People

This part of the two epic stories concerns comparisons to be made between Christ and the twin heroes when both are in their prime. However, here there are significant differences. First, in the biblical tradition the story brings forth a new figure, Jesus, who represents a new generation. Although he did do some rather violent things, like throwing a group of dishonest money changers out of the Jerusalem temple, Jesus was basically a teacher and a healer throughout his thirty-two years (most say) of his life on earth. Jesus was a leader who had little personal experience with physical fighting. He certainly did not ride a horse, carry a sword, beat up school children, lock women up, or fight hand-to-hand with a group of forest hunters, let alone kill any of his challengers. That is in stark contrast to the twin heroes' record of aggression against numerous types of local adversaries (clansmen, the clansmen's children, an artisan, the Chola king, and a big group of forest hunters). But if we allow for a large gap between the twins' birth stories (between numbers 1, 2, and 3, and numbers 4 through 11 in the list just below) then the overlap does become quite stunning.

At the beginning of their lives, Christ and the Ponnar-Shankar duo exhibit some similarities. These can be easily described. In one case a single divine character (Christ/Jesus), and in the other a divine set of brothers (the god-backed twin sons of Kunnutaiya), all exhibit the following common traits:

1 In both epics the leaders' births are announced in advance – via an *annunciation*. Both also experience an *immaculate conception* by a great god (God the Father or Lord Shiva) who has no sexual contact whatsoever with their devout and very pure mother (Mary or Tamarai).
2 Both Jesus and the twins are *hidden at birth* because they are males who are subject to a plot by jealous rivals who want them killed.
3 Both are graced with *magical abilities* that aid in their search for justice.

At this point there is a gap during which these heroes' lives clearly do diverge. Jesus walks a middle line that lies somewhere in between the twins' contrasting personalities. Like Ponnar, Jesus is gentle in most situations. He cites the rules of proper behaviour and tries to follow them. He is also known as a counsellor, leader, and teacher. He is contemplative and respectful. But there still a few times when he becomes angry or violent, for example in the well-known scene when he throws the money changers out of the temple. Although Jesus Christ is more like Ponnar than Shankar, their disparate traits are merged in him, making him a singular and outstanding leader, rather than those qualities being split into the two different types of leaders that the twin brothers embody.

As the two brothers and Christ near the end of their lives, the similarity between their stories returns in a striking fashion:

4 Both Jesus and the twins are fed a *ceremonial last meal.*
5 Both are able to *realize the moment when their personal end is near.*
6 Both submit to a *sacrificial death* without resistance, seeing it as a gift to others.
7 All three deaths involve a *piercing* of the leader's body by an external metal object (or objects).
8 Both Jesus and the twins undergo *a brief earthly resurrection*, in order to talk briefly with a female associate.
9 Both *rise up to heaven*, to stand proudly by the side of their "father."
10 Both have a *shrine* built in their honour and that temple (church) tradition grows in importance over time.
11 All three are worshipped using *an image (or a ritual) representing their sacrificial death* that is incorporated into their ceremonial veneration.

There is no need to summarize the biblical evidence for the above eleven points of correspondence. That account will be common knowledge for most readers. But some elaboration on how these eleven themes apply to the Ponnivala Nadu heroes is, of course, needed.

1 Lord Shiva announces to Tamarai, the mother who struggled for twenty-one years to reach his council chambers, that she will soon be gifted two sons and one daughter (the *annunciation*). This event is preceded by a much earlier announcement by Lord Vishnu, also made directly to her, that she can expect this gift, a set of triplets in embryo form that will be placed inside her, at the successful conclusion of her long pilgrimage, when she finally speaks with Lord Shiva in person. At that moment Shiva places three life spirits magically in Tamarai's womb, lodging them there one by one with just the raising of his right hand while he looks straight at her.[9] The first two, both males, are to be reincarnations of two famous Mahabharata heroes, Arjuna and Bhima. The third is a girl, the youngest of the seven Pleiades sisters. She is called into Shiva's presence and asked if she will agree to go to earth for a time. The girl consents. Shiva then magically transforms her into a beam of light that will also become a little embryo once it penetrates Tamarai's belly. This completes the *immaculate conception* and makes Lord Shiva the divine father of all three of Tamarai's children-to-be.
2 There is an evil midwife, complete with a hunched back, who has previously promised Tamarai's husband's lineal cousins that she will faithfully kill any sons born to the queen at the very moment of their birth. That mischievous midwife places a blindfold on Tamarai when her labour pains start. With this act she hopes to avoid allowing the queen to ever learn that she birthed any male children. But, as in many other instances in this story, Lord Vishnu intervenes at a key moment. When the midwife is outside the birthing room

sharpening her knife, this god steps in. Then, without the midwife seeing him, he performs a quick magical and bloodless Caesarian on Tamarai. When the twin boys then jump out, fully clothed and each carrying a small hand-held weapon, they run and kick the unsuspecting midwife. Right after that, the local Ponnivala Nadu goddess Cellatta steps in and grabs them. She whisks the two little boys through a secret tunnel that she has just dug. It connects the palace birthing chamber to a small cave situated directly under her local temple. This is the *hidden at birth* scene. There the goddess raises both boys in secret for five years. The midwife, meanwhile, removes the blindfold from Tamarai and hands her a little girl, the third of the triplets. This little girl, unlike her brothers, is delivered via a natural birth just a few minutes after her two brothers have been carried off. Tamarai and her husband subsequently raise that little girl, without realizing that she has two brothers until a full five years have passed.

3 The twin boys, named Ponnar and Shankar, have a variety of magical powers. First, they are raised on tiger's milk by the goddess. They also have magical horses that can run as fast as the wind. Their swords carry extra power, a magic transferred to them by their chaste, virgin sister. This is the *magical abilities* theme. And these twins also have Lord Vishnu at their side during many of their exploits, especially at times when they challenge family enemies and try to defend their kingdom against the lies, assaults, and other injustices they believe their rivals are responsible for. Not the least of the twins' acts of justice is their killing of an abusive and cruel Chola king. The same twin heroes also send an entire village of lineal cousins into exile because they (or their parents) had earlier unnecessarily ruined Ponnivala Nadu's fine crops, demolished Kunnutaiya's birth palace, secretly toasted seeds before giving them to Kunnutaiya for planting, and more. These same heroes also kill an artisan, likely a goldsmith, who tries to steal their fine swords from a palace storeroom late one night. The same two siblings also fight an imagined war against the members of a neighbouring hunting community, the Vettuvas. These men are believed to have struck an alliance with their arch anti-farm enemy, a very big and black wild boar whose name is Raja Komban.

4 The twins are told by their magical, all-seeing sister Tangal that they will not return from their next and last great expedition, the boar hunt they have been plotting and which they hope will bring down that wild beast named Komban. To her brothers' distress, their sister tells them both that they will not survive the hunt. Tangal then insists that her two brothers sit down for a last meal with her in their joint palace. It is a special treat that she personally prepares and then serves to them with loving tenderness. This is the triplets' *ceremonial last meal* together.

5 After the twin heroes leave the battlefield where they believe they have just fought viciously with group of hunters from the adjacent forest, they

quickly go to a river nearby to wash their swords. There, while they stand in its flowing water, Lord Vishnu secretly shoots a flowered arrow at younger twin Shankar while perched on a tree limb nearby. He uses a sugarcane bow and an arrow made of flowers for this attack. That arrow removes Shankar's protective chest thread (an act reminiscent of Kama, the Hindu cupid). The young hero reads this gesture accurately, realizing that he and his brother must now declare their own (implicit) love of god (and also perhaps of the goddess) and sacrifice their lives to them. The twin brothers do not question Lord Vishnu's message but rather rapidly act on it. Thus, they *know when death is near*. The twins agonize only very briefly over the message, just as Christ did when listening to God tell him that he would soon be crucified. But both sets of heroes comply and submit to that ultimate truth, quietly and rapidly.

6 and 7 The two heroes climb a small bank bordering the river where they have just washed what they believe to be the blood of a great battle off their swords. They then plant the heels of those same two swords firmly in the ground and fall forward deliberately. The very sharp points of the swords penetrate their chests with ease. The two slump to the ground, both dying quickly, side-by-side. This constitutes their *sacrificial deaths* and *the piercing* of their bodies. Shankar takes the initiative in this and Ponnar quickly follows suit.

8 Tangal finds her brothers' two corpses deep in the forest. They still lie at the exact spot where they fell. She sprinkles a sacred watery liquid on them while chanting some prayers. Following Tangal's gesture, the heroes come to life briefly. For a few minutes they stand and talk with their sister as if they were in normal good health. This is their *brief resurrection*. Tangal begs her twin brothers to return with her to their beloved Ponnivala Nadu. But the two men refuse saying that they must die where they are now standing and that they are willing do this. They tell their sister that they are knowingly passing the leadership of Ponnivala to others. They are, at that moment, jointly renouncing their position as the twin rulers of the kingdom known as Ponnivala Nadu.

9 The two men fall back on the ground and die (figure 4.21). Then Lord Vishnu appears along with his customary vehicle, a great eagle named Garuda. That god quickly takes these men's two spirits, puts them in a little golden box and carries them skyward, heading for the council chambers of Lord Shiva high above. This is their *rise up to heaven*. There the two brothers are re-embodied and can be seen to stand, to this day, next to their great father, who resides in Kailasa, a Hindu version of heaven.

10 and 11 The heroes' sister Tangal commissions a small temple built in her brothers' honour (figure 4.22). It is built just at the edge of the forest, not far from where the two heroes earlier gave up their lives. Thus, *a shrine is built*. Tangal is the first person to worship (conduct a puja) at this humble temple. This first and primary place of the heroes' worship still exists today.

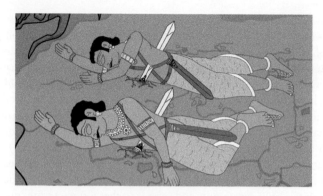

Figure 4.21. The two heroes lie still after falling forward deliberately on their own swords.

Figure 4.22. The shrine the heroes' sister built for them, as depicted in this story's animated version.

> Inside there are two terracotta sculptures depicting the twins, each one being shown in the very act of committing a ritual suicide. Hence one can see an explicit *image of their sacrificial death* at this all-important temple built in their honour (see Hiltebeitel, 1999, plate 5). This is not so different from the standard Catholic crucifix that shows Christ dying on the cross.

The Growth of a Tradition of Shrines and of Rituals Focused on the Heroes' Story

In recent years, many other temples or folk shrines honouring these same two heroes have sprung up in the Ponnivala area. They usually also contain pottery statues of other members of the heroes' family or their associates, other characters familiar to those who know the story well. Around the edges of many such shrines, one often finds additional pottery figures, such as Komban, the wild boar, or his rival, the tiny female palace dog named Ponnacci. Occasionally, one also finds statues of the heroes' magnificent and much beloved horses.

At many of these shrines, furthermore, a major festival is held each year. This event happens on Shiva's great night (Shiva Ratiri). At that time, many serious devotes undergo a kind of dedicatory death experience that lasts several hours until they are revived by a young virgin girl who sprinkles water on them. Often, she uses a wand similar to the one described in the story's actual resurrection scene. This late-night ritual sequence compares nicely to the Via Dolorosa rituals in Jerusalem, held on Good Friday, where devotees carry crosses larger than their own bodies along a route representing the stations of the cross. That route memorializes Jesus' own struggle as he walked to the Calvary, the place of his certain death so long ago, carrying his own heavy cross. The Ponnivala Nadu heroes' deaths are memorialized once each year in much the same way.

Theme Seven: Revelation – And Lastly, a Promise of Renewal

Aside from the founding of a temple or church tradition at the end of both the biblical and the Ponnivala Nadu stories, there is also a similar if oblique prediction of a second coming. In the biblical case this is a genuine forecast, a **revelation** that Jesus himself will return and reign on earth for a thousand years. It is believed that Christ's return and his subsequent personal rule will blanket the earth with peace and righteousness. In the Ponnivala Nadu case a similar kind of prediction is made, but this time it surfaces in the form of a blessing offered by the bards who sing this story to a live audience. Those singers end their tale by describing the world's coming renewal. They tell of this as a time when the roots of lovely green grasses and fine clumps of healthy bamboo will spread (figure 4.23). This is the way, the story singers imply using very poetic words, that our earth will once again prosper and humans will finally find peace. This is the parallel Ponnivala Nadu version of a concluding **revelation**. The frame concept is the Hindu belief in the four yugas (the Hindu concept of cyclical time). The central idea there is that the renewal described will create a new sequence of ages or yugas, as the world begins once more, issuing forth a fresh, moist burst of new vegetation. According to this folk tradition, it will be a very cool and very green new beginning.

The two sets of heroes celebrated by the two stories under discussion further resemble each other in terms of their own personal, sexual virginity. Christ never weds, and at least overtly never has a female girlfriend. The twin heroes do marry but never, ever touch their brides. Hence a principle of extreme sexual abstinence applies to both sets of heroes. However, the two stories' hugely different time frames offer a big contrast. The Bible covers some forty-two generations while

166   Multiple Epics Compared

Figure 4.23. One of the images of renewal used by the lead Ponnivala Nadu story artist to illustrate the end of this epic story.

the Ponnivala epic covers just three. Hence one would expect any structural comparison between these two legends to involve significant telescoping in the much shorter folk story's account of events. That is indeed the case. But where the two stories overlap most strikingly is in the lead up to and respective deaths of their heroes. At this point the similarity between these two epic legends is quite remarkable.

Conclusion

In sum, there is an obvious correspondence between many details in Christian Bible and the Ponnivala story. However, in another sense this overlap, though present, is quite subtle. Reading through or hearing the legend of Ponnivala just once is not enough to really perceive that there are deep themes embedded there that reverberate with Christian traditions in many ways. Having lived with the Ponnivala account for more than fifty years now, I have finally come to appreciate and to viscerally feel those connections. The overlaps between the Old Testament and the Ponnivala Nadu legend are vaguer than they are where the New Testament is concerned. In comparisons with the Old Testament, discovering the similarities requires using generalizations and metaphoric connections that exist at a high level of abstraction. But there can be no doubt that even there, a surprising consistency in basic themes is present. And there are similarities in the structure of how these parallel themes progress. The basic messages of both stories also contain a fair degree of similarity, a resemblance that can be described loosely as follows: The earth and its peoples have struggled mightily to build a just, peaceful, and tolerant social order. But the history of that communal effort, and especially the effort of those peoples' leaders, has always been countered by the forces of greed, self-aggrandizement, and the desire to violently subdue, and conquer rivals. However, both epics end by featuring their leaders' ultimate endorsement of humility and recognize that the only honourable path, in the end, is to offer up one's own life willingly, referencing alongside of that theme, a vision of broad community service. Both stories state a wish for a greater, future good that can stem from one's service to a higher morality, a loftier goal than individual self-gain. Just when and how that greater state of wellness and joy will come about, is left largely to the imagination, in both cases. The poets and writers of both these stories present this idea poetically. In the Ponnivala case, the presentation is musical as well. It is set out as a kind of pleasing dream, itself a kind of **revelation**.

The deep symbolism of sacrifice has captured the imagination of millions, across many regions and cultures. The two stories discussed in tandem here hold the potential for enriched cross-cultural teaching along these lines. The many possibilities embedded in the comparisons noted above can expand our empathy and our understanding of others' perspectives significantly. These overlaps point to how so many have found differing ways of celebrating our great human heritage under one wide conceptual umbrella. In the next two chapters these lofty goals shift somewhat, turning to issues of family well-being and personal achievement. In the Icelandic Saga that follows there is little reference to a great god, or even to an initial creation event. Although the church was becoming established in Iceland at the time of this saga's construction, this story's broad message is more limited. Personal loyalty and family identity are key to the next account, especially as these two themes become interwoven with ideas about justice. At the same time, the landscape surrounding the Saga heroes also becomes more foreboding. The landscape here has fewer humans. Instead, more wild forces are at work. The Icelandic tale to be studied is filled with witchcraft, curses, and dark places where malicious spirits lurk. Close family bonds between kinsmen, rather than the approval of one or more gods living in a distant heaven, are what offers a person security in this next story setting. Primary kin bonds, especially male ones, will be especially important as they constitute an individuals' prime fortress against attack by external and unpredictable dangers.

5 Landscapes and Identity Formation: The Vatnsdaela Saga

(An Icelandic Heritage Legend)[1]

Icelandic sagas are famous all over the world as founding legends on which later Western literature has built. Furthermore, Iceland's marvellous tales are presented in a very direct prose style, unlike many other legends that belong to a larger corpus of European literary legends. The saga tradition is considered to have preserved an important record of this island's early culture. Together, the many sagas that have been documented represent a significant and unique storytelling achievement. Here we will discuss just one sample tale: The Vatnsdaela Saga. This colourful story describes the very first people to settle one specific region of Iceland. The task will be to compare this beloved legend with the Ponnivala Nadu epic. The Vatnsdaela Saga depicts the early settlement of one locale in Iceland that is similar to an area of South India known as Kongu Nadu. Iceland's saga immigrants came from Norway and were backed by the Norwegian king of their time. That powerful ruler was hoping that the handful of wealthy land-owning men who had decided to leave his kingdom to find and build an even better fortune elsewhere would remain loyal to him. He reasoned that their success in establishing fine farms abroad would eventually reflect on Norway, adding to his own influence and fame. In the parallel Ponnivala Nadu story, a group of pioneer farmers from outside that area were encouraged by a similarly influential king to enter and begin to farm an equally remote region lying outside that king's immediate area of control. Both kings nursed similar ambitions. However, there was one key difference; Iceland was not inhabited at the time, while Ponnivala Nadu was.

In 2014, while driving across the northern part of Iceland during a summer visit, I stopped at a small, local store. And there, on a display shelf, was a very colourful brochure in English describing the heroes of a local epic known as the Vatnsdaela Saga. That pamphlet, laid out in the form of a large local map, instantly attracted my interest and I purchased it. Embedded along the edges of the map were a number of images depicting the scenes and characters featured

The Vatnsdaela Saga 169

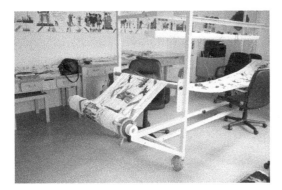 

Figure 5.1. Huge 2014 local embroidery project honouring the heroes.

Figure 5.2. Folk statue of Shankar, a Ponnivala Nadu hero, on his horse, along with some human-faced demons displayed below the horse's chest.

in this tale. Curious to learn more, I traveled to various places marked on this convenient map and visited several of the sites mentioned there. Not long after that, while stopping in a larger town in that area, I found a full translation of the saga for sale in a major regional bookstore. My curiosity was heightened further when I found I could also visit a local cultural centre where a group of local artists were working on a very large, embroidered banner featuring the same tale (figure 5.1). Later still, I visited a major museum in Reykjavik that featured this same saga in a large exhibit hall. It became clear by then that an in-depth comparison of similarities between the Vatnsdaela saga and the Ponnivala Nadu epic would yield interesting results.

As one might imagine, at first glance it seems very unlikely that the Vatnsdaela and Ponnivala Nadu legends could have any direct cultural links, even though the Vikings and the Tamil traders of South India both came from skilled sailing traditions. What is clear is that both these populations had a zest for foreign adventure. Furthermore, as far as is known, these two folk traditions thrived during roughly the same time period (800 to 1500 AD). Yet there is no evidence that they ever encountered one another, even through intermediaries. What the following comparison attempts to show is that despite a presumed lack of contact, these two stories have much in common. Both build around a group of larger-than-life social ancestors whose memory lives on inside their own culturally distinct area, to this day (figure 5.2).

Theme One: Roots

Arrival of the First Pioneers

The Vatnsdaela Saga and the Ponnivala stories both begin with a clan forefather. Both legends then focus on the descent line that grows from that ancestor through several additional generations, tracing the significant impact of this initial figure on the local region. In the Icelandic case we hear briefly about Ketil the Large and his son Thorstein. Later the story proceeds to describe the key clan founder named Ingimund. To allow comparison, we will largely ignore Ketil and just briefly mention Thorstein, the man who sired the main characters featured in the Vatnsdaela epic account. Skipping past these two, who both lived in Norway, we will start with Ingimund, the saga's main character who moved to Iceland and is central to this comparative study. Honoured as Vatnsdaela's founding father, Ingimund travelled from Norway to Iceland as a Viking, looking to start a pioneer farm in a new, wild, area that was completely without human presence at the time (figure 5.3). Because Ingimund was a man of stature in Norway, he had been able to bring three fine ships, a crew, and ample supplies along with him to Iceland. Furthermore, Ingimund carried with him an array of spoils obtained from previous wars, all given to him by King Herald. Of course, Herald expected Ingimund's political support and loyalty in exchange for this help.

Just as with the Norwegian ruler, so too did South India's (unnamed) Chola king expect Kolatta to remain a loyal ally. Kolatta was leader of a group of immigrant brothers who were the first plough farmers to enter Ponnivala Nadu according to that story. Both epic accounts imply that the wealthy king who backed a hand-picked set of pioneer heroes was primarily interested in expanding his own power and territory by sponsoring those intrepid explorers. Both kings were committed to opening up and settling a new area beyond their own kingdom's current borders. Furthermore, both pioneer expeditions followed water and used that as a signpost that pointed towards where they should go. In the case of the saga, the adventurers sailed northwest across the Norwegian Sea. In the Ponnivala Nadu case they moved northwest by moving upstream along the south bank of a major river, the Kaveri. In the first account three boats were used, while in the second, the nine brothers appear to have walked to their new land, possibly accompanied by a few ox carts filled with tools and supplies. The outcome was the same. In both cases these well-supplied envoys were successful in gaining a toehold in a foreign land. Both groups then began to farm. In the Ponnivala case the land Kolatta staked out was soon divided into two adjacent parcels, one for him and one for his eight younger brothers. It seems likely that the lands in and around the Vatnsdaela valley were also soon divided in much the same way.

The Vatnsdaela Saga   171

Figure 5.3. Ingimund's ship reaches Iceland.

Figure 5.4. Kolatta and his eight brothers confront a group of artisans already resident in the area they have just entered.

One important difference in these two epic accounts, as already noted, is that Ingimund found himself in a truly empty land while Kolatta found other people living there (figure 5.4). Those first inhabitants, in Kolatta's case, were skilled artisans who understood how to market their goods using a broad trade network already established in the area. There were also indigenous hunters living in this new land they called Ponnivala Nadu. Those forest-dwelling people, unlike the artisans, were more secretive, and they did not reveal their presence to the newcomers right away. Despite such differences, however, both Ingimund and Kolatta were founding fathers. As a result, both their reputations have been richly embroidered with mythical imagery by their storytellers. Each epic wraps these first pioneers in a story cloak that links them to the land's local soil, providing each with special roots and a strong mission (figures 5.5 and 5.6). Furthermore, their goals were near

Figure 5.5. Kolatta prepares for his rise from the earth.

Figure 5.6. Ingimund finds a buried magical ring.

identical: each dreamed of establishing a new agricultural domain in a remote and unknown area where little or no farming activity had existed prior to their arrival.

In the Ponnivala case a short mythical tale describes Lord Vishnu placing Kolatta inside a pit in the ground. Later, Vishnu causes him to rise up in front of an audience of local residents already living there (figure 5.5). Coming magically out of the earth helped Kolatta claim he had a god-given right to plough that local soil. But this did not please those who watched. This controversial incident quickly became a source of tension and dispute. Ingimund was wrapped by his storytellers in a similar myth that helped him to establish his land claim as well. He came to know of a sorcerer's prediction that a ring has been buried in this new land and that whoever found it would have the right to rule there (figure 5.6). Accordingly Ingimund found the buried ring and then decided to settle and build his home on that exact spot. But in Ingimund's case, unlike in the Ponnivala Nadu story, the place he selected had not been claimed already by others.

The Vatnsdaela Saga   173

Figure 5.7. Lovely hills surround the Vatnsdaela Valley.

Figure 5.8. Ponnivala area showing crop land with hills behind.

The Beloved Land

The lands of the Vatnsdaela Valley are surrounded by beautiful green hills that are celebrated by the saga tellers. These hills are also featured on the tapestry that was being prepared at the Icelandic Textile Center at the time of my visit. The clear link between this core Icelandic legend and its landscape is made quite clear in this artistic rendering of events. The Ponnivala Nadu story provides a similar landscape overview. There, the hills that border the ploughed land that the heroes opened up represent a place where these men underwent many of their most challenging adventures. In both stories these nearby hills are dangerous places. They are locations where the main story characters meet their fiercest foes. Meanwhile, each area's lowlands are located near a reliable water course and lie in a welcoming area that is considered safe and desirable. In both legends these flatlands provide an attractive place to begin cultivation. In sum, the core landscape is tame in both legends, but it becomes more and more chaotic as one approaches that area's boundaries (figures 5.7 and 5.8). There is one obvious contrast, however, that cannot be ignored:

Figure 5.9. Vatnsdaela with its natural waters featured.

While Iceland is cool all year round and very cold in the winter, Ponnivala Nadu is a tropical land, warm all the time and especially hot during the summer months. The style of agriculture practised in these two locales is thus bound to be different. Nonetheless, the lifestyle these stories share in most other ways is surprisingly similar. Both legends feature cattle, sheep, and the importance of the plough. Furthermore, each story is centred on a largely self-sufficient peasant homestead, at least at first.

Theme Two: Reclamation

A Clear Clean Source of Water

In this modern photograph of the Vatnsdaela valley the area still retains its homestead look (figure 5.9). The beautiful body of water seen in the foreground is known as the Vatna Fjord, but what is featured in the photograph is an attached inland bay called Hop. It is a peaceful and beautiful scene that conveys the feeling of being a serene homeland. In the Ponnivala Nadu story, similarly, the Ponni River is the key to the heroes' pride in their lovely homeland (figure 5.10). Again, this place is portrayed by its story artist as peaceful, cool, and clean. Just as in the Vatnsdaela image, the lighting is soft and pleasing. We see a calm stretch of river water glowing under a full moon. A local homestead is not seen in the picture, but many activities described in the Ponnivala Nadu story take place here: ceremonial bathing, collecting good drinking water, and the like.

In both epics the very name of the body of water that is key to the story is used by its poets to give the story an identity and stature. This water represents the core, the centre, what one might call the symbolic lifeblood of the place. Perhaps not surprisingly, water also becomes a source of death in both stories. In each, a

Figure 5.10. Ponnivala Nadu with its key river featured.

Figure 5.11. Jokull used his sword on this enemy who had magical powers and left him to die in the river.

key villain is slain and left to die in the water. In both cases, the victim who dies in water is also a deserter, someone who has fled from an earlier confrontation. So, not surprisingly, both men are described as falling into water, not at a central place but rather in a liminal place right at the edge of each heroes' featured kingdom. This is, symbolically, exactly where a deserter belongs. In a scene from the Vatnsdaela Saga shown in figure 5.11, we see an enemy who had negative magical power fleeing from the hero Jokull by diving into water. The man, known as Leather Cap, was unsuccessful in his escape attempt. He was crippled by the fact that Jokull had already cut off his buttocks using his extra sharp sword. As a result, Leather Cap could not swim properly. In the Ponnivala Nadu story, the villain is an artisan who tries to deceive and ultimately to kill Ponnar, Kolatta's grandson and one of the twin heroes. The artisan dies when he is beheaded and his body falls into an irrigation sluice that, similarly, lies right at the edge of the Ponnivala Nadu area (figure 5.12).

Figure 5.12. The beheaded artisan's body falls into an irrigation sluice.

Hence, both villains die in water, almost as if that liquid has the power to cleanse and reverse the evil and pollution involved in the bloody event that has just occurred. Similar folk motifs occur worldwide, but here we see that even the underlying logic of the two stories appears to match in a surprising way.

The Pioneer Homestead

The pioneer homestead is an important concept in both the Vatnsdaela and the Ponnivala Nadu epic universe. The original Icelandic homestead portrayed is a modest but well-built structure with a sod roof. Solid wooden planks have been used for the front entrance. Ingimund stands proudly in front of his home, assuming the stance of an elder who combines both authority and wisdom (figure 5.13a). This is the family's proud location, the core of their territorial claim and their first home. It is intended to mark their dominance of the region and their position at the base of long lineage-to-be of fine men. Ingimund's wife Vigdis is also seen standing appropriately right by the homestead's front door, guarding the inner womb if you like (figure 5.13b). Ingimund is the son of Thorstein but was adopted and lived with his father's friend (Ingjald) from boyhood onward. Ingimund and his father, Thorstein, grew up in Norway, the foreign land far from Iceland where the Vatnsdaela story begins. But then Ingimund left his foster father Ingjald's home to strike out on a life of Viking adventures. He conducted daring raids early in his teens, but his exact age is not given at that point. The saga describes him as an already brave, handsome, and physically talented man who was always gentle towards others. It was only after Ingimund's marriage that he decided to leave for Iceland and start a new life in an unknown land.

Figure 5.13a. and b. a) Ingimund in front of the family homestead. b) Ingimund's wife Vigdis in front of the family homestead.

The parallel the Ponnivala Nadu hero Kunnutaiya presents makes for a striking comparison. He led a similar homestead life early on, soon after his marriage. Kunnutaiya, like Ingimund was also an adopted son. Kolatta was Kunnutaiya's guardian and social father when he was a young boy, like Ingjald had been for Ingimund. And, like Thorstein, Kolatta is the Ponnivala Nadu story's clan ancestor. He was created by the goddess Parvati in a mysterious place called Vellivala Nadu, far from Ponnivala itself. Ponnivala Nadu was a place no one, at that point, had ever heard of. Kunnutaiya also became independent early in life. This happened suddenly when both his "parents" died. The gods simply declared that those two had lived their lives and that their time on earth was up. Kunnutaiya was six years old at this point and his uncles soon began to taunt him. He ran away and became a self-reliant orphan, experiencing many adventures and hardships. Those youthful adventures tried his spirit and built his character, much as the adventures of the young Viking raider Ingimund moulded him. Like Ingimund too, Kunnutaiya was an exceptionally handsome and talented young man, but he was also gentle, thoughtful, and kind. It was only after Kunnutaiya's marriage that he left his place of work to rediscover his father Kolatta's old family lands. It was only then that he would start a new life in Ponnivala Nadu, the place he had been born in but had left at age six. Kunnutaiya's first home after his marriage was humble, just like Ingimund's was (figure 5.14). In both cases the roof was made of local grasses, though because of the climate of South India, grass thatch rather than grass sod was used. Both homes were built from local wood (probably driftwood in Ingimund's case). Kunnutaiya and his wife had one cow, similar to the way in which Ingimund must have started his own first dairy herd.

178 Multiple Epics Compared

Figure 5.14. Kunnutaiya in front of his first homestead.

The Story Tellers

Scholars think that the Vatnsdaela Saga was probably written down by monks associated with the ancient church at Pingeyrar, sometime between 1270 and 1320 CE. The saga itself was only preserved in later manuscripts, however, the earliest fragments of which can be dated to between 1390 and 1425 CE. The story is based on events that are estimated to have occurred between 875 and 1000 CE. Overall, the text reads like a narrative with just a few lines inserted here and there to represent conversational exchanges between its many characters. This particular saga, furthermore, is just one of a large collection of stories derived from Icelandic oral tradition. Like many of the others, it was converted into written form by those interested in preserving local Icelandic history for future generations. It's not known if the earlier oral versions contained songs and extensive conversational passages, but it seems likely that this was the case. The Ponnivala epic is also part of an oral tradition, and one that was only written down, at least with the intention to circulate it in print, quite recently.[2]

The Vatnsdaela Saga was traditionally narrated to a live audience, quite possibly by men who also worshipped at the Pingeyrar church (figure 5.15). The Legend of Ponnivala Nadu is sung by local bards to this day and was transmitted orally, at least until quite recently. The version referenced here was tape recorded during a thirty-eight-hour performance in 1965. It was delivered to a village audience of eager listeners over eighteen nights by two live singers and then later transcribed (figure 5.16). A parallel version of the same story, this time dictated by the same singer who led the live performance is also important for this analysis. That dictated account can be said to stand midway between a fully oral performance and an ancient manuscript. Accurate dating of the Ponnivala Nadu story is impossible but its core events roughly reflect the inscription-rich history of the area (found on stones and on copper plates). Several events that occurred between about 1000 and 1500 CE are the ones that best (though only very roughly) echo the details of this story.

The Vatnsdaela Saga 179

Figure 5.15. Church at Pingeyrar where the Vatnsdaela Saga may have been written.

Figure 5.16. The village temple wall, with its red and white stripes, against which the Ponnivala Nadu Legend was sung and tape recorded.

Figure 5.17 shows a pair of men who might have been engaged as scribes at the Pingeyrar church. They could have been active tellers of historical stories about the region that were conscientiously preserved and handed down through many generations in just this type of church setting. The Vatnsdaela story text, as far as can be assessed from the English translation used here, does not read like epic poetry. It is more like a string of narrated adventure tales. Furthermore, it is a tale which is clearly grounded in the region where the Pingeyrar church is located. There are no obvious song passages and no repeated stanzas. The Ponnivala Legend is different. In this tale there are a lot of character voices, supplemented with a limited amount of narration that functions to bridge the various scenes and conversations presented. There are also many songs, some of which (with a certain amount of variation) are used multiple times. The Ponnivala Nadu story is driven forward by the main bard, but he regularly sang with an assistant who was an advanced apprentice (figure 5.18). This second singer repeated the lead singer's phrases in

Figure 5.17. Pingeyrar monks possibly associated with recording the Vatnsdaela story.

Figure 5.18. Traditionally dressed bards singing the Ponnivala legend.

order to give them more emphasis. He sometimes added extra lines, questions, or exclamations of pleasure or surprise as well. This makes the Ponnivala story stylistically different from its Icelandic counterpart, though content wise there is a lot of overlap, as has already been demonstrated above. Still more examples of overlap will be detailed below.

Theme Three: Resistance

Heroes versus Villains

Many people feel that the rich have a duty to redistribute or share their wealth. Giving one's assets away can sometimes bring rewards but can also be a dangerous task. In both the Icelandic and the South Indian epic legends examined here, the duty to share good fortune is taken seriously by at least one central story character. In the Vatnsdaela Saga Ingimund first kills a wealthy robber. Then he

The Vatnsdaela Saga 181

Figure 5.19. People are joyful when their stolen goods are returned.

Figure 5.20. Tamarai shares her new wealth with surprise visitors: One thousand beggars.

returns the goods the robber stole to its rightful owners. In the Ponnivala Legend several clansmen try to ruin Kunnutaiya's maize crop by having their cattle trample it. But with Lord Vishnu's help those plants spring back. When Kunnutaiya's wife Tamarai then examines the plants closely, she finds that each and every cob now contains jewels, not mere kernels of corn. Tamarai then declares that she will share all this surprising and unexpected wealth with the thousand beggars who suddenly appear at her homestead door. Clearly, both epics make sure that the principles of generosity and social responsibility find illustration through the actions of at least one important story character. In the Vatnsdaela Saga the generous parent is male, while in the Ponnivala case, this role is given to a devout female, someone who worships god regularly. There are several other ways in which females are given a heightened and more visible role in the South Indian story than in its Icelandic counterpart. That difference, of course, fits with other clear gender contrasts between these two legends. Furthermore, in each case there is someone watching this redistribution, someone who is displeased because their own assets (and perhaps potential inheritance) stand to be diminished in the process. This is an age-old dilemma well illustrated by the current day debate about whether there should be progressive taxation brackets imposed on the society's richest citizens, or heavy fines placed on corporations that break official rules in order to make extra money. Both the traditional stories being discussed here take a firm stand on this matter and project the moral conviction, still relevant today, that the richest members of one's community have a moral duty to share.

In both the Ponnivala Nadu and Vatnsdaela legends, the sons of celebrated and generous senior figures reject or ignore a rule of benevolent generosity advocated by their parents. Thorstein and Jokull from the Vatnsdaela Saga and Ponnar and Shankar in the Ponnivala Nadu story show little interest in charity. These youthful heroes, especially the younger of the two brothers in each epic account, grow into aggressive young men and instead focus their energies on killing a variety of villains. Jokull kills a man thought to have negative magical powers (figure 5.21), while Shankar kills an (unnamed) Chola king who also wields his power in inappropriate ways. Jokull sometimes destroys several men at a time, even killing multiple thieves simultaneously. Shankar also kills multiple men, in his case in quick succession. In one example Shankar attacks a group of clansmen who are jealous of the fine crops that grow in fields he believes are rightfully his. In a roughly parallel episode, the Icelandic Jokull kills the son of a known sorceress. Significantly, his powers to accomplish good, and his rightful superiority are demonstrated by the fact that only he (and not his adversary) rides a horse. In a significant parallel, when the Ponnivala account describes the heroes' enemies they are never once depicted riding a horse, while the twin protagonists in that legend often ride their magnificent steeds.

In the Ponnivala case the heroes kill a variety of adversaries, from clansmen to a Chola king, several forest hunters, and even a lone unarmed artisan who is a thief. The most dangerous opponent in this story, however, is a wild boar named King Komban.[3] He has magical powers as well as enormous physical size and strength. Komban wears a star sign on his tongue, a ring through his navel, and a small garland of flowers on his tail (figure 5.22). Komban, furthermore, believes he is destined to kill both Shankar and his brother Ponnar with his two sharp tusks. In this South Indian case these magical attributes likely reflect a much wider folk preoccupation with the supposed sinister powers of Nath yogis, a religious cult whose members roamed right across India in the Middle Ages. Overall, the central heroes in both epics have parents who resist greed and self-aggrandisement but their sons, Thorstein and Jokull in one case and Ponnar plus Shankar on the other, seem to counter those values by placing a contrasting emphasis on personal fame and power. Komban, as an animal raja or "forest king," embodies these latter two themes as well.

The Vatnsdaela Saga 183

Figure 5.21. Jokull killing the son of a sorceress.

Figure 5.22. The wild boar Komban shown with his three magical attributes.

Feuds and Arguments

In the Vatnsdaela tale every hero including Ketil, father of Thorstein the Elder, plus every generation of males to follow, kills at least one other man. And in almost every one of these violent encounters, the saga depicts the heroes' family as the one fighting for justice. Their adversaries, meanwhile, are depicted as thieves, sorcerers, or wild men of various types. For the most part, each of these encounters is almost a black versus white event. Right and wrong are clearly distinguished in this story. Furthermore, almost every encounter is between two individuals, or else describes one brave hero taking down several unrelated challengers at one go (figure 5.23). And notably, too, in this saga cousins and clansmen do not engage as adversaries (with the possible exception of a scene referred to as the Borg incident). The Ponnivala Nadu story differs from the Icelandic one in that cousins and clansmen do confront one another repeatedly (figure 5.24). More important, in the Ponnivala Nadu case enemies almost always embody mixed value messages. Evil and good are not so black and white in this South Indian case where contests are more evenly balanced and, if one looks under the surface, enemies can be seen to share many of the same values that protagonists claim as theirs.

The saga has considerably more genealogical depth that the Ponnivala story. Furthermore, one central man starts off the heroic Icelandic story while nine brothers are present at the beginning of the Ponnivala legend. These different beginnings generate a lot more opportunity for descendants of Ponnivala Nadu's original group of nine to get into arguments. They are competitors who are alive at the same time, and are men of the same generation. The Ponnivala story is also structured slightly differently in terms of its central disputes. There, the story's main feud lasts for three generations. An initial unequal division of the land between the nine brothers starts things off and then lies behind much of the rest of the story. The eldest sibling, Kolatta, is given the best and largest territory while his eight younger brothers must share a single, smaller, second parcel. The clansmen who descend from the younger eight thus nurse a grudge and try periodically to get back some of the original land they feel their forefathers had been cheated out of. That key Ponnivala disagreement lies at the heart of repeated raids and attacks, fights that get initiated in a see-saw fashion, by both sides. This major tension ends only when one of the two heroes in the third generation, Shankar (aided by his assistant Shambuga), finally kills off all his remaining male cousins. Not only is that feud nasty, but it is also not black and white. Both sides present reasonable points of view. No one can easily argue that one or the other was completely right.

In the Vatnsdaela case there is also an ongoing enmity between two important men. The dispute begins at a wedding and builds gradually. It concerns a groom-to-be (affiliated with the Borg line) and a girl from Ingimund's family. Just before the ceremony, Bergur the Bold of Borg insults Ingimund (who is the head of Bergur's family clan and host at Bergur's daughter's wedding). Bergur simply and physically shoves Ingimund to one side, but the anger generated by this insult lasts long beyond the wedding day. Finally, a duel between the two sides is proposed but the weather is terrible. The Borg group is represented by a man named Finnbogi, a friend and ally of Bergur the Bold. When Finnbogi fails to show up to fight, Jokull, the heroic son of Ingimund, goes to Finnbogi's sheep shed, drags a post taken from it out to a nearby horse field and then kills a mare there. Next, he impales the bloodied corpse of that horse on the post he brought with him. This is a vengeful act intended to shame the Borg group. Significantly, the anger generated centres on killing the opponents' female horse, which must have been a focus of their pride. Interestingly, the two horses that the Ponnivala Nadu heroes ride were also mares. This shared symbolism metaphorically suggests, in the Icelandic case, that the heroes' mare was something like his wife. Impaling that horse's head would have been the symbolic equivalent of raping her. In sum, these repeated, violent scenes have to do with the disposing of bizarre or unwanted members of society in insulting ways and, unlike in the Ponnivala story, tend to focus on the one "bad" character, in this case Bergur

Figure 5.23. Jokull killing thieves.

Figure 5.24. The clansmen begging mercy after being beaten by the twin heroes, helped out by their assistant Shambuga.

the Bold as represented by his friend Finnbogi. Often these individuals are overtly killed (or in the Borg case their family symbol is murdered and then raped). But if not, they are at least pushed out of the Vatnsdaela region forever (figure 5.25). Either way, such acts do more to cleanse the homestead valley of negativity than to extend a feud into successive generations.

The Ponnivala story is much less about individual bad apples and much more about the struggle for dominance between three types of social groups: farmers, artisans, and tribal hunters. These three communities are not treated as castes so much as they are described as representing different socio-economic clusters of people. In general, communities of non-kinsmen confront the heroes as undifferentiated social groups. Furthermore, each such group has at least some portion of "right" on their side. Take the example of the artisans. They are deprived of their land early in the story and an unfair contract is then imposed on them. No wonder they are angry. Consequently, neither the farmers nor the craftsmen have

186 Multiple Epics Compared

Figure 5.25. Jokull attacks Bergur, the man who snubbed his brother.

Figure 5.26. A group of forest hunters preparing to attack the heroes.

a monopoly on right or good. Similarly, the forest hunters in the Ponnivala story constitute a more or less undifferentiated group of adversaries (figure 5.26). Except for one female, an unmarried forest princess named Viratangal, these people are depicted as a uniform cluster of fighters. And their grudge is reasonable: for the hunters, the farmers have destroyed much of their former forest habitat as well as the animal and bird population that lived there. Thus, they have a right to be angry. As a result, the Ponnivala epic presents a more sophisticated view of society and its many woes than does the ethically much simpler Vatnsdaela story

Negative Powers and Curses

In the Vatnsdaela story there are two striking examples of women able to act negatively on others from a distance. One contorts herself, placing her head upside down and then walking backwards. The other walks counter clockwise

Figure 5.27. Komban vows to kill the twin heroes with his two tusks.

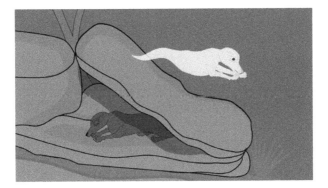

Figure 5.28. The heroine's pet dog sends a curse.

around her home (an inauspicious way to circle) while swinging a cloth full of gold back and forth. But despite these occasional examples, most of the negative magic in the Vatnsdaela story comes from men. This contrasts with the Ponnivala legend where no human male embodies negative magical power. Women, however, several times curse their own relatives. For example, the heroine Tamarai curses a group of children to punish her own brothers, making them appear to be dead for a time until she revives them later when the brothers apologize. Another difference from the Icelandic tale is that in the Ponnivala story animals generate curses too. Perhaps the most important curse of all is issued by a great black boar, an animal who vows that the twin heroes will die when pierced, one by each of his two sharp tusks (figure 5.27). Ponnacci, a tiny, magical female dog in the Ponnivala story, has the power to curse too. She sends an illness to her mistress's two brothers that cripples them and causes them lie helpless in their hunting tent while their wild adversary, the boar, roams free (figure 5.28).

188 Multiple Epics Compared

Animals and women may be more active in these magical ways in part because the animals are more humanlike in that story and many of the humans are part divine by birth. In general, identities are more fluid and are seen to cross divides like good versus bad more freely and more often in the Ponnivala case than in the Icelandic one.

Magical Tools

The topic of magical tools also touches on Icelandic and South Indian story similarities. In the Icelandic epic, the core family has its own magical ally in a sword named Aettartangi. It is believed that this sword's power has carried over, inside the heroes' family, from generation to generation. Even the hilt of this special sword is imbued with importance (figure 5.29). Swords are also important in the Ponnivala legend. But in this case their power derives from a virgin's blessing, one that must be reapplied each time the heroes leave on a new mission (figure 5.30). A separate tool used by women in this epic, the winnowing fan, has to do with prediction. The winnowing fan helps to ascertain if the blessings she is planning to give are warranted at all. The heroes' sister, Tangal, uses her winnowing fan to determine if her brothers will die when they leave for the hunt they are planning. Their goal is to seek out and kill their greatest adversary, a huge wild boar. Standing in front of the family's local temple before they leave, Tangal tosses a handful of seeds in the air. Her brothers are to swing their swords and split each seed in half as it falls. When the test is over, she picks up the results from the ground at their feet and places them in her winnowing fan (figure 5.30). She notices that two of those seeds did not get split, which to her indicates that her brothers' lives will soon be lost. In other words, the winnowing fan helps Tangal to recognize and separate different kinds of outcomes, just as a winnowing fan is normally used to separate grain from chaff. In this case, she learns the future through this ritual and realizes that it would be pointless to bless her brothers' swords knowing that they are going to die anyway. Figure 5.31 shows that she did bless her brothers' swords earlier in the story, but there is no mention of her doing this before the final battle they fight, precisely because she never does so!

To sum up, the Vatnsdaela story portrays multiple human male sorcerers, but only a few female ones. In the Ponnivala epic, by contrast, all acts of magic or sorcery stem from women or certain animals who are also endowed with this power. In general, the powers of women are given greater importance in the Ponnivala case than in the Icelandic epic. **Resistance**, of course, lies at the heart of many stories, worldwide, and can be intertwined with supernatural powers. But the details that accompany such acts vary significantly between these two culture areas discussed above.

The Vatnsdaela Saga 189

Figure 5.29. The hero Jokull blesses others with his magical sword.

Figure 5.30. Tangal conducts a divination ritual using her winnowing fan.

Figure 5.31. The heroes' virgin sister blesses the heroes' swords before an early battle.

Theme Four: Resilience

Climate Struggles

The comparison between South India's Ponnivala legend and Iceland's Vatnsdaela Saga appears to be quite straight forward where climate is concerned. Iceland is cold and snowy. Therefore, to establish a toehold in this new land the story's characters must confront the hardships of deep snow and cold temperatures, especially during their first winter. That physical reality causes the young heroic family to suffer. They have to live together in one simple home just to keep warm, and also because of a scarcity of trees, a key source of building materials (figure 5.32). However, when summer does finally arrive, this first family is able to begin their farming efforts right away. The hardship is that there are no nearby human settlers at all in this vacant land, rather than what the Ponnivala heroes had to face, that is, multiple hostile neighbours.

In both Iceland and in South India, the first challenges facing the newcomers are environmental, ice and snow in one setting versus drought and heat in the other. The nine brothers that the goddess created and set down in a forest begin their new lives by sharing a single home. But very soon they face a serious climatic challenge when the land around them becomes hot and dry. Although these nine men start to plough and irrigate, all their work turns to naught and everything green withers and becomes brown (figure 5.33). As a result, all nine men have to pull up stakes and relocate. Kolatta leaves first but eventually his other eight brothers all follow. In a twist of good fortune, these nine siblings find a neighbouring kingdom where the drought has not hit. They are taken in there as labourers by a kind king. After pleasing this monarch with their hard work, the king decides to thank the immigrants by suggesting they become pioneers. He would like to give them a fresh assignment: opening up a new region. To do this he sends all nine men upriver, ordering them to begin cultivation in an uncharted area he has heard of and which he calls Ponnivala Nadu.

The nine brothers were told to cut down the trees and tame this wild and remote region by ploughing the land there for the first time. But a surprise awaits. The land in question is not empty! Instead, there are many artisan families already living there. Furthermore, these artisans believe that this local area belongs to them so, naturally, they confront the farmers and complain. These local resisters, plus a group of tribal allies who inhabit the nearby forested hills, soon make plenty of trouble for the newly arrived ploughmen (figure 5.34). Their joint animosity towards plough-farming runs deep and it colours the entire story. Thus, in both epics a harsh climate shapes the heroes' early actions, but the kind of resilience required is different in each case. In the Icelandic story it is other settlers from Norway who arrive just a bit later and then compete with the heroes' family (figure 5.35). In the Ponnivala case it is the indigenous

Figure 5.32. First winter home for the Vatnsdaela pioneers.

Figure 5.33. Heat plus a serious drought during the first summer for the nine South Indian pioneers.

occupants of the land in question who resist and argue that the land belongs to them. In the Icelandic case it is the heroes who are the resisters and who do not welcome further immigrants to the area., Still, the harsh environment both groups of settlers find themselves in has an unspoken positive influence: in each situation the harsh climate helps to mould a **resilient** forefather who later makes his descendants proud.

Prominent and Resilient Women

The Vatnsdaela Saga and the Legend of Ponnivala Nadu each feature a prominent and very resilient woman who becomes mother to a set of male heroes in the next generation. In the saga we learn very little about Vigdis except that she is clearly a strong and good person who undergoes (at least one) childbirth alone

192   Multiple Epics Compared

Figure 5.34. The ploughmen prepare for local resistance.

Figure 5.35. The landing of additional settlers is resisted by the heroes who had arrived first.

in a forest under difficult circumstances. That first child is a daughter, but she also, later, bears two sons. This is very similar to the Ponnivala Nadu heroine Tamarai (figure 5.36) who also has a daughter and two sons. The difference is that this time the three are all born at once as a set of triplets. Tamarai's life also differs in that she suffers years of barrenness while Vigdis has no problem at all with fertility. However, Tamarai's determination to bear children despite her perceived handicap, is exceptional. This is illustrated by her twenty-one-year quest to obtain help from Lord Shiva himself. Prior to being granted that gift, Tamarai's resilience while sitting on a pillar praying, through sun, wind, rain and cold, is striking. When she eventually does give birth to triplets, that scene, too, is also memorable for its hardship. An evil midwife blindfolds her and plans to kill Tamarai's two male heirs-to-be, but instead the two boys are taken and hidden by the local goddess until they reach five years of age. Unaware of this intrigue, Tamarai suffers during this entire period believing that Shiva's gift of

Figure 5.36. Kunnutaiya's wife Tamarai.

sons had never materialized! Of course, as discussed before, she eventually learns the truth, which makes her very happy.

In both epics, then, motherhood is honoured through richly textured scenes. Both epics describe their core heroines as mothers who have great courage and the willingness to make self-sacrifices for the benefit of their close family members. In addition, as described previously, Tamarai was born magically from a red lotus flower, and hence it is no accident that her name means lotus in Tamil. The flower is her symbol and it is certainly one of resilience. The lotus, as it grows up from the mud through water, produces a single bloom that sits atop a long stem. That stem provides this flower with its own personal pillar as it tries to reach the sky, which makes the reasoning behind her name even more appropriate. The final chapter will discuss the lotus image and unpack its significance as a central Ponnivala story symbol in much more depth.

The two epics under study are also similar at their core because both describe a struggle over the issue of inheritance. Who will inherit the main leadership position? In the saga this struggle is heightened by the fact that a girl is born first. In the Ponnivala story the problem arises because the potential heir is an adopted son rather than a biological one. No one even knows who his parents were because he was simply found under a pile of stones in a back field. In the Ponnivala case, furthermore, barrenness is featured as key and recurring issue. But moving to a somewhat higher level, both epics revolve around the definition of a central family line and its members' many struggles to retain its local status. This issue hangs over both stories like a dark grey cloud.

Furthermore, the issue of adoption is important in both the Vatnsdaela Saga and in the Legend of Ponnivala Nadu. And the imagery used to describe this situation is surprisingly similar. One of Ingimund's great grandsons, Goat Thigh, was born out of wedlock to the mistress of Ingimund's grandson Thorgrim (figure 5.37). On the command of Thorgrim's wife, that baby boy, who was named Thorkel, was

Figure 5.37. Thorkel, nicknamed Goat Thigh, the orphan adopted by Thorir eventually becomes a respected elder.

Figure 5.38. Kolatta finds a baby under a rock pile and adopts him. He eventually becomes king Kunnutaiya.

left out in the cold to die. But Thorstein, another son of Ingimund, felt compassion for this little baby who was nearly dead when found. Thorstein spoke with another brother, Thorir, and asked him to raise the child. Significantly, in terms of its symbolism, Thorkel was discovered lying on bare earth, but his body was somewhat hidden, and his face was covered. Did this mean he was born of the land itself? Thorir agreed to take on the responsibility of caring for the boy, while his brother Thorstein called on the sun to help him out.

In the Ponnivala Nadu story every descendant of the pioneer grandfather Kolatta was created at least in part by Lord Shiva (who himself bears several mythological links to the sun). In the Ponnivala parallel we have earlier noted that Shiva created a male child whom he hid under a rock pile. Kolatta found that babe with the help of others, and in particular, with the help of a cow (figure 5.38). This gives Kunnutaiya a mythological link to the soil as well, and more expansively,

The Vatnsdaela Saga   195

Figure 5.39. Kunnutaiya's two sons, raised by a goddess for five years.

to the fields and pastures of Ponnivala in general. Kolatta and his wife raise their adopted son with love and care, calling him Kunnutaiya or "boy of the rock pile."

In the next generation the goddess Cellatta secretly adopts the queen's twin boys at their birth (as mentioned above) and quickly carries them through a secret tunnel to a cave under her temple. There the goddess's personal tiger plays with them regularly and nurses them on tiger's milk. This cave gives these two boys a further link to the land, and to the local goddess living there (figure 5.39). The two boys are also orphans, in large part, as they were adopted by this goddess at their birth and no one (locally at least) knows where they came from. After the five years are up the goddess delivers the twins to their biological birth mother plus their social-but-not-quite-biological father. However, no one (except the gods) knows that they are really the birth-children of Tamarai herself.

Ingimund, Thorstein's only son, becomes a main story hero at the start of the saga. He matures early and is both handsome and talented. As a young man, we have learned above, he became Viking raider (figure 5.40). Later, however, Ingimund became a wealthy farmer after successfully settling in Iceland, and importantly, he always remained loyal to the king of Norway. When he later made a return trip to Norway, he took gifts to the king and in turn, received various material rewards from that monarch. Ingimund also received a talisman that he used to mark his identity as an ally of his Norwegian benefactor. Soon after this Ingimund married a high-status Norwegian woman whom he took back to Iceland with him. Similarly, Kunnutaiya was Kolatta's only son and he matured early too. When still young Kunnutaiya had to resist the attempts of several mean clansmen who tried to abuse him and take advantage of his pitiful condition after he was suddenly orphaned at the age of six. But Kunnutaiya defied all odds and fended for himself as he grew into adolescence. He, too, eventually married a woman of high status, and soon after that he managed to locate and reoccupy his father's old homestead lands. Kunnutaiya re-established the family line there and accumulated substantial wealth as he aged (figure 5.41).

196 Multiple Epics Compared

Figure 5.40. A young Ingimund on horseback.   Figure 5.41. Kunnutaiya as an adult.

Figure 5.42. Ingimund as a senior, wise leader.   Figure 5.43. Kunnutaiya giving advice in his senior years.

A Leader Loyal to the King

Ingimund and Kunnutaiya were both loyal to a great king, in the former case this was the king of Norway, in the latter it was an unnamed Chola monarch from whom the hero eventually received honours and a small crown. Both men were loyal allies who the two respective monarchs could trust, and both controlled territory in an outpost area that the king, somewhat tentatively, held sway over. Both Ingimund and Kunnutaiya, furthermore, were even-handed rulers who cared deeply for their subjects (figures 5.42 and 5.43). Each was also a heroic father and a clan hero, and both grew wise in their later years. To top off all that, both had a set of two sons, men who inherited some of their father's reputation and honour. There are many ways, then in which the key

Figure 5.44. Ingimund's wedding.

heroes of the second generation, in both stories, bear a striking resemblance to each other.

Theme Five: Relationships

Weddings – Creating a New Relationship

Weddings are a key means by which kin bonds are created. In the Vatnsdaela Saga a giving his daughter away in marriage is understood to be an important gift that a father makes to his future son-in-law (figure 5.44). This is an old Indo-European tradition with wide reach, and it is linked to the concept of dowry. The same tradition is also prominent in India. However, this custom was not previously the norm among non-Brahman groups in the South Indian Kongu Nadu area where the Ponnivala Nadu story takes place. There, in past centuries, wedding gifts conventionally travelled in the opposite direction, that is from the groom's family to the bride's, a custom known as bride price. To further accentuate this difference, in the Ponnivala heroes' wedding (described previously in chapter 2), the twins undergo what is called a "uniting ceremony" (innai cir). Their sister, Tangal, holds a winnowing basket on her head during this ritual and it contains both the wedding sari and necklace that the groom will give his bride at the high point in the rituals to come. A sari is also held between the brother and sister, under their arms. That cloth is used to symbolize the idea that this specific brother-sister relationship is expected to remain intact in the years to come (figure 5.45). Indeed, it is hoped that brother's marriage will only make this bond stronger, because it is hoped that the daughter of that brother will one day marry his sister's son (called a cross-cousin marriage). The two epics studied here, then, endorse opposing, but related, wedding gift concepts: one where the

Figure 5.45. Uniting ceremony for Ponnar and his sister: these two are marked with a white oval.

bride is given to the husband along with gifts and the other one where the bride is exchanged for gifts from the husband's family. That difference stems from the two very different cultural milieus in which the two stories were nurtured. However, in the end, both epics emphasize that marriages create important future bonds between two families.

In-Law Animosity

Relationships created at marriage, however, can also bring animosity and it is often up to the women of a family to try to smooth these over. There is a long tradition, seen in many cultures, of women acting as intermediaries to resolve tense family problems, especially those created through marriage. There is just one good example of this in the Vatnsdaela Saga but there are many in the Ponnivala Legend. In Vatnsdaela there is enmity between the hero Ingimund and the father of the woman he wishes to marry (figure 5.46). This is because Ingimund had earlier murdered this man's son, the brother of his own hoped-for bride. The bride's mother then interceded on Ingimund's behalf and cooled her husband's animosity. The wedding proceeded. In a similar vein, there is a very direct intercession by a female advocate on behalf of someone else's interests in the Ponnivala Nadu case. However, that incident occurs, not on earth but among the gods. There we see the Parvati speaking to her husband Shiva at the request of her brother Vishnu (figure 5.47). She asks him to soften his attitude towards Tamarai for the sake of her brother, Shiva's brother-in-law. Significantly, she succeeds in this request. Shiva listens to her pleas and acts accordingly.

Later in the Ponnivala Nadu story Kunnutaiya's wife Tamarai advocates on the behalf of beggars, persuading her husband to soften his resistance to her spending

The Vatnsdaela Saga   199

Figure 5.46. Ingimund tries to win hand of Vigdis but her father resists.

Figure 5.47. Parvati intercedes with Shiva on her brother Vishnu's behalf.

the family fortune on alms. This pattern of providing go-between services is less pronounced in the next generation where the key females (Tangal and her hunter counterpart Viratangal) operate more as visionary advisers who try to help their brothers specifically, rather than advocating for generosity by all. As sisters rather than wives, one of a woman's central responsibilities is to uncover and hand along useful information to the males who are a part of her family. As seers both Tangal and Viratangal have access, through visions, to situations evolving outside the palace. Speaking abstractly, these young women also help to mediate between the outsiders' and the family's points of view.

Horses

The cooperative team composed of a magnificent horse and its rider function as an important prestige symbol in both the Vatnsdaela and Ponnivala epic stories.

Figure 5.48. The mature leader Ingimund on his horse (see also figure 5.40).

Figure 5.49. Shankar riding his magical horse.

In each epic the heroes' horses (and/or those of their close allies) are thought to have special powers. In the Vatnsdaela Saga horses with magical attributes are always seen working for the heroes, but not for the villains (figure 5.48). In the Ponnivala story the twin heroes of the third generation are the only ones to ride horses. These fine animals are blue-black in colour and lovely songs describe their unique speed and deft footwork (figure 5.49). The forest-dwelling hunters who live in the hills nearby are described as having a horse stable, too, but the hunters never ride these animals themselves. One suspects this reflects the (unstated) fact that multiple Chola kings were known to own horses and elephants that were grazed by their forest keepers in the hills nearby, but that those caregivers were not given riding privileges.

Horses in both stories are used to either pull or carry important things. In the Vatnsdaela Saga a magical horse (Freyfaxi) is described as pulling a winter

The Vatnsdaela Saga 201

Figure 5.50. The magical horse Freyfaxi pulls a sled.

Figure 5.51. Ponnar carries tribute to the king on his magical horse.

sled that several of the heroes ride in (figure 5.50). In the Ponnivala case the heroes' two magical steeds never pull anything, but Ponnar does carry all-important tribute to the king on his featured horse (figure 5.51). Also interesting is the fact that Shambuga, the Ponnivala heroes' key assistant, never ever rides a horse although he is the stable keeper and knows these prize animals' ways very well. Instead, Shambuga is a man who embodies the magical powers of those horses in his own body. He is often described as running after his masters' two galloping steeds and, surprisingly, he is always able to keep up with them (figure 5.52). Shambuga also fashions halters made from viper skins for his masters' two horses. Those skins possibly transfer the power of the feared viper snake to the heads of the horses wearing that gear, perhaps lending them powers such as those Freyfaxi has in the Icelandic story. Thus, the relationship between horse and hero is all-important in both contexts. The horse the hero rides functions as

Figure 5.52. Shambuga runs behind Shankar's magical horse.

a prime prestige symbol, but also as an extension of his unique personality: This steed embodies the hero's strength, valour and, no less important, his handsome self-presentation. Furthermore, these horses are supremely loyal to their masters in both epics.

Divination and Prophecy

It is also interesting to compare the concepts of divination and prophecy depicted by descriptions provided in these two epic legends. In Norway and Iceland both, magicians and sorcerers were largely male, although at least one female described by each story does share some related traits. In Iceland, a fair proportion of those marginalized and dangerous sorcerers were thought to come from Lapland, a place even farther away than Norway and a locale with a significantly different culture. And in addition to that, several other Vatnsdaela Saga characters are described as "berserks." This label is quite possibly linked to their habit of using hallucinogenic mushrooms to aid them with their divination work. Three close male friends, for example, follow the consumption of magic mushrooms with a "flight-via-the-mind" from Norway to Iceland, a journey considered possible only with the help of shamanistic powers (figure 5.53). The three friends hope to locate a gold ring they believe a sorceress previously buried there as discussed earlier. But in the end, it is Ingimund himself whose heroic stature allowed him to find that golden treasure, thus showing that his own special powers supersede those of any ambitious outside visitor.

In the Ponnivala story, by contrast, it is only the women who have shamanistic power. The most important female who is endowed in this way is the heroine Tangal, sister of the legend's twin heroes. As her story unfolds her powers grow. At first, she simply exhibits a surprising ability to see what is happening

Figure 5.53. Would-be shamans preparing to fly.

Figure 5.54. Tangal flies on the back of a goose.

at a distance through dreams, but this visionary gift gradually develops into still other magical gifts. Eventually Tangal, like the berserks, exhibits an ability to fly (figure 5.54). She too can divine the future using specific ritual gestures. Just before her two brothers leave for an important battle, for example, she performs a very specific divination rite as seen earlier in figure 5.30. Other examples of her magic are discussed elsewhere. In Ponnivala then, women monopolize all the local shamanistic power available, unlike in the Icelandic case where those powers are shared by both genders. Why is this important in relationship terms? It takes a special kind of skill to interact with non-human powers and be able to influence, manipulate, and repel them, according to the need at hand. This shared body of beliefs and understandings about spirit powers provides a key to understanding the heroes and heroines of both epic legends.

Figure 5.55. Three-eyed Finnish fortune teller Finla hides the ring Ingimund must later find.

Figure 5.56. Tangal tells her brothers she cannot bless their swords.

The Vatnsdaela story mentions several female fortune tellers, the most prominent being the Finnish woman Finla. She had the power to steal and then bury a gold ring belonging to Ingimund, using it to mark the place in Iceland where she predicts he will build a future homestead as per the gold ring story above (figure 5.55). Tangal is also able to manipulate the future by refusing to embody an important object with a special power its owner wishes for. Tangal uses her special powers of perception in an especially amazing way, late in the epic story. This occurs just after she learns, in the winnowing fan divination rite discussed previously, that her brothers will never return home from their next adventure. Tangal is always expected to bless her brothers' swords before their departure on a new adventure, but now, for the first time, she denies them this magical aid. Tangal makes a secret decision not to not bless the heroes' principal weapons before they leave the palace. Then she cleverly notes, in conversation, that her two

Figure 5.57. A sorceress.

Figure 5.58. Tangal with her magical pet dog, Ponnacci.

Figure 5.59. Jokull ready to kill his enemy named Leather Cap.

brothers failed to ask her to do this before they placed their powerful swords in the scabbards they had strapped to their waists. She tells them that it is now too late (figure 5.56). Then, in line with that winnowing fan omen, the two heroes die on this last mission and never return home. They only see their sister one final time after their demise deep in the forest, the moment when she finds their bodies and magically brings them back to life for just a few minutes.

It is interesting that sorcery or negative magic finds differing styles of symbolic expression in the two epics being discussed. In the Vatnsdaela case the sorceress delivers a negative spell by inverting her body and then walking backwards (figure 5.57). She does this to try to overcome the hero, Jokull, and the power she presumes he has to take revenge on her son. Jokull was angry at the boy because of an insult. In contrast, in the Ponnivala tale Tangal's more subtle anger is directed at her own two brothers. This happens when they cease expressing concern for her welfare. Her fury is then expressed through (perhaps projected into?) her tiny, female, earless dog (figure 5.58). The dog, Ponnacci, sends a message to her brothers in the form of a dream-curse that makes both brothers sicken in their war tent. The heroes are then essentially incapacitated until the younger, Shankar, makes amends for them both, expressing his humility via a humble apology to Ponnacci for their oversight.

It is interesting to note that swords and other long vicious weapons also have special magical powers in both these epic stories. In the Vatnsdaela case, as mentioned earlier, Jokull uses the sword passed down in his family, which has its own personality and also its own name, Aettartangi (figure 5.59). In the Ponnivala story the heroes' swords do not have names or personalities but they do take on special powers due to sister's blessings, notably when the Tangal gives them fresh power just before their use (figure 5.60).

Figure 5.60. Tangal, in this instance, blessing her brothers' swords.

Theme Six: Reflection

Elder and Younger Brothers

The contrast between a pair of elder and younger brothers is an important theme that can be found widely in the world's folklore. It is not a surprise, therefore, to discover that this concept is present in both the Vatnsdaela Saga and the Legend of Ponnivala Nadu. Indeed, the similarities in how twinship functions in these two stories is quite striking. In each account the brothers frequently appear and act together as a set, even though they differ significantly in their individual personalities. In both stories, as well, these two prominent brothers are heroes in the third generation, not counting (as reasoned earlier) the mention of several additional Vatnsdaela ancestors who appear briefly, before Ingimund himself steps onto the stage. Why do they each enter the story so late, if they are such important characters? The answer appears to relate to what a pair of twins really represents. As mentioned earlier, a paired set of leaders stands for a principle of balance. A good leader must have many abilities. He should be kind, thoughtful, generous, and empathic on the one hand, but also at times he must be physically aggressive, even domineering, in order to vanquish challengers. Twins embody this dilemma by acting together as a set. Notably, in both tales, it is the elder brother who is the more passive, attentive, and considerate of others. The younger, by contrast, is faster to anger, physically stronger, and more sensitive to insults. For example, Phorsteinn (the elder, on the left in figure 5.61) holds a sword but it is still in its sheath. His cape is blue in the original image and there is no blood around him. Standing right beside him on the right is the younger brother Jokull, in a red cape. He grasps an unsheathed sword that is covered with blood! Furthermore, Jokull stands in the centre of the picture while his elder brother stands to one side. In a parallel illustration from the Ponnivala legend, we see the two brothers in a similar pose. Ponnar, the elder (on the left), wears blue pants while Shankar, the younger

The Vatnsdaela Saga 207

Figure 5.61. Elder and younger brothers Phorsteinn and Jokull.

Figure 5.62. The Ponnivala twins run towards danger with Shankar in the lead.

(on the right) wears red ones (figure 5.62). Furthermore, Shankar runs in the lead, is seen closer to the centre, and his arm positions are more energized than are his twin's whose arms are lowered. It just takes one image, in each case, to clearly convey the idea that the elder twin is a follower while his younger brother is the lead, always the instigator when it comes to new adventures. Not only is the elder brother contrasted with the younger in these images: in each case the younger is also subtly favoured.

Describing a set of twins can be like studying one character but seeing it twice, once straight on and once in a curved circus-style mirror. The image seen in the latter mirror is distorted, sometimes more and sometimes less so. This reflection concept answers a long-standing question the Ponnivala story raises: why is the younger and more violent hero, the one who breaks the law and does outrageous things, the popular favourite? He would be the one seen in the circus mirror, more interesting, more mercurial, and more entertaining. But thought about

Figure 5.63. Ponnar and Shankar lie dead, with Shambuga close beside them.

more deeply, this aggressive younger twin gives voice to many individuals' inner, personal drive to affirm their own self-importance, as well as to control those who are more timid and humble. This is a drive all humans struggle with. Both stories, in sum, hide deep paradigms inside their paired male heroes. They also lay some of these deep assumptions bare whenever that set of twins appear side by side.

The Death of a Hero

Ingimund dies of a sword wound. Then two of his close friends quickly pierce their own breasts with swords as well, expressing their loyalty to him. (No image is available for this act in the case of the saga). Both friends die, of course, right alongside the epic hero himself. Their mutual and shared ending closely resembles the deaths of the two heroes in the Ponnivala story. Ponnar and Shankar die a heroic double-death, when they fall on the tips of their own swords (figure 5.63). Quickly following this, their loyal assistant Shambuga also kills himself, right at their side. Even though the death of the main saga character, Ingimund, and the death of the twins of the Ponnivala legend are not precisely parallel in religious terms, the hero(es) in both epics do die from sword wounds. Even more similar are the deaths of their closest supporters who, in each case, take their own lives in a similar way. By their own dramatic actions, then, each symbolically reflects a deep loyalty felt towards a beloved leader or, in the Ponnivala case, a pair of leaders.

Birds

Ravens are important in both the Vatnsdaela and the Ponnivala epics. In the former they appear just as the hero Ingimund kills a wealthy robber. They

Figure 5.64. Ravens associated with death of a robber killed by Ingimund.

Figure 5.65. Tangal feeding ravens as part of the rituals for her brothers' funerals.

represent the spirit of the deceased departing towards the sky the moment it is released from the corpse (figure 5.64). In a related Icelandic tradition from the same period the Norse pagan god Odin befriends two ravens Huginn and Muninn, two birds that liked to sit on his shoulders. They were his messengers, and they are linked by scholars to various shamanistic practices of the period. In addition, a raven banner was flown by several Viking and Scandinavian rulers during the nineth, tenth, and eleventh centuries. Birds, especially crows, are important in a similar way in South India as they represent a family's ancestors coming back for a visit (figure 5.65) In South India there is, furthermore, a similar and very well-known image visible on the famous sculpted rock cliff at Mahabalipuram (figure 5.66). There two birds sit near the left shoulder of the famous image of the Mahabharata hero Arjuna. In that carving, we see Arjuna as an extremely emaciated penitent. He is likely

Figure 5.66. Arjuna's penance, Mahabalipuram sculpture, South India, showing two birds near the hero's right shoulder.

near death's door. Although these two South Indian birds do not have a raven shape, they echo another segment of the Ponnivala story where Tamarai (Arjuna's double) is doing penance and two parrots, previously nesting inside her, leave her body.[4] In the Ponnivala story, furthermore, we see not two but a whole flock of ravens arriving for a funeral feast of cooked rice that the heroes' sister throws to them in a ritual that follows her two brothers' deaths. Those birds are believed to be feasting on behalf of those twin heroes' departed spirits. This striking set of parallels between the old Norse and Dravidian South Indian traditions surrounding ravens and death is quite surprising. The similarity likely reflects a pan Indo-European set of symbolic traditions regarding birds and the concept of the spirit separating from the human body during the final moment of life.

Special Gifts

Giving gifts that show respect is another important theme in both the Vatnsdaela Saga and the Legend of Ponnivala. Gift giving helps to bind the two parties to a transaction and creates a sense of future obligation implying that more transactions will also occur in time. The most famous gift in the Vatnsdaela story is Ingimund's discovery of two polar bear cubs on the sea ice, along with those cubs' mother. He decides to take all three to the king of Norway to thank him for his support and as gesture of his intention to remain the king's loyal ally (figure 5.67). Although not nearly as grandiose, in the Ponnivala epic Kunnutaiya takes a gift to the Chola king, the distant ruler who earlier sponsored his settlement in the Ponnivala Nadu area. Kunnutaiya gives the king a gift of fine curds made from the milk of his family cow (figure 5.68). He also

Figure 5.67. Ingimund's gift of a mother polar bear and her two cubs to the king of Norway.

Figure 5.68. Kunnutaiya on his way to make a gift of fine curds to the Chola king.

plans to report on the progress of the fine maize crop he has planted. He had just measured the impressive yield generated by that first crop and (with a little help from Lord Vishnu) he wants to thank the king for his help in backing this pioneering agricultural effort. Both kings are pleased with these gifts and recognize the importance of maintaining their positive political alliance with their distant regional leader. In the Vatnsdaela case the king gives Ingimund a marvellous ship in return, one of the finest of its day, and even puts wind in its sails (figure 5.69). He also gives his visitor some gold and a stash of fine building wood to take home in his new vessel. Ingimund brings all this back to Iceland and builds a fine shelter for his boat on the inlet near his home. He hopes it will weather the hardship of many winters. Of course, this is an ostentatious gift, a fitting exchange for the receipt of a fine mother polar bear and her cubs! Kunnutaiya receives something equally grand from the Chola king,

Figure 5.69. The Norwegian king gave Ingimund a very special boat.

Figure 5.70. The Chola king gives Kunnutaiya a very special crown.

though in size it is much smaller. The reciprocal gift he receives is a small crown that he can wear proudly and show off to the residents of Ponnivala Nadu (figure 5.70). It symbolizes the Chola's respect for Kunnutaiya's success and his acknowledgment of this hero's proven power as an entrepreneur. Of course, he is also in the process of building up a new local economy that will benefit the Chola directly. Neither king mentions the expectation that taxes or tribute will be generated and brought to him regularly in the future, but that is an obvious and likely assumption that a king might make. We can certainly suspect that both monarchs had already thought about the potential future revenue that Vatnsdaela and Ponnivala might generate. Whatever the case, in both stories acquiring a new outlying region managed by an important and friendly ally represents a fresh and positive political extension, a new arm so-to-speak, of that king's own growing power.

Theme Seven: Revelation

Insiders and Outsiders: Social Rights

In both the Vatnsdaela Saga and the Legend of Ponnivala Nadu there are stories about outsiders arriving and being resisted by locals. In the Ponnivala case it is the hero who must overcome the threats of residents who were already living there when he and his brothers arrived. In the Vatnsdaela scenario, the hero got there first and then must resist an ambitious man who arrives later at the same locale and has similar pioneering plans. A foreign boat lands near Ingimund's homestead, and as a leader and first man of the area, Ingimund goes to meet at vessel and its skipper, Hrafn, as it is docking. Ingimund politely offers to let this new arrival stay in his home as a guest and Hrafn accepts. But there was a custom requiring the first man to meet any ship would be allowed select from its wares whatever item he fancied most. Hrafn had a fine sword with him that Ingimund admired and which he asked to have given to him. Hrafn refused and Ingimund nursed that rebuff as an insult. Sometime later the two men went to Ingimund's homestead shrine together. Ingimund went in first. Then he turned around and found Hrafn coming at him with his sword drawn. Ingimund was now doubly angered and announced that no sword should ever be drawn inside a sacred temple. He then asked that Hrafn hand over his sword to pay amends to the gods, which Hrafn did this time. However, soon afterwards, knowing he had been outsmarted, he left the area for good. His fine sword was treasured by Ingimund (figure 5.71). and was later handed down to his two sons and, from there, on to their descendants. This is the same sword, named Aettartangi, that Ingimund eventually passed to his son Jokull.

There is a somewhat similar but inverted set of stories about Kolatta and his grandsons that also describes a sword fight. Again, a god gets involved. This time, the test is one where an outsider (newcomer) confronts an insider (an existing inhabitant). But now the outsider, not the earlier resident, is backed by divine will. As has already been noted previously in this book, the Ponnivala Nadu story suggests that artisans, not farming pioneers, were the first settlers to inhabit this area. Furthermore, the artisans were specialists in smelting and forging, so they were likely sword makers as well.[5] Kolatta was the newcomer and he had arrived with a plough, not a sword. Ponnivala's resident artisans resisted Kolatta's desire to plough their lands and, therefore, threw their swords at him, attempting to behead this newcomer (figure 5.72). But Lord Vishnu quickly stepped in and rendered those artisans' swords ineffective against the story's clan ancestor, Kolatta. Vishnu then announced a social contract that he intended to enforce on all. In that contract, Vishnu awarded the heroes' family the sole right to plough the lands of Ponnivala. That pronouncement significantly diminished the artisan's social status and handed leadership, prestige, and power to the farmers. Later the grandsons

214   Multiple Epics Compared

Figure 5.71. Hero Ingimund with the magical sword he obtained from Hrafn.

Figure 5.72. An artisan throws his sword at Kolatta.

of Kolatta carry fine swords while the Vettuva hunters carry only sticks. Even the artisan thief in this story is made fun of by the story tellers on account of a sword he tries to steal (see figure 5.73). It is as if the right to bear a sword became an exclusive privilege claimed by the area's immigrant farmer-kings, and that swords were no longer an appropriate weapon that any other category of person had the right to use.

In Ponnivala Nadu furthermore, the power of the sword did not determine the hierarchy of social rights, instead the gods did. They favoured progress and backed the Chola king's plan to colonize the area. When Vishnu intervened soon after the first-generation pioneers entered Ponnivala Nadu, he managed to lessen the power of the artisans' swords by manipulating the outcome of Kolatta's contest with the prior residents of this area. Vishnu not only protected Kolatta from the swords those prior residents threw at him, he also devised a special contract; every

Figure 5.73. An artisan tries to steal Ponnar and Shankar's special swords.

time the artisans made a new wooden plough they were to be paid with three full measures of farmers' grain. That might sound fair, but in fact it made the artisans into occasional service providers who did not even have the power to set a price on their own labour. Perhaps the difference between the Ponnivala Nadu and Vatnsdaela Saga's sword stories, then, is not as great as it might seem. In each case the sword become a vehicle of a god's own greater will. Most notably, in both legends one great sword (or a set of twin swords) protects the hero and affirms his superiority and his local control, in the face of all his angry adversaries.

The sword in both stories, furthermore, can be seen to be a kind of symbolic vessel. That vessel contains a hidden fate, a knowledge that is beyond the power of its owner to fully grasp. In other words, the sword itself gets to decide who should win a contest. The Ponnivala story goes even further in this matter. In the third generation, Kolatta's grandsons both own swords. The twin boys were born with the weapons already in their hands, swords which we can assume must have grown larger as the twins matured. Meanwhile, the original inhabitants' descendants who still lived there, the artisans, continued to hold a grudge against the farmer-heroes' family. Afterall, they had taken away the prior residents' land and caused it to be ploughed. Now, as we shall see, the swords themselves tell the reader (or listener) that fine swords automatically know when they have been disrespected. In the relevant story chapter, a wicked artisan tries to grab Ponnar and Shankar's swords by sneaking into their palace storeroom in the dead of night (figure 5.73). But the thief fails. One of the swords in question suddenly acquires moral agency and itself wounds the thief who is trying to steal it (figure 5.74). Skipping a few in-between events, the tables turn even further the next morning. Shankar arrives on horseback and beheads the thief during a subsequent trick he tries to pull off, one that directly threatens the life of Shankar's elder brother Ponnar. In successfully beheading the artisan in this latter scene, Shankar uses the exact same palace sword that the villain had earlier tried to steal!

216   Multiple Epics Compared

Figure 5.74. The sword wounds the thief in response to his treachery.

Wild Lands and Magic

In both the Vatnsdaela Saga and the Legend of Ponnivala, the area's wild, upland, mountainous areas are symbolically important. In the Icelandic case these hills present a major contrast with the much flatter farmed or grazed lands the heroes are actively cultivating. Here we see a lovely homestead valley that is hemmed in by rocky hills of volcanic origin (figure 5.75). Those hills are where the magicians, sorcerers, and spirit beings roam and thus are dangerous areas not to be entered without due thought. The flat lands of Ponnivala are a little more expansive, but nonetheless they are also surrounded by high hills that the story describes as filled with wild animals and fierce tribal hunters (figure 5.76). The paths leading into that forested area, furthermore, are filled with thorns. A wild boar living there threatens all intruders and a fierce goddess (Kali) reigns supreme over this area. It is a no man's land that is shadowed in mystery. As a result, in both stories the underlying, spatially distinct categories are quite obvious. These are wild versus civilized, chaos versus order, and danger versus safety.

The Vatnsdaela Saga speaks of Porolfur (the dark-skinned troublemaker) who lives in a fortress in the hills, a man suspected of sorcery and related acts that involve multiple animal sacrifices. The story hero in the third generation, Jokull, manages to scale Porolfur's defensive hill fortress in an attempt to destroy him (figure 5.77). In the Ponnivala Legend, events in the third generation also involve a fortified dwelling situated deep in the forest. Shankar has an assistant who visits that awesome, fortified place on his behalf. Though Shambuga does not scale the hunter's palace (figure 5.78) or enter inside it, he does manage to talk with the princess there using cleverly chosen words. Using deception, he persuades her to let him take away a valuable stash of iron rods. But that expedition is dangerous. Tigers and cobras live in the forest that surrounds the hunters' palace. It is

The Vatnsdaela Saga 217

Figure 5.75. The wild, rocky cliffs of Vatnsdaela.

Figure 5.76. The forbidding, forested hills that surround Ponnivala Nadu.

Figure 5.77. Jokull climbs a fortress wall in pursuit of Porolfur.

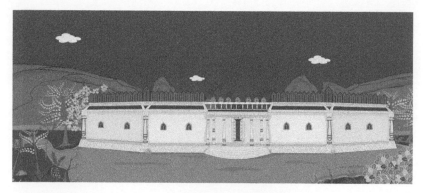

Figure 5.78. The hunters' palace with mountain visible behind it.

also interesting to learn that the princess there can speak to these fierce animals and that she has befriended them. Indeed, she has them agree to function as her guards. Among other things, Viratangal asks that five thousand tigers and five thousand cobras protect her two most treasured parrots, a pair mentioned earlier in discussions about birds and about Tangal and her twin brothers' funeral. When the farmers eventually outwit these animals and steal the female half of that that semi-human parrot pair, a war is started. Eventually, if only symbolically, the Ponnivala princess herself is kidnapped, even if the hunters mistake a palace maid for the real princess and so Tangal's honour is saved. But what is important is that her reputation was almost besmirched. The heroes' actions in stealing that forest parrot, clearly represent a trespass of the hunters' rights and the hunters in turn realize that this travesty merits reprisal.

In both stories, we see third-generation light-skinned heroes fighting their darker-skinned forest-dwelling adversaries. In the Vatnsdaela case, dark-skinned Porolfur has been on the run and is exhausted (figure 5.79). Jokull's kill is relatively easy, though the lead up to it was challenging. In the Ponnivala Nadu case the forest adversaries are also darker skinned. Just like Jokull, Shankar is the better armed and he wins this confrontation with those rivals, or so it seems (figure 5.80). But in truth, the outcome in this case remains somewhat mystical. Vishnu creates a grand vision before the heroes' eyes (discussed elsewhere) that makes them believe they have victoriously killed many hunters, when in fact those forest dwellers have stood back in safety, due to Vishnu's advice, and they have not been harmed. In the Vatnsdaela case it is clear that the cultured, civilized Saga heroes had better tools and that Jokull triumphed over the mountain-dwelling Porolfur and his negative magic. The stereotype the heroes hold of the forest-dwelling hunters in the Ponnivala Nadu story is similar. There too, those characters (now a whole community) are darker-skinned, and do not farm. But this time, if one considers the story carefully, there is no real win. Instead

The Vatnsdaela Saga 219

Figure 5.79. Jokull pursues and then kills the dark-skinned Porolfur who is suspected of magic and sorcery.

Figure 5.80. Shankar attacks and tries to kill a hunter.

the forest hunters survive and a cosmic balance between field and forest is maintained, thanks to Vishnu's intervention. The Ponnivala legend is sociologically more advanced and the outcome more nuanced. But the description of the heroes and their own principal motives remain very similar across both stories.

Finally, in the Vatnsdaela case there is a tenacious wild boar named Beigad. Ingimund chases this beast until it jumps in the water and then runs up a hill. There, exhausted, the boar dies. In the Ponnivala story there is also a wild boar of great significance. Komban is a magical beast, a devil, and a sinister yogin. He is eventually killed by Shankar's huge boar spear after a long chase. Hence both stories point to a common wider, deeper paradigm: agriculture, social norms, and bright sky-dwelling gods rule and are superior in might and right to their darker, hill-dwelling forest adversaries. The boar, however, has far greater prominence in the Ponnivala account and he has his own seat on the other side of a grand balance scale. The Vatnsdaela Saga does not share that wider and more cosmic tapestry where there are two sides to everything.

Morality and Divine Justice

In both the Vatnsdaela Saga and the Legend of Ponnivala there are references to the orthodox and prevailing religion of the time. In the Icelandic case this reference is to Christianity. A bishop and his assistant both appear briefly in this epic, though they do not play a very big role in it. Instead, this popular saga is full of references to pre-Christian beliefs and, in particular to sorcery, witchcraft, and various other kinds of magic. Divination and spirit flight (from Norway to Iceland and back) also have a role to play. Speaking broadly, the Icelandic epic presents themes that mix these two traditions. One could almost say that two worldviews operate here simultaneously. It is important to remember that this story was redacted and preserved in written form by Christian monks. They no doubt did have some influence in shaping its occasional references to the cultural themes of Iceland's later and profoundly Christian history.

In the case of the Ponnivala story, local folk traditions that are marginally Hindu are balanced with the respected power of two main Hindu gods, Lord Vishnu and Lord Shiva. Vishnu is by far the more active of these two gods in this legend. Vishnu intervenes in many events by visiting the earth to influence the main characters' decisions. Furthermore, Vishnu serves as a human-divine go-between in many situations (figure 5.81). This is very much in keeping with this god's basic personality and mythology as depicted in a much broader and deeper set of text-based Hindu traditions. Shiva, on the other hand, is an ascetic and a loner. He enters the story only a few times, and only by request, usually only after outright pleading by one of the story's principal characters. Nonetheless, Shiva's role cannot be discounted. In the legend of Ponnivala Nadu, Shiva is most certainly *the* Supreme Being. It is he who makes all, or almost all, of the key life-and-death decisions.

In the Vatnsdaela story the bishop is the great power representing the church on earth (figure 5.82). Like Shiva in the Ponnivala Nadu case, he backs some (if not all) of the actions taken by the story's human characters. For example, there is a scene where we learn of a group of guests who are enjoying a feast when two berserks enter the longhouse by surprise and attack them. Later in revenge the berserks are caught and forced to walk through three fires burning in a trench on the floor of that great home as a test of their faith (figure 5.83). It was only after they suffered burns, indicating their lack of adequate faith in the gods, that they were attacked and killed, and this was done with the backing of the bishop. Similar tests of faith by firewalking can be seen to this day in South India, and although no one is killed should they get burnt, they certainly do feel humbled and embarrassed by that outcome. Nonetheless, the backing of these story characters by the religious institutions of the day is certainly present in both accounts. In the

The Vatnsdaela Saga 221

Figure 5.81. Vishnu, the more compassionate god, and Shiva, the much fiercer one, speaking with one another.

Figure 5.82. The bishop and a colleague: two men who were among Iceland's first missionaries.

Figure 5.83. The people of Vatnsdaela kill two berserks with the backing of the bishop.

Figure 5.84. The wild boar Komban, a kind of anti-Christ in the Ponnivala story.

Ponnivala Nadu case, the great Hindu god Shiva plays a role similar to that of the Christian god's representative in the Vatnsdaela story. In being a divine messenger, Lord Vishnu's role in the story is at times somewhat like that of the bishop in the Icelandic saga as well. One can also argue that the great wild boar Komban is to the Ponnivala story something like what the anti-Christ is to Christian folk tradition (figure 5.84). He denies the rights of the godly, which in this story would be the heroes' family whom Vishnu always backs. Even when Vishnu backs the Vettuva hunters and saves them from harm he still finds a way to save the heroes' pride by making them believe they have just won a great battle

Each a Keystone Story

In this final segment of this chapter, it is important to stress the important role of both the Vatnsdaela Saga and The Legend of Ponnivala Nadu in popular folk tradition today. Both are keystone folk stories and the importance of their role as such cannot be stressed enough. Both celebrate foundational events that oral tradition has long associated with a specific geographic region. Figure 5.1 presents an important expression of local pride, the Vatnsdaela Saga in the process of being retold in the form of a huge embroidered folk banner. It had been under production for several years when I first came across it. At that time, it was located in a community textile centre in Blondos, Iceland, where it was being embroidered by a large team of students. Figure 5.85 presents part of a comparable mural that I spotted in 1965, right in the middle of the area where the Ponnivala story is celebrated today. As is commonly the case for foundational legends, related folk art, folk architecture, and local customs predictably spring up around them. They serve to mark and celebrate such stories in visible ways. As one moves through the two local landscapes just described one sees, hears, and sometimes viscerally

Figure 5.85. A temple wall mural in the Kongu area of Tamil Nadu depicting the Ponnivala story.

experiences reminders of each of these legends with remarkably frequency. Those reminders are embedded in various features of the landscape that are naturally associated with each story's most popular scenes. These stories are also celebrated through the use of local names that pin-point specific spots singled out for mention that relate the story to a specific local geography. The same themes find further celebration in folk art and even in the logos and names of business enterprises important in each area. Inns, as well as gas stations, tea shops, and other locally popular spots can be found, both in the Vatnsdaela area and in parallel Ponnivala locales. All these local businesses reference their areas' traditional legends with pride. It is abundantly clear that both epics still play an active role in the formation of local identity in each of their respective regions, even today.

The next chapter turns to a discussion of a native North American bundle of stories all focused around one major cultural hero, known as Nanabush. Unlike in the Icelandic Saga, which mainly highlights contentious human encounters, Nanabush zeros in on specific natural elements found in his environment: a specific species of tree, a particular animal, a rock, a body of water, a unique bird, etc. In keeping with this broad pattern, we will see that this premodern, largely self-reliant hero lives out in the bush. This native North American cultural tradition takes a keen interest in what makes humans, well, ... human beings. Nanabush lives in a world where animal-human contrasts are made into puzzles or games. As a great trickster, a being that relishes his super-human reputation, Nanabush negotiates his travels through the natural world skilfully and moves light-heartedly among an entire range of differences that separate animal from human norms. The Icelandic Saga just discussed is much more serious with stronger overtones of fear and catastrophe, while what we will encounter next is more playful and more explorative, as it looks at animal, plant, and human relationships as part of a wonderous world overall.

6 Human versus Extra-Human Powers: The Nanabush Story Cycle

(Ojibwa First Peoples, North America)

In this final chapter of part 1 we will be juxtaposing the South Indian Ponnivala narrative to a cycle of stories told about a well-known North American Aboriginal culture hero named Nanabush. Nanabush is an Ojibwa hero celebrated by many communities of First Peoples located in eastern and central Canada and also in a variety of locations in the northeastern United States. Today the Ojibwa can be found in small, dispersed communities as well as in most large- and medium-sized cities in this large region. The Ojibwa constitute a distinctive branch of a larger Anishinaabeg cultural grouping. Most scholars would say that Ojibwa traditions do not feature just one epic story, but rather many smaller legends that are strung together in multiple ways depending on the context in which they are referenced. Why then would one choose Nanabush, of all examples, to include in a book about epics? This Ojibwa heritage has been selected precisely because this important cycle of short tales lies at one extreme of a much larger story continuum. It is an example of an important Indigenous story tradition that has no clearly defined edges.

Ojibwa tales feature animals, trips into the forest, concern with food scarcity, and other commonplace themes that relate to a life lived on the land. But heritage stories are never simplistic, though they might appear so on the surface. Of course, the Ojibwa, like the rest of us, convert their daily experiences into symbolic tools that help advance their thinking about much larger issues. The Ojibwa, for example, are more succinct and more abstract than most non-Native groups in the way they use natural forest-based imagery to express important thoughts. They have an ability to freshly capture ideas with metaphors in ways that seem quite new, especially when encountered by the average student raised in a community that has no significant Indigenous representation. The previous chapters have exclusively discussed a wide variety of so-called classic epic examples, all of which stem from European, Middle Eastern, or South Asian cultural foundations. By contrast, the Ojibwa stories about Nanabush belong to a symbolic tradition that has a strong, and ancient, hunting-and-gathering history. The stories about Nanabush are a good example of a cluster of tales, generally called a cycle, that all reference a single culture hero but do not have to be told in any specific, logical order. The Ojibway stories selected here come from just one book of Nanabush tales. The reader will easily be able to find many other legends about Nanabush that have been published in other sources. Out of the sixteen tales recounted in just that one book, we will focus on eight in the discussion that follows.[1] This is enough to illustrate that even a limited sample of tales, taken together, will address all seven core analytic dimensions of epic story telling that have been referenced repeatedly throughout the first half of this work. Those seven topics will now be discussed in relation to Ojibwa thinking in the hopes of throwing light on their unique and perceptive approach to worldview issues.

Theme One: Roots

Kongu Tamil farmers and the Ojibwa First Peoples approach the theme of roots in a surprisingly similar way: they both give importance to the Pleiades star cluster. These two cultures each ground their epic hero's heritage by referencing this one constellation in particular. And in each case, that highly visible cluster of seven closely spaced stars represents a group of seven women. Both traditions believe these seven stars mark a hole, or perhaps a gateway, into another realm, a secret door that makes travel between two different worlds possible (figure 6.1). Ojibwa artists have a brilliant way of reducing their graphic statements to the essentials, compressing several profound ideas into one seemingly simple image. In one Ojibwa story these seven sisters, all young women, ignore father moon's instructions and descend through that Pleiades' hole, in a basket, in order to dance on earth. But on their trip, one sister falls in love with a human and so she takes him back to the sky world with her, where she plans to get approval for a marriage. Grandfather Sun disapproves but, nonetheless, he does allow the marriage to proceed. After this, the couple make further visits to earth from time to time. However, the girl's other six sisters are sent to a place farther from earth so that they will not be tempted by a similar encounter that the Sun does not wish to see repeated. The Pleiades and several other star constellations, even today, provide a key to Ojibwa thinking about the sacred. And a belief that these seven stars can influence human life underlies much in Ojibwa culture, helping to frame this community's broader sense of meaning. Strong evidence for the fact that the Pleiades play this role can be seen in common Ojibwa rituals. These seven Pleiades maidens are represented by, perhaps even embodied in, the seven stones used to surround the Ojibway sacred sweat lodge fire, a ceremony that is central to traditional Ojibwa life. The seven sisters are also represented by the seven poles that hold up a round cone-shaped tent made of skins. That distinctive structure has a roof-hole at its peak, and it is used, among other things, for Ojibwa so-called shaking tent ceremonies.

Figure 6.1. Ojibwa sacred fire and its seven stones that represent the Pleiades. Author's sketch.

Tamils in the Kongu area of Tamil Nadu also place great importance on the same seven sisters, a set of young girls who are said to form the seven stars associated with the Pleiades constellation there as well. One of those seven, the youngest maiden, also travels to earth and back in the Ponnivala story. She is sent down to earth by the great god Shiva, as an embryo in her mother's womb where she is joined by two male fetuses whose very different spirit lives Shiva recruits from elsewhere. This female lives on earth for sixteen years, protecting and advising her co-born brothers throughout that entire time period. At the end of the epic, after both of her brothers die, this lone sister travels back to heaven in a chariot, returned there by Shiva to live again alongside her other six sisters. This one Pleiad who spent sixteen years on earth, Tangal, is central to the Ponnivala epic legend. She is the secret force who dwells largely in the shadows behind her two brothers, but who influences their fates in many ways. Furthermore, Tangal is the only major character in the Ponnivala story who does not experience death. And in the Ojibwa, as well as in the South Indian case, all seven Pleiades girls are symbolized together in a unified cluster form (figure 6.2). It is as a unified group that, according to both cultural traditions, these seven maidens wield an important divine influence over human lives present on earth.

In the Tamil case Tangal is an important figure in a powerful local ritual practised during festivals, an event used to retell her story as attentive devotees watch. To honour the story of her brothers, several self-selected men from the Kongu area undergo a temporary death in an annual ceremony that re-enacts these twin Ponnivala heroes' final sword fight. The men who die during this ritual are then brought back to life in a dramatic fashion by a ritual novice, who must be a local pre-puberty girl, an obvious parallel to the legend where Tangal magically resurrects her two brothers from their suicidal death. As well and just as important, the

Figure 6.2. Frieze depicting the seven sky sisters, the Pleiades, on the gateway of a temple dedicated to the heroes of the Ponnivala story.

seven sisters are the goddesses that oversee the cow pen (patti Pongal) ceremony that farmers celebrate at harvest, which occurs very close to the time of the winter solstice.[2] In that South Indian ritual a square shallow pool is temporarily dug in the family's cattle pen. Along one edge overlooking that freshly dug pond, seven white stones are set out that represent the seven sky girls that reference the Pleiades constellation. This pond is much like the sweat lodge fire associated with the seven sisters in the Ojibwa case (figure 6.1). In both examples, this ritual space (composed of fire in one and water in the other) serves like a gate or hole through which spirits or dreams can reach the sky. In the South Indian story this small pond is something like a reflecting pool that further resembles the sky because it mirrors the heavens, both at night and during the day. What is important and interesting here is that the stars, in general, and the Pleiades constellation, in particular, provide a foundation or root symbol on which both story traditions build.

The Ojibwa and Ponnivala Nadu stories each base their larger legend on a local creation event, not on an ultimate "in the beginning" account explaining where the entire universe came from. Instead, both can be called regional creation tales. In the Ojibwa case that story describes many of the animals Nanabush created, animals the wider culture depicts as clan ancestors. In the Ponnivala case, too, the goddess creates ancestors for the epic heroes. In that case, however, there are no animal intermediaries. Rather the goddess directly places nine adult men in a forest, asking them to plough and grow food. These men later turn out to be the clan ancestors of the twin male heroes-to-be. Nanabush, by contrast, is seen to recreate life by taking control of an earlier world ruled by a serpent woman and her two human brothers. He drowns all three by creating a great flood and then re-forms the world to his own liking. He then produces the new earth by using a single handful of recycled mud that he had held back when he destroyed the old earth.[3]

228   Multiple Epics Compared

Figure 6.3. The Ojibwa turtle that causes the stars to adhere to the sky.

This wonder-hero, Nanabush, also creates a turtle who soon placed the stars where they belong in the sky (figure 6.3).[4] The turtle does this by using his tail to slap the surface of the lake where he swims; water drops then fly off in a way that allows them to lodge in the heavens above and sparkle there. This story is one of many that depicts Nanabush as the creator-god responsible for the natural features of the forested environment where the Ojibwa traditionally lived.

In the Ponnivala Nadu epic there is also a local creation myth. As mentioned above, nine adult brothers are first created by a goddess in the sky, Parvati. They are then sent down to earth where she asks them to start clearing land so that they can then plough an otherwise well-treed area. This mother goddess gives them the tool that they need to use and instructs them to begin ploughing. They are to grow abundant food crops using their new, important, and highly specialized tool. The nine brothers try hard to do the bidding of the goddess, but they suffer in the process and eventually must move to another region. However, in the end they manage to establish a homeland for themselves (Ponnivala Nadu) that combines a mix of forested foothills with fine open farmland. In figure 6.4, note that there are seven dots near the goddess's head seen in the upper right corner. She lives in the sky near these dots (the Pleiades) and also near her husband Lord Shiva. Together these two principal gods cause all subsequent human figures central to this epic also to be born-of-the-sky in some way or another. Thus the goddess Parvati (in her multiple forms) is responsible for this first creative act that establishes both an ancestral line and the key features of the basic lifestyle that the heroes will endorse. In the Ojibwa case a magical male trickster, Nanabush, is the ultimate creator, but in one of his first acts he forms a turtle whose tail places the stars in their rightful place in the sky where they are responsible for much that helps guide the traditional Ojibwa way of life. In summary, in both these stories an origin myth lays out the **roots** or basic framework on which both of these epic stories will then grow, or build.

Figure 6.4. Parvati creates nine human brothers.

Figure 6.5. Nanabush carried by a goose.

Theme Two: Reclamation

The second topic of discussion here has to do with Ojibwa and Ponnivala story themes describing the hero or heroine returning to a place important to his or her ancestry. However, if that is not possible, then they reclaim and reassert their own personal ancestry in some related way that is then used to help claim and assert their group's unique cultural identity. This is made very clear in the Nanabush story cycle when the culture-hero is himself twice carried away by a goose and dropped in a new land (figure 6.5). The first time Nanabush is displaced he returns to the locale that he came from, but the second time he is left in that new land for good (figure 6.6).

Figure 6.6. Nanabush falls to earth in a different place that becomes his new home.

In the Ponnivala Nadu epic, the heroes are also displaced twice, but now the order of the two events seen in the Ojibwa case are presented in reverse. The first time the heroes are forced to move they do not return to their place of origin, a remote forest. But the second time is somewhat different. They now move at the behest of a king who sends them out to plough a new area. Later, after the first generation farming that new land dies, their young son is banished from his family lands by cruel cousins and he too must wander for many years. That young hero finally marries and is then motivated to return to his father's homeland. Returning there, he rebuilds on top of the ruins of the old family palace, an act that allows him to start anew. In both cases the hero's return home is symbolic (figure 6.7). And in both cases this serves as a substory about rebuilding a heritage that allows the heroes' family to claim the land they now live on as rightfully theirs. In the Ojibwa account the return to an original locale happens first, and then later the hero gets uprooted and must settle in a new place for good. In the Ponnivala Nadu example, life in the land that will soon be abandoned is described first, and then the new homeland is found as step two. The **reclamation** of that final homeland is a third step, something that follows the heroes' temporary exile from it. In sum, the Ojibwa case makes this group's homeland something that lies in a distant mythical past that can now only be referenced and **reclaimed** via a story. In the South Indian case, the parallel story makes the homeland contemporary and places it right at the listener's feet. The heroes' father **reclaimed** it long back and then left it for its current occupants to enjoy.

Theme Three: Resistance

A third topic these two stories have in common has to do with subduing and punishing a mean challenger. In both cases there is at least one standoff that serves to establish the skill, trickery, and outright courage displayed by the key protagonist

Figure 6.7. The son of the first ancestor finds his father's old lands.

Figure 6.8. Nanabush punishes the bald eagle.

when he or she is challenged. In the Ojibwa case the challenger is a nasty bald eagle that ignores Nanabush's polite request for directions. This great bird is just flying by but Nanabush faults him for being rude and uncaring because this great bird simply ignores Nanabush's request for help. In revenge for that uncalled-for treatment, Nanabush chases that uncaring eagle through the sky. He gets it to turn around but then flies beside it, preventing it from landing. He also punishes it by declaring that this bird and all its descendants will henceforth be bald, never again being able to wear proud feathers on its head (figure 6.8). This is an insult because the Ojibwa wear feathers on their heads during special ceremonies. The story is about civilized behaviour and how one should not ignore legitimate requests for help from others. It also reflects the fact that, in the Canadian forests where the Ojibwa live, various large birds are often seen to chase each other using very mean attack techniques. They do this in an effort to try and protect their own home territory.

The Ponnivala Nadu substory that seems appropriate for comparison here is about humans, not a bird. For years, the heroes' parents have been taunted and challenged by a malicious set of cousins. The cousins believe that their ancestors received an unequal share of good land when the matter was first negotiated and therefore try to alter that early contract, using nasty tricks. This starts an intrafamily feud that runs through much of the broader epic account. The cousins continue to taunt and be mean to the heroes' family. Being good and wise citizens, however, the heroes' parents counsel their twin sons not to take revenge. But the two boys do not listen. Instead, just as Nanabush teaches the eagle a lesson, so the twin boys decide they need to teach the cousins and their families a lesson. They start a fight in their cousins' children's school, hoping to do settle the score (figure

Figure 6.9. The Ponnivala heroes punish their cousins and their cousin's children.

6.9). The cousin's families end up being pushed into exile by the two young men, just like the eagle was forced to turn around and then was not allowed to land. The heroes of both stories win in these brave singular encounters. But the issue is never fully resolved. The cousins reappear and then find new ways to take revenge for all their recent suffering. And bald eagles still pester other animals whom they chase and threaten. Moral issues remain in both cases. Who was really in the right? Was Nanabush right to chase the eagle away simply for ignoring to answer his request for directions? Were the twin heroes of Ponnivala Nadu right to attack their cousin's children while they studied at school, simply because their parents had previously challenged their own father's land claims? These are moral dilemmas, questions that have no simple answer. More fundamentally, is revenge a legitimate form of resistance? Both legends pose similar questions, each describing such encounters in their own way. But the Ojibwa story is the more symbolic, the more magical, and the more metaphorical. But no matter what one concludes in terms of specifics, anger aimed at characters who behave in cruel and inhuman ways is a theme common to the heroes of both epics. At heart in these two very important but also very different story legends lie a similar set of human dilemmas, one of which is how to express **resistance** and defy a cruel or unfair challenger.

Theme Four: Resilience

This fourth topic focuses on the resilience needed to successfully pursue a cherished goal despite repeated hardships. The Ojibwa example described here tells of a Giant Beaver who Nanabush and his grandmother chase across the land. They know that they have a quarrel with him though they do not know exactly why or how it started. Eventually, tired, the grandmother and grandson camp on the shore of a lake. The beaver has built a dam on that lake and, when he arrives to inspect his

Figure 6.10. Nanabush's grandmother holds on to the great beaver's tail.

work, the grandmother grabs his tail. She holds on to that beaver for days, but she does not have the strength to pull his heavy body from the water. Then suddenly one day the dam breaks due to a tunnel the beaver had earlier constructed under it. In the commotion that followed, the beaver manages to pull his tail free of the grandmother's grasp. He then swims out to sea (figure 6.10). Nanabush could not catch the beaver after that, but he did have the presence of mind to shout at him. Trying to use trickery, he praised the beaver's cunning and asked for a peace treaty. To his surprise the beaver agreed and the grandmother, Nanabush, and the beaver end up becoming friends. After that the beaver begins to build dams that the Ojibwa people find useful and so these once staunch opponents now collaborate.

In the Ponnivala Nadu story there is similar heroine who has an equal degree of patience and who displays a degree of resilience at least equal to that shown by Nanabush's grandmother. Tamarai is barren and very distressed by her lack of children, as discussed previously, although she doesn't really know why this has become her fate. So, she climbs a pillar and does penance to Lord Shiva for twenty-one years, begging this great god for the gift of a child. Nonetheless, Shiva continues to torture her in various ways, ignoring her sincere request. But then Vishnu, Shiva's sometime rival and brother-in-law, comes to Tamarai's aid. He shoots a stream of hot fire at Shiva. This burns him and awakes him from his deep forest meditation. Shiva is angered at being disturbed but he does recognize how patient Tamarai has been (figure 6.11). Finally, he invites her into his heavenly courtroom and grants her wish: an immaculate conception. In addition, Tamarai obtains magical powers from Shiva that enable her to pass her own gift of pregnancy on to others when she finally returns to earth. To do this she distributes drops of magical water from a pot Shiva gave her before she left his council chambers and returned to earth. Tamarai's family and the whole kingdom of Ponnivala Nadu now become fertile. Shiva and Vishnu, meanwhile, make peace as well. In

Figure 6.11. Tamarai prays to Lord Shiva while perched on a pillar.

both stories, then, the **resilience** of an important female heroine leads to the reconciliation among warring protagonists, as well as achieving a degree of increased prosperity for all the human families involved.

Theme five: Relationships

Relationships between story characters are key to any legend or tale. There are many types of hero and heroine experiences that fall under this heading. Both kinship bonds and political or economic ties can be relevant. We will consider just one example for each story. In each this will be an incident where the hero violates a relationship of trust. As a result, the offender receives punishment. The Ojibwa tell a story about the day Nanabush placed his trust in a birch tree that grew near his home. He was about to leave on a short trip and therefore stored some uneaten fresh meat high up on the poles of his large tent. Then he left on his errand, taking his grandmother with him. But before departing, Nanabush asked his birch tree neighbour to guard his tent and the precious food he had left within it. However, it was a warm day and the tree fell asleep. Soon after that, a flock of birds swooped down and flew around Nanabush's wigwam. They discovered the meat inside and consumed every last bit of it. When Nanabush returned he was shocked and demanded an explanation from the sleepy birch tree. But the birch tree could not find a good excuse for failing keep its promise. So Nanabush ripped a branch off a neighbouring balsam fir and beat the birch hard, leaving scars on its bark (figure 6.12). One can see those scars to this day.

This birch tree's oversight is not the simple story that it first seems to be. Was Nanabush right to place his trust in a tree when it came to guarding human food, especially when guarding it from the birds who would normally be a tree's friends and allies? After all, birch trees let birds perch on their limbs and nest in

Figure 6.12. Nanabush whips a birch tree.

their hollow trunks when they get old. Ultimately one must wonder whether it was reasonable for Nanabush to place his trust in that particular neighbour, and whether it was right to punish a tree that was not realistically able to help, either morally or physically?

A similar incident occurs in the Ponnivala Nadu epic when the twin heroes are invited to worship at a distant shrine at the invitation of a powerful king. The king takes his two guests there and has them climb a ladder in order to reach the shrine, which was located at the very top of the cliff. But after the two brothers had climbed up the ladder and stepped onto the cliff's summit, the king suddenly ordered his men to pull the ladder away. This cruel action left the two brothers stranded. The men cried out for help and finally a wandering mendicant heard their pleas. The beggar who had come to the rescue was actually Lord Vishnu in disguise. This god/beggar rolled his hair into two long coils and threw them to the stranded men, then he held the two hair-ropes taut. This allowed the two heroes to slide down and reach the ground safely. The twin heroes thank the wandering beggar for his help and then rush back to the king's palace where they kill him in anger over how he had so treacherously tricked and disrespected them (figure 6.13). That same king had already shown his animosity towards the two heroes in other ways and had secretly tried to kill both brothers earlier the same day. Were the two heroes right to place their trust in him after all that and thus allow themselves to be stranded when they already knew he was untrustworthy? And were they right to wreak such a harsh punishment on him, their own overlord, over just one added insult? Both stories provide an example of unreasonable trust being placed on someone (some being) whose loyalty to their cause is clearly in doubt. Both the Ojibwa story and its Ponnivala Nadu counterpart are about human relationships and neighbours who can or cannot be depended on. Both accounts highlight this issue by choosing a time when the person who needed help could suffer harm should that trust be broken.

Figure 6.13. Twin heroes escape from a clifftop and kill the Chola king. The event seen in figure 2.1 is here re-represented within its larger story context.

Nanabush would go hungry if his meat were to be stolen and the Ponnivala Nadu brothers could have died had they been stranded for days on that high cliff. The similarity lies in the fact that both stories advocate careful thought before relying, at a critical moment, on a **relationship** that has not proven dependable in the past.

Theme Six: Reflection

This is an important story theme that has many permutations. Basically, the term reflection, as used here, refers to the doubling of the hero or heroine in some way that highlights a difference between them and the person or thing they are paired with. In the Ojibwa case, the story describes Nanabush admiring a woodpecker's ability to tap on a tree with his beak, especially when he notices two raccoons (two tasty dinners) drop out of that tree, seemingly as a result of that tapping action. The woodpecker roasts both animals. Then he proceeds to eat a piece of one, alongside Nanabush, who eats the rest. Later Nanabush tries to tap on a similar tree, imitating the woodpecker by using some wooden pins as his beak, but that effort fails miserably. Instead, Nanabush himself falls out of the tree and lies unconscious on the ground until the woodpecker decides to sit him up. The woodpecker then chuckles, knowing that a human cannot peck for food as a woodpecker does. Nanabush is humbled by those woodpecker words. As a sign of thanks for saving his life, Nanabush then gives the woodpecker some of the blood that dripped from his nose while he lay on the ground, helpless. He gently places this blood on the woodpecker's crest, colouring it a brilliant red (figure 6.14). That has been the woodpecker's trophy-mark ever since and is a sign of its inner natural power. But the story is about more than just "how the woodpecker got its red crest." It is about the triumph of a hidden force: the woodpecker is the smaller and, seemingly, humbler creature, at least when compared with Nanabush who

Figure 6.14. Woodpecker is gifted a red tuft by a submissive Nanabush.

is the size of a full-grown man. But this little bird displays an awesome natural power. In the end it is he who wears the crown and becomes marked as superior. The woodpecker was also the one who knew how to readily find food, and in particular, he was the one who knew how to roast it to create a feast. This act of cooking suggests that woodpecker was some sort of human being in disguise since birds do not cook their food as humans do. The story thus has a surprise ending. The woodpecker seems to deserve his new red hat. He must be respected.

In the Ponnivala Nadu story a wild boar named Komban plays a role somewhat similar to that of the Ojibwa woodpecker. Komban has two sharp tusks and he repeatedly taunts the two story heroes with them. Komban calls himself a "raja," meaning a king, and he is a forest dweller who sides with the fearsome goddess Kali who lives there as well. Komban, furthermore, destroys the twin protagonists' farm fields and tears open their prize irrigation dam. The two Ponnivala Nadu heroes fight back, eventually spearing that huge forest beast in the heart. They then convert his flesh into a forest offering. But the goddess who dwells nearby is allied with the god Vishnu, and she uses his help to secure that great boar's severed head. Of course, a head is largely a skull and does not have enough meat on it to make a meal for forest spirits to enjoy. Instead, the head symbolizes something far greater: a magic seed that the great goddess will use to restart life on earth itself. Thus the goddess ends up getting the real trophy that two hunters (the story heroes) foolishly overlook. Both of these tales use reflection as a key to their deeper meaning. And in both cases that reflection in seen to reside in an animal companion. The woodpecker, though seemingly small, has secret strengths. It can source food at will and cook it as well when it wishes to do so. Komban, larger than the heroes in body size, has a head desired by the goddess herself, that is full of magical power (figure 6.15). Similar to the woodpecker, as well, Komban behaves like a human being, disguised in animal form. He knows how to talk and how to tease. Komban

Figure 6.15. Komban's head is gifted to the goddess.

represents a hidden divine power, a seed that can reproduce itself and create new life over time. In both stories, we see that the hero's own prowess is trumped by a seemingly lesser being, a forest animal. Both stories, therefore, involve helping listeners think more deeply about animal-human relationships. Each legend helps the story listener think about which types of being really contain the most spirit energy. Thus animals sometimes **reflect** human traits, enhancing them in that **reflection,** which can sometimes add to that being's own non-human or counter-human significance.

Theme Seven: Revelation

Revelation, as used here, refers to the power of epic stories to unveil deep hidden meanings. Now we provide two Ojibwa examples. In the first, a story called Granite Peak, Nanabush goes to visit his father, the great west wind Mudjekewis. But four warriors from back home miss him and, when summer starts, they set out to search for Nanabush. When they find him, the great hero invites them inside and his granddaughter offers them all food. Her pot is very small, but she feeds them all without difficulty, as her magic vessel seems to be inexhaustible. Next, the warriors ask Nanabush to use his own special powers to individually grant each one a special gift. The first asks not to be killed in battle, the second wants never to starve for lack of food, and the third needs a wife. Nanabush grants the first two what they ask for but acts differently towards the third. He gives the third his own granddaughter as his wedding partner but with a special requirement. That lucky man is not to talk to this woman, ever, or at least not during the time it takes the two of them to reach home together and thus become man and wife. The man agrees. Then the fourth warrior speaks up and his request is quite different. He wants to live forever. Nanabush becomes angry and replies that his wish is greedy. "Your request is impossible to grant," Nanabush says. As a punishment he turns that fourth warrior into a huge rock, a great granite peak that will never move but that will certainly last forever. And sadly, the third warrior also makes a mistake, forgetting his promise of silence. Therefore, part way home, the beautiful girl at his side vanishes and returns to her grandfather's distant abode. This is how Nanabush taught the Ojibwa about the consequences of greed and about what can happen if one breaks a vow.

A similar story, found in the same corpus of Nanabush stories from which all the examples discussed here are drawn, concerns the great hero himself rather than his warrior companions. This time Nanabush himself is promised a wife by the Great Spirit Gitchi-Manitou. This impressive being tells Nanabush that he must walk east and then cross a great river to win her. Nanabush does this bravely and the woman appears. He then lives with her and together they raise many children (figure 6.16). However, in one important respect, his children are not like him – they are the first human beings to live on earth. So, in the version of the story we told just above, the river crossing is done by a warrior who is subordinate to the great Nanabush. There the story is about greed and about keeping one's word. The second version of the story is about Nanabush himself crossing a river. This time that river is even more symbolic as it is not just a set of rules about good behaviour, it is symbolizing the actual divide between the gods (who live forever) and humans who live only for a short time. Here a seemingly simple tale becomes a story about how human life got separated from divine life to begin with. This more philosophical version tells us how all human life became limited and must thus be concluded with each human's ultimate death. This is a case where the same basic tale, told in a slightly different way, can take on a very significant added meaning overall. It is said that Nanabush hesitated while crossing that great river. He paused just long enough for the great spirit Gitchi-Manitou to realize that his word had been doubted. Thus, Gitchi-Manitou made death become inevitable for Nanabush's wife and his children. Nanabush himself, however, had special powers and was able to avoid death. He would live on forever at the side of Gitchi-Manitou.

In the Ponnivala Nadu story the approach to death is not that different from what we just saw above. When the Ponnivala twin heroes finally die, they do so by committing a voluntary suicide by falling forward on their own swords. Then their sister Tangal (who, as was explained earlier, is a human multiform of the youngest of the seven Pleiades stars) learns of their deaths and begins to search for their bodies (figure 6.17). On her way she acquires seven pots filled with magical substances. When Tangal finally locates her brothers' bodies, deep inside the forest, she sprinkles the contents of her pots on their corpses, reviving them, but only briefly. Back on their feet, the heroes speak to their sister and explain that they cannot live forever. They tell her that their status and responsibilities must now pass to others who will replace them and take over the rulership of the kingdom of Ponnivala. Tangal accepts this, letting her two brothers fall back into death. Then she builds a small set of shrines in their honour and worships their

240 Multiple Epics Compared

Figure 6.16. This story is told in two different ways. In the first account an Ojibwa warrior is seen crossing the river, whereas in the second it is Nanabush himself who is crossing that waterway, which is now a cosmic-scale divine/human divide. In both cases, that crossing is made in order to greet a new wife.

Figure 6.17. Tangal crosses a deep forest to find her brothers' bodies.

memories. Finally, the great lord Shiva sends down a chariot and returns her, still alive, to heaven where she joins Shiva, her brothers, and also the other six Pleiades maidens. Tangal is the only character in the Ponnivala Nadu story to avoid death. All others must experience life's end. Both this substory and the Ojibwa one above deal with the reality that human death is inevitable. At the same time both stories point to another kind of truth: that some humans may also have superhuman or semi-divine qualities. In these examples Nanabush is one such being and Tangal is another. Each is understood to be a divine spirt in disguise. Thus, the two need not die but can rise directly into the sky and live on there forever. In both stories these intriguing correspondences contrast the forest with a human surround. Both present a kind of nature versus culture puzzle: a natural world that appears to live on forever, even though all human and animal beings living in that earth-bound space must age and die.

It is also important to note that both the Ojibwa and South Indian story legends involve a young female who carries a magical pot. In both contexts that pot's contents appear to be inexhaustible and the liquids within bestow life on those who share something of its nourishing essence. Both stories contain the idea that there is a magical elixir somewhere, a liquid force controlled by a female mother or sister figure, that can mysteriously renew the gift of life. And looking at the theme of male/female bonding, both story traditions also suggest that humankind is significantly dependent on cross-gender kinship ties, be they due to marriage or to siblingship, and that these bonds must be honoured and sustained through time. And both stories also take note of a still greater truth: the impermanence of everything humans enjoy. This fundamental truth is one important thread that broadly energizes all the epics studied and compared in the first part of this work. And digging still further, we find one more surprising theme that the Ojibway and South Indian Ponnivala Nadu traditions share: the central importance given to a set of seven Pleiades star sisters. That cluster of sky maidens offers a communication channel that allows humans to exchange energy and gifts with extra-human powers dwelling above. Somehow, that extra human energy seems to be embodied by the stars we can see at night. These ideas, referenced several times in earlier chapters, will surface again in chapter 8.

This concludes part 1 where six different epic traditions have been surveyed and studied. One, the Legend of Ponnivala Nadu, has been taken as the baseline or template to which the other five have been compared and contrasted. The similarities help us to grasp some of story telling's universals, while the differences highlight the various specifics of the multiple and rich cultural traditions that these six epics have their roots in. Each has flourished due to support provided by a distinct historic and cultural landscape. We first explored the complex character and plot structures that underlie the Mahabharata's forceful and ongoing influence on India and also on several adjacent nations. Next the Epic of Gilgamesh was considered, including its particular focus on the grand set of balances life presents, including everyman's end point: death. The surprising similarities between this story and the Ponnivala Nadu epic from Kongu area of South India were discussed. Following that, the extremely influential biblical tradition that grew from ancient Middle Eastern roots was studied. There, too, we saw how similar much of that tradition is to ideas found buried deep within South India's Ponnivala Nadu story as well. In the case of the Vatsendaela Saga the central impact that the near barren landscape has had on early Icelandic sagas was examined, and the variety of ways that a story's geographical and ecological foundation play out in an epic context were discussed. And finally, we have explored a first peoples' cycle of hero stories, focusing on its supernatural visions and emphasis on a variety of nature-culture contrasts, all of which are found to be featured in at least one specific example, the Nanabush Legend cycle.

Next, in part 2, this study turns away from comparisons across stories to a further and deeper examination of just one case: The Legend of Ponnivala Nadu itself. Now the intent and the focus of discussion is different. The second half of this work will first examine how this singular story presents and crystalizes a variety of themes already prominent and well known to people living within its specific cultural milieu. It will ask how and why these themes find themselves embedded in a grand local story, and in what ways surprises emerge. Instead of just depicting popular attitudes and action structures in direct, well-known ways, the Ponnivala Nadu story is subtle. It plays with some of the most popular themes found in that parent culture. For example, we will see how this story divides a popular local divinity in two, in order to reverently and rather secretly play with and further celebrate the values, meanings, and magical powers he represents. Themes of doubling and tripling characters through disguise and displacement will also be studied. The ways in which various nature-culture assumptions are expressed through the description of the pervasive farmer-hunter conflict found there will be unpacked further. After that, three separate broad models that help explain this story's unique shape will be examined. A complex map of the constellations, in both its Babylonian and its ancient Hindu form will be explored first. Following that we will look at a sketch of a great cosmic lotus and ask how that diagram helps us to understand the extensive visual imagery the Ponnivala epic's lead bard employed in his poetic songs. Finally, this work will turn to a discussion of the ecological reality with which locals in the Kongu area have lived for millennia: the oscillation of extreme dry weather with the downpours that accompany the monsoon rains. The final hidden paradigm discussed will show how this reality of a farmer's life, so fully dependent on copious periods of rain, has coloured this story's many musical interludes. We will end with a study of the emotive praise-poems describing rain, songs that this legend's very talented bards love to sing.

PART TWO

Hidden Paradigms

7 Splitting, Replicating, and Twinning of Gods and Animals

This second part of the book will consider the nature of hidden paradigms and flesh this idea out with numerous details. Basic cultural concepts that underlie an epic story, however, rarely announce themselves. One has to dig in order to identify them. These are assumptions, images, and main ideas that normally form a part of a story audience's subconscious thinking. They are concepts and metaphors that sketch out a broad view of the world and that are largely taken for granted, such as the need to give gifts to gods to demonstrate one's underlying faith in that divinity's special powers and to show that one endorses a general worldview focused on respect, generosity, and goodwill towards others. Another example would be the belief that human life involves striving, climbing, and meeting constant challenges. A common image used to express this is the vision of a huge tree or post that stands at the centre of the universe. That tree works hard to push upward and as a result of those efforts it helps to hold up the sky. The interpretation of the image can be literal, but it can also be metaphorical. The sky can represent morality, goodness, and clarity of principle. Climbing up a pillar can, furthermore, be a way to reach the gods and thus to imbibe some of the magical liquid goodness that resides in the sky. Rain or a soft breeze, even a pleasing dream, can be understood as a sign than one has climbed up into the clouds and that they are therefore releasing their approval, guidance, or blessings in collaboration with one or more great unseen beings that reign on high.

Still another hidden paradigm is the idea that prosperity on earth begins with the fertilization of the atmospheric waters of a great sea-that-is-the-sky. The night sky suggests such a sea, filled with fish that sparkle like tiny lights, just like a heavy black cloud can suggest that a great store of wealth is building up and swirling about. It portends a great event, the day that wealth will shower down in the form of rain. When the monsoon finally arrives, health, goodness, and fresh energy will descend alongside that rush of water. Rain is sent to earth as a divine blessing from the goddess herself, as she works to regenerate energy in all forms of being that dwell below. There are multitudes of ideas like the ones just cited, but some are more central and have more inspirational power than others. Some root themselves deeply in an individual mind, but just lie there quietly, dormant for years. Sometimes, many years later that nascent paradigm will find fresh nourishment through some active form of human ritual activity. Hidden paradigms are often given strong support when an individual participates in a ritual procedure that reawakens old feelings, allowing such a seed, previously hidden, to sprout. Ritual procedures provide symbolic ways of expressing deep beliefs, and as a ritual is repeated, various underlying paradigms a person may have acquired in their youth may be energized and given new importance. This is how, gradually, many paradigms come to manifest themselves more openly in the elderly, as new symbolic actions that reference a deeply held idea gradually get added to an individual's daily routine.

The previous chapters have shown how the comparative use of seven key concepts can help uncover core themes hidden within specific epic stories. But an epic tale's core themes can still be difficult to identify with any certainty or clarity. It took more than fifty years to uncover a variety of interesting concepts that will now be identified in the ensuing pages, concepts that lie deep within the Legend of Ponnivala Nadu. Much of what a researcher finds in a story, of course, will be determined by the specific assumptions and frame concepts that are unconsciously brought to bear when studying it. This first chapter of part 2 will point out some very novel insights pertaining to the Legend of Ponnivala Nadu that were discovered only slowly, most often by repeatedly questioning various specific details that seemed incongruent or troubling. Why was a particular scene or set of images there to begin with? Some of these story scenes haunted me. What did they signify? Some of those troubling spots will be identified below and then an answer will be attempted. Later chapters in part 2 explore specific pre-existing paradigms that could be buried in this epic and then ask if they add some new meaning to the whole. Does the idea or theme provide any fresh, helpful insights? Each time the answer will be affirmative. Each cosmic vision studied will open new doors and reveal important added understandings. But first we must consider some basic ideas that emerge when we simply ask why and then wait for observations to emerge that will contribute, bit by bit, to finding a useful answer.

The Birth of Murugan (Also Known as Kartikeya or Skanda)

We begin this second section with an observation about the two main male characters in the Ponnivala Nadu story: Ponnar and Shankar. Why do devotees who listen to this story repeatedly love these two men so much? Furthermore, why do they live just sixteen years and why are they so different from each other, one a confirmed warrior who often initiates trouble while the other is a kind and quiet observer who is rarely critical of others and almost never presses for change? Both men are reincarnations of even greater heroes, two major figures in the Mahabharata, Arjuna and Bhima. But this local set of twins does not look much like those earlier heroes, nor do they act like them. Furthermore, everyone who knows anything about the two sets of classical heroes, which is almost every local resident who listens to this popular oral epic, knows that Arjuna carried a huge bow and Bhima had a large club, each a unique and much favoured weapon. But Ponnar carries neither of these tools and instead holds a long, grain-harvesting-style of knife called an aruvadai katti when portrayed in many local shrines. His sibling and fiercer counterpart carries a huge spear called a vel. Because this is a story from Tamil Nadu, where Lord Murugan, second son of Shiva, is the most popular god, these differences suggest that the twin Ponnivala Nadu heroes' interests relate to agriculture but also to war. The favorite local god, never mentioned directly in this story, is Murugan. Could these twin heroes be two faces or two sides of Lord Murugan, expressing his secret presence in this story via a novel bodily form?

This chapter will argue that many of Lord Murugan's core traits have been built into the two Ponnivala Nadu heroes' background descriptions in clever ways. But there is a catch. If these local heroes are a form of Murugan, then why, in this story would his traits be split, some being allocated to Ponnar and some to Shankar? Over the years the reason for this bifurcation has gradually become clear me. Reincarnating Murugan as twins is not a travesty. The Ponnivala story's apparent representation of a most beloved god as a set of twins is a subtle and effective way of expressing the nature of this god's rich and complex personality. Indeed, this approach or way of thinking transforms the Ponnivala epic into a huge devotional enterprise, albeit in something of a clever disguise. Murugan is both wild and tame, fierce and sympathetic, youthful and mature. Murugan, like this story's two adolescent heroes, is an aggressive, even a fearful warrior at times, but he can also be as vulnerable as a young child or as romantic as a handsome lover.

We begin this argument with one version of Murugan's birth story, the one that explains the most because it blends a variety of themes together. There is wide agreement that Murugan was born from the semen of the great Lord Shiva, but in a complex way. There are many variants of this tale but basically what happened was that Shiva paused his meditation work because he was temporarily overcome by lust. In this state of intense desire, he threw his arm around his wife and wanted to unite with her. But she rejected his advances and hid herself in the bodies of the wives of seven sages who just happened to be meditating in a nearby forest. Unsatisfied, and now intent on pursuing his wife Parvati, Shiva shrewdly took the form of fire (the god Agni). Reaching the place where the seven sages were meditating, he then signaled his interest in meeting those seven women who were hovering patiently not far from their meditating husbands. Six of the sages' seven wives showed some interest in satisfying Shiva's "fire of desire." That was because, as a magician, Shiva managed to enter these women's minds and influence their thinking. But there was one wife, the seventh, whose mind remained steadfastly focused on her own husband and so she experienced no lustful thoughts. However, the six women who were attracted by this intruder, still wished to retain their chastity and good reputations, despite this temptation caused by a romantic visitor. They did not want their bodies violated. Supportive of these women's wishes, Shiva's own wife Parvati continued to keep herself hidden within each of the six. As Shiva approached each one with desire, Parvati reached out her hand and each time she managed to catch the fiery semen Shiva ejaculated, receiving it in her cupped right palm. Later, after leaving the six women and taking the form of a bird, this fine goddess flew out of that forest, directly to the very summit of the Himalayas. Still holding her special treasure, she went right to the place where she and Shiva shared a home. Reaching the summit of the sky's great vault, Parvati then put all of the semen she had collected into a single golden pot for safe keeping.

This all happened on the first day of the lunar fortnight of the yearly period called Krittika, when the sun rises at dawn in the constellation known as the Pleiades. This association of the spring equinox with the Krittika will be further discussed in the next chapter. For now we need only note that Agni or fire resides specifically in the Krittika constellation. To continue with the story; the precious and fiery seed that Parvati had placed in her storage pot soon began to take on form. It developed into the shape of a young boy. That infant's growth from an embryo into a full-blown young boy took a mere four days. When that small child finally stepped out into the open, however, he had six heads. This was because the semen that had generated him had been ejaculated at six distinct, separate moments. Six separate hands had collected it and it had then been carried upward in the form of six distinct gelatinous balls. Furthermore, the result of the merger of these six gel-balls created no ordinary baby. Instead, a miraculous young boy now emerged and was holding a great bow in one hand and a spear in the other. All the other gods were terrified when they saw this miracle. They wanted that young child killed because they feared his power. But this young child, who of course was Murugan, now immediately shot arrows towards his father's home. That home was the great white mountain where Shiva both lived and liked to meditate. Next the same young boy hurled his other weapon, the spear that he held in his second hand. It flew towards the same mountain where it promptly split it into equal halves. The gods were amazed, and the all the mountains nearby bowed down in awe before that newborn child.[1] There is more to the story but let us pause here for now.

Next consider the birth of the twin heroes in the Legend of Ponnivala. It was Lord Shiva who first placed the essence of the twin heroes' spirits in Tamarai's womb. The two life-energies he chose, as mentioned above, were those of Arjuna and Bhima, key heroes in the Mahabharata story. Here comes the first parallel. We know that in Murugan's story Parvati placed Shiva's semen in a golden pot for safe keeping. In the Ponnivala Nadu story the heroes' mother, Tamarai, caries a near-identical golden pot back to earth with her that Shiva gave her when she visited his council chambers in Kailasa. When Tamarai gave drops of the liquid in that pot to barren women on earth, they all become pregnant. We can presume, of course, that this Ponnivala Nadu story pot was full of the same magical substance: Shiva's own semen. When baby Murugan leapt out of his golden pot, in the Murugan myth, he carried weapons and was instantly able to speak and fight. In the Legend of Ponnivala Nadu Vishnu performs a magical and bloodless Caesarian on Tamarai and two little heroes then jump out of their mother's womb fully dressed and they are carrying weapons as well. This time one boy holds a dagger-like knife and the other a small spear. These seem to be near-multiforms of the arrow and spear Lord Murugan held at birth and quickly used to split Mount Himalaya in two. According to the classic myth, Murugan first shot an arrow at this mountain peak but then, deciding that one arrow was not enough, he also used his spear. The desired effect came to pass on his second try, and thus the spear became his weapon choice. Nowadays, everywhere in Tamil Nadu, one can find icons of Lord Murugan standing tall and holding a great spear in his right hand.

In Figs. 7.1 and 7.2 we see two images, both photographed in 1965 in the local Kongu area where the text of the Ponnivala story studied here was first collected. Figure 7.1 is a painting of the twin Ponnivala Nadu heroes seen on the exterior wall of a temple that at the time was devoted to these dual folk divinities. Note that their sister, Tangal, is shown seated between them. She is given extra prominence and a larger shrine than they are. Figure 7.2 is a photograph of a stone statue honouring Lord Murugan that resided in the local Shiva temple nearby. There Murugan was housed in a separate building, not far from the main shrine in the same complex, which was dedicated to his father, Shiva. Murugan's mother Parvati and his elder brother, Ganesh, also had their own shrines within the same big temple compound. This is the standard layout for a Shiva temple complex in this area. Note that in this classic layout the Murugan icon occupies the centre of the sacred space and that he is then framed by statures of his two wives, whose height is much less. But the reverse is the case in figure 7.1 where the female (now a sister) is in the centre and it is she who is framed by her two smaller-scale brothers. As is typical of many, many examples, Murugan's spear is pointing upward (a resting pose) in the Shiva temple context where we find him, while in the shrine dedicated to these two folk heroes their very similar knife-like weapons point downward (an active, more violent position). The similarity between the two sets of deities, one classical and folk, is clearly visible yet certain features have been inverted. These icon sets are different, yet also similar in several suggestive ways.

Note that in the high-class Shiva temple setting Murugan has his first wife to his right. Her name is Devayanai, while on the other side we see his secondary wife, a forest-dwelling concubine-spouse named Valli.[2] In figure 7.1, the folk temple parallel, there is a reflection of this same idea. There we see the heroic younger brother Shankar (labelled Cinnannan in the Tamil script seen) standing to his sister's right. That is the place of honour. Meanwhile Ponnar (Periyannan on the label, a name for the elder brother) is presented standing on her left. Hence, the

250   Hidden Paradigms

Figure 7.1. The Ponnivala triplets, showing the two heroic brothers with their sister Tangal between them. This is a painting on the exterior wall of a folk temple dedicated to all three.

Figure 7.2. Lord Murugan framed by his two wives. The conventional, high-status wife is placed to Murugan's right. These stone statues were located inside a large, high-class shrine primarily honouring Murugan's father, Lord Shiva.

right-side left-side contrast is maintained across the classical-folk divide. In the folk epic it is the younger brother who is most loved and most worshipped and we see that he is accorded that extra right-side status even though he is always addressed as the younger twin. Significant, too, is the fact that in high status, classical, iconography where one finds two females, usually wives, they represent split roles, one elder and formal, the other younger and more informal, often a girl of the forest, a concubine or similar love-wife. Two males play this contrast out in the folk heroes' iconography employed in another localized Ponnivala Nadu folk temple. Figures 7.3 and 7.4 present two additional examples of the portrayal of that younger, much beloved twin in a visual form. Note how these images both focus on his best known and most violent action of all, the killing of the wild boar. By contrast,

Figure 7.3. Cast bronze statue of the younger twin, Shankar, spearing Komban, a wild boar demon-like figure.

Figure 7.4. Terracotta image of Shankar spearing the wild boar Komban.

Murugan is universally portrayed in a far calmer and less threatening pose. In temple settings his spear always points upward, and in addition, it is often capped with a protective and cooling lemon fruit.

The Ponnivala Twins

Now it is time to continue with the epic story told about the Ponnivala Nadu twins. As we shall see, the folk account of these two heroes' arrival on earth suggestively parallels Murugan's own birth history as recounted by multiple myths. In the Ponnivala case, no time is lost in emphasizing the folk heroes' ferocity and bravery from the first minutes of their lives. The instant the twin brothers jump out of their mother's womb danger confronts them. Remember that Murugan, too, was threatened by the gods of Kailasa who were jealous of him and feared his strength from the start. In the folk epic rival male cousins are the first threat the twin heroes face. Those cousins fear they will lose their lands if those twin children are ever allowed to mature and take back their family lands. Therefore the cousins bribed a local midwife to kill them at birth. But the boys were born faster than expected (due to Vishnu's caesarian) and as they jumped out they both ran into the neighbouring palace room where they found the local midwife sharpening her knife. She was hoping to murder them at birth before their mother, Tamarai, even became aware of their existence. The midwife had blindfolded Tamarai soon after her labour pains began, with this violent plot in mind. The two Ponnivala boys' first act, after they emerge from their mother's womb into the light of day, was to rush into the birthing room's side chamber and kick the evil woman hard. She is described as a hunch-back, a familiar mythical theme representing evil intent. But when Shankar, the younger twin, kicks her hump her back magically straightens

252   Hidden Paradigms

Figure 7.5. Shankar kicks the hunch out of the midwife's back.

Figure 7.6. The twin heroes are fed tiger's milk by the goddess Cellatta

(figure 7.5). This act exorcises the midwife's evil nature and her frightening wish to kill the two new-born brothers and the two boys can now run safely back to the queen's larger birthing room nearby. There they are quickly grabbed by the fine family goddess, Cellatta, who has just emerged from a secret tunnel she dug earlier that day. The tunnel's exit lies hidden under a wooden box, strategically placed inside the birthing chamber. Cellatta quickly grabs the twin boys and carries them, without a sound, back through that hidden passageway. Once she reaches her temple, she places both boys in a wide cave-like space located directly beneath her own shrine. The two heroes live in this special area, hidden from all around them, for a full five years. During this time Cellatta dedicates herself to teaching the two a variety of martial arts. Furthermore, this divine foster mother, feeds them both on tiger's milk (figure 7.6).[3] In early myths about Murugan, it must be noted, a tiger serves as his mount, another possible parallel with the folk story account of the twin's early life. And the same mount is also used by

Splitting, Replicating, and Twinning of Gods and Animals 253

Figure 7.7. The seven Kannimar, linked by the story to the Pleiades or seven Krittika maidens.

Cellatta. The two boys thus become tiger-like almost from the moment of their birth. Both brothers also learn to ride an elephant under Cellatta's careful watch, another animal strongly associated with Murugan's broader story.

The elephant fits nicely with Murugan's wider mythology as he also rode an elephant as a young child.[4] But the elephant's most common depiction is as a mount for the ancient god Indra. And, indeed, many have noted that Lord Murugan seems to have more or less taken over Indra's role in the wider Hindu pantheon as his own mythical tradition developed. Very much in keeping with that historical suggestion is the interesting fact that Indra often expresses ambivalence towards Murugan. Perhaps he had a sense that Murugan would become a rival and feared being overpowered by this newcomer. When Murugan demonstrates his strength by shattering several mountains, Indra's multiple expressions of anxiety seem to be justified.[5] Therefore, when we hear that Ponnivala Nadu's own local hero, Shankar, also rode an elephant in his early years, it suggests, once more, that this younger brother is growing up to become an unspoken double, a kind of beloved folk avatar of Lord Murugan worshipped at the local level.

Another set of clues that suggest there may be a deep resonance between the Ponnivala Nadu twins and Lord Murugan can be seen in the role their sister Tangal plays in this folk epic. Tangal is explicitly described as the youngest of the Kannimar (figure 7.7) and the youngest of the seven sisters of the Pleiades constellation, locally known as the Krittika. This constellation (Nakshatra) spans two of the zodiac's key symbolic figures, Aries and Taurus. In Babylonian sky drawings, as will be seen in the next chapter, the Pleiades are placed right above the hairy hump of the great sky bull where they are, most certainly, intimately linked to that great bovine male.[6] Although story listeners know that a third child, a sister-triplet, is also born at the same time as these two brothers, this little girl is never mentioned side by side with her twin brothers' story, at least not for the first five years. At birth the sister stays hidden inside her mother's womb until after her brothers have left the scene through that tunnel. Then she exits through her mother's cervical passage, following normal birth procedures. There is a reason for this. Tangal is not threatened by the cousins and did not need the local goddess' protection in the same way her two brothers clearly did.

The association between a bull and the seven entities pictured above its hump is depicted now and then in a much wider context, being part of a pattern of associations that emerges very early in Indo-European art. Though there is some variability in whether the seven Pleiades characters are male or female, there is wide agreement that they embody both aggressive and protective styles of energy and are, in an important sense, androgynous. Ancient sailors around the globe depended on this constellation's movement across the night sky for navigational guidance. Somewhat similar myths about this very particular star cluster can be found in almost every culture around the world, including in native North American legends (see figure 6.1 and 6.3).[7] Using the Pleiades as a kind of compass was a navigational skill likely spread by ocean-going sailors. And various mythical tales about them must have travelled alongside. Indeed, the Pleiades' association with a bull or a cow is widespread in Europe and in the Middle East, as well as in South Asia. Milk is boiled for these seven maidens during the winter solstice rituals (called the patti pongal) and also for the sun, for whom Shiva may be a stand-in (figure 7.8). These seven women are mentioned in ancient Indian astrological records and are also seen, pictorially, in early Indus Valley seals that archaeologists have uncovered. There are multiple examples of this same star cluster in art traditions popular for millennia with the peoples of ancient Mesopotamia as well.[8]

The Krittika are associated with birth in Hindu tradition, and most specifically with the birth of Lord Murugan. Many different myths mention that there were six Krittika maidens hovering around this god at his birth, a critical event that occurred at the time of the spring equinox, the time when the new year was believed to begin. According to stories told in India, six maidens picked up the glowing young Murugan as he miraculously came into sight. They then nursed him with their own milk which, unaided, began to flow from their breasts. Hence the Krittika are believed to have served as Murugan's nursemaids and protectors, right from the beginning. Although that is the standard myth, there are other versions where Parvati, wife of Shiva, Murugan's mother in all but a biological sense, herself picked up the baby Murugan and nursed him. When this happened milk suddenly flowed directly from her breasts into his mouth.[9] There are also many variants of the Murugan story that describe the Krittika constellation as representing the six sages' wives and in some very popular stories these six women nursed Murugan at his birth, a possible explanation for why he manifests himself with six heads (perhaps so he can nurse from six women at once).

Splitting, Replicating, and Twinning of Gods and Animals   255

Figure 7.8. A farmer's wife boiling milk for the patti pongal ritual.

It is also important to clarify that Murugan is an ambivalent god with multiple personalities. For example, Kamil Zvelebil has translated a part of one well-known poem describing Lord Murugan as follows:

You who have form and are formless
You who are being and non-being
who are the fragrance and the blossom
who are the jewel and its luster
who are the seed of life and life itself[10]

The numerous oppositions expressed in the above poem are obvious: form/formless, being/non-being, smell/look, solid object/reflected light, and potential/actual life-energy. Another well-known author states that "Skanda-Kumara may be a composite deity linked to the Greek gods ... given the numismatic overlap in their iconography and their similar warrior-god mythologies."[11] Another well-known Murugan scholar, Fred Clothey, has written: "Murugan is a uniter, championing the attributes of both Shaivism and Vaisnavism."[12] Therefore, finding a folk form of Murugan expressed as a twinned pair or set of dual heroes is not so far-fetched when we consider that the orthodox iconographic form of this god shows him with one body but six heads. In sum, diversity and complexity are used to express the very essence of Murugan's inner being.

The Vaisnavite-Shaivite mix found in the folk symbolism associated with Ponnivala Nadu's two heroes is similarly remarkable. Both Shiva and Vishnu are featured in this epic folk tale where they collaborate as brothers-in-law much as they do elsewhere in Tamil folk tradition. Indeed, these two deities are seen interacting several times in this story. They collaborate but there is also some tension, and they tease each other regularly. The insight the Ponnivala Nadu story provides into this deep paradigm is useful and it has contemporary implications: here we see Lord Murugan quietly hidden within two bodies. He projects and displays himself, in this epic account, through the bard's repeated and reverent description of a collaborative pair of male twins. These two have very different personalities and contrasted skill sets. One brother is peaceful and contemplative, while the other is active, violent at times. Although this duality of the divine is celebrated here, in the broader folk tradition Murugan remains a singular deity. Thus, this idea that Murugan could manifest himself in a very popular folk epic as a set of twins may seem surprising. There are numerous lifetime devotees of the Ponnivala twin deities, as well as of Murugan as a separate god. Yet none have described this overlap to me in words. But as a long-time observer and ethnographer, I am convinced that the hidden paradigm just described is real. Indeed, it is manifest not only in the divine Ponnivala twins' actual behaviour patterns but this similarity is also displayed in the enormous emotive expression of affection and devotion locals feel for these two heroes of their favourite regional story.[13]

The Ponnivala Nadu twins are always two separate heroes who move about together (most of the time) in the Ponnivala Nadu story. They are never described as six rather than two, just as Murugan himself is never spoken of as six gods who are multiples of each other in some way, even though Murugan often has six heads. Many readers will have already thought of these two heroes' likely association with the famous Vedic Aśvin twins. This is a pair of early heroes described as having horses' heads and whose job was, among other things, to faithfully pull the sun's chariot across the sky daily. And the Ponnivala Nadu twins are indeed famous for their horsemanship, too, just like the Aśvins were. The next two chapters will discuss this parallel in more depth. Here it is sufficient to say that the sun fathered the Aśvins, while Murugan was sired (in many variants of his mythology) by Agni who is the god of fire. The sun and Agni, of course, are closely related entities. But more interesting is that many variants of the Aśvin's story give them a sister named Usas or "Dawn." As we know, Tamil folk twins Ponnar and Shankar also have a sister, Tangal, who is a key player in the brothers' life stories. Tangal also has sun associations and is the direct re-embodiment of one of the Krittika sisters, the Pleiades star-based constellation that rose just before dawn at the time of the spring equinox during the period just before and just following 2200 BCE.

The vernal equinox was once considered the starting point for a new annual cycle of the Hindu Nakshatras, twenty-eight constellation patterns that fill the sky according to Hindu astrological tradition. Although the starting point of this ancient system has now been shifted to an earlier appearing constellation called Ashwini (named after the Aśvin twins) due to a well-documented physical phenomenon called "the procession of the equinoxes," the role and symbolism of the Krittika remains prominent even now. Tangal, as a Krittika, can thus be thought of as a star cluster associated with fire that both helps engender new life and serves to protect and nurture it. The Krittika are also associated with the farmers goat, sheep, and cattle pens where new life is birthed in the spring. Tangal is also the Ponnivala story triplet selected by Shiva himself as a secret form of the goddess that he places in Tamarai's womb along with the twins. Her mission will be to guide and advise those two co-born brothers throughout their lives. And Tangal (the Krittika maiden) is also the one who repeatedly blesses the heroes' swords, lending them the magical power that helps them to defeat others at critical battle moments.[14]

At the end of the Ponnivala Nadu story Tangal briefly resurrects her two brothers, an event discussed previously, especially in the chapter that discusses this story's significant biblical parallels. This resurrection happens when she finds their dead bodies and yearns to talk to her two siblings one more time. Tangal offers the twins a drink of milk as she briefly resurrects them. In local rituals performed one day a year, local devotees become possessed by these twin heroes' spirits and soon fall to the ground, as if dead. One or more pre-puberty girls are then drafted to revive them, a critical procedure that local worshippers depend on to return their community members to life.[15] Tangal, an earthly representation of the Pleiades, is also strongly associated with milk and with all its symbolism related to nurturing, caring for, and protecting young children that special liquid suggests. Mother's milk is ritually replaced in local ceremonies by cow's milk, and a central event focused on the boiling and drinking of sweetened cow's milk is woven directly into rituals performed in association with the telling of the Ponnivala Nadu story. Note the ritual vessel prominently positioned at the side of this set of constellation-linked females (the Kannimar) in figure 7.9. There will be more on this below.

After her brothers' final demise, Lord Shiva returns Tangal to heaven to rejoin her other star-sisters. She does not immediately appear to be anything like the fierce Krittika group of male divinities that others describe in accounts of ancient Mesopotamian tradition. But a "male" side to the Krittika's temperament is certainly made clear in several collections of Tamil poetry dedicated to describing these seven women.[16] For example, Tangal becomes very fierce after her brothers die. It is only then that she decides to burn down her own family palace

Figure 7.9. A temple icon for the Kannimar, seen with a direct reference to the ritual pot painted on the right side of their small shrine.

as well as the secondary palace where her two sisters-in-law live while they are still inside it.[17] Tangal then proceeds to conduct a brief joint funeral ceremony for her two dead brothers by feeding crows cooked rice. She also takes the burnt bones of her cremated sisters-in-law to the river and lets them float away there. Although feeding the crows is generally a woman's responsibility, placing human remains in a river is a man's job according to Hindu tradition more generally. Afterwards Tangal embarks on a long forest journey alone, wandering through unknown territory in search of her brothers' dead bodies. That is a dangerous excursiion that normally only a very brave man would undertake. For a girl, travelling alone is far from usual or acceptable. In sum, after her brothers' deaths Tangal's character shifts from being mostly female to one that is largely male. When one considers this phase of her life one can say that Tangal now becomes an androgynous figure at heart, part male and part female. She thus presents another kind of doubling, different but also clearly related to the doubling her own brothers portray.[18]

O'Flaherty writes that the Krittikas at times appear as loving women with breasts full of milk but that at other moments these same girls act as hideous mothers who try to kill Murugan. In that latter case the Krittikas resemble Kali. O'Flaherty goes on to say that the instant the Krittikas were born was itself a moment fraught with danger and a swirl of oppositions, a moment when the sun opposed the moon and fire opposed water. It was also a moment of dangerous astrological ambivalence, one where there was a clear reversal of pairs, particularly of male and female behaviours.[19] This could be a major reason why we see Tangal (the Krittika) displaying both female and male traits. This finding reinforces the larger argument presented here, that ambi-valence (sitting on two sides of the same scale) is a key theme associated with all three triplets. The earlier reference to the spring equinox becomes more meaningful now as it too is a moment of balance between opposites, the dark and the light halves of the year, the cool and the hot periods in this cycle, etc. Murugan, too, displays a mixed bundle of character traits in his many myth-based stories. All these findings align nicely with the earlier suggestion that Murugan, himself, is hidden inside this most interesting Ponnivala Nadu folk epic, as a pair of twins.

Cows

The second hidden paradigm this chapter will focus on is the centrality of cows in the Ponnivala Nadu story. This may sound like a truism for a legend from India, since popular wisdom has it that every Hindu believes that cows are sacred, but in fact, the importance of cows in this epic account is not nearly as obvious as one might think. Instead, the role of cattle constitutes an additional deep paradigm underlying this entire legend, However, just like the secret presence of Murugan and the broad theme of the doubled or combo-set of personalities he embodies, the importance of cows does not rise to the surface of this account easily. It is a topic that needs further exploration in order to highlight its full significance. To begin, we can first note that the two bards who sang the Ponnivala Nadu story, at least as collected during my fieldwork stay in the area, used the following ritualized sequence of phrases repeatedly:

> In the land of fulfilment, the land of cows,
> (In) the beautiful country where the Kaveri flows.

In these words we find fulfilment, cows, and the lovely Kaveri River merged. These words belong together and as a unit they express one basic thing: contentment and prosperity. As further evidence of this, when the heroine Tamarai began to worry that she was barren, she looked to the landscape around her before crying out in despair. The first thing she noticed was that the cows of Ponnivala Nadu were all barren as well. She then decided to test that discovery and so she asked a servant to find and buy two fine calves. He was told that these must be beautiful animals, of opposite sex, and of fine ancestral stock. They were to have big eyes, small ears, and short tails. The servant found two animals that fit that description, purchased them, and handed them over to the queen. She immediately passed the two fine animals on, one cow and one bull, to the family shepherd. Tamarai ordered him to raise both with loving care.

The outcome of all Tamarai's effort was sad indeed. One year later she observed that there had been no successful mating between those newly purchased animals and thus, no young calves had been born. Afterwards Tamarai tried mating other animal pairs, like a handsome billy-goat with a lovely nannie, but the outcome was always the same. A state of complete barrenness had blanketed her entire kingdom. Tamarai's first concern lay with the reproductive prowess of Ponnivala's cows. This was of central symbolic significance and she gave it primacy. The infertility of Ponnivala Nadu's cows was a key sign that the family kingdom, as a whole, was in dire trouble. What she also knew was that when her husband Kunnutaiya was much younger, things had been different. He had once worked as a shepherd for two powerful farmer-landowners of a different male lineage, the one her father belonged to. After Kunnutaiya was hired, those two bosses noticed that their herd of cows started to grow rapidly and that there were plenty of calves being born. Kunnutaiya, their young shepherd, was credited with that success. His goodness had brought fertility to their lands. His skills, his attitude of honest service, and his inner magic had combined to bring well-being to all around him. Once Tamarai married Kunnutaiya and they returned to his ancestral farmlands, everything had changed. She knew something must be wrong and she blamed herself. What had she done to cause this family calamity? She believed that she must herself be the ultimate barren cow, the misfit that lay at the base of all this misfortune.

The true reason that cow welfare is considered to be at the root of human prosperity in this story, however, surfaces much earlier, during the lifetime of the first generation of Ponnivala Nadu story heroes. As already described, seven beloved cows had met their deaths by trying to jump a fence that Kunnutaiya's foster father Kolatta had built. Kolatta had only meant to protect his first sugarcane crop from harm and had never envisioned, of course, that the new fence he had built would kill any cows. But later this error in judgement became all too plain and simple. Kolatta had not done enough research to try to discover what kind of animals had been grazing in his sugarcane field and trampling down his prize plants. This pioneer ancestor had been overly hasty in deciding to order the construction of a vicious spiked barrier. He had only wanted to protect those precious plants from further harm but had not thought about the welfare of others. The result had been catastrophic.

Those seven dead cow spirits rose to Shiva's Kailasa council chambers high in the Himalayas and there they complained bitterly. As a result, Shiva had cursed Kolatta saying that his entire family line would now undergo seven generations of barrenness as a punishment for that mistake. Shiva's rule of compensation, it would seem, was that future suffering would have to match the crime. Hence he decreed that human birthing by the females in Kolatta's family line would stop until seven generations had passed, one for each cow that had died. As a result Kolatta's wife found herself barren after her marriage, although she herself did not know the reason for this. But as we know, there is more. Shiva's brother-in-law then pleaded with him and managed to soften Shiva's heart. Somehow the founders of the Land of Ponnivala Nadu had to have descendants. To resolve this problem Shiva decided to hide a baby of his own creation under a pile of rocks in a back field, a place where Kolatta, if he was sufficiently attentive, could find it. Furthermore, a cow was involved in that key event.

It was a kind-hearted cow that led the hero to the pile of rocks where the baby lay hidden. How? After some time Kolatta noticed that this cow, a member of his own herd, was discharging her milk into a pile of rocks. Kolatta was curious and ordered his workers to investigate. When they started removing rocks from that pile, they found a young baby lying there underneath. The workers handed that child to Kolatta, who was overjoyed at his unexpected find. He and Tamarai quickly adopted the little boy. They named him Kunnutaiya (roughly meaning "man of the hillock" or "man from the stones"). In sum, Shiva's gift of a child and the act of the cow who fed that child milk are treated as connected. Cows and human women are seen to be multi-forms of each other throughout this story. They are also part of a visual art tradition: images of divine cows that are shown in folk art as giving their milk to the earth are commonplace, as in the painting on a local temple wall shown in figure 7.10. We will return to these points shortly.

Bulls

On the reverse side of this human-cow match up, however, are negative consequences. Cruelty to cows on earth is followed up with complementary acts of cruelty by the gods, at least in the Ponnivala Nadu story. As an example of this we can examine the case of a merciless, bull-like Shiva who taunts Tamarai while she is trying to perform a serious penance, asking him for a pregnancy. This determined Ponnivala queen finally succeeds in her quest, but only after Shiva has put her through seven horrific deaths. The harsh god orders his assistants to burn her, to have her chewed up by an elephant, to have her trampled until she becomes nothing but mush, and finally asks his assistants to cut off her head. It would seem that Shiva is seeking retribution for those seven cow deaths

262   Hidden Paradigms

Figure 7.10. Painting of a divine cow seen on the exterior wall of a Shiva temple in the area.

that occurred much earlier in the story. That bout of cow suffering was not of Tamarai's making. This was a mistake made by her father-in-law long back, before she had even been born. But Shiva had equated the cows' lives with human ones. Now one poor human female, a queen no less, is made to suffer one death for each of the seven cows.[20] Tamarai undergoes those seven deaths at the hands of Shiva's helpers. But each time Vishnu counters this cruelty by wetting her bones in a nearby stream and reviving this poor woman. Shiva's anger and the punishment he meted out are reminiscent of a powerful sky bull who snorts and charges at an innocent bystander. Since Tamarai is seen to be a metaphorical cow, it seems likely that Shiva is her metaphorical equivalent here, a dangerous bull-like sky-god. He may well reflect the constellation, Taurus, seen in early sky maps and known to both the Egyptians and the Babylonians.[21] Shiva is also Tamarai's mythical father, the god who disguised himself as a deer to chase his wife, and whose semen then fell on to a lotus plant below, from where Tamarai emerges as a tiny baby in one of this epic's most vivid and charming side-stories.

In these scenes where Shiva orders Tamarai attacked, we see sky and earth responding to each other and interacting. This is especially so when cow welfare is at issue. To make this linkage even clearer, in the third generation we see something more happen. The story's heroic twins have been formed by Shiva from the spirits of two great Mahabharata figures, Arjuna and Bhima. Both embryos are birthed by Tamarai as young magical children and then two grow gradually into the story's twin heroes, both of whom serve as great bull-like human warriors. Eventually when they decide to give up their lives by falling forward on their swords, the two men are understood to be giving their spirits back to the sky for recycling in the divine realm high above. What came from the sky now

Figure 7.11. The seven Kannimar with a cobra hood stretched over the group. The photograph was taken inside a local temple dedicated to honouring this story's epic heroes.

goes back to the sky. In sum, when one looks carefully at the background themes in this folk epic, it becomes clear that cow prosperity and cow deaths, provide both an engine and a backdrop to all that happens in the larger Ponnivala Nadu story. Bovines and humans are also intimately intertwined in ancient Tamil poetry. There we see human warriors likened to fierce bulls and human females with young offspring compared with lactating cows. One could go on to discuss the symbolism of human breast milk and of cow's milk within this same poetic universe. That is another equivalent symbolic theme that derives from pairing humans and cattle. But the core point has already been made.

Cobras

What should be further noted, however, is that the cow seen in figure 7.10 is releasing her milk onto a snake mound, likely one housing cobras. It is very common to see portrayals of the seven Kannimar with a wide cobra hood stretched over them as shown in figure 7.11. Cobras are strongly associated with milk, which is thought to be their favourite food. This species of serpent is especially sacred, and people often set out dishes of milk for them. Further, if a cobra is killed it will then be given a ceremonial, human-style cremation. Perhaps this is because cobras are major representatives of the underworld. They serve to complete this picture of milk (also of nourishing rain) travelling from the heavens above, to earth and then to underground rivers which constitute the cobra community's main home. It is as if the universe is understood to have a sandwich construction with gods both above and below. Flowing milk, poetically equated with abundant rain, serves to connect these three domains. Both the spirits above and the frightening forces below will protect mankind if treated with empathy but both will also punish humans if ignored or abused.

In at least one local shrine dedicated to the heroes of this local epic, the initial deity worshipped is a cobra snake called "mother." She receives first honours, even before Shiva and Parvati are offered foods, though they stand next in line. After that comes the goddess Lakshmi and then Saraswati, followed by a line-up of the seven Kannimar. After that, the first Ponnivala Nadu character worshipped is the heroes' younger sister Tangal. Only after all these preliminaries does the priest reach the heroes Ponnar and Shankar themselves. These two are presented, with great pride, sitting on their fine terracotta horses (see figure 7.12). In sum, the entire temple presents an interesting folk model of the cosmos writ large. There is a clear recognition of the underground deities, in this case a cosmic cobra mother, next the folk epic's key characters who inhabit middle earth, and finally we see an array of grand deities that dwell in the sky, the great gods Shiva, Parvati, Lakshmi, Saraswati, and even Brahma. The heroes stand in the middle, between an underground and an upper realm. Thus, this temple, like many others, places this important epic legend in a middle ground that is seen surrounded by what lies both above and below. The story may be presented simply in this local folk shrine, but the layout visually acknowledges its link to some very deep underlying paradigms about the universe at large. And there are some interesting further details to note as well. Although it is difficult to see in figure 7.12, both brothers hold swords, but only the younger brother, Shankar (on the right), has a lemon stuck on the tip of that weapon. This is because he is the fiercer of the two men and hence his weapon is the more dangerous one, an implement that needs some cooling protection applied to its fierce, deadly point.

The Cattle Pen

Why is the cattle pen such an important symbol? It is, for the most part, because of an interesting matchup between the importance given cows in the Ponnivala story and some parallel facts found to permeate ancient Babylonian beliefs. Gavin White, in his enthralling book, *Queen of the Night* (2014b), addresses the Babylonian cattle pen concept in some detail. White shows clearly that all

Splitting, Replicating, and Twinning of Gods and Animals 265

Figure 7.12. The twin story heroes on terracotta horses featured in the folk temple discussed.

Figure 7.13. The cattle pen where Kunnutaiya cared for his master's most significant animals as a young boy.

human life, and much animal life as well, was believed by Babylonians to originate in a great cattle pen that had two parts, one on earth and the other in the sky. The sky was the lead-off pen where life was created in embryo form. It was where the great bull of heaven dwelt and, now and then, where he cast his semen among the stars. Some of that birthing power, people believed, fell to earth (or was carried there by intermediaries) where it then entered the cattle pens of men. The result was the appearance of new calves in each pen, early in the spring. That same gift of fertility was also thought to enter human wombs and cause pregnancies. At least this is the persistent metaphor widely seen in Mesopotamian art, according to White. Sometimes young calves are shown in the illustrations during the moments when they are being carried down to earth by eagle-like birds. When those calves reach the land below, the art further suggests that they then become lodged inside human wombs so that human women can birth them. Indeed, human birthing may have commonly happened outside the home, in the family cattle pen anyway. If this were South India, the reasoning would be that the cattle pen is a place where the blood and disorder of a new birth can be tolerated and its pollution contained. In Ponnivala Nadu the gods above are seen as the life-givers, offering their life-giving benefits both to humans and to cattle. Cows and humans, in ancient Babylonia and as also as seen in the Ponnivala Nadu epic to a lesser degree, are metaphorically merged. The concept may seem magical to modern readers, but it fits well with the evidence White presents. His book contains numerous Babylonian-sourced illustrations of this principle.[22] The cattle pen was a point of intersection, a place where sky, cow, and human female met.

There is one more important point: What highlights this well-hidden Ponnivala epic theme of the cattle pen's centrality can be seen in a ritual that is performed each January in association with a larger harvest festival in the Kongu area referred to as the Pongal festival (a term associated with the verb "pongi," meaning to be abundant or to overflow.) Locally, the "patti pongal" or a pongal performed in the cattle pen was an event I first encountered during my early fieldwork carried out in this region in 1965–6. But its central significance only became highlighted in my thinking much later, when a local Ponnivala bard stressed its link to the story studied here, in an interview.[23] This singer spontaneously pointed to the fact that it was his personal habit to urge all his story listeners, immediately upon having heard his story, to perform a patti pongal. In his mind this entire legend was intended as a precursor that led up to and necessitated the ceremonial completion of this specific ritual in order to properly complete this story's telling.

The Patti Pongal

Unfortunately, the patti pongal rite is no longer widely performed. This has likely happened because people wealthy enough to own cows nowadays also

Splitting, Replicating, and Twinning of Gods and Animals 267

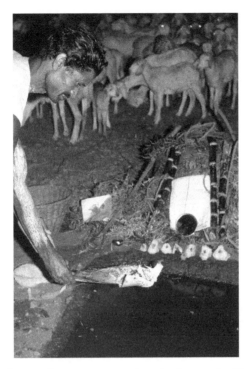

Figure 7.14. Worshipping the seven sisters in the animal pen, a ritual known as the patti pongal that I attended in 1966. Here the pen happened to contain sheep.

tend to prefer spending their money and time sponsoring more orthodox rituals that have Vedic links and that are managed and presided over by Brahmins. But there is little doubt that patti pongal ceremonial procedures were once very popular among farmers living in the hinterlands of the Kongu region. Here is a brief summary of the central steps involved in the patti pongal ritual (figure 7.14): 1) A shallow square depression is dug inside the farmer's cattle pen enclosure and filled with water; 2) Seven small white-quartz rocks are then set along this pool's western edge so that these stones face east, and also so that they look across this watery pond, perhaps surveying it and keeping it safe; 3) Either the farmer himself or a hired non-Brahman ritual specialist then performs a worship of those seven stones with an offering that includes the burning of a vegetal torch made from a large palmyra palm leaf; 4) A vine is strung across the eastern end of the pond between two upright stakes; 5) An uncastrated male calf (in other words, a young bull) is then driven through that vine so that he breaks it in two. That calf is then chased across the watery pool that is situated just behind that now-broken vine; 6) The animals in the

268   Hidden Paradigms

cattle pen, which may also include goats and sheep, are sprayed or sprinkled with red-coloured water; 7) Milk is boiled in a pot in or near this entire layout and that milk, which can be mixed with rice or other grains plus a little sugar so as to form a gruel, is allowed to boil over the pot's edge; 8) The sweet hot milk, after being boiled, is then offered to the seven stones before being shared by the entire family of onlookers as a sweet conclusion to this patti (cow pen) event.

If we try to read some meaning into the above sequence of actions, taken together, they appear to point to the following broad concepts:

1) The pond represents or mirrors the vast ocean believed to be the sky above, a vast moist expanse in which the stars (metaphorically fish, called meen in Tamil) reside. Significantly, the shallow pond that is dug for the patti pongal is always square in shape, as are almost all Hindu ritual representations of the universe at large.[24]

2) The seven white stones aligned along the pond's western edge represent the Krittika (Pleiades constellation), locally referred to as the seven Kannimar. Those seven stars are the seven virgin maids, previously discussed, one of whom descended to earth to become the sister and protector of the heroic twins featured in the Ponnivala Nadu story.

3) In the sky, as mentioned, the Krittika constellation sits just above the hump of the great sky-bull known in the west as Taurus. He may well be watching this ceremonial event taking place on the surface of the world below. From the Tamil poetry about these young Krittika girls, we can further surmise that they appear to supervise and perhaps now and then limit or constrain the activities of that great bull, the grand fertilizer of all life. This would nicely parallel the role that Tangal plays in relation to her two brothers, Ponnar and Shankar, in the Ponnivala Nadu story. In any event it would seem that all lives, both animal and human, begin their journey through time as a small spark of light in the heavens above and that they gestate there while the Krittika watch over and help to protect these precious beginnings of new life.

4) The vegetal torch that is lit helps the worshipper and his/her family communicate with the Krittika, asking that they add new energy to their efforts and extend their protective watch. The same torch may also help light the way for any Krittika who wish to visit the earth as Kannimar maidens, as they frequently are said to do in local poetry collected in this area. Lighting the way would also help any carriers of new bright sparks to descend safely to earth and facilitate any subsequent births that may occur in the chosen cattle pen below. The red water thrown across the animals' backs is surely a signal that these beasts are thereby being fertilized, mysteriously, with new life. Meanwhile, the young bull that breaks the hymen-symbol of the vine, joins with the womb waters of a surrogate sky-pond to accomplish this magical fertilization task.

5) The boiling of milk and its overflow references the nursing and motherly care that will be given to all newborns, while the sweetness that is added reflects the

genuine joy participants anticipate they will feel when the many hoped-for births occur. Although human women in the area now give birth in hospitals, there is reason to think that many of their ancient grandmothers once went to their family's nearby cattle pen for their moment of delivery. If a woman went there to birth her child, the blood would easily have been soaked up by the earth, and the placenta would also have been left there. The hidden paradigm is that the stars in the sky are cows, and a bull (a star constellation) is roaming around amongst them. Their fertility and the consequent production of new sparks of life is what is ultimately responsible for the fecundity of human life wished for on earth.

The Great Sky-Cow and Sky-Bull

In the Ponnivala Nadu story the core cow-plus-bull theme performs several important practical functions as well as some mythical ones. The great goddess Parvati, herself, was thought of as the cosmic cow and as the primal creatrix. Afterall, it was she who, at the beginning of the story, creates an ancestral group of nine brothers and sees to it that they are placed safely on earth below. She then hands these nine a plough and instructs them to begin farming. Her male counterpart, Shiva, is pictured as a source of cosmic sexual energy, energy stored up by his incessant yogic-style meditation. He is vital to generating those first sparks of life that populate the sky, as well as to making sure that the entire cosmos stays energized. But his earthly counterpart, the neutered oxen, was vital to the ploughing process and to the transport of agricultural goods by oxcart. Oxen have been used as a principal draft animal all over South Asia since at least Vedic times. They are also critical for traditional irrigation, at least as it was practiced in the Kongu area up until 1970 or later. The oxen's great strength was needed to lift water up from deep wells. In addition, two-wheeled oxcarts were extensively used in village areas to transport humans as well as goods. I rode in these two-wheeled carts many times between 1964 and 1966 and, with athletic young oxen pulling them, those carts can move surprisingly fast.

The presence of cows is evident elsewhere in the Ponnivala Nadu legend as well, largely because their milk serves to nurture new life. The first generation of heroes arrives as a set of adult male brothers that descend to earth directly from the skies due to Parvati's creative powers. But in the second and third generations the gods supply, as a special gift, every baby that the lead lineage will require to ensure succession. Kunnutaiya arrives as a direct gift from Shiva and a cow feeds him while he lies beneath a pile of stones waiting to be discovered. In the next generation Shiva takes two existing spirits that float about in the sky, Arjuna's and Bhima's life essences, and places them in Tamarai's womb where they grow into the twin heroes. Once born they are protected and fed by the goddess Cellata, using the milk of a tiger, and of an elephant, which seem to be her super-powerful counterparts for the ordinary temple cow. The third triplet is fed by her foster mother on local cows' milk. As a foster mother Tamarai's breasts are not producing milk, so a local cow provides the backup she needs. This set of circumstances has the resulting benefit of giving each key protagonist a significant degree of divine parentage. But this story's logic does more than just offer each hero a part-divine ancestry. It also provides evidence of a deeper belief that all human life ultimately owes its origins to the magical fertility sent to earth by divinities who inhabit the skies above and gives each male access to magical milk that flows from heaven as well, something suggestively similar to the Vedic concept of a life-giving liquid called soma.

Cows in the Ponnivala Nadu story are gentle milk producing creatures who nurture others. Bulls, on the other hand are hero-helpers who protect their human masters but, if needed, can also help threaten their masters' enemies. In one central example a bunch of cattle (it is not clear if they are oxen or bulls) are driven across Kunnutaiya's finest field by a group of cruel and jealous cousins. The intent is to ruin his nascent crop. Fortunately, Lord Vishnu then appears on the scene and helps the trampled plants spring back to life. In a second case, two bulls take on the role of Ponnivala Nadu boundary guardians. When the Chola king sends an envoy to the collect tribute owed to him, those bulls challenge the outsiders and forbid them entry. Significantly, the bulls in question are able to speak, and when the king's envoys say unkind things about the twin rulers, they become angry and threaten to kill them both. This brings the two bulls very close to being human themselves. That same pair of bulls are also absolute loyalists who will not allow anyone to insult either the lands and the cattle of Ponnivala Nadu or its two rulers.

An interesting iconographic pattern that parallels the above can be observed on the walls of just about every local Shaivite temple found in the Kongu area. Many of these historic temples have prominent sculpted bulls seated at the four corners of that shrine's outermost compound wall (in figure 7.15, see the small, circled animals). In very modest shrines that have no outer compound this can mean these bulls sit on the four corners of the primary shrine itself. Using some imagination, this iconographic tradition seems to suggest that a group of bulls guard a cattle pen that is spatially and metaphorically identical with the temple's central compound. This again supports the idea that Shiva is metaphorically likened to a great sky-bull who dwells in his own grand cattle pen. This god's residence on earth, then, becomes not only a temple, but simultaneously evokes the image of a fine cattle pen. The god inside is the family head of that pen as well as the commander of a co-located temple space. By extension that same god, the great bull-of-heaven, is also the leader of an entire earth-based (human) family and the symbolism seems to state that the community worshipping there is his local cattle herd.

Just as a cattle herd can be seen to serve as a visual metaphor for a group of human families, so god's family in metaphoric terms consists of devotees who rest and feel at home inside his sacred pen. His devotees live there with him,

Splitting, Replicating, and Twinning of Gods and Animals 271

Figure 7.15. Local temple showing bulls on a Shiva compound wall, plus a (male) shrine with a central cupola.

Figure 7.16. The cupola summit on the local Cellatta temple, displaying a row of five pots plus a set of horns.

and he is their guardian. There is also a noticeable and consistently related pattern that references the central cupola-style summit used on the top of local Shiva shrines. The dome on a modest Shiva temple seen in this area will have a round form above its central shrine that looks like a pot with a spike on top of it (figure 7.15). But a temple dedicated to a goddess will have what looks like a row of pots, framed on each side with a shape that looks like a set of horns (figure 7.16). The male version reaches higher, is sky-oriented, and is singular, while the female version is horizontal, a row of duplicates (like her children) appearing to reference general abundance and perhaps the home of multiple children (little pots) guarded by a male with horns. The vessels depicted on the summit of these shrines always come in uneven multiples (three, five, seven, or nine) and are always aligned in a straight row. The situation depicted in ancient Babylonian art is not exactly the same, but there, both deities and kings wore crowns that look as if they could be cattle horns.[25] In this Kongu region of South India, Shiva is architecturally honoured with multiple male bovine guardians seated on the four corners of his temple compound wall, while counterpart goddesses have a bovine set of horns guarding the multiple pots that decorate the shrine's summit.

Shambuga and Shiva

Shambuga is a dark-skinned low-caste ally of the heroes who is half wild and sometimes unpredictable. It is interesting, considering Shambuga's low social rank, that he seems to bear some similarities to Shiva. For one, both Shiva and Shambuga are depicted riding a bull from time to time (figure 7.17). As mentioned earlier, Komban, the great wild boar in the Ponnivala Nadu story, seems to have some interchangeability with a wild bull.[26] One could suggest that Nandi is a kind of ascetic wild bull who is very loyal to Shiva and might also be his pet. The same cannot be said for Komban who is Shambuga's adversary. However, Komban is explicitly the pet of the forest maiden Viratangal. Shambuga knows the forest well and feels at home in the wild. He knows how to track and find a wild boar in his cave. His ancestors could well have once belonged to this forest dwelling group, but later found a job working for the Ponnivala Nadu kings, at which point that family would have switched its loyalty over to them. Since the wild boar is the pet of Viratangal, a woman who is possibly a distant sister to Shambuga, his possible forest ancestors would likely have had considerable regard for a wild boar, just as Shiva has considerable regard for Nandi. In sum, it is argued here that Shambuga acts as if he might be Shiva's secret agent, so-to-speak,[27] and perhaps represents his darker underside?[28] Shiva is a kind of outcaste himself, matching nicely with the fact that Shambuga is explicitly a Dalit.

Cows versus Horses

Other references to cows and bulls in the story revolve around farming scenes. Cows are linked to all three generations of the Ponnivala epic, but they are mostly seen in substories that relate to Kolatta and Kunnutaiya. In contrast, in the third and final generation the story's young heroic twins are fed by a female tiger and elephant, not by a cow. That may give them some divine energy, but their real personal interests lie in their family's two colts. The two youthful heroes spend much of their time as young boys learning to ride a set of fine mares. Those two magnificent horses eventually become the heroes' pre-eminent animal companions. This shift in the story's key animal characters in generation three, from bull

Splitting, Replicating, and Twinning of Gods and Animals 273

Figure 7.17. Shambuga riding a bull in front of a local temple dedicated to the epic heroes.

to stallion is significant. It reflects a slow historical change in the culture itself, from kings like Kunnutaiya who were proud of their fierce bulls, to rulers whose key status symbol revolved around their fine horses and related equestrian skills (figure 7.18).

Bulls and horses are both represented in the form of folk statues in many Ponnivala Nadu temples. Sometimes these bulls, statues made of terracotta and fired in pieces, just stand alone in front of a shrine. Their typical posture suggests they are patiently waiting for an opportunity to serve as a mount for the invisible travels of the god or gods within (figure 7.19). These bull statues mirror the purpose of Shiva's own great bull Nandi, however Nandi is not presented in the same way. While the folk bulls always stand proudly on all four legs, Nandi is generally seen lying down with at least three of his legs folded under him (figure 7.20). More interesting, many of the standing bulls seen in folk shrines have a rider, a man who sometimes carries a drum as we saw in figure 7.17. When a drum is present this instantly identifies the mounted figure as Shambuga, the twin heroes' outcaste assistant. The heroes, themselves, by contrast, always ride horses.

To sum up, this chapter has singled out a bundle of key concepts that act as hidden paradigms, all of which have something to do with the symbolic splitting, doubling, or twinning. These are: 1) The idea that the Ponnivala epic's twin heroes may present an underground, secretive, unspoken set that portrays two different and vibrant sides of the locally beloved god Murugan. This would constitute a symbolic splitting of his multiplex personality into two counterbalanced bundles. Taken together, these epic twins embody and express much of who this god really is. Stated in reverse, the great god Murugan blends into one being a wide range

274 Hidden Paradigms

Figure 7.18. The story's heroes ride through town on their magnificent horses.

Figure 7.19. A horse and a bull, standing outside a local temple, waiting to serve the story heroes.

of values and symbolic themes that the twins, taken together, represent. This folk epic deliberately explores two separate and sometimes contradictory principles and explores how they balance out, sometimes struggling against one another. However, taking a broader view, they can be understood to be working together. Murugan is a very popular and very complex god much beloved by the Tamil people. It is understandable that Murugan's key characteristics and behavioural patterns, therefore, would have worked their way into this story, even when not explicitly identified as a multiform of this great god. Second, we have seen that

Splitting, Replicating, and Twinning of Gods and Animals 275

Figure 7.20. A Nandi statue that is part of the Royal Ontario museum's Asian collection in Toronto. Photograph by the author.

this emphasis on duality extends much further into the story and pertains to several of this legend's other features as well. Tangal represents the opposite of splitting, which could be called blending, as she is really two: the male and female rolled into one. Third, the god who sired the twin heroes, Shiva, also enters this story in secretive ways. Shiva is lord of cattle, a very important theme. People are frequently compared to bovines and the cattle pen serves as a metaphorical human home. Examples have been given here of how Shiva is secretly doubled when he becomes a grand bull who oversees his worldly cow pen which is also his local temple. Shiva is also secretly doubled a second time, specifically in relation to the Ponnivala Nadu story of the Dalit character Shambuga. Bulls and wild boars are also twinned by this folk legend, the bull being a key symbol for farmers, and the boar for the hunters. The bull gifts pregnancy to local cows, but also fiercely protects Ponnivala Nadu's farmlands from invasion by outsiders, especially from those demanding demeaning gifts of tribute for their Chola king. The wild boar serves to protect and fertilize the forest where a different kind of power lurks. There is still further complexity here since Shiva, as a bull, contrasts with Vishnu, in his form as Varaha the great earth-rescuing boar. Thus this principal Shiva-Vishnu pair are symbolized as a bull and a boar, but they are also brothers-in-law when viewed in a different light. Paradigms can be shifty, easily taking on complex mythic forms.

Horses, however, also have a prominent role in this story's third generation, being the real pets of the twin heroes themselves. In Tamil Nadu, horses were and have been from medieval times forward, a classy means of transport, especially for warriors. The last hidden paradigm discussed in this chapter is that the heroes appear to serve as mythical, symbolic doubles for the ancient Aśvin pair of horse-brothers. In the following three chapters we will carry the exploration of hidden paradigms that underlie much of this Ponnivala Nadu epic account still further. First, we will explore an ancient Babylonian view of the world through an examination of a very helpful constellation star chart and its related myths. Following that enquiry, we will look at a paradigm that relates the same epic to a great lotus, a plant that has been a deep and ancient Hindu emblem for millennia. Last of all, we will explore an ecological paradigm, that of the monsoon rains. When one looks carefully at the songs the bards sing intermittently, throughout this grand legend, one discovers how truly important periodic downpours of rain are to Kongu's local farmers. In the bards' songs images of rain predominate when times are good and the heroes' family is prospering. Recognizing the power the rain songs embody will surprise many and present to us what is perhaps the deepest and most meaningful hidden paradigm of all.

8 The Story Told by the Stars: Babylonian Star-Lore and the Hindu Nakshatras

It is not very often that an epic story can be said to reflect patterns seen among the stars and, in this case, the importance of Babylonian starlore seems particularly surprising. Nonetheless, there is a unique and very interesting hidden paradigm buried in the Ponnivala story that can be uncovered through studying ancient Middle Eastern mythology and examining how those stories link certain specific events to star patterns seen in the sky above.[1] This correspondence was discovered more or less by accident while I was researching the history of the wild boar Komban, clearly a featured animal in the Ponnivala Nadu legend. Komban has a star on his tongue, indicating his connection to the heavens and the night sky. The obvious question is why is this connection mentioned and why is it specific to Komban and no other character in this story? Furthermore, to the best of my knowledge, no other epic legend in Indian folk tradition so far published, either in Tamil or any other Indian language, features a huge, wild, forest boar.

In my search to understand Komban better, I stumbled on an ancient Babylonian star map and found a very interesting wild boar depicted there.[2] On the reconstructed map of mythical Babylonian motifs a large beast fitting this folk epic description is embodied in a constellation associated with autumn. After he disappears from the autumn night sky, he is said to hide underground to await spring. Months later, as the days start to grow longer once again, this boar re-emerges from the abyss below as a young piglet.[3] Further overlaps between the Babylonian map of the heavens and various details in the Ponnivala Nadu story were then also discovered. In exploring these connections, Gavin White's amazing 2014 dictionary of myths and other information on the ancient Babylonian story world proved to be of great help. The set of correspondences uncovered has been mapped out, in some detail, using the three charts shown in figures 8.2, 8.3, and 8.5.

In figure 8.2 the horizontal axis represents the positioning of the spring equinox vis-a-vis the starry backdrop seen at sunrise, on the day of the spring equinox in roughly 2200 BCE. The specific constellation that rises just before dawn on the eastern horizon, at a given equinox or solstice moment of each year, changes slowly over

278   Hidden Paradigms

Figure 8.1. Vishnu, in the form of a humble washerman, drags the sacrificial boar head away, saying he is taking it to his pregnant wife (who, by implication, is Bhudevi).

time due to a known wobble in the earth's axis. The stars seen at night shift their position, seeming to rotate clockwise, but very slowly. That change adds about one degree of rotation every seventy-two years. Thus, even a very observant individual is unlikely to be detect such a subtle change within their own lifetime. On the other hand, the entire sky rotates counter clockwise very noticeably each night, accomplishing a 360 degree rotation every twenty-four hours. What was important, in both Indian and Babylonian traditional astrology/astronomy was determining which constellation had just risen in the hour or so just before sunrise on any given day. That was the system used for marking the passage of the seasons and the beginning of a new cycle each year. The point at which the length of the day and night are exactly equal (half way through the six months when the sun rises slightly further north each day) is what we know as the spring equinox. That point was accepted in ancient Babylon as being the day when the calendrical cycle was considered to restart. It was the point of a new beginning. Put another way, this day marked the beginning of the bright half of the year when every day would last longer than its opposite half, its matching night.[4]

Some careful observers, having listened to their predecessors and consulted their notes, must have noticed that the constellations their teachers had taught them to refer to were not rising at the same moment they used to but instead were now showing up weeks later. This meant that the equinox, in time, came to be marked by the preceding (earlier rising) star cluster. Those scholars, then, eventually had to adjust their larger reference system to match that new reality. In sum, the equinox that used to be marked by the rising of the head of Taurus, now became linked to the rising of the star cluster we know as the Pleiades. As a result, some constellation figures and the myths related to them were also adjusted, redrawn, or shifted in position. Sometimes a constellation was even eliminated as observers tried to tweak matters and thus preserve their underlying system of

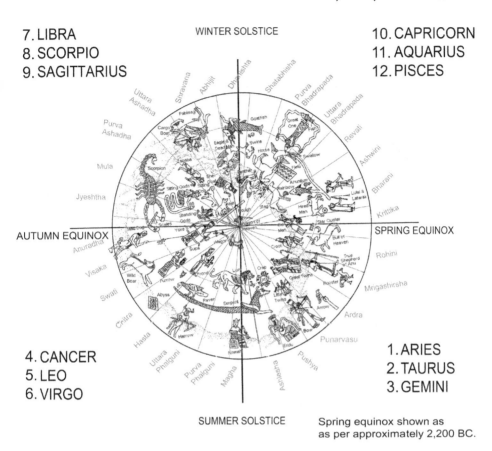

Figure 8.2. Chart 1: An array of Babylonian star signs and the approximate position of the rising sun against this mythical backdrop, as seen just before dawn on the day of the spring equinox in 2200 BC. The image includes the location of the Indian Nakshatras as a reference frame.

thought. These necessary adjustments were essentially maintenance work. White traces many of these adjustments, and their outcomes, but those changes are not focussed on here. The main point is that, if we restrict our gaze to a high level of abstraction, much of this system's core logic remained intact for many centuries. It is those core concepts and their match with deep paradigms embedded in the Ponnivala Nadu legend that we will now attempt to explore further. There are four quadrants in figure 8.3 (Chart 2) and we will briefly discuss each of them in turn with reference to White's sketches, starting with quadrant #1.[5]

280   Hidden Paradigms

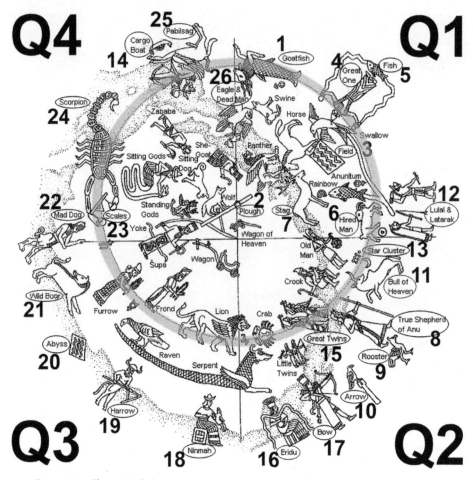

Figure 8.3. Chart 2: Babylonian star map with twenty-six different constellations named. The numbers refer to their individual position in terms of discussion in the text. The grey circle locates the zodiac. Based on White 2014.

Quadrant One

1 **Plough**: In Babylonia, the plough sign signified the work of cultivation and was strongly associated with cereal farming. The plough lay at the technological core of the most highly evolved and most prestigious human food production system known in early times and is still very important today. In the Ponnivala Nadu story the goddess Parvati gave a plough to the nine

human males she had newly created as her first act. She then instructed them to begin farming their forested land in order to make it bountiful and full of foods men could harvest. I have started this discussion of the Babylonian star map with the plough because it was the central tool both for that early culture and for the primary characters in the Ponnivala Nadu story. Furthermore, the plough was a circumpolar constellation that never rose or set. All the other constellations to be discussed rose and set in a regular fashion, in synchrony with the season shifts they were associated with. The only other Babylonian constellation to be discussed that did not rise and set is the Stag (#6), a cluster of stars associated with the sun. Like the plough, the sun was also a very central entity for agriculturalists, and one critical to any farming enterprise.

2 **Goatfish**: In Babylonia, the Goatfish was the ruler of the fertile waters. It was strongly associated with new beginnings. Around 2200 BCE its head and horns would have risen just before dawn at the time of the winter solstice. Its fertile horns linked it to the watery sea in the sky, believed to be the place where goats, cattle, and humans were all generated before their tiny embryos descended to earth to mature, perhaps falling from the sky along with the spring rains. In the Ponnivala Nadu story the Goatfish, known in the West as Capricorn, is very important. It is the mythical equivalent of the Makara, a legendary sea creature seen in Hindu iconography that is the vehicle of the sea god Varuna and the river goddess Ganga. The star sign known in Tamil (and in Sanskrit) as Makara is linked to the winter solstice too and thus is also related to the concept of renewal. The Makara is also the symbol which the god of love, Kamadeva, has emblazoned on his flag. It also sometimes appears as a gargoyle, a guardian, or as spout attached to a natural spring. These associations with love, with the beginnings of life in a watery womb, and/or in a river or in the rain drops descending to earth from the sky give it special significance. It is a starting point. If marriage and conception are linked to the spring equinox, then this point, which occurs exactly nine months later, matches well with the idea of life stepping forth from a womb. No wonder the Tamil Pongal festival appears to celebrate the idea of new births-in-the-cow-pen at this time. The goddess Parvati floats in the clouds at the beginning of the Ponnivala Nadu epic, where it is described as a great sea filled with many fish, which are the nighttime stars. While hovering up there in the rain-generating clouds, Parvati creates this epic's first people, nine men who are the heroes' ancestors. The association of her first act with the moment of the winter solstice and with the constellation of Capricorn, or Makara, thus seems entirely appropriate.

3 **Great One**: In Babylonia, the water bearer was Gula or Aquarius. His waters brought progeny to all creatures. Gula's great powers included governing human reproduction and providing fertilizing rain. In the Ponnivala Nadu story the heroes' grandfather, Kolatta, had to leave his original forest home due to a severe drought. So he migrated to a neighbouring area, looking for work in a locale

where there was no problem with the rains. Kolatta was hired by a (Chola) king and not much later that ruler realized his good luck. He believed that this newly arrived refugee had brought his kingdom more rain than normal and increased his fields productivity. Kolatta appeared to be gifted, and his presence, the king soon realized, was a kind of special blessing. His trust in this new ploughman he had hired, grew rapidly. He, like Gula, seemed to have brought beneficent rains with him, a sign that his kingdom would prosper. Kolatta thus functions as a water bearer.

4 **Fish**: In Babylonia, a popular ancient fish-figure (similar to Pisces) dwelt in the freshwater sea located below the earth. In a related Mesopotamian myth, the fish living there discovered a large golden egg, which they brought to shore for brooding. Eventually that egg hatched into a goddess.[6] In the Ponnivala Nadu story the successor to the first ancestor, the childless Kolatta, was a magical boy who was hidden as a baby just below earth under a rockpile. Kolatta found that child, raised him, and named him Kunnutaiya. The boy had a fine character and was devoted to the golden goddess Cellatta, a local divinity deeply interested in the productivity of the fields in her area. Eventually the orphan boy became a wealthy farmer and a highly respected ruler of Ponnivala Nadu. Significantly, he was found underground as a newborn baby, much as one might discover a fish in a local field well, born of the mass of egg jelly birthed by a fish and then accidentally dropped there by a bird wanting a drink. Hence Kunnutaiya, Kolatta's son, is the equivalent of a hatched golden egg.

5 **Field**: In Babylonia, the Field constellation stood for a watery, well-irrigated plot of land. White also describes it as a reservoir where the chief Mesopotamian god Enki liked to sit. Many mermen sat near Enki, along with seven sages, who were at times dressed in fish skins, which made them look like fish themselves. In the Ponnivala Nadu story the heroes' ancestors start cutting down trees, laying out fields, and beginning their farm-focused activities almost immediately. They also set up a local irrigation system to make sure that their fields will always be well watered. These activities make the Field a central symbol in both cultural traditions.

6 **Stag**: In Babylonia, the stag was a somewhat mysterious animal. It had a strong solar association as its rack was considered to be a sign of the radiant heavens. In the Ponnivala Nadu story the gods foresaw a need to find a spouse for young Kunnutaiya. Echoing several ancient Hindu myths, Lord Shiva and his wife decided to take the form of two deer, or possibly antelope (a stag and a doe) and copulate to help create the needed young girl. This allowed some of Shiva's semen to fall (radiate down?) from the bountiful heavens (as do rays of the sun). As a result, a baby girl was born in a lotus flower from a drop of that semen. She would eventually become Kunnutaiya's bride and assist him in reclaiming the Ponnivala Nadu family lands earlier lost to a set of greedy cousins. Like the plough, the stag constellation,

too, constantly circled the pole star of its time. It never rose or set. Just like Shiva and Parvati, the Stag was a constant feature of the night sky and a reminder of a shining divine energy located there. The ancient Tamil goddess Kottravai was traditionally represented by the figure of a black buck that had a lovely set of horns. Kottravai could possibly be a female counterpart of that early Babylonian concept of a great Stag-in-the-sky. Kottravai is also referred to in several places in early Tamil literature as the mother of the god Murugan. This would equate her with Parvati who is the mother of Murugan most often mentioned today. Kottravai is also represented in a famous rock carving at Mahabalipuram, in the same panel as the great wild boar Varaha. That boar, a form of Vishnu, is deeply connected with the folk epic discussed here. Using mythical reasoning, perhaps Kottravai could even be the black buck Shiva dallied with to produce that special drop of semen used to create the mother of the Ponnivala heroes, Tamarai.

7 **Hired Man**: Babylonians believed in a celestial Ram, a creature linked to the constellation we know as Aries. The constellation of the Ram was understood to be a child (a lamb who grew to greatness) under the care of the great shepherd god Dumuzi. In the Ponnivala Nadu story, Kunnutaiya, who first appeared as a baby beneath a rock pile, was later orphaned at age six when his parents both died suddenly. For years following that misfortune, Kunnutaiya had to wander and work to sustain himself, first as a shepherd and later as a multi-talented hired hand. As a child he had cared for others' animals, especially for sheep, goats, and cows. Because of this Kunnutaiya acquired a broad knowledge of farming and he was known to always bring good luck to the farm of his masters, not unlike the way a fine sheep is sometimes thought to bless its keeper. The constellation of the Ram, here called the Hired Man (and possibly also the Crook seen just a bit later), are two symbols that reference good shepherds. Both bear possible links to the father of Ponnivala's twin heroes, Kunnutaiya, who was a skilled in animal husbandry. But the imagery linked to this idea (see figure 8.3) changes somewhat when that shepherd matures into a fine king (see True Shepherd of Anu below).

8 **Lulal and Latarak**: In Babylonia, Lulal and Latarak was a constellation located somewhere near that of the True Shepherd of Anu. It featured two men with lion-like faces and likely rose concurrently with the Hired Man (above) and just a short while before the True Shepherd constellation appeared. According to White it is not entirely clear whether the two men pictured in this constellation were related and worked together, or if the two names reference the same figure known under different labels or monikers at different times. Nonetheless, what is clear is that the two were equally fierce, and that they both had lion-like heads. It seems that these same two characters may also have wielded magic that could be used

Figure 8.4. Two assistants to Yeman, the god of Death, as seen in Ponnivala Nadu story illustrations.

to counteract the work of evil demons. Importantly, they also seemed to have been guardians, perhaps related to the beginning of the Babylonian new year, which started just around this time. Thus they may have also had a role in banishing evil influences from the year just past (White 2014a, 192). There is no clear correspondence with the Ponnivala Nadu story but a possibility for comparison are the figures of Yeman's two unnamed assistants mentioned there. These two (see figure 8.4) had the unenviable responsibility of notifying living characters, notably Kunnutaiya's parents, that their time of death had arrived. As a result, Kunnutaiya quite suddenly became an orphan. The two assistants were a fearsome duo who marked the transition to a new era by announcing the death of the story's first-generation couple. The Ponnivala Nadu story's animation director depicted them as having horns rather than lion faces, but the idea is similar. The appearance of such fearsome guardians of the gateway to a nether world, the mysterious region where this family's clan founder will now reside, marks Kolatta's death and is an appropriate end to Quadrant One.

The progression of these eight Babylonian constellations provides a close match with the characters and themes emphasized in the early chapters of this South Indian epic text. Four of the constellations are somewhat unique to Babylonia while the other three have now been incorporated into the Western zodiac. Most readers will recognize them as Capricorn, Pisces, and Aries respectively. The story we have been studying unfolds like a textbook overview of the first seven Babylonian star groups, circled for emphasis, in quadrant 1 of figure 8.3. Even the order of these seven constellations' appearance on the eastern horizon matches nicely with the order of themes seen to emerge and grow in importance in the Ponnivala Nadu account. Now let's see how good the alignment is when it comes to the other three quadrants of the year.[7]

Quadrant Two

9 **Star Cluster:** In Babylonia, the star cluster was the name for the ancient and well-known Pleiades constellation. It is depicted many times over in ancient Babylonian art and is likely visible on at least one Indus Valley Seal (M1186) as seven young girls. This group of women constitute a fierce and battle-ready group of deities. As a cluster they are traceable back to old Sumerian poems where they are described as a group of seven stars given to Gilgamesh by the sun god. According to Sumerian tradition they were male and their role was to guide Gilgamesh eastwards and help him in his quest for immortality.[8] We have already discussed the fact that the same star cluster is also well known in South India where it is called the Krittika constellation, is considered female, and is locally known as the seven Kannimar. There the youngest Kannimar is sent to earth by Shiva where she becomes the twin heroes' sister. Tangal is dreamy and spiritual, and possibly the open courtyard swing she sits on hangs down directly from those stars. The Pleiades provide a clear link between Babylonian tradition and the epic of Ponnivala Nadu. And, of course, it makes sense that this constellation's story should follow immediately after referencing a set of twins that belonged to Anu, the Babylonian creator god. These twins birth sister, Tangal, is clearly described as the youngest of the seven Kannimar in this epic story. These seven served as guardians of doorways and passages, and in particular, it seems that they were embryo guardians. But according to South Indian mythological tradition, these seven maidens have the added responsibility of being nursemaids. The Great Bull and the Star Cluster are both a part of a cultural tradition that tries to visualize, in terms farmers can identify with, the idea that a powerful creative energy resides high in the sky and that this energy is responsible for periodically re-inseminating and re-growing life (likely through rain) just as fresh embryos begin to grow in the wombs of women down on earth. These two constellations have everything to do with fertility, germination (to use a seed metaphor), and with re-beginnings. When they rise, they serve as an omen that new life is beginning but has not yet become visible and manifest to all.

10 **Bull of Heaven:** In Babylonia, one of the earliest constellations mentioned in the written records is the Bull of Heaven (Taurus). Taurus was originally depicted on this star-map as a bull-calf, symbolizing the spring equinox. Somewhat after 3500 BCE, however, local tradition appears to have decided to transform that visualization into a full-grown bull. This change probably took place in order to accommodate the fact that the bull's appearance at dawn was gradually occurring later and later in the calendrical cycle, now happening well after the equinox and rising nearer to the start of the summer drought. Later still, the Bull of Heaven was mythically killed, as per the Gilgamesh story told in chapter 5, because he had sucked up all the river water

in Dumer and caused a terrible drought. Perhaps due to the popularity of that story the bull image, as seen in the heavens, got cut in half leaving only its front portion visible when it was depicted on a later star map. This butchering of the bull's body, symbolically speaking, may reflect the story of his being killed in the Gilgamesh story. However, it is equally likely that this was done in order to accommodate new constellations created at about this same time. Those new constellations were assigned a spot in the great sky dome just a bit to the west of the fine bull himself.[9] The comparison one can make between this great bull and Ponnivala Nadu themes fits best with the middle phase in how the great bull was visualized in Babylonian accounts. This is the point where the Bull of Heaven is understood to be mature, fierce, and wild, but before he is described as having been killed by Gilgamesh. In his full form, this bull stood for a great sky god, associated with the sun, prosperity, and abundant herds of cattle. He was a wild, natural power ready to inseminate an entire cattle herd. That set of associations matches well with the personality, deeds, and high position Lord Shiva is accorded in the Ponnivala Nadu story. Both Tamarai and Vishnu wanted Shiva to abandon his ascetic pursuits, and instead expend his energy fertilizing her. He also needed to pay attention to all the other infertile females resident in Ponnivala Nadu who were suffering too. Here we likely see a mythical connection between the traditional role assigned the Bull of Heaven in Mesopotamia and Shiva's role as the principal creator of central characters featured in the Ponnivala Nadu account. Shiva eventually bends under the pressure exerted on him by his sister and his brother-in-law. He then agrees to immaculately impregnate the chaste queen. In addition, as we saw earlier, Shiva also gives Tamarai a golden pot to take back to earth. The magical liquid contained in that vessel (a form of his semen) served to fertilize every barren woman in the queen's entire kingdom. Similarly, the main duty of a healthy bull, when kept as such by a farmer, is to inseminate all the cows living in his cattle pen. This kind of metaphor is one we can easily relate to the west's zodiac sign known as Taurus. The sign of Taurus is one that any experienced farmer, both in Mesopotamia and in Kongu Nadu, can still easily relate to today.

11 **True Shepherd of Anu**: In Babylonia, the god An was a figure similar to Orion. He regularly travelled between heaven and earth to relay messages from the gods above to the people below. This god then returned to the skies with the people's prayers and requests. In the Ponnivala Nadu story the True Shepherd of Anu makes metaphorical sense if we think of him as a match for An, adult son of the Bull of Heaven. That would be Kunnutaiya (born of Shiva's semen). He would be represented as a young boy in quadrant one, as the Hired Man. But after his marriage to Tamarai, Kunnutaiya became an independent farmer and grew to old age as an increasingly respected Ponnivala king.[10] He was honest, genuine, and he worked hard to help his people.

He blessed them, met with them, and listened attentively to their requests. Although he did not manage animals directly after his marriage, he remained a True Shepherd in the sense of being an influential leader who cared for his local flock, both human and animal, in other words, all the residents of his nadu. He was a good "lamb" that had matured well and grown into a fine and powerful Ram, a son of the Great Bull (who could, of course, sire beings of any species or create a mix of himself and that person's other, human parent).

12 **Rooster**: In Babylonia, the True Shepherd of Anu was accompanied by a Rooster who followed at his heels. That rooster was likely the announcer, carrying his master's messages to the people, just as a rooster announces the arrival of each new day at dawn. In the Ponnivala Nadu story both Kunnutaiya and his two sons were assisted by a trusted first minister. In fact, there had been a line of Ponnivala first ministers. Shambuga-the-father and Shambuga-the-son were both drummers by caste. One of these two men's many jobs was announcing important local events like weddings, funerals, and hunting expeditions. Drummers were important, much as town criers were in medieval Europe. They spread the news of the king's latest decisions, using a drum to draw attention to that fresh public news. Metaphorically speaking, Shambuga was Kunnutaiya's rooster. That is why you see the Rooster standing at the feet of the True Shepherd of An.

13 **Great Twins**: The Great Twins are a pair of Babylonian warriors who are dressed to the hilt. They guard an important entrance to the underworld and are responsible for preventing demons from rising up to trouble the human world. Like the Greek myth about Castor and Polydeuces, these twins are destined to die in unison. White suggests they are likely linked to the Little Twins who stand just behind them, and they both portend the downfall of the land and the death of the king. I propose that Ponnivala Nadu's heroic twins reflect many of the themes that the Great Twins represent. Possibly the Little Twins express the childhood these two underwent, in the same quadrant. If so we see the same principal characters represented twice, but at different times in their short lives. Whatever the case in that regard, I only discuss them once here. We do know for certain that this Ponnivala duo not only portend the death of their unjust ruler, the Chola king, they also proceed to execute him soon after their parents die of old age. Also like the Great Twins in Babylonian mythology, these two heroes represent a fierce pair of warriors who believe they are charged with guarding the moral order of their time. They die together as well. Shankar sacrifices himself first, and within minutes, Ponnar follows his lead. In terms of the Babylonian calendar the New Year started in the spring and marriage also happened during this period (of course with a number of annual cycles presumed to take place in between these two events for any particular character). White has tried his best to place each of

the figures he has sketched where he believes the Babylonians saw them in the sky, using ancient texts as his primary source material. I suggest, at least reading the same sky map from a South Indian perspective, that the second quarter's Great Twins best represent the Ponnivala Nadu story's principal parental characters, that is Kunnutaiya and Tamarai, after their marriage. We have already described Kunnutaiya as the True Shepherd of An. Tamarai will be discussed below in connection with the Arrow. Ponnar and Shankar fit in best just after their parents' demise, as they take over and inherit their family's nadu as its two ruling kings.

14 **Arrow**: In Babylonia, this was the name for the star we know as Sirius, the brightest star in the sky. Sirius was depicted as a bird perched on a pillar and astrologers used this constellation as a marker of the summer solstice, the day when the sun reaches its highest point in the sky. In that earlier era Sirius stood in the east just before dawn on this important day, the longest one of the year. In Babylon, the Arrow was also associated with the god Ninurta, an agricultural deity linked to rain and to flooded fields. The most fitting Ponnivala character to link with this constellation is Tamarai, the twin heroes' mother, who would have risen just after her husband, Kunnutaiya, the True Shepherd of Anu. Here again we uncover one of the more surprising and important Babylonian mythic overlaps we can find with the South Indian epic themes being discussed. Tamarai, barren and distraught, spent twenty-one years sitting on a pillar, constantly begging Lord Shiva to grant her children. Eventually she is impregnated, high in the sky, by this great god himself. Like a bright star, she was a beautiful, sincere, and chaste lady. The parallel with a bird perched on a pillar is also fitting, since a bird is a common simile for a woman used by Tamil poets. We can also point to the fact that Tamarai was the woman who was born in a lovely lotus flower, one that had a long stalk-like post supporting it along with roots that lay deep under water.

15 **Bow**: In Babylonia, the Bow represents the third maiden in Whites' trilogy of female constellations. She is a warrior-virgin equivalent to the Greek huntress Artemis. White envisions her as a kind of oracle who issues omens that predict war. Equally, she can also serve as symbol suggesting the potential for a fragile peace. The Bow constellation conjures up thoughts of Tangal's forest twin, who is appropriately named Viratangal, the brave and fierce younger sister. Viratangal tries to co-exist with Ponnivala Nadu's twin kings, but was deceived three times by them (they stole her family's stash of iron rods, then her most beautiful parrot, and lastly, the twins slaughtered her huge pet boar). So, leaving aside any prospects for peace, Viratangal finally turns on these two heroes. She does this by calling on her one-hundred forest-dwelling-hunter brothers to initiate a war. Viratangal represents the forest, while Tangal represents the farmers and their ploughed fields. These two women are mirror opposites, both are virgins, they are of the same age,

and both have a special power to bless their brothers. But they are otherwise quite different. Viratangal is fierce, practical, and very defensive of her forest domain, while Tangal is gentle and dreamy. It is likely that the Bow also symbolized a wild goddess of the forest who stood in contrast to Eridu who was associated with well-irrigated fields.

16 **Eridu**: In Babylonia, Eridu was a maiden whose two hands held an overflowing water vessel. She is one of three constellations that White groups together as a possible forerunner of the triple goddess concept made familiar later via Greek and Roman mythology. White further suggests that the middle female of the three, Eridu, may represent a fertile maiden who embodies the potential for new life in the period just before the autumn rains. She is an eminently attractive maiden, but one who is not yet pregnant. This would make her very similar to the twins' young sister Tangal, a woman whose essence lies in possibilities that are expressed through her dreams. The fact that Tangal always sits on a swing, furthermore, makes her both attractive and unpredictable. She is Ponnivala's potential cornucopia, a forerunner of future prosperity, and of hope for descendants not yet born to the ruling family. Of course, it is appropriate to tell her story immediately following that of her two elder brothers who exited their mother's womb just a short while before she did.

This survey of quadrant 2 reveals Babylonian parallels for a whole cluster of Ponnivala Nadu family members. The ideas here relate to the concept of a leading family and its members, while the symbols used relate nicely to each one's most memorable back story, the queen impregnated after sitting on a pillar, for example, and the aging King Kunnutaiya as his region's great shepherd. This very significant quadrant traces out a grand family that possibly includes grandparents; the old man Kolatta as clan founder and perhaps also as a shepherd named The Crook. Plus, the Bull of Heaven is also evident in this quadrant, the grand male whose semen sired Ponnar and Shankar (namely Shiva). Finally three women are also represented who may relate to Tamarai, the twin's mother, as the Arrow (a sign of where she received impregnation), Tangal, the twin's sister, as Eridu (a source of the regenerative liquid that resurrected them), and Viratangal, the twin's shadowy second sister-of-the-forest, as the Bow (because she belongs to the Vettuva community). The western zodiac is simpler here with the main surviving characters in this quadrant comprising Aries, possibly the True Shepherd of Anu, as grandfather (number one), Taurus the Bull as father (number two), and Gemini, the Great Twin Grandsons (as number three). The ancient Babylonian version of this modern star map was both richer in content and conceptually better structured, but there is, nonetheless, an important degree of overlap between the two. Most important, in quadrant 2 there is a haunting similarity of elements and characters featured in the Ponnivala Nadu story. The star-based characters popular in ancient Babylon reflect the concept of a heroic family-in-the-sky and their varied and moving stories about imagined human lives. I have allowed myself some liberty in suggesting these links. The purpose of this comparison is to outline a broad and suggestive shared structure, a kinship paradigm that possibly underlay both traditions. Particularly striking in quadrant 2 are first, the importance given to twins, second, that two principal women appear to be twins as well and stand suggestively close together, and third, that there is overarching three-generation family paradigm implicated in this basic layout.

Quadrant Three

17 **Ninmah**: In Babylonia, Ninmah is the first female in a trilogy of constellation-based goddesses discussed by White. Ninmah is the mother goddess, patron of midwives and a mother to all creatures. In the Ponnivala story this same description also applies nicely to the mother of Ponnivala's triplets, Tamarai. But just like we found Kunnutaiya represented twice, and the twins also presented twice, Tamarai may be seen twice as well. Unlike in quadrant two where the arrow represents her experience of impregnation stemming from her sitting on a pillar, the context is different now. In quadrant two Tamarai was anguished by the thought of barrenness. Her fear was that she would never be able to birth children. After Lord Shiva stepped in and granted her a set of triplets during her visit to his sky-based council chambers, she became a different woman. The pot she brought back to earth was filled with a liquid that she then shared with each female in Ponnivala who was hoping for pregnancy. Now Tamarai became a mother-to-all. Thus she began what was essentially a new life. Her new personality and role after that long pilgrimage make Tamarai look much like Ninmah. In keeping with this new position, quadrant 3 shifts the focus from the human family nucleus to community welfare at large. Ninmah and Tamarai are both goddesses whose role is to help engender and guard over all young life, not just to protect their own personal children.

18 **Harrow**: In Babylonia, the Harrow was a key agricultural implement associated with making preparations for planting. The figure associated with this tool on the Babylonian star map is the body of a bull. White says, and I concur, that this symbolic motif likely stood for an ox, that is, a mild-mannered, subservient, castrated bull. As White also writes, the name for a harrow, if one reads it in reverse (not an uncommon practice in ancient Sumeria), also yields the secondary meaning of "son or child of the house." This is exactly how a field worker or hired hand would have been described. Also interesting is that White provides a sketch of the harrow that is an almost exact inverse image of how the plough was represented by Mesopotamian carvers and artists.[11] The harrow and the plough were thought to be similar tools. White suggests that the name for the harrow

constellation, "Bison-Man," links this tool with an epithet for a very strong man, one whose role is to seed the fields. The Babylonian constellation called the harrow maps nicely onto the Ponnivala Nadu story, too, that is, if it we consider it to refer to the many field workers that surround the king. These would be the men who undertake the heavy field labour needed to sustain a kingdom and its agricultural wealth. Thus, the harrow, when used as a part of a sky map like this one, likely stands for a group of workers, making it a community concept rather than a reference to any one character. This same idea also illustrates the dual-purpose of such sky maps: they project a broad frame concept, one that can reference various forms of magical energy and multiple legends and stories, unifying local variations in tradition that may be popular across a wide, multi-ethnic area. What we see here is a common concern, featured in both ancient Babylonia and in medieval South India: everyone was dependent on maintaining and valuing the area's local economic base, a plough-and-irrigation-reliant economy. It is worth noting as well, that the shape of both the plough and the harrow seen in the Ponnivala Nadu story (and that are still used in the area today) very closely resemble the shape of these same two tools as they are seen on this Babylonian map of the starry night sky.

19 **Abyss**: In Babylonia, the symbol of the Abyss referred to a hole or access point that led to a watery underworld thought to be a part of middle earth. That abyss lay just below the earth's surface and was governed by largely beneficent but fanciful beings. Below that was another level where ancestors and various evil-intentioned spirits dwelt. White says that the abyss was juxtaposed to the fertile Field discussed in quadrant 1. That Field was a symbol of early spring, and the Abyss was its autumnal opposite. In the Ponnivala Nadu story there is a prominent pond-cum-irrigation tank, where the kingdom's war drum was kept. When war was declared, that drum was raised from the watery depths and refreshed with new animal skins. That rite involved the sacrifice of two young male buffalos and the meat of those two animals was then set out for various forest beings to feast on. These fanciful creatures exit from that pond to feed on these sacrificial offerings. Similarly, in ancient Babylonia, a square, watery pond was understood to serve as the gateway that allowed spirit beings that normally dwelt below, to revisit earth. An exit from the Abyss in the spring was generally considered auspicious and natural, like a plant pushing its way out of the soil or an animal emerging from its cave with new pups. But an exit from the Abyss at other times could be a cause for fear, especially if an exit was made during the hot season, before the rains, when many forms of life were expected to remain dormant, retreating from life to sleep.

20 **Wild Boar**: In Babylonia, a constellation located quite near the Abyss was referred to as the Wild Boar. Wild boars' natural behaviour is to plough the

ground around them with their tusks, as they look for roots and tubers to eat. Obviously, then, the activities of a wild boar are likely to have planting and seeding overtones, just like the Harrow does. This is especially so since fresh green shoots commonly appear just days after a wild boar has dug around in a specific place. Their digging seems to cause a rapid regeneration. Wild boars, furthermore, are known to disappear during the winter months, and then to reappear with multiple nursing piglets the following spring. Hence death and rebirth link easily to boar-related themes. Furthermore, Babylonians used piglets for sacrificial purposes in many ritual settings, just as piglets are still used for this purpose in the Kongu area of Tamil Nadu. As stated earlier, it was this important Babylonian boar constellation that originally suggested to me that I should explore the Babylonian star map more deeply. Readers will already know that the Ponnivala Nadu epic features a huge wild boar who digs up the heroes' finest fields, causes a flood by breaking open their irrigation tank, and then challenges them to war. When Komban is killed, Vishnu drags away its head, and appears to give it to the earth goddess, Bhudevi. Under her care his head becomes a seed that she, the creatrix, will later replant in order to jump start a cosmic renewal. In sum, the Hindu mythology surrounding the story of Varaha, overlaps with this part of the Babylonian star map particularly well.

This survey of quadrant 3 suggests that this period of the year was focused on community needs and farming concerns, reasonable since it coincided with the start of the autumn rains in Babylonia and thus was the planting season. The same period of the year links nicely with the start of the monsoon season in South India. One sign that has not yet been discussed, Cancer (the Crab), signals the onset of quadrant 3 likely because it is a creature that seems to be able to walk backward. The moment of the summer solstice, of course, is the critical point, each year, when the sun reverses its path and starts rising further south again, each day. The sign of the Lion also appears at the start of quadrant 3, representing a fierce beast that is likely expressive of warfare. This is the time of year when men often left their families to fight communal battles organized by their patrons or overlords. The Wild Boar, mentioned above, also likely suggests warfare and violence. Quadrant 3 is also a time when the spirits of the dead visit the earth, rising out of the Abyss, linking the underworld to the earth humans know, expressed equally by the Serpent and the Raven. Nonetheless, this important quarter of the year is also a time of ploughing and of placing seeds or seedlings in the freshly overturned sod, as per the references to Furrow and Frond. In every way, then, this is a period focused on the community, both on its nourishment and growth, and on its anguish and warring factions. These are themes that fit well with the Ponnivala Nadu heroes struggle with a wild boar and the chaos visited on their fine lands and fertile fields by this beast.

Quadrant Four

21 **Mad Dog**: The Mad Dog constellation rose in the autumn months just on the cusp of quadrant 4, at around 2000 BCE. In Babylonia, the mad dog was a dog-lion combination, an animal considered to be the gods' private exorcist. The angry dog was able to dispel disease and demons and cure the sick. In contrast to a normal dog, however, the mad dog was a creature that had lionlike elements and also some affinity with hot, dry summers. In the Ponnivala Nadu story the female dog named Ponnacci appears to parallel this male canine character seen on the Babylonian star chart quite nicely. Ponnacci brings disease down upon the twin heroes in order to get their attention and then cures them of their illness (dispelling the demons she earlier called into service). Ironically, she is very small and earless, unlike the mad dog of Babylonia who is likened to a huge bison-headed human. However, Ponnacci does have very sharp teeth and certain magical qualities just as her Babylonian counterpart did. She becomes hot and angry when the heroic twins ignore her fighting skills. And Ponnacci is especially skilled at hunting wild boars. Ponnacci, furthermore, is the heroes' sister's pet, and she is a hidden multiform of the local goddess Kali. Appropriately, perhaps, Ponnacci's teeth contain a poison, and she does seem to have the personality of a lion or a tiger, rather like Kali herself who is specifically associated with these two animals. Ponnacci defeats Komban by biting his testicles, embodying the larger idea that a little female has the innate power to conquer a huge male bully. Like the mad dog on the Babylonian star map, Ponnacci is able to bring a gigantic demon to its knees, thoroughly intimidating a cosmic monster like Ponnivala's wild boar named Komban.

22 **Scales**: In Babylonia, the Scales were a balancing tool, a symbol appropriate to the autumn equinox when day and night were once again, just for a day or two, equal in length. An omen attributed to the scales said that "If the moon and the sun are in balance the land will be stable." It was a moment for justice and this constellation was believed to directly counterbalance the presence of the star cluster that rose in the spring (the Pleiades), a constellation also associated with self-control and balance. Both equinoxes were a time to pause, plan and consolidate. In the Ponnivala Nadu story, Tangal insists that her brothers undergo a small ritual before they leave on their grand boar hunt. She has the skills of a visionary and she knows it is her responsibility to advise her brothers and provide accurate predictions of what lies ahead for them. Tangal knows that this great black boar is a form of the god of death. She believes that her brothers are risking their lives by chasing him and for this reason she insists that they submit to a magical test before they leave. From the results of her test Tangal learns, for certain, what she has long suspected: her brothers will die in the forest and never return from their

hunt. But she does not tell them this, fearing their anger at hearing such terrible news. And so, the two men proceed without taking their sister's warning seriously. It is as if they are crossing a threshold into the darkness of winter. Death is in the air. Astronomically speaking, the scales now tip towards darkness and days start to grow ever shorter. The magical test initiated by Tangal marks this turning point. It signals the same outcome, that the heroes' last days have arrived in the Ponnivala Nadu story. Again, this theme matches nicely with this part of the year as it is portrayed on the Babylonian star map.

23 **Scorpion**: In Babylonia, the Scorpion constellation was associated with autumn and, of course, this little creature has an extremely painful, often deadly, sting. Significantly, the scorpion men (and women) in Babylonian mythology act as guardians of an all-important mountain. That mountain is the huge hill behind which the sun descends each night, seeming to undergo death before rebirth the next day. Deeply significant, however, is the fact that this frightening little creature was also associated with the act of impregnation, as White points out.[12] In the Ponnivala Nadu story there is also a scorpion. It bites the heroes' father Kunnutaiya one night while he and his wife Tamarai are starting their pilgrimage towards Kailasa. That scorpion bite happens at exactly the moment when these two are about to climb up the great Himalayan Mountain slopes. Kunnutaiya never fully recovers from the weakness that results from that painful scorpion sting and hence never climbs those mountains. Instead, he is eventually put to sleep and converted into a stone by Vishnu, which means that Tamarai will have to proceed alone. Kunnutaiya had to stop there, but the omen the scorpion provides still comes true. His wife will become pregnant, but by a different and infinitely more powerful male, Shiva himself. Perhaps it is a good thing that he does not know how to read that bite's deeper and very painful significance. Twenty-one years later, after Tamarai has wrested a magical and immaculate pregnancy from a reluctant Lord Shiva, she returns via the same path and Kunnutaiya reawakens. This broad scenario matches nicely with what White presents when he describes beliefs about the character and meaning of the scorpion in ancient Babylonian. It is a symbol of impending death, but also a symbol of likely new life to come.

24 **Cargo Boat**: In Babylonia, the Cargo Boat was a name for the crescent moon. It was seen as a boat that sailed among the stars. The moon was also associated both with the boat-of-the-dead and with a human-embryo believed to be the Babylonian hero-to-be sailing in a boat before his birth. It was a womb-boat where the hero was first rocked on (or in) the waters of his mother's pregnancy sac, much like a boat rocks as it floats on the sea. Though still in the womb, the hero here is fully formed and already has the weapons he will need, by his side. In the Ponnivala story this cargo boat looks as if it is out of sequence on the star chart, but for good reason. If one

thinks of Tamarai as having been impregnated by Shiva around the time of the summer solstice, then at the ensuing winter solstice she would be six months pregnant, enough for her condition to be quite visible. Hence now there is a realization that a cargo boat lies hidden in the queen's womb. But that child will only step forth into the sunlight at month nine, as the sun reaches its next spring equinox point. Meanwhile, the world will be waiting patiently for the hero's birth. Notice that the Cargo Boat constellation lies directly opposite the Arrow, which is the star group that we have just suggested may have been intended to indicate the actual moment of the queen's conception. Furthermore, if one draws a straight line between the Cargo Boat and the pillar-plus-Arrow sign, one easily sees that this line intersects the constellation of the Great Twins. The Star Cluster, the potential nursemaids, are also waiting, ready for the immanent birth of the heroic twins. This set of start themes suits Babylonia and medieval South India equally well. Everyone knows spring is not far away and that something great is about to be born. The Cargo Boat is the positive omen that predicts this future, momentous, outcome.

25 **Pabilsag**: In Babylonia, Pabilsag was the equivalent of Sagittarius in the western zodiac system. This familiar character is an archer, but the rest of his iconography varies, especially how the lower part of his body is depicted. In Babylonia Pabilsag was sometimes seen as a horse below the shoulders or even as a bird or a scorpion. Pabilsag presided over the final month of the year and was considered to be a guide that helped deceased souls in their subsequent travels. He was frequently depicted as having a scorpion-like tail, which could certainly suggest that he might play a role in impregnation and renewal as well as being a hunter able to cause both animal and human death. There is an equivalent to Pabilsag in the Ponnivala Nadu story that presents a very interesting comparison. There we see Lord Vishnu himself taking up this role. To do this Vishnu sits on the branch of a suma tree, which is the same tree that the Pandava brothers of Mahabharata fame hide their weapons in (or under) during the twelfth year of their exile. A branch of this tree overhangs a river called the Vani, another name for the goddess of wisdom, Saraswati. It is here that the twins wash the blood off their war swords after their last battle. Then, without warning, Lord Vishnu shoots at the younger brother from his perch on that suma branch, using a sugarcane bow and a flowered arrow. Vishnu even looks a little bit like Pabilsag as he does this. But he uses a weapon generally ascribed to Kama, the god of Love in Hindu mythology. That gentle arrow takes away just one thin protective thread that hangs around the neck of the younger twin and Shankar knows the meaning of this: his own death is now at hand. Just a short time later Shankar and his elder brother Ponnar respond to that message by committing suicide, standing on a small hillock located very close to the banks of

the Vani river. Vishnu's actions as well as the symbol he uses to send his message to the heroes appear to reference what Pabilsag also represents: a rapid death followed by some form of spiritual guidance that helps the deceased pass through the underworld. On the Babylonian star map, Pabilsag's raised and thickened penis is visible. Thus the theme here, as elsewhere in quadrant 4, combines omens of death with clear signs of potential transformation, the injection of new energy, a fresh fertilization, and hence hope for a possible rebirth.

26 **Eagle and Dead Man**: In Babylonia, the Eagle and Dead Man constellation rose in the month leading up to the winter solstice, the moment at which the souls of the dead were believed to ascend into the heavens. Two stars are referenced by the Babylonians here, and they both appear on the horizon together. White connects this set of images to the story of the Anzu-bird, a deity that carries or brings children and animals down to earth at their birth. Like Pabilsag, this next star cluster to rise has overtones both of death and of rebirth. Very significantly, the dead man carried in the eagle's claws is associated with a story about the mythical king Etana. The eagle carries Etana into the heavens to find the plant that will procure him a son and regal heir. After an initial failure he carries Etana up into the heavens a second time, now to seek an audience with the goddess Ishtar, a deity closely resembling Shiva's wife Parvati. When this fails as well, Etana attempts yet another journey ... alas the ancient text here is broken. However, White is able to cite an independent piece of magical lore which describes a stone of pregnancy that reputedly assured previously infertile couples a pregnancy. Etana visits that stone. The Ponnivala story provides a stunning overlap that mirrors this exact story: Tamarai and her husband also visit a stone for childless women wishing for pregnancy.[13] Just at that moment, Vishnu appears and notices that Kunnutaiya is suffering (from a scorpion sting) and having difficulty walking. Vishnu directs him to sit on that stone and wait there for his wife's return. Unbeknownst to him, she will not come back to that spot for twenty-one years. There is never any explanation of why this stone is there in the case of the Ponnivala Nadu epic. But White's description of the Babylonian parallel suggests that an ancient and well-matched folk tradition also existed there. Both the Sumerians and the Akkadians, White says, describe a similar stone in their texts. Significantly, this was called the eagle stone, linking it to their word for pregnancy.[14] In the Ponnivala Nadu story it is called the "stone of the childless" (varadi kal).

There are many eagle-related scenes in the Ponnivala epic because this is the vehicle, called Garuda, that Vishnu uses to move between earth and sky. Lord Vishnu arrives on his eagle, for example, exactly at the moment when the heroes chose to commit their double suicide. He then opens a tiny golden box and places both heroes' life spirits inside.[15] Next Vishnu flies upward into the sky on his trusted bird, with that little box in hand. His mission is to deliver its precious contents directly to Lord Shiva, who awaits him inside his famous council chambers.[16] The eagle, in the Ponnivala Nadu story, is thus present at the very moment when old, used-up lives get stored away in a little box, albeit in their spirit form. Resting there, these bodiless energies await god's next call. It is generally believed, by both cultures compared here, that eventually those spirits will get recycled and sent back to earth for a new round of duty down on earth.

The degree of overlap observed between a medieval South Indian folk legend and a wide range of ancient Babylonian beliefs described above is truly surprising. The examination of twenty-six separate star-based constellation clusters and their stories has uncovered an extensive set of parallels. An entire map of the Babylonian star-linked belief system has been surveyed and its core themes, as well as its specific details, have been shown not only to progress logically but also to correspond with the Ponnivala Nadu story in significant detail. These findings suggest that some form of ancient contact likely occurred long ago between the area surrounding ancient Babylon, a place which lay within reach of the Arabian sea, and the southern tip of the Indian peninsula. The early Tamils were famous for their long-distance trading networks, reinforcing the suspicion that some form of early contact is probable.[17] However, the specific historical record in this regard needs further exploration and is, in any event, not the main focus of this book.

This completes the mythological survey of many, if not all, of the of characters present on White's ancient Babylonian star map. The significant parallels found with the Ponnivala Nadu epic story make it seem reasonable to assert that the worldview of the ancient Babylonians somehow reached South India at an early date, though it is not quite clear how. Furthermore, this similarity has been identified not so much via the specifics of individual stories directly, but rather by examining the larger pattern that these mythic tales exhibit. There are many interesting parallels embedded in White's a grand Babylonian sky map, a map full of thematically organized mythical images that represent the full human life cycle, on the one hand, and in parallel, an annual calendrical one as well. Hindu traditions commonly identify a human body with the nature of the cosmos in general. The Babylonian calendar does not consider the body as human per se, but rather appears to depict the full human life cycle. Furthermore, it appears to merge that important theme with agricultural references and the larger solar-linked environmental cycle that determines a community's local planting and harvest schedule. The similarities seem amazing and the overlap is far greater than what a generic mapping of similarities between two cultures, so randomly matched, might be expected to produce. These deep paradigm similarities amount to what I suggest is a totally unexpected and seemingly significant discovery.

The Main Quarters of a Suggested Ponnivala Nadu Storied-Sky

It is now time to introduce another diagram, one that it is hoped will help readers to think about the yearly cycle of constellations in the sky more generally. The Hindu equivalent of a Babylonian star map, what most would identify as the ancient Nakshatra system, also describes and gives meaning to the cycling of identified star groups seen in sky. The Babylonian star groups and the South Asian Hindu ones, of course, rotate in the same way over the course of a year. But their names, and the way they are described and counted is very different. The Babylonians did not specify an exact number of star groups, but they did visualize them, as well as give them names. The Hindu Nakshatra system is equally ancient, but it appears to be more abstract and, at least as far as I can tell, does not reference mythical stories to the same extent though they are present in this second culture-linked system as well. However, one approach to the Nakshatras that does provide some helpful systematization will now be studied with the Ponnivala epic in view. There are twenty-seven Nakshatras and each one is linked to a specific human body part.[18] But there is also an intercalary space called Abhijit, which is used to make adjustments that allow the stars' year cycle to stay in sync with the sun's all important and nearly matching cycle. Abhijit represents a small window in terms of days, and the size of this space varies a bit from year to year. Abhijit has very few personal characteristics and is not linked to any specific body part. It is the next-to-last Nakshatra before the winter solstice and can be seen just a little to the left of the summit of the broad circle depicted in figure 8.5. The name means victorious or conquering completely, which gives some clue as to what it signifies. In addition, this is the one time of the year where an individual can write their own destiny and is considered to be the most auspicious period of all. Abhijit is known to coincide with the moment when the sun enters Capricorn, which used to mark the start of the winter solstice festival in Tamil Nadu. The date for this festival has now shifted to 14 January due to various calendrical modifications that have occurred over the centuries, but its association with the winter solstice remains very strong. At least one bard studied has said that Ponnivala story listeners should perform their traditional patti pongal cow pen ritual immediately after the bard brings the Ponnivala story to a close, asserting a clear link between its concluding verses and the start of a new beginning on the winter solstice day.

Examining the implications of the body part imagery provided by the rotating Nakshatras as sketched out here also proves interesting. A specific association between each Nakshatra and its body part has not been provided, so as not to clutter an already dense diagram. However, the main points of this match up need discussion. First, the body part system starts with the top of the head which is linked to the Krittika Nakshatra (the Pleiades). To remain In line with the earlier analysis of the Babylonian star map, the Krittika constellation has been placed in the same position

The Story Told by the Stars 299

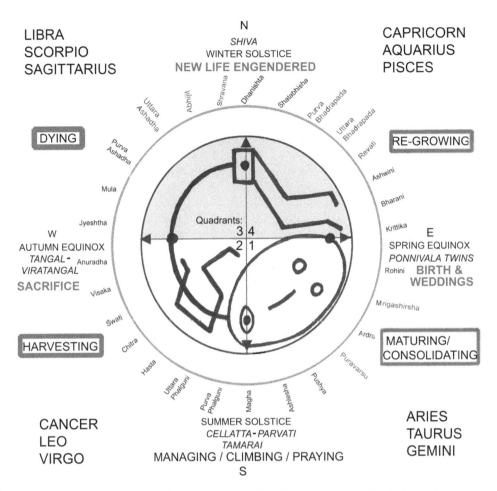

Figure 8.5. Chart 3: The four basic quarters of the Nakshatra star map in relation to the solar year.

as in figures 8.2 and 8.3, namely at the moment of the spring equinox occurrence in about 2200 BCE. The sketch here has been oriented to match this same frame.

That the Krittika constellation was traditionally used to start the sequence and the solar year is significant, though it is not the constellation used to start the year now. This selection of the Pleiades to begin the cycle aligns perfectly with Babylonian thinking. Today, because of the precession of the equinoxes, astrologers describe the year as beginning with Ashwini, since this is the Nakshatra that now rises at the spring equinox. For our purposes, however, it makes sense to stick with the older patterns and the presumed thinking that lay behind it which focused on the Krittika. When we do this, everything else lines up nicely. But there is another issue that could confuse readers. The top point on the head of the human sketched in figure 8.4 aligns with the spring equinox and it is clearly marking the moment this child or foetus is born. But that is not the moment this new life began. Look to the bottom of the chart, the summer solstice, for the moment of its conception. Then, six months later, the winter solstice, marks the moment its presence is visibly announced as the mother's belly swells. If we use a different analogy, this is the moment the egg is laid. It will then go through a further incubation period and hatch at the spring equinox. We have to understand the diagram in this way in order to line up these two different, but still eerily similar, conceptual systems.

The next striking thing about the Nakshatras in relation to human body parts is that the first seven Nakshatras (starting with the Krittika) all describe parts of a human head, but they do not unfold in a very predictable way. For example, the seventh part named is the ears, possibly reflecting the moment (late in the creation process according to related myths) when sound begins to fill the universe. Whatever the case, it is certainly clear that a sketch of this body's parts does not depict an adult human. The many parts of the head that are listed makes it clear that the head of this being has been allocated a huge space in relation to the rest of its body. And then we come to the eighth part, which starts off the following quadrant. Its initial point is assigned to the body's lips and chin, formally matched up with the Magha nakshatra. What seems to be implicated here is what lies between the lips and the chin which is, of course, a mouth. That mouth has been aligned with the summer solstice point. Six other parts follow. These are the hands, neck, chest, etc., but again these elements are not listed in any seemingly logical vertical order as the hands come first. Indeed, the drawing required to illustrate this area seems compressed. This is because of the need to squeeze every part of the body that is now listed, each of which sits somewhere between the mouth and the navel, into this one quadrant.

The next quadrant starts with the Anuradha Nakshatra. It is associated with the moment of the autumn equinox and is linked to the stomach. It seems very likely, though it is not specifically stated, that this point of the body refers to its navel. Six more Nakshatras again follow, and the list here includes the intercalary period called Abhijit. The last Nakshatra that falls in this quarter of the circle is Shravana, which is linked to the genital area. What is still more interesting is that the ensuing and last quarter does not begin with the genitals (as one might expect) but rather with Dhanishta which is joined to the anus of this circular body. Note that the anus, basically a hole, now lies directly opposite to another key opening which we have suggested is this body's mouth. Obviously, what goes in the mouth largely exits via the anus. That direct correspondence does not appear to be accidental.

We can also clearly see that the top of the head in figure 8.5, is important. Of course, this is the place where a newborn baby has a soft spot, that is, the spot where the skull bones have not yet closed. This more subtle opening matches nicely with the navel, also a sort of half-hole, located on the opposite side of this diagram. That opposition, though not as biologically obvious as mouth and anus, may well stand for a secondary channel understood to run through the body, something like the entry and exit points of the body's spirit being. We can speculate that the idea suggested here is that life enters the unborn child through its umbilical cord, of which the remainder is a belly button, and then leaves through the top of the head at death. This last thought is tentative but basically matches several central yoga concepts and is something that readers might want to explore further.

The last quadrant, what is left to mention, consists of the anus plus six other body parts that relate to the legs and feet. What is most interesting now is that the next to last part named is the "upper part of the feet" while the very last item is the "lower part of the feet." That idea is represented in figure 8.5 by the way the two feet have been positioned. Note how this portrayal of the two feet completes the circle very neatly. One foot, the one that comes first in terms of the Nakshatra cycle, seems to make contact with the edge of the circle, perhaps signalling that the fetus is about to leave the womb, while the second seems to hover above that soft spot on the newborn's head. It is as if this body is blessing what will be its replacement in the next cycle with foot one before leaving the circle or womb, and saying goodbye with foot two, just as it leaves to join the external world via its birth. This connection would seem to be a gentle and reasonable way to imagine how the next cycle might begin. Of course, the head of newborn child normally exits the mother first. This biological fact also matches the diagram nicely, confirming that the body seen is that of a child in the womb. The enormous size of the head compared with the rest of the body is another indicator of this. This body, whose parts are listed in astrological texts, must be doubled-up to fit the circle shown, which is yet another indicator that this body is indeed a fetus depicted in its prenatal state. In sum, this deep paradigm can be said to conceive of the stary sky as one giant embryo, a nascent human child. This idea is more abstract than the Mesopotamian view of a sky map where we see the same prebirth period (quadrant 1) populated with a cargo boat, water, fish, a deep tunnel, freshly seeded fields, an infant wild boar, and so forth. Nonetheless, the underlying worldview that structures the Nakshatra plan blends comfortably with that earlier, richly embellished, story-based Babylonian vision of the same creation process.

Both the Hindu and Babylonian universes were basically conceived of as sitting on a set of layered squares.[19] In the charts in figures 8.2, 8.3, and 8.5, the centre of the left edge of that square has been used to locate the autumn equinox and implicitly references the west. Following the same logic, the top of the square represents the north and the winter solstice, the centre of the right edge represents the east and spring equinox, while the bottom point marks the south and summer solstice and is strongly linked to the anticipation of the heavy rains that will follow. The rains come after a prolonged period of great heat. We know, however, that the spring equinox event has moved gradually counter-clockwise at the rate of about one degree of the larger circle every seventy-two years. Seen another way, the starry backdrop rotates clockwise at that same exact speed. The stars themselves, however, do not alter their positions relative to one another as seen from earth during this rotation process. We have seen, above, that the mapping of imagery done by a culturally trained observer singles out clusters of star points within the larger array and then connects the dots. This mapping of constellations differed when it was done by ancient Babylonians as opposed to ancient South Asians. Nonetheless, there is something similar about two mapping systems. Both are structured such that there are four quadrants or phases to the sun's journey each year.

The sun's movement, relative to its starry backdrop, is what defines time in both the Mesopotamian and South Asian views of the world. It is the basis of the calendar and marks the important ritual and agricultural phases of each annual cycle. The stars themselves provide a mental chart that helps to signal where we humans stand in the grand cycle at any given moment. Through myriad associated mythological stories, charts of the sky also help astrologers, soothsayers, mystics, and seers predict how our current circumstances are going to change. Culturally based visions of the sky provide us with some of the deepest paradigms of all, and by the same reasoning, this unique way of thinking can be grasped by anyone who is patient enough to seriously study the night sky.[20] The description that follows will help clarify the patterning implicit in the Nakshatra version of an ancient star-mapped worldview and uncover its links to the Ponnivala Nadu epic story,

Quadrant 1: The period after the winter solstice marks a watery new beginning. The theme here is that of potency and possibility. Fish and other aquatic life appear and are featured. But human life is still hidden, growing mysteriously within the greater cosmic womb. This is a time of fluidity, a time of hope, a period of gradually increasing sunlight and longer days. It is a time used to harvest but also time to begin fresh planting, and a time when piglets and lambs are born. In sum, this is a quadrant of the year filled with anticipation. It is also the time, according to both the Mesopotamian and the South Indian Nakshatra understanding of a sky-mapped world, when the foetus takes on human form in its mother's womb. In terms of the Ponnivala Nadu epic this would be the time of Tamarai's visible pregnancy with the twin-heroes-to-come. In would also be the time, in the previous generation, when Shiva is thinking of hiding a small child under a pile of rocks who will become Kunnutaiya. It is also the time when Shiva and Parvati were courting each other in the form of two deer. And finally, it could even be the time when Parvati herself was contemplating placing nine healthy young brothers on earth, hoping they would use the plough she gave them.

Quadrant 2: At or near the spring equinox things begin to find a fresh balance and thus a new beginning. The nights and days gradually become more equal. It will be the time of a great birth. In South India's broader festival tradition cycle, the spring equinox heralds the birth of Lord Murugan. In the case of the Ponnivala Nadu story this will involve the birth of triplets, certainly a rare event. Taking a more general view, this will be a time of abundance, and thus of multiples more generally. For example, at his own birth Lord Murugan will have not one but six, separate heads. And in the Ponnivala Nadu story male twins plus a sister will all be born together. Furthermore, there will be other births that double this set of three, in some way. The twins' birth is doubled by the birth of a wild boar who will later grow up to challenge them. Meanwhile, their sister will also have a double form, because a fiercer and wilder female is born at the same time in the forest, and even her name will match the sister's. There will also be a female pup born in the palace who is destined to have an important future role. The Ponnivala Nadu triplets, therefore, are themselves matched by three equal but more mystical figures (Twins vs Murugan, Tangal vs Viratangal, and Ponnacci vs Komban). All six will grow up as a generational set with their own families and there will be tales of mirrored personalities, complex attractions, and interpersonal jealousies. This second quarter is thus a period of family identify formation. Ponnivala Nadu marriages are also linked to this quadrant, or at least that association seems likely. Marriage is another symbol of family identity and solidarity. Conducting a wedding involves rites that look forward to the creation of still more family bonds in the future. Tamarai marries and then the twin heroes themselves marry. Both weddings seem to be linked to the beneficent light rains that fall in the spring, However, those showers will gradually come to a halt sometime after the equinox period has passed. Discomfort will start to grow. The period of greatest heat is about to begin. The family living space now starts to feel constrained and human emotions, especially quarrels, begin to heat up. Another event that seems suitable to this second quadrant is when Tamarai develops anxiety because she has not become pregnant. Furthermore, in the next generation there is the moment when the twin's wives are locked in a separate palace where their husbands never visit them. Barrenness threatens the land by the end of the second quarter.

Quadrant 3: This is the moment of full summer, the period when the sun is highest in the sky. The third quarter also carries with it several sets of special symbols. For one, this is the period directly opposite the winter solstice. Now low, field-rooted plants with tender sprouts are described, as opposed to lofty, cloud-swept mountains where the gods sit to debate great matters. Here on earth life is troubled. Cousins challenge each other. Women carp and bully one another. Those who suffer seek a way out. They look to the sky and wish to travel upwards into what looks like a cooler life in the gathering rain clouds. This is when Tamarai and her husband begin to search for solutions. First Tamarai thinks of suicide, but Vishnu persuades her to look for ways to help others instead of focusing on her own troubles. The summer solstice is associated with the sun sitting high in the sky, as if it were on a post. Tamarai is encouraged to be strong-willed and determined. She is advised to ignore her suffering. Furthermore, in the Ponnivala Nadu legend this third quarter is a period of female dominance, and a period of great power for the lone goddess Cellatta. In Babylonia many beasts that appear to be female appear on the Babylonian star chart during this time. On the southern and hottest part of that star map we see animals with heavy teeth or sharp claws such as the lion, serpent, and crab. There are also images in this quadrant of mothers caring for children and a woman holding a pot whose liquid content endlessly pours out for the benefit of others. This reminds us, in the Ponnivala story, of the moment when Tamarai herself brings a golden pot filled with a life-giving liquid, down to earth with her, after visiting Shiva's Kailasa council chambers. There are many more agricultural references in quadrant 3 as well, more so here than in the other quadrants. The fields, the earth, and the ploughed furrow are all signs that carry significant female connotations. On the Nakshatra map, in parallel, the breast is located here, as are the body's helpful arms. And at the end of this quadrant is a reference to the navel and hence to the mother's umbilical cord.

Quadrant 4: This quarter begins on the day of the fall equinox, when the harvest is underway. It is the second point of balance in this grand circular diagram. However, this is also the time when indications that death and/or various kinds of sacrifice start to take on importance. The harvest is, itself, a kind of sacrifice, a sacrifice of plants and their seed-kernels as they are reaped by humans or else begin to die off on their own. We find a predominance of references to animal sacrifice in this quarter, as well. Both Komban in the Ponnivala story and Humbaba in its Gilgamesh parallel die during this period. And the Great Bull of Heaven is also sacrificed, it would seem, at this time. After this consequential killing Gilgamesh begins to wander, looking for everlasting life. It seems likely that, the twin Ponnivala heroes sacrifice themselves during this same period, gifting themselves to an all-powerful earth goddess, likely Bhudevi. Much plant life dies and animals hide for the winter. Now a divine female energy is at work, applying her powers to recycling and to rebirth efforts. In the Ponnivala Nadu story the heroes' sister Tangal takes control at this point. Here she is the goddess linked to the Pleiades constellation, but now reincarnated as a female on earth. She embodies the power of resurrection, an ability to bring new life to the dead. Eventually Tangal manages to briefly revive her own two brothers, before they continue with their journey and hope to rejoin Shiva in the sky. But Tangal stays behind to build them a temple so that others can remember their greatness.

The presence of a rough correspondence between the seven terms used throughout the earlier parts of this book and these four quadrant descriptions may also interest readers. With this in mind, it is suggested that following (rough) associations apply: quadrant 1: **roots** and **reclamation**; quadrant 2: **relationships**; quadrant 3: **resilience** and **resistance**; and quadrant 4: **reflection** and **revelation**. These seven terms do not fit perfectly with figures 8.2, 8.3, and 8.5. Nonetheless, there are similarities suggesting some degree of basic agreement exists across all the charts presented: an underlying logic intended to describe a life-generating process. That logic has long infused humankind's efforts to systematize our understanding of the heavens.[21] Humankind has repeatedly exhibited, from very ancient times forward, a persistent need to create a meaningful pattern of pictures sketched out as a kind

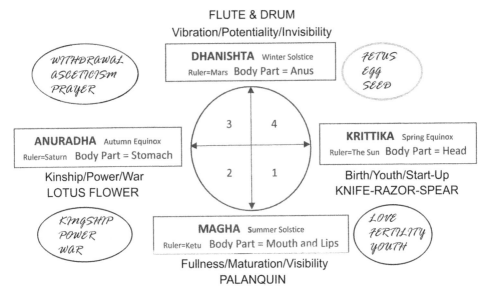

Figure 8.6. Further implications of the Nakshatra structure for understanding the symbolism of the solar year.

of broad vision that references story characters seen in the stars. That search for a pattern is reflected in art, myth, and ritual throughout Babylonia. The same aspiration also existed in ancient India. There, the ancient Nakshatra system was used to bring meaning to the same stars, although in this instance, the stars were connected in different ways. Anyone who has slept under a starry sky where there is no electric light and little local air pollution for nights at a time, as I did in South India while doing research, will know how compelling a backdrop the heavens can be. It is no wonder that many ancient humans, whether sleeping on solid ground or tossed about as sailors on ships at sea, turned to this amazing display of gradually rotating little lights. Many, many generations of humans have tried to tease the awesome, larger-than-life meaning from those twinkling stars above.

One more diagram should help highlight still further aspects of the Nakshatra system that appear to have some relevance for the Ponnivala Nadu story. The four ovals in figure 8.6 express what has just been described above: a progression in all life from conception, through birth, adolescence, adulthood, and finally to death. Here we see two axes of opposition that mark the start and end of each quadrant in this larger cycle. Dhanishta, rising just before dawn during the second half of the third millenium BC, marking the moment of the winter solstice, is associated with the body's anus. This seems odd until one realizes that, using animal symbolism, especially that of a bird or a crocodile, this is where a new egg comes from.

Of course, that egg laying precedes its hatching, an event that will happen later, around the time of the spring equinox. Laying that egg or planting a seed is step one and can be said to be the moment that something new gets started. As a result, there is some confusion in Tamil Nadu about whether the new year starts with the winter solstice or the spring equinox. Seeds planted will later sprout, just like eggs laid will later hatch or like a human, where impregnation will eventually lead to a human birth. Both the ancient Babylonian and the South Asian Nakshatra calendar began the year at the spring equinox. This is the official reasoning in marking the new year at this time of the year in Tamil Nadu today.[22] But the symbolism that surrounds the winter equinox certainly suggests that there is a strong competing option available. Thus a reasonable degree of ambiguity exists due to the very nature of the underlying deep paradigm involved. The idea of beginning the year at the winter solstice does have some appeal, but the idea of starting the year with the actual birth, be it hatching, sprouting, or exiting a human womb, is also appealing. This is a joyful moment and it does coincide with spring according to ancient thinking. Nonetheless, the winter solstice is a better marker of potential newness, as it nicely anticipates the happiness of an arrival yet to come.

Magha is the Nakshatra that opposes Dhanishta, the winter solstice marker according to the ancient Nakshatra calendar. Again, there is some confusion as the point of the appearance of winter solstice sunrise shifted due to precession. Magha now occurs around the time of Shravana, in late July or early August, but the symbolism referred to has not changed. Dhanishta is a Nakshatra dedicated to the Eight Vasus who represent the eight aspects of the sun, which makes them appropriate deities to worship during this important solstice event, a reversal in the direction of the sun's path of travel. Dhanishta's symbols are the flute and the drum. What it is important to note is that both of Dhanishta's symbols create musical sounds, but the sounds themselves are invisible. The symbol for Magha, the palanquin, contrasts with sound in that it is highly visible, but even more important, it makes special people very visible. Palanquins are used by high status humans for comfort, but also to claim respect and show off the prestige of its travelling occupants. Thus, invisibility versus visibility is a theme that contrasts two opposing parts of the calendrical cycle. Thinking in metaphorical time, rather than in real months, the child in the womb is invisible during Dhanishta but by the time Magha, the opposite sign, is rising in the predawn sky, that child has not only been born but has grown and is now highly visible as a young, handsome, marriageable male. Ponnivala Nadu's male twins, along with other family members, ride inside a palanquin when travelling to their marriage site. The only other time they ride in a palanquin is when their sister wants to show them off as their spirits transition to the sky above soon after their deaths.

The Krittika are equally interesting as they mark a balance point in the sun's yearly cycle. The Nakshatra that celebrates the Krittika is associated with the spring equinox and its symbols are the razor or blade, the knife, and the spear.

What do these items have to do with birth and with spring? They are all metallic tools that will flash if held in the sun. They are also all symbols of alertness, and of youth, especially if considered very broadly. Those sharp tools contrast very clearly with the opposing Nakshatra, Anuradha, whose soft and gentle symbol is the lotus. The lotus opens to light in the morning but begins to close its flower in the late afternoon, before shutting or folding completely at night. It is like an oracle: it sees the darkness ahead and begins to prepare for nighttime, and thus (metaphorically) for death. The metallic tools of spring are hard and assertive. A lotus, by contrast, is empathetic and peaceable. It is also a more feminine symbol. In sum, it can be helpful to consider the symbolism of the Nakshatras in relation to Ponnivala Nadu story events, especially those Nakshatra symbols that relate to the four key transition points that link to days of special significance in the sun's broad circular cycle. The first axis relates to the sun's winter and summer solstice positions and contrasts the hidden with the highly visible (the darkness of night versus the brightness of midday). The second axis connects and contrasts the spring and autumn equinox points. The key idea is the difference here between the shiny and hard metallic qualities of powerful weapons with the soft, enveloping, and nurturing qualities of a lotus flower. This makes the second axis begin with a sudden exit from darkness, followed by a gradual retreat back into hiding, thus completing the year's cyclical journey. The second axis has more to do with relationships, and the need to seek a balance between competitive, socially ranked interactions on the one hand and unifying, welcoming relationships that are infused with mutual love. This too, fits the symbolism of the solar cycle since both equinox points are characterized by the important idea of finding the balance point where night and day are equal. Here one end points to wealth and to heroic battles with knives and swords, while the other suggests loving care and tenderness, making mediation, collaboration and the need to adapt to changing circumstances, primary. A reference to both axes can be found in the Ponnivala Nadu story. We see the first when we connect the heroine's invisible gift of pregnancy received from Lord Shiva is contrasted with her twin sons' later very visible display of grandeur as they ride to their double wedding, Ponnar traveling in a fine palanquin with Shankar following a bit later on a magnificent horse. The second axis is also well represented, this time by the twin brothers' glorious sword fights with their adversaries on the one hand, and their gentle interactions with their sister Tangal on the other.

Nonetheless, the strongest parallels with events described in the Ponnivala Nadu are to be found in studying the Babylonian star map, rather than in a close examination of Nakshatra patterning. The Nakshatras do not contradict that early Mesopotamian map layout, but they are focused on a much more abstract set of insights. The Babylonian star map exposes an entire universe of stories in a structured, progressively unfolding, paradigmatic way (figure 8.3). However, the Nakshatra universe more closely resembles the thinking outlined in the previous chapters; a conceptual style that fits well with the four key theorists discussed earlier, namely Frazer, Campbell, Lincoln, and Witzel (table 1.1). The next chapter will discuss a perspective that lies in between these two types of worldviews. It will uncover a highly visual paradigm, but one that exhibits only a very subtle link to the ideas just discussed. The lotus plant starts to grow underground and, in that sense, can be linked to the symbolism of the winter solstice where new life still lies hidden from view. But when it flowers, it is very grand and beautiful, floating and swaying like a palanquin being carried by attendants. The lotus flower can also be compared with a human navel. Like a belly button, it is a soft, round form with a depression at its centre, a shape with folded skin that looks a bit like a set of lotus petals. The lotus also retains a history of attachment to a long stem, its umbilical cord, reminding us that it has grown up through the waters of its pond-mother's womb until it found light as it burst forth and blossomed. But the lotus is also like the soft spot at the top of the head where its soul resides. The lotus is glorified in Hindu temple designs that link these many themes together more fully yet. We will discuss this lotus paradigm in depth in the next chapter and link that broader imagery to the several important concepts we have discussed so far.

9 The Shining Lotus Plant: A Visual Approach to Finding Hidden Paradigms

Chapter 1 discussed the approach of four grand theorists: Frazer, Campbell, Lincoln, and Witzel, and their somewhat related approaches to discovering underlying themes. As stated in that chapter, these approaches may work as rough predictors of a few common structural features of epic stories. But for the reader interested in understanding a specific story they leave much to be desired. The theoretical frames generated by such universal inquiries are by necessity superficial, and also somewhat vague, in order to allow them to apply to a vast corpus of epic and mythic story examples. These theories lack colour and cultural flavour almost by definition, which is what makes individual epics enthralling and entertaining. There is, however, a fifth theorist who restricts his overarching frame theory to a much smaller universe, drawing examples solely from Hindu and Buddhist sacred art. In his book *The Golden Germ*, F.D.K. Bosch uses an approach that is both informative and productive.[1] His scheme, which will be discussed at length below, allows us to discover and appreciate a core symbolic structure that lies deep inside the Ponnivala story. Bosch's approach stands alongside the four theorists previously discussed but employs a fresh perspective that yields quite a different understanding of this story considered as a whole. Bosch's approach is highly visual and thus uses what many would call the brain's right half, which scientists report is structured around non-verbal sensory clues. The other theorists rest their cases on a view from the brain's left side, which mainly employs highly analytical verbal tools to extract story themes. A further strength of Bosch's approach is that it aligns well with the seven questions used throughout this book to explore how the Ponnivala Nadu story relates to a variety of other epic legends. Bosch's fascinating book falls under the general category of art history. Nonetheless, his work relates well to a broad range of South Asian myths and stories and their many beautiful thematic threads. He has discovered and extracted many themes from his extended study of temple architecture and carvings. Bosch's work is so interesting that it is worth delving into his conclusions at some length. His extensive corpus of photographs gives his work a special richness and a grounding that references

310 Hidden Paradigms

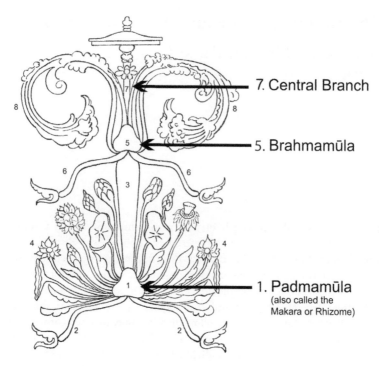

Figure 9.1. Bosch Diagram of his lotus paradigm, showing its many parts (adapted from Bosch 1960, 79, figure 11).

a specific cultural area of the world. Since our goal is still comparison, all of his ideas under investigation can be illustrated anew by drawing on parallels found in Ponnivala Nadu story materials.

Bosch's ideas are intended to draw attention to a core paradigm, a broad underlying belief structure that references the shape of a mature lotus plant. Bosch has sketched that sacred lotus and named its eight parts (figure 9.1). Note that Bosch numbers the lotus's various segments vertically,[2] starting with the plant's roots, which reflects, of course, the dynamic underlying how most plants grow. Furthermore, Bosch identifies three key locations on his plant sketch. Taken together, his segments 1, 5 and 7 clearly reference what we can call the lotus plant's primary spine.[3]

The Lotus and Its Many Parts

1. The *padmamūla* (meaning the rhizome or root ball): My **roots**.
2. The *lateral branches* at the plant's base: My **reclamation**.

3. The *main stem*: My **relationships**.
4. The *lotus vegetation* branching off the lowest node: Also my **relationships**.
5. The **brahmamūla** (meaning the elixir of life, or soma): My **resilience**.
6. The *lateral branches* extending out from the central node: My **reflection**.
7. The *central branch* which constitutes the highest segment of the stem: My **revelation**.
8. The *main branches* curling up to form a protective roof over the central node: My **resistance**.

Bosch's basic scheme draws on an in-depth study of the artwork he photographed while documenting the grand Barabudur Temple located in Central Java. He presents an extensive library of graphic images to illustrate his ideas, and fortunately, an equally large number of drawings are available that depict similar scenes in the Ponnivala Nadu legend. These latter images were generated while producing an animated video series dedicated to telling this story in a uniquely visual way. Because of that fortuitous correspondence in reference materials, a very graphic set of similarities can be investigated. It may seem surprising to think of applying Bosch's thinking to such a distant Hindu setting. Although Central Java is a long way from South India, many residents of both areas identify with a broad, Hindu-Buddhist universe of symbolic concepts. And the two locations taken together do seem to substantiate the hypothesis that a very general Hindu-Buddhist worldview has been visualized for centuries by exploring how it corresponds to the form of a sacred lotus plant. That insight may not seem especially novel if one were to ask an Indologist, but what is surely unique is the possibility of using this plant-like image to better understand the essence of an epic length Hindu story.

The principal purpose of any artist-story-teller-illustrator's work in depicting a great myth or heroic legend must, first of all, be to tell that tale. Furthermore, almost any artist will want to praise and glorify the central characters of the story being referenced. Those characters will usually include a set of gods and goddesses. The correspondence is simple: the lotus diagram has a central spine and two roughly symmetrical sides, just as a human body does. It also has two vertically aligned power nodes which could represent (though Bosch does not state this), its genitals, and its heart.[4] In his terminology these two key nodes are the lotus *padmamūla* and the brahmamūla. My focus will be on those two points and Bosch's illustration of the way that they have been conventionally represented by sculptors and architects in the South and Southeast Asian context.[5] Numerous right and left branches clearly extend outward from these central nodes. However, we will treat that branching as generating somewhat secondary, supplemental, supportive appendages. It is also important to note, at the outset, that there is a certain mystery pertaining to the likely presence of a third node, poised either somewhere on the *central branch* or just above it. In other words, does this lotus body have a head? Indeed, Bosch seems to indicate that there is a superior node. He represents this using a small flower medallion located just above his segment number 7. We will return to this problem at a later point to suggest that, at least according to the Ponnivala Nadu story, there are likely two such heads or else two faces of one head that are located vaguely adjacent to one another in this area of his diagram, taking into account the grand scheme of things. Furthermore, there is a small parasol, never discussed, that sits atop Bosch's entire illustration. Here too there is likely ambivalence, perhaps even some confusion, over what that parasol represents and how it functions. That mystery will be set aside for the moment but will be returned to later.

Before proceeding, we must first connect Bosch's core concept map[6] to a second fundamental element in most temple settings: the torana or honorary arch. Bosch discusses this torana theme here and there but leaves its affinity with the lotus diagram largely implicit. For our purposes that relationship needs to be set out clearly. The torana arch is clearly intended to accent, encompass, and honour the heart or centre of the lotus plant, specifically its brahmamūla or shining core. If we were to enlist a human analogy, that spot would be the heart. The torana frame clearly forms a roof over the central node or icon but what else, above that, is also covered by it is less clear. In figure 9.2a there is a benign and contemplative figure shown above the Buddha that is clearly included under the arch. But in figure 9.2b the arch rests immediately above the Buddha's head and is capped by a frightening figure, a *kāla* head, which, similar to father time, references the idea that eventually all will be swallowed up and revert to dust. We'll return to the discussion of kāla heads at a later point.[7]

Consider what happens to the central stem when using the lotus plant as the source concept thought to inspire a deity's icon design. But, to insert a lotus concept into a shrine context, its stem must recede into the background, or by a related logic, step aside. Simply put, to make room for a deity, the stem of the plant, which originally would be seen to support the base of the sanctuary, resting directly under its key deity, in this context gets split, or doubled. Now a matching set of left and right supporting posts are used to hold up a soaring torana arch. Usually, these posts are decorated with a vegetal motif that looks something like a climbing vine. Along with this being a practical solution for how to reference a plant base as the primordial source of the deity represented by the icon to be worshipped, this splitting of the primordial stem also adds an element of symmetry to the shrine as a whole.[8] The two posts are usually decorated in a similar manner but, nonetheless, are rarely exactly the same. Furthermore, what was once a single root or rhizome sometimes becomes two serpents instead of two vines, each of which holds something valuable at its summit, something placed just before the point where the curve of the arch or torana begins. Most often this point is depicted as a makara head. But what is a makara head and what does a pair of them, atop two parallel posts or pillars, look like?

Figure 9.2a and b. Two Buddhist shrines that employ the torana frame (Bosch 1960, plates 39b and 9a) with both their arches accented in this text in white to clarify the argument being made.

The Padmamūla

The lowest node in Bosch's diagram (figure 9.1) is labelled the padmamūla or rhizome bundle. As this is the lotus plant's point of origin our first question must be why Bosch deliberately chose the word makara to describe the rhizome. The meaning of the botanical term is clear, but why does Bosch so quickly relate it to the idea of a makara, a motif which is best known as a fanciful animal form suggestive of a crocodile head? It is likely that his choice stems from the term makara being used earlier by other art historians. But Bosch does not just borrow the term, he also states that he understands why there is resemblance between this makara symbol (figures 9.3a and b) and the look of a lotus's rhizome. Bosch believes that many early poets and writers imagined a strange and wonderful animal was concealed within this basic botanical shape. And he acknowledges as much when he writes that "from its first appearance in Indian art, over the entrance to the cave of Lomas Rishi in Mihar (ca. 350 B.C.) the makara was pictured as a fantastic quadruped with a crocodile-like head, a snout curled backwards and a scaly crest on its tail."[9] After that Bosch lists and discusses later examples and describes how this form gradually develops an open mouth, then loses its back legs, and also develops very prominent teeth. The same basic motif was also sometimes given ram-like horns. As well, some artists morphed the makara body so that its tail looked like that of a fish.

By the medieval period, at least in South India, the makara motif shifted again, this time to become strongly associated with the head of an elephant with a curled-up trunk. In addition, the makara's body now starts to look rather like a rhino or other large animal with a thick skin.[10] So this is clearly a creature whose

314   Hidden Paradigms

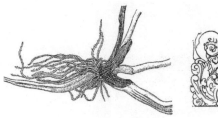

Figure 9.3a. The visual form of a lotus rhizome; a typical makara design (Bosch 1960, 33, figure 6). Figure 9.3b An image of an actual 'mugger' crocodile head, a species that is native to the plains of South Asia.

Figure 9.4a, b, and c. Three examples of the makara motif presented by Bosch (1960, 30, figure 4j, plate 8d, and figure 4l respectively).

specific attributes have shifted over time. Nonetheless, this imaginary being has always retained a strong association with water. The makara[11] is also known as an important vehicle for the great sea god Varuna, and perhaps more interesting still, is popularly regarded as the prime means of transport for the god of love and desire (Kamadeva). Furthermore, its association with a cave in early times is very fitting. As we will later see, the creature that will be identified as a makara-like being in the Ponnivala Nadu story, lives in a cave.

The makara also bears a significant link to one well-known sign of the Zodiac, Capricorn. Capricorn is explicitly a constellation associated with the winter solstice and hence with the rebirth of the sun. However, there is yet another set of important associations for those interested in the makara. In ancient Egypt, the crocodile was also sacred animal. It was, in fact, considered to be the true source of a pharaoh's supreme power and strength. It is also highly likely to have been considered sacred in the ancient Indus Valley during the third millennium BCE (figure 9.5).[12] The Indus Valley, a cultural antecedent to South Asian civilization more broadly defined, quite possibly served as the source that inspired an early carving of a makara-crocodile style shrine, seeming to honour a male and female crocodile pair, which has been spotted more recently in a tribal area of Southern Gujarat. References to the crocodile are found on Indus Valley seals, sometimes

Figure 9.5. Indus Seal M482B (enhanced by the author for better visibility) as per Joshi and Parpola 1987, 116.

placed in the upper register of the layout in juxtaposition with an animal sacrifice taking place just below it.[13] Here, in the seal shown, the crocodile is either eating a fish or, perhaps more likely, disgorging a fish as a way of symbolizing that this is a powerful underwater creator. Bosch provides a number of sketches and photos of the makara's importance in Southeast Asian art.

We now turn to the relationship of the makara to the torana and to Bosch's wider symbolic frame (figure 9.6). The four circles mark the key points that correspond with Bosch's basic lotus model. The brahmamūla is located roughly at the location of the goddess' womb. That key creative locus is framed by two makara heads, one on either side, each on top of a post. On the posts themselves the vine theme is not apparent until one looks closely. It is disguised by two matching mythical creatures that suggest a horse version of the basic makara concept. These twin creatures face outward and each holds a vine in its front hooves, while the vines they hold up appear to be exiting from their mouths. Just behind each horse is a nicely executed vine design that ascends each pillar to the point where the more conventional makara motif sits. Figure 9.7 consists of several key details extracted from the larger photo of the goddess Durga seen in 9.6. Each extract looks something like a makara, or a makara's head. On each side of Durga's garlanded figure, we see two parallel posts, each capped by a makara (seen within the added white circles). The two makara face the goddess, reversing the orientation of the two horses just below them. Looking carefully, one can see their open mouths, but the vines that grow upward from them now appear to rest on their backs rather that to issue from their mouths, as in the case of the horse-like makaras beneath them. These makara are meant to symbolize the creative force that permeates the universe at large and is responsible for generating new life replacing what is constantly dying out. This is why the makara motif is most commonly positioned parallel to the goddess' womb, or in the case of a male deity, adjacent to his genitals.

316 Hidden Paradigms

Figure 9.6. A temple icon dedicated to the goddess Durga, Richmond Hill, near Toronto, 2021. Photograph courtesy of Raj Balkaran.

Figure 9.7a to d. Details drawn from figure 9.6. (a) A kāla head at the summit of the torana frame; (b) and (c) Two near-matching makara heads, one on each side of the goddess at waist level; (d) The head of the buffalo demon the goddess Durga is known to conquer, a creature described in numerous popular myths.

But these odd makara creatures also express the idea of life's continuation, as new generations take over at regular intervals from previous ones. Hence, in the case of the makaras seen in this mid position, the organic plant vines that represent growth appear rest on their backs, rather than issuing from their mouths.

The idea of a deity's power to regenerate as well as to protect life at large is further enhanced in a second way if we now consider the role of two additional heads, one seen at the top of the torana and the other beneath her feet (figure 9.7a and d respectively). The kāla head, as mentioned earlier, is not very well defined in this instance but we will see more examples of it below. Basically, this motif type is frightening to look at. It has large teeth, often accompanied by tusks, an open mouth whose lower jaw is sometimes missing, big swollen eyes and a long, lolling tongue. It is again a mythical creature, but one that in some instances looks somewhat like a very fierce pig. The kāla head is always seen head-on and it does

The Shining Lotus Plant 317

Figure 9.8a to d. The torana of the Buddhist shine seen in figure 9.2b (repeated here) compared with the toranas seen in three folk shrines dedicated to the twin Ponnivala heroes.

not have vegetal vines issuing from it. No clear explanation of this kāla head motif is given in Bosch's work, but Gautama Vajracharya (discussed further in chapter 10) has offered some interesting observations. He calls this the kirtimukha and suggests that this type of image symbolizes the face-like patterns that many see in the dark rain clouds just before the monsoon rains arrive. The kāla (or kirtimukha) and the makara shown here are key to understanding an important hidden paradigm that lies beneath the Ponnivala story.

Before the underlying connection between the kāla head, the makara head, and the Ponnivala Nadu epic can be revealed, however, we must demonstrate that this same set of motifs is also present in local temples dedicated to the folk heroes honoured by that legend. Figure 9.8 provides three examples of toranas encountered early in 2020, each inside a separate local shrine dedicated to this story's main characters. Two roughly matching makara images, one on each side of the central statue(s) can be discerned in every case. Only the left side of each has been marked, in the interests of simplicity. In figure 9.8c, because the two brothers and their sister are being honoured side-by-side, these two makara forms, each set on a pillar, have been placed at the extreme right and left sides of the entire icon group, while the centre support (marked with an extra circle) has been given a more abstract theme, possibly referring to a leaf of the sacred pipal tree. We are suggesting that there is a key parallel with Bosch's work here. In each case the Ponnivala Nadu story heroes are presented in the centre of a torana frame, corresponding to the location of the brahmamūla, thus likening the heroes (and heroine) to a golden core or primal seed.

Again, as before, in the Ponnivala Nadu temples shown here, the makara image rests halfway up the torana frame, at the point just before that arch begins to curve. Now its placement lies roughly at the same height as the shoulders of the two male gods, perhaps making a reference to their physical or muscular power, by contrast to the generative female womb. Another way to describe this, however, is to say that each makara head sits on a post or pillar that serves as a pair of legs. In that case there may well be a more general parallel being sought with the genital area. As with most symbolic bundles, absolute consistency is rare and is never insisted on. Artistic flexibility and interpretation are a hallmark of such traditions, exactly as we have seen above when discussing the ways in which the makara form itself has changed over time. It is only a consistency in the basic idea or concept that is at stake. Building on the concept of an underwater rhizome, we can now say that the side pillars of the torana frame can be equated to the stem of a lotus that rises under the water but that this stem has morphed into a pair of supports needed to hold up the torana arch. The reflection of this near universal shrine design is fully present in local temples dedicated to Ponnivala Nadu story, even where a pair of heroes or a set of triplets are being honoured.

By examining the torana that conventionally frames a deity's statue, many of Bosch's ideas attain a sharper focus.[14] The torana is an important feature of a wide variety of Hindu temples, both in humble and in high status settings.[15] However, it doesn't appear that this cluster of motifs has (yet) been identified in a South Asian folk context and, more important, that it has ever been used to help analyse a long and complex Hindu story. As was argued previously, highly generalized theories of story form, like the one attributed to Joseph Campbell in his *Hero with a Thousand Faces*, or Michael Witzel in his *Origin of the World's Mythologies*, do little to advance our in-depth understanding of specific epics or mythical structures. Identifying thematic clusters specific to cultural regions, themes such as the one Bosch has proposed, can do considerably more to advance our understanding of the underlying foundations of an area's entire belief structure. We now turn to a deeper discussion of the various segments identified in Bosch's scheme, one-by-one.

First let us further consider the makara that corresponds to the lotus rhizome. Figure 9.8 presented three recent examples of Ponnivala hero statues located in temples dedicated to this story's popular set of divine twins. Now, in figure 9.9 we see a close-up of the left pillar's makara image in each case. Of course, these are folk images, and the artwork is not as precise as in the illustrations Bosch provides. Nonetheless, the depiction of this beast is fairly consistent: there is an open mouth, an eye, some kind of upper jaw, and a leafy or swirly tail.[16] Furthermore, we may note that the third image in this sequence of examples is purely vegetal. Nonetheless the suggestion of an eye can still be seen, along with the shape of an open mouth next to it.[17] All three examples, therefore, reflect the motif of an animalistic makara-shaped aquatic being. These illustrations will take on added meaning towards the end of this chapter when we examine more fully the peak of each torana, where a kāla head is consistently seen.

The Deeper Meaning of the Makara and Its Equivalence to Ponnivala's Wild Boar Character

Clearly, the concept of the makara form is present in many Kongu region folk temples, but now the discussion turns to its place and representation in the Legend of

The Shining Lotus Plant 319

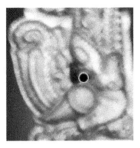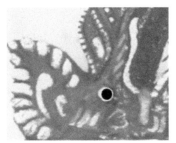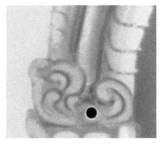

Figure 9.9a, b, and c. A close-up view of the three left-side makaras seen in the folk temple icons displayed in figure 9.8.

Ponnivala Nadu. Here, it would appear that a substitution has taken place. The wild boar, a water-loving creature that is also strongly associated with fertility, is the mythical beast given equivalence with a makara-creature. The bard who sang the Ponnivala Nadu story locally in 1965, described this boar, whose name was Raja Komban or king of the tuskers, many times and in many ways. First, he is sixty feet tall and seventy feet long. Of course, that description has fantastical overtones, but a little bit of the fantastic fits very easily within the larger makara tradition. Komban, as previously discussed, is very black and knows how to write a message with his tusks on the muddied back of a human. He can converse with the story's human characters and has a remarkable star on his tongue suggesting that he is somehow linked to a constellation in the sky. Like the crocodile, the wild boar is dangerous. Both animals are capable of killing and of carrying off young children. Hence, the wild boar appears to function as a localized equivalent of a makara-being.[18] Note that Komban hides and usually operates at night, while a crocodile also hides in a dark cave-like place, in this case under water. The association of both these animals with water is important. Crocodiles spend most of their lives in or near water, possibly a water source used for crop irrigation, while Komban's most consequential act is to create a serious flood by breaking the dam that holds back the waters of the hero-family's principal water storage tank, which is also a central local resource used for crop irrigation. In the Ponnivala Nadu story, the head of the wild boar is recycled by the gods and then made ready to serve as a new life-seed.[19] Komban appears again later in this argument at the point where the symbolism of the kāla node is further discussed. During the story's climatic ending, Komban's head is given a central role.

In the discussion above, we focused specifically on how the wild boar reflects the makara concept traditionally portrayed in South Asian temple art. There is clearly a basic fit here with what Bosch has discerned. Wild boars are known to tear up farmers' fields. Using their tusks, they rip up the earth and raise large clumps of it

Figure 9.10. Three images taken from the animated version of the Ponnivala Nadu story, each showing how the head of the wild boar Komban has been illustrated by the story's folk artist, a village man from the area who, to the best of my knowledge, was totally unaware of the term makara, or of its existence as an abstract concept.

in the air. These chunks of rooted plant life are strongly associated with the boar's mouth. Boars may even eat bits from the plants they tear up. The illustrations of Komban shown in figure 9.10 are drawn directly from the Ponnivala story.[20] In that account Komban soon starts to play around in the vast sea of flood water he creates by breaking apart the farmers' irrigation dam. This is a mythical wild boar. Komban is far too big and too skilled in human habits to be a real animal. But wild boars are considered to be demons and their destructive power is well known to local farmers, even today. The makara, similarly, is a mythical creature of darkness, a creature that loves chaos and swirling waters. But the boar and the makara also share the idea that they embody a creative, recycling form of energy associated with new life born from flooding waters. Furthermore, the shape of a boar's head reflects the creepy, scorpion-like shape of the lotus rhizome itself.[21]

In Hindu mythology more generally the great boar Varaha, a well-known incarnation of Vishnu, is also fearsome. Varaha embodies a fundamental life force that serves to recycle life, just as the crocodile is associated with Kama, the classic god of love and the Hindu form of Cupid. Varaha and Komban both bring large clumps of earth up from the waters and expose them to the sun. Those clumps of earth will then function like well-watered seeds, perhaps even like new lotus flowers. Reinforcing this idea is the story in which Varaha famously brings up his own sweetheart. He finds her during his grand, mythic, underwater dive. This woman, his sweetheart, is mother earth, widely known by the name Bhudevi. Komban's birth was generated by a vow closely related to the heroine Tamarai's parallel vow to herself that she would steadfastly pray for a pregnancy. It is Tamarai's constant pleading that finally leads to her becoming pregnant with this story's two epic heroes. When those heroes reach the age of sixteen and become adults, Komban emerges from the dark forest nearby, for the very first time. The heroes marry at this point, at their mother's urging. And meanwhile Komban initiates his own mission to flood the earth. The potential for recreation, for new life, is present in both these events. Like the lotus rhizome hidden under water, the wild boar Komban lurks in the forest shadows, not very far from Ponnivala's fine fields. Story listeners know that he will eventually emerge and wreak havoc. Thus, the wild boar is a story form of the makara or crocodile known to Indian temple artists. Komban's real meaning was a question that plagued me for many years. Looking deeply into Bosch's cosmic lotus has allowed me to uncover where he fits into the Ponnivala story's larger cosmic scheme. This is one of several key paradigms hidden deep within the Ponnivala Nadu epic that will be further discussed below.[22]

The Lateral Stems

In Bosch's diagram the next principal component that needs explanation in relation to the local epic (component) are the **lateral stems**. These can be seen to grow horizontally outward from the lotus's rhizome base. Because these branches develop in the mud and in darkness, we have called this energy a kind of reclamation. That process of development can be linked to the need to affirm a family's base or roots, in other words, its ancestral line. The lateral stems represent the point where the earliest family branching takes place and the clan ancestors emerge, to use a human analogy. In the Ponnivala Nadu story this event equates nicely with the emergence of nine male ancestors, each of which soon begins to create a separate family line. It also parallels the point where the first in-law cluster appears, meaning a separate family whose females are therefore potential marriage partners, from the heroes' perspective. Figures 9.11a and b illustrate the Ponnivala Nadu equivalent where the nine original ancestors first find marriageable women and then each welcomes one of those females into a marital bond with a symbolic flower garland. This illustration demonstrates the general correlation between Bosch's botanical sketch of a lotus plant's lateral stems and the concept of starting a separate human descent line.

However, there is a second significant parallel that also requires mention. A tunnel is featured just after the two heroes' birth. It is a tunnel dug by the goddess of the family lands, Cellatta. She knows this precious set of newborn male twins is under threat. Those two young boys, born already clothed and carrying small weapons they can use to defend themselves, have been threatened by jealous relatives. It is the old story of male cousins who do not want the children of a rival uncle to grow to maturity and inherit fine lands they might otherwise claim for themselves. To protect the boys from these threats, the goddess Cellatta carries the newborn twins through an underground tunnel that she has just finished digging. It leads from the birthing chamber inside the family palace to a secret cave under her own local temple, where they will live for five years. They drink the milk of her personal tiger and from her personal elephant until they have gained strength and self-confidence, at which point they return to their rightful mother. These images

322 Hidden Paradigms

Figure 9.11a and b. Images of the nine clan ancestors who established the Ponnivala family line and of their first marriage alliance with women from a separate, marriageable descent group.

Figure 9.12a and b. The underground tunnel the local goddess carries the newborn heroes through, and the cave under her temple where they are nursed by a tigress (and, unseen, a cow elephant).

provide an interesting parallel with the underwater tunneling shoots the rhizome of the lotus plant sends out. The image of moving through a tunnel drilled in the mud of the earth and then living in a dark nest or adjacent cave where they feed on rich, energizing growth-producing liquids, fits Bosch's vegetal parallel quite well.

Main Stem and Lotus Vegetation

Parts three and four of Bosch's diagram, the **main stem** and **lotus vegetation**, taken together for our purposes, equate well with the concept term **relationships** in this study. Here the same word can be used to denote the development of kinship bonds that grow strong as a family matures. The diagram under discussion here clearly has a central stem, the family descent line, and a wide-spreading set of shoots that cluster around that family spine, representing its known universe of relatives. There are so many family images found in the Ponnivala Nadu animation

Figure 9.13a and b. Two kinds of family relationships featured in the Ponnivala Nadu story: A broad cluster of relatives who inhabit the same region (as many parrot families may inhabit the same tree) and the loving bond between a husband and wife (as described in the loving bond between the specific two parrots in the story).

series that it is challenging to select just one or two to illustrate this simple idea. Hence, the metaphor of a great family tree, in this case the Ficus benghalensis or ala maram, was chosen to illustrate this story's link to these two lotus plant segments. This fig species is the famous one that sends down numerous aerial roots. Furthermore, such trees often harbour many parrots, all of whom belong to the same large family (figure 9.13a). The banyan or ala maram (Ficus benghalensis) with its aerial roots grows well in ancient, natural forest settings. So too, the cosmic lotus which is thought to dwell in its own, private, and primeval pond. The second image, figure 9.13b, presents a close-up of two specific parrots living in a banyan tree and belonging to the forest-dwelling Vettuva hunters in the Ponnivala account. According to the story, these two are a loving couple that harbour a very positive warm sense both of family and of romantic love. In one of the tragedies of this epic, this parrot pair gets torn apart. The legend, furthermore, makes clear that these two lovers should never have been forcefully separated. The twin heroes that severed their family bond caused the parrots great suffering. The Ponnivala Nadu's epic's broad support for family bonds, furthermore, is a central theme in this folk account. In the same way, security, well-being, and mutual aid are all suggested by the strong stem that grows upward from the rhizome of the main lotus plant. In the plant world this stalk and its multiple branches represents a lotus plant's bundle of close relatives. The parallel is clear and needs no further explanation.

The Brahmamūla

The set of family relationships described above is not very remarkable. But the next element in Bosch's diagram, the brahmamūla, certainly is. The Ponnivala story illustrations provide a remarkable set of correspondences with Bosch's brahmamūla

 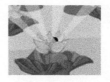 

Figure 9.14. The Ponnivala Nadu story of the creation of the heroine Tamarai: A drop of fertile semen created by Shiva and Parvati (who took the disguise of two deer to make love in the clouds), fell onto a lotus flower below, and a lovely baby girl soon emerged.

node, which is perhaps the most important segment of the lotus plant overall. As already noted, the brahmamūla rests directly above the rhizome and directly below the central branch. These three parts of the lotus, considered together, represent the spine or backbone of Bosch's entire plant diagram. The brahmamūla, furthermore, is the intermediate stage between the origin of a new lotus plant in the mud and its demise as death takes over somewhere near the upper limit of its growth towards the sky. Bosch does not say much about this, but death certainly appears to be referenced by the torana's kala head. That ominous and frightening head, full of teeth and presenting a wide-open mouth, seems akin to the dark starry sky that becomes visible behind the lotus plant after it has closed its flower for the night. Light energizes the lotus and causes it to grow. What happens at night, under the cover of darkness, is not so well illustrated in Bosch's diagram but we will return to that problem later. First we should consider the joyful brahmamūla. Each new lotus plant eventually reaches the surface of the pond, but only after it has been growing upward for some time. The very top of the plant will then exit its watery womb and begin to absorb the rays of the sun that now shine directly on its leaves. Of course, each lotus flower sits on top of a very long stem. It is like a maturing female, who soon after marriage will likely give birth to her first child. That child begins as a bud but will soon blossom as it learns to walk and talk. Maturation would be the appropriate metaphor for the time period during which a lotus plant bud opens and begins to show off its lovely colours. Although a lotus flower always rests on or very near the pond surface and does not go higher, one's imagination can picture how it might continue to grow as an adolescent and then as an adult. This leads to Bosch's metaphor of a great cosmic tree, one that rests on the surface of the earth just beside that lotus pond. Meanwhile, as the adolescent grows, its loving lotus parent will work to provide its lovely flower(s) with continued support. We will consider that tree metaphor further below, but first, there is still more to be said about the lotus brahmamūla analogy itself.

The brahmamūla is the place of the golden germ, the title of Bosch's work. It is now time to turn to the several points in the Ponnivala Nadu story that very clearly and visually reference this exact theme. It is surely significant that all of the

Figure 9.15. Lord Shiva, seated in his Kailasa council chambers, magically creates a golden pot filled with fertility water and asks the heroine Tamarai to carry it to earth for distribution drop by drop to women throughout her kingdom.

Ponnivala substories which celebrate a golden node revolve around women. The first and most important example is that of the heroine's own magical pregnancy. Finally, after many years of being tested, Tamarai is at last invited for a personal audience in front of Lord Shiva himself. Once there, and while she stands in front of all his associates in his sacred council chambers, Shiva immaculately places three embryos in her womb. He also provides Tamarai with a golden vessel filled with an unnamed magical liquid. That ambrosia has been first empowered by this great god such that it will create a new pregnancy inside any female who drinks just a drop or two of its magic. Shiva instructs the heroine, whose name of course actually means lotus flower, to take that special pot back to earth with her. When Tamarai arrives home in Ponnivala Nadu she very soon calls out to all the females in her kingdom who have been wishing for pregnancy. She then carefully pours a few drops into the palm (or mouth) of each one, both humans and animals, giving every female who wishes for conception the opportunity to ingest some of it. Furthermore, Tamarai herself is destined to give birth to Shiva-sired triplets just nine months later, two boys plus one girl. In Fig. 9.8c one can see these three depicted as a set, in their temple icon form.

One more reference to the brahmamūla symbol needs mention: the repeat of the magical pot symbol once again in the third generation of Ponnivala Nadu heroes. There we can see this theme featured through the actions of Tamarai's daughter, Tangal, although there is a difference. Tangal climbs a pillar located deep in the forest and remains there only briefly, whereas Tamarai climbed a pillar that was located somewhere in the sky, halfway between heaven and earth, and stayed there for twenty-one years. Nonetheless, the time Tangal spends atop that special post also bears fruit, and this time there are no significant trials or tests that this prayerful woman must undergo. While wandering in the forest Tangal comes across a mysterious character, a woman who is described as a sun maiden (Arukandi). This woman, who comes from nowhere and seemingly has no relatives, cedes her perch to Tangal for only a short while, but long enough for Tangal to obtain what she wants. After an hour or so she descends from that high perch with a golden wand

Figure 9.16a to d. Tamarai returns to the Ponnivala Nadu palace with her husband after receiving the gift of pregnancy from Lord Shiva. She carries a golden pot full of fertility water which the god gave her and then distributes drops to every female in the kingdom who wishes to become pregnant.

in hand. It is a magical tool that is given to her by Shiva but hand-delivered by Vishnu who flies to her perch using his famous eagle-like vehicle, Gaurada. When Tangal climbs down Arukandi then instructs her to go and find a tiered set of seven pots. As Tangal soon discovers, she needs her new wand to accomplish this.

Tangal wanders further, and after a time, finds potter who lives in a small nearby village. But this man refuses to give her any pots because she has no money to pay for them. So, Tangal curses that reluctant artisan and destroys all of his wares by conjuring up a huge rainstorm with her new wand. That downpour floods and dissolves all the work this poor man has just finished and set outside his home for his wife to sell. Like the great flood discussed earlier that was caused by Komban, the wild boar, this new inundation creates a similar chaos and readies the scene for Tangal's next step. Now, this powerful young woman commands the sun to reappear and, like magic, the potter's entire display springs back to its former lovely and completed state, although now newly reconstituted and magically cleansed. The potter is amazed and, recognizing that this woman has magical powers, willingly gives Tangal a set of tiered pots as a gift. There could be no better symbol of renewal: those seven pots (or brahmamūlas), first destroyed by a watery chaos and then remade as shiny new vessels, will revive her two brothers' lives soon thereafter.

Fertility is also a theme where pots are concerned. In the story just told there is not just one vessel, but rather a whole family of pots that are featured together. These can be compared to a group of seven children, all born very neatly, each just one year after the last, and with the youngest one being the smallest (the top pot in the stack). Also, these are no longer just randomly scattered individual vessels but rather they form a single group, just as human children normally form family clusters. Tangal carries her new pots back to the forest pillar where Arukandi awaits her. The sun maiden descends her pillar once more and magically fills Tangal's seven pots with fine liquids (and also several types of seeds or grains). These marvellous substances flow freely from her open right hand as if her own body was, just beforehand, filled with soma (a sacred ancient drink referenced in the Vedic texts) while she sat atop her post worshipping the sun. Finally, this mysterious maiden lends Tangal her goose-like vehicle so that this grieving sister

The Shining Lotus Plant 327

Figure 9.17a to e. Tangal on the sun pillar, the Sun Maiden praying, the Sun Maiden placing magical substances in Tangal's pots, Tangal's flight on a golden goose, and her revival of her two brothers by sprinkling them with a magic elixir.

of the two heroes can fly over the forested mountains nearby and discover where her two brothers' dead bodies lie. When Tangal does find those two corpses, she quickly goes to work sprinkling the liquids she has carried with her onto their bodies (figure 9.17). That act causes the two men to spring back to life, just like the pots themselves sprang back out of raw mud just a little earlier. What better image of a life-giving bundle of brahmamūlas could one find? That tier of seven pots contained the elixir of life-renewal itself, the very secret to overcoming death.

There is yet one more item in the Ponnivala Nadu epic story that evokes the brahmamūla theme. This is the great war drum that the heroes raise from the mud at the bottom of a local, irrigation pond. They need it so that they can announce to all the residents of their kingdom that they plan to enter the forest to fight the great wild boar, the very beast that had earlier so badly flooded their farm fields that all the crops had been destroyed. The family war drum had been left at the bottom of this pond for years and had been guarded all that time by a fierce set of demons that lived there under the water. These local water-loving demons remind one of the makara-crocodile and its propensity to spend much of its time under water too. The drum, meanwhile, cannot speak until it is raised from that watery abyss, given a new buffalo skin, and then beaten with heavy, firm strokes (figure 9.18). After this, its voice will be heard, for the first time in many years, across the entire Ponnivala Nadu kingdom. The sounds that emanate from it will be so powerful that they will shake up the gods themselves, even though they reside in the heavens far above. Indeed, the loud, rhythmic "tum, tum" this drum produces

328   Hidden Paradigms

Figure 9.18. (a) The war drum that lives in the mud at the bottom of a pond, (b) the demons that guard it, (c) the raising of that drum, (d) offerings made to the drum's guardians in thanks for their service, and (e) the satisfied demons, no longer needed to guard the drum, ascend to the sky.

rattles everything in the cosmos to its core. Its voice resembles the first sounds said to have once filled a silent universe.[23] It also seems likely that this drum's fine voice can be related to the most sacred of all Hindu chants, the sound of the sacred syllable "Om."

After the drum rises to the surface and is given a new skin, its guardians also rise to the surface and are thanked for their work by being offered the meat of an animal sacrifice. Satisfied, these multiple beings then depart skyward. This cluster of water demons seem to have a dual role as they also belong to the kāla doorway of a fearful fire-filled tunnel that Tamarai encounters during her own pilgrimage quest much earlier (see figure 9.30 on page 342). Their fierce-guardian faces look much like the familiar kāla motifs seen elsewhere, as is shown in figure 9.25 on page 338. More kāla heads stand at the exit from that tunnel, each of their mouths awaiting its special chance to swallow a life and end that being's existence in its present form. It is unstated but likely understood that each person whose present form of being is thus extinguished will be whisked off by just such a kāla-like guardian, who will take it back into darkness, preferably to the bottom of a deep lotus pond. There that lonely soul's head will perhaps someday burst open as a fresh seed, and then sprout and rise again as a new lotus stem which will, in its turn, produce a new brahmamūla and more new lives.[24] In this world of metaphor, that corpse's head is like a drum and when it does regenerate as fresh, sprouting seed it will also be capable once more of making sounds that can attract listeners and communicate meaning.

Instead of proceeding laterally, we now move to discuss the very top of Bosch's sacred lotus diagram. That is, we next move up this plant's central stem, following its central branch, to the highest point shown. Bosch has given this pinnacle of the plant something of a parasol or an umbrella shape, mirroring what can be observed more generally in much Southeast Asian architecture and art. This crown jewel, so-to-speak, is merged, in many cases, with the summit of a temple icon's torana or with the top of an entrance to a cave or other dark place. It can even be used to cap the summit of a temple tower. Bosch compares this position to the noonday sun. This makes sense because the sun reaches its zenith at noon, as it temporarily rises to the top of the sky. If the brahmamūla or heart of the lotus is bright and joyful, this parasol occupies the place where kāla heads are often seen.

The top of the sky can easily be considered too bright, a place where fire reigns and where it is too hot for comfort. This concern with excessive heat is especially germane if we consider the perspective of residents located on India's hot plains during the dry season just weeks before the much-wished-for monsoon rains arrive. Reaching the summit of the sky during daylight represents danger.[25]

There are endless temple examples of a kāla head in this summit position and Bosch illustrates many of them in the photographs he has attached to his work. But the reader never gets a very clear idea from this writer-theorist as to exactly where on his lotus diagram a similar head for this paradigm plant is to be found[26] Logically it must occupy the very top position as that is where architects and artists always locate the kāla head. This would mean that this fearful visage is represented, in the Bosch sketch, as that nondescript parasol form he places at the summit of his theoretical drawing (figure 9.1). Perhaps he envisioned this to be a cloud, a body of water, or even a cooling parasol which has a duty to protect what is below from the dangers of what may dwell way up high up in the sky.[27] The two round forms seen just beneath that parasol, furthermore, could suggest golden pots that hold the amrita-like liquid known as soma, which is akin to what clouds full of rain produce. Again, Bosch is silent on this detail in his drawing as well. Just below the two pots there is also a small flower design that has seven petals. Perhaps this flower is a sweet euphemism for the kāla head whose mouth swallows the spirits of recently deceased beings on their way to entering a blissful state of nothingness, something so high up that it lies beyond even the stars? We can never be sure what Bosch intended to suggest with these unique details, but what seems likely is that the Ponnivala Nadu, as a folk account, provides a less abstract interpretation. Pairing uneasily with the learned idea of Moksha or release extensively referenced in orthodox literary texts, many folk temples simply have a very scary kāla head perched on the summit of their local temple tower.

The main argument behind what has been suggested above can now be clarified. The great wild boar in the Ponnivala Nadu story represents both a necessary end to life, and its possible rebeginning, just as a kāla head does. Figure 9.10 shows the wild boar Komban, in his makara or kāla form. There he is seen lifting vegetation from the flood waters, giving it a new start in life, a kind of rebirth one might say, generated by his fearful but also loving and playful actions. This is the concept of the padmamūla or rhizome, where life originates (figures 9.4 and 9.5), being transferred to the brahmamūla position, where it usually becomes a part of the torana frame designed for that shrine's icon. As Bosch himself writes, the makara and the kāla heads are two parts of one concept. Put into the terms being used here, the kāla swallows life and sends it back down to the roots of the cosmic lotus. There it will regenerate, much as a lotus creates new rhizomes that will soon begin to spread out laterally from its original padmamūla, perhaps an old head now issuing forth new life. This is exactly the fate of Komban's own head which the goddess uses after his death to create a new yuga. When seen at the bottom of the lotus plant, at its root, the kāla head, and equally the padmamūla, always seem to face forward. This same tradition can also be observed, for example, in the case of the buffalo head the goddess acquired in her form as Durga (figures 9.6 and 9.7d).[28] But when moved to the side of the torana arch (that is shifted along the lotus root system in the regenerative mud, the kāla head morphs into a profile view and becomes a life-generating makara head (as seen in figure 9.3a). We will look at this theme more closely later, where kāla heads will again be discussed.

The Lateral Branches

There would seem to be good reason that the brahmamūla has two lateral arms, extremities that resemble the two parallel pillars seen in temples where a torana is used. For Bosch this is segment 6 (Fig. 9.1) of the larger lotus plant and he calls these extensions the **lateral branches**. This terminology links easily to the concept of **reflection**, for good reason. The lateral arms in Bosch's diagram stretch out towards both sides of his sketch, much like the arms of a human person. But this idea can be expanded beyond just making a reference to the human form. These laterally structured arms likely also refer to a set of divine forces that are believed to pull the sun through the sky. These are traditionally imagined to be a pair of horses that pull the swift chariot in which the sun rides. Figure 9.19 shows these two steeds as they appear in the Ponnivala Nadu story. All the adornments seen on these horses are gold coloured. More interesting still, the artist has used bright orange for their ears as if the sun is always shining brightly on them as they pull it across the sky. But what happens at night? It is significant that the bard describes how the brothers' lives, after they die by falling deliberately on their swords, were captured in a special tiny gold box by Lord Vishnu. That was the equivalent of putting those (two) suns into a dark box. Later these twin heroes are resurrected by their sister and their spirits are then seen to be mobile and bright once more. So too, the sun eventually rises from darkness at the dawn of each new day. The brahmamūla's round shape and central location suggest that it further serves as a symbol for the sun, something Bosch also mentions. Summarizing several Hindu mythical references, he discusses the idea that stem of the lotus (segment 3 of his diagram) equates to an unseen cosmic pillar which holds up the entire sky, with the sun at its zenith. We have already seen that the torana itself is also held up by vegetal posts, this time one on either side of the brahmamūla. Those spots where the makara heads sit are the very places where the sun appears (left) at sunrise and then disappears (right) at sunset each day. These are also two locations where the mythical golden goose, the same bird Tangal is seen flying on in the epic account, likes to rest.[29] Note that these two torana makaras are therefore clearly associated with the only two liminal times that occur each day, the moment when light and dark exchange roles and all things are briefly in flux.

Also of interest in the study of the Ponnivala Nadu legend is its relationship to the oldest of all Hindu texts, the Rg Veda. There is plenty of textual material

Figure 9.19. The heroes' fine horses, portrayed as shining and bright, like the sun itself. They bear a remarkable symbolic resemblance to what I suggest may be the Aśvin twins, a set of brothers who are mythically referenced as having once pulled the sun's personal chariot.

suggesting that the two Ponnivala Nadu brothers are likely a covert reference to twins mentioned there as the Aśvin twins. In the Rg Veda these two young men, both sons of the sun, help their father move from East to West each day by pulling him using their horse form. There is ample evidence that these sons of the sun secretly resurface in the Ponnivala Nadu story as its two great heroes, Ponnar and Shankar. Just like the Aśvins, the twins in this great folk epic display many complimentary characteristics: bright versus dark, contemplative versus aggressive, and more. These complex beings, perhaps stand-ins for the sun and the moon on one level, also serve the gods and help advance the much grander process of basic cosmic recycling.[30] Their similarity to the two complementary arms of Bosch's lotus diagram is obvious, as is their link to the broad concept of the need for social and political complementarity or duality in leadership, a concept already discussed elsewhere in this book.

If we return to the idea that the brahmamūla is mostly female, then likely its primary reference in the Ponnivala Nadu story is Tamarai, while its flower is her daughter Tangal. But Tamarai bore triplets, and the other two in that set are male twins. Their presence, in this lotus paradigm, I argue, is symbolized by the lateral branches in Bosch's basic lotus diagram. They are the men who will become the guards who serve that central node, which now stands for their sister who represents the brahmamūla. Here we can clearly see how the lateral branches and the concept of reflection (especially a reflection in terms of kin relationships) nicely overlap. Two brothers frame, guard, and may even at times propel, the air borne vehicle in which their sister (the sun) rides. Could this heavenly vehicle, in the Ponnivala Nadu story, be the sister's swing, the surface that she sits on for hours each day?

We can now see that the lotus plant's lateral branches and the reflection theme are intimately linked to a larger symbolism that focuses on balancing alternative forces. The two Ponnivala Nadu brothers have contrasting personalities, and often very different reactions to the same event. As such, the lateral branches represent one of the more interesting parts of the grand cosmic lotus paradigm. If the brahmamūla stands for the midpoint between two pillars, one in the west and one in the east, one where the sun regularly appears at dawn and the other where it disappears at dusk, then the centre, the padmamūla, acts as a fulcrum serving, as it were, as the balance point of a cosmic seesaw (or also of a cosmic swing). And not only does this idea relate to the sun's daily and yearly movements, but it could also serve as a symbol of the moon's and the stars' movements as well. The sun travels underground at night and retraces its steps using a tunnel. Meanwhile the moon and the stary night sky take its place. Since Tangal is an earthly manifestation of the Pleiades star cluster, she could also represent the stars in the night sky, giving her two distinct faces. In sum, there are two sides or aspects of the sun's power. The first is associated with the right side of a larger being, that is, with day, heat, new life, and energy. The other, the left, is linked to night, coolness, and rest. The topic is too vast to explore fully here, but this symbolism nicely embodies the essence of the twin heroes and their sister Tangal, the three central figures featured in the Ponnivala Nadu legend.

There are still more overlaps between the two Ponnivala Nadu heroes and how locals understand of the structure of the heavens and its prominent solar cycles. The first-born twin, Ponnar is easily compared with the daytime sun. Indeed, his name means gold and he behaves like the golden sibling. In figure 9.20 we see him standing on a dais and giving orders to all who listen from a few feet below. Ponnar is depicted as the local leader in many songs, and he is always described as wise and gentle. He behaves like the virtuous and empathetic king most people would like to have. Furthermore, Ponnar wears a blue lower cloth, while his brother (the hot second-born twin) wears red. Ponnar is non-violent and thoughtful by nature. He is the twin who is celebrated in every epic poem that describes a ruler, poems that simultaneously reference prosperity and the lush growth of the region's fine crops. Indeed, one can say that he resembles Vishnu in so much as he is a benevolent and kind character who is trusted by his companions. The other brother is named Shankar, a moniker that references Shiva, the darker and more violent god who is also associated with night and with the moon. Shankar is righteous and impatient, eager to confront wrong while using violent actions to ensure the rule of principles he believes to be right. Although both brothers carry swords, it is Shankar's sword that does much of the work in the many battle scenes described. He is the one to physically fight for the brothers' joint kingdom while Ponnar is Ponnivala's ceremonial ruler. Shankar's sword is often held out in front of his body while Ponnar's hangs down and is often not visible at all. Shankar is the one to violently cut through an opponents' resistance. The images selected for figure 9.20 express this idea of the twins' complementarity in terms of their physical presence.

The Shining Lotus Plant 333

Figure 9.20a and b. (a) The senior twin Ponnar serves as ruler of the kingdom and its ceremonial head of state. (b) The junior twin, Shankar, serves as Ponnivala Nadu's' main defender and lead warrior.

Figure 9.21a and b. The two key temples in the Ponnivala Nadu story: (a) The one dedicated to Cellatta, the goddess the two heroes worship, and (b) The one dedicated to Karukali, where the hill-dwelling Vettuva hunters worship.

Figure 9.21 suggests how the same contrast between the Ponnivala brothers that opposes bright versus dark, or peaceful versus violent, is also captured by the Ponnivala Nadu story in many additional ways. For example, of the two key goddesses described, the goddess that protects the land, Cellatta, is seen in the first image. Here the countryside is peaceful and quiet, with the temple sitting in the middle of ploughed farmland. In contrast, the second image depicts a temple dedicated to Karukāli, the black goddess of the forest. Before her shrine stand many fighters, forest hunters who contest the hero-farmers' rights to the flat lands that lie near their own hilly domain. In this frame, also taken from the animation, we see Viratangal, the hunters' brave and outspoken sister. She provides a near-exact mirror image of the heroes' own sister Tangal, even down to her name. Viratangal is a fierce version of Tangal, a woman who calls her one hundred forest brothers together and asks them to attack the two Ponnivala Nadu heroes and their farmlands. There are many more mirrors in this story, all of which express the same basic principle of complementarity that we see expressed in Bosch's diagram as a set of paired Lateral Branches. Bosch remarks that sometimes animals appear in the place of those lateral branches when it comes to temple torana designs. He also notes that such animals, when present, are generally given functions assigned to horses such as pulling a chariot. He has suggested that the forms on the right and left of the toranas he has found might reference the Aśvins, just as has been suggested here. Significantly, in the context Bosch references, namely several Vedic texts, these horses have a wife (or a sister), a female sun-goddess named Sūryā (daughter of her father Sūrya, the sun itself).[31] This makes Sūryā a sister of the Aśvins, and it includes a romantic undertone in instances where her brothers try to woo her.[32] Again the presence of a possible parallel between the Aśvins' story and the central characters of the Ponnivala Nadu account is very clear. Also interesting is the fact that Bosch comments that those same horses are never visible in contexts where a reference to the sun is absent.

Even more significant in this context of sun imagery is Bosch's comment that the Aśvins have now sunk into complete oblivion in India, but that they remain a memory that predates the Vedic period itself. In sum, they belong to India's most ancient heritage.[33] Yet here in this practically unknown oral folk epic, the Ponnivala Nadu story, there is a remarkable set of twin heroes that strongly evoke the Aśvin pair. This is perhaps one of the most significant findings of this larger study overall, a discovery that was significantly bolstered when an exploration of this epic legend's larger worldview began and used Bosch's work as a starting point. Such an important insight suggests that studying a range of basic concepts and related cosmic understandings that may be woven into a relatively unknown epic can be a worthwhile endeavour. This search for hidden paradigms has led to an exploration that has made discoveries reaching well beyond what Joseph Campbell could have found using the paradigm he favours in his work: *The Hero with A Thousand Faces*. Who would have guessed that lying concealed within an oral folk epic collected with a tape recorder in a remote area of South India nearly sixty years ago, one could find strong traces of an essential idea that stretches back further into the mists of human history than even the very earliest of the Vedic texts?[34] The resonance of the ideas just discussed with figure 9.23 is striking. This figure shows an Indus Valley seal dating back to at least as early as 1900 BCE, but likely even earlier. This idea along with a few other, closely related insights, will be revisited at a later point.

And there is more. Note that the two symmetrical arms in Bosch's principal diagram curve slightly downward. Why is that? As has already been mentioned, a number of South Asian stories suggest that the sun enters a tunnel each night in order to traverse the world underground, from west to east. Thinking about these possible mythic connections inspired a re-examination of a very particular episode

The Shining Lotus Plant 335

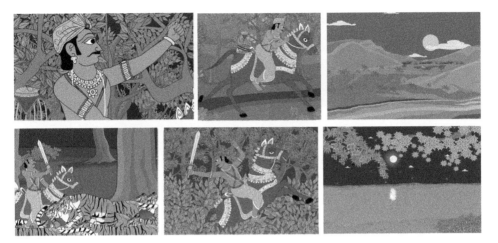

Figure 9.22. Upper row: The hero Ponnar who is equated with the sun; and lower row: The hero Shankar who is equated with the moon.

Figure 9.23. An Indus Valley seal M296, showing what looks like a central sun symbol flanked by two horse heads (from Joshi and Parpola 1987, 72).

in the Ponnivala Nadu story that had always posed a puzzle ... that substory involves a devious artisan who, as one of the heroes' main rivals, tries to trick (and threaten) Ponnar by asking him to protect a fake golden vessel of his overnight as a favour. That vessel, already known to the listeners as fake, is presented by the artisan as the equivalent of any of the many true gold vessels the heroes keep in their palace storeroom. Metaphorically this fake vessel belonging to the artisan is like a false sun. The story begins as the artisan cuts down an ancient and very sacred family tree, clearly a serious moral transgression. He then uses a part of the trunk

 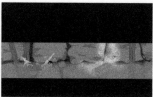 

Figure 9.24a, b, and c. The Ponnivala Nadu sluice gate showing Ponnar. guided by Vishnu, swimming with the flow, then against the flow, and then his brother throwing his sword that will cut off the head the adversary who demanded this test in the first place. That artisan is seen wearing white pants in the first image.

of that tree to carve himself a wooden vessel. Next, the artisan coats this vessel, ever-so-lightly, with a layer of gold leaf his wife buys in the village market. It now looks very grand. Next, by trickery, that artisan places his fake golden pot next to a burning lamp in the heroes' palace storeroom overnight. The lamp always stays lit and the heat from that little flame, in an effect anticipated by the wily artisan, melts the gold leaf on his fake pot overnight and leaves behind just a plain wooden vessel. But the next sequence is even more interesting. When the artisan and Ponnar enter the storeroom together, the artisan, feigning surprise, claims that his fine golden vessel has been secretly switched out and replaced by a wooden one. He then bullies the hero, claiming that Ponnar secretly stole his valuable golden pot in the dark of the night, replacing it with a cheap substitute. Ponnar, of course, swears that the artisan's cruel accusation is untrue.

Responding to Ponnar's protestation, the artisan then insists he needs proof of Ponnar's honesty. To achieve this, he demands that Ponnar successfully pass a great truth test (figure 9.24). To this end he asks Ponnar to swim through the sluice gate found at the lower end of his family's huge irrigation tank. The first part of this test is for Ponnar to successfully swim with the flow of water, downstream. He is to exit out the sluice gate and into a channel used to water the fields below. But when Ponnar succeeds in this, the wily artisan then announces that he must now swim back through that same sluice gate, this time against the current's natural flow. Ponnar achieves this feat too. He thus successfully passes both parts of the artisan's test. But his success is not accomplished alone. Ponnar enjoys some help from Vishnu who volunteers to secretly lead this hero through that dark and watery tunnel, the dangerous path upstream that he must travel to complete his truth test. A metaphor can be read into this that equates Ponnar with the sun at night. It must pass through a dark tunnel as well. The first half of the sun's voyage replicates Ponnar's passage downward through that tunnel, with the flow of its water, at sunset. The second half reflects the sun's rise the next day at dawn, when it must now struggle back up and out of the tunnel. Ponnar, of course, has been asked, in the second test, to buck the natural flow of water through the sluice gate in the very same way. Ponnar is thus being tested by the artisan to see if he is as strong and brave as the sun itself. Can he survive a journey through a dark flooded tunnel like the sun does each night? It is also significant that Vishnu leads the way in this grand test. Vishnu himself stands for the bright or sunny half of the famous Vishnu-Shiva divine pair. Furthermore, the whole incident ends when Shankar (the darker sibling) arrives on horseback. Shankar quickly throws his sword at the artisan who is just then preparing to drown Ponnar by dropping a heavy stone on him as he exits that upper sluice gate.[35] The bard telling the story describes Shankar's palace sword as flashing with rays of light as it flies through the air, preparing to strike the artisan and thus put an end to his lies. As such it is being suggested here that his sword operates as a symbol of the morning sun's rays. They flash and glint as they accompany this primal orbs' valiant rise, up and out of the rushing water, symbolizing the moment the artisan is killed. This is, of course, the very same moment that the sun appears at dawn and replaces the darkness of night.

Perhaps surprisingly, there is still more to reveal. Pillars have already been featured, as they appear in some of Bosch's photographs (not shown) and in relation to torana images showing the use of pillars in relation to the arch that appears above many icons. But pillars are a genuine feature of the Ponnivala Nadu epic story as well. A pillar first appears as a tall tower that Tamarai has built when she is thinking of suicide. Fortunately, Vishnu dissuades her from jumping off its summit at the last minute. Then, just a little later, he instructs her to light a light a fire on top of a pillar as one of the tasks she must complete before leaving on her long-planned pilgrimage to heaven. That fire-in-a-pot clearly references a major Tamil festival celebrated during the dark month of Kartikai (November-December) when people place pots of fire on pillars hoping to light a path upward into the night sky. This is a ritual celebrated at the main gate of each Shiva temple, throughout Tamil Nadu. One can also argue that nursing a fire and getting it to burn in a pot is possibly a metaphor for life that is gradually growing in a woman's womb. Furthermore, this ritual conveniently precedes the winter solstice, the moment when the sun is reborn and then proceeds to reverse its rising and setting movement along the horizon, by just a few weeks. It has been moving steadily southward and now it shifts back and starts to move north once again. In sum, placing a pot filled with fire on the top of a high post can be compared with lighting a fire in the womb of the sky. That this occurs just before the winter solstice seems to suggest that it is a rite or ritual gesture intended to anticipate the sun's rebirth at the moment it reverses its course.

Now consider the symbolism of a bundle of opposing images in the story, ones that relate to the moment of death. Consider the perspective of a flame-in-a-pot analogy. How does that image get reversed at the moment of the heroes' deaths, when a person's life essence, its personal flame, is reduced to nothing more than

338   Hidden Paradigms

Figure 9.25a, b, c, and d. (a) Vishnu collects the heroes' bright spirits after their deaths; (b) Vishnu then places these life flames in a small rectangular box; (c) Next, Vishnu returns to Kailasa with that box in hand; (d) Finally, Vishnu presents that little box to Shiva.

a glowing ember? The inspired Tamil folk artist who created the images used for the Ponnivala Nadu story's animation followed the bard's descriptions and graphically represented this idea. Just after death, a small glowing light exits each hero's chest. In essence these are their two spirits seen in the form of two flames (figure 9.25a). Those flames are called or beckoned by Vishnu (while in other cases it is Yeman who stands nearby and beckons the spirit flame to come to him). In the twin heroes' case Vishnu takes (or catches) those two embers and makes sure that they land inside a small rectangular box that he conveniently carries with him (figure 9.25b). Using that container, Vishnu quickly carries those two tiny spirits upwards into the sky (figure 9.25c). Perhaps, in the afterlife, the little box serves as a womb-like place for a person's never-totally-extinguished, spirit-ember to rest. The pot on a pillar and the little hinged box function as parallel but also contrasted enclosures, one a round and open-to-the-sky earthen rebirthing pot, the other a rectangular metal death-box that has a firmly closing lid. The womb during pregnancy is round and warm and the mother's cervix must greatly expand to allow her child's birth. The little decorative box (roughly the same size as a womb), however, is cold, rectangular and has a hinged lid that allows the divine being carrying it to access it at will. Those after-life spirit embers can be compared with tiny suns, and each living person has his own version residing in his or her own chest.[36] Thus we can say that the sun, the womb, the heart, and life itself are all represented in the Ponnivala Nadu story in a way that easily connects them to Bosch's suggestion that a vital brahmamūla or great seed lies at the cosmic lotus plant's core. At death it gets a hard rectangular box, but at rebirth it gets placed in a nice, gentle, well-rounded pot.

The Kāla Head

It is time to further explore the imagery of the uppermost segment that is labelled, in Bosch's diagram, the kāla head (which must surely constitute an unlabelled subsegment of Bosch's lotus element 7). The illustrations Bosch has used in his book when he discusses the kāla testify to its being the most fearsome

Figure 9.26a, b, and c. Three Bosch examples of a kāla head (jacket, figure 9, and plate 9b).

element in his grand lotus scheme. To begin with, compare the three heads in seen figure 9.26 (all borrowed from Bosch) with three similar kāla heads seen in figure 9.27. The latter composite image features a live crocodile head plus three kāla heads extracted from torana photos taken in folk temples honouring Ponnavala Nadu's heroes. Note that all seven examples show heads that have fearsome and very prominent eyes along with mouths, teeth, and/or tusks.[37] It can be argued that these kāla are makara or fanciful crocodile-like beings now seen head-on, in their most fearsome pose. In their (normal) kāla location at the top of an arch, the heads are presented in their portrait pose which looks much more unsettling than when they sit on a post in their makara form and are seen in profile. Sometimes the tusks are featured, in other images the teeth. Sometimes the tongue lolls out and appears to be unnaturally extended. No matter what the details, however, in each case we see that kāla head in solitary splendor, prominently displaying either its teeth or its tusks if not both. In addition, each one is without any kind of softening vegetal surround.

In one more row of examples (figure 9.28) we see several kāla heads drawn from frames used in the animated story itself. The first is easily recognizable as the head of the featured wild boar Komban. He is shown in the stance he takes when he threatens to destroy the twin heroes' two lives. The second is the head of one of the guardian demons that flew up into the sky after the release of Ponnivala Nadu's great war drum from the bottom of a small lotus pond located on the heroes' own land. The third and fourth heads are located at the summit of the torana that arches over a frightening tunnel that the heroine Tamarai had to walk through during her pilgrimage to meet Shiva in his Kailasa council chambers. That tunnel is located part way between earth and heaven and is filled with fire. Its main purpose seems to be to test a human devotee's perseverance and courage during their trek that leads up into the sky. The third in this sequence of kāla heads looks rather like an upside-down makara, and it possibly even has the elongated snout of a wild boar. Like the kāla head in figure 9.26c, one cannot tell if it is swallowing something or, instead is spitting or vomiting something out.[38] Nonetheless,

Figure 9.27a, b, c, and d. Photograph of a real mugger crocodile head compared with three different kāla heads seen on local temple toranas honouring the Ponnivala heroes. Note that (c) in this array of examples looks suggestively similar to a wild boar, that is, it is a possible reference to Komban, the wild boar character in the Ponnivala Nadu story.

it is this upside-down position holds the most interest. This is because it makes a powerful reference to chaos, confusion, and general disorder. Each of these several Ponnivala kāla heads, furthermore, relies on an image that suggests opposition to all that is natural and nicely ordered. All these examples reference death, both as a state of being and more broadly as a cosmic concept. Note that Komban's head is prominent among these examples.

The kāla heads found in local fold temples that honour the epic story heroes exhibit a wide range of imaginative variation. The image seen in figure 9.27c) is particularly striking because of it seems to so closely resemble the face of a pig with tusks. This helps confirm the argument being made here: that Komban, the wild boar in the Ponnivala Nadu epic account, is not just any asura-like demon but more specifically, a makara-kāla being. In addition, it is not just the idea of death that we see in these kāla heads. They also express two very natural human primal fears: the fear of being bitten, that is, of being pierced by sharp teeth or tusks, and the fear of being swallowed, cosmically speaking, by an infinite abyss that lies behind all existence. Both anxieties are triggered by these multiple illustrations, which clearly activate one's mythic imagination.[39] Indeed, it may be that the idea of being eaten and digested by an attacker is truly at the heart of all these kāla head images. They seem to all suggest the wildness of life in a jungle where large beings largely live to eat one another up. The photograph of a living crocodile of the mugger species in figure 9.27a allows readers to judge for themselves what confronting one of these real beasts might feel like.

And there is one further point well worth noting. Heads are prominently featured in the depiction of death throughout the Ponnivala Nadu story. Tamarai, mother of the heroes, provides a vivid example of this. Her lovely head is cut off by Shiva's assistants, following his orders, and this is just one among several

The Shining Lotus Plant 341

Figure 9.28a, b, c, and d. A variety of kāla heads encountered in the animated version of the Ponnivala Nadu story: (a) Komban's pose as he threatens the two heroes' lives; (b) The face of one of the underwater beings that guarded the great Ponnivala Nadu drum before it was raised and beaten in advance of the great hunt to kill Komban; (c) and (d) Two heads seen on the arch Tamarai had to pass under to enter the fiery tunnel on the path to Kailasa that she had to follow.

forms of torture she must endure on her way to Kailasa. Very near the beginning of the story seven cows meet an accidental death by falling on the sharp points of an iron fence which had been deliberately capped with a line of sharp points. Those poor cows, who were very hungry at the time, tried to jump over that barrier but failed and fell on its multiple spearheads instead. Shiva was very unhappy about this catastrophe. He later remembers this and makes Tamarai suffer dearly as compensation for the loss of those seven cow-lives. The twenty-one years Tamarai spends on the pillar appear to be calculated as three years of prayer and penance for each cow killed. These are magical numbers, popular in Hindu mythology generally, and they do not realistically measure time. However, this calculation does help describe the amount of extreme suffering the heroine is forced to endure. It also highlights seven very special moments of regeneration that the heroine undergoes, one each time that Vishnu generously revives her. The loss of her head, the last and most significant of her seven trials, is illustrated in figure 9.29. The posts seen in the 9.29c are the ready-made posts on which many other heads have been placed previously while enduring a similar bout of suffering. Thought of another way, however, all of this is Shiva's deliberate way of purifying the heroine before he, eventually, sees to her immaculate impregnation. But focusing solely on her head, we can easily see that this body part can, metaphorically, be likened to a seed and that this seed is what Vishnu is magically revivifying a full seven times.

Now compare the fate of the heroine's head, seen above, with the fate of the head of the wild boar in this same story. It too, after being severed, is taken away by Vishnu. Later it seems that Komban's head is set before the goddess of the earth herself, Bhudevi.[40] The story indicates that this goddess, wife to Vishnu, is about to give birth, a birth that will serve to start a new cosmic cycle. But Komban's head is not regenerated and put back on his body in this epic, in contrast to

Figure 9.29a, b, c, and d. Tamarai on her penance post, Tamarai's severed head being placed in a basket that is destined to sit on one of the nearby posts, Shiva's assistants carrying her severed head to this display spot, Vishnu restoring Tamarai to her full-bodied form after bathing her dried bones in nearby river, water said to come from an underground tributary of the Ganges itself.

Figure 9.30a, b, and c. Three images of the wild boar Komban chasing, trapping, and then violently attacking the heroes' fighters, creating chaos. His acts include fighters' being tossed in the air upside down, expressively linking chaos with death and the idea of one's entry into an abyss when life ends.

Tamarai's head which Vishnu reattaches to her body each time he revivifies her. Instead, Komban's head goes towards the goddess's grand cosmic recycling work, something she periodically undertakes. That scene is briefly described by the bard in a concluding song that sketches out his broad concluding vision for the future (see figure 10.35 in the next chapter).

There is, however, a further important concept that underpins all this kāla symbolism. That is the idea of being swallowed up by a great abyss, a darkness which can be imagined only by comparing it with the black depths of the sky at night, or by thinking about tunnels, wells, and caves, all of which find a place in this long epic story. This abyss concept is a liminal space related to nightmares, where the mind conjures up images of sliding down into the belly of a fearful demon and then being digested there. There are also images of being turned upside down and/or of bodies falling through a vast vacuum. Add to this the several scenes of dead warriors whose bodies are thrown into chaotic heaps where human body parts are jumbled and scrambled beyond recognition. A few of those themes have been captured in figure 9.30 with the intent of illustrating how Komban's actions compare with those of a great kāla demon. Komban is first shown killing all the loyal villagers who accompanying the heroes into the forest to support the hunt. His act of human slaughter seriously weakens the Ponnivala Nadu twins' ability to continue their wild boar chase. But soon after the two brothers do succeed in killing Komban himself and then a little later the boar's head is dragged off for recycling. It will be put to good use. His severed cranium will help to end a long era of suffering and injustice: the Kaliyuga. As this folk epic ends, the listener comes to understand that a completely new era (a new entire yuga cycle) is about to begin and the old one, with all its chaos, is now over.

Earlier, in figure 9.10, several images were presented that showed Komban rooting in the mud and turning plants in the heroes' fields upside down. These acts immediately follow his breaking through the farmers' key irrigation dam, causing a great flood. Komban then extends this chaos by uprooting these farmers' finest crops. Komban is a forest creature who lives in a cave, as many wild boars do. If wild boars are dangerous, however, they are also known for their fertility. They reproduce quickly. In fact, wild boars often produce two litters per year, each containing up to ten piglets. And they love rooting around in the forest for mushrooms. Wherever they have dug these up, experienced mushroom hunters will tell you that the very spot they excavated will quickly produce a great wealth of new green sprouts. In ancient Indian rock art, similarly, there are many wild boars depicted. Those Mesolithic designs display sacred associations, making it clear that boars have been linked to divine power on the Indian sub-continent for many millennia.[41] Our discussion has shown that makara and kāla themes are closely connected in folk art as well as in classical temple imagery: we repeatedly see references to rebirth used in combination with images of death, or of divine magic and hunting trophies intertwined. This early rock art affirms that in South Asia, the wild boar has been a beast strongly associated with ritual death and renewal for a very long time. Scenes of hunting these creatures appear to associate their demise with magic, with the idea of travel across the sky, as well as with ideas about the renewal of life. At least one such Mesolithic hunting scene actually depicts a wild boar standing on its nose as if that drawing is actually referencing a boar constellation, that is as a powerful divinity in the sky.[42]

Within the framework of this story, specifically, a fire burning on a pillar serves to prefigure or foretell Tamarai's own destiny. A fire, like a kāla head, easily digests whatever it swallows. In a sacrificial context what is thrown into a fire is said to feed it. Various forms of human food are often used for this purpose. In figures 9.32c and d we see Tamarai's own body serving as a kind of fire offering to a kāla-style being (the ominous dark clouds that surround her). Shiva's violent assistants that attack Tamarai (figures 9.29a, b, and c) can also be understood to be kāla like monsters.[43] Perhaps Tamarai's own flesh will burn, much like the bright Kartikkai flame mentioned earlier, as she sits on that penance pillar for

Figure 9.31a, b, c, and d. (a) The tunnel Tamarai must enter on her way to Kailasa; (b) An image of the post that not only swallows and then holds up a severed head, but also (spits it out) to regenerate life; (c) An image of a well that a bundle of enemy Vettuva hunters are dropped into by their Ponnivala assailant (a forest version of the abyss idea); (d) The entrance/exit to Komban's own cave where he lies, at birth, next to his devoted mother.

Figure 9.32a, b, c, and d. (a) Tamarai entering the root-entwined base of a great sacred tree (Ficus religiosa); (b) Tamarai praying on her pillar of penance adjacent to that tree; (c) and (d) The constant cycle of sun and moon who witness her travail as they pass by her day after day while she silently prays.

twenty-one years.[44] After all, she must constantly endure the harsh heat of day, as well as the cold of night, while all of her seven deaths are a mere precursor to the final outcome, the gift of new life via her pregnancy. Her pillar parallels those seen topped by makara heads used to support a torana. Her position on that high pillar reminds us that she, herself, is like a sun. The story artist has even included additional pillars in the background (figure 9.32) that await their next occupants, other prayerful penitents who might arrive at any moment.

An explicit makara figure is often seen sitting on top of a torana pillar. This makara, a symbol of re-creative power, is always located near the torana's mid-point (at least in local folk shrines I have visited). That placement, of course, associates it with the brahmamūla or with whichever divinity happens to sit under the torana arch in the shrine. In the Ponnivala Nadu story, when Tamarai sits on her penance pillar she is praying to Lord Shiva. It is he who testing her and who will, eventually, invite her into his council chambers. In sum, all the various forms of being seen sitting at that midpoint location, just to one side of the brahmamūla itself, are addressing the power expressed by and contained in that central spot. As we have

The Shining Lotus Plant 345

seen, the sun, vegetal life, and/or the makara-head are all there with a purpose. Each is offering assistance to and expressing reverence for the brahmamūla. Each is there to help produce new growth. But the vital spark, the key energy needed to ignite that new life rests within that sacred node itself.

As can be seen in figure 9.32a, before beginning to climb her penance pillar, Tamarai enters the root-encircled hollow of this sacred tree that is located right beside her pillar of penance. This tree is named in the story and is, quite appropriately, a grand Ficus, called the king tree (arasa maram) in Tamil. Botanically known as a Ficus religiosa this tree is one of the most sacred known on the Indian subcontinent. There, in between its tangled roots, Tamarai finds and quickly puts on the saffron cloths that she needs to wear for her twenty-one years of penance and prayer. Unstitched saffron colored cotton clothing is a culturally recognized dress code used by people who are undertaking extended ascetic pursuits. Significantly, the clothes that Tamarai finds are not just there for the taking but are guarded by a huge cobra. That creature, here as elsewhere in Indian art and sculpture, is commonly portrayed standing in an upright position with its head-hood spread wide open. Such images are common in folk art as well as in more classical settings. The idea, it seems, is that it can judge one's inner state of purity and it will only allow the worthy penitent to pick up the clothes it guards.

Often the bodies of two cobras with open hoods are portrayed intertwined, as if they are intended to form a symbolic pillar using their own bodies for its construction. Metaphorically speaking, this wrapping resembles the behaviour of many real species of fig trees that send their seeds through the air, or via the intestines of birds, to nest and take root in the crevasses of other trees. They have good luck when they find a comfortable nesting spot in the crotch or pocket which forms where a branch starts a new stalk. Once having landed in such a spot, a fig seed will grow there comfortably. That one little fig seed will soon send out tendrils that will gradually encompass and then, in the end, completely choke its host tree. Eventually the conquered tree rots away, leaving the new tree, now a fig), with a hollow core. In sum, a young fig that lands in such a spot can actually "swallow" its host tree and, given enough time, slowly replace the original tree trunk with one of its own. This natural process provides a powerful metaphor for the kāla head which is similarly able to eventually swallow its prey or whatever it strikes or decides to settle on (figure 9.31b).[45] Tamarai is, in a symbolic parallel, swallowed by heat, cold, wind, and other atmospheric assaults that swirl around her for twenty-one years. Note that this kāla-headed pillar is considerably shorter than the others the artist has portrayed. It is as if whatever tall post and resident penitent were once resident at that spot has now been swallowed up by the grotesque head and replaced by it. The cobra that Tamarai encounters has its own hood spread open as she takes the clothes from the hollow base of that great tree (figure 9.32a). Perhaps that image serves as a harbinger, or even a direct representation, of the idea that she will herself be swallowed by time (the precise meaning of the word kāla) as she waits patiently on her own penance post, hoping to receive an eventual audience with the great Shiva himself.

This sequence of interesting images can be taken still further by comparing them with the remarkable capturing and swallowing ability of several species of fig, as well as with the behaviour of serpents themselves, who swallow their food whole. When a snake swallows a frog, for example, that unfortunate victim can be seen as a visible lump that quickly appears just beyond the snake's head. That lump gradually moves towards the snake's tail, growing smaller and smaller as it progresses and then gradually disappearing when the frog has been fully digested. These similarities between snakes, fig trees, and fire are not lost on the Indian imagination. The short post that supports the parasol (alternately a dark kāla rain cloud that has a scowl and an open mouth on its underside) in Bosch's diagram (figure 9.1) could also be imagined to be the head of a cobra. Bosch's examples support both ideas. Several of his selected photographs depict the presence of a round, umbrella-like form above the central divine figure.[46] That umbrella can be interpreted as being the formalized representation of the open hood of a cobra or, alternatively, as a rain cloud. In other Bosch images it is seen to be just an upward extension of the great fig tree itself usually with a deity like the Buddha or else a Hindu god sitting underneath.

Bosch provides illustrations of several similar serpent designs that have been carved on the temple posts of Barabudur. Often these are composed of two snakes, usually with hoods, that twist around each other, creating a singular hollow interior similar to what the fig creates when it swallows its host. Every cobra met in the long Ponnivala Nadu epic, however, behaves with goodwill, usually offering a protagonist both help and protection.[47] Any more sinister meaning is always covert. However, it seems likely that most cobras encompass a double meaning, just like the kāla motif itself. Seen one way, the kāla head is associated with fertility, rain, abundance, and birth. But seen in another way, it has vicious and sharp-pointed teeth (or tusks) that can be deadly. Much like the makara, which when seen in profile appears to have a benign and procreative intent, but seen in portrait, that is, face-on, its visage conveys a much more ominous message.

The Lateral Branches

So far, we have discussed pillars that support the two sides of a torana. But in Bosch's main diagram there is just one pillar located in the centre of his design. In the diagram this post looks like an extension of the lotus plant's main stem, but its main purpose seems to be to support the heavy weight of two big lateral branches that spread, one to each side, and then downward, almost reaching close enough to touch the brahmamūla itself. The shape of those extensions, element 8 in Bosch's diagram, is rather squat, forming a rectangle that is wider than it is high. This same structure also supports the parasol which we have earlier identified as a kāla motif. This upper portion of Bosch's sketch, furthermore, does not look like a lotus plant anymore. Instead of being tall and slender like a lotus, this part of the diagram is broad and looks less delicate than what stands under it. And it almost appears to flow downward, pulled in that direction by its heavy lateral branches. If we take our guidance from the Ponnivala Nadu story, this tree is the sacred fig tree, specifically the Ficus religiosa seen in figure 9.33b. How do we know this? The singers of this magnificent epic specify that exact species by name when they mention it. Furthermore, this impressive and ancient-looking tree is located at a very sacred spot, the point where the heroine will perform her twenty-one-year long penance. It is also a tree with a hollow space inside its roots that contains the guardian cobra described earlier, as well as the saffron robes Tamarai will put on. Named the arasa maram or "king tree" in Tamil, this is the national tree of India. Its mission is to hold up the sky itself, assuring that airy dome's ongoing separation from the earth below. This same tree also acts like a great umbrella that shields (and cools) all that lies under it. Medieval Tamil kings always carried a ceremonial umbrella with them when they travelled. That umbrella was not meant for the monarch so much as it was meant to symbolize that the king carrying it would provide cool shade for all whom he ruled, those who served and also honoured him. The main branches in Bosch's diagram are depicted in just this way. They originate from a place that is high up, but they then curl down around the brahmamūla, also the location of a king's throne. Kings were also considered to be deities, and a king's central position was taken for granted in such a diagram.

Tamarai's association with this grand tree matches well with her role as Ponnivala Nadu's queen and provides an important symbolic theme which runs through the story at large, a theme she personally embodies. After her penance she will become the mother of heroes, the twin-kings-to-be who are the focus of the story at a later point. Great mothers are like great trees. They spread their arms to wrap around and protect the young, the innocent, and the vulnerable. Tamarai exhibits a similar loving attitude, but she is also tough, and resilient. She cannot be defeated, even by Shiva's own confederates. Those vicious henchmen kill her briefly seven times, but after each of these deaths Tamarai springs back to life and then settles once again on her pillar of penance to continue her prayers. A strong tree, even if a few of its branches have been lopped off, can often regenerate itself in just such a way. And like a great tree, Tamarai, too, is destined to touch the sky. She stands out above the story's lesser characters because of her amazing degree of perseverance in the face of threats. This same pluck is also reflected in her determination to bear a child so that her family line can continue to prosper and to rule Ponnivala Nadu.

Looking at this great Ficus religiosa tree from a different perspective, it must also be noted that on Bosch's diagram it seems perched on top of a lotus flower

Figure 9.33a and b. Two forms of protection: (a) The king of the cobras holds his great hood over Tangal during her forest journey; (b) The great king tree spreads its grand branches over the world at large.

that is supported by just a single, solitary stem. Everything else grows on its own from deep under water, generated by the padmamula itself. Why does the top part of Bosch's model morph in this way, into something so surprising? There doesn't seem to be a good explanation except to suggest that this idea must represent some early merger of several different concepts, including the possible myths that that were associated with them. Bosch recognizes this unnatural plant union without discussing its oddness. However, he does note that the Buddhists call this the tree of Dharma,[48] meaning something like duty, rights, laws, and ethical behaviour all rolled into one. We must simply accept that this grafting of one plant onto another is what Bosch intended to portray in designing his model. However, it can and should be noted that this union is totally in keeping with the biological nature of this specific fig species. This particular tree species always nestles, as a seed, in the crotch of another plant and then gradually takes it over. Bosch's model may express this idea, that the grand tree of heaven somehow absorbs and takes over the primal lotus, perhaps at the very early moment when the creation myth states that earth and sky first became separated. Indeed, this tree has functioned as mainstay of Hindu religious art for centuries and Bosch argues it may well date back to a theme he believes is referenced on a Mohenjo-daro seal from the Indus Valley civilization that more or less ended around 1900 BCE.[49] It is totally appropriate, furthermore, that this tree represent kings, and that Tamarai climbs a pillar that sits right next to it. In the next chapter we will see a photograph of a local Ponnivala Nadu temple gateway (figure 10.10) that clearly suggests this same concept, showing the great tree with a lotus painted just beneath it, is present in folk art to this day. One can also find this tree, which can live for hundreds of years, growing right next to a temple tank or pool. Such ritually important locations likely replicate this same idea, that the great Ficus religiosa is partnered with the lotus such that its watery home and the great tree of life co-exist in harmony, side by side.[50]

The Shining Lotus Plant 349

Figure 9.34a, b, c, and d. Shiva is very often depicted as having a cobra wrapped around his neck: (a) When in his council chambers giving an order; (b) When angry and on fire,'; (c) When meditating in the forest; and even (d) When just dreaming of the forest while still seated in the snowy Himalayas.

Figure 9.35a, b, and c. Vishnu's association with an open cobra hood or equivalent, the shade of a grand fig tree: (a) He floats among the clouds on a sea of milk; (b) He displays his visvarupa grandeur before a devotee, blending his form with a background of cobra bodies; (c) His resting place in a garden found inside a green, cool forest where a great Ficus religiosa tree provides him with ample equivalent shade.

Switching to the related theme of trees and the cobras that lie under them, it is also worth noting that both major gods in the Ponnivala Nadu animation series are depicted as having a strong association with cobra heads as well as trees. In figure 9.34 Shiva is always seen, at least in the illustrations developed for this story, as having a cobra wrapped around his neck. It does not matter whether he is seated in his council chambers, is burning with fiery anger, is in the forest mediating, or is dreaming of a deep lush forest while seated high in the Himalayas on an icy rock shelf. Most images featuring Shiva seated show that he also rests on his beloved tiger skin, providing yet one more marker of his general association with makara fierceness. Vishnu also has strong associations with a cobra, especially with one that has its hood open (figure 9.35). Vishnu appears repeatedly in the story while seated on a cobra floating on a great sea of milk, looking down and monitoring what is happening below. This same cobra hood is also seen straight on in a visvarupa moment Vishnu sometimes offers his devotees (a brief but powerful visual revelation of his cosmic grandeur, granted only on special occasions to special people). Though difficult to see in this tiny reproduction, note that in figure 9.34b he is not just shaded by a cobra hood but that the bodies of several snakes are wrapped around each other and that they blend in with his body as they hover behind him.

For Vishnu, a backdrop of water, trees, and greenery is common. In figure 9.35c, for example, his bed is barely seen (indicated by the arrow) because it is somewhat concealed behind a large, wide-spreading tree. That tree, a Ficus religiosa, has strong associations with water and with the great water-god Varuna. It also has powerful links to fire, to the mythology of the Aśvin twins and to the act of impregnation.[51] These associations all match nicely with the position of the Brahmamūla (#5) in Bosch's diagram, including its two branches (#6) which have already been linked to the Aśvins in the discussion above. Shiva, by contrast, never sleeps. Instead, he engages in powerful, focused meditations, that most often take place deep in a forest. Even there, however a watchful cobra guardian is always wrapped tightly around his neck. In sum, trees, cobras, and the great gods all bear some association not only with pregnancy and renewal but also with the kāla head that haunts the pinnacle of the heavens. This is where lives get swallowed up and where a great abyss (the vast night sky) looms behind all. Some lives find peace, escape, and eternal bliss leaving earth to float in a space that has no time and no clear shape. But most await a slide back down to the base of the lotus[52] where a new life, or an almost-new flame, can then be reborn in the next cycle, one yet to come.

One more association seems so striking that I feel it is worth a mention, even though it is speculative. There is one seal available from the Indus valley excavations, M296 (see figure 9.23, page 335), that bears a haunting resemblance to the idea of the Aśvin twins pulling the sun, the brahmamūla in Bosch's lotus diagram (figure 9.1). Compare Bosch's diagram with the ancient Indus image and suddenly it appears that horse-like heads, rather than vegetal branches, reach outward on the two sides of the central lotus stem in a balanced fashion. These two are likely twins, and the iconography can certainly be understood to reference horse heads and vigorous movement. Their unicornlike horns are an Indus valley style-marker. Now we see them in association with a peepul or Fiscus religiosa tree which will be further discussed below but that also has divine, sky-dwelling association. It is also worth comparing both the above images with the photograph of a contemporary Durga icon located in a Toronto temple (see figure 9.6, page 316). Though very distant in time, and also in location, the same motif of two horse-like beings prancing outward from a sacred core that is female is present there too. This time the horses have a much more modern look and they are placed a bit below the goddess's womb area, but the idea is still suggestive of a very ancient iconic theme. The brahmamūla is embodying the source of life, both as a sun and as a womb. And since the Aśvin twins learned the secret of life-giving soma from the head of a horse these associations only multiply. The suggestion is speculative, of course, but worth pursuing further.

There is yet another interesting insight to be gained from working with Bosch's core diagram. Basically, that sketch depicts a living plant-like entity. But with a little imagination we can say that its shape also reflects or somewhat resembles that of a human being. In Bosch's diagram that body has two feet that spread out (element 2), a heart, navel, womb or central core (element 5), two arms (element 6) and a head (a part included in element 7). One can even suggest that element 8 is the equivalent of a set of huge ears and or else a huge mop of hair that surrounds a rather abstract face. This comparison is suggested for two reasons. First, it is very common in Indian Hindu thought to imagine that the cosmos at large has the basic shape of a human body. And second, this additional metaphor gives Bosch's diagram three axes and thus a full, three-way dimensionality.

These qualities seen in Bosch's basic lotus form are important because they reinforce the idea that the Ponnivala Nadu story is concerned with its female characters' desire, in particular, to move upward. Tamarai spends years reaching towards the sky while trying to contact Shiva in his council chambers high above. But before finding her penance pillar, she had to pass through a dark tunnel. Her daughter, Tangal, passes through an equivalent darkness, a deep forest, and then also ascends a pillar, if only briefly. Later she flies across high mountains riding a magical goose. It is notable, however, that before this Tangal had spent most of her earlier life sitting on a palace swing in an open courtyard, symbolically suspended directly from the sky above. At the end of the story furthermore, she is the only story protagonist never to experience death. Instead, she is magically transported back up to Shiva's abode in the sky. She ascends to that spot in a lovely flying chariot sent down to earth to fetch her by the god himself.

The story's twin males, by contrast, first experience a dark tunnel right after birth, a passage that leads to a cave directly beneath the temple that belongs to the local goddess Cellatta. In contrast to Tamarai's tunnel, which is a passage leading upward into the sky, the tunnel these twin boys pass through is horizontal and carved through the earth itself. After they return to their home on earth, the heroes begin to move about their family lands on horseback. Later still they start to fight battles while riding their magnificent steeds. Hence their travels are mostly horizontal with very little vertical movement. Also significant in this the story is that very near the beginning of this long epic seven very hungry cows who fail to jump over a dangerously spiked fence and die impaled there instead. Soon afterwards, their female spirits ascend upward to complain about this injustice to Lord Shiva himself. Although Tamarai's own suffering eventually compensates for the loss of those poor cows, their sad fate continues to loom over the story. And, at the end, the two heroes die on sharp metal points themselves, impaling their bodies on their own swords. Their mythical adversary, the wild boar Komban, also dies by the spear. Indeed, all the key male deaths in the story occur while the heroes are moving across the world without ever lifting themselves more than a few feet off the ground. This dimensionality is reflected in Bosch's diagram, where both horizontal and vertical growth are depicted. It is also expressed in two contrasted trees, the Ficus religiosa that rises to the heaves adjacent to where Tamarai performs her penance (figure 9.33b), and the Ficus benghalensis, buried deep in the forest (figure 9.13a). The latter tree has many associations with a progression in the opposite direction, downwards from the sky to the earth below. This reversal in directional movement finds expression both in its hanging aerial roots and in the fact that two parrots fly down from heaven to nest there, part way through Tamarai's climb upward. She stretches towards the gods' council chamber, in unison with the Ficus religiosa that stands near her. These two tree species apparently complement one another, the one being a very grand tree that reaches upward and is surrounded by an open and airy space, while the Ficus benghalensis appears to be a tree that conveys gifts from the gods downwards towards earth, specifically seeking an environment where a womb-like (enclosed, well-forested) space can be found.

In sum, the interpretation of Bosch's basic diagram, as presented above, points to two circular cycles, both embedded in Bosch's lotus paradigm. One movement is predominantly female and involves an upward progression similar to what is frequently referenced in the discipline of yoga. The other is male and is focused on side-to-side movement, an oscillation not unlike the route traced by the rising and setting sun, half of which is above and the other half below the ground. Joined together these two types of movement make up a whole that is dynamic and processual. Seen this way, Bosch's cosmic lotus model is not a static diagram at all, but rather an enlivened human body that has both vertical movement from the base to its summit via a spine and side-to-side movement that one could liken to its working arms or simply to its regular breathing. This second dynamic is basically horizontal, a back and forth, like the alternation of night and day. But what about the first type of movement? It more closely resembles the yearly oscillation between the winter solstice moment when the sun zenith lies its southern-most point, and the summer solstice when it rises to its most northerly summit of the year. Many who study traditional Hindu calendrical cycles and its well-known nakshatras or star-based constellation patterns, speak of the sun as being occasionally swallowed by the tail of a huge beast, either a dragon, snake, or crocodile. That is also the story of the makara, the sign linked to the zodiac constellation known as Capricorn and strongly associated with the winter solstice.

Our entire interpretation of Bosch's diagram now comes full circle. The kāla head, which references the portrait view of a makara, may originate from an early fear of a crocodile's head and its prominent teeth. In Indian mythology that head swallows the sun at the winter solstice, a story that includes the fact that the sun soon manages to exit that abyss and be reborn.[53] This swallowing and then disgorging process correlates with the sun's ability to reverse its gradual southward movement and begin to progress northward once again each year. And when it rises at the winter solstice it is understood to be a young sun once more, a newborn. When

Figure 9.36a, b, c, and d. (a) Tamarai kneeling on needles atop her pillar of penance; (b) Her daughter Tangal's ride back to Kailasa seated in Shiva's golden chariot. These two examples depict females rising into the sky while alive, in contrast with two further scenes that involve important males in the story: (c) Tangal's younger brother falling on his own sword; (d) The demise of the great wild boar Komban who also dies while on earth from a similar impalement.

the sun starts to move northward again, following the solstice, it is also moving upwards in terms of Hindu geography, because it is moving towards the Himalayas. A northerly movement gradually draws the sun's zenith closer to Shiva's council chambers. That new cycle, that dramatic rebirth, begins when the kāla head swallows the sun and then spits it out, making it young and re-energized once more.

The most striking insight of all is one that came to me only recently as a result of studying Bosch's diagram further. I had been wondering, "what more can one say about the padmamūla" when I suddenly realized that Tamarai herself was the lotus bud equivalent in the Ponnivala Nadu story, while her daughter was a form of the sun. Remember that Tangal's two brothers, Ponnar and Shankar, were earlier compared with the two Aśvin horses that pull the sun's chariot. Tangal spends all her time on a palace swing, inside her family palace compound. The swing is in an open central courtyard and thus she is able to see the sky above. Her swing moves gently back and forth, just as the sun repeats its course across the sky each day and returns to its starting point through a tunnel each night. Tangal is the shining orb, the living, giving force within the heroes' palace. She is like the sun itself and her brothers' mission is to guard her safely through her time on earth, just as their horses, metaphorically, labour to pull the sun's chariot (her swing) back and forth across the sky.

Tangal is one of the seven maidens of heaven, one of the Kannimar who serve Shiva. She was sent to earth by this great god to accompany and guide her two brothers. In a local temple near the town of Vellakovil, near where the Ponnivala Nadu story was first tape recorded and transcribed, there is a temple dedicated to a lone ascetic male. He is a brave warrior and a form of Murugan who is unmarried and known to lead an ascetic lifestyle. He is a loner, not part of a twinned male set. Nonetheless, he stands for the same core ideas expressed by the Ponnivala Nadu heroes themselves. Just at the back of this god's temple, which

Figure 9.37a and b. Outer south wall of the Vīrakumaraswamy temple's central shrine, Vellakovil, Tamil Nadu 2021. Photograph courtesy of Hari Harapriyan of Coimbatore. (a) The dark open slot is where the sun enters its tunnel and turns around at the winter solstice. (b) The sun's face as it exits that tunnel after morphing into a newly born being. Note the all-swallowing kāla head carved in stone just above it.

stands just next to the shrine for the seven Kannimar sisters, there is an interesting architectural detail, an image of the sun (figure 9.37b). The kāla head that hovers over it is easily seen, while, less clearly visible are two makara shapes, one situated on each side at neck level. What is the sun doing carved above a hollow doorway on the back of this shrine to Vīrakumaraswamy? This god's basic purpose is to guard and protect the entire region around his temple. But could he also, implicitly be understood to be the son of the sun itself, the deity whose image has been carved on the rear wall of his temple? Vīrakumaraswamy is a form of Murugan, son of Shiva, which would make the sun seen here a multiform of Shiva himself. Given its location above the hollow doorway, this carving might represent the night sun entering its underground tunnel. There are also many terracotta horses to be seen in this temple courtyard, all donated to Vīrakumaraswamy so that he can ride around at night and at will. He might just decide to use one or more of those horses to help pull the Sun through that dark tunnel. But the real surprise comes when we look a bit further south, just another few yards behind this key Vīrakumaraswamy shrine. There we find a very ancient and huge cobra mound, which according to this temple's origin story was the reason for its being built at this exact location. The god rose out of that mud home, long back, in snake form. He was recognized by the farmer who owned the land there to be a miraculous apparition of Lord Murugan himself.[54]

The farmer wanted to honour this spot and thus built a temple at the site that is known as the Vīrakumaraswamy temple today. However, a much humbler shrine, also intended to honour this origin story, was built over that mound then (figure 9.38). This little shrine is called the Puttu Kannu. That term has several meanings, puttu being a snake mound and kannu referring to a hole, to a young calf, or even a young baby human. The shrine features a bright earthen image of the sun (figure 9.38a) made of dried mud. It is painted a bright yellow. Next to it and just slightly lower stand two terracotta cows, one on each side of this little shrine to the (newborn) sun. And under each cow is a snake mound, also made of clay. Each cow is seen releasing her milk over that snake mound, just as Kunnutaiya was fed by a similarly generous cow as he lay alone hidden by Lord Shiva under a rock in Kolatta's back field. Note that in figure 9.38d and e, we see the sun framed by a huge open cobra hood in the position where the kāla head is normally seen, plus lower down, the standard makara head is seen birthing something new. This modest shrine is located at the very southernmost edge of the larger temple compound, exactly where the sun itself would rise at the winter solstice point. It is as if this sacred cobra mound functions as a makara from whose mouth a fresh baby sun emerges each year, after the resident cobra in that mound has briefly swallowed it. It is not surprising that this temple celebrates one of its biggest festivals of the year at the winter solstice. To the north stands the brave hero, Vīrakumaraswamy, surrounded by his horses. And to the east stands a shrine to the seven Pleiades or Kannimar. If needed, these young maidens can help the new-born sun, assisting and nurturing it until it grows strong and independent once more. They are Vīrakumaraswamy's own shining sisters, his astro-siblings.

This chapter has tried to show how this seemingly simple, sometimes almost fairy-tale-like, Ponnivala Nadu epic story exhibits strong links to many of Hinduism's greatest ideas. In the previous chapter we focused on this huge legend's key characters and linked them to a whole bundle of ancient Babylonian constellations and their related mythology. That exploration introduced us to an astral category of hidden paradigms. But when it comes to core symbolic themes like golden seeds, sacred trees, and lotus plants, Bosch's truly Hindu-Buddhist vision of the world, is even more helpful. So while the previous chapter focused on characters and events, this chapter has focused on metaphors buried within the story that visually express a set of core beliefs that relate to a world likened to a lotus plant. These beliefs are deeply held but rarely verbalized. These hidden paradigms build on vegetal, astral, and cosmic imagery. This chapter has uncovered an entire range of metaphors well known in South Asia, core symbolic themes that are widely shared by millions of Hindus living both on the Indian subcontinent and well beyond. The analysis just presented has helped to show how fully integrated into the wider culture of India the thinking behind this regional folk epic actually is. Yet at the same time its uniqueness has helped us to develop a fresh perspective regarding some familiar religious paradigms, expressing them vividly through the

Figure 9.38a, b, c, d, and e. (a) The Vīrakumaraswamy Puttu Kannu shrine honouring the new-born sun; (b) The horses ready to assist in pulling it through its night-time tunnel; (c) One of the cows feeding the snake mound in which that new sun/son is re-born; (d) and (e) The kāla and makara heads shown on the torana that frames the new baby sun. All five photographs, 2021, courtesy of Hari Harapriyan of Coimbatore.

use of a variety of non-verbalized but popular folk constructions. The final chapter will take this exploration one step further, attempting to study some of the key songs and poetic epithets found in this same unique South Asian legend. We will see how those images, mostly buried in songs that are also poems, point to a different set of underlying core paradigms. We will now move in a different direction, referencing climate patterns and the concerns of farmers, especially highlighting the importance of the area's seasonal rains. This next and final chapter also explores some striking architectural parallels that embody a quite different type of non-verbalized paradigm thinking than do the ideas just surveyed above.

10 The Monsoon Rains: Filling a Lotus Pond and Nourishing a Golden River

In previous chapters we have discussed many different aspects of the Legend of Ponnivala Nadu, otherwise known as the Land of the Golden River. The focus has been on the many diverse scenes and characters that are expertly woven into the fabric of this grand epic story. Now we turn to the actual words of the text, in order to examine the special significance of this story's songs and their own unique hidden paradigms. It is the bard's poetic and melodic interludes that best capture the true emotional texture of this tale. The singer used these melodic breaks to highlight several of the core values which underlie the story from his perspective. He did so in a rhythmic, memorable, and highly expressive manner. The songs lead us to yet one more fundamental concept, an underlying worldview that beautifully frames the entire epic narrative. It has taken fifty years for me to realize how important the words of the bard's songs are. They are like the water in which fish swim. They articulate a perspective that is so central that it is taken for granted, known but not articulated by listeners. In my case, it took the reading of the works of a very perceptive South Asian religious scholar and art historian from Nepal, Professor Gautama Vajracharya, to alert me to the centrality of the several key ideas that will now be discussed. The first is the importance of the monsoon rains. At least twenty-eight songs in the Ponnivala Nadu epic feature rain in one way or another.[1] Here is one typical example:

Ponnayyā's rule of justice, sweet rule,
The king ruled with authority, he ruled there,
Ponnayyā[2] ruled with a golden (signet ring on his) finger, a sweet rule,
The brothers ruled alone, they ruled there,
Ponnayyā, the farmer, ruled with a golden ring, ruled there,
They ruled as masters of the country, they ruled there,
As farmers of the country, with golden rings, farmers there,
Lords of the earth, sweet Lords of that country,
Ponnayyā's good age,

It rained, it rained there,
Kaṭuku sampa paddy grew on the land, paddy grew there,
Poṉṉayyā's land was covered with rain,
Miḻaku sampa paddy grew on the land, paddy grew there,
In Poṉṉayyā's country **it rained three times a month, it rained there,**
In that land there was a shower of hailstones once a year, it poured there,
Oh, Lord, elephants were used to thresh the paddy,
To thresh the paddy,
Oh, lovely Country, lovely Land Where the Kāveri Flows,
Oh, flourishing country there!
See the faggot bundles in the **Land Where the Kāveri Flows,**
See the black-tipped paddy.
Gold grows like fine paddy; pearls grow like the first paddy crop.
Where elephants are used to thresh grain,
The beautiful **Land Where the Kāveri Flows.**

References to ripe paddy and to elephants are additional obvious takeaways. In fact, had the references to rain not been highlighted in bold here, you might not have noticed this core theme, since it is just one of many images provided that reference wealth and prosperity. But these other themes can be taken as largely subsidiary or emergent, because they all result from the farmer's location in a moist, fertile landscape nourished by abundant rain. In this Kongu area of South India, even now, there is relatively little paddy grown due to a lack of sufficient water. This, plus the idea of elephants being needed to do the threshing constitute largely wishful thinking. Indeed I have never seen a farmer use an elephant to conduct any farming chores in this area. Using oxen is a different matter. I have seen plenty of oxen used for tasks where copious muscular energy is needed. But oxen are secondary to rain. Everyone prays for rain and feels grateful when it finally arrives. The underlying idea is very evident: rain is an atmospheric response, a gift from the clouds on high. The presence of a strong and virtuous ruler, however, is the ultimate cause of that desired prosperity. It is his presence that causes the clouds to release their watery gift. Of course, this broad concept is somewhat circular. The moral tenor and empathic rule of a fine monarch is believed to cause the rain to fall, and rain in its turn causes prosperity and a happy, contented human community. It also makes for a contented king. Happiness in the region as a whole, then, stems from having a fine, virtuous ruler. Thus, the many rain references in songs of the Ponnivala Nadu story are used to poetically highlight the stature of Poṉṉayyā himself, as well as to describe the state of prosperity that emanates from his body due to his sheer presence in this locale. This monarch is likened to the sun itself, a point that is also made in other similar songs. Poṉṉayyā radiates warmth and comfort. People seek darshan when they enter his presence.[3] Listening to the bard sing the words of the song text seen above transmits similar benefits to all the listeners who hear its words spoken in lovely melodic phrases, accompanied by a happy rhythm played on a hand drum.

Some of these rain songs speak of love, of sweetness, and of general spiritual goodness.[4] That general sense of joy is closely related to rain and to rain clouds. One need only think of the dark clouds so often shown in depictions of Krishna and the love dances he enjoys with his many gopis.[5] There is also an auspicious personal Tamil name for a male, Karmēkam, which literally means "black cloud," a positive name in a Tamil cultural environment, though the same term would certainly carry negative tones if applied to someone using the equivalent in an English-speaking context. This whole ensemble of poetic images refers to the beneficent and much anticipated monsoon rains. Vajracharya discusses the importance of the monsoon rains on the Indian subcontinent and suggests that this climate-linked reality is key to understanding ancient Indian farmer thinking, and that it inspired prayers, causing people to pray for rain while fearing drought. Vajracharya writes that clouds were described using metaphors of fertility and that, as they swelled, they were thought to foster new life. He argues that it is this central idea that helps him to distinguish what he argues was originally a South Asian bundle of religious attitudes from what people belonging to the early Vedic culture of the nomads of the Asian steppes knew well. The nomads were understandably focused on fire and on the sun's radiant heat, two positive attributes emanating from the natural world that were vital to melting the winter snows. That heat was required to convert the huge fields of ice that covered the mountain valleys into water that would flood local rivers and, in turn, herald the arrival of spring. Both cultures, one situated on the plains of the Indian peninsula and the other on the steppes, appreciated the importance of rivers, but the symbols these two cultures used to highlight that goodness were different. The so-called Aryan culture that spawned the early Rigvedic texts was highly mobile. It was a society dependent on horses for transport and on grazing animals for food. This tradition emphasized fire sacrifice and many animals' lives were offered to the gods in thanks, through the smoke of sacred fires. These gifts were carried upwards, it was believed, by the fire's rising trails of smoke. The people of the plains, by contrast, used fire and appreciated sunlight too, but what mattered to them most was abundant water. Hence symbols of water were highly valued and this spawned worship traditions based on green plants, seeds, and pots that could hold precious water for later use. These were the ancient symbols central to religious traditions located on the plains of the subcontinent and considered central to the varied local traditions of worship found there.

Vajracharya further suggests that, as the nomadic Indo-Aryan speakers descended from the steppes onto the plains of South Asia, they absorbed many indigenous ideas. He believes that he has uncovered many examples of this blending together of two initially rather different worldviews, while studying many of the early Vedic texts. Of course, fire and water are natural opposites that work together in a complementary fashion, just as heating and cooling are paired in other contexts. But Vajracharya suggests that it matters which side of that opposition was given primacy; heating themes and bright light were highlighted by the steppe nomads, while deep shade and cooling opportunities were all-important for those living on the hot plains. This same author extends his argument to discuss a third key difference, that between the more aggressive, horse riding and raiding culture of the steppes, and the more ascetic, withdrawn, yogic practices related to aestivation (a term referring to torpor or dormancy during a hot or dry period that he uses frequently)[6] This set of traditional behaviors was better understood and more admired on the plains. Vajracharya suggests that ancient South Asian agrarian traditions thought of the sky as a kind of ocean that replenished its waters by soaking up moisture from the earth via the heat of the sun. The sky was, furthermore, likened to a great womb. At the start of the dry period (around November in most parts of India), that womb became pregnant due to the fertile energy of a great sky bull who absorbed and concentrated the rising moisture in order to re-inseminate the great ocean known as the sky. New, fresh life invariably unfolded due to the bull's energy, and that, in turn, would kick-start a new cycle of cloud growth that would result in the heavy monsoon rains eventually returning all that goodness to earth.

The sky's new pregnancy, Vajracharya writes, could be seen in its clouds. Although the fresh life engendered in the sky was invisible at first, it grew more and more visible as the months passed and the monsoon season approached. All kinds of life could now be detected in the ever-changing cloud patterns which gradually grew darker in colour as well as larger in size. Some saw aquatic animals like fish and crocodiles, others saw birds, and more important, still others thought they saw four-footed beasts like bulls and lions, and even human fetuses, way up there on high. The babies seen in the clouds were generally light coloured and rotund, like little cherubs.[7] These multiple forms of life were understood to descend to earth with the rains and to enter the flooding rivers as they filled with fresh water. These beings were understood, Vajracharya argues, to descend from the heavens to take up earth-based lives. As they appeared on earth, they were considered striking testimony to the life-giving properties of rain. Of course, it is important to understand that this thinking was largely metaphorical in nature. It is not that these early South Asian farmers were caught in the grip of some version of fantastical, mythic illusions. They knew that cows did not literally rain down from the sky. But these people were poetic. They spoke, using metaphors, about the wonders of life on earth, admiring how nature always seemed to spring up with fresh energy as a result of the rains. These cloud-centred images gave their lives added beauty, especially when poets sang about their love of rain. The songs of the Ponnivala Nadu epic story must be understood in the same vein. References to needing elephants to harvest fancifully abundant crops is but one of many examples of such thinking. The extensive references to paddy in the song quoted here would be another. Actually very little paddy was grown in the Kongu area before the advent of tube wells. There was just not enough water available to nurture this very desirable but also very thirsty crop. Poetic metaphors enrich life by embellishing our thoughts using imaginative references and images. Poetic metaphors and epithets are not meant to be scientific formulae.

Vajracharya also writes about sky pillars and references a number of early Vedic myths where a pillar is used to prop up the sky and separate it from the earth below, leaving the sun to traverse a mid-space between those two domains. Before this separation occurred, chaos reigned. Everything was mixed up together. That initial pushing apart of sky and earth was what brought about orderly life as we know it today. But that important pillar, an axis mundi, had a second and equally important purpose. It functioned as a channel of communication. People and gods, when needed, could travel up and down using this mythic pillar, as it was essentially something like a big pipe that rose vertically from the inner earth and into the sky above.[8] Most important, from Vajracharya's perspective, that grand pillar provided an orderly way for water to come down to earth during the monsoon season and to rise back up during the dry period. He writes extensively about the symbolism of water pillars supporting upside down pots at their top end and, sometimes, upturned pots at their base as well. He then sees this idea turned horizontal in the design of the many fantastical water fountains that are a unique heritage feature of Nepal, his home country. The water that flows into towns and village centres in Nepal's central valley via these amazing fountains provides a locus for cultural celebration. What is of special interest is that most of these fountains feature mythical animals, especially cows and calves, that visually flow forth from the mouths of those fountains.[9] Seen from my perspective as a South Asian anthropologist, one especially familiar with the non-Brahmin rural communities of the Kongu region of Tamil Nadu, Vajrachraya's ideas resonate well. They have caused me to notice features of local life in Kongu Nadu that I had never paid much attention to before. What follows illustrates some of these correspondences and links them to parallel images that are deeply embedded in the Ponnivala Nadu story, starting with the idea of a pillar connecting heaven and earth, and then proceeding to pots and seeds, and finally to a discussion of vegetal vines and lotus ponds.

The Pillar

Vajracharya speaks repeatedly of water imagery related to posts, particularly as they can be seen in architectural settings. Posts are also quite prominent in the Ponnivala Nadu story, though seen there in natural environments rather than in a village or temple setting. Three of these pillars are of special significance because the heroines climb them. The first pillar is the outlier. It is a suicide pillar that

Tamari, later the mother of the twin heroes, has built because she intends to jump off it. She is desperate, due to her barren, childless condition. This pillar's significance lies in what does not happen. After Tamarai climbs this post on her ominous mission and starts to pray, Lord Vishnu hears her cries and tries to rescue her. He is able to talk her down with his promise of help, and then he further manages, quite skillfully, to redirect her thinking. Essentially, Vishnu turns Tamarai's mind around, persuading her to stop focusing on her own suffering, due to her barrenness. As she climbs the pillar her thoughts are all about her lack of fertility, her dryness, and her emotional heat due to her sense of desperation.

Significantly, the seven chores Vishnu assigns are fully focused on helping others. Vishnu counters Tamarai's self-centred, self-degrading anxiety about being barren by setting her seven tasks and promising help after she has completed each and every one of these assignments. He asks her to do things like hire workers to dig wells for thirsty travellers, construct places that provide shelter and food for animals, create shaded resting spots for weary travellers, organize a feast for hungry beggars, and so on. These various work assignments can be equated with cooling and beneficent acts of social charity. All, furthermore, place the needs of the community above her intense anxiety about her own failings. In this case, Tamarai's climb of a suicide pillar helps lead her to an inner mental conversion: she moves from hot to cool, from self-centred to a focus on others' needs, and from death to finding a new inner purpose that will carry her forward. Eventually she is rewarded with three children. They will be triplets granted to her, via an immaculate conception, by Lord Shiva himself. This is the most abstract of the three pillar stories the epic presents, but it clearly serves to illustrate the basic idea. Here climbing a pillar becomes a metaphor for following a path that leads to goodness for all. Her dedication to a new sense of social responsibility provides a way for her to discover a new state of being, essentially a way to undergo rebirth and thereby begin a new and better life.

The second pillar climbed by Tamarai is a central part of her pilgrimage quest to locate Shiva's council chambers and, once there, to beg him in person for a gift of fertility. Here the imagery is less abstract, though still metaphorical at its core. Tamarai climbs this, a much higher pillar, and then sits on top of it praying to Shiva for a full twenty-one years. Meanwhile, unlike Vishnu at the first post, this other great god, Shiva, treats Tamarai quite cruelly. He has Tamarai tortured and essentially killed seven times over, all while she waits patiently for the moment this great divine being will finally invite her to enter his esteemed Himalayan council chambers. What is interesting, in the context of the water pillar concept being discussed here, is that every time Tamarai dies on that high post, it is due to some kind of violence (a form of severe heat) ordered by Shiva himself, although carried out by his subordinate and very loyal henchmen. Every time these assistants attack her, Tamarai's body is reduced to little more than dry bones. But then Vishnu somehow magically appears, and he quickly dips her dry bones in a nearby river.[10] As a result of that brief bath, Tamarai's full body is speedily reconstituted and her life revived. Her seven transformations from a ritual death and back to life, therefore, are always accomplished via river water, albeit with a little help from Vishnu who acts as her personal magician. The rest of the story will be known to those who have read the other chapters of this work: Tamarai is finally immaculately impregnated by Shiva in front of his full council of advisers. This fulfils her lifetime wish. But equally important, the three new lives now implanted in her womb have a counterpart in the magical pot of water Shiva also gives this heroine. Tamarai carries that golden vessel back down to earth with her and then, following Shiva's instructions, she gives out one drop of its "pregnancy inducing liquid" to every woman in her kingdom, both human and animal. Thus, the second pillar climbed in the Ponnivala story essentially yielded the womb full of new life that Tamarai had wished for. When climbed by a sincere penitent, this pillar gave that seeker the gift of several new watery lives, plus the ability to pass this precious gift on to all the other women seeking pregnancy in her kingdom. As the heroine leaves Kailasa, all that watery potential for new life, found both in her womb and in her pot, descend back to earth with her.

The third pillar is a tall post in the forest that is used by a local female ascetic who has been worshipping the sun by climbing it on a daily basis. Her name is Arukandi or Sun Maiden. As Tamarai's daughter, Tangal, wanders the forest searching for her dead brothers' bodies, she comes across this Sun Maiden sitting high above on her pillar. Arukandi is kind enough to share that post and allow Tangal to climb it and sit alone there for a few hours. Tangal does this and as she prays, she receives a special golden wand as a gift from Lord Shiva. That wand is then used several times: first to bring on heavy rain that reduces a potter's work to mud, demolishing all the pots he has recently set out on the ground ready for sale. Then, that same wand stops this destructive rain, and brings on the sun. All the potter's work is restored and as a result he is awed by her power and offers her a tier of seven fresh pots as a free gift. She will later use those pots in her own mission to revive her dead brothers. Tangal is assured that her new pots are absolutely pure because they have just been remanufactured from fresh mud, on the spot. Tangal returns with her new set of seven pots and Arukandi then fills them with seven wonderful substances: some liquids, some grains, and the one pot that she filled with sweet local berries. All are magical gifts that Arukandi retrieved from on high, perhaps given to her by the sun itself. Each gift is a symbol of local plenty, of life, of liquid wealth, and of sweetness. Tangal will soon sprinkle all these substances on her two brothers' corpses. With that sprinkle she will manage to bring them both back to life. Like visiting the water fountains of Nepal, climbing this third pillar yields multiple life-giving items. These liquids and grains, including a stream of milk, are all fruits of the Sun Maiden's added austerities. She obtains these only after her climb up a pillar and into the sky. Those many gifts to Tangal can together be symbolically compared with a gift of cows and calves and, of course, of sacred sky-sourced water. They are all things that symbolize well-being and prosperity. A very similar bundle of goodness is symbolically offered to those who visit Nepalese water fountains where the symbolic presence of cows and calves is directly represented by the figures found on those fountains' highly decorated spouts.

Water Fountains and Waterspouts

Exploring the concept of sacred, wish-fulfilling water pillars should not stop with story-based examples. A local temple complex dedicated to the goddesses Kaliyamman and Mariyamman is located just next door to the village where the Ponnivala Nadu story was first tape recorded. The complex contains shrines to the goddesses that provide significant visual reinforcement for the ideas just discussed.[11] In this case the colours painted on these temples' pillars provide important clues and thus readers are asked to think in colour while reading the paragraphs below. The first example (figure 10.1) depicts one of two matching pillars found at the entrance to the Kaliyamman temple. Each has a very watery look. The entire base of both posts has been painted a water-blue colour accented with lighter blue design work. The swirly wave-like motifs seen on each of these two pillars contrast with a burnt orange background. It would be hard to miss the core concept being presented here, that these pillars are filled with water. As well, it seems likely that given their common orange background, both pillars are to be imagined as seen against an early morning, orange-coloured sky or perhaps a seared, hot landscape.

The Mariyamman temple next door also has a set of two matching pillars framing its entryway. But these two pillars are quite different from those described above. Both pillars of this second set are painted bright pink but are otherwise quite plain, except for their remarkable summits. Both rise from identical, unremarkable, and unpainted stone bases. But this only serves to highlight their matching capitals, which are quite stunning and certainly eye-catching (figure 10.2). At the top of each of these pillars, just under a square slab that is painted a striped but dull yellow, is a large bright red lotus flower that has been accented with decorative little water droplets. Those droplets are shown forming around the edges of each flower and they are painted white. Beneath each lovely flower is a round, squat, blue pot, decorated with white blossoms. And just as Vajracharya has described, this pot appears to be upside down. Beneath the blue vessel is an orange rim leading into what looks like a lotus bud that has been given a purple colour. Still lower on the column is a kind of skirt of petals that are multicoloured and encircle the bright pink pillar holding all this decoration up. Most notable of all is the gold-coloured cube seen at the very top of each pillar (figure 10.2, area 1). It looks like a gold box one might find in a king's treasure room, a box in which he stores all his fine jewels. This orange-yellow

The Monsoon Rains 365

Figure 10.1. A temple entranceway pillar decorated with flowing water motifs.

Figure 10.2. Top portion of a temple entranceway pillar decorated with a lotus motif, plus several other related symbolic designs.

box, it is suggested, references all the wonderful treasures held by the clouds in the sky. Beside that, jutting out to the right (figure 10.2, area 2) is a bright green fountain-like spout, very reminiscent of those Nepalese fountains Vajracharya describes. This fountain-like spout has a green surface that has been further decorated with small white dots. It is possible that those dots represent flowing water. And at the tip of each spout is a large golden drip-bulb embellished with a little white nipple at its tip.[12] Metaphorically, water from this fountain is constantly "dripping" on those who pass through this temple entrance way, blessing them with a sprinkling of heavenly liquid, much like Tangal, seen in the epic story, sprinkles her brothers to bring them back to life. I had never expected to find such a direct correlation with Vajracharya's writings about Nepalese water fountains in a very local temple found in the heart of the Kongu region of South India. To my knowledge no one else has yet described a similar match between a local story and local architecture anywhere else on the subcontinent, at least not in modern times.[13]

This interpretation is strongly re-enforced by the presence of what is called the makara spout, found on north or west exterior wall of the inner shrine of this and all other high-status temples in the Kongu area. This spout is usually carved in stone and functions as a sacred drain or exit pipe for liquid offerings earlier gifted to the god or goddess inside. The design of this spout (figure 10.3) replicates the almost identical look of the pillar-top fountains just discussed. But now there is an added detail. The join between the spout and the temple's exterior wall looks very much like the mouth of makara type of being. It is known by all to be a station where a devotee should pause at the end of his or her circumambulation of that inner shrine. Convention holds that one should walk round that sanctum

Figure 10.3. A typical carved waterspout on a shrine's exterior wall where liquids first poured over the deity inside are then channeled to an exterior courtyard or passageway accessible to devotees. The spout here belongs to a Shiva temple in the Salem area of Kongu Nadu. Photo courtesy of Raj Rajendran.

sanctorum barefoot, moving clockwise through the exterior space that encompasses the core building, the one housing the idol of that temple's principal deity. The last stop on this journey is where the devotee will collect a cupped handful of the liquid exiting from such a spout. A person will then drink and/or sprinkle that ambrosia over their own head. The shared understanding is that this is a way of receiving a liquid form of the deity's personal divine blessings. The most common design for this spout is a makara-pranala, where the faucet is carved to emphasize that this liquid is exiting directly from a maraka's mouth.

Moving inside the same Mariyamman temple and looking at what might be called the goddess's inner front courtyard, the same motif, that of a fountain located on top of a pillar, is now seen to be repeated (figure 10.4). But this time the idea has been given added three-dimensional splendor. Now, at the top of the pillar there are three green fountain spouts visible, each displaying its own golden bulb and accented golden droplet. But this pillar is also somewhat different. Here there is no lotus motif and the pillar under it is not bright pink. Instead, it has just a dull grey surface. This courtyard is adorned with four matching pillars, each holding up one corner of a most interesting ceiling that looms over this entire open space. First, consider this new set of pillars as a single ensemble. Each one is decorated with golden water drops that seem to slide downward from the square red motif located at its

Figure 10.4. A wide view of a pillar, one of four seen at the corners of the inner courtyard of the Mariyamman Temple, Gannapuram.

summit (figure 10.5a and b). The square is painted red and its curls are its vegetal accents, each leaf being painted white. It is eye-catching against the dull grey of the pillar it is attached to. It seems hot and it has two golden drops carved, as a side-by-side set, just beneath that vegetal square. One can image these gold drops as descending liquids that exit from that hot square. They appear to descend from it. Figure 10.6a and b contrast the square seen at the top and at the bottom of each pillar. Note that the bottom square is different. It is bright green, looks cool and has a pair of golden "wings" attached just above it that reach upward. This contrast makes sense. The first square, high up on the pillar, looks vegetal but is red and also a bit watery. The bright red suggests it could be an aquatic plant, perhaps a lotus flower that has golden water drops descending from it. But the bottom square is the colour of leaves and seems to have tendrils or small growing extensions above it that reach upwards. Seen together these motifs suggest the two ends of a lotus stem, one which starts under water in the mud but grows upwards and then has a flower at its summit. Plus, there is the added hint, via the colours chosen, that this lotus stem is cool at its base but very warm at the top where its red flower is in constant sunlight.[14] Furthermore, these pillars not only signify the lotus plant specifically, but also the gold or wealth that falling water carries with it. All four pillars function like heavenly fountains, linking their showers to sky-sourced rivers, to waterfalls, and to rain in general.

368 Hidden Paradigms

Figure 10.5a and b. Two views of the details of a pillar's summit design, as seen in the interior courtyard of the Mariyamman temple, Gannapuram. Note the square vegetal motif at the top and plus the pair of golden drops that run down that pillar on either side.

Figure 10.6a and b. (a) A bright red square attached to the top of the pillar seen in figure 10.4; and (b) a bright green square attached to the bottom of the another pillar belonging to the same set of four. Note the golden coloured drops that seem to flow downward from the red square at the top of the pillar, but which have a different design and appear to reach upward from the green square at the bottom.

Figure 10.7a and b. Two motifs found halfway up each of the four Gannapuram Mariyamman temple's inner courtyard pillars, one an elephant and the other a makara-style being with huge teeth in its mouth that could also be water drops issuing from it, plus an elephant's trunk for a nose, and a lush, vegetal style tail.

There is one more element is worthy of note on the four pillars just discussed above. Midway up each one there are two additional design motifs (figure 10.7a and b) which alternate, depending on which side of the pillar is being viewed. One of these motifs is an image of an elephant, possibly referencing the idea (as Vajracharya has suggested) that elephants will often spray water using their trunks as they play and bathe in lotus ponds. On an adjacent surface, situated at a ninety-degree angle to the first, one can find a makara design that looks very much like the makara figures Bosch has discussed at length. These have vegetal vines issuing upwards from their fanlike tails. Most other temple-related designs that feature makaras look somewhat similar. Both the elephant and makara designs feature four golden water drops, two below the design that flow downwards, and two above that flow upwards. This suits their position at the midpoint of each pillar very well. Water is flowing downward during the monsoon season and upward during the dry periods that both precede and follow those life-giving downpours. In sum, the four pillars that define this temple's inner courtyard, help reinforce the interpretation already proposed: these pillars provide a metaphorical statement that brings to light a hidden background paradigm. All the pillars discussed depict the transfer of water downwards from heaven to earth and then its return upwards, less visibly, at a later date. However, each pillar features falling water more prominently than its counterpart, rising water vapours. There are more downward pointing drips and droplets than upward pointing ones. Falling water is auspicious and joyful. The monsoon season is the most joyous period of the year. Everything turns green. This is what everyone prays for. Above we have seen that this same basic idea is also extensively referenced in Ponnivala Nadu story songs. There we find three pillars that the various heroines climb. All three resemble the Ficus religiosa tree growing near Tamarai's penance post, a prop reaching into the sky, emphasizing upward movement. But all the falling water and the spouts associated with a great lotus pond above, link even more comfortably to the Ficus benghalensis and its auspicious, downward hanging, aerial roots.

The Lotus Pond and The Sacred Tree

We now turn to the ceiling supported by the four posts just described. Here we see a very beautiful, if highly stylized, lotus flower (figure 10.8). It is huge, bright red, and surrounded by a kind of woven mat motif, very similar to what Vajracharya has described and the way he has predicted a lotus motif should be depicted. This huge round flower pattern, which can also be called a lotus-style mandala, is situated high above all viewers, each of whom must walk under it if they want to view the goddess in her inner sanctum. Framing this lotus motif is a square whose four corners are bright green. Each has been given a decorative motif suggestive of lotus leaves. As well, there is a bright red and yellow woven-mat motif, looking as if it might hold up the water stored above but is porous enough to allow a little bit to drip down. Furthermore, the edges of this large area have been framed with resting lions who are likely the guards of this beautiful scene.[15] Under that, on each wall, lovely lotus flowers can be seen floating on the pond's bright blue and slightly wavy surface. But this is not the end of the distinctive parallels one can find with Vajracharya's work. In the same courtyard, just beyond the lotus flower, and also high up on the ceiling, are paintings of three huge and very recognizable animals, each either standing in or lying right next to the waters of that same pond. These are a lion, a bull, and an elephant respectively (figure 10.9a, b, and c). These exact animals are what Vajracharya describes as the important animals that flow from the sky to earth during the rains but that first grow from seeds or divine semen scattered throughout the sky above, a process he calls "atmospheric gestation." In their cloud forms these beasts often have vegetal or fish-like tails and thus they are metaphorical beings that reference the farmer's dependence on community life and seasonal renewal.[16]

One final example is called for, this time drawn from a well-known temple that sits right on the south bank of the Kaveri River.[17] In this temple dedicated to the goddess Periyakandiamman, the main characters from the Ponnivala story are honoured in several places. The gateway through which one enters this temple's main pre-shrine courtyard is unique and worth studying. Here one must pass under a wide, flat lintel that has a large lotus design painted on its underside (figure

Figure 10.8. Ceiling of the inner courtyard, Gannapuram Mariyamman temple.

Figure 10.9a, b, and c. Three paintings adjacent to the lotus medallion at the centre of the inner courtyard, Gannapuram Mariyamman temple.

10.10a, sketch, and 10.10b, photograph). Hence, like in the Mariyamman temple just described, one can only pass into this special space by, metaphorically, walking beneath a lotus pond situated high above. But here, in this unique display, one can also see what lies above the lotus pond. Unlike in the Mariyamman temple, where the lotus pond is on the ceiling (figure 10.8) here there is no solid ceiling, just a gateway with a lotus motif seen on its underside. What is remarkable is that here we can see the heroic set of triplets, Ponnar, Shankar, and Tangal, as described in the Ponnivala Nadu story, shown worshipping the goddess Durga above the lotus flower (circle A, figure 10.10a). Celandiamman (circle B, figure 10.10a) is a regional variant of Durga and of Cellatta, the same goddess that appears in the story itself. A group of additional characters, likely just residents of Ponnivala Nadu, are shown worshipping her. This scene is interesting for many reasons, not

372 Hidden Paradigms

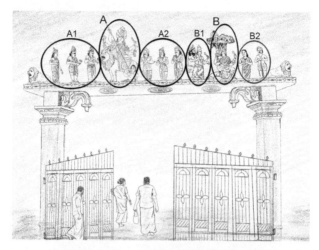

Figure 10.10a. Sketch of the gateway arch built across the entrance path leading to the famous Celandiamman temple at Madukkarai, adjacent to the Kaveri River. The waterspouts, seen to the left and right of the arch are nearly identical to the spouts seen in the Mariyamman temple courtyard (figures 10.4 and 10.5). I have an original photograph that shows exactly this, but it was taken at an angle that does not make the layout of the whole very clear. Thus, I commissioned this sketch in order to show more clearly how this entire gateway display is organized.

Figure 10.10b. My photo of the right side of the arch seen in Figure 10.10a. Note the downward facing fish outlines seen at the far right inside the box marked #1. This does not show up clearly in the artist's sketch.

Figure 10.11. A close-up photo of the goddess, Celandiamman, seen as circle 'B' in figure 10.10.

the least of which is that it shows how the story is understood to be linked to the grand mythology of Hinduism and to the famous goddess Durga. On this frieze Durga, seated on her lion, is killing her demon challenger with a spear, much like the twin Ponnivala heroes kill the demon Komban in the local epic story. This is the most formal, or perhaps one could say highest class, temple in the region that explicitly references this epic legend. It does so by overtly expressing these core characters' link to a pan-Indian Durga mythology. But it does more as well. This gateway essentially incorporates two ideas into its display: 1) Scene A shows the three heroes on one side of Durga and the three best known dynasties in South India (the Chola, Chera, and Pandya) on the other, each dynasty being represented by a non-specific king. As such it ties the story into a large south Indian history and links the local legend's royal family to the three great dynasties of this region's history. All three dynasties have links to this area, although none of them ever controlled this region for a significant time period, lending even more prestige to this local story about these people's own, home-grown leaders. 2) Scene B features this local goddess and seems to reference her incorporation into the local epic by showing her at ease, presumably resting and praying under a great pipal (Ficus religiosa) tree which is painted bright green. She corresponds nicely, in this particular pose, to the heroes' own mother, Tamarai, who spent twenty-one years praying right beside this same type of tree, before receiving the gift of pregnancy from Lord Shiva that created the twins and their sister, seen to the left as A1.

The half wall behind the characters (visible in figure 10.10 and 10.11) is painted a light blue, as if all these characters are either standing in the sky itself or else just adjacent to a pond which features lotus flowers. That both the heroes and these two goddesses reside above the surface of that water body is made clear by the lintel and lotus emblems seen beneath their feet. In other words, this gateway lintel clarifies that the gods, and the devout people of this area who worshiped this story's associated characters, all now dwell (after their deaths) in a space situated near or just above a heavenly lotus pond whose waters drip (or rain) down on the earth below. This position allows the water to touch them first and then to bless all story listeners and devotees who frequent this temple complex, including those just passing through the gateway as shown in this sketch (figure 10.10a). Furthermore, there are two spouts, just under the gateway lintel, one on the left and one on the right that are shaped and painted in a manner that is nearly identical to the ones seen in the Mariyamman temple courtyard described earlier. However, this time these two fountain spouts have been attached to the underside of this very symbolic doorway.[18] This scene provides yet more evidence for the idea that devotees must pass under the heavenly lotus pond in the sky in order to enter the main temple, and while doing so they may receive a sprinkle of the beneficial waters which drip slowly downward from it. More interesting still is the location of the goddess Celandiamman just above the lintel's lotus mandala, along with her story entourage. Note that she sits under a great green tree, very likely a Ficus religiosa. Indeed, her tree looks quite similar to the one seen growing at the spot where Tamarai climbed her own pillar of penance (figure 10.12, box 1). The branches of this tree have also been shaped, by the artist, so that they resemble the hood of a cobra, much like the one seen over the heads of the seven Kannimar in many temples. Tamarai also expresses special empathy towards a female cobra wishing for pregnancy, offering her a drop from the golden pot filled with a magical liquid Shiva had given to her to take back to earth. There seems to be a special relationship between women, cobras, and the gift of fertility, throughout the Kongu region. In accordance with this link, images of cobras that stand upright, carved in stone, are worshipped under similar large trees in many places, especially by women wishing for a child.

This highly revered tree is the exact species understood to act as the axis mundi that separates heaven and earth according to a much broader corpus of traditional Hindu imagery. In the configuration seen here, drawn from illustrations used for the Ponnivala Nadu story animated series, we find the same species depicted. Now, instead of growing up from the centre of a lotus flower, this tree grows up from a non-distinct cloudlike base. In the gateway shown in Fig. 10.10, the brahmamūla (here tripled to form a row of lotus blossoms) floats just below the lintel's upper surface. But in Fig. 10.12 the lintel is replaced by a cloud-laden sky. Though never specified, these clouds likely hold the monsoon's rainwater.[19] The mother of the heroes, Tamarai, was born in the centre of a floating lotus and her name is the term used in Tamil for a lotus flower. When Tamarai matures, she sits on her own pillar (figure 10.12, box 1), a post that is imaged by the artist

Figure 10.12. The great Ficus religiosa tree seen adjacent to the magnificent pillar (box 1) on which Tamarai sits while calling on Lord Shiva for twenty-one years. Also shown, still higher in the clouds, is the location of Shiva's council chambers (box 2) and one of the other pillars used by penitents that includes a fire pot at its summit (box 3).

Figure 10.13. Wider view of figure 10.12 showing that the entire structure on which the tree and pillars stand appears to float and that there is a staircase leading to this platform, seen at the far right.

to be shaped much like a lotus plant, a plant which is firmly rooted but that is gradually growing upwards on a tall slender stem. She is praying to Shiva, Lord of the Kailasa council chambers (seen here as figure 10.12, box 2). But where is this entire scene located? Figure 10.13 presents a wider view revealing that the artist imagined the entire ensemble as if it were a scene resting on a lotus leaf. Viewed in this light the staircase becomes the stem of that leaf (figure 10.14). Carrying this analogy just a bit further, the seeker, the truthful penitent, climbs up out of the watery surround of life on earth, passes thru a gateway and finds herself now in the world above. This can be imagined as a passage that uses the stem of a lotus

Figure 10.14. The shape of an actual lotus leaf.

Figure 10.15. Three-dimensional lotus on the ceiling of the inner courtyard of the Gannapuram Kaliyamman temple.

leaf as the necessary path. Climbing onto that leaf gets one to the great tree and a variety of waiting pillars (figure 10.12, box #3), any one of which one can then use to climb up further, that is if one's grand goal is that of eventually reaching the doors of Kailasa itself.

Just to put a fine point on the idea that there is a lotus pond in the sky that drips water on devotees who visit the temple of a goddess, we need only look back at the Kaliyamman temple where we started. There, the reader will remember, is a pair of fine water pillars standing next to the entrance. But that does not complete the set of symbolic references to sky ponds and water seen flowing down to earth in this setting. Again, this Kaliyamman temple has an inner courtyard which is located just before the doorway to the inner sanctum area, the space worshippers must traverse if they wish to pray and take dharshan of the deity inside. Here the ceiling has a magnificently sculpted, three-dimensional lotus, brightly coloured in many shades of red, which is dripping water (symbolically) off many points around its circumference (figure 10.15). The watery theme is everywhere!

Kāla Symbolism

Now it is time to look a little more closely at the counterbalance to water, which is the theme of fire, dryness, and heat. A second look at figure 10.13 will confirm that there are several other pillars to be seen in this scene. When viewed in its original, coloured version, it is very clear that each of these pillars holds a large bowl of fire on its summit.[20] Just like the squares at the summit of the pillars seen at the Mariyamman temple pillar that are all painted red, so too a prayerful person meditating on a pillar will be hot due to the intensity of their accompanying ascetic practices. That fire of the seeker rises up, and the divine response, when this person is successful, is a cool rain that that then falls upon them. If we think of a lotus mandala on the underside of a gateway lintel (as seen in figure 10.10), we can imagine that the space below it is filled by a great lotus growing up out of the mud of the earth, while the lintel represents its flower as it rests on the surface of the pond where it grows. Under that flower is life on earth. Above it is a grand tree whose branches accompany those who seek to go further as they climb still higher, this time into the clouds. But before one reaches this tree there is a tunnel of fire to pass through. It is significant that Tamarai, on her pilgrimage to Kailasa, climbs a fair distance up a staircase but then reaches a tunnel full of fire that contains multiple scenes of human suffering. Perhaps this is a passage through the lintel holding up the lotus pond, a passage required in order to reach the pond's surface? If so, then Tamarai must pass through that lintel-like-gate, and withstand the fires burning within that tunnel, in order to reach the great tree in the clouds. There, beside that tree, she will finally complete her twenty-one-year journey. The entrance to the tunnel she must pass through is covered with kāla heads. The scene is one of chaos. All the heads feature open mouths and fierce, sharp teeth (figure 10.16). The upward rising streaks seen inside the entrance, furthermore, are bright red flames in the original design.[21]

Before proceeding to discuss other related issues there are some important further thoughts to share which were gleaned from a 2014 article written by Vajracharya. For one, he uses the Sanskrit term kīrtimukha rather than the Javanese term kāla that Bosch employed to refer to the image of this head. The two terms reference the same basic set of faces so often seen at the top of a toranam arch. But kīrtimukha is a bit more pleasing because it means something like "glory face" rather than "face of time," the latter being a term that contains overtones of death. Vajracharya describes this as a cloud face, something seen in the darkening rain-pregnant clouds that gather before the monsoon rains start. He speaks of this face as being a symbol of an entrance to the world of the gods and as something seen on gateways to ancient temples. That position would lend such a frightening head roughly the same meaning. The term "glory" (kīrti) in the compound kīrtimukha refers to the cloud of glory that precedes or emanates from a great, virtuous person, something such as a great light or fine sound that might be felt to come directly from them.

378   Hidden Paradigms

Figure 10.16. Entrance to the cave full of fire and other means of torture that Tamarai must pass through on her way to the great Ficus tree where she will pray. The entrance is lined with kāla images.

Vajracharya also cites evidence that such heads are often three dimensional and that they can have four or even five faces intended to address all four directions of space, plus have one face gazing upwards in order to reference the vertical dimension as well. And the kīrtimukha face is associated with rain because it also often includes one or more chains of pearl-like drops that are often seen issuing from its stretched-out tongue. Those drops suggest, according to Vajracharya, that it is as if a shiny, watery, liquid elixir exits from each cloud, which then falls like a soft rain on all the devout souls who are passing through the gate below and hence entering into that sacred temple space.[22] I would add that those drops could also suggest that the face is salivating or drooling in anticipation of swallowing a meal, as the makara seen in figure 10.7b, whose teeth seem to have multiple symbolic overtones. This would be in keeping with the head having a clear double meaning, one positive and the other terrifying. Vajracharya does not mention that the kīrtimukha face is somehow associated specifically with Dravidian or South Indian iconography, as opposed to being familiar throughout India. However, the only examples (outside of Nepal) in my experience are from Karnataka, Tamil Nadu, and Southeast Asia, or are associated with Buddhist shrines. This may explain why these kāla/kīrtimukha images, seen frequently in Bosch's examples, have not been reported by other ethnographers who focus on folk traditions elsewhere in India itself.

The kīrtimukha also has associations with the head of a snake. This does not seem surprising. Wikipedia describes images referred to by this term as monstrous faces with bulging eyes and suggests that they reference the idea of an entity's reabsorption by all-devouring divine force. This may also be extended to the idea that one can reabsorb oneself, as in bringing on personal death via the practice of extreme yogic austerity. Others say the kīrtimukha references a story from the Skanda Purana where Shiva creates a hungry demon who ends up eating himself.[23] Still others reference the two planetary nodes, Raku and Ketu, which are the points where the paths of the sun and moon intersect and thus are the locations where solar eclipses occur. The shadow that passes over the sun at the moment of the eclipse is understood as a swallowing event and is imagined to be a moment when the sun is swallowed by a snake. Raku is pictured as the head of a snake and Ketu is its tail. Somehow the sun escapes permanent dissolution by exiting the snake's belly, leaving in place only a remnant, Ketu, which is a snake's tail. One can find plenty of iconographic representations of snakes rising upwards, their bodies ending in large heads that can either protect or swallow other beings that they encounter.[24] The game of snakes and ladders provides a good example of this idea. There, an unlucky player will be swallowed by a snake head but then exit onto the playing board once more from its tail, the part of the snake that rests near the bottom of that board. The totality of that board, furthermore, represents a high hill that the player, a virtuous penitent, is trying to climb.[25]

The kīrtimukha has also come to be associated with Lord Vishnu's vehicle, the Garuda, which is an eagle-like bird that can kill and eat snakes. That iconography references death, both because of what this bird itself can do to serpents, and by the fact that this is the very vehicle that Lord Vishnu rides when he collects the souls of the twin heroes, at their moment of death, in the Ponnivala Nadu story. In sum, the kīrtimukha / kāla head is clearly an ambivalent, two-faced way of referencing the broader process of recycling. It is a glory face but also the face of death and dissolution. The two are complementary points in that the ending of one life paves the way for its eventual rebirth just as a period of drought and aestivation necessarily precedes the monsoon rains.

Frogs and Mud

It must also be mentioned that Vajracharya goes to some length to discuss the role of frogs in his understanding of Nepalese religiosity. Unlike kāla heads, which are frightening and ominous, frogs are worshipped and respected because they are said to be the cause of rain. Their songs or hymns make the clouds release their monsoon heavy waters and they are praised because their magical powers are believed to be able to make that downpour happen. The situation is similar to that of a human king, whose great virtues are spoken of as being the cause of heavy rains that will bring forth prosperity. Frogs are not central to the Ponnivala Nadu story but there is one interesting frog scene. This occurs while Tamarai is on her way to Shiva's council chambers, near the start of her long pilgrimage. At the time she is accompanied by her husband, although later he must give up, due to weakness while Tamarai proceeds onward alone. But before that separation from her husband happens, the two are resting on the trail to Kailasa, when her husband is bitten by

Figure 10.17. The frog in the Ponnivala Nadu epic story.

a scorpion while he naps.[26] When he wakes up, he is not only in pain but also weak and thirsty. Tamarai sets off to find water in hopes of being able to revive him.[27] She finds a pond nearby but is frustrated that its waters appear to recede each time she approaches. Finally, there is nothing but mud left to be seen at the bottom of the depression where she saw water just moments earlier. But then, a frog calls out her name. Tamarai is startled and puzzled. She tries to catch it, thinking it might yield a few drops of liquid if she were to grasp it, carry it back and then squeeze its moisture into her husband's mouth. But that frog stays just out of reach. Feeling helpless and disappointed Tamarai climbs back up out of that muddy depression. Oddly, the water starts to appear again and follows her back up, rising with each step she takes but remaining just out of reach. As she reaches the rim of that deep hole Tamarai has another surprise. Now she suddenly sees that a wandering ascetic has seated himself nearby, under a tree. Tamarai has the power to see certain things others cannot, and she soon realizes that this ascetic must be a form of Lord Vishnu himself, so she bows to him and shows him respect. Then Vishnu reveals his true form and asks her to collect some water from the pond behind her, which she is now able to reach and touch. Tamarai does this and returns to her husband with some of this precious liquid. She sprinkles some of that water on him and he is, indeed, immediately revivified and re-energized. The full meaning of this small incident is never revealed, but again there appears to be some overlap with what Vajracharya reports from Nepal. Tamarai did not respect that frog, did not worship it and hence it did not allow her to fetch water from that magical pond. Only when Tamarai recognized that the ascetic sitting nearby was a form of Lord Vishnu and worshipped him, was she able to obtain water. The water was magical and had the power to bring her husband's health back. It seems that Vishnu had made himself into a frog, but not recognizing this, Tamarai had wrongfully thought about catching and then squeezing it instead of showing him her respect. This is not exactly what Vajracharya describes as worshipping frogs, nor is it recognizing their power over the monsoon rains. Nonetheless, there is a suggestive echo of that idea to be found in this story. Locally, in the Kongu area, frogs are honoured and their songs are welcomed, even if they are not specifically worshipped.

There is another aspect to a frog's life, however, that it is useful to mention here. Frogs love mud, and Vajracharya claims that they aestivate in the mud during the hot season in order to retain their needed body moisture. He also speaks of mud as an elemental substance out of which life and goodness can emerge. The importance of mud is highlighted in the Ponnivala Nadu story as well. As described above, Tangal reduces all the potter's pots she finds to mud by calling on a torrential rain using her magic golden wand. Then, when she stops the rain and calls on the sun, those pots spring back to their original form. The potter is in awe of her powers and now agrees not to charge her for the seven pots she has requested. But her real purpose in doing this, it would appear, is not to avoid paying for his wares, but to ensure that the pots she gets are absolutely pure and that no human hand will touch them other than her own. These become perfect vessels, now ready to carry the seven magical substances she will soon receive from the Sun Maiden and then use to revive her two dead brothers. Those pots had to be made of mud. Nothing else would be pure enough for the life-saving task that lay before her. This long-standing belief in the superiority and sanctity of mud pots, in contrast to metal or plastic ones, survives to this day. People in the Kongu area still prefer to use clay pots for ritual purposes, wherever possible. Mud, it seems, is able to bring forth life, something metal cannot do.

Before leaving the topic of mud, another example of forming new, beneficial things from raw earth, requires mention. Tangal, in the Ponnivala Nadu story, has to perform a set of funeral rites for her two brothers and also for her two sisters-in-laws. For this it is conventional to set out a feast for the crows who are thought to embody the spirits of the recently deceased. But because the palace kitchen where she once lived is no longer operative, there is no cooked rice available. So, instead, Tangal picks up a handful of sand and prays to Vishnu saying: "Oh Lord! Let me see this sand turn into cooked rice!" The sand heats up and is quickly transformed into moist, cooked rice that the crows gather and enjoy as she throws the soft grains on the ground for them.[28] This short scene provides a springboard to advance this exploration of hidden paradigms to a new level. In the discussion above a number of examples of water flowing downward along a pillar were presented, symbolizing the potential falling rain has to reinvigorate life below. This parallels the blessings that clouds and a heavenly lotus pond also provide, if and when they release the monsoon rains. But that "drip down" theme, up to now, has been described in a rather passive and season-specific way. The drip, drip perspective is that of humans who live on the earth below those clouds. Fortunately, this interesting paradigm can now be given added meaning. Humans do not just sit and wait for the rain to fall. They actively strive to encourage seeds and plants to grow, carefully using and conserving the water they collect to water important plants and to irrigate the most important farm fields.

382   Hidden Paradigms

  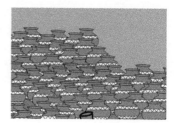

Figure 10.18a, b, c, and d.   (a) The potter's wife with her display of new pots for sale; (b) The sudden downpour turns all to elemental mud; (c) Tangal brings out the sun and restores all and finally; (d) Tangal carries off her pristine new pot set.

Figure 10.19a and b.   (a) The heroine Tangal reaches for a handful of muddy sand and then (b) magically heats it in her hand to turn it into cooked rice.

Milk Posts and Water-Filled Pots

The imagery of milk posts and pots can easily be found in the Ponnivala Nadu legend, but both themes are best elaborated on, and their purpose better seen and understood, when local rituals are carefully examined. Multiple varieties of seed (often nine) are planted in some rituals, or else tied in a small bag that is attached to a post, or thrown into a watery pond.[29] For example, nine types of seeds are thrown into the teppa kulam, a deliberately constructed earth-based reflection of a cosmic lotus pond, during the winter solstice ceremonies farmers perform.[30] Though symbolic in this ritual context, the larger idea is surely to reference human efforts to encourage and foster seed-germination. This attempt to engender fresh life through human action is an especially appropriate symbolism when seen in a farming community context. The acts of ploughing and seeding are both given considerable emphasis in the Ponnivala Nadu story itself. It is significant, however, that extended descriptions of planting the fields occur only in that part of the story that pertains to the first and second generations of the heroes' family. Such references are absent in the third generation when the twin heroes themselves turn away from any direct involvement in farming. Instead, the twins decide to focus on warfare and initiate contests for supremacy that challenge their neighbours. As a result the concluding song and prayer in this epic legend praises the father of the heroes rather than the twin brothers themselves. He, not they, is the great king who upheld the traditional values of the farming community in the Kongu area.

One rite amongst many stands out as a penultimate expression of the Ponnivala Nadu story's central planting and growing themes. That is the description this account provides of a ritual where a milk post is erected. This happens twice, once when the family builds a new palace and once when the family's twin grandsons undergo their wedding ceremony. In both instances a branch is cut from a tree that has a very milky sap and then planted at the spot where the ritual in question will take place.[31] The branch is first held jointly by multiple family participants (figure 10.21a) and a little seed bag, prepared earlier (figure 10.21b, and c), is tied to it and then water is gently poured over the whole. Finally, to complete the ritual, that branch is tied to the nearest upright object, usually a house pillar, where it stays until the end of the ceremonies, overseeing the entire event (figure 10.21d). Again, the core symbolism is that of seed germination and growth. Family expansion and fertility is also referenced, a theme appropriate to both house warmings and wedding events. Significantly, milk is the "sap" in this branch, a reference to feeding and nurturing new growth inside the family, as well as new growth in the fields that surround it. A larger version of this milk post can also be erected, in a prominent way, high over the entire home (figure 10.21e). This second, larger post extends the symbolism and suggests that this post will spread its blessings and hopefully waft or sprinkle its liquid "milk" ambrosia over the entire wedding area.[32]

384   Hidden Paradigms

Figure 10.20. A pot of milk ready for a ritual boiling ceremony

Figure 10.21a, b, c, d, and e.   (a) The ritual milk post being installed prior to a wedding; (b) The sacred seed before being tied-up; (c) The seed pack attached to the post; (d) The same post now tied to an existing house pillar; (e) A second huge post erected above the entire house expressing the same idea of auspicious seed packets (this time whole coconuts) tied to a central pillar that literally looms over the whole event.

Pots, especially earthen pots, are a core ritual object used in ceremonies throughout the Kongu area and far beyond as well. The concern here is to highlight the fact that this is yet one more way of referring to the life of the earth itself which the Kongu farmers honour and nurture at every turn. It is, in essence, their life calling to do so. Of course, similar kalsam pots and their related symbolic meaning as wombs that nurture and foster growth can be found in many settings, but their significance may be most prominently featured in Kongu Nadu. Rituals include pots holding four basic types of ingredients that have a cooling and highly auspicious aura: milk that has or will soon boil over, green leaves that are moist

The Monsoon Rains 385

Figure 10.22a, b, c, and d. Four versions of local ritual pots that emphasize vegetal bounty: (a) A single pot filled with coconut flowers; (b) Four tiered pots topped with coconut flowers; (c) A pot filled with cooling margosa leaves; (d) A pot topped by a whole coconut plus an array of betel leaves. The is the most common form of a sacred vegetal pot and it is very widely used for ritual events throughout the subcontinent. The other three styles are likely local to the Kongu region.

and cooling, a pot filled with coconut flowers, and another lined with betel nut leaves with an intact coconut fruit sitting on its rim (figure 10.22d). There are also a variety of local rituals that feature a pot filled with hot embers, a fire pot, which provides a symbolic counter theme that contrasts with the cooling pots listed here and, more generally, with the dripping of divine waters falling from the lotus pond in the sky.[33] Hot embers reference human efforts to contain and utilize personal energy both for general social good and for personal moral betterment. I have heard local non-Brahmin priests complain that they were burnt by a fire pot (or by walking on fire) when either their secret intentions or their physical bodies were not pure enough for undertaking an ordeal that involved fire.

The pot containing water and green leaves represents the fertile world, a world full of new life believed to spring forth from fresh seeds that will sprout as the waters of the sky pour down. By contrast, Brahmin fire sacrifice rituals, fed (nowadays) with vegetarian items thrown into its flames, are of course Vedic in their cultural style. Fire offerings invigorate gods like Indra and Varuna, rather than nourishing fetuses growing in the sky's dark clouds. In the first of four images of local sacred pots, shown (figure 10.22a), we see a simple earthen pot filled with coconut flowers and used in a farmer's celebration of the winter solstice. In the second image (figure 10.22b) we see a stack of four ritual pots, topped by a similar bunch of coconut flowers. These pots are part of a local wedding ceremony and seem to refer to the wish for a rapidly expanding family that will stand tall, proud and beautiful. The third photo (figure 10.22c) presents a pot that provided the background to a family shrine worshipped inside their communal home. The

Figure 10.23. A Brahmin priest at the Ponnivala Nadu heroes' wedding. He is offering a tray that holds a sacred pot with a coconut in its mouth, to a sacred fire.

neck of this pot was filled with cooling margosa leaves, a tree whose foliage is considered to be especially cooling.[34] This cooling pot likely parallels the wish for a cool, peaceful, and united family life. The fourth image (figure 10.22d) is of a very common kind of ritual pot, the whole coconut surrounded by betel leaves resting on the lip of the pot beneath., This configuration is given a central position in many, many ceremonies, both in Kongu Nadu and far beyond. All four types of pots present a clear contrast to the sacred fire theme that represents the feeding of unseen divine power and features rising smoke that carries the foods placed in the fire pot to specific named divinities who reside high above.[35]

To conclude this section on the importance of vegetal pots one additional scene from the Ponnivala Nadu story is worth examination. When the twin heroes, grandsons of the original farmer, Kolatta, are married, a Brahmin priest is invited to conduct certain central rituals, including, of course, the lighting of a sacred fire. Thus the sacred fire tradition from farther afield and the vegetal pot ritual more prominent locally have been integrated by the bards of story into one overall scene of worship. In figure 10.23 the Brahmin places the primary vegetal symbol (as seen in figure 10.22d) on a tray along with other offerings such as flowers, incense, and a coconut broken into two halves. He lifts these and presents them as a symbolic offering of respect to the sacred fire. This scene visualizes what has already been suggested above, an interpretation that blends nicely with what Vajracharya has written about in much greater detail from the perspective of someone who is a learned Brahmin himself. It seems very likely that the influx of Brahmin priests into the Kongu area resulted in their positioning at the very top of the social hierarchy, at least ritually speaking. The vegetal symbolism embodied in the pots has been retained and is given respect, but this imagery is now accorded a subordinate position vis-a-vis the sacred fire. The priest's gesture in this image says it all. The two religious traditions, a Vedic one that likely originated on the steppes of

Central Asia and the other from the plains far below, have merged in a non-conflictual, gradual, and seamless way. At the same time, however, a hierarchy between these two sets of symbolic traditions has become subtly, but very firmly and clearly, established. This symbolism and the rank order embedded in the merger of these two ceremonial traditions persists in the Kongu area to this day.

Rain versus Drought and the Midday Sun

The central idea of life brought to earth via heavy rain can now be discussed in the light of the Ponnivala Nadu story's central theme of dual kingship. Indeed, the duality and differences between the two heroes in the Ponnivala Nadu account involves a similar kind of collaborative duality. This idea is very clearly embedded, at a deep level, in the lovely poem quoted at the beginning of this essay. The character of the twin heroes is both separated and combined, quite subtly, in numerous other songs that the bard sang. The core idea is that these are two men with very different roles and personalities were born as twins and are thus entangled as one.[36] The contrast between those two key men can now be understood in a new light. The elder twin is the ruler who is praised consistently in these songs. In many instances one might surmise that he alone is the king being referenced. This is because a good king was, in the bard's mind, thought to be responsible for good rains, and for fertility and prosperity resulting from that goodness. It is notable that on four occasions in the Ponnivala Nadu story, good rains literally follow the hero Kolatta as he moves around: Kolatta's presence caused good rains to fall on the lands of the Chola kingdom, but then when he moved on to settle in Ponnivala Nadu, the good rains followed him there, leaving the Chola king in dire straits.

Later, to recap the next part in this story, Kolatta's young son, Kunnutaiya, becomes an orphan because his parents die a natural death when he is only six years old. However, he is a good, sincere boy and a hard worker. Kunnutaiya then wanders and is eventually taken in as a farm helper by two wealthy distant relatives who are themselves brothers. Kunnutaiya brings good rains with him because he is such an honest and honourable man. The brothers are pleased. They acknowledge this valuable boy and treat him well. Kunnutaiya is respected and appreciated as a fine young shepherd and becomes a general helper who milks cows, cuts firewood, and performs many other necessary tasks. But then, with secret help from Lord Vishnu, Kunnutaiya is married to these same two brothers' younger sister whose name is Tamarai. This marriage angers the brothers, who believe that Kunnutaiya, though a good man, is far beneath them in terms of social status. They expel the young couple and the newlyweds have to wander in the heat, suffering from thirst and from the many thorns that pierce the young girl's feet. But eventually the two find Kunnutaiya's place of birth, Ponnivala Nadu, and begin to farm there.

Figure 10.24. Tamarai finds jewels inside the cobs of maize.

Once again, the rains follow, and though life is somewhat primitive, this young married couple prosper, and their local goddess Cellatta also becomes happy. Significantly, Kunnutaiya's wife Tamarai has the power to see things others cannot. When Kunnutaiya's first crop of maize appears ready to harvest he is distressed because he cannot find seed grains where they would normally be, inside the large sheaves attached to the plant stalks. But then Tamarai has a look and soon finds that those sheaves are filled with jewels, where the grain would otherwise be. It is like a shower of gold for the young couple and they become rich and can now rebuild the family's old home in the form of a lovely new palace. Kunnutaiya and Tamarai are *showered* with wealth and there is now prosperity all around them. The bard's songs, at every point in this development, have stressed water, rain, and seeds that grow like gold. There is so much abundance that the maize grains left behind on the threshing floor start to sprout by themselves, even without planting. In sum, Kolatta and Kunnutaiya were good men at heart and, thus, everywhere they went, good rains and prosperity followed.

In the third generation, however, the story shifts and a set of twin heroes now inherit the family's wealth and prominence. We already know that both officially inherit their father's status as a king. But only one son really rules. He is the "golden one," Ponnar, the one with the shining face whose presence is auspicious and who brings goodness to all. His younger brother, Shankar, by contrast, is a warrior and a horseman whose role is that of this kingdom's principal defender. He is the primary fighter and the one who wields the sword with great skill. His brother may stand beside him but Shankar is the real warrior, often assisted by his helpmate Shambuga. Shankar wears the red turban. He is the *hot* one. Indeed, it is possible to argue that the elder twin inherits and expresses the peaceable and often ascetic ruler ideals Vajrachraya equates with ancient pre-Sanskritic India-of-the-plains, while the younger brother embodies the aggressive, physically skilled qualities of a horse rider, the Vedic warrior who attacks his neighbours and succeeds, via this means, in expanding his kingdom. Of course, the principal idea in this epic story is that there is a need for balance between these two very different brothers. Eventually, it is the younger twin who leads the kingdom deep into a war that eventually brings on death (through suicide) for both siblings at the young age of sixteen. Their deaths are then converted into renewal, as has been seen in previous chapters. The poetry itself expresses this duality. For example, in the two lines repeated below which the bard recites together, one directly following the other, just one brother is king, and then in the very next line, both are kings together:

Ponṉṉayyā, the farmer, ruled with a golden ring, ruled there,
They ruled as masters of the country, they ruled there.

Ponnar (Ponṉayyā) is the calm brother, the wise one, the golden one. He appears to rule alone. But these two brothers have inherited the kingship together. So does just one rule or do they rule together? The text is purposefully ambiguous when it comes to this matter.

Consider the opposite of the monsoon rains, the period of heat that precedes this, the time when the sun dries and burns all who move about beneath its piercing rays. The bard telling the story is very specific about this point in time, speaking repeatedly of the exact moment of the day when the sun is at its zenith. He uses this image to describe several difficult and painful moments in the heroic family's three-generation story. For example, when Kunnutaiya and Tamarai are secretly married by Vishnu, they then set out on foot to find the groom's ancestral lands. The walk is very hot. The sun is high in the sky. The couple experience extreme thirst. Thorns pierce their feet. The bride pants and says her face has never experienced so much direct sunlight before and is burning. When, later, the bride tries to return to her natal home, a place she has been banished and exiled from, the imagery is similar. On top of heat and sun, she is attacked and beaten by a palace guard the moment she arrives and tries to re-renter her natal home. Similar images are used to introduce other moments of extreme danger. Another example is the scene where Kunnutaiya decides to visit his clansmen's village to ask those adversaries for a sack of seeds. He needs this help in order to plant his first crop. But those clansmen are dishonest and secretly roast the seeds first before handing them over, hoping that they will not germinate. This encounter between rival families again happens under the noonday sun. When Tamarai returns from her twenty-one-year pilgrimage to visit Lord Shiva as he reigns in the gods' council chamber, furthermore, her return to Ponnivala Nadu occurs at noon. The imagery is appropriate because all the people of her kingdom are suffering, and all the women there are barren. The same happens again when Tamarai is in labour and suffering extreme pain. Kunnutaiya must go to seek a midwife to help her, under the hot noon-day sun.

The examples cited above by no means exhaust the use of scenes set in the midday sun to describe a character's pain or anguish. The twin brothers, for example, attack their clansmen's children in their village school, at midday, at the hottest time. Those poor, innocent children are tied up and thrown out of their classroom after being viciously beaten. They and their parents both suffer from the outcome of this cruel attack, becoming refugees and having to leave their village altogether. In a similar vein, Shambuga sets off to find the enemy boar, named Komban, at midday. When he finally finds this huge forest pig, dozing at the entrance to his local cave, Shambuga is teased and humiliated by the wild beast. The bard uses terms referencing dryness and heat to describe his anguish as well.

When women are wronged and become angry, they are described as becoming very hot. They beg Lord Shiva for ball of fire to use as a tool, and when he grants them that wish, the women throw the fire ball at their tormentor. Such scenes merge a heroine's internal emotional heat with images of the actual act of anger, which, to the person being attacked, surely resembles being hit with a ball of fire. Metaphorical or real, the bard frequently describes a heroine's anger as exactly that, a form of fire that emerges from deep within her physical body, most often described as a fire lurking in one or both of her breasts. Anger, of course, easily relates to depression, feelings of being lost, and a sense of being untethered or confused. Heat is thus also a kind of chaos, a mental state that Tamil poets widely express through referencing an angry woman's unkempt hair. In the following song the heroine, Tangal, is searching for the bodies of her two dead brothers. Significantly, in this song, the bard chooses the metre of a funeral dirge. Furthermore, Tangal's mental chaos is now translated into images of thirst:

> Oh, brothers, young ones born with me
> **My hair hangs in tangles**
> I am coming in search of you, my siblings
> Oh, brothers, the chaste one is coming.

And in another adjacent song:

> **I am thirsty for good water**
> I go with my tongue parched
> I am thirsty for cool water
> My teeth are dry
> For my thirst not even a spoonful of water
> Is available, oh, brothers!

In this state of extreme thirst, the heroine stands facing north and prays to Vishnu: "If it is true that I was born in the gods' council chamber, then for my thirst let there be a needle-like flash of lightning and some clouds. And let there be a measure of rain enough to fill this small depression with a mouthful of water, oh, Lord of Conjeepuram!"

In further poems misfortune and death are equated with dust and dry leaves, just as drought is. When dust is remoistened with rain, everything is brought back to life. There are many examples of this theme embedded in the Ponnivala Nadu story. Seven such examples relate to the seven times Vishnu revives Tamarai from near death as she dries up while perched on her penance post, praying for the gift of a child. The excerpt from the story below once again mixes tangled, unkempt hair with suffering, heat distress, and death:

> Vishnu arrived in the great, golden Benares,[37] and he noticed the figure of Tāmarai on the pillar of penance. She was dried up and hanging like a finger. Vishnu brought her body down and saw that there were huge termites living in her hair ... Vishnu took Tāmarai's body to the bank of the Ganges[38] and moistened it with water. Then he brought it out [of the water] and gave it [new] life.[39]

This final set of examples presented to illustrate this theme, how extreme heat precedes remoisturizing, can be seen in a set of images that describe the heroes' sister Tangal. They are discussed here because they, too, link nicely to Vajracharya's many references to rain clouds, lightening, and thunder, all of which are important precursors of the monsoons. When the rain begins people experience a major sense of relief, both psychological and physical. In the passage referred to, Tangal is walking through a forest, and she is alone. She is very thirsty and so she calls on Vishnu to let her have some water. He answers Tangal's prayers by generating a momentary rain cloud and a small depression in a boulder found along her path that quickly fills with water. But what happens immediately after the depression fills is even more interesting. As Tangal stops and water appears, the king of the cobras draws near and gently offers her his help. This appearance fulfils a prediction made by the serpent's mother directly to Tangal's mother many years earlier. He will help her. This handsome cobra king then leads the heroine on through the forest generously opening his hood above her head to shield her body from both the sun and the rain. Cobras are strongly associated with moisture and rain. They also serve as go-betweens, beings capable of bringing exhausted life down from the skies and reviving it underground. Cobras can be thought to act like a chute or passageway guiding a bolt of energy down through the atmosphere for recycling inside the womb of the earth. When treated well, cobras are lifegiving and beneficent creatures, both in this story and elsewhere in South Asian tradition. Tangal's prayers bring her water in a time of great thirst, but also produce an impressive protector that will guide her in her onward travels. He will ensure that she soon meets the magical Sun Maiden, also doing penance in the forest. The Sun Maiden will then give Tangal the substances needed to revive her two brothers from death. She will also lend Tangal her magical goose, a bird that will offer to fly Tangal to where her brothers' bodies lie.

392   Hidden Paradigms

Figure 10.25. Tangal walking through the forest, protected from the sun and the rain by the king of the cobras.

Figure 10.26a, b, and c. Tamarai reaching upwards, illustrating the complexity of her journey: (a) She is held up on her meditation pillar by her own stiff braids which together outline a kind of cube-like space; (b) A powerful mystic design depicted in the epic's illustrations, showing that the same heroine praying in the middle of a sacred mandala; (c) A terrifying kāla head expressing the horrors of the fiery tunnel she must pass through and the various other types of torture that still await her.

Figure 10.26 vividly illustrates how suffering and self-denial are practised in anticipation of an eventual spiritual reward, poetically experienced as being like a metaphysical shower of cooling rain. Tamari is seen against a backdrop of rain clouds, but they have not yet released their waters upon her. Vajracharya mentions this same idea in the context of yogic prayers. He talks about physical stasis and a withdrawal from normal social life, usually accompanied by various additional forms of personal denial. This same idea is made abundantly clear in the Ponnivala Nadu artist's visual portrayal of Tamarai as she sits for many years on top an array of needles that themselves stand upright atop the summit of a high pillar. Tamarai has only her very long hair, divided into four stiff braids, to hold her on that perch as she practises her intense concentration. Essentially, she manages to spin a kind of protective spell, a mandala pattern, around her carefully balanced body. Nearby are several kāla heads, clearly suggesting that she may have to pass through death itself before she reaches her final goal.

The Square or Cube and Its Central Point, a Post

There is a second theme to be seen in this imagery, which is the role of the three-dimensional quincunx, or more specifically a cube that has a significant centerpiece embedded in it. In Tangal's case this centerpiece is a post. We see this almost universally in Hindu temple layouts, a topic Kramrisch has discussed at length.[40] Tamarai's case is especially interesting because it is her braids that outline the special and sacred three-dimensional square that surrounds her. A few local temple examples of this are provided in figure 10.27. They portray the look of local temple architecture and are shown here in order to further clarify the idea being discussed. The first photograph (10.27a) is typical. Shiva's bull Nandi who here has been given a special three-dimensional cube outlining his own private space as he waits patiently in front of a shrine dedicated to his master. In figure 10.27b, we see a more localized example, an icon of Tangal seen inside a local temple where she has been given her own private, sacred space. In the third example (figure 10.27c) we see a pillar, typically found just near the front entrance of a local Shiva temple. This pillar always has four sides. It is embedded in a cube-like space, and each side has direction-specific imagery carved on it. Tangal's parallel pillar clearly cross-references this idea, as it stands close to the entrance to Shiva's Himalayan council chambers (figure 10.13). What is interesting here is where the pillar originates. It is as if the cube at its base represents a watery well, perhaps a lotus pond, out of which the pillar rises. Many Hindu bathing tanks where devotees go to bathe and cleanse their souls have large, sacred trees growing nearby, so that visitors can pay homage to or even hang a prayer on their branches after their bath. Some even have a pillar rising out of the middle of the tank itself. We know that there is a huge tree, likely a Ficus religiosa, just next to where Tangal prays on her solitary pillar (also seen in figure 10.13). There is even a cobra inside the trunk of that tree, according to this epic story. That cobra steps out from this tree's entangled roots to help Tangal prepare for her penance. Vajracharya presents an interesting parallel in one of his own published photos. In an image he took of the tank in Durbar Square, Bhaktapur, Nepal, apparently built in 1688, there is a huge metal serpent rising up, high and alone, from the very centre of a very large, square, manmade stone pool.[41] It is as if cobras are also considered to be praying ascetics, especially during moments when they raise themselves up on their own tails.

394 Hidden Paradigms

Figure 10.27a, b, c, and d. Four examples of square pillared canopies in temple settings: (a) A pillared canopy outside a Shiva temple that honours his devoted bull, Nandi; (b) A pillared canopy that honours the heroine, Tangal, holding a lotus bud, seen in a local shrine specific to the Ponnivala Nadu story; (c) A pillar that holds a pot of fire used to light up the sky during the month of Kartikkai; (d) A sketch of a similar pillar. It holds a pot of fire at its summit evoking an ascetic's burning desire to ascend into the sky, and perhaps helping to light the way.

Climbing Vines and Dangers That Lurk in the Dark

These examples lead to another paradigm, one that is central to the Ponnivala Nadu legend. This is the idea that the main female characters in this story (the grandmother, mother, and daughter, in turn) are often referred to poetically as climbing vines. Vajracharya discusses the idea of water descending from atmospheric clouds extensively, including the downward plunge of other magical liquids like soma and amrita. Kathmandu fountains extensively feature milk bearing cows (or calves) carved on these waterspouts, at or very near their mouths. Figuratively speaking, those bovines exit from those fountains right alongside the water itself.[42] But it is also important to consider in more depth the opposite type of movement: themes that depict ascent. The central pole, post, or icon of a divine figure seen frequently in the illustrations provided above, are not only versions of a great prop that separates sky and earth or conduits for the downflow of water. They also represent an upward-directed channel via which humans aspire to ascend to the world above. Often these pillars (or fountains in Vajracharya's case) are associated with a meditating ascetic that resembles figures honoured in local temple icons.[43] Virtuous women, in particular, are compared with climbing vines in the Ponnivala Nadu story, referencing the same theme.

Figure 10.28a, b, c, and d. Examples of fast-growing or climbing vegetation given special significance in local rituals and in the Ponnivala Nadu story: (a) Devil's ivy or Epipremnum aureum climbing stairs in a private home; (b) The heroine Tangal as a vine that has climbed a pillar; (c) Marriage of a Pipal to a fast-growing Neem tree seen in front of it; (d) The vine-like milk post that is tied to a tree or post at a wedding.

This idea of a climbing vine as a key poetic phrase in the Ponnivala Nadu epic requires further discussion. In figure 10.28a we see a good example of an actual physical vine being honoured in a real-life setting. The plant shown is a betel leaf vine that is been treated with love and is growing well. It is located on the exterior porch of the home of my long-time research assistant Krishna Sundaram, who originally wrote down by hand the version of the Ponnivala Nadu legend that I have worked with for many years. The betel leaf vine is an honoured plant that is commonly found in local homes. Indeed, it is considered to rival the importance of the Brahmin tulasi plant. Both are given respect and considered to exude benevolence, creating an atmospheric mood that can benefit family well-being. Earthen pots, holding water and dressed with flowers or green leaves, serve as central ritual symbols and are given a status equal to that of the Brahmin priest's sacred fire in the area where the Ponnivala Nadu legend is celebrated to this day. So, too, is the centrality accorded a betel vine in many Tamil homes. Figure 10.28b provides an illustration drawn from the Ponnivala Nadu epic that shows the heroine Tangal against a rich background of greenery. Here she sits atop a pillar in the forest where she has been wandering. She is a female renouncer who has turned her back on her own lovely palace, leaving behind a comfortable and protected life to wander in search of her two dead brothers' bodies. Pictorially, Tangal looks like a lotus atop a high stem, in other words like a green plant in search of sunlight and a new life. Her search, furthermore, is not for herself but for the future welfare of her two dead siblings. Referring to Vajracharya's work, we can say that Tangal looks much like an ascetic sitting under a Nepalese water fountain. Here is a specific example of how the term climbing vine is used by the bard of the Ponnivala Nadu story in one of his songs (note that the vine climbs upward in this song but that the tears, being a liquid generated by that climb, flow downwards):

The one born as a **climbing vine** is coming
On the face of that fine **climbing vine** tears of coral flowed downwards
The fine **climbing vine** dreamt truthful dreams
(But) evil dreams, that is what Tangal, the golden **climbing vine**, saw now.

Tangal experiences evil dreams as well as peaceful ones, because she knows that many difficulties and tests of her character lie ahead. This premonition provides a clear parallel with what her mother previously endured (see figure10.26).

The term climbing vine is clearly a term of praise and admiration, as is shown by the frequent addition of adjectives like fine or golden to the basic epithets used in this song. Figures 10.28c and d take this climbing theme one step further by noting its relevance to the theme of marriage. There is a small segment of the Ponnivala Nadu story where the heroine Tamarai commits to sponsoring a special rite that marries two trees that were earlier planted next to one another. These two trees are usually a Ficus religiosa commonly called a pipal, and an Azadirachta Indica or neem. While the first is equated with the strong and muscular, prop/post thought to hold up the sky, the latter is equated with cooling greenery and is a species that has important medicinal qualities. The pipal grows slowly but lives a very long time while the neem is fast growing, hence its comparison to a climbing vine. The pipal can live up to fifteen hundred years while the neem only lives up to about two hundred years. These two trees are very compatible. The first is usually treated as the male because it is very strong, its trunk is wide and stout, and it can live a very long life. The neem is considered the female in this partnership. It is often found planted inside the temple compound of a goddess. It is cooling, and is used to treat fevers and blisters, especially in the case of smallpox. But it is not nearly as strong or large as the pipal and does not live nearly as long. When these two trees grow together, they are treated as an auspicious expression of a beneficent and fertile marital union. Essentially, the neem is attracted to the pipal and grows up quickly alongside it, symbolizing its interest in climbing or reaching up. It is imagined as aspiring to join with its much larger partner at the top of the sky. In the context of the above discussion, the pipal provides the benevolent support post that its female counterpart will climb.

The final image in the set, figure 10.28d, also drawn from the Ponnivala story, shows the milk post used in the wedding of the two epic brothers. The plant chosen must have a milky sap. A bag of seeds is tied to it, and then it is attached to an adjacent pillar, tree, or (preferably) a support post of the actual house where the wedding will take place. The milk post is a similarly auspicious symbol that is said to watch over the wedding rituals and bless the new union that is about to occur. The importance of this post has already been discussed (see figure 10.21). Here the purpose is to suggest its climbing vine associations. The branch selected for the ritual appears to represent the female half of a broader pairing symbolism, because of its milk-like sap and green leaves. The seed sac is the male counterpart that gets attached to it. The whole is then tied to a post and water is poured over it with the idea that this marriage it represents will flourish and quickly produce further generations of life. In figure 10.28d one can readily see that two other symbols that may also reference upward movement, a set of tiered pots and a lamp with a small burning flame, have been placed beside this milk post for the marriage ritual, creating an ensemble of three auspicious signs each of which represents the same core idea: growth and upward movement.

All the above examples, each of which relates to a climbing vine and its support pillar, suggests a set of emotions and actions that precede and contrast with the much-awaited period of monsoon rain. First, moisture and hope must rise up, aided by human efforts. That upward movement is directed at a greater power believed to be embedded in the sky, a power that holds within itself blessings that will potentially return to earth by way of a heavy rain. This is a power whose presence and potential is made clear through the awesome periodic event we humans know as lightning and thunder. This idea is nicely expressed in an episode from the Ponnivala Nadu story. At one point during the couple's pilgrimage the heroine is forced to leave her weary husband behind due to his frailty. This happens at the foot of a staircase, which the heroine will then precede to climb alone. Her disciplined yearning leads her to continue her journey upwards, no matter what adversities befall her. A terrible, fearful, and dangerous period of struggle, and also one of great heat, always precedes the monsoon's cooling relief, as do fearsome lightning and thunderstorms. Figure 10.29 expresses these feelings nicely. As Tamarai starts up the staircase into the clouds, even the four pillars that hold up a normal pavilion are crumbling while the steps of the path itself grow ever thinner and less sturdy until they disappear entirely. A dark tunnel filled with fire and then seven deaths await her. But finally, she will reach her goal and obtain the gift of a magical liquid, placed both in her own womb and in a pot she will carry back to earth by the great Shiva himself. That gift is the equivalent, for her, of a beneficent monsoon rain.

We now turn to a different set of concepts that are associated with scenes that take place just after sunset. This second time period, when referenced by the bard, is quite different in its ambient emotions. The period just following dusk is a time when things happen in secret, a moment of uncertainty. The events that may happen at this time can be ultimately beneficial, but they can also have a more immediate and negative flip side. In other words, the moments after sunset are liminal and transitional. It is a time when energy shifts its state, a time when live beings are able to cross boundaries. Our first example concerns a bunch of poor hungry cows, mentioned in earlier chapters, who, early on, managed to sneak into Kolatta's sugarcane field to surreptitiously graze in a field where they did not belong. These hungry animals

398 Hidden Paradigms

Figure 10.29. A staircase leading into the clouds and to the council chambers in Kailasa as well as to the pillar where Tamarai did her twenty-one years of penance.

ate their fill, making a true feast out of this secretive visit. But when they returned a second time, the next night, they encountered a surprise fence. This time all seven cows died, quite abruptly, trying to jump over that new barrier. A second example, similar in some respects, occurs just after darkness descends as well. This is when Vishnu looks down from the sky above and suddenly decides to marry the hero Kunnutaiya to the young sister of his two wealthy bosses. Because Kunnutaiya was working for these two men as their farmhand, Vishnu's plan is socially radical. As a god, of course, Vishnu will eventually succeed with his plan, but it results in Kunnutaiya first receiving a severe beating from his two bosses when he first requests their sister's hand. As we have seen, that marriage will finally be accomplished, despite their resistance, but both Tamarai and Kunnutaiya suffer greatly while the arrangements are being negotiated.

A third example can be seen in a scene where Kunnutaiya's rival clansmen, in the darkness that precedes the dawn, harness their oxen and set off to plough a set of fields they have deceitfully claimed are now theirs because Kunnutaiya's parents have died. These men do some ploughing, but their work is superseded by an order from the Chola king that they return those fields to Kunnutaiya now that he has matured, married, and returned to claim what rightfully belongs to him. In sum, the outcome of this act, started in darkness, has an unfavourable ending as far as the clansmen are concerned. They lose those fields. Dawn, by contrast to dusk, is a much more favourable time to start something new. This period, the time when the sun is rising, is considered auspicious. This is the pleasing moment when all the scenes in the Ponnivala Nadu story that involve important acts of worship, occur. Of course, this is not a surprising observation.

It is widely known that Hindus almost always choose dawn to celebrate very auspicious events, especially weddings.

Ritual Blessings: Local Architecture and the Stylized Porch Pillar

The way a worship ceremony is conducted, albeit at any time of day, is worth mentioning as well. As an example, take the description of the first worship Kunnutaiya performs for the local Ponnivala Nadu goddess, Cellatta. She has not been worshipped for many years at this point, and her temple has been sorely neglected. That neglect is the equivalent of chaos. It stands as a symbol of humanity's lack of care for their own community, for the land, and for all life that exists under the purview of this goddess. In other words, Cellatta's lands have just experienced a long period of drought. Now Kunnutaiya begins his efforts to reverse this unfortunate state of neglect. Cellatta first addresses him saying: "Blessings to you, Kunnutaiya Kavuntar! For the past twenty-five years, ever since your father's death, I have had no puja. Do a puja for me now!" Right then, Kunnutaiya prepares and presents her with eighteen decorations. He then breaks open a coconut and sets it before her along with a few with bananas. With this he begins a puja.

SONG:
"Ting, ting!" He rang the bell,
From below he **lifted the pot of water** on high,
A bath of milk, a bath of honey,
A bath of rose water, a bath of sacred ash,
It was all performed properly.

When Kunnutaiya had finished the puja, he paid his respects to the goddess. He was then blessed by her. To express the hero's relief, the bard describes how Kunnutaiya's shoulders straightened and how the hall of his heart became peaceful. He was now happy. Note that this entire ritual is described as a series of baths, all created by specific liquid or powdered substances that have been poured over the icon of the goddess. As she is worshipped so too is the land moisturized and the fields fertilized anew. Worshipping the local goddess Cellatta and honouring the lands she oversees are here understood to be one and the same thing. The substances are poured onto her are like offering her a moment of great rain. The event is done in an orderly fashion. There is no chaos. As a result, Kunnutaiya's heart becomes peaceful. Indeed, in Tamil, a popular way of expressing this feeling is to say that one's heart has turned green (rather than its normal colour red).[44] Here are two images of this idea that are quite expressive. In figure 10.30a we see a home shrine, decorated for the

400 Hidden Paradigms

 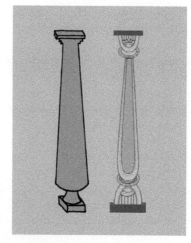

Figure 10.30a and b. Symbols of heavenly showers: (a) As suggested by two stalks of sugarcane erected over a family shrine; (b) In the shape of two popular pillar styles found in village homes of prosperous families, both expanding as they descend in a way that suggests abundant, downward flowing liquid goodness. One looks like a narrowly focused rain shower, the other like a huge, elongated droplet. The second perhaps expresses the idea of a constant, if slow dribble.

Figure 10.31. The palace of the Ponnivala heroes' family. Note how the multiple pillars on the front porch all widen towards their stone base. Furthermore, the palace has a backdrop of lovely greenery, blooming flowers, and a pleasing dawn sky overhead.

Figure 10.32a, b, and c. Three examples of a sacred lotus pond: (a) In the Ponnivala story as the place where the heroine Tamarai was born (b). A teppa kulam sprinkled with flower petals, dug during the winter solstice ritual performed by farmers in the Kongu area; (c) A temple pool supplying water drawn to worship the Ponnivala heroes' icon.

winter solstice festival. Two stalks of local sugarcane have been set so that their leaves hang down over the table-top shrine. Those lithe green fronds have been arranged to resemble a gentle release of rain from the skies above. In figure 10.30b two styles of porch pillars are shown, both suggesting the abundant down-flow of water in such a way that the pillars themselves symbolize a form of rain, thicker at the bottom because they are holding extra moisture there, set to release it on the ground. In figure 10.31 we see a broader view of how these suggestive water-pillars are set out at the front entrance of local homes. The example presents the porch design of the story heroes' own palace. Here the many pillars on display are nearly identical and all have the same special shape, carved to resemble elongated drops of water, or perhaps small waterfalls. These are physical portrayals, carved in wood, that essentially represent water exiting a sky-based waterspout. These homes have porches whose canopies are supported by an entire row of such pillars, all of which widen as they reach a small base of stone. Each pillar provides that home with a small blessing by symbolically pouring water on it.

One final set of images can be presented in conclusion. Scenes that resemble lotus ponds occur in many settings: at temples, near villages, in ritual settings, and in the epic story as well. Figure 10.32 provides three examples: figure10.32a Is the place where the heroine Tamarai was born, sent down to earth by the gods, figure10.32b is an actual if temporary lotus pond constructed by a farmer's family to celebrate the winter solstice (called the patti pongal), and figure10.32c is a well adjacent to a temple where the heroes' family is remembered and honoured. Lotus ponds are soothing, cooling, and hopeful symbols of beauty. They represent positive feelings and plentiful rains, all gifts from the sky that it is hoped will continue to flow downward through the eons and many yugas yet to come. In these images we can see the same themes evoked a) in a birth scene, b) in a seasonal family ceremony, and c) in the importance given to local wells in a temple setting. The pillars seen in prosperous private homes provide yet one more expression of this same basic idea.

Figure 10.33. King Kunnutaiya, wearing his crown and ruling the land of Ponnivala Nadu with a just heart and firm hand.

Figure 10.34. The three siblings, born as triplets, are pictured here at the end of the story. They are imagined meeting in Kailasa after the spirits of the two brothers ascend and their sister, who has been carried upward in a golden chariot, joins them. They presumably look down together and bless those on earth who have heard their story.

Chapter Closing Comments:

The sister of the twin kings, Tangal, has been discussed in detail elsewhere, but here is the song that concludes her work, as she performs the first rite of worship at the shrine for her two, now deceased, brothers that has just been built:

> The bell she rings goes "kiṇi, kiṇi"
> She sprinkles water upwards from a pot below
> There are offerings of milk, offerings of honey
> There are offerings of rosewater, offerings of wood-apple
> See her make the eighteen proper offerings
> See her ring a bell that goes "kiṇi, kiṇi"
> She sprinkles water upwards from a pot below.

Note the emphasis on sprinkling water, her use of a pot (an earthen one), and also the nature of the offerings. These are all conventional items offered in temple worship today, but here the bard's emphasis on sweetness and on the beauty of the little bell she rings is notable. There are just a few lines left to the story. The concluding words of the bard are:

> Tangal finished the god's puja, the puja for the family deity, and the fifty-eight lingam puja for her brothers. Then Shiva saw this and thought, "Oh, Tangal! She has finished

The Monsoon Rains   403

Figure 10.35a, b, and c. Three images of perpetual moisture and growth mentioned in the last poem of the Ponnivala Nadu story: (a) A river that never dries up; (b) A banyan tree that grows and multiplies itself; (c) Spreading clumps of bamboo that surround residents and promise prosperity for all.

Figure 10.36a, b, and c. Milk is the everyday manifestation of the broader concept of soma or amrita as a magical elixir that renews and sustains all forms of life. The idea is symbolized: (a) As an overflowing pongal pot; (b) As the cow being milked in the cow shed; (c) As the heavenly kamadhenu whose flow of milk issues from the sky. That cow's udder is so abundant that it reaches all the way to the serpent beings who live deep beneath the earth (seen inhabiting the hill under her udder).

all the business matters for her brothers. Now she must be brought to the gods' council chamber." So, he sent a flowered palanquin to earth. When the palanquin touched down, Parvati climbed in and left for the abode of the gods.

A final song used to bless the listeners, immediately follows:

Those who read the story of **the farmer Kuṉṉuṭaiyā Kavuṇṭar**,
those who teach it, and those who hear it,
**Let them be eternal, like the golden hall at Chidambaram,
and like the gods' council chamber** itself,
Whatever the country and time, let them reign **like an undiminishing milk well**,
Like a little river that never dries up, like a banyan tree that grows and multiplies itself,
They shall be firm, like the well-rooted aruku grass,[45]
while their relatives prosper and **surround them like clumps of bamboo**.

This epic's concluding message of hope is clear. Listeners can look forward to: 1) Kind rulers who resemble a group of just gods that share a collaborative council chamber; 2) Abundance equal to a well of milk that can never be emptied; 3) Constant moisture provided by a river that will never stop flowing; and 4) Luxuriant family expansion likened to bamboo and grass, both pleasing types of vegetation that grow quickly and spread rapidly (figure 10.35). These are primarily agricultural images of well-being, not images of power referencing individual fame or status. Milk (referred to in the poem above) is understood to be a very important cosmic, life-supporting, liquid essence. Some important images that are used to express this theme at the local level are provided in the final figure 10.36. They are intended to sum up this chapter by referencing one last and very important hidden paradigm: Milk. Heaven-sourced liquors (soma or amrita), be they offered in the form of milk or just plain rainwater, are basically equivalent in their power to sustain and renew. Like the Kaveri River, these divine juices provide the humans who walk this earth with a very nourishing liquid form of gold.

Conclusion

I knew, from the day the two local story singers finished their eighteen-day performance of the Ponnivala Nadu story way back in 1965, that this legend would inspire me and that I would one day want to share its essential meaning with others. However, my early wish to obtain a deeper grasp of this magnificent epic's core revelations, its *hidden paradigms*, took longer than expected. But the energy and magic embedded in this very long tale wrapped themselves around my heart when I first encountered it. After some fifty-five years of thinking about this wonderful oral narrative, I finally felt ready to tackle this early project with renewed gusto. This book is the result of that journey. In this large tome, I have explored many different ways to examine a given epic's many non-verbal underpinnings. *The Land of the Golden River*, the title of my recent translation of the text, is a very rich legend. But it has only been through the process of studying this story comparatively that I have learned so much more about its significance than I was initially aware of. Comparison pushes one to ask new questions and allows one to re-examine something already known from multiple fresh perspectives.

By unpacking this one very singular epic I have tried to extract and present the reader with a multilayered view of its underlying paradigms, its themes, and its deeply embedded metaphors. This story speaks to what human life represents in general, and also to how individual lives are believed to follow broad patterns as they progress through time. The result is a thickly woven, multi-dimensional tapestry. What I have presented in the foregoing chapters has many threads. Pulling one or two of those threads at a time helps both to deepen one's understanding of the cultural specifics this legend describes and also to reveal its general construction methods. Isolating those various techniques helps us identify the story's symbolic foundations, as well as the principles employed by poets and singers to develop it over time, so as to more fully embellish its basic scenes and key characters. When generalized, the questions asked here can be used to reach across all cultures and all historical time periods, helping us learn along the way a little bit more about how human minds use stories to highlight basic, underlying largely non-verbal aspects of a larger, widely shared worldview.

I hope that the chapters of this book have provided some guidelines and examples that students or scholars of any age can employ in their own attempt to extract themes from any long legend. I also hope it will help others appreciate how important this particular Tamil folk epic is. I also believe this study demonstrates how much oral epics in general have to contribute. I do not claim that everyone born or raised in a particular culture will share a specific worldview presented by any specific tale, but the symbolic themes that mark a group's core identity are both real and discoverable. When such themes get expressed through story it also means that they on their way to becoming heritage concepts. One striking discovery that has proved very helpful to me, but that was only made clear near the end of this journey, is the importance of rain in this epic. This was something that was right there in the story's songs and poetic passages, which I had both read and listened to many times. But I didn't think much about this theme until I read Vajracharya's unique and stimulating work *Frog Hymns and Rain Babies*. Like cows and bulls, I had taken rain for granted. Only now, after completing the final chapter of this book, do I feel I have really reached this story's deep paradigmatic core. The idea makes a lot of sense: the Kongu area is basically one large and quite dry, upland plain. Until the advent of tube wells there was not enough surface water in most areas to allow for the growing of rice, at least not without the labour-intensive construction of very elaborate irrigation reservoirs and very deep wells. Only that, plus strong bullock teams used to raise buckets of water from such wells and a means of distributing that water across a small and limited set of fields using an elaborate system of irrigation channels could have created the conditions for growing even a acre or two of rice. Water was, indeed, the gold that farmers in this area needed to survive.

There are sometimes major disagreements about what core story themes mean and how one can or should react to them. This is one of the major challenges of living in today's media rich world. We wander through a wide universe composed of the tattered remnants of many important stories and central concepts. Some, perhaps many, such ideas may now feel out-of-date. Nonetheless, we all need to explore and come to better understand our own roots. Fundamental paradigms are by their very nature rich and flexible clusters of meaning. Finding new ways to understand, interpret, and apply these building codes can yield powerful results. We should not neglect epic stories. Major cultural legends often intertwine many smaller mytho-poetic tales, serving to tie them together into one large, memorable, and well-structured bundle. Epic stories constitute an important aspect of our human heritage. We need to try to better understand them and explore how their essential messages can best be recycled and reused. Then we need to creatively re-apply their insights to the new needs and fresh challenges that face us today. The importance of forest preservation and the water vapours that dense clusters of trees can capture and re-release into the atmosphere is one such insight, an issue that remains extremely relevant to the huge issue of climate change facing humanity today.

Roots are important to any social community. Given time and a favourable environment they will grow and spread, and support the larger entity they underpin, helping it to survive. A well-rooted plant can sometimes accomplish the **reclamation** of its former place in the sun, even if it has lost a few branches along the way due to competition or to a climate-related surprise. A set of roots can also contribute to a plant's strong **resistance** in the face of an external challenge. The same foundation can also give a plant fresh **resilience** and help it to build a network of supportive exchange **relationships** with other entities in its neighbourhood. Those other entities often serve as a **reflection** of a given plant's own individuality but also help state the role it plays within a larger communal cluster. Understanding how a shining lotus manages to duplicate itself can also be a **revelation**. A lotus plant, for example, can replicate itself either sexually or asexually. All lotus species are able to use either seed dispersal or their local root system for reproduction, an interesting and relevant survival strategy.

In conclusion, the roots of the lotus plant contribute to their defence structure but in equal measure they also enable a lotus to replace itself with a new, refreshed plant entity over time. A lotus rhizome protects its offspring, allowing each new node to eventually blossom into a unique and lovely lotus flower. Furthermore, the lotus plant closes for rest each night, giving it an ability to flourish for many days. Rain is similar. The wish for abundant rain is commonplace, especially for farmers, precisely because its regular reappearance is at times lacking or at least somewhat unpredictable. I have heard pleas addressed to the local goddess Mariyamman to please bring forth rain, every time I have attended her festival. But I had never given much importance to that simple observation until I began to write the last chapter of this book. Sometimes the simplest things take the greatest amount of time to discover but that makes the recognition all that more meaningful when it does finally arrive. Epics are worth studying deeply. Like a great milk well, or a cornucopia, the wealth of insights buried in an epic are there for the curious and the determined to uncover. Furthermore, a rich and long legend's underlying ideas can ever be fully exhumed. There is always more to discover, more to learn. It is my hope that readers of this work will find new ways to apply the insights found here to new projects. If the new ideas and understandings gained from this work are used productively, then this book will find new life by living on in minds of others. Creative energy and fresh questions grow the most beautiful blossoms of all.

Appendix: Names of the Central Ponnivala Nadu Story Characters

In this listing these names have been spelled with the appropriate diacritical marks added. The names as they appear in this book are listed in parentheses.

This list will be useful for anyone wishing to do an electronic search for these characters as they appear in the book *The Land of the Golden River* (published in paperback in 2023, Victoria BC: Friesen Press).

Cāmpukā (Shambuga) – Also Cāmpukaṉ, the twin heroes' key assistant, sometimes addressed as their first minister.

Caṅkar (Shankar) – A key hero in the third generation of the story. He is also known as Caṅka, Ciṉṉa, Ciṉṉāṉ, Ciṉṉacāmi, Ciṉṉaṉṉacāmi, and Ciṉṉayyā. He is almost always with his twin brother, Poṉṉar, and is a brother to his triplet Taṅkāḷ.

Cellāttā (Cellatta) – The goddess of Poṉṉivaḷa Nāḍu. She is a form of the great goddess Pārvati.

Kāḷi (Kali) – A great Hindu goddess, a fierce form of Pārvati. Her forest form in this story is named Karukāḷi, which means the black Kāḷi.

Kaṉṉimār (Kannimar) – A set of seven sister goddesses who are said to represent the Pleiades constellation, called the Krittika in Tamil. Taṅkāḷ is the youngest of the seven, sent to earth by Shiva, where she becomes the heroine of the story in the third generation.

Kōḷattā (Kolatta) – Name of the clan founder, representing generation one of the heroes' family lineage.

Kompaṉ (Komban) – Also called Kompā, name of the wild boar who is a pet of the Veṭṭuvās.

Koṟṟavai (Kottravai) – An ancient Tamil goddess mentioned in the earliest body Tamil literature. Taṅkāḷ is compared to her near the end of the story.

Kuṉṉuṭaiyā (Kunnutaiya) – Son of Kōḷattā and a key figure in the second generation.

Pārvati (Parvati) – Goddess, wife of Shiva, sister of Vishnu. Also, a name of endearment used by the twin brothers for their sister Taṅkāḷ.

Piḷḷaiyār (Ganesh) – An important god, son of Shiva, who is worshipped everywhere in India, especially before one starts something new. He is also known as Ganesh, Ganapati, or Vinayakar.

Poṉṉar (Ponnar) – One of the twin heroes of the third generation. Alternate names include Periyaṉṉacāmi and Poṉṉayyā.

Poṉṉācci (Ponnacci) – This name translates as "little golden one." Poṉṉācci is a tiny dog who is the pet of the heroine Taṅkāḷ, sister to the story's twin brothers in the third generation.

Tāmarai (Tamarai) – The wife of Kuṉṉuṭaiyā in the second generation and the "mother" who immaculately conceived the twin heroes of the third generation and their sister and triplet, Taṅkāḷ.

Taṅkāḷ (Tangal) – Also known as Taṅkā. The sister of the twin heroes in the third generation. Taṅkāḷ is their "triplet" as all three were born from the same womb and of the same pregnancy. She is also addressed as Pārvati by her brothers towards the end of the story.

Veṭṭuvā (Vettuva) – The community name for indigenous hunters in the story. They live in a large, mountainous, heavily forested region.

Vīrataṅkā (Viratangal) – Also called Vīrataṅkāḷ. She is the sister of one hundred (sometimes said to be a thousand) Veṭṭuvā brothers.

Notes

Introduction

1 See Beck 2011 for a detailed description of how I made this discovery.
2 In Tamil this epic story is called the Annanmar Kathai (Story of the Elder Brothers) or sometimes the Ponnar Shankar Kathai, a title which references the two male heroes of the third generation, by name. Either way, these monikers describe only two brothers and, sadly, leave out their all-important sister Tangal who was born at the same time as their triplet. So, in most of my later writings (since about 1995) I have referred to this epic story using a poetic term its singing bards employ to describe the specific area where the story takes place: Ponnivala Nadu. This translates (roughly) as The Land of the Golden River. This is because Ponni (golden) is a name for the lovely Kaveri River, which supplies life-giving nourishment to the entire area through which it flows. For my two-volume graphic novel (2013) telling this story visually, I made the further decision to call this epic account *The Legend of Ponnivala*. However, Tamil speakers are more comfortable with the more complete phrase Ponnivala Nadu, nadu being the Tamil word that denotes a well-known region or administrative area. But as this is a mouthful for English speakers, in that work as in this one, I will sometimes use "Ponnivala" as a stand-alone term, for simplicity.

1 Summarizing an Epic Legend: The Legend of Ponnivala Nadu

1 Copies of the original display panels can be accessed by contacting the author.
2 This is the Ficus bengalensis fig species, botanically speaking. But another species of fig, the Ficus religiosa is also very important in the story. It is discussed at length in chapters nine and ten.
3 The reader will not see blood in the illustrations provided here. This is because these drawings were developed several years ago with a different application in mind. Children were to be a part of the audience and the author was strongly advised to keep blood out of the images for that reason. But blood is copiously mentioned in the text

of the epic itself. See Beck 1992, vol. 2, 760–1 for an example: the bards' description of blood spilt as the two heroes died.
4 See Beck 2023 for a full text of this story that can be used in a classroom. The story is also available as a set of graphic novels, Beck 2013 and as a twenty-six-episode set of animated videos.
5 These generalizations refer to the discussion of paradigm concepts found in chapters seven, eight, nine, and ten respectively.
6 Bruce Lincoln, Caroline E. Haskell Distinguished Service Professor Emeritus of the History of Religions, University of Chicago.
7 Wikipedia, 15 January 2021 (https://en.wikipedia.org/wiki/The Golden Bough).

2 Character and Plot Structures: The Mahabharata

1 This chapter compares the Ponnivala story with the northern and best-known version of the Mahabharata. There is a Tamil version but to my knowledge it has not been fully translated into English and I have not had much access to it.
2 The earliest preserved parts of the Mahabharata story, as a text-based document, date to around 300 or 400 BCE according to a variety of scholars whose work and research are widely accepted at the present time. A limited few have laid claims for an earlier date, but that is a not a dispute that is relevant here.
3 According to Hiltebeitel 1999, oral epics "innovate from the darker areas" that the Sanskrit epics leave open. In particular, he has studied a Draupadi cult in the Gingee area where Draupadi re-emerges as an angry, vengeful, and dangerous character. Hiltebeitel also speaks of a sort of sub-text welling up relating to the Liebestod mythology of Kali (as it relates to the story of the goddess Durga and the buffalo demon she is attracted to and then kills). Local Mariyamman festivals in the Kongu area provide a good illustration of this point. However, taking a wider view, I believe that the Ponnivala Nadu story does much more than just innovate from the darker areas of the larger Mahabharata story.
4 Hiltebeitel 1999. It is interesting that this initial link to the Mahabharata in the story's invocation is given more emphasis in the bard's dictated version of the story that I tape-recorded and preserved than in an actual oral performance that pays somewhat less formal attention to this connection. In the oral performance Lord Murugan is added to the list of praise poems that start the story, a difference that reflects the fact that this son of Shiva (not Saraswati or Vinayakar) is the most popular local deity of this area. See chapter 7 for further discussion of the importance of Murugan.
5 In RgVeda, verse 10.90, the Brahmin is associated with the head of the great cosmic body (Purusha) and the Kshatriya are his arms.
6 It is a kingdom of widows because, earlier, the great boar Komban has killed all the village men who volunteered to help hunt him down.
7 Beck 1982, 182.
8 Of course, Komban is likely a form of Varaha, one of Vishnu's famous incarnations, the great wild boar of Indian mythology. In Varaha's story the gods

complain, saying that he is causing the earth too much trouble. Varaha agrees to die but says that he needs help, as he cannot kill himself. Shiva then agrees to do the needful after taking the form of the great Sharabha. In the folk epic Ponnacci does not completely kill Komban, but she brings him close to death and then lets the twin heroes finish the job (one of this pair being a form of Arjuna). Ponnacci, likely a form of the goddess Kali, would then be Parvati in her more violent form, or Shiva's other "half" in this important replay of an ancient contest.

9 Because the two sons are kept in a secret cave under Cellatta's temple during their first five years, this generalization really applies only after the three children are raised together, beyond the age of five. The two parents do not even realize that they have two sons until that point. Consequently, all of their attention and love go to their sole daughter during the first five years.
10 Beck 1992, 444–7 (slightly paraphrased).
11 Doniger 2009, 611.
12 This is true today only if the couple being married decides to follow a local tradition that the major landed caste in the Kongu area upholds. This particular rite is referenced in the epic story (Beck 1992, 2:441) but not described. It is more fully illustrated in the animated version of the story and in the related graphic novel set.
13 This right that a groom can present to a young woman's family is called his urimai claim.
14 The two women have magically retained their youth. Their time as statues is not counted in the maturation process. The same is true of Tamarai's twenty-one years of penance. They do not age her. She is the same youthful woman when she returns from Kailasa as she was when she left her palace home over two decades earlier.
15 Khangai, 2.
16 This may be one more indication that the story was gradually constructed backwards, starting with a local tale about two brothers that gradually got expanded to include these two men's parents and grandparents. It was likely in that expansion that an effort was made to connect it to the more famous Mahabharata account.
17 This is another reason to think that Komban might have been a form of the great god Vishnu in his well-known incarnation as Varaha in the wider corpus of Hindu myths.
18 This similarity is also mentioned at the very beginning of this chapter, but there Shambuga's similarity to the monkey leader Hanaman, was highlighted.
19 Beck 1992, 2:700–1.
20 Pattanaik 2010, 388.

3 Human Life as a Balancing Act: The Epic of Gilgamesh

1 White 2014a, 412. The most recent research suggests this date could even be a bit earlier. The corpus is considered to have originally been a collection of independent stories that were later combined to create a longer and more unified epic legend.

2 For an in-depth discussion of this transformation see Scott 2017 and Beck 2019a. Many early Sangam Tamil poems speak about the significance of cattle, too, expressing a similar worldview.
3 White has written extensively about this theme. Using examples drawn from widely different sources he has been able to generalize to describe a symbolic tradition shared throughout the ancient Near East. Many other creatures are also depicted, but he sees the cow as especially central to this highly visual worldview because it, along with a nursing calf, pointed to the concept of a mother goddess. Perhaps the best way to get a quick overview is to go to White's *Symbol Index* (2013, 178–9) and selectively consider the illustrations he has grouped under the headings Cow and Calf, Descending Calf, Calf, Bull Head, Calf Head, and Bull Sacrifice. Goats and sheep are bundled in with cattle and can substitute for cows and calves in this metaphoric universe, as would be appropriate to a world where animals of several kinds may be herded into a single home pen to spend the night.
4 Shambuga is a Dalit, a Paraiya by caste, in the key Ponnivala Nadu text referenced here. This group was classified as outcaste and its members were forced to live in a separate settlement outside the boundaries of normal village life.
5 Because of his low status, Shambuga did not carry a sword like his two masters did.
6 These are traits clearly described in local poetry that I collected about the Kannimar.
7 Beck 2016a and 2016b plus White 2014a, 296–8.
8 The cooling tulasi plant. Considering where it is placed on Komban's body, it may play a role in controlling and cooling his wildness.
9 https://en.wikipedia.org/wiki/Humbaba.
10 Lombardo, 160. However it must be noted that all versions of the story mention Humbaba's tusks. In most early illustrations Humbaba's head has a fearsome appearance, much like the Hindu kāla or kirtimukha head extensively discussed in chapter nine. Komban's head is similarly frightening in the key artistic representation used in the animated version of this epic (figure 9.27a).
11 Beck 1981 discusses a related local village ritual for the goddess where a buffalo head is severed and then buried like a seed.
12 George, 46–7: Lombardo, 38.
13 One can also appreciate this human or divine theme as it relates to a total yuga cycle restart, when thinking about this ritual planting scene.
14 George, 2.
15 Of course, various modern-day political parallels for this kind of popular adulation as a bully are not lost on me. Here is an excellent point of entry for teachers who can use this to launch a classroom discussion of the relevance of this epic story in its modern context.
16 Beck 2023.
17 Some would argue that an even deeper meaning buried here is that the goddess must eventually triumph over all male aggression towards her, even by a lover, and that her ultimate responsibility is to maintain control of the birthing and nurturing forces of

the cosmos by ensuring that attacking males submit and do not harm that goal. Berkson (1997) makes this larger point in great detail.
18 George, 70.
19 George, 205.
20 This uniting ritual is called the innai cir in Tamil.
21 According to traditional custom in this area of Tamil Nadu, it was quite acceptable, even desirable, for a woman to marry her mother's brother. The cook who lived with me while I was doing my doctoral research had been married by her parents to a brother of her mother. So, the idea that Vishnu might have been interested in Tamarai, his sister's daughter, is not at all surprising in this cultural context.
22 Woods. Note that Woods spells Innana as Inana.
23 Ibid., 91.
24 Ibid., 90.
25 Ibid., 85.
26 It is possible that this killing of the Bull of Heaven also reflects a natural phenomenon: the gradual precession of the equinoxes. There was a natural shift in the specific constellation that once rose at the time of the spring equinox. At that specific moment of the year as seen from Uruk, around 2200 BCE, the Pleiades would have started replacing the wild bull as the constellation that rose last in the eastern horizon, just before dawn's new light would no longer allow any further study of the stars. It would have taken some time for careful observers of the heavens to admit this change had occurred, however, and then to invent a myth to try and explain it. If this speculative idea is right, then this story of the great bull's death may reflect the natural progression of that just-before-dawn shift from Taurus to the Pleiades. It was the custom to pay close attention to which constellation rose during the last half hour or so of night at the time of the spring equinox, because that constellation was thought to signal the start of the new year. Furthermore, according to what we will discuss in chapter 8, there were two constellations, one depicting a bull, and the other a boar, and they were located on opposite sides of the night sky. Thus, at about 2200 BCE, the boar would have been setting at dawn just as the bull rose, that is, until things started to change. Due to the phenomena of precession, the Pleiades were rising and although the bull was still very close behind it could no longer be seen due to dawn's increasing light. Similarly, the bull would have set earlier than it did in 2200 BCE. Early rock carvings from central India also indicate an ancient and seemingly close association between a bull-like figure and a boar-like one, another that reason that these two constellations may have been considered related. The evidence is from Erwin Neumayer (2013, 118–21) but he does not discuss the relationship between these two animals in this way, nor does he mention the fact that one boar seen in a rock carving he has photographed, is seen standing on its nose. That unnatural posture would seem to indicate that this boar image refers to a constellation seen in the sky. Another related rock carving places emphasis on a boar's semen, a suggestion that it, like the

bull, may have embodied the idea of the sky's fertility and that these two animals, in particular, were capable of impregnating it with new life.
27 Woods, 94.
28 Nehemiah 2.8.

4 Seven Great Phases of History: The Bible's Old and New Testament Stories

1 Augustine lived between 354 and 430 CE.
2 Hindus also greatly value the number seven. The importance given to this special number is not unique to the Bible, nor even to traditions held in common by the entirety of Western Europe and the Middle East, including ancient Babylonia. However, given the importance of the seven Kannimar maidens in the Ponnivala account, where six are always grouped together but the seventh is treated separately, makes this particular detail of special interest. These women are the Pleiades, seven women who are important in this folk epic, in local ritual contexts, and in Hindu thought more generally as the Sapta Matrika or seven mothers are said to be married to the seven Rishis. These women and their significant gender ambiguity as well as their confusing count as either six or seven is discussed further, at many other places in this work.
3 Augustine (to the best of my knowledge) was the first to formally describe the biblical story in this way. He recorded his thoughts in his *Works*. I have tried to read the relevant section of his extended treatise, using Philip Schoff's edited translation (1887, 302–10), but this is a difficult source to fully understand if one is not a trained a biblical scholar. Thus, a helpful discussion of Augustine's argument provided by Frei (1974, 1–3, 173–82) has been heavily relied on. A further reduction of these seven eras or stages of man's history is nicely presented, using true laymen's terms, in much more recent book (Fahs 1952, 63–75). That discussion further compresses the seven basic stages into short, meaningful units. That work, aimed largely at classroom Sunday school teachers, uses very direct language. After outlining the basic seven stages referenced above, Fahs goes on to critique this standard interpretation. She proposes a more modern, more rebellious, and more creative approach to the western world's biblical story heritage. However, her larger contribution pertains to innovative childhood religious curriculum development. Due to a need to focus on this book's own core theme, neither Frei's nor Fahs' interesting commentaries are addressed in the arguments presented here.
4 This comfortable match-up does not feel accidental but it is also not a deliberately constructed one. Some might attribute the likely overlap to my own pseudo-Christian perspective on life, since that is the worldview within which I was raised. However, the same set of categories is at least equally the framework chosen by the multiple native American-Canadian authors whose book these terms were borrowed from: (Doerfler et al. 2013). Although the Nanabush tales themselves are Indigenous, Christian missionaries heavily influenced Native religious thought on the North American continent for centuries. Therefore, this match appears largely due to a

deep (but mostly unspoken) paradigm which accepts a vaguely Christian perspective, something Indigenous cultures on this continent have long been exposed to. This is especially true of highly educated North American Indigenous peoples, many of whom owe their early education to time spent studying in overtly Christian-managed schools.

5 In the Tamil realm of symbolic thinking, ploughing is itself often used as an explicit metaphor for the male sexual act. Furthermore, in Tamil this same act is also described by the identical everyday word for doing work because it is commonly used by farmers going out to their fields for the day (vēlai ceyvatu).

6 The implication could be that the goddess Parvati (unwittingly?) placed her nine first men in an unenviable position. They would have to choose between preserving their lovely Eden-like environment and following her wish that they use the plough she gave them. That plough would (implicitly) convert them from their initial state as wild forest inhabitants into civilized, cultured beings whose key tool for survival would be that very implement. There is further evidence, provided later in the Ponnivala Nadu story, that the forest (at least the surviving patches of it) is ultimately a place of sacred power that should never be mistreated or destroyed. Like the Christian Adam and Eve, therefore, these first men must confront a complex moral choice. Furthermore, they, again like Adam and Eve, are led by their desire to prosper (reinterpreted as a reproductive or sexual imperative to bear and then feed copious offspring) and are thus driven to employ new strategies for food acquisition. The plough, which was clearly one such strategy, entailed some degree of consequent environmental destruction. Perhaps the drought was caused by gods' hot anger over the loss of a primeval, lovely, and cool forest environment. See chapter 10 for an extensive discussion of the symbolism of heat, anger, and drought in this story, as opposed to the cool, moist, and fertile impact of monsoon rain.

7 The outer coating (hull) of the castor seed contains a deadly poison called ricin. This outer coating can cause nausea, vomiting, diarrhoea, abdominal pain, dehydration, shock, and more. This was an act that had ominous overtones of ill will.

8 The singing bard ends this story with a special song-blessing (a mangalam) about how death will become the source of new life so that the land of Ponnivala can continue to flourish.

9 In the animated and graphic novel versions of this story the symbol of a beam of light emerging from Shiva's right palm is the symbol used to indicate this key transfer of life spirits and their special energies, from his hand to her womb. The text does not specify how this transfer of life energy is accomplished.

5 Landscapes and Identity Formation: The Vatnsdaela Saga

1 All details here, and in the following pages of this chapter, are taken from Andrew Wann (2001, 185–269) and from an Icelandic tourist brochure entitled *Vatnsdaela Saga Heritage Map* (Iceland 2010). This map is also the source of many (but not all)

of the illustrations of this saga provided in the pages below. I was unable to identify the artist, nor to contact the map's publisher, even after many tries. However, I acknowledge the source and am thankful for the lovely illustrations it provides. These drawings were coloured in their original form, but they have been converted to black and white for use in this publication. The rest of the Icelandic illustrations are photographs that I took of the wonderful, embroidered banner telling this epic story, which I discovered while exploring the story area (and mention a few paragraphs below).

2 There is one possible palm leaf manuscript in existence but just how authentic it or its published version is has been questioned. See Caktikanal (1972) for more detail on the written variants that exist today.

3 The presence of a similar character is abundant in pre-Hindu rock art. See Neumayer 2013. For more discussion of the significance of the wild boar in the Ponnivala Nadu story see Beck 2016a and 2016b. Various details of the heroes' final funeral ceremony and momentary resurrection also exhibit unique features that are too complex to further detail here. For more discussion of this topic see Beck 2016c.

4 These parrots fly to earth and settle in a tree near the hunters' forest palace. Then one parrot (the female) is captured and brought to the Ponnivala Nadu palace for their sister to enjoy. It is as if one half of Tamarai's spirit (in bird form) finds a new life residing with her daughter Tangal, while the other half remains with this daughter's (reflected) forest double, Viratangal. It is also significant to note that it is the female parrot in the pair that is housed with the story's civilized female while its male partner remains with this girl's very fierce, wild, and stereotypically warrior-like counterpart. It would be worth asking whether the theme of bird-spirit doubles for key characters can be found in other Tamil folk legends as well.

5 There is ample archeological evidence from the Kongu region that skilled artisans were forging high quality metals, using advanced smelting techniques, well before evidence of wide-spread plough farming in this region can be documented. The archeological dig at Kodumanal is one prime example.

6 Human versus Extra-Human Powers: The Nanabush Story Cycle

1 The key resource on which this analysis relies is a book of stories told by Sam Snake, Chief Elijah Yellowhead, Alder York, David Simcoe and Annie King. This 1980 collection was compiled by Emerson Coatsworth and David Coatsworth and illustrated by Francis Kagige.

2 Beck 2020.

3 We will see in the final chapter that mud is also a key symbolic element used to form new things, in the Ponnivala Nadu case.

4 This and all subsequent Ojibwa sketches in this chapter are taken from original (coloured) artwork created by the Ontario Ojibwa artist Francis Kagige (1929–2014). All were published in Coatsworth, Emerson, and David Coatsworth, *The Adventures*

of Nanabush: Ojibway Indian Stories, New York: Atheneum, 1980, and have been rendered here in black and white.

7 Splitting, Replicating, and Twinning of Gods and Animals

1 There are many myths describing Murugan's birth. What has been cited here follows O'Flaherty, because she conveniently combines several stories she translated (1975, 104, 109–15) each basically drawing on a particular section of the Mahabharata. The key themes we see are that Shiva's amorous advances are rejected by a goddess (who has several forms and names in different stories), but that he ejaculates anyway. His semen is magically collected but it is hot and hard to hold. It is, therefore, deposited somewhere, often in a wetland or swamp of some kind. From that clump of semen, Lord Murugan springs forth.
2 See Beck 1975 and 1982b for two extensive discussions of the significance of Murugan's two wives.
3 Van Bakel (2019) sees the tiger, at least on Indus Valley seals, as a form that Kartikeya took when wooing his second wife, Valli, in a forest. He cites several Indus valley seals as examples. Here the goddess Cellatta could be considered to be a form of Valli who feeds these young boys while matching her lover-husband's tiger form.
4 Van Bakel believes he sees a depiction of Kartikeya as riding an elephant in several Indus valley seals. The elephant is a symbol for his first wife, Devasana.
5 O'Flaherty 1975, 105.
6 This relationship can be seen in early in European rock art as far back as the Lascaux cave paintings in France, circa 14,500 BCE.
7 Andrews 2004.
8 Black and Green 2011, 162, 190. See chapter 8 for more details about the Krittika constellation.
9 O'Flaherty 1975, 168. In this translation the milk is said to flow from Parvati's breasts due to her joy.
10 Zvelebil 1973, 243.
11 Mann and Fleming 2014, 234–46.
12 Clothey 2019, 3–4.
13 There are a range of local rituals performed in honour of these twins that go well beyond what is seen in other temple festival settings, including dramatic actions that involve death and then resurrection as devotees express their feelings about the two heroes. See Beck 1982 for more details.
14 See Beck 2018 for an interesting parallel along these lines with the Living Goddess, called the Kumari, of Kathmandu.
15 Beck, 1982a, 46.
16 M.N. Srinivas (1944) published the only printed corpus of these very interesting songs that I am aware of, and a large collection of my own transcripts of songs describing these young girls is also available (in Tamil) through the University of Toronto Library, Scarborough branch.

17 Readers familiar with Hindu traditions more generally will recognize this as a "suttee" or wife-immolation moment, in this case not a voluntary suttee but one forced upon these two wives by the heroes' sister Tangal.
18 This is particularly true if one considers that Ponnar and Shankar themselves represent, symbolically, a kind of female-male pair.
19 O'Flaherty 1975, 104.
20 This equation seems apparent although it is not explicitly stated to be so by the story's bards.
21 Taurus is not a constellation identified by name in the Hindu Nakshatra sky-mapping tradition, but this bull sits very close to the Krittika or Pleiades, a constellation located just over this bull's shoulder hump. Taurus, of course, is a key figure important to all Zodiac sky maps.
22 White 2014b. He also has a second, slightly earlier book, published in 2013, that discusses many of these same ideas but is accompanied by a different set of illustrations and comments. An extensive further discussion of Ponnivala-Babylon similarities can be found in the next chapter.
23 See the Krishnaswami archive, an excellent resource.
24 For a further discussion of the significance of the square in Hindu thought see Beck 1976.
25 Indus valley seals, an important corpus of early South Asian iconographic images, are also replete with characters (both male and female) who wear a "set of horns."
26 Neumayer argues, using multiple illustrations, that bulls and boars were equivalent kinds of beings in early South Asian Mesolithic art (2013, 118 ff). Thus this interchangeability appears to have a very long history. Neumayer provides a variety of very early Mesolithic rock art examples documented from areas across peninsular India.
27 This pattern of complementarity seems to hold true both in Babylonian culture and in Ponnivala Nadu. There the wild boar (Figure 8.3) sits almost directly opposite the bull of heaven on the Babylonian star calendar. The bull would be the equivalent of Shiva in his beneficent and tame form, while the boar would represent his wild and fertile but unpredictable form.
28 This would parallel Shiva's decision to disguise himself as a hunter in the famous Shaivite myth where this great god challenges Arjuna in a contest over who can successfully spear a wild boar. In this story Shiva is a wild man, a forest hunter who is skilled with his bow. This is a test which Shiva's darker side wins, but then he turns to praise Arjuna's penance and hands him his critical weapon of war, the Pasupata.

8 The Story Told by the Stars: Babylonian Star-Lore and the Hindu Nakshatras

1 India also has an important starlore tradition (the Nakshatra system of time reckoning). It is significant, too, but the correspondences to be found there with the Ponnivala Nadu story specifically, are less compelling. There is no wild boar seen in the Indian system of reading the stars and many other character-correspondences are also

missing. The Indian system is less visual and relates more to a mapping of a generalized human body onto the sky (Beck 1976), than to the mapping of specific stories on to the same.

2 There is also a wild boar on the earliest known Egyptian star map, the Dendera zodiac.
3 White 2014a, Frontispiece. White's Babylonian star map has been an inspiration to me and very helpful in thinking about what seemed at first to be a very unlikely set of Tamil and Babylonian story tradition correspondences. The author is very grateful to White for his support and helpful correspondence. The boar is actually mentioned twice in White's diagram, once at the autumn equinox and again in the early spring when he emerges from darkness as a reborn, youthful, and gentle being. Although he states that some elements of his star map are speculative, the details concerning the specific placement of certain figures in the sky are not important details to me. It is the overall correspondence of his work with the underlying themes of the Ponnivala Nadu story that are of interest here.
4 Although the equinox can be determined by carefully accessing the length of each day in relation to the length of each night, the common habit was to use the rising of a specific star pattern just before sunrise as the main sign of its arrival.
5 All of the information provided in the sections that follow, whenever the Babylonian star signs are discussed, has been drawn from White's encyclopedic work (2014a). I do not footnote each detail as his discussion of each item can be easily found using White's well-alphabetized presentation.
6 This Mesopotamian story makes me think of the story of Varaha who raises the goddess of the earth (Bhudevi) up out of the waters on one tusk. If we link Varaha to the boar constellation of (autumn) and think of him as bringing up an egg-earth-goddess from the deep, it would appropriately hatch at around the time the Makara-Capricorn constellation appeared (the winter solstice discussed above).
7 I have also studied the Nakshatra system of star constellations, known in India since ancient times, quite extensively. As best as has so far unearthed in my search, there is nothing like this kind of amazing match-up to be seen when that equally important star-based system is examined for parallels.
8 White and many others say that these seven, in Babylonia, were generally spoken of as males. But one author, Verdamme, who specializes in this subject says there were also seven females who held a similar position, assisting the Hendursaga, a complex Sumerian god who had both positive and negaltive qualities. He was assisted by three hepads, one of which was made up of female goddesses (Verdamme, 111).
9 White 2014a, 89–91.
10 White discusses these shifts in the understanding of the Bull of Heaven, which he associates with the winged gate (something like a passageway used by a go-between that is half human and half divine). This newer version of the Bull of Heaven seems to appear late in the 3rd millennium BCE, when grand animal is depicted as crouching in front of a god. He or goddess in a posture that looks much more like Shiva's Nandi.

I think we can equate this with the idea of the bull being a king who is an aid or associate of the gods. He is a great leader of the people, and is thus referred to as a "great bull" who respects the gods and serves them through his work on earth. Kunnutaiya, a human son born of Shiva's semen, and then placed on earth by that god, became that sort of highly respected leader after his marriage and his return to Ponnivala Nadu.

11 It must be made clear to readers that White is not just sketching these many star groupings using his own imagination. On the contrary, he consistently references actual examples found in ancient Mesopotamian art that he has faithfully replicated in his drawings. He also identifies the sources he has used for each of these images.

12 White (2014b, 74–6) provides some very interesting sketches of ancient tablets, dating back as far as the mid 3rd millennium BCE, where a scorpion is seen under a bed where human copulation is occurring, and also one where it is seen under what appears to be a birthing couch.

13 Beck 1992, 326–7.

14 White 2014a, 127.

15 See chapter 9 for a further discussion of this imagery.

16 Beck 1992, 726–7.

17 This is not a topic that can be explored here, but the possibility of some direct contact, given the amazing degree of overlap with Babylonian star-lore that has just been outlined, is certainly probable. Some, including White, have suggested that this must have been due to Greek and Roman contacts, but I am not convinced. There are many details described here that fit better with Babylonian traditions than with Greek and Roman ones, as best as can be discerned at this point. The issue of still earlier contact having occurred between the Tamils and Babylonia requires further careful research. What we do know is that the Tamils were famous for their sailing skills and for their travels as traders, at least by the time of documented Greek and Roman contact.

18 I follow Sutton's information on this, although she does not give the description of these body parts much importance (2014). The references are scattered through her book, which is organized to follow the standard Nakshatra sequence, making these details easy to find.

19 The core concept being discussed, the constellations seen in the sky, naturally involves their very visible rotation that can be seen on any clear night. Thus it would be reasonable to represent the whole using a circular layout. Nonetheless, a diagram of these principles can be expressed in either a circle or square form and both cultures seem to have preferred to use a square. No matter which form was chosen, however, these two ways of mapping constellation movements can be understood as more-or-less interchangeable.

20 It must also be said that the Babylonian star map, at least as sketched by White, is far more visual. His use of illustrations to identify the twenty-six motifs linked to those various map segments is very helpful in advancing one's understanding of their significance. Unfortunately, I have never found any equivalent visualization of the

twenty-seven Nakshatras (twenty-eight if one includes Abhijit, as done here in figure 8.4). And the link to various mythical stories, though present, is also not nearly as clear. (Sutton is the best source this author has yet found for this). This lack of visualization has, unfortunately, restricted my ability to make a list of much more specific comparisons.

21 White is well aware of this basic logic. He writes about this in several places, and I am not claiming any new insights in this regard. What is new with this research project, however, is the discovery of a significant crossover between this ancient Babylonian system and the Legend of Ponnivala Nadu story. One could argue that this is because the Indus Valley civilization displays links to both these cultures and that it is the uniting factor. I would disagree, but the Indus Valley materials are still opaque due to the lack of a definitive deciphering of the writing displayed on the wide array of seals found in that area. Where the Indus Valley sits in this cultural mapping is complex and that discussion must be left for another time.

22 The Tamil Nadu New Year now falls about three weeks after the actual moment of the spring equinox. This is likely because of the stars' precession. That is, the star patterns have rotated clockwise over time. The festival's core symbolism became linked to a particular constellation, which once rose just before dawn around 2200 BCE, but the festival's calendrical positioning likely became fixed at a later date, perhaps around the beginning of the Christian era. The result is confusing but means that now these days of winter solstice celebration happen three weeks after the technical winter solstice occurs, just as the spring festival occurs three weeks after the official spring equinox date.

9 The Shining Lotus Plant: A Visual Approach to Finding Hidden Paradigms

1 Bosch 1960. Figure 9.1 reproduces his figure 11: The Basic Form (79).
2 Ibid.
3 This spine concept relates well to certain key assumptions very familiar to Indic tradition, themes referenced by many yoga philosophers; that the goal of such practices is to move or assist the ascension of the body's energy upwards with its end position being located at the centre of the human forehead, readied for is eventual release. In sum, the shining lotus plant also serves as a grand metaphor for the human body itself.
4 Bosch does, however, discuss his concept in relation to a very pervasive Hindu vision of the body as a microcosm of the universe at large (1960, 80–1).
5 Bosch's very rich library of examples have not been included, as space is at a premium. Instead, the author has decided to note some of the most helpful plates in his work, ones that best illustrate the most important parallels being discussed.
6 Bosch does not name his concept as a whole, just its pieces. But it would be fair to say that his diagram represents the visual canonization of a form that he believes embodies the basic structure of a sacred lotus plant.

7 The kāla head can equally be called the kirtimukha (translated as glorious face), the term Bosch seems to prefer. We have stuck with the term kāla, believing that these two terms reference the same motif: a scary face with huge fangs, a gaping mouth, often a lolling tongue and bulging eyes as well.
8 Bosch discusses this in relation to his underlying sense that the lotus is a human body metaphor that has, of course, a right and left side. I also, coincidentally, discussed this important right-left symbolism at length in my 1972 book.
9 Bosch 1960, 21.
10 Bosch 1960, 21–2.
11 Also known as the Gharial crocodile or Mutalai (in Tamil).
12 Figure 9.5 is an enhanced version (for better visibility of the underlying idea) of Seal M482 as documented in Joshi and Parpola 1987, 1:116.
13 The topic of the importance of the crocodile as a symbolic creature for the early residents of the Indus Valley civilization is a fascinating one and worthy of further research. But that must be left aside as being too lengthy a diversion for discussion here. See Parpola 2011 and Ganesan 2016 for further tantalizing details. The association in Bihar with the entrance to a cave also bears further enquiry. I especially note the link between cave entrances and a makara in the Ponnivala Nadu story, something that will be discussed further, at a later point.
14 The recent renovations to the Mariyamman temple in Gannapuram have given heightened emphasis to this same idea, and more generally to the great cosmic lotus concept. Chapter 10 will discuss these parallels in detail.
15 This may be something more commonly seen in Shaivite settings, or Shaivite regions of South Asia. I am not sure about this.
16 They are also photographs I took before I realized that these details would be of real interest. That is why close-ups of these features were not obtained on site.
17 The eye has been slightly enhanced in each case for added clarity.
18 Robert Beer has rightly written about the makara as a composite animal, saying that it is composed of several beasts that collectively reflect the essence of a crocodile. He specifically mentions that two of the key components in this are the parallels to be seen between a crocodile's lower jaw and the tusks and ears of the wild boar (2003, 77).
19 A whole young boar was also a desirable animal that could be sacrificed, at least that was the case in this area where I lived some fifty-five years ago.
20 All the folk images seen in these illustrations were drawn without my input, nearly twenty years ago. The artist knew nothing of Bosch or of any other general theories attempting to describe Hindu themes and principles. He was a village boy who knew the story well and who simply drew on ideas he held in his own heart.
21 Significantly, in Tamil, the term makara refers to a crocodile. Among other things it is the vehicle of Kama, the god of love and desire. It is also a significant animal in the Indus Valley, a key source of India's heritage culture. Scorpions are also associated with fertility (White 2014b, 74–6). In the Ponnivala Nadu story a scorpion bites

Kunnutaiya just as the future mother of the heroes prepares to venture further on her pilgrimage to Kailasa to obtain an audience, and a pregnancy, from Shiva himself. It is as if that scorpion signals to him that a (immaculate) pregnancy for his barren wife, is close at hand. The scorpion is also associated with water and is known to appear when it rains. All these similarities link nicely with the shape and significance of the lotus rhizome.

22 During a visit to Assam a few years back, I was struck to learn that the wild boar is also a key figure in the folklore of that region. He was named Varaha there and it seems possible that the boar theme emphasized in these two very disparate areas of the South Asian continent are both related, in principle, to the symbolism of the lotus rhizome.

23 That is, its sounds can be likened to the voice of Vac, the goddess associated with the origins of speech and of the concept of communication using sound more generally.

24 Bosch himself admits that there is a strong equivalence between the padmamūla and the brahmamūla. Both nodes lie on the central stem and each has a creative force buried deep within itself. Both have the power to create new life. A possible analogy is that one is the parent and the other its child or seed, but like the chicken and the egg, these two seem most likely to recreate one another and thus depict an endless regenerative cycle.

25 Vajracharya (2014), discussed in the next chapter, equates the kāla head with an atmospheric cloud and/or a heavenly lotus pond. Pond water and clouds are not hot concepts, nor does either conjure up especially frightening images. But when we reference either in the context of death and transformation then both concepts do become scary. Reaching Nirvana and escaping rebirth still involves a passage through a deathlike dissolution according to the broad Hindu worldview. This is a dissolution into a liquid or airy state in which one becomes transparent or invisible. Because of the kāla head's open mouth imagery there is also a suggestion that one may well be eaten and digested during this passage to that ultimate state of eternal existence in a heaven high above. Hence it seems reasonable for the folk artist to reference frightening forms like large teeth and open mouths if they associate a kāla head with that passage. Surely it is scary to imagine oneself, currently a living entity, being converted into either some kind of atmospheric moisture or even just thin air. Both states of being suggest near-nothingness and with that, the total loss of personal identity. Nonetheless, Nirvana, Moksha, non-self, emptiness and the like all refer to a core Hindu and Buddhist concept that receives positive treatment in many philosophical texts, although these texts may display many subtle variations depending on the specific school of thought referenced.

26 Although the kāla head is not see on the summit of all temple towers, by any means, there is now a prominent kāla head on the top of the recently renovated Mariyamman temple in Gannapuram. Earlier this temple had a row of three kalasam-like pots framed by what the author took to be two paired half crescents, perhaps the horns of a sky-bull seen to be protecting the goddess. But it now, in the light of Bosch's work,

seems possible that those two shapes might also have been meant to reference the tusks or fierce teeth of an invisible kāla head. The next chapter discusses some interesting insights which Gautama Vajracharya has to offer on the subject of this head (2011–12). But it is worthy of note here that Vajracharya talks of the kāla head as a fearsome face-seen-in-the-clouds just before the monsoon rains begin. Certainly, the top of Bosch's diagram, which we have likened to a protective umbrella, could equally be interpreted to be a very dark rain cloud, something that expresses both a frightening and a hopeful new day to come, all wrapped into one.

27 Vajracharya, in the next chapter, makes the argument that these heads can be seen in the dark monsoon clouds and cites many examples although he does not specifically reference a lotus plant in his somewhat parallel reasoning.

28 This idea is strongly reinforced by the local festival for the goddess Mariyamman. In this annual festival, a buffalo was traditionally beheaded (paralleling Komban's severed head in the Ponnivala story) and then that head was pounded into a hole in the ground in front of her temple and left there for the goddess to use for her regeneration work (Beck 1981). The ground in front of this shrine surely holds many buffalo heads that have been buried there in years past. Those skulls likely resemble the kāla head seen at the base of an icon of Durga (figure 9.6). It may also be that this form of the rhizome/makara relates to the goddess Ganga (a form of Durga/Mariyamman?) who was traditionally seen to ride on a makara that serves her, just as Durga rides on the buffalo that serves her.

29 Bosch 1960, 242–6.

30 There are also important antecedents of this Aśvin pair in early Mesopotamian myth where they are known as Mitra and Varuna respectively in the ancient Avesta texts. The Aśvin twins are also magical healers, which can be understood as another way of advancing renewal and even rebirth.

31 Bosch 1960, 183, and Doniger 2009, Rg. Veda, mentioned in her index-glossary.

32 The twin heroes, who resemble the Aśvins, live together with their unmarried sister in the Ponnivala Nadu legend, but any romantic attraction between them is very firmly suppressed and, if indeed present as a possible undertone, is never alluded to.

33 Bosch 1960, 184. He includes a footnote which makes his point about the Aśvins' antiquity even more forceful.

34 The Indus Valley seal (M296 as seen in Fig. 9.6b) has already been discussed. It appears to represent a plant paradigm very similar to the one Bosch presents. Furthermore, the two arms that lead outward from its Brahmamula look quite a bit like horses' heads. We have already noted the presence of the makara concept in this civilization's bundle of key symbolic elements. There is certainly more to explore here.

35 That stone is a statue of Ganesh, itself a significant choice. The artisan tries to kill Ponnar with the help of an icon of this beloved god. Of course he does not succeed and he looses his own life in the process. The gods prevail and the sun stays its course, rising from the waters of night as usual.

36 This is a common Hindu image. I have been to a Hindu primary school in Canada where they celebrate a special ritual in the gymnasium each morning in which the

children are told to carefully nourish the tiny little flame that burns inside each one of them.
37 In some examples the eyes are excessively large, in others they are tight and angry, while in still others they bulge out in a very unnatural way.
38 Vajracharya, to be discussed in the next chapter, argues that faces like these that have extended tongues are cloud-based beings that are spitting out pearls, or perhaps rain drops as they bless or send gifts to those below. Certainly this is one possibility, but it is hard to dismiss the ambivalence many must feel in looking at these faces. At best they have two sides. It is hard to believe that these kāla are just benevolent beings that mean no harm.
39 The head shown in figure 9.27d also appears at the summit of the Mariyamman temple in Kannapuram, a temple that the residents of the village where I lived visited frequently. Both there and as shown here, the design of the head exhibits a strong similarity with kirtimukha faces seen in Nepal (Beer 2003, 79) where jewels descend from the upper jaw of this head and the lower jaw is missing.
40 In the scene where this occurs Vishnu is present in the disguise of a washerman and is claiming that his wife has pregnancy cravings. When he secures Komban's head and drags it off saying it is for her we can guess the goddess in question is Bhudevi because Vishnu, in his boar form (Varaha) is married to her (the goddess of the earth). There is also the possibility that this wife he is referring to may also be a form of Kottravai, an ancient Tamil goddess of the forest related to both Durga and Kali.
41 Neumayer 2013, 109, 118–23, and Beck 2016a and b.
42 Beck 2016a and b. In some scenes the boar's testes are referenced, suggesting the idea of magical fertility. Infant boars are sometimes depicted as well. And the rock art appears to show humans collecting a boar's back hairs. This is also something that Komban's hunter, Shambuga, does in the Ponnivala story. These back hairs seem to contain curative magic. For example, Shambuga burns some of the hairs he stole from the boar while standing directly in the doorway of the tent where the twin heroes lie sick. Shankar suddenly feels better as he breathes in that acrid aroma.
43 These same assistants appear in the animated version of the epic as Yeman's helpers, as well (see figure 9.4). Vajracharya stresses the idea that kāla faces appear in dark rain clouds. Those monsoon clouds are black and ominous at first but eventually produce new vegetal and animal life resulting from the copious rains that everyone knows will follow.
44 South Asia is replete with stories of women who pass through fire to be purified and born anew, the most famous of course being the heroine of the Ramayana, named Sita.
45 Being able to swallow something large and being hollow inside seem to be mythically related. Handelman and Shulman (1997) discuss this process of becoming hollowed out, at some length. Also note that Tamarai can be understood to be dramatically hollowed out, too, while she sits meditating on that pillar. This is the moment when two

428   Notes to pages 345–54

parrots who were earlier nesting inside her, depart through her nose. Clearly those two birds leave empty the cavity inside her where they once had nested.

46   For example, as seen in Bosch's plates 15a, 19, 20, and 21 (1960).

47   The role of serpents, especially cobras, is worthy of a separate enquiry. There is much to say on this topic but there is no room for that discussion in this chapter. A cobra's open hood can also be compared, visually, with a creature showing the world its open mouth or even the idea of their having a huge hollow tube that connects to that gateway (figure 10.25 provides a vivid example of this). Snakes swallow their prey whole, another indication that they may have a huge hollow inside. Note, as well, that in the ancient Indian game of snakes and ladders, a player caught in a cobra's mouth quickly slides all the way down to its tail where he or she must then start their journey upward all over again.

48   Bosch 1960, 123. He writes "the primal lotus is hidden in the darkness of the waters from which root sprang the organism of the cosmic tree and which is at the same time the bearer, the Dharma of the universe."

49   Ibid., 68. Bosch's comment likely refers to Indus seal M296, figure 9.6a in this text.

50   There are also references by Bosch, and many others, suggesting that a great upside-down tree also exists, one whose roots reach into the sky while its branches grow downwards. While this does not match well with the banyan tree whose aerial roots hang down (not up) and nor with any other actual botanical species of tree we are aware of either, it is certainly possible that the great Ficus benghalensis could be referenced here as seen reflected in a lotus pool next to which it stands. In that inverse position, mirrored on the surface of the pool, it would appear to be growing downwards, perhaps even to merge with a lotus plant seen there, while those aerial roots would appear to stretch upwards as if the tree were rooted in the sky. Such a vision would be most likely to occur at sunrise or sunset, when reflections are at their best, and which is also a liminal and mysterious time in general, a moment when mythical thinking is very likely.

51   Parpola, 2015, 126–7. Parpola provides Rg. Vedic and other classical text references that document the early importance of these ideas.

52   At times this slide can be down the steep incline believed to be a tunnel-like passage inside the body of the snake. See footnote 49.

53   The Nakshatra specialist Komila Sutton references these ideas nicely in relation to the star cluster named Uttara Ashadha (Sutton 2014, 198–9). It is notable that she states "between Sagittarius and Capricorn the Sun is in a state of flux. The ingress between Sagittarius and Capricorn is the point where the sun is reborn every year," which is the exact point of the winter solstice according to popular South Asian astrological thinking. As mentioned earlier, this day is called Makara Sankranti in Tamil, literally meaning the point where the crocodile crosses over between constellations, and more figuratively, the point where it transforms the sun. It seems that it does so by swallowing it whole.

54   This is a very common temple origin myth. See Shulman (1997) for other examples.

10 The Monsoon Rains: Filling a Lotus Pond and Nourishing a Golden River

1. Ample rain is praised in about 6 per cent of the total corpus of songs the bard sang while telling this story. Many more speak of fine cows, ripe paddy fields, and other related agricultural topics that are important local themes celebrating well-being and prosperity. The Kāveri River is mentioned 294 times, for example, largely as a translation of the Tamil term for the area where the heroes live: Ponnivala Nadu or "Land of the Golden River." The metaphor suggests that abundant flowing water is the equivalent of liquid gold. This is the fundamental idea behind the image highlighted by that name.
2. Ponnar (Poṇṇayyā) is the elder twin, in the story. His name literally translates into English as "The Golden One." At several points this song groups the two brothers together and speaks of them as one. But it also emphasizes that this land springs from true gold, gold hidden beneath the earth itself. The elder twin is named as golden, and the same term is used in the description of at least twenty different objects, including ploughs, fingers, garlands, and more. The Ponnivala area is said to belong to Ponnar, the one chosen to rule it. In songs he wears a signature gold ring, a symbol of the grand monarch who sits on the throne. Even today young grooms are often gifted a gold ring at their wedding, a reference to this same idea, that they are a king-to-be. We will discuss the purposeful ambiguity of whether there are two brothers/rulers, or just one, after a few other ideas have been discussed first.
3. Darshan refers to beholding an auspicious sight and the merit bestowed on the observer as a direct result of seeing or sensing that holy presence.
4. This is an important theme mentioned in many Sanskrit texts and in Sangam literature, the earliest corpus of Tamil poetry. Love, in particular, is linked to rain and to flooding in that body of literature. This is a time of joy, a period when there is also a certain degree of chaos and sexual freedom not seen at other times of the year.
5. Gopies are the many intimate female friends of Radha, Krishna's wife, as well of Krishna himself.
6. Aestivation is the act of going dormant, that is, of being dried out and still during the hot season that precedes the rains. Frogs bury themselves in the mud to aestivate, during this period and then come out croaking (singing) as the world begins to flood around them. Some fish, turtles, and other aquatic creatures do the same thing.
7. Vajracharya points to a number of these babies in illustrations that can be seen on the ceilings of the Ajanta caves.
8. This paraphrases and simplifies some of Vajracharya's work in my effort to communicate his central concepts to readers of this work. Vajracharya's thoughts are fresh and innovative, and his thinking has inspired some of my own recent observations. Readers should consult his writings directly and discover his massively detailed examples for themselves.
9. Makara-like animals are also carved on many of these fountains, linking them nicely to ideas discussed by Bosch and featured earlier in chapter 9. Here these open mouths

flow with liquids carrying new life, rather than swallowing up the living, a theme discussed extensively in the previous chapter.
10 That river is metaphorically referred to as the Ganges. A connection with the real Ganges is accomplished via a mythical underground channel.
11 Both these temples are located on the outskirts of Gannapuram, and they share a common wall.
12 These makara spouts do, of course, have droplets of water flowing out of them from time to time. Devotees deliberately circle the temple's exterior in order to be able to slide their right hand under such a spout to collect this holy water which they will then sprinkle on their own head, and/or drink as a liquid blessing.
13 Architectural features are the subject of discussion here. Of course, folk paintings that describe mythical stories can be noted in many temple contexts, and sometimes (at least in the Kongu area), painted pottery statures of various story characters can be seen as well.
14 Hot and cool are an extremely important pair of concepts in local life in the Kongu area. The idea is especially applied to foods, the majority of which are classified as having either a heating or cooling effect on the human body when consumed. See the appendix of Beck 1969 for additional details. A lotus is considered an edible food.
15 The lion is also the vehicle of the goddess Mariyamman.
16 It is worth noting that in many traditional Tamil homes the wooden pillars that hold up the veranda are much wider at their base than at the top, Yet they rest on a slender neck of stone that swells into something round (rather like a stylized pot) underneath. That slender neck actually emphasizes the fact that the foot of such pillars have a swollen look. I had always wondered why this odd pillar shape existed as, to my eye, it did not have any particular added beauty or special function. Now the idea becomes clear: the pillar is shaped to suggest that it is auspiciously swollen with water which, due to gravity, has flowed downward and thus has enlarged or expanded its base.
17 This is the Madukkarai Celandiamman temple, which is important to the Ponnivala epic story tradition and references the heroes in several of its shrines. See figure 10.10a for a sketch of its main gate and the story characters that sit on top of that entrance arch.
18 If one looks closely at an actual photo (figure 10.10b) one can see a fish-like shape swimming inside this fountain spigot (look carefully at box 1), again suggesting that it is intended to represent a waterspout that directs water downwards from a heaven-based lotus pond on to people walking beneath it as they enter this temple sanctuary. It also suggests that this water may have life-like creatures swimming in it, confirming that that this is a life-giving elixir par excellence.
19 See chapter 9 for more details. Here the tree parallels what Bosch has labelled the Central Branch in his diagram (1960).
20 Each of these pillars resembles a Karthikai deepam, a high post on which a pot or bowl holding burning embers is placed during the Tamil month of Kathikai (mid-November–mid-December). Tamarai and her husband set out on their pilgrimage to Kailasa to meet

with Lord Shiva just after this important festival, which takes place on the full moon day of that special month. For a detailed discussion of fire and water symbolism as these themes are employed in numerous Sanskrit texts, see O'Flaherty 1971.
21 This would seem to locate the kāla heads discussed by Bosch adjacent to the brahmamūla. Bosch and Vajracharya, however, both largely avoid discussion of this negative kāla imagery and its associated fiery heat, likely due to their keen sense that such themes have inauspicious overtones.
22 Vajracharya 2013, 20.
23 There are further possible associations here, especially with Shiva in the form of Bhairava, who at his fieriest is called Kāla Bhairava. Kāla Bhairava is often represented by a head that is associated with and said to guard Saivite goddess temples, like those dedicated to Mariyamman and Kāli. Furthermore, idols of Bhairava are generally situated on the north side of a larger Shiva temple compound and face west. In such temples the larger ritual routine begins with the Sun or Surya and ends with Bhairava, a god whose idol often has protruding teeth and terrifying looks. Adding to this frightening demeanor, the image is often garlanded with red flowers (referencing its ferocity and its association with death and blood). See Handelman and Shulman, 1997, for a wealth of additional information on this subject. This whole layout echoes multiple ideas presented in chapter 8, including the idea of a core annual cycle linked to death and rebirth both of humans and of the sun at the winter solstice moment.
24 Tangal, as seen in figure 10.25 is a good example of this.
25 Vajracharya also cites a story of the snake that formed Shiva's bangles being asked to stop pouring rain and instead create a ladder. This set of double images suggests that snakes can nurture life from above, in the form of falling rain, but also assist its assent from below via a ladder. Figure 10.29 seems to be an interesting reference to how Tamarai's staircase to Kailasa has been designed to look like the body of a snake, but in this case with its tail, rather than its head, pointing upward, and with the gate she passes through being the gateway built over the path leading to the god's realm high above. Perhaps she is about to be swallowed as she heads for the snake's tail. She has yet to undergo the seven rebirths that will occur as she sits on the pillar she will shortly find.
26 Babylonian traditions, seen linked to the story in chapter 7, associate scorpions with fertility and a subsequent pregnancy (White 2014b, 74–6). This singular scorpion bite, the only one recounted in this story, may presage the fact that Tamarai will eventually be impregnated by Lord Shiva when she finally reaches his council chambers.
27 This episode can be found in Beck 1992 and 2021a. Unfortunately, a plant version of this frog scene replaced this frog in the story's animated and graphic novel equivalents. This was done at the lead animator's suggestion. He felt very uncomfortable drawing images of a squished frog. He also felt that children watching or reading these versions might be upset by the same.
28 Louis Dumont speaks of productive "handfuls of mud" taken from the location of an old temple to a new location by the Kallar community whenever they begin to build a new shrine (1957). Tamarai does something similar when she takes mud from near

her old family palace and uses it to curse (and purify) that palace after her brothers refuse her entry, which is one of her basic female rights. Mud is also important in the annual Mariyamman festival rituals where devotees pour water over and over again around the entire temple exterior, making everything near its walls very muddy (Beck 1981). This surely refers to the idea of a new beginning and the possible rise of a new life energy from the mud itself.

29 Hiltebeitel 1991b. It may be that the ritual of planting seeds in a square shallow tray is primarily associated with Brahmin-supervised temple activities. I do not remember seeing that specific kind of ritual planting in situations where a Brahmin priest was not involved. The erection of a milk post, however, is very common and does not require a Brahmin.

30 See Beck 2020.

31 The northwest corner of the ritual site is especially valued as the spot for a milk post's erection.

32 In Beck 1964 we see in detail how this milk post is more popular and given more and more centrality, the farther down in the caste hierarchy observations are made. The lower-ranked castes have no sacred fire, do not engage a Brahmin priest, and instead have the newly wedded couple circumambulate this important post making it into the central ritual symbol of the entire event. This finding also matches with Vajracharya's reasoning about themes that were likely central to South Asian ritual activities on the plains well before the arrival of the Vedic poets, whose attention was, instead, focused on the importance of a sacrificial fire, being as they were, a people who hailed from the snowy steppes of Central Asia.

33 The Mariyamman festival pots make this opposition clear. That festival deliberately alternates a pot of green, cool leaves set on an upright post during the day with a hot pot full of embers set on the same post each night (Beck 1981).

34 Azadirachta indica, a leaf used in medicines and its flowers are valued for local ritual use. These leaves are considered to be cooling and to have curative properties, especially for the pox category of diseases thought due to excessive bodily heat. Significantly, this is said to be a very drought-resistant species. The leaves can be eaten as a vegetable as well. This photograph has been modified in order to insert a traditional clay pot as would have been originally used but which is now difficult to find.

35 Beck 1994 clearly demonstrates, based on detailed marriage ritual descriptions provided by the British ethnographer Edgar Thurston in 1906, that the importance given to sacred vegetal pots increases as one descends the social hierarchy, while the centrality of feeding sacred fire lessens in importance. Further, the reference to a sacred fire is absent entirely wherever a Brahmin priest is not hired to be present to care for it and to provide the appropriate accompanying chants.

36 This idea has already been discussed, in some detail, in the previous two chapters.

37 This means: the place where Tamarai is doing penance, the place where she has gone to die.

38 Again, not the actual Ganges but a stream near her penance pillar that is poetically equated with that great river.
39 Of course, there is an obvious parallel here with the traditional Hindu funeral where a body's remaining bones are extracted from the funeral pyre and then emersed in a river (preferably the Ganges) as the mourner hopes for his loved one's rebirth at a later point.
40 Kramrisch 1946, vol. 1, 40–3, and elsewhere in the same volume.
41 Vajracharya 1913, 144, figure 7.2.
42 Vajracharya, significantly, remarks on the fact that images of meditating ascetic figures are often seen placed under or very near these water fountains. He has captured an image of one of these stone-carved ascetic figures (Vajracharya 2013, 148, figure 7.8).
43 We include in this generalization about images of rising serpents, a theme deeply embedded in yoga. The peaceful Nandi, usually seen with his legs folded under him, rather like a seated human ascetic with legs crossed, is another animal form suggestive of this. Nandi is a virile bull, not a castrated ox. But his sexual energy is controlled and directed inward. His sole desire is to serve his master Shiva. Both animal forms are understood, through these common and very popular image forms, to have set aside their own ego in order to redirect their personal energy such that it feeds into a broader life-generating force believed active in the universe at large. The serpent seen in figure 10.25 is doing just that. Tangal, the lady he protects, embodies that creative life force and will soon use it to bring new life to her two deceased siblings.
44 This is called having a paccai manacu. The substances used for these baths exit the temple through a channel described above and pictured in figure 10.3. Other worshippers can partake of these substances by imbibing a cupped handful of this liquid blessing, which they are free to collect from this exterior spout.
45 This is the Tamil name for Durva grass or Cynodon dactylon. The term is a synonym for sun, and it is a very sacred herb. It is a symbol of revival, like the phoenix bird. It can grow anywhere and at any time.

Annotated Bibliography of Primary Epic Story Sources, by Chapter

The Epic of Ponnivala Nadu (A Story with Many Names) – Chapters One, Seven, and Eight

No one has published a full-length text, in English, of the Ponnivala Nadu story except myself and I have produced several versions of the story that students can and should consult. These are:

Beck, Brenda. 2023. *Land of the Golden River: The Medieval Folk Epic of Ponnivala Nadu,* Victoria, BC: Friesen Press (available via Amazon.com).

An almost identical version of this story was published in 1992 under the title *Elder Brothers Story* (known as the *Annanmar Kathai* in Tamil), vols. 1 and 2. Madras: Institute of Asian Studies. (If one can read Tamil this is a good way to source the original text of this story, told directly in the words the village bard used to dictate his account, over many days, to my local Tamil scribe). This work, spread over two volumes, provides the Tamil original and the author's English translation on facing pages for easy reference. Unfortunately, this book set is very hard to find these days, but some libraries do have copies. The 2023 version only provides a translated English version of the text but has the convenience of being contained within one relatively inexpensive volume that can easily be purchased from several internet sources. It also has a long, original Introduction, new diagrams and maps, a glossary, story summaries, and the convenience of having a thorough index.

Beck, Brenda. 2013. A thirteen-hour animated video program comprised of twenty-six separate half hour segments. This serial video version of the story was broadcast in Canada in 2013 on the Asian Television Network (in English and in Tamil) and in South India (in Tamil) on Thanthi TV in 2014. To watch these animated episodes, go to https://ark.digital.utsc.utoronto.ca/ark:/61220/utsc1. You can also use the adjacent QR code to access these online video episodes. Access to these videos is free of charge.

Beck, Brenda. 2013 and 2015. *The Legend of Ponnivala: A Graphic Novel in Two Volumes*. Amazon: Create Space.

Presented in 26 segments, each substory being 36 pages long, told with full colour illustrations that use a traditional South Indian folk-art style. Order in Tamil or English. Published in 2013 via Create Space and available as a print-on-demand purchase at Amazon.com. Republished by N.I.A. Educational Institutions Pollachi, Tamil Nadu, India in 2015 (also in both languages). Each of the 26 segments of this graphic novel is also available separately on Amazon in Tamil and in English as a small, young student-friendly, graphic "comicbook." Some of these materials can also be partially viewed online at http://www.ponnivala.com. A different selection is available at http://www.sophiahilton.ca. Two further websites provide a variety of teacher-friendly materials that build on the Land of the Golden River story. Go to www.ponnivala.com and www.sophiahilton.ca to access these resources. Other resource materials can be obtained by contacting the author.

Beck, Brenda. 1965. Unpublished.

A tape recording of an actual performance. A short except from the thirty-eight hours of audio can be heard online at https://folkways.si.edu/erucanampalayam-ramasami-and-olappalayam-palanisami/annanmar-katai-the-birth-of-the-queens-triplets-six-excerpts/india-world/music/album/smithsonian. These excerpts provide a listener with a feel of the bard's presentation, as he sang. (A request to make access to these recordings free for students is pending.)

Caktikanal, Palaṇicāmi. 1972. *Aṇṇaṇmār Cuvāmi Katai*. Coimbatore, Tamil Nadu: Veṟṟivēl Patipakam.

This work is entirely in Tamil. It is a reprint that includes added introductory essays but that cites a palm leaf manuscript as its primary source. It provides access to another variant of the Ponnivala Nadu story. Some key differences with the version collected by the current author are discussed in Beck, 1982.

Krishnaswami, P. 2012. "Interview with Singer Devanampalayam Mylasamy."

This constitutes one small part of an excellent and much larger research archive developed by P. Krishnaswami who served as Principal Investigator. He is an Adjunct Professor,

Languages, Christ University, Bangalore. The archive is housed there and is titled *Floating Cultures. Voices from the Hinterland: Many Shades of India's Oral Traditions – A Study of a Tamil Folk Epic, Annanmar Kathai* (the AMK Project).

The Mahabharata – Chapter Two

The Mahabharata is to Hindu India a little bit like what the Bible is to Christian countries in the West. It is sacred and beloved, and most of the people resident on the subcontinent know quite a bit about the stories contained within it. There are also many, many versions available in a variety of languages. Also similar is that there are substantial differences in what various devotees and story fans think the Mahabharata's main message is. There is even more variation, however, in the story details known to scholars, especially when all the folk renditions that are performed in a wide variety of festival settings are considered. The Mahabharata is also different from the Bible in that it is usually paired and contrasted with the Ramayana, a second great story known across the subcontinent and beyond. The most authoritative, classical version of the Mahabharata that I know of in English is:

Van Buitenen, J.A.B, trans. and ed. 1973–8. *The Mahabarata*. 5 vols. Chicago: University of Chicago Press.

Two more volumes, numbers 6 and 7, have been completed since then by translator James L. Fitzgerald who took over this huge work after van Buitenen's untimely death. Three more volumes are still anticipated in order to complete this ambitious project. The work is very useful if one is searching for an authoritative translation of specific paragraphs or small segments of the story. Furthermore, the books that are available are well indexed.

Another well-known translation is a ten-volume boxed set, available in paperback but still expensive due to its vast size:

Debroy, Bibek, trans. 2014. *The Mahabharata*. 10 vols. Gurgaon, Haryana: Penguin Books India

For an introductory reading, however, I recommend two lively but greatly condensed versions that make for easier and more pleasurable reading. These are:

Narayana, R.K. 1978. *The Mahabharata*. New York: Viking Press.
Pattanaik, Devdutt. 2010. *The Mahabharata*. New Delhi: Penguin India.

The Pattanaik edition has many entertaining hand-drawn sketches added that were drawn by this multi-talented author himself.

The list goes on. One can find many, many more editions of this major story with a simple search of the internet. In addition, a significant (now iconic) series of film episodes telling the Mahabharata story was broadcast via India's national TV, *Doordarshan*, between October 1988 and June 1990. That broadcast included ninety-six episodes, each approximately one hour long. Animators have built on this success to develop animated versions of various story excerpts. Other dramatic versions have also been produced for mass media consumption.

Perhaps the most comprehensive critical work discussing the Mahabharata in its many versions makes a useful read for those seeking an overview and some perspective on this great story:

Hiltebeitel, Alf. 2001. *Rethinking the Mahabharata: A Reader's Guide to the Education of the Dharma King.* Chicago: Chicago University Press.

This study does not depend on any one version of the Mahabharata. Instead, it focuses on the kinship structure of the story and the contrastive characteristics of the key protagonists since these features remain more-or-less constant across versions. My intention has been to focus on commonalities across the best-known text-based versions, not on the details of variation. I cannot recommend a book or article that does a good job of comparing versions as, to my knowledge such a thorough study of this kind has not yet been published.

The Epic of Gilgamesh – Chapter Three

The Epic of Gilgamesh is perhaps the earliest epic for which we have a recorded text. It is extremely important for the history of Western civilization and has been translated a number of times and studied by many scholars. There is a lot of information available on the internet about it.

Translations

PRIMARY TRANSLATIONS CONSULTED

George, Andrew R., trans. 1999. *The Epic of Gilgamesh: The Babylonian Poem and Other Texts in Akkadian and Sumerian.* Penguin Classics Series. London: Penguin.

This work represents the primary translation used in this study. George's book includes a long and especially useful introduction, a map, a few sketched illustrations drawn by the translator, plus a range of other Babylonian texts and poems, an appendix and a glossary but no index:

Another translation that was also consulted is:

Mitchell, Stephen. 2004. *Gilgamesh: A New English Version.* New York: Simon and Schuster.

A few of many other translations that are available are:

Jastrow, M., *and A.* Clay. 1920. *An Old Babylonian Version of the Gilgamesh Epic: On the Basis of Recently Discovered Texts.* New Haven, CT: Yale University Press.
Kovacs, Maureen Gallery. 1989. *The Epic of Gilgamesh: An English Version with an Introduction.* Stanford: Stanford University Press.
Foster, Benjamin R. 2001. *The Epic of Gilgamesh: A New Translation, Analogues, Criticism.* New York: Norton.
Mason, Herbert. 2003. *Gilgamesh: A Verse Narrative.* 1970. Reprinted, Boston: Mariner Books.

Annotated Bibliography of Primary Epic Story Sources   439

A very helpful and well-acclaimed visual resource on Mesopotamian mythic and artistic traditions from the Gilgamesh period, as well as added traditions that are dated somewhat later is:

Black, Jeremy, and Anthony Green. 1992. *Gods, Demons and Symbols of Ancient Mesopotamia*. Austin: University of Texas Press.

Two helpful additional resources providing more general information on Mesopotamian religious beliefs during the Gilgamesh period are:

Jacobsen, Thorkilld. 1976. *The Treasures of Darkness: A History of Mesopotamian Religion*, New Haven: Yale University Press.

and

Dalley, Stephanie, ed. 2000. *Myths from Mesopotamia: Creation, the Flood, Gilgamesh, and Others*. Oxford: Oxford University Press.

Plenty of further information is available via the internet, all of which is accessible using common research procedures.

The Bible (Old and New Testaments Combined) – Chapter Four

There is a vast literature available about the Bible, and a great many alternate versions exist nowadays. These include ones available in almost all the world's numerous written languages, due to extensive missionary activity throughout the nineteenth and twentieth centuries. It is difficult to select just one or two translations or adaptations to recommend. Students are advised to select a version that is easy to obtain and that makes them comfortable given their own religious background and perspective. Some versions have simplified grammar and vocabulary, some choose more modern sentence forms. Some follow the language used in conventional church services. The King James version is the standard reference, but even that has many versions: This is one reasonable choice:

The King James Study Bible (Kindle Edition). 2017. Nashville, TN: Thomas Nelson (A division of Harper Collins).

This same text can also be purchased in hardcover. There are many variations available. An alternative approach is to select the following:

Metzger, Bruce, ed. 1982. *The Reader's Digest Bible*. Pleasantville, NY: The Reader's Digest Association.

The title of this work does not sound very scholarly, but I find it to be a very readable and relatively unbiased version that is useful for general study. It particularly suits those looking for a basic introduction to biblical studies and the central but very long and challenging text the Bible represents. This version has not been greatly abbreviated or condensed and contains an index, which is a very useful addition, particularly if the reader is hoping to pursue a very specific topic. If one is going to quote specific passages, then it is important to select one or more well-known versions and cite those references because the wording of individual sentences and phrases can vary widely. Bruce Metzger's work is a reliable reference point. He was a well-respected biblical scholar, translator and critical thinker who spent nearly a lifetime affiliated with the Princeton Theological Seminary. He died in 2007.

An additional book that is useful for interpretation and for an understanding of changing perspectives through the centuries is:

Frei, Hans. 1974. *The Eclipse of Biblical Narrative: A Study in Eighteenth and Nineteenth Century Hermeneutics*. New Haven: Yale University Press.

I reference this work in my own comparative discussion, as presented in this book.

The Icelandic Epic of Vatnsdaela – Chapter Five

There is only one modern version of the Vatnsdaela Saga available in English at present, the version used for this study (just below). This same work also provides the text of nine other sagas. plus additional Icelandic tales that reflect this same early oral story genre. This excellent book will introduce any interested reader to a wide range of saga texts:

Thorsson, Örnólfur. 2000. *The Sagas of Icelanders: A Selection*. New York: Penguin Books.

This book also includes several helpful appendices, a glossary and a good index.

There has been a lot of research done on Icelandic sages and a number of good articles on specific topics can be found on the internet. Two broad modern compilations of scholarly essays that cover a wide range of topics can be found in:

Jakobsson, Armann, and Sverrir Jakobsson, eds. 2017. *The Routledge Research Companion to the Medieval Icelandic Sagas*. New York: Routledge.

and

Ross, Margaret Clunies, ed. 2000. *Old Icelandic Literature and Society*. New York: Cambridge University Press.

A fairly extensive synopsis of the Vatnsdaela story, in English, is also accessible via the internet using straightforward search techniques.

The Ojibway Cycle of Stories about Nanabush (whose alternate name is Nana'b'oozoo) – Chapter Six

Coatsworth, Emerson, and David Coatsworth. 1979. *The Adventures of Nanabush: Ojibway Indian Stories* Illustrated by Francis Kagige. Toronto: Doubleday.

This is the book referenced in this study. It is an easy and pleasing read and has excellent illustrations.

Jones, William (collector), and Truman Michelson (editor). 1917. Ojibwa Texts. Vol. 7, pt. I, *Publications of the American Ethnological Society*, ed. Franz Boas. Leiden: E.J. Brill.

This is the authoritative collection of Ojibway stories about Nanabush. It is well worth a read by any student who wants to specialize specifically on Ojibway traditions.

Other books that focus on Ojibway stories that feature Nanabush and make excellent reading include:

Johnston, Basil. 1995. *The Manitous*. Illustrated by David Johnson. Toronto: Key Porter Books.

and the much shorter but also informative and entertaining:

Johnston, Basil. 1995. *The Bear-Walker*. Illustrated by David Johnson. Toronto: Royal Ontario Museum.

Two additional books that provide a broader overview of Ojibway storytelling and link these tales explicitly to modern issues concerned with Ojibway identity, independence, and pride are:

Broker, Ignatia. 1983. *Night Flying Woman: An Ojibway Narrative*. Illustrated by Steven Premo. St. Paul, MN.

Doerfler, Jill, et al. 2013. *Centering Aneshinaabeg Studies: Understanding the World through Stories*. East Lansing, MI: Michigan State University Press / Winnipeg: University of Manitoba Press.

It was while reading this work that I discovered the seven questions used that I have applied to this study: Roots, Reclamation, Resistance, Resilience, Relationships, Reflection, and Revelation. This interesting work provides a very helpful overview, from a Native perspective, of modern North American First Nations issues. Anishinaabe, it should be noted, is common term used by the Ojibway people to describe their unique identity.

General Bibliography

Andrews, Munya. 2004. *The Seven Sisters of the Pleiades: Stories from Around the World* North Melbourne: Spinifex Press.

Balkaran, Raj. 2020. *The Goddess and the Sun in Indian Myth.* London : Routledge.

Beck, Brenda E.F. 1964. "The Examination of Marriage Ritual among Selected Groups in South India." B.Litt. thesis. (Available to be read (on site) at the Bodleian Library, Oxford, Aleph System Number 019282038. A copy of the same is also available through the American Folklife Center of Library of Congress, Washington D.C., and via the University of Toronto Library, Scarborough as a part of the Beck research collection available there.)

— 1965. "A Thirty-eight Hour Taped Performance of the Annanmar Story," unpublished, fully transcribed, in Tamil only. Available by contacting the author.

— 1969. "Colour and Heat in South Indian Ritual." *Man* 4: 553–72. https://doi.org/10.2307/2798195.

— 1975. "A Praise Poem for Murugan." *Journal of South Asian Literature* 11, no. 1, 2: 95–116.

— 1976. "The Symbolic Merger of Body, Space and Cosmos in Hindu Tamilnad." *Contributions to Indian Sociology* 10: 213-43.

— 1981. "The Goddess and the Demon: A South Indian Festival in Its Wider Context." *Purusartha: Recherches de sciences socials sur l'Asie du Sud*, part 5, 82–136. Paris: Ecole des Hautes Etudes.

— 1982a. *The Three Twins: The Telling of a South Indian Folk Epic*, 248 pages. Bloomington: Indiana University Press. Now available as a download (due to an ACLS re-publication project) at: https://quod.lib.umich.edu/cgi/t/text/text-idx?c=acls;idno=heb33132.0001.001.

— 1982b. "The Courtship of Valli and Murugan: Some Parallels with the Radha-Krishna Story." In *The Divine Consort: Radha and the Goddesses of India*, ed. J. Hawley and D. Wulff, 262–77 and 360–2. Berkeley, CA: Berkeley Religious Studies Series.

— 1992. *Elder Brothers* Story (Known as the *Annanmar Katai* in Tamil), vols. 1 and 2, a folk epic of TamilNadu (in Tamil with English on facing pages), col., trans., and ed. by Brenda Beck, ca. 780 pages. Madras, TamilNadu: Institute of Asian Studies.

- 2011. "Discovering a Story." In *Hinduism in Practice*, ed. Hillary Rodrigues, 10–23. Oxon, UK: Routledge.
- 2013. *The Legend of Ponnivala: A Graphic Novel.* Amazon: CreateSpace. Available from Amazon.com (both Tamil and English versions) and via http://www.ponnivala.com.
- 2015. *The Legend of Ponnivala: A Graphic Novel.* Pollachi, TamilNadu, India: N.I.A. Educational Institutions.
- 2016a. "Divine Boar to Sacrificial Pig: References to Swine in the Sangam Texts, in Tamil Folk Tradition and in Ancient Astrological Art," part 1. *Pandanus* (Charles University, Prague) 16, no. 1: 29–54.
- 2016b. "Divine Boar to Sacrificial Pig: References to Swine in the Sangam Texts, in Tamil Folk Tradition and in Ancient Astrological Art," part 2. *Pandanus* (Charles University, Prague) 16, no. 2: 17–58.
- 2016c. "A Tamil Oral Folk History: Its Likely Relationship To Inscriptions & Archaeological Findings." In *Medieval Religious Movements and Social Change: A Report of a Project on the Indian Epigraphical Study*, ed. Noboru Karashima, 87–123. Tokyo: Toyo Bunko.
- 2018. "Becoming a Living Goddess" *The Oxford History of Hinduism: The Goddess*, ed. Mandakranta Bose, 201–41. Oxford: Oxford University Press.
- 2019a. "Resistance versus Rebellion in a South India Oral Epic: Two Modes of Opposition to an Expansionist, Self-Aggrandizing, Grain-Dependent State." *Asian Ethnography* 78, no. 2: 311–39.
- 2019b. "Kannimār Shrines and Iconography: A Set of Tamil Folk Goddesses Interpreted in a Pan-Indian Context." *Religions of South Asia* 13, no. 2: 188–229.
- 2020. "Women, Cows, and the Cosmic Womb: A Tamil Winter Solstice Festival." *Nidan: International Journal for Indian Studies* (South Africa) 5, no. 2: 27–50 (July and December).
- 2023. *Land of the Golden River: The Medieval Tamil Folk Epic of Poṉṉivaḷa Nāḍu.* Victoria, BC: Friesen Press.

Beer, Robert. 2003. *The Handbook of Tibetan Buddhist Symbols*. Delhi: Serindia Publications.

Berkson, Carmel. 1997. *The Divine and the Demoniac: Mahissa's Heroic Struggle with Durga*. Oxford: Oxford University Press.

- Bisht, R.S. 2015. "Excavations at Dholavira 2089–2005." https://www.scribd.com /document/422632739/Excavations-at-Dholavira-1989-2005-RS-Bi.

Black, Jeremy, and Green, Anthony. 2011. *Gods, Demons and Symbols of Ancient Mesopotamia: An Illustrated Dictionary*. Austin: University of Texas Press.

Bosch, F.D.K. 1960. *The Golden Germ: An Introduction to Indian Symbolism*. 'S-Gravenhage: Mouton and Co.

Campbell, Joseph. 1949. *The Hero with a Thousand Faces*. New York: Pantheon Books.

Caktikanal, Palaṇicāmi. 1972. *Aṇṇaṉmār Cuvāmi Katai*. Coimbatore, Tamil Nadu: Verrivēl Patipakam.

Clothey, Fred. 2019. *The Many Faces of Murugan: The History and Meaning of a South Indian God*. Berlin, Walter de Gruyter.
Coatsworth, Emerson, and David Coatsworth. 1980. *The Adventures of Nanabush: Ojibway Indian Stories*. New York: Atheneum.
Debroy, Bibek. 2010–2014. *The Mahabharata*, vols. 1–10. New Delhi: Penguin Books India.
Doerfler, Jill, Heidi Kiiwetinepinesiik Stark, and Niigaanwewidam James Sinclair, eds. 2013. *Centering Anishinaabeg Studies: Understanding the World through Stories*. East Lansing: University of Michigan State Press; Winnipeg: University of Manitoba Press.
Doniger, Wendy. 2009. *The Hindus, An Alternative History*. New Delhi: Penguin Books India.
Dumont, Louis. 1957. *Une Sous Caste de L'Inde du Sud, Organisation sociale et religion des Pramalai Kallar*. Paris and La Haye: Mouton.
Fahs, Sophia Lyon.1952. *Today's Children and Yesterday's Heritage*. Boston: Beacon Press.
Frazer, Sir James George. 1976. *The Golden Bough: A Study in Magic and Religion*. 3rd ed. 1900. Reprint, New York: Macmillan Press.
Frei, Hans W. 1974. *The Eclipse of Biblical Narrative: A Study in Eighteenth and Nineteenth Century Hermeneutics*. New Haven: Yale University Press
Friese, Kai. 2018. "4500-Year-Old DNA from Rakhigarhi Reveals Evidence That Will Unsettle Hindutva Nationalists." *India Today* (10 Sept.): cover story.
Ganesan, Naga. 2016. "Indus Crocodile Religion as Seen in the Iron Age Tamil Nadu," 16th World Sanskrit Conference Proceedings, Bangkok, Thailand. https://archive.org/details/IVCReligionInIronAgeTamilNaduByNGanesan-2016-16thWSC.
George, Andrew. 1999. *The Epic of Gilgamesh*. London: Penguin Press.
Handelman, Don, and David Shulman. 1997. *God Inside Out: Siva's Game of Dice*. Oxford: Oxford University Press.
Herbert, Vaidehi, trans. 2012. *Pathitruppāttu: English Translation with Meanings*. Troy, MI: Digital Maxim.
– 2014. *Pathupāttu: English Translation with Meanings*. Troy, MI: Digital Maxim.
Hiltebeitel, Alf. 1991a. *The Cult of Draupadī: Mythologies from Gingee to Kurukṣetra*. Chicago: University of Chicago Press.
– 1991b. *The Cult of Draupadī: On Hindu Ritual and the Goddess*. Chicago: University of Chicago Press.
– 1999. *Rethinking India's Oral and Classical Epics: Draupadi among Rajputs, Muslims and Dalits*. Chicago: University of Chicago Press.
Iceland Tourism. 2010. *Vatnsdaela Saga Heritage Map*. Reykjavik: Landnam Ingimundar Gamla.
Joshi, Jagat Pati, and Asko Parpola. 1987. *Corpus of Indus Seals and Inscriptions*. Vol. 1 of 3 volumes. Helsinki: Suomalainen Tiedeakatemian Toimituksia.
Karashima, Noboru. 2009. *Ancient to Medieval: South Indian Society in Transition*. Oxford: Oxford University Press.
– 2014. *A Concise History of South India*. Oxford: Oxford University Press.

Khangai, Ravi. 2013. "Aborigines in the Mahabharata: A Case Study of Hidimba and Ghatotkacha." In *Anthropology in India: Retrospect and Prospect*, ed. Gautam Kumar Bera, and K. Jose, 213–30. New Delhi: Abhijeet.

Kramrisch, Stella. 1976. *The Hindu Temple*, vol. 1 and 2. 1946. Reprint, Delhi: Motilal Banarsidass.

Krishnaswami, P. 2012. "Interview with Singer Devanampalayam Mylasamy." *Floating Cultures: Voices from the Hinterland: Many Shades of India's Oral Traditions – A Study of a Tamil Folk Epic, Annanmar Kathai* (the AMK Project). Archive at Christ University, Bangalore.

Lincoln, Bruce. 1986. *Myth, Cosmos and Society: Indo-European Themes of Creation and Destruction*. Cambridge: Harvard University Press.

Lombardo, Stanley, 2019, *Gilgamesh*, Indianapolis, Hackett Publishing Co. Inc.

Malaya Gounder, Palanichamy. 2014 "Tamil Merchant in Ancient Mesopotamia." *PLoS One* 9, no. 10: e109331. https://doi.org/10.1371/journal.pone.0109331.

Mann, Richard, and Benjamin Fleming. 2014. *Material Culture and Asian Religions*. Abingdon, UK: Routledge.

Mitchell, Stephen. 2004. *Gilgamesh*. New York: Simon and Schuster.

Moorjani, Priya, et al. 2013. "Genetic Evidence for Recent Population Mixture in India." *The American Journal of Human Genetics* 93, no.3: 422–38. https://doi.org/10.1016/j.ajhg.2013.07.006.

Neumayer, Erwin. 2013. *Prehistoric Rock Art of India*. Oxford: Oxford University Press.

O'Flaherty, Wendy Doniger. 1971. "The Submarine Mare in the Mythology of Siva." *Journal of the Royal Asiatic Society*, no. 1: 9–27.

– 1975. *Hindu Myths: A Sourcebook Translated from the Sanskrit*. Harmondsworth, UK: Penguin Classics.

Pattanaik, Devdutt. 2010. *Jaya, An Illustrated Retelling of the Mahabharata*. New Delhi: Penguin Random House.

Parpola, Asko. 1994. *Deciphering The Indus Script*. Cambridge: Cambridge University Press.

– 2011. "Crocodile in the Indus Civilization and Later South Asian Traditions." In Occasional Paper 12, ed. Toshiki Osada and Hitoshi Endo. *Linguistics, Archaeology and the Human Past*, Kyoto, Japan: Research Institute for Humanity and Nature.

– 2015. *The Roots of Hinduism: The Early Aryans and the Indus Civilization*. Oxford: Oxford University Press.

Scott, James 2017. *Against the Grain: A Deep History of the Earliest States*. New Haven: Yale University Press.

Schoff, Philip, trans. and ed. 1887. *Augustine, in The Nicene and Post Nicene Fathers of the Christian Church*. 1st series, vol. 3. New York: Christian Literature Society.

Shah, Sayid Ghulam Mustafa, and Asko Parpoa, eds. 1991. *Corpus of Indus Seals and Inscriptions*. Vol. 2 of *Collections in Pakistan*. Helsinki: Suomalainen Tiedeakatemia.

Shuman, David Dean. 1980. *Tamil Temple Myths*. Princeton: Princeton University Press.

Srinivas, Mysore Narasimhachar. 1944. "Some Tamil Folksongs." *Journal of the University of Bombay* 12, pt. 1: 48–86.

St. Augustine. 1887. *The Nicene and Post Nicene Fathers of the Christian Church*. 1st series, vol 3, ed. Philip Schaff. New York: Christian Literature Society.

Sutton, Komila. 2014. *The Nakshatras: The Stars beyond the Zodiac*, Bournemouth, The Wessex Astrologer Ltd.

Vajracharya, Gautama V. 2010. "Unicorns in Ancient India and Vedic Ritual." *Electronic Journal of Vedic Studies* 17, no. 2: 135–47. https://www.academia.edu/40209555/Unicorns_in_Ancient_India_and_Vedic_Ritual.

– 2011–12. "Mattavaraṇa: A Key Word for Understanding the Significance of the Toraṇa in South Asian Art." *Jñāna-Pravāha Research Journal* (Centre for Cultural Studies and Research, Varanasi 221 005) 15: 46–56.

– 2012. "Newari Woodcarvings." *Marg* (Mumbai, The Marg Foundation) 64, no. 1: 88–96.

– 2013. *Frog Hymns and Rain Babies*. Mumbai: Marg Foundation.

– 2014. "Kirtimukha: The Serpentine Motif and Garuda: The Story of a Lion That Turned into a Big Bird." *Actibus Asiae* (Museum Reitberg, Zurich) 74, no. 2: 311–33.

– 2020. "Sculpted Spouts of Nepalese Fountains and Vedic Evidence: Dolphin Deified – A Review Article." *Electronic Journal of Vedic Studies* 25: 1–23.

van Bakel, Tom. 2019. "Spectacular images of Kartikeya on Indus Seals," https://www.academia.edu/38576442/Spectacular_images_of_Kartikeya_on_Indus seals, 1–9.

Verdamme, Lorenzo, 1916. "Pleiades in Ancient Mesopotamia," *Mediterranean Archaeometry* 16, no. 4: 109–17.

Wade, Lizzie. 2018. "Ancient DNA Untangles South Asian Roots." *Science* 360, no. 6386: 252. https://doi.org/10.1126/science.360.6386.252.

Wann, Andrew, trans. 2001. "The Saga of the People of Vatnsdal." In *The Sagas of the Icelanders*, Örnólfur Thorsson, series ed. *World of the Sagas*, 185–269. New York: Penguin.

White, Gavin. 2013. *The Queen of Heaven*, London: Solaria Publications.

– 2014a. *Babylonian Star-Lore: An Illustrated Guide to the Star-Lore and Constellations of Ancient Babylonia*, 3rd ed. London: Solaria Publications.

– 2014b. *Queen of the Night: The Role of the Stars in the Creation of the Child*. London. Solaria Publications.

Witzel, E.J. Michael. 2012. *The Origins of the World's Mythologies*. Oxford: Oxford University Press.

Woods, Christopher. 2012. "Sons of the Sun: The Mythological Foundations of the First Dynasty of Uruk." *Journal of Ancient Near Eastern Religions* 12: 78–96. https://doi.org/10.1163/156921212X629473.

Zvelebil, Kamil. 1973. *The Smile of Murugan: On Tamil Literature of South India*. Leiden: Brill.

Image Credits

Front Cover: Two bards singing the Legend of Ponnivala Story sit under a great sacred tree. This image attempts to capture the connection felt between a pair of great tale tellers, their magnificent story, and the sacred universe that connects it all. This tree, the *Ficus religiosa*, draws energy from a deep watery pool of underground energy, embodied in a wild boar head. This fresh vigour then travels upwards through its branches, establishing a connection with the sun's rays by day and the entire starry sky at night. This is the tree that the epic heroine described in the Ponnivala Nadu epic legend joins as she sits upright beside it on a pillar, engrossed in prayer for twenty-one years. Her efforts generate new human life in an embryo carrying the spirit lives of a set of triplets. Lord Shiva has chosen three previously active beings whose separate essences he reformulates and sends to earth to perform great deeds. This interplay of human effort with a mesh of existential forces is captured and expressed through multiple hidden paradigms lying beneath the surface of the specific South Indian legend this book discusses at length.

Back Cover: This folk painting expresses more or less the same core principles displayed on the front cover but here expressed through an authentic and ancient South Indian storytelling style. In this image, the interaction of human and divine forces are portrayed horizontally with a combination of cosmic forces depicted on the right, two sacred trees placed in the middle, and cattle, a strong metaphor for humanity itself, placed on the left. The female cow featured in the foreground portrays alert and conscious beneficence. She serves as a metaphor for a fine human woman, while her male counterpart seen in the background is looking upwards, hoping for the divine guidance he believes can be seen in the stars. Meanwhile, the wild boar threatens domestic life and the farming lifestyle that both these bovines embody. The left-versus-right structure organizing this scene conveys a key theme that underlies many folk epics. Its core significance is documented and thoroughly explored in the present work.

450 Image Credits

Chapters 1 through 4

All figures courtesy the author.

Chapter 5

Figures 5.1–5.8, 5.10, 5.12, 5.14, 5.16, 5.18, 5.20, 5.22, 5.24, 5.26, 5.27, 5.28, 5.30, 3.32, 5.33, 5.34, 5.36, 5.38, 5.39, 5.41, 5.43, 5.47, 5.49, 5.51–5.55, 5.57, 5.59, 5.61, 5.63, 5.64, 5.66, 5.67, 5.69, 5.71, 5.73, 5.74, 5.75, 5.78–5.81, and 5.83, all courtesy the author.

Remaining figures from Vatnsdaela Saga Heritage Map, published by Landnam Ingimundar gamla, Reykjavik, 2010.

Chapter 6

Figures 6.3, 6.5, 6.6, 6.8, 6.10, 6.12, 6.14, 6.16 by Francis Kagige, in Emerson Coatsworth and David Coatsworth. 1980. *The Adventures of Nanabush: Ojibway Indian Stories*. New York: Atheneum.

Remaining figures courtesy the author.

Chapter 7

All figures courtesy the author.

Chapter 8

Figures 8.2 and 8.3 from Gavin White. 2014. *Babylonian Star-lore: An Illustrated Guide to the Star-Lore and Constellations of Ancient Babylonia*, 3rd edition. London: Solaria Publications.

Remaining figures courtesy the author.

Chapter 9

Figures 9.1 and 9.2 adapted from F.D.K. Bosch. 1960. *The Golden Germ: An Introduction to Indian Symbolism*, figure 11, p. 79 and plates 39b and 9a, respectively. 'S. Gravenhage: Mouton and Co.

Figure 9.3 (a)–(c) Bosch, figure 6, p. 33, and (d) adapted from online source.

Figure 9.4 (a) and (c) Bosch, figure 5j and l, p. 30; (b) Bosch, plate 8d.

Figure 9.5 adapted from Jagat Pati Joshi and Asko Parpola. 1987. *Corpus of Indus Seals and Inscriptions*, vol. 1, p. 116, Indus Seal M482B. Helsinki: Suomalainen Tiedeakatemian Toimituksia.

Figure 9.6a Indus Seal M296 as per Joshi and Parpola 1987, p. 72 (see credit 9.5 for full reference).
Figure 9.6b courtesy of Raj Balkaran.
Figure 9.7 courtesy of Raj Balkaran and the author.
Figure 9.8 (d) is a detail from figure 9.6; remaining images in figure courtesy of the author.
Figure 9.9 are details from figure 9.6.
Figure 9.23 as per figure 9.5, p. 72, Indus Seal M296.
Figure 9.26 (a) from Bosch jacket, (b) Bosch, figure 9c, p. 44, and (c) plate 9b.
Figure 9.37 and 9.38 courtesy Hariharapriyan Loganathan of Coimbatore.
Remaining figures courtesy the author.

Chapter 10

Figure 10.3 courtesy Raj Rajendran.
Figure 10.10 sketch courtesy of Hariharapriyan Loganathan of Coimbatore.
All remaining figures courtesy of the author.

Index

Abhijit, 298, 423n20
Abraham (Bible), 148
Abyss constellation, 291
Adam (Bible), 138–41, 417n6
adoption: of Kolatta and Kunnutaiya, 61–2, 78, 96, 194–5; in Vatnsdaela Saga, 193–5
aestivation, 360, 379, 429n6
Aettartangi sword, 188, 205, 213
ala maram, 12, 16, 323, 352
amrita (magical liquid), 394, 403–4
An (progenitor-god), 129, 131, 286
anger, 390, 417n6; Gilgamesh at the Bull of Heaven, 119; Ingimund being insulted, 184; Komban, 36, 105; Kunnutaiya and Tamarai, 83; Nanabush, 232; Ojibwa story, 232; Ponnacci, 75, 205; Shankar and Vishnu, 51; Tamarai at her brothers, 55, 124; Tangal, 27, 125, 205
animals/birds, 208–10; barrenness in Ponnivala Nadu, 259–61, 325; bovines, 262–3; bulls, 112, 261–2, 269–72; capturing of, 44–5; celebrated during Gilgamesh period, 111–12; cobras, 263–4; cows, 145, 259–61, 269–72, 325; cows versus horses, 272–6; cows as religious symbols, 112; crocodiles, 319;

cursing, 187; death of, in Kolatta's field, 14, 81–2, 144–5, 260; deer, 44–5, 262, 282, 302, 324; elephants, 358; and epics, 44–5; horses, 272–6, 330–1; oxen, 269, 358; sacrifice, 117; woodpecker, 236–7
Annanmar Kathai (Story of the Elder Brothers). *See* Ponnivala Nadu
annunciation, 160–1
anti-Christ, in Ponnivala story, 222
Anu (Babylonian god), 118, 285
Anuradha Nakshatra, 300, 307
Aquarius, 281
arasa maram, 344–5, 347–9, 352, 373–5, 378, 396
Ardhanarishvarar, 129
Ariyanacci (Ponnivala Nadu): and adopted son Kunnutaiya, 61–2, 78, 96, 146, 194–5; born from clouds, 15; and Kolatta, 78, 81, 140; leaves home due to drought, 143; and Shiva's curse and infertility, 82
Arjuna (Mahabharata), 48, 54, 209–10; and Krishna, 67–9; Pasupata weapon, 77; and Ponnar, 99–100, 161, 246–7, 262; and Shiva, 75; Tamarai analogy, 76–8
Arrow (Sirius) constellation, 288, 295
Artemis, 288

artisans (community), 11, 70, 162, 171, 185; attack Kolatta, 214; beheaded trying to kill Ponnar, 175–6; and farmers, 190; and fence built for Kolatta, 144–5; against Kunnutaiya, 18; stealing twin brothers' special swords, 215–16; testing Ponnar, 335–7; and trade goods, 47, 110, 171; and Vettuva hunters, 89–90, 105

Arukandi (sun maiden), and tiered pots for Tangal, 27–8, 36–7, 325–7, 362–3, 381, 391

aruku grass (Durva grass/*Cynodon dactylon*), 403, 433n45

Aryan culture, 359

ascetic renunciation, 54

Ashwini constellation, 257, 298

Asvathama (Mahabharata), 72; versus Shambuga, 100–2

Aśvin twins: compared with Ponnivala Nadu brothers, 276, 331, 334, 350; and Usas (Dawn) sister, 256–7

atmospheric gestation, 370

Augustine, St., 137, 416n3

autumn equinox, 293, 300, 301, 304, 307, 421n3

Azadirachta Indica (neem), 395–6

Babylonia star map, and Hindu Nakshatras, 277–308; 1st quadrant, 280–4; 2nd quadrant, 285–90; 3rd quadrant, 290–2; 4th quadrant, 293–7

banyan tree (*Ficus benghalensis*, ala maram), 12, 16, 323, 352

Barabudur Temple in Central Java, 310

bards, 42, 178, 358–9; and creative story engineering, 45–6

barrenness. *See* childlessness

Beigad (wild boar), 219

Bergur the Bold: and Finnbogi, 184–5; insulting Ingimund, 184; and Jokull attacks, 186

betrayal, 95, 114–15

Bharata (Mahabharata), 43

Bhavagad Gita, 67

Bhima (Mahabharata) vs. Shankar, 99–100, 161, 246–7, 262

Bhishma (Mahabharata), 58

Bhudevi (goddess), 26, 52, 106, 116–17, 121, 237–8, 278, 291, 304, 320, 427n40

Bible (Old and New Testament): prophets warning, 158; reclamation and chosen survivor after disaster, 146–51; reflection: and leaders, 158–65; relationships, within God's favoured family, 155–8; resilience, 153–5; resistance, 151–3; revelation, promise of renewal, 165–6; roots, beginnings and original sin, 139–46; ten plagues, 152, 153

Bison-Man (harrow constellation), 291

black boar. *See* Komban

Black Kali (Karukāli), 48

Boar: Beigad, 219; Varaha, 283, 320, 421n6. *See also* Komban

Borg incident, 183

Bosch, F.D.K., 309–56

bovines, 262–3

Bow constellation, 288–9

brahmamūla, 311, 315, 323–30, 331–2, 350

Brahmins, 44, 100–1; fire sacrifice rituals, 385–6

brother-brother relationship, 22–3, 133; Vatnsdaela Saga, 206–8. *See also* twin brothers

brother-sister relationship, 91–3; Mahabharata, 92, 95; ritual wedding sari, 91; Vishnu and Parvati (Cellatta), 94–5, 127, 130, 198–9

Bull of Heaven (Taurus) constellation, 117, 119, 131–2, 285–6, 304; killed with spear, 120, 131, 415n26

caesarean, Vishnu delivers twins by, 87, 161–2, 249, 251
Campbell, Joseph, 32–3, 318, 334
Canaan (Bible); conquered by Israelites, 157; great famine, 151
Capricorn constellation, 281, 314, 352
Cargo Boat constellation, 294–5
cattle herd, as status marker, 111
cattle pen, 110–12; Babylonian, 264, 266; Kunnutaiya, 265
Celandiamman temple, at Madukkarai, 371–3
Cellatta (goddess, form of Parvati), 18, 48; and Kunnutaiya's worship, 399; and secret tunnel, 195; and tiger's milk, 195; and twin brothers (under tunnel), 21, 63–4, 100, 162, 252, 321–2, 351; and Vishnu, 94; versus Krishna in Mahabharata, 100
Central Java, 310
chants (Om), 328
childlessness, 14, 17–18, 145, 152, 193, 259–61, 325, 362
Chola king, 29, 69–71; death of, 70–1, 80, 88, 182, 235–6; and Kolatta, 170, 282; and Kunnutaiya, 17, 58, 78, 149, 196, 210–12; and Ponnar giving tribute, 201; and twin brothers against, 47
Christianity, 220; Judgement Day, 138. *See also* Bible (Old and New Testament)
Cilappatikaram, 45
Cinnannan. *See* Shankar (younger twin, Ponnivala Nadu)
Clansmen: and Kunnutaiya, 158, 181–2, 195, 389–90, 398; schoolhouse attack, 97, 119, 159; threatening Tamarai, 64; twins aggression against, 80, 159–60, 182, 184–5, 390; in Vatnsdaela Saga, 183
climate change, 6, 406

climate struggles, 190–1
climbing vines, 394–9
Clothey, Fred, 255
clouds, 375, 377, 425n25; dark, 31, 342, 359, 385, 426n27, 427n43; and Kailasa, 77, 128, 134–5, 397–8; kala head in, 329, 426n26; and Kollata's wife's (Ariyanacci) birth, 15; and Parvati floating in, 281; rain-generating, 31, 281, 358–60, 374, 381, 391; songs or hymns to, 379; and Vishnu floating in, 349
cobras, 218, 263–4; and Shiva, 349; as hood for Tamarai, 348; Tangal protected by king of, 134, 391–3: and Vishnu, 349; women and, 348, 374, 391–2
conch tool, 50–1, 128, 130
cooling pot, 385–6
cosmic power, 12
cosmic renewal, 28, 107, 292
cousins rivalry, 11, 18–19, 41, 58, 62–3, 69, 87, 96–7, 270, 321
cows, 259–61, 269–72, 360; barrenness of, 259–61, 325; death in Kolatta's field, 14, 81–2, 144–5, 260, 341; death of and seven generation curse, 14, 17–18, 48, 82, 152, 261–2, 344, 397; killing of, 145; Kunnutaiya fed by, 61, 261; religious symbols, 112; versus horses, 272–6
cradle of Tangal, 24, 125, 134, 353
crocodiles, 313–15, 319–21, 327, 339–40, 352, 360, 424n18
cross-cousin marriage, 35, 91, 197

Dalit caste, 37, 43, 64, 100, 102, 272, 275, 414n4
dangers, in dark, 394–9
dark clouds, 31, 342, 359, 385, 426n27, 427n43
Dasharatha (Ramayana), 43

death(s): of artisans in Ponnivala Nadu, 175–6; of Chola king, 70–1, 80, 88, 182, 235–6; and cosmic renewal process, 28, 33; of hungry cows in Kolatta's field, 14, 81–2, 144–5, 260, 341; of Ingimund, 208; of Jesus Christ, 161; of Kunnutaiya, 60; of Leather Cap in Vatnsdaela Saga, 175–6; of Pandu, 60; of Shambuga, 53, 208; of twin brothers, 27, 33, 52–4, 72, 101–2, 106, 161, 163, 208; water as source of, 175–6. *See also* Yeman (Yama)

deer: in Ramayana, 44–5; Shiva and Parvati disguised as, 262, 282, 302, 324; and Sita, 44

Devil's ivy (*Epipremnum aureum*), 395

Dhanishta Nakshatra, 300, 305–6

Dhritarashtra (Mahabharata): birth of, 57–8; father of Kauravas, 62

dicing, 23, 51–2; in Mahabharata, 52; and twin brothers, 51–2, 80

divination, 189, 202–5; and prophecy, 202–5; ritual of Tangal, 189; and spirit flight, 220

dowry (wedding gifts), 197

Draupadi (Mahabharata), 52; born of fire, 65, 75; cult of, 41; cursed dogs, 75; disrobing of, 73; insults/humiliation of, 65–6, 72; joint wife of Pandavas, 54–5, 65, 71; life in exile, 72–3; poetic lament over dead sons, 74; and Tamarai, 65–6, 71–2; and Tangal, 66, 72–5

dreams/visionary powers, of Tangal, 26, 66, 74, 79–80, 125

drought, 190–1, 359, 379; in Canaan, 151, 158; and Gilgamesh epic, 132; in Ponnivala Nadu, 32, 81, 118, 142–3, 145, 281–2, 285–6, 399, 417n6; versus rain, 387–93

Dumont, Louis, 431n28

Dumuzi (god), 129–30, 283

Durga (goddess), 24, 41, 316, 373; head of buffalo demon, 316; temple icon dedicated to, 316

Durva grass (*Cynodon dactylon*), 403, 433n45

Duryodhana (Mahabharata), 104

Eagle and Dead Man constellation, 296–7

earthen pots, 384–5

earthly marriages, 55

Eden garden, 115

elephants, 358, 369

Enkidu (Gilgamesh epic), 112–14, 119; Humbaba cursing Gilgamesh and, 114, 119

Enlil (forest god), 116–17

Enmerkar (Uruk founder), 125–6

Epic of Gilgamesh (oldest epic in world). *See* Gilgamesh epic

Eridu constellation, 289–90

ethnic communities, 7

Eve (Bible), 115, 138–41, 417n6; created from Adam ribs, 140–1; and forbidden fruit in Garden of Eden, 141–2

Fahs, Sophia Lyon, 138, 416n3

family rights, 32, 57–60

family survival, 6, 18

famine/drought, 190–1, 359, 379; in Canaan, 151, 158; in Gilgamesh epic, 132; in Ponnivala Nadu, 32, 81, 118, 142–3, 145, 281–2, 285–6, 399, 417n6; versus rain, 387–93

farmer-heroes. *See* twin brothers

female power, in Ponnivala Nadu, 11, 19, 48–9. *See also* Tamarai; Tangal, Virutangal

female resistance, 65–6

female suffering, in Mahabharata, 41

fence, around Kolatta's sugarcane field, 14, 81–2, 144–5, 260, 341
feuds and arguments, 183–6
Ficus benghalensis (ala maram), 12, 16, 323, 352, 411n1
Ficus religiosa (arasa maram), 344–5, 347–9, 352, 373–5, 378, 396
Field constellation, 282
Finla (fortune teller, Vatnsdaela Saga): and hidden ring of Ingimund, 202
Finnbogi (Vatnsdaela Saga), 184–5
fire pot, 375, 385–6
first minister. *See* Shambuga
Fish constellation, 282
forbidden tree, Eve picks fruit from, 141–2
forest: massacre in, 101–2, 105; sacrifices, 26–7; versus ploughed fields, 24. *See also* Vettuvas
forest garden, nine (ancestral) men of Ponnivala placed in by Parvati, 139–40, 321–2
Frazer, James, 33–4
Frei, Hans W., 138, 416n3
Freyfaxi (magical horse, Vatnsdaela Saga), 200–1
frogs, in Ponnivala Nadu, 379–82

Gandhi, Mahatma: orphans/Dalits as children of god, 64
Ganesh (Ganapati/Vinayakar, god), 12, 103–4, 249
Garden of Eden: and Eve with forbidden fruit, 141–2
Garuda (Vishnu vehicle), 163, 296, 379
gender differences, 141, 143
Gilgamesh epic: background, 109–10; brother-sister relationship in, 126; Enkidu (partner-helper), 112–14, 119; gateway to Enlil's sanctuary, 117; Humbaba (wild boar), 114–15, 119–20, 131–2, 304; and killing of Bull of Heaven, 119; powerful and prominent king, 118; reclamation, 114–18; reflection, 131–3; relationships, 125–31; resilience, 123–5; resistance, 118–23; revelation, 133–6; roots, 110–14; tyranny, 118–19; wandering, 123
Gitchi-Manitou (great spirit), 239
Goat Thigh, 193–4
Goatfish (Capricorn), 281
Golden Bough, The (Frazer), 33–4
Golden Germ, The (Bosch), 309
golden magical pot, 21, 71, 156, 233, 248–9, 324–6, 363
Gondwana alternative, 34
Good Friday, 165
Goose: Nanabush, 229; as Tangal's vehicle, 28, 134, 203, 326–7, 330, 351, 391
Great One, 281–2
Great Twins constellation, 287–8
Gula (Aquarius), 281–2

half-brothers, 41
Ham (Bible), 148
Hanuman (Ramayana), 43
Harrow constellation, 290–1
Hastinapura, 53–4, 57
heaven-sourced liquors, 404
hell, 54, 107, 134
Herald (king, Vatnsdaela Saga), 170
Hero with a Thousand Faces, The (Campbell), 318, 334; stages compared with Ponnivala Nadu, 32–3
Hidamba (Rakasha), 95
Hiltebeitel, Alf, 40
Hindu Nakshatra system: Anuradha Nakshatra, 300; autumn equinox, 293, 300, 301, 304, 307, 421n3; Dhanishta Nakshatra, 300, 305; and human body parts, 300; Magha

Nakshatra, 300, 306; Shravana Nakshatra, 300; spring equinox, 248, 254, 257, 259, 277–8, 281, 285, 295, 299–302, 421n3; star map, 298–302; summer solstice, 288, 292, 295, 301–4, 307, 352; winter solstice, 227, 254, 281, 295–6, 298, 301–3, 306, 314, 337, 352–5, 383, 385, 401, 423n22
Hired Man constellation, 283
homeland, 47–8, 119, 143–5, 174, 228, 230
homestead, 176–8
horses, 184, 199–202, 272–6, 330–1
Hrafn (Vatnsdaela Saga), and Ingimund, 213–14
human behaviour, 7, 136
Humbaba (wild boar), 114–15, 131–2, 304; cursing Gilgamesh and Enkidu, 114, 119; killed with a knife, 120
hunter-gatherers, 6, 63, 109
hunters, 11, 26, 30, 52–3, 63, 171, 185–6; and kidnapping of Kunnutaiya's maid, 18

Iceland: first missionaries, 220–1; and sorcerers from Lapland, 202. *See also* Vatnsdaela Saga
immaculate conception, 99, 124, 128, 155–6, 161, 233, 286, 290, 325, 362, 431n26
immigrants, 28–30, 70, 151, 168, 170, 190–1, 214
immortality, 132–3, 285
Indra (god), 73, 253, 358
Indus Valley civilization, 254, 285, 314–15, 334–5, 348, 350, 423n21
Ingimund (Vatnsdaela Saga): and arrival in Iceland, 171; Bergur the Bold insults, 184; death of, 208; and family homestead, 176–7; finding magical ring, 172; and fortune teller Finla hiding ring of, 202; generosity and social responsibility, 180–1; and horse riding, 200; and Hrafn, 213–14; and king of Norway, 196, 211; marriage, 195, 197; Norway to Iceland as Viking, 170; as Viking raider, 195–6; wooing Vigdis, 199
Ingjald (Vatnsdaela Saga), 176–7
innai cir (uniting ritual), 91, 93, 197
Innana (goddess), 123–4, 129–31
Ishtar (goddess), 117; Bull of Heaven, 119, 121; temple for, 118

Japheth (Bible), 148
Jayadratha (Mahabharata), 67
jealousy: of cousins in Ponnivala Nadu, 11, 18–19, 58, 62–3, 69, 87, 96–7, 270, 321; against Murugan, 251
Jerusalem (Via Dolorosa rituals), 165
Jesus Christ, 160; crucifixion of, 139; earthly resurrection, 161; hidden at birth, 160; last meal, 161; sacrificial death, 161
Jews (Passover festival), 153
Jokull (Vatnsdaela Saga), 216–17, 219; and attack on Bergur, 186; and magical sword, 189; and negative magical powers, 175, 182–3, 205
Jordan river, 144
Joseph (Bible), 148; and honours by Egyptian pharaoh, 150; as a slave in Egypt, 148–9

Kaikeyi (Ramayana), 43
Kailasa (Shiva council chambers), 18, 33, 349; and demands of penitents, 50; and Pleiades sisters, 73, 134; Ponnivala heroes in, 101, 122, 130; staircase leading into, 77, 128, 397–8; and Tamarai, 20, 48, 57, 233, 248 (*see also* Tamarai); and

Tangal, 134–5, 353, 402 (*see also* Tangal)
kāla (kirtimukha), 317–18, 328–9, 377–9, 424n7; head, 312, 329, 338–46, 379, 392, 426n26; at summit of torana frame, 316; symbolism of, 377–9
Kāla Bhairava, 431n23
Kali (goddess), 26, 48; and Komban, 116; Krittikas resembling, 259; "Liebestod mythology" of Kali, 41; Ponnacci curse to twin brothers, 101
Kaliyamman temple, Gannapuram, 364, 376
Kama (Hindu form of Cupid), 122, 163, 320
Kamadeva, 314
Kannagi (Cilappatikaram), 45
Kannimar (seven dancing maidens, as Pleiades), 23–5, 45, 73, 116, 124, 130–1, 248, 253–4, 257, 259, 268, 285, 299–300, 306–7; and cobra hood, 263; and pongal milk boiling ritual, 257–8, 383–7. *See also* Tangal
kanyas (virgins), 73
Karmēkam (black cloud), 359
Karna (Mahabharata), 60–1, 64
Kartikkai month, 394
Kathmandu fountains, 394
Kauravas (Mahabharata), 71
Kaveri river, 144, 170, 259, 370, 411n2
Ketil (Vatnsdaela Saga), 170, 183
Ketu (planetary nodes), 379
Kichaka (Mahabharata), 67
kin relationships, 331
kirtimukha, 317–18, 328–9, 377–9, 424n7
Kolatta (Ponnivala Nadu), 16, 32, 78, 118, 172, 184, 282, 397–8; and Ariyanacci (wife), 15, 140; attacked by artisan, 214; and Chola king, 170, 282; and eight brothers, 62, 96, 171, 190; and grandsons' sword fight, 213; and Kunnutaiya, adopted son hidden by Shiva, 14, 16, 35, 61–2, 78, 85, 96, 146, 147–8, 194–5, 261, 282; and rains, 387; settling in Ponnivala Nadu, 144; and seven generations curse, 60
Komban (black boar), 32–3, 36, 52, 75–6; and aggression, 342–3; demise of, 105, 106, 250–1, 353; versus Ganesh (god), 103–4; and irrigation dam, 105; and twin brothers, 103–4, 105, 120, 187; and magical attributes, 116, 182, 183, 277–8; and makara, 318–21; in his mother's cave, 344; protector of wild domain, 114; Shambuga's failure to kill, 101, 113; shrine to, 165; Vishnu's giving head of to Bhudevi, 52, 106, 121, 237–8, 278, 291, 427n40
Kongu Nadu, 47, 100; and cattle pen theme, 111; local life in, 36; predominant Shiva-worshipping region, 129; and sacred vegetal pot, 384–6; weddings in, 90, 197
Kongu Vellalar caste, 44
Kottravai (goddess), 26, 283
Kramrisch, 393
Krishna (Vishnu avatar), 49, 100; and Arjuna, 67–9; dark clouds in depictions of, 359
Krittika. *See* Kannimar (seven dancing maidens, as Pleiades)
Kshatriya, 44, 58, 66
Kunnutaiya (Ponnivala Nadu), 61–2, 63, 69, 261; adoption, 61–2, 78, 96, 146, 194–5; as adult and senior years, 196; and advice for sons/twin brothers, 79, 158; beaten by uncles, 148; becoming respected leader, 69, 150; and Cellatta worship; and

460 Index

Chola king, 17, 58, 78, 149, 196, 210–12; and cousins', 43, 70; death of, 60; fed by cow, 61, 261; found under rock by Kolatta, 14, 16, 35, 61, 85, 147–8, 261, 282; homestead life, 177–8; marriage to Tamarai, 16, 35, 55, 64, 387; orphaned, 58, 61, 69, 78, 86, 96, 177, 387; as a servant to brothers of Tamarai, 148–9; as a skilled cattle manager, 111; status of minor king, 17, 58, 78, 149, 402; Vishnu converts to stone, 57, 77, 128, 154
Kunti (Mahabharata), 60–1, 64

Lakshmi (goddess), 264
Land of the Golden River. *See* Ponnivala Nadu
lateral branches, 310–11, 321–2, 346–56
Laurasian archetype, 34
Leather Cap, 175
Levi-Strauss, Claude, 42
"Liebestod mythology" of Kali, 41
life-giving liquid (soma), 15, 28, 36, 270, 304, 311, 326, 329
life-seeds, 107, 117
Lincoln, Bruce, 34
Lomas Rishi in Mihar, 313
long line of animal pairs waiting to board Noah's ark, 147
lotus flower, 370; Bosch diagram, 310; *brahmamūla*, 323–30; lateral branches, 330–8; lateral stems, 310–11, 321–2; main stem and vegetation, 311, 322–3; as meaning of Tāmarai's name, 15; *padmamūla*, 310, 311, 313–18; rhizome (makara) design, 314; sacred pond, 370–6, 401; shape of actual leaf, 376; symbol, 6
lotus-like tree, 31
lotus-style mandala, 370

loyalty, 196
Lugalbanda (Gilgamesh epic), 126
Lulal and Latarak constellation, 283–4

Mad Dog constellation, 293
Madri (Mahabharata), 84
Madukkarai (Celandiamman temple), 371–3
Magha Nakshatra, 300, 306
magical pot (life-giving liquid), 21, 71, 156, 233, 248, 304, 325, 363
magical tools, 188–9
Mahabharata, 7
 – Arjuna, 54; versus Ponnar, 99–100
 – Ashwatthama, 72
 – Asvathama, 100, 102
 – Bhima vs. Shankar, 99–100
 – Bhishma, 58
 – Dhritarashtra; birth of, 57–8; father of Kauravas, 62
 – dicing in, 52
 – Draupadi: born of fire, 65, 75; cursing of dogs, 75; disrobing of, 73; and insults/humiliation of, 65–6, 72; as joint wife of Pandavas, 54–5, 65, 71; and life in exile, 72–3; poetic lament over dead sons, 74; and Tamarai, 65–6, 71–2; and Tangal, 66, 72–5
 – Duryodhana, 104
 – Jayadratha, 66
 – kanyas (virgins), 73
 – Karna abandoned by mother, Kunti, 60–1, 64
 – Kichaka, 66
 – Madri, 84
 – marriages, 54, 57
 – on brother-sister relationship, 92, 95
 – Pandu, 57; childhood, 69; death of, due to curse 60
 – versus Ponnivala Nadu, 39–43

- reclamation: of family rights to lands and leadership, 57–60; jealousy, 62–3; male blood line, 60–2; reproduction aided by gods, 63–5, 71
- references to Ramayana: capture of animal and consequent regrets, 44–5; midwife, 43; "monkey god" Hanuman, 43; Rama and Laksmana brothers, 44
- reflection, 98–104; Arjuna/Ponnar and Bhima/Shankar, 99–100; Asvathama/Shambuga, 100–2; Komban/Ganesh (god), 103–4; Ramayana character named "Shambuga," 102–3
- relationships: brother versus brother, 96–8; parents versus children, 78–81; rulers versus subjects, 88–96; wife versus husband, 81–8
- resilience: Arjuna and Tamarai, 76–8; Draupadi and Tamarai, 71–2; Draupadi and Tangal, 72–5; Draupadi, Tangal, and dogs, 75–6
- resistance: Draupadi vs. Tamarai/Tangal, 65–6; female, 65–6; Krishna and Arjuna vs. Shankar and Vishnu (Mayavar), 67–9; Kunnutaiya as boy and as emerging leader, 69; male, 67–9; sons of Kunnutaiya and Chola overlord, 69–71
- revelation, 104–6
- root of, 62
- roots, 47; deaths of twin brothers, 52–4; dicing, 51–2; and goddesses, 48; of Lord Shiva, 49–51; of Lord Vishnu, 49; marriages and romance, 54–7; and women power, 48–9
- suttee, 84
- Vichitravirya, 57, 62
- Vyasa sage, 57, 62
- women king makers, 64
- Yudhishthira, 54, 66

makara (rhizome), 281, 313–14, 316, 364, 369; and Ponnivala's wild boar, 318–21
Makara star sign, 281
male blood line, 60–2
male resistance, 67–9; Krishna and Arjuna vs. Shankar and Vishnu (Mayavar), 67–9; Kunnutaiya, 69–71
male-to-male relationships, 21–2
Mantara (Ramayana), 43
Mariyamman (goddess), 117, 118; Gannapuram temple, 364, 370–1
marriages/wedding, 303; Adam and Eve, 139–40; Arjuna, 55; creating new relationship, 197–8; cross-cousin, 35, 91, 197; Draupadi and Pandavas, 82; in-law animosity, 198–9; Ingimund, 176–7; Kolatta and Ariyanacci, 81, 139–40, 322; Kunnutaiya and Tamarai, 16, 35, 55–6, 81–3, 86–7, 91, 149, 177, 193, 286–7, 387; with no children, 93–4; Pandavas in Mahabharata, 54; Pandu and Kunti, 60–1; pipal to neem tree, 395; ritual of brother-sister bond, 91, 127; and romance, 54–7; rules of, 90–1; of twin brothers, 21, 56, 74, 83–4, 306; Vichitravirya, 57
Mayavar (Vishnu), and Shankar, 67–9
Meski'ang-gasher (Gilgamesh epic), 126
Mesopotamia, 110
midday sun, 387–93
Middle Eastern mythology, 277
Midwife: blindfolding Tamarai in labour, 161, 192–3, 251–2, 389; in Ramayana, 43
milk, 403–4; boiling ritual, 255, 257–8, 268, 383–7; posts, 383–7
mirrors, 98–9
"monkey god" Hanuman, 43
monsoon rains, 6, 357–61

morality and divine justice, 220–2
Moses (Bible): and God, 151; out of Egypt, across Red Sea, 154; and stone tablets (ten commandments), 155–6
motherhood, 192
mud, 379–82
Murugan (Kartikeya/Skanda), 274–5; birth of, 246–51; elephant riding, 253; and Indra (god), 253; and Krittika as nursemaid, 254; and Shiva, 247; versus twin brothers, 249–59; and wives Devayanai and Valli, 249, 250
Myth, Cosmos and Society (Lincoln), 34

Nakshatras, 257, 277–308
Nanabush story cycle (Ojibwa First Peoples, North America), 7, 223; and birch tree, 235; creation of turtle, 228; crossing waterway, a cosmic-scale divide, 240; falling to earth, 230; and four warriors, 238–9; grandmother and great beaver, 232–3; Granite Peak, 238–9; and greeting wife, 240; punishing bald eagle, 231; reclamation, 229–30; reflection, 236–8; relationships, 234–6; resilience, 232–4; resistance, 230–2; revelation, 238–42; roots, 225–9; and woodpecker, 236–7
Nandi (Shiva's bull), 112, 272–3, 275, 393–4, 422n10, 433n43
Nath yogis, 182
negative magic (sorcery), 205
negative powers and curses, 186–8
Nepal, 361
Neumayer, Erwin, 415n26
Ninmah constellation, 290
Ninsun (goddess), 112, 129
Noah's family (Bible), 146–51
nomads, 359

North America, 7, 30
Norway, 170
Norway king (Vatnsdaela Saga): Ingimund's gift of polar bears to, 211

Odin (god), 209
O'Flaherty, W., 259
Ojibwa Peoples, North America, 224; culture, 7; warrior crossing river, 240
Om chants, 328
oral epics, 41, 405–6, 412n3
Origin of the World's Mythologies (Witzel), 318
original sin, 14, 145–6
Origins of the World's Mythologies, The (Witzel), 33, 34
Orion, 286
oxen, 111, 269, 358

Pabilsag constellation, 295–6
padmamūla (rhizome), 310, 311, 313–18, 329, 332
Pandavas, 40, 47; dice game, 52; Draupadi, joint wife of, 54–5, 65, 71
Pandu (Mahabharata), 57; childhood, 69; death of, due to curse, 60
Paraiyar caste, 37, 43, 100–1, 102, 272, 275, 287, 414n4
parrot, conflicts since Taṅkaḷ wants, 44–5, 89, 95, 105, 115–16, 120, 135, 218, 288, 323, 418n4
Parvati (goddess), 12, 23, 48, 198; creation of nine brothers, 16, 35, 46–7, 84–5, 139–40, 177, 190, 228–9, 280–1, 321–2, 417n6; floating on clouds, 281; Murugan, birth, 246–51; Tamarai, Shiva and, 15, 35, 74. *See also* Cellatta; Mariyamman
Passover festival, 153

Pasupata weapon, 77
Pattanaik, Devdutt, 107
patti pongal, 254–5, 257–8, 266–9, 298, 401. *See also* winter solstice
Periyakandiamman (goddess), 370
Periyannan. *See* Ponnar/Ponnayyā (elder twin)
Pharaoh of Egypt, 150–1
Phorsteinn (Vatnsdaela Saga), 206–7
pillars, 361–4
Pingeyrar church, 178–80
Pisces, 282
place of origin, 139–43
Pleiades constellation, 248, 253–4, 268, 285; as compass navigational skill, 254; and Ojibwa First Peoples, 225; in Ponnivala Nadu, 225–6. *See also* Kannimar (seven dancing maidens, as Pleiades)
Plough constellation, 280–1
ploughed fields, 6, 63, 70–1, 85, 108, 173, 215, 333; and Kolatta, and Ariyanacci, 143, 147; versus forest, 24
Pongal festival, 5, 266
Ponnacci (Tangal's pet), 24, 26, 293; cursing twin brothers, 75–6, 187–8; shrine to, 165; Vishnu to twin brothers about, 32–3; against wild boar, 32–3, 36, 105, 132
Ponnar/Ponnayyā (elder twin, Ponnivala Nadu), 11, 123; and concerns about Tangal, 95, 133–4; equated with sun, 335; jailed by Chola king, 70; and killing of Chola king, 70–1, 80, 88, 182, 235–6; as reincarnation of Arjuna, 99–100, 161, 246–7, 262; as reincarnation of Yudhisthira, 99; and sari ritual with sister, 91, 127; and Shankar arguing, 97; tested by artisan, 335–7; and tribute to Chola king, 201; wise and gentle, 332–3, 388. *See also* twin brothers

Ponnivala Nadu, 3; anti-Christ in, 222; artisan death in water, 175–6; bards singing about, 179, 180; brother-sister relationships in, 91; colonial conquests, 29–30; and core message of Bhavagad Gita, 68–9; cows barrenness in, 259–61, 325; crop land behind hills, 173; death of ruling king, 88; death of twin brothers, 27, 33, 52–4, 72, 101–2, 106, 161, 163, 208; drought, 142–3; female power, in Ponnivala Nadu, 11, 19, 48–9; first peoples versus colonizers, 29–30; forested hills in, 217; frogs in, 379–82; and immigrants, 28–9; importance of cattle in, 111; in-law animosity, 198–9; jealousy of cousins in, 11, 18–19, 58, 62–3, 69, 87, 96–7, 270, 321; and Kannimar (Pleiades sisters), 23–5, 45, 73, 116, 124, 130–1, 257–8; and other authors' paradigms, 31–8; and rains, 357–8; ravens, 208–9; reclamation, 16–18, 32, 35; reflection, 23–6, 33, 36; relationships, 21–3, 32, 35–6; resilience, 19–21, 33, 35; resistance, 18–19, 32, 35–6; revelation, 26–8, 33, 36; river featured in, 175; roots, 12–16, 32, 35; stages compared with *The Hero with a Thousand Faces*, 32–3; temple wall mural of, 223; triplets, 16, 21, 60, 78, 124, 128, 156, 161, 250; Vaisnavite-Shaivite mix of, 256; war drum, 291, 327–8, 339; Witzel's and Lincoln's analysis to, 35–7; and women king makers, 64. *See also* Ponnar/Ponnayyā (elder twin); Shankar (younger twin); Tangal; twin brothers
porch pillars, 399–402

Porolfur (dark-skinned troublemaker), 216–17, 219
pots, 384–6
"procession of the equinoxes," 257
prominent and resilient women, 191–6
prophecy, 202–5
Puttu Kannu, 355

quadrants, of Babylonia star map, 280–97
Queen of the Night (White), 264

rain: versus drought, 387–93; -generating clouds, 31, 281, 358–60, 374, 381, 391. *See also* dark clouds
Raku (planetary nodes), 379
Ram (Ramayana), 43
Ram constellation, 283
Ramayana: character called Shambuga, 102–3; Mantara versus the hunchback midwife, 43; "monkey god" Hanuman versus Shambuga, 43; Rama and Laksmana brothers, 44; Sita and the deer, 44–5
ravens, 208–9
reclamation
 – Bible, 146–51
 – Gilgamesh epic, 114–18
 – Mahabharata: family rights to lands and leadership, 57–60; jealousy, 62–3; male blood line, 60–2; reproduction through gods, 63–5
 – Nanabush story, 229–30
 – Ponnivala Nadu, 16–18, 35
 – Vatnsdaela Saga: clean source of water, 174–6; pioneer homestead, 176–8; story tellers, 178–80
Red Sea, 154
reflection, 98–104, 330–8
 – Bible: hero's sacrifice, 160–4; leaders sent by god, 158–65; shrines/rituals, 164–5
 – Gilgamesh epic, 131–3

 – Mahabharata: Arjuna/Ponnar and Bhima/Shankar, 99–100; Asvathama/Shambuga, 100–2; Komban/Ganesh (god), 103–4; Ramayana character called Shambuga 102–3
 – Nanabush story, 236–8
 – Ponnivala Nadu, 23–6, 36
 – Vatnsdaela Saga: birds, 208–10; death of hero, 208; elder and younger brothers, 206–8; special gifts, 210–12
regional epics, 39–43. *See also* Ponnivala Nadu
reincarnation, 42, 74
relationships, 311, 322–3
 – Bible, 155–8
 – Gilgamesh, 125–31
 – Mahabharata: brother vs. brother, 96–8; parents vs. children, 78–81; rulers vs. subjects, 88–96; wife vs. husband, 81–8
 – Nanabush story, 234–6
 – Ponnivala Nadu, 21–3, 35–6
 – Vatnsdaela Saga: divination and prophecy, 202–6; and horses, 199–202; and in-law animosity, 198–9; and weddings and new relationships, 197–8
reproductivity: given by gods, 55, 63–5, 124
resilience, 323–30
 – Bible, 153–5
 – Gilgamesh, 123–5
 – Mahabharata: Arjuna and Tamarai, 76–8; Draupadi and Tamarai, 71–2; Draupadi and Tangal, 72–5; Draupadi, Tangal, and dogs, 75–6
 – Nanabush story, 232–4
 – Ponnivala Nadu, 19–21, 35
 – Vatnsdaela Saga: climate struggles, 190–1; leader loyal to king, 196–7; prominent women, 191–6

resistance
- Bible, 151–3
- Gilgamesh, 118–23
- Mahabharata: Draupadi vs. Tamarai/Tangal, 65–6; female, 65–6; Krishna and Arjuna vs. Shankar and Vishnu (Mayavar), 67–9; Kunnutaiya as emerging leader, 69; Kunnutaiya as young boy, 69; male, 67–9; sons of Kunnutaiya and Chola overlord, 69–71
- Nanabush story, 230–2
- Ponnivala Nadu, 18–19, 35–6
- Vatnsdaela Saga: feuds and arguments, 183–6; heroes vs. villains, 180–3; magical tools, 188–9; negative powers and curses, 186–8

resurrection, of twin brothers, 27–8, 36–7, 122–3, 161, 163, 226–7, 325–7, 363, 381, 391

Rethinking India's Oral and Classical Epics (Hiltebeitel), 41

revelation, 165–6
- Bible (Jesus return), 165
- Gilgamesh, 133–6
- Mahabharata, 104–6
- Nanabush story, 238–42
- Ponnivala Nadu, 26–8, 36, 213, 222–3
- Vatnsdaela Saga, 222–3; morality and divine justice, 220–2; and social rights, 213–16; wild lands and magic, 216–20

Rg Veda, 330–1

rituals/ceremony, 246; blessings, 399–402; innai cir (uniting ritual), 91, 93, 197; Kannimar pongal milk boiling, 257–8; sacred threads, 58–60; suttee (Indian female widow's suicide act), 84, 93; Via Dolorosa in Jerusalem, 165

Rooster constellation, 287

roots, 46–57, 310, 311, 313–18, 329
- Bible: finding homeland, 144–5; original sin, 145–6; pristine place of origin, 139–43
- Gilgamesh, 110–14
- Mahabharata: deaths of main heroes, 52–4; and dicing, 51–2; goddesses, 48; human heroines, 48–9; Lord Shiva, 49–51; Lord Vishnu, 49; marriages and romance, 54–7
- Nanabush story, 225–9
- Ponnivala Nadu, 12–16, 35
- Vatnsdaela Saga: arrival of first pioneers, 170–3; beloved land, 173–4

sacred liquids, 28
sacred mandala, 392
sacred threads ritual, 58–60
sacred tree, 370–6
sacred vegetal pot, 384–6
sacrificial offering, 32–3, 36, 167
Sagittarius, 295
salvation, 137–8
Saraswati (goddess), 25, 264, 295
Sati, 124
Scales constellation, 293–4
Schoff, Philip, 416n3
Scorpion constellation, 294
Second Coming, 137
seeds, 383, 396
seven tiered pots, from sun maiden, 27–8, 36–7, 325–7, 362–3, 381, 391
sexual attraction, 55, 126, 130
sexual purity, 126–7
Shamash (Utu), 129
Shambuga (Ramayana character), 102–3
Shambuga (first minister, Ponnivala Nadu), 18, 37, 43; versus Asvathama, 100; versus Enkidu (Gilgamesh), 113; and bull,

272–3; Dalit (Paraiyar) caste, 37, 43, 100–2, 272, 275, 287, 414n4; death of, 53, 101–2, 208; and failure to kill Komban, 101, 113; and killing of Chola king, 88; and misguided forest hunt, 101–3, 106, 113; resemblance to Hanuman in Ramayana, 43; runs behind Shankar's horse, 201; and schoolhouse attack, 97, 119, 159; secret affinity with Komban, 113; and Shiva, 272; steals local hunters' iron rods, 89, 105, 120, 216, 288
Shankar (younger twin, Ponnivala Nadu), 11, 44; killing artisan to protect Ponnar, 337; killing of Chola king, 70–1, 80, 88, 182, 235–6; killing of Komban, 105, 115, 250–1; and Mayavar (Vishnu), 67–9; and the moon, 335; and Ponnar arguing, 97; reincarnations of Bhima, 99–100, 161, 246–7, 262; removal of chest thread, 53, 122; resemblance of Gilgamesh, 119; riding horse, 200; righteous and impatient, 332–3, 388; and schoolhouse attack, 97, 119, 159; and Shambuga, 102–3; statue of, 169; and Tangal, 95, 133–4; and Vishnu shooting arrow, 51, 53, 122, 163. *See also* twin brothers
shared human roots, 38
Shem (Bible), 148
Shiva (god), 48; Ardhanarishvara (bisexual) form, 129; and bow and arrow contest with Arjuna, 75; and cobra wrapped around neck, 349; as a fiercer god, 220–1; Mahabharata vs. Ponnivala Nadu, 49–51; and male bovine guardians, 271–2; and son Murugan, birth of, 246–51; and Nandi (bull), 112, 272–3, 275, 393–4, 422n10, 433n43; and penitents,

50; seven generation curse on Kolatta, 14, 17–18, 48, 82, 145–6, 152, 261–2, 344, 397; and Shambuga, 272; and Tamarai, 20, 48, 57, 233, 248 (*see also* Tamarai); and Vishnu, 23, 50–1, 128–30, 338 (*see also* Vishnu). *See also* Kailasa (Shiva council chambers)
Shiva Ratiri festival, 165
Shravana Nakshatra, 300
Shrine: Komban (wild boar) in, 165; Ponnacci (Tangal's pet) in, 165; of twin brothers, 74, 106, 125, 161, 163–4. *See also* temples
Shudras, 58
Sinai Peninsula, 154, 155
Sirius, 288
Sita (Ramayana), 44
Skanda Purana, 379
sky pillars, 361
slave labour, 7
snakes and ladders game, 379
social rights, 213–16
socialization, 62
soma (life-giving liquid), 36, 270, 304, 311, 326, 329, 394, 403–4
sorcery (negative magic), 205
spring equinox (Krittika), 248, 254, 257, 259, 277–8, 281, 285, 295, 299–302, 421n3
square/cube central point (post), 393–4
Srinivas, M.N., 419n16
Star Cluster, 282–3, 285
story engineering, 45–6
"Story of Salvation," 137
story tellers, 178–80
Sumeria, 110; Early Dynastic period, 112
summer solstice, 288, 292, 295, 301–4, 307, 352
sun maiden (Arukandi), 27–8, 36–7, 325–7, 362–3, 381, 391
Sundaram, Krishna, 395
Sūryā (female sun-goddess), 334

suttee (ritualistic Indian female widow's suicide act), 84, 93
Sutton, Komila, 48n53
Symbol Index (White), 414n3

Tamarai (Ponnivala Nadu), 20, 48, 57, 76–7, 124, 233, 248; and advice for twin brothers, 79, 158; and arasa maram, 344–5, 347–8, 352, 378; Arjuna analogy, 76–8; and barrenness, due to Shiva's seven generation curse, 14, 17–18, 48, 82, 152, 261–2, 362, 344, 397; beaten by brothers' guard, 66, 92, 127; birth of, due to love liquid falling on lotus, 15–16, 19, 35, 65, 74, 85, 193, 262, 282, 302, 324, 401; and Draupadi, 65–6, 71–2; empathy of, 16; and feast for poor, 152–3; finding jewels in crops, 16–17, 388; and frog, 380; generosity and social responsibility, 152–3, 181; as heroic mother figure, 21; immaculate conception of, 15, 99, 124, 128, 155–6, 161, 233, 286, 290, 325, 362, 431n26; insults/humiliation, 66, 72, 87; and king of cobras, 348; Kunnutaiya, marriage to, 16, 35, 55–6, 64, 76–7, 82–3, 86–7, 91, 149, 193 (*see also* Kunnutaiya); life in exile, 72–3; magical pot (life-giving liquid) from Shiva, 21, 71, 156, 157, 233, 248, 304, 324–6, 363; and midwife during labour, 161, 192–3, 251, 389; and natal home, 55, 87, 91–2; and penance pillar, 16, 21, 234, 298, 343–5, 351, 353, 362, 375, 392; pilgrimage, 16, 19–20, 21, 35, 48, 71, 76, 77–8, 83, 155–6, 161, 344, 351, 362, 375, 389, 397–8; and Ponnivala Nadu, 49–50; and Shiva, 14, 15, 20, 48, 57, 233, 248 (*see also* Shiva); and suicide, 152;

and Tangal, 23–4, 79–80, 87, 254; and triplets, 16, 21, 60, 78, 124, 128, 156, 161, 325, 362; and twins' brides turned to stone, 92–3, 127; and Vishnu, 18, 20, 35, 50–1, 57, 152, 161–2, 249, 251, 342, 362 (*see also* Vishnu); and vision of hell, 54
Tamil Nadu New Year, 423n22
Tamil traders of South India, 169
Tangal (Ponnivala Nadu), 18, 28, 226, 264, 285, 289; and blessing of twins' swords, 26, 65, 189, 204; builds temple in memory of twins, 122; and burning of sisters-in-law, 45, 83–4, 93, 115, 125; cobras' protection of, 391–2; and divination ritual for twins, 188–9; and Draupadi, 66, 72–5; dreams/visionary powers, 26, 66, 74, 79–80, 125, 134, 162; and finding her brothers' bodies, 239–40; and forest parrot conflict, 44–5, 89, 105, 115–16, 120, 135, 218, 288, 323, 418n4; and funeral rites for twins, 27, 66–7, 83, 208–9; and golden wand from Lord Shiva, 325–7, 363, 381, 391; and goose as vehicle, 28, 134, 203, 326–7, 330, 351, 391; and innai cir (uniting ritual), 91, 93; as Krittika, 254, 257; and magical power, 64–5, 382; normal birth of, 87, 254; and palace swing, 24, 125, 134, 353; and Parvati, 128; and Ponnacci (pet of), 24, 26, 32–3, 36, 75, 205; and resurrection, 27–8, 36–7, 42, 74, 122–3, 161, 163, 226–7, 325–7, 363, 381, 391; riding to Kailisa in Shiva's golden chariot, 125, 353, 402; and ritual wedding sari, 91, 127; and seeing the future, 48–9; seven tiered pots from Arukandi, 27–8, 36–7, 325–7, 362–3, 381,

391; and Shiva, 125, 326, 353, 363, 381, 402 (*see also* Shiva); and shrine for, 74, 106, 125, 161, 163–4; and Tamarai (mother), 23–4, 79–80, 125; and Viratangal, 25–6, 135; and worship of Cellatta, 135
Taurus (Bull of Heaven), 131, 268, 278, 285, 420n21
temples: Barabudur (Central Java), 310; Celandiamman (Madukkarai), 371–3; Ishtar, 118; Kaliyamman (Gannapuram), 364, 376; Mariyamman, 364, 370–1; Virakumaraswamy (Vellakovil, Tamil Nadu), 354–6; temple built by Tangal for twins in memory, 122; temple gateways, 117, 348; temple pool, 401; temple, torana frame in, 318; temple, wall mural in, depicting Ponnivala story, 223
ten commandments, 155–6, 157
teppa kulam, 383, 401
Thorgrim (Vatnsdaela Saga), 193–4
Thorir (Vatnsdaela Saga), 194
Thorkel (Vatnsdaela Saga), 193–5
Thorstein (Vatnsdaela Saga), 170–7, 194
Thurston, Edgar, 435n35
torana frame, 312–13, 330; of Buddhist shrine, 317; important feature of Hindu temples, 318; *kāla* head, 316
triplets (Ponnivala Nadu), 16, 60, 78, 99, 124, 128, 155–6, 161–2, 233, 250, 259, 286, 290, 303, 325, 331, 371, 402, 431n26
True Shepherd of Anu constellation, 286–7
twice-born status, 58–9
twin brothers, Ponnar and Shankar (Ponnivala Nadu), 21, 104–5, 120, 133; artisan stealing swords of, 215–16; as folk gods in Kailasa, 123, 161; birth of, clothed and armed, 87, 162, 215, 249, 321; Cellatta as caretaker, 63–4, 100, 160, 162, 252, 321–2; and claim of Kshatriya status, 58–60; and female parrot kidnapping, 44–5, 89, 105, 115–16, 120, 418n4; death of, 27, 33, 52–4, 72, 101–2, 106, 161, 163, 208; dual kingship, 387; and killing of Chola king, 70–1, 80, 88, 182, 235–6; and last meal, 161, 162; and local hunters' iron rods, 89, 105, 120, 216, 288; and magical horses, 159, 162; marriages of, 21, 56, 74; and parents advice for, 79, 158; punishing cousins, 232, 390; resurrection of, 27–8, 36–7, 106–7, 122–3, 161, 163, 226–7, 325–7, 363, 381, 391; and sacred threads, 58–60; sexual purity of, 126–7; and shrine for, 74, 106, 125, 161, 163–4; symbolism of, 97–8; and Tangal, 27, 66, 67, 204 (*see also* Tangal); and tiger's milk, 21, 162, 252, 321; twice-born status, 58–9; and magical horses, 159, 162; and violence after parents' death, 80; Vishnu, 51–2, 235, 236 (*see also* Vishnu); war drum, 291, 327–8, 339; wives' fate after their death, 83–4, 93. *See also* Ponnar, Shankar
twin characters, 31

untouchables (Paraiyar/Dalit by caste), 37, 43, 64, 100, 102, 272, 275, 414n4
Uruk city, 111
Usas (Dawn), 256–7
Utu (Sun god), 116, 126, 129

Vajracharya, Gautama, 317, 357, 359–61; about yogic prayers, 392
Valavandi Nadu, 90
Vāṇi river, 295
Varaha (boar), 283, 320, 421n6

Varuna (god), 314
Vatnsdaela Saga (Icelandic heritage
  legend), 7
 – adoption, 193
 – and berserks, 202, 220–1
 – death through water, 175–6
 – and dispute at wedding, 184
 – embroidery project honouring
  heroes, 169
 – and in-law animosity, 198–9
 – Ingimund first kills wealthy robber,
  180
 – inland bay (Hop), 174
 – Porolfur (dark-skinned
  troublemaker), 216, 219
 – reclamation: clean source of water,
  174–6; pioneer homestead, 176–8;
  story tellers, 178–80
 – reflection: birds, 208–10; death
  of hero, 208; elder and younger
  brothers, 206–8; special gifts,
  210–12
 – relationships: divination and
  prophecy, 202–6; and horses,
  199–202; in-law animosity, 198–9;
  weddings and new relationships,
  197–8
 – resilience: in climate struggles,
  190–1; of leader loyal to king,
  196–7; and prominent women,
  191–6
 – resistance: feuds and arguments,
  183–6; heroes versus villains, 180–3;
  magical tools, 188–9; negative
  powers and curses, 186–8
 – revelation: and insiders and outsiders
  and social rights, 213–16; and
  morality and divine justice, 220–2;
  wild lands and magic, 216–20
 – roots: and beloved land, 173–4; first
  pioneers, 170–3
 – Vatna Fjord, 174
 – wild, rocky cliffs of, 217
Vatnsdaela Valley, 172–3
Vellivala Nadu, 90, 177
Vettuvas, 48, 70, 89–90, 116, 344;
  conflicts over forest parrot, 44–5, 89,
  105, 115–16, 120, 135, 218, 288,
  323, 418n4; weapons, 214
Via Dolorosa rituals, in Jerusalem, 165
Vichitravirya (Mahabharata), 57, 62
Vigdis (Vatnsdaela Saga), 191, 199; and
  family homestead, 176–7; and
  marriage, 195, 197
Vikings, 169
Virakumaraswamy temple, Vellakovil,
  Tamil Nadu, 354–6
Viratangal, 24, 105, 288; brother–sister
  relationships, 95–6; and forest parrot
  wanted by Tangal, 44–5, 89, 105,
  115–16, 120, 135, 218, 288, 323,
  418n4; and Komban as special pet,
  121; as mirror image of Tangal,
  25–6, 116, 333–4; worshipping
  Kali, 135
Vishnu (god): and cobra hood, 349;
  as compassionate god, 220–1;
  converting Kunnutaiya to stone,
  57, 77, 128, 154; convincing Shiva
  to grant Tamarai children, 50–1;
  disguised as washerman, 52, 106,
  278, 291, 427n40; floating on
  clouds, 349; and forest massacre,
  101–2; and his Garuda (vehicle),
  163; illusion of artisans/hunters
  conflict, 26, 30; giving Komban's
  head to Bhudevi (goddess), 52, 106,
  121, 237–8, 278, 291, 427n40;
  and Krishna (avatar), 49; and
  Kunnutaiya and Tamarai's marriage,
  86–7, 91, 149; Mahabharata vs.
  Ponnivala Nadu, 49; illusion of
  artisans/hunters conflict, 26, 30; and
  Shiva, 23, 50–1, 128–30, 338 (see

also Shiva); shooting arrow against Shankar, 53, 122, 163; and Tamarai, 18, 20, 35, 50–1, 57, 152, 161–2, 249, 251, 342, 362; and twin brothers, 32–3, 235, 338, and visits to Ponnivala Nadu, 49–50
vision of hell, 54
Visvarupa vision, 67
Vyasa sage (Mahabharata), 57, 62

walking on fire, 385
Wann, Andrew, 417n1
war drum, 291, 327–8
water, as source of death, 175–6
water-filled pots, 383–7
water fountains and waterspouts, 364–70
water pillars, 362
wedding gifts, 197–8
wedding rituals, 91
White, Gavin, 264, 277, 279, 287; Symbol Index, 414n3
Wild Boar constellation, 291–2

wild lands and magic, 216–20
winnowing fan, 188–9
winter solstice, 227, 254, 281, 295–6, 298, 301–3, 306, 314, 337, 352–5, 383, 385, 401, 423n22
Witzel, Michael, 33, 34, 318
women: and anger, 390; and childbearing pain, 141; and cobras, 374; cursing own relatives, 187; generating protection, 21; as hidden source of resistance, 18–19. *See also* female power, in Ponnivala Nadu
Woods, Christopher, 130, 134

Yeman (Yama), 81, 284, 338, 427n23
Yeravan land (Bible), 146
yogic prayers, 392
Yudhishthira (Mahabharata), 54, 67, 75, 98, 107
yugas, in Hindu tradition, 165

Zvelebil, Kamil, 255

Milton Keynes UK
Ingram Content Group UK Ltd.
UKHW012230190424
441406UK00003B/297